A PRACTICAL GUIDE TO

U.S. TAXATION OF INTERNATIONAL TRANSACTIONS

Third Edition

Robert E. Meldman
Michael S. Schadewald

CCH INCORPORATED
Chicago

The Hague • London • Boston

Co-published by **CCH INCORPORATED** and
Kluwer Law International

Sold and distributed in North America by:

CCH INCORPORATED
4025 W. Peterson Ave.
Chicago, IL 60646-6085
1 800 248 3248
http://www.cch.com

Sold and distributed outside of North America by:

Kluwer Law International
Distribution Centre, P.O. Box 322
3300 AH Dordrecht
The Netherlands
http://www.kluwerlaw.com

ISBN 0-8080-0491-3 (CCH)

ISBN 90-411-8851-7 (Kluwer)

To my wife, Sandy Meldman, who has put up with my absence and allowed me to travel overseas as part of my international tax practice, my children, Saree Beth Peltin and Richard S. Meldman, and my grandchildren, Bradley Peltin and Lindsay Peltin, whose lives and work will be in a new global society.

Robert E. Meldman

To my sons, Doug and Tom.

Michael S. Schadewald

Acknowledgments

I gratefully acknowledge the efforts of Robert J. Misey, Jr., a colleague at Reinhart, Boerner, Van Deuren, Norris & Rieselbach, S.C., for his participation in the updating and editing of the "Transfer Pricing," "Tax Treaties" and "International Tax Practice and Procedure" chapters. Rob's previous experience as an attorney in the Office of Chief Counsel, Internal Revenue Service (International) was invaluable.

Robert E. Meldman

I wish to acknowledge the support of my wife, Claire Schadewald, while I was preoccupied with writing the book.

Michael S. Schadewald

Preface

This book is designed to provide the reader with a practical command of the tax issues raised by international transactions and how those issues are resolved by U.S. tax laws. The book emphasizes those areas generally accepted to be essential to tax practice. The book is written primarily as a desk reference for tax practitioners and is organized into four parts. Part I discusses two fundamental principles of U.S. taxation of international transactions, which are tax jurisdiction and the source-of-income rules. Part II explains how the United States taxes the foreign activities of domestic corporations, U.S. citizens, and other U.S. persons. This part includes chapters on the foreign tax credit, the deemed paid foreign tax credit, transfer pricing, controlled foreign corporations, foreign sales corporations, foreign currency translation and transactions, income tax treaties, and planning for foreign operations. Part III describes how the United States taxes the U.S. activities of foreign corporations, nonresident alien individuals, and other foreign persons. The chapters in this part deal with the taxation of a foreign person's U.S.-source investment-type income, and the taxation of a foreign person's U.S. trade or business activities. Finally, Part IV provides an overview of international tax practice and procedure.

March 2000

Robert E. Meldman
Michael S. Schadewald

About the Authors

Robert E. Meldman, J.D., LL.M., is a shareholder in the law firm of Reinhart, Boerner, Van Deuren, Norris & Rieselbach, S.C. Mr. Meldman received his undergraduate degree from the University of Wisconsin, his law degree from Marquette University, and a Master's of Law in taxation from New York University. He is admitted to the Wisconsin, Florida and Colorado Bars. His practice focuses on the aspects of general business and international transactions. He is co-author of CCH's *Federal Taxation Practice and Procedure* and CCH's self-study course, *Practical Tactics for Dealing with the IRS,* and has written numerous articles for journals and law reviews. He is an editorial board member for the *Journal of Property Taxation* and *Tax Litigation Alert.* He is an adjunct professor in the Master of Taxation and Graduate International Business programs at the University of Wisconsin-Milwaukee and has served as taxation section chair of the Milwaukee Bar Association and the State Bar of Wisconsin.

Mr. Meldman frequently speaks before U.S. and international legal and accounting organizations. He has led business development missions to Southeast Asia and received the 1992 Outstanding Tax Professional Award presented by *Corporate Reports Wisconsin* and the *UWM Tax Association.* He is listed in *The Best Lawyers of America, Who's Who in American Law,* and *Who's Who in the World.* He also served as Moot Court Judge in the Jessup International Law Moot Court Competition Midwest Region and the Thomas Tung National Moot Court Competition. He is a member of the American Bar Association and the International Bar Association, and is the U.S. representative to the LAWASIA Joint Venture and Investment Law Standing Committee of the Law Association for Asia and the Pacific.

Michael S. Schadewald, Ph.D., CPA, is an Associate Professor of Accounting and Director of the Deloitte & Touche Center for Multistate Taxation at the University of Wisconsin-Milwaukee. He holds a Ph.D. from the University of Minnesota, an M.S. from the University of Wisconsin-Milwaukee, and a B.B.A. from the University of Wisconsin-Whitewater. He has co-authored a book on international taxation and has published over 25 articles in accounting and tax journals, including *The Journal of the American Taxation Association, The Accounting Review, Contemporary Accounting Research, International Tax Journal, The Journal of Taxation, The Tax Adviser, International Tax Notes, TAXES—The Tax Magazine,* and *Journal of State Taxation.* He serves on the editorial boards of *The Journal of the American Taxation Association, The International Journal of Accounting, International Tax Journal, Issues in Accounting Education,* and *Journal of Accounting Education.* He has been awarded numerous research grants and fellowships by Big-Five accounting firms and worked in the Milwaukee office of Arthur Young (now part of Ernst & Young) prior to entering academics.

Table of Contents

List of Appendices

Chapter 1

Tax Jurisdiction

¶ 101 JURISDICTIONAL ISSUES

Bases for Asserting Jurisdiction

A government must answer two basic questions in determining how to tax international transactions: Which "persons" should be taxed? and What "income" is subject to tax? One basis upon which countries assert tax jurisdiction is a personal relationship between the taxpayer and the country. For example, a country may wish to tax any individual who is either a citizen or a resident of the country. The concept of a personal relationship also applies to corporations and other types of entities. A corporation may be considered a citizen of the country in which it is organized. Similarly, a corporation can be considered a resident of the country in which its seat of management or principal place of business is located.

A second basis upon which countries assert tax jurisdiction is an economic relationship between the taxpayer and the country. An economic relationship exists whenever a person derives income from property or activities that are located within a country's borders. The set of persons deriving income from sources within a country includes not only citizens and residents (those persons who already have a personal relationship with the country), but also foreign persons who are neither citizens nor residents of the taxing country.

Under the current U.S. system, personal relationships are the basis for taxing U.S. citizens, resident aliens, and domestic corporations, whereas the source of income is the basis for taxing nonresident aliens and foreign corporations.

Territorial vs. Credit Systems

A double taxation problem usually arises when a taxpayer who has a personal relationship with one country (the home country) derives income from sources within another country (the host country). The host country usually will assert jurisdiction on the basis of its economic relationship with the taxpayer. The home country also may assert jurisdiction over the income on the basis of its personal relationship with the taxpayer. In these situations, the countries involved must decide whether and how to adjust their tax systems so as to avoid international double taxation. Traditionally, it has been up to the home country to solve the double taxation problems of its citizens and residents. The home country can accomplish this only by forfeiting part or all of its jurisdictional claim over the foreign-source income of its citizens and residents, either through a territorial system or a credit system.

Under a territorial system, the home country taxes citizens and residents on income derived from sources within the home country, but allows them to exclude from taxation all income derived from foreign sources. For example, the home country would tax a citizen's wages that were earned domestically, but would exempt from tax any wages earned abroad. This leaves only the host country to tax the citizen's foreign-source income. Therefore, under a territorial system, the foreign income of a citizen or resident is taxed only one time at the host country's rate.

Under a credit system, the home country taxes the foreign income of its citizens and residents, but allows a credit for any foreign taxes paid on that income. In effect, the home country asserts secondary jurisdiction over the foreign income of its citizens and residents. The claim is secondary in the sense that taxpayers are allowed to claim a foreign tax credit to the extent their foreign income is taxed by the host country. The net result is that foreign income is taxed only one time at the higher of the host country's rate or the home country's rate.

Example 1.1: ABC Corporation has taxable income of $100 (all numbers in thousands), all of which is derived from foreign sources. Assume the home country tax rate is 30% and the foreign tax rate is 20%.

Case 1—No mechanism for mitigating double taxation: If the home country provides no mechanism for mitigating international double taxation, the total tax on ABC's $100 of foreign-source income is $50 [$30 home country tax + $20 foreign tax], computed as follows:

Home country tax return	Foreign tax return
Taxable income . . . . $100 Tax rate . . . . × .30 Tax . . . . $ 30	Taxable income . . . . $100 Tax rate . . . . × .20 Tax . . . . $ 20

Case 2—Territorial system: Under a territorial system, the total tax on ABC's foreign-source income is $20 [$0 home country tax + $20 foreign tax], computed as follows:

Home country tax return	Foreign tax return
Taxable income . . . . $ 0 Tax rate . . . . ×.30 Tax . . . . $ 0	Taxable income . . . . $100 Tax rate . . . . × .20 Tax . . . . $ 20

Case 3—Credit system: Under a credit system, the total tax on ABC's foreign-source income is $30 [$10 home country tax + $20 foreign tax], computed as follows:

Home country tax return	Foreign tax return
Taxable income . . . . $ 100 Tax rate . . . . × .30 Pre-credit tax . . . . $ 30 Foreign tax credit . . . . . . − 20 Tax . . . . $ 10	Taxable income . . . . $ 100 Tax rate . . . . × .20 Tax . . . . $ 20

A credit system and a territorial system both solve ABC's double taxation problem, but they do so in fundamentally different ways. A territorial system eliminates the $30 home country tax on ABC's foreign-source income, resulting in taxation once at the lower foreign rate. In contrast, a credit system effectively eliminates the $20 foreign tax on ABC's foreign-source income, resulting in taxation once at the higher home country rate.

As Example 1.1 illustrates, territorial and credit systems produce different results when the host country tax rate is lower than the home country rate. Under a territorial system, the taxpayer pays only the lower host country tax. Under a credit system, the taxpayer pays not only the host country tax, but also any home country tax in excess of the lower host country tax. In contrast, when the host country tax rate is higher than the home country rate, territorial and credit systems produce equivalent results. Under a territorial system, foreign-source income is taxed once at the higher foreign rate. A credit system also results in taxation once at the higher foreign rate, since the foreign tax credit completely offsets the pre-credit home country tax on the foreign-source income. Therefore, no home country tax is collected on the high-tax foreign-source income under either system.

Example 1.2: The facts are the same as in Example 1.1, except now assume that the foreign tax rate is 40%, rather than 20%.

Case 1—Territorial system: Under a territorial system, the total tax on ABC's foreign-source income is $40 [$0 home country tax + $40 foreign tax], computed as follows:

Home country tax return	
Taxable income	$ 0
Tax rate	×.30
Tax	$ 0

Foreign tax return	
Taxable income	$100
Tax rate	× .40
Tax	$ 40

Case 2—Credit system: Under a credit system, the total tax on ABC's foreign-source income also is $40 [$0 home country tax + $40 foreign tax], computed as follows:

Home country tax return	
Taxable income	$100
Tax rate	× .30
Pre-credit tax	$ 30
Foreign tax credit	− 30
Tax	$ 0

Foreign tax return	
Taxable income	$100
Tax rate	× .40
Tax	$ 40

Tax Treaties

Territorial and credit systems represent unilateral solutions to the international double taxation problem in the sense that they are created by individual countries. Tax treaties, on the other hand, represent bilateral solutions to the international double taxation problem since they are created by and apply to both of the countries that are parties to the agreement. In general, tax treaties mitigate double taxation through reciprocal tax exemptions and lower tax rates for income derived by residents of one treaty country from sources within the other treaty country. For example, under the income tax treaty between the United States and the United Kingdom, the United

Kingdom agrees not to tax U.S. residents on any interest derived from sources within the United Kingdom. In exchange, the United States agrees not to tax U.K. residents on any interest derived from sources within the United States.[1] Thus, tax treaties shift the claim of primary tax jurisdiction from the host country to the home country, thereby saving a larger share of the tax on international transactions for the home country. The increase in the home country's tax revenues comes at the host country's expense, however, which explains why tax treaty provisions are always reciprocal in nature. Tax treaties are discussed in more detail in Chapter 9.

¶ 102   OVERVIEW OF U.S. JURISDICTIONAL SYSTEM

Foreign Activities of U.S. Persons

The United States taxes U.S. persons on their worldwide income.[2] U.S. persons include the following:[3]

(i)   *U.S. citizens*

(ii) *Resident alien individuals*—Citizens of foreign countries who meet either the green card test or the substantial presence test.[4]

(iii) *Domestic corporations*—Corporations created or organized under the laws of one of the 50 states or the District of Columbia.[5] Although the location of a corporation's headquarters office or seat of management is a pertinent factor for determining corporate residence under the laws of some foreign countries, it is irrelevant for purposes of determining whether a corporation is domestic or foreign under U.S. tax principles.

(iv) *Domestic partnerships*—Partnerships created or organized under the laws of one of the 50 states or the District of Columbia, unless the Secretary provides otherwise by regulations.[6]

(v)   Any *estate* other than a foreign estate. An estate is foreign if its foreign-source income, other than any income effectively connected with a U.S. trade or business, is not subject to U.S. taxation.[7]

(vi) Any *trust* if a U.S. court is able to exercise primary supervision over the administration of the trust and one or more U.S.

---

[1] Article 11 of the U.S.-U.K. Income Tax Treaty.
[2] Code Sec. 61(a).
[3] Code Sec. 7701(a)(30).
[4] Code Sec. 7701(b)(1)(A).
[5] Code Sec. 7701(a)(4) and (a)(9). A corporation organized or created under the laws of a U.S. possession is considered a foreign corporation.
[6] Code Sec. 7701(a)(4) and (a)(9).
[7] Code Sec. 7701(a)(30)(D) and (a)(31)(A).

persons have the authority to control all substantial decisions of the trust.[8]

The United States uses a credit system to mitigate international double taxation. Therefore, a U.S. person can claim a credit for the foreign income taxes imposed on foreign-source income.[9] Under this credit system, foreign-source income is taxed one time at the higher of the U.S. tax rate or the foreign rate. In other words, the United States collects any residual U.S. tax due on foreign-source income that the host country taxes at a rate lower than the U.S. rate. On the other hand, if the foreign tax rate exceeds the U.S. rate, no U.S. tax is collected on that foreign-source income because the available foreign tax credits are more than sufficient to offset the pre-credit U.S. tax on that income.

A key feature of the U.S. credit system is the foreign tax credit limitation, which restricts the credit to the portion of the pre-credit U.S. tax that is attributable to foreign-source income.[10] The purpose of the limitation is to confine the effects of the credit to mitigating double taxation of foreign-source income. The limitation accomplishes this by preventing U.S. persons operating in high-tax foreign countries from offsetting those higher foreign taxes against the U.S. taxes on U.S.-source income.

Example 1.3: USAco, a domestic corporation, has $200 of U.S.-source taxable income, and $100 of foreign-source taxable income (all numbers in thousands). Assume that the foreign tax rate is 45% and the U.S. rate is 35%.

Case 1—Credit is limited: If the foreign tax credit is limited to the U.S. tax on foreign-source income (i.e., 35% × $100 = $35), the total tax on USAco's $300 of worldwide income is $115 [$70 U.S. tax + $45 foreign tax], computed as follows:

U.S. tax return	
Taxable income	$ 300
U.S. tax rate	× .35
Pre-credit tax	$ 105
Foreign tax credit	− 35
U.S. tax	$ 70

Foreign tax return	
Taxable income	$ 100
Foreign tax rate	× .45
Foreign tax	$ 45

Case 2—No limitation: If there were no limitation on the foreign tax credit, the total tax on USAco's $300 of worldwide income would drop from $115 to $105 [$60 U.S. tax + $45 foreign tax], computed as follows:

---

[8] Code Sec. 7701(a)(30)(E).
[9] Code Sec. 901(a).

[10] Code Sec. 904(a).

U.S. tax return	
Taxable income	$ 300
U.S. tax rate	× .35
Pre-credit tax	$ 105
Foreign tax credit	− 45
U.S. tax	$ 60

Foreign tax return	
Taxable income	$ 100
Foreign tax rate	× .45
Foreign tax	$ 45

Without the limitation, the net U.S. tax on the $100 of foreign-source income is negative $10 [$35 pre-credit U.S. tax − $45 credit], which reduces the U.S. tax on USAco's domestic profits from $70 in Case 1 to $60 in Case 2.

One major exception to the U.S. credit system is the deferral privilege, whereby the United States does not tax foreign-source income earned by a U.S. person through a foreign corporation until those profits are repatriated by the U.S. shareholder through a dividend distribution. The deferral privilege is the result of several features of U.S. tax law. First, U.S. consolidated reporting rules take a "domestic" consolidation approach, whereby affiliates organized in foreign countries are not allowed to join their U.S. counterparts in filing a federal consolidated income tax return.[11] Second, the earnings of a regular corporation are not taxed to its shareholders until distributed as a dividend. Finally, the United States does not tax the foreign-source income of foreign corporations. Therefore, as long as a foreign subsidiary derives only foreign-source income, those earnings will not enter the U.S. tax base until they are distributed to the U.S. parent corporation as a dividend.

> **Example 1.4:** USAco, a domestic corporation, owns 100% of FORco, a foreign corporation. FORco operates a factory in a country that has granted FORco a 10-year tax holiday. In its first year of operations, FORco has $10 million of foreign-source income and repatriates $4 million of those earnings to USAco through a dividend distribution. Because FORco is a foreign corporation, the United States does not tax FORco on its $10 million of foreign-source income. However, the United States does tax USAco on the $4 million dividend that it receives from FORco.[12]

The policy rationale for deferral is that it allows U.S. companies to compete in foreign markets on a tax parity with their foreign competitors. However, deferral also opens the door to tax avoidance, particu-

---

[11] Code Sec. 1504. In contrast, U.S. accounting principles require a "worldwide" consolidation, whereby all majority-owned subsidiaries, domestic and foreign alike, must be consolidated with the U.S. parent corporation for financial reporting purposes. Statement of Financial Accounting Standards No. 94, *Consolidation of All Majority-Owned Subsidiaries* (Financial Accounting Standards Board, 1987).

[12] USAco cannot claim a dividends-received deduction because FORco is a foreign corporation. Code Sec. 243(a).

larly with respect to passive investment income, the source of which can easily be shifted to a foreign country. Therefore, Congress has enacted a variety of anti-deferral provisions, including Subpart F, as well as the passive foreign investment company and foreign personal holding company provisions. Under these provisions (which are discussed in Chapter 6), certain types of unrepatriated earnings of a foreign corporation, such as passive investment income, are subject to immediate U.S. taxation.

A second major exception to the U.S. credit system is the foreign earned income exclusion. Under the general rules, the United States taxes U.S. citizens and resident aliens on their worldwide income, even when they live and work abroad for extended periods of time. To provide some relief, a U.S. expatriate who meets certain requirements can exclude from U.S. taxation a limited amount of foreign earned income plus a housing cost amount.[13] The foreign earned income exclusion is discussed later in this chapter.

Before discussing how the United States taxes the U.S. activities of foreign persons, it is worth noting how the jurisdictional scheme for domestic corporations impacts tax planning for foreign operations. Because the foreign earnings of U.S. companies are subject to both U.S. and foreign income taxes, a commonly used metric for evaluating these tax costs is the total effective tax rate on foreign earnings. When evaluating a U.S. corporation's effective tax rate, the de facto benchmark is the top U.S. statutory rate of 35 percent.[14] However, it is quite common for the total tax rate on foreign earnings to be greater than or less than 35 percent. The total tax rate can exceed 35 percent when the foreign jurisdiction taxes corporate income at a rate in excess of 35 percent (as, for example, in Canada, France, Germany, Italy and Japan), and the foreign tax credit limitation prevents U.S. companies from claiming a credit for those "excess" foreign taxes. In contrast, the total tax rate on foreign earnings can fall below 35 percent when the foreign jurisdiction taxes corporate income at a rate less than 35 percent (as, for example, in Hong Kong, Ireland, Singapore and Switzerland), and the U.S. company takes advantage of its ability to defer the residual U.S. tax on low-tax foreign earnings until such time as those foreign profits are repatriated by the U.S. parent corporation through a dividend distribution. Tax planning for foreign operations is discussed in detail in Chapter 10.

---

[13] Code Sec. 911. The exclusion amount is gradually increased from $70,000 for 1997 tax years to $80,000 for tax years beginning in 2002 and thereafter. See ¶ 104.

[14] Code Sec. 11.

U.S. Activities of Foreign Persons

U.S. tax law contains a two-pronged territorial system for taxing the U.S.-source income of foreign persons. Foreign persons include the following:

(i) *Nonresident alien individuals*—Individuals who are neither citizens nor residents of the United States.[15]

(ii) *Foreign corporations*—Corporations created or organized under the laws of a foreign country or U.S. possession.[16]

(iii) *Foreign partnerships*—Partnerships created or organized under the laws of a foreign country or U.S. possession.[17]

(iv) *Foreign estate*—Any estate that is not subject to U.S. taxation on its foreign-source income which is not effectively connected with a U.S. trade or business.[18]

(v) *Foreign trust*—A trust is foreign if no U.S. court is able to exercise primary supervision over the administration of the trust, or no U.S. persons have the authority to control all substantial decisions of the trust.[19]

The United States taxes foreign persons at graduated rates on the net amount of income effectively connected with the conduct of a trade or business within the United States.[20] On the other hand, the United States taxes the gross amount of a foreign person's U.S.-source nonbusiness (or investment-type) income at a flat rate of 30%.[21] The U.S. person controlling the payment of U.S.-source nonbusiness income to a foreign person must deduct and withhold the 30% U.S. tax.[22] Withholding is required because it is the only sure way to collect taxes from passive offshore investors. In order to withhold, the withholding agent must be able to readily ascertain both the tax base and the applicable rate. This explains both the gross basis taxation and the use of a flat tax rate since it would be difficult for the U.S. withholding agent to determine the foreign person's allocable expenses and appropriate tax bracket based on worldwide income.

There are several major exceptions to the general rules for taxing foreign persons. For example, income tax treaties usually reduce the withholding tax rate on interest, dividend, and royalty income from the statutory rate of 30% to 15% or less. In addition, the United States generally exempts from taxation portfolio interest income.[23] Capital gains also are generally exempt from U.S. taxation,[24] except for gains from the sale of U.S. real property, which are taxed in the same manner

---

[15] Code Sec. 7701(b)(1)(B).
[16] Code Sec. 7701(a)(5).
[17] Code Sec. 7701(a)(5).
[18] Code Sec. 7701(a)(31)(A).
[19] Code Sec. 7701(a)(31)(B) and (a)(30)(E).

[20] Code Secs. 871(b) and 882(a).
[21] Code Secs. 871(a) and 881(a).
[22] Code Secs. 1441 and 1442.
[23] Code Secs. 871(h) and 881(c).
[24] Reg. § 1.1441-2(a)(3).

as income effectively connected with the conduct of a U.S. trade or business.[25] Table 1.1 summarizes the general rules regarding U.S. taxation of international transactions.

TABLE 1.1. U.S. TAXATION OF INTERNATIONAL TRANSACTIONS—GENERAL RULES		
Type of person	*Type of income*	*U.S. taxation*
U.S. person	Foreign-source income	U.S. collects the excess of the pre-credit U.S. tax over the related foreign tax credit
Foreign person	Income effectively connected with a U.S. trade or business	U.S. taxes the net amount of income at graduated rates
	U.S.-source nonbusiness income	U.S. taxes the gross amount of income at 30%

¶ 103   DEFINITION OF RESIDENT ALIEN

The United States taxes resident alien individuals on their worldwide income, whereas nonresident aliens are taxed only on their U.S.-source income. As a consequence, the taxation of alien individuals depends critically on whether the person is considered a U.S. resident. An alien is considered a U.S. resident in any calendar year that he or she meets either the green card test or the substantial presence test.[26]

Green Card Test

Under the so-called green card test, an alien individual is treated as a U.S. resident for a calendar year if, at any time during that calendar year, the individual is a lawful permanent resident of the United States.[27] An alien qualifies as a lawful permanent resident of the United States if he or she has been lawfully accorded, and has not revoked or abandoned, the privilege of residing permanently in the United States as an immigrant.[28] Such "green card" holders are treated as U.S. residents for tax purposes, regardless of whether they are actually physically present in the United States during the year.

This rule forces aliens who have obtained a green card but have not yet moved to the United States on a permanent basis to pay U.S. taxes on their worldwide income. These individuals are expected to pay taxes on the same basis as U.S. citizens, since they have rights in the United States similar to those of U.S. citizens. In particular, they have the right to exit and reenter the United States at will.

---

[25] Code Sec. 897(a)(1).

[26] Code Sec. 7701(b)(1)(A).

[27] Code Sec. 7701(b)(1)(A)(i).

[28] Code Sec. 7701(b)(6).

Substantial Presence Test

An alien who does not hold a green card is considered a U.S. resident for a calendar year if he or she is physically present in the United States for 183 or more days during that year.[29] This substantial presence test is based on the premise that spending more than half of a year in the United States establishes a stronger connection with the United States than with any other country for that year.

> **Example 1.5:** T is not a U.S. citizen and does not hold a green card. However, T is physically present in the United States from January 1 through September 30 of the current year. T is a U.S. resident for that year because she is physically present in the United States for 183 or more days.

A day is counted as a day of U.S. presence if the alien is physically present in the United States at any time during that day.[30] Thus, presence for part of a day, such as the day of arrival or departure from the United States, counts as a full day. However, certain types of U.S. presence are disregarded, including commuters from Mexico or Canada,[31] travelers between two foreign points,[32] individuals with medical conditions,[33] and certain exempt individuals.[34] Exempt individuals primarily include qualifying students, teachers, trainees, and foreign-government-related individuals.[35]

A variant of the substantial presence test, called the carryover days test, extends U.S. residence to aliens whose stay in the United States is prolonged, but is less than 183 days in any given calendar year. For example, under the general rule, an alien could be physically present in the United States for the last 182 days of one year and the first 182 days of the succeeding year (for a total of 364 consecutive days in the United States), without establishing U.S. residency. The carryover days test addresses these situations by taking into account days spent in the United States during the two preceding calendar years. Under this test, the 183-day standard is applied by counting a day of presence during the current year as a full day, a day of presence during the first preceding year as one-third of a day, and a day of presence during the second preceding year as one-sixth of a day.[36] In all cases, an individual must be present in the United States at least 31 days during the current calendar year to be considered a resident for that year.[37]

> **Example 1.6:** T is not a U.S. citizen and does not hold a green card. However, T is physically present in the United States for 90

---

[29] Code Sec. 7701(b)(3)(A).
[30] Code Sec. 7701(b)(7)(A).
[31] Code Sec. 7701(b)(7)(B).
[32] Code Sec. 7701(b)(7)(C).
[33] Code Sec. 7701(b)(3)(D)(ii).

[34] Code Sec. 7701(b)(3)(D)(i).
[35] Code Sec. 7701(b)(5).
[36] Code Sec. 7701(b)(3)(A)(ii).
[37] Code Sec. 7701(b)(3)(A)(i).

days during year 1, 150 days during year 2, and 120 days during year 3. The primary 183-day test is not met in any year of the three years. However, the carryover days test is met for the first time in year 3 [120 days + (1/3 of 150 days) + (1/6 of 90 days) = 185 days].

Under the carryover days test, an individual who consistently spends just one-third of the year in the United States (122 days to be exact) is treated as a U.S. resident.[38] This potentially unfair result is mitigated by an exception to the carryover days test for an alien who satisfies the following requirements:

(i)   the alien is present in the United States for less than 183 days during the current year,

(ii) the alien's tax home (i.e., principal or regular place of business) for the current year is in a foreign country, and

(iii) the alien has a closer connection to that foreign country than to the United States.[39]

This exception does not apply, however, if the alien has applied for a green card.[40] Determining whether a taxpayer has a closer connection with a foreign country than with the United States requires a consideration of all the facts and circumstances, such as the location of the individual's family, permanent residence, and personal belongings, as well as the location of the individual's social, political, cultural, and religious relationships.[41]

Another exception applies for determining "presence" with respect to foreign vessel crew members. Under these rules, the days that such individuals are present in the United States as a member of a regular crew of a foreign vessel engaged in transportation between the United States and a foreign country or a U.S. possession are disregarded unless the individual is otherwise engaged in a trade or business in the United States on those days.[42]

First Year of Residency

If an alien establishes U.S. residency after January 1, that individual is generally treated as a nonresident alien for the portion of the calendar year preceding the residency starting date, and as a resident alien for the remainder of the year.[43] An alien's U.S. residency starting date depends on whether residency is established under the green card test or the substantial presence test. If residency is established under the substantial presence test, the residency starting date is the first day

---

[38] 122 days + (1/3 of 122 days) + (1/6 of 122 days) = 183 days.

[39] Code Sec. 7701(b)(3)(B).

[40] Code Sec. 7701(b)(3)(C).

[41] Reg. § 301.7701(b)-2(d).

[42] Code Sec. 7701(b)(7).

[43] Code Sec. 7701(b)(2)(A)(i).

the taxpayer is physically present in the United States.[44] For this purpose, visits to the United States of 10 days or less, such as a house-hunting trip, are ignored if at the time of the visit the individual had a closer connection to a foreign country than to the United States.[45] If residency is established under the green card test, the residency starting date is the first day the taxpayer is physically present in the United States with a green card.[46] If the requirements of both residency tests are satisfied in the first year of residency, the residency starting date is the earlier of the two starting dates.[47] Finally, to prevent a gap in residency when an alien is a resident in two consecutive calendar years, the residency starting date for a taxpayer who was a U.S. resident in the preceding year is January 1, regardless of when the green card test or the substantial presence test was first met for the current year.[48]

A special first-year residency election is available to certain qualifying aliens. Under this provision, in the first year that an alien satisfies either the green card test or the substantial presence test, he or she can elect to be taxed as a U.S. resident for a portion of the preceding year, if any, in which he or she was present in the United States.[49] This election allows the alien to itemize his or her deductions and claim a foreign tax credit, beginning with the entry date into the United States. However, it also exposes all of the alien's income to U.S. taxation, including his or her foreign-source income.

Last Year of Residency

An alien's U.S. residency termination date depends on whether the alien qualified as a resident for the current year under the green card test or the substantial presence test. If the alien qualified as a U.S. resident under the substantial presence test, the residency period extends until December 31, unless an exception applies.[50] Under the exception, the residency termination date is the last day of the year on which the individual was physically present in the United States, provided the taxpayer establishes that for the remainder of the year he or she had a closer connection to, and a tax home in, a foreign country.[51] If this exception applies, the alien is taxed as a U.S. resident from January 1 to the residency termination date, and as a nonresident for the remainder of the year.

Similar rules apply to an alien who qualified as a U.S. resident under the green card test. Generally, the residency period extends until December 31. However, under an exception, the residency termination

---

[44] Code Sec. 7701(b)(2)(A)(iii).

[45] Code Sec. 7701(b)(2)(C).

[46] Code Sec. 7701(b)(2)(A)(ii).

[47] Reg. § 301.7701(b)-4(a).

[48] Reg. § 301.7701(b)-4(e)(1).

[49] Code Sec. 7701(b)(4).

[50] Reg. § 301.7701(b)-4(b)(1).

[51] Reg. § 301.7701(b)-4(b)(2). If the closer connection test is met, visits to the United States for 10 days or less which take place after the residency termination date are ignored. Code Sec. 7701(b)(2)(C).

date is the first day during the year that the individual is no longer a green card holder, provided that the taxpayer establishes that for the remainder of the year he or she had a closer connection to, and a tax home in, a foreign country.[52] If an alien qualifies as a resident during the current year under both the green card and the substantial presence tests, the residency termination date is the later of the termination dates under the two residency tests.[53]

To prevent a gap in residency when an alien is a resident in two consecutive calendar years, the normal residency termination date rules do not apply if the alien is a U.S. resident in the succeeding year. In such cases, the residency termination date for the current year is December 31, regardless of when the green card test or the substantial presence test was last met for the year.[54]

Filing a Joint Return

A married couple is not eligible to file a joint return for a given taxable year if, at any time during that year, one or both spouses was a nonresident alien.[55] However, an alien who becomes a U.S. resident during the year and is married to a U.S. citizen or resident can elect to be treated as a U.S. resident for the entire taxable year.[56] In addition, an alien who is a nonresident for the entire year, but is married to a U.S. citizen or resident, also can make a special election to be treated as a resident alien.[57]

¶ 104   EXCLUSION FOR FOREIGN EARNED INCOME

The United States ordinarily taxes U.S. citizens and resident aliens on their worldwide income, even when they live and work abroad for an extended period of time. To provide some relief, a U.S. citizen or resident who meets certain requirements can elect to exclude from U.S. taxation a limited amount of foreign earned income plus a housing cost amount.[58] A double tax benefit is not allowed, however, and a taxpayer cannot claim a credit for foreign income taxes related to excluded income.[59]

Exclusion vs. Credit

Because the foreign earned income exclusion is elective, an expatriate must decide whether to elect the exclusion or to rely on the foreign

---

[52] Reg. § 301.7701(b)-4(b)(2).
[53] Reg. § 301.7701(b)-4(b)(2).
[54] Reg. § 301.7701(b)-4(e)(2).
[55] Code Sec. 6013(a)(1).
[56] Code Sec. 6013(h) and Reg. § 1.6013-7.
[57] Code Sec. 6013(g) and Reg. § 1.6013-6.
[58] Code Sec. 911.
[59] Code Sec. 911(d)(6) and Reg. § 1.911-6(c). The foreign earned income exclusion does not apply to

FICA taxes. A U.S. citizen or resident alien employed abroad by an "American employer" (as defined in Code Sec. 3121(h)) is subject to FICA taxes on his or her wages, unless there is a social security totalization agreement (a type of tax treaty) between the United States and the host foreign country. Code Sec. 3121(b). Expatriates who do not work for an American employer normally are exempt from FICA taxes.

tax credit.[60] A key factor in deciding which option is more advantageous is the relative amounts of U.S. and foreign taxes imposed on the foreign earned income before the exclusion or credit. The exclusion completely eliminates the U.S. income tax on the qualifying amount of foreign earned income. This allows expatriates who work in a low-tax foreign jurisdiction, or who qualify for special tax exemptions in the countries in which they work, to benefit from the lower foreign tax rates. In contrast, under the foreign tax credit option, the United States collects any residual U.S. tax on lightly taxed foreign income, and the expatriate derives no benefit from the lower foreign rates.

The exclusion also eliminates the U.S. tax on the qualifying amount of foreign earned income derived by an expatriate working in a high-tax foreign jurisdiction. The credit option also achieves this result, since the higher foreign taxes are sufficient to fully offset the U.S. tax on the foreign earned income. In addition, under the credit option, the expatriate receives a potential added benefit in the form of a foreign tax credit carryover. Foreign taxes in excess of the foreign tax credit limitation can be carried back up to two years and forward up to five years.[61] Therefore, an expatriate can use these excess credits in a carryover year in which he or she has foreign-source income that attracts little or no foreign tax.[62] For example, expatriates who return to the United States may be able to use their foreign tax credit carryforwards to the extent their future compensation is attributable to foreign business trips.[63]

Qualified Individuals

The foreign earned income exclusion is available only to U.S. citizens or resident aliens who meet the following two requirements:

(i) the individual is physically present in a foreign country for at least 330 full days during a 12-month period or (in the case of a U.S. citizen) is a bona fide resident of a foreign country for an uninterrupted period that includes an entire taxable year, and

(ii) the individual's tax home is in a foreign country.[64]

In applying the 330-day physical presence test, every full day in a foreign country is counted.[65] Therefore, a series of foreign stays, including foreign vacations, can be pieced together to meet the 330-day test.

---

[60] It also is possible to deduct foreign income taxes. Code Sec. 164(a). Typically, however, a credit or exclusion is more advantageous.

[61] Code Sec. 904(c).

[62] Under the separate-category-of-income foreign tax credit limitations, excess foreign tax credits related to foreign earned income ordinarily are assigned to the general limitation basket and can only offset an excess limitation from that basket. Code Sec. 904(d).

[63] Compensation is treated as foreign-source income to the extent the related services are performed abroad. Code Sec. 862(a)(3).

[64] Code Sec. 911(d)(1).

[65] Reg. § 1.911-2(d)(2).

For this purpose, U.S. possessions are not considered foreign countries.[66] U.S. citizens who are unable to meet the objective 330-day physical presence test must satisfy the subjective bona fide foreign resident test. Whether an individual is a bona fide foreign resident is determined by his or her intentions with regard to the length and nature of the stay.[67] Factors which suggest that an expatriate is a bona fide foreign resident include the presence of family, the acquisition of a foreign home or long-term lease, and involvement in the social life of the foreign country.[68]

The second requirement is that the individual has a foreign tax home.[69] An individual's tax home is his or her principal or regular place of business, provided that an individual is not treated as having a tax home in a foreign country during any period in which the taxpayer's abode is in the United States.[70] An individual's abode is in the United States if that is where his or her economic, social, and personal ties are closest.[71]

When both spouses are working abroad, qualification for the foreign earned income exclusion is determined separately for each spouse, and each spouse individually makes an election to claim the exclusion.[72] Therefore, it is possible for one qualifying spouse to elect the exclusion, while the other qualifying spouse chooses not to exclude any foreign earned income.

Computing the Exclusion

For tax years beginning on or before December 31, 1997, the maximum annual exclusion is $70,000, and is prorated for the number of qualifying days in the taxable year.[73] A qualifying day is any day within the period during which the individual meets the foreign tax home requirement and either the bona fide foreign resident requirement or the 330-day physical presence requirement.[74]

> **Example 1.7:** During 1997, T satisfies the requirements for claiming a foreign earned income exclusion and has 292 qualifying days for the year. Thus, T's maximum foreign earned income exclusion is $56,000 [$70,000 × (292 days ÷ 365 days)].

For tax years beginning on or after January 1, 1998, the limitation amount increases as follows:

---

[66] Reg. § 1.911-2(g).

[67] Reg. §§ 1.911-2(c) and 1.871-2(b). An individual with earned income from sources within a foreign country is not a bona fide resident of that country if the individual claims to be a nonresident of that country for local tax purposes. Reg. § 1.911-2(c).

[68] For example, see *G.H. Jones v. Comm'r*, 927 F2d 849 (5th Cir. 1991), *rev'g and rem'g* 58 TCM 689 (1989).

[69] Code Sec. 911(d)(1).

[70] Code Sec. 911(d)(3) and Reg. § 1.911-2(b).

[71] For example, see *J.T. Lemay v. Comm'r*, 837 F2d 681 (5th Cir. 1988), *aff'g* 53 TCM 862 (1987); and *Lansdown v. Comm'r*, 68 TCM 680 (1994).

[72] Reg. § 1.911-5.

[73] Code Sec. 911(b)(2)(A).

[74] Reg. § 1.911-3(d)(3).

For calendar year—	The exclusion amount is—
1998	$72,000
1999	$74,000
2000	$76,000
2001	$78,000
2002 and thereafter	$80,000

For tax years beginning after 2007, the $80,000 amount will be indexed for inflation.[75]

The exclusion is available only for foreign-source income that was earned during the period in which the taxpayer meets the foreign tax home requirement, and either the bona fide foreign resident or 330-day physical presence test.[76] Therefore, when identifying compensation that qualifies for the exclusion, the determinative factor is whether a paycheck or taxable reimbursement is attributable to services performed during the qualifying period, not whether the expatriate actually received the compensation during that period.[77] A deferred payment, such as a bonus, qualifies for the exclusion only if it is received before the close of the taxable year following the year in which it was earned.[78] Pension income does not qualify for the exclusion.[79]

Employment-related allowances, such as foreign housing and automobile allowances, also qualify for the exclusion if the allowance represents compensation for services performed abroad during the qualifying period. In this regard, any taxable reimbursements received for expenses incurred in moving from the United States to a foreign country ordinarily are treated as compensation for services performed abroad. On the other hand, any taxable reimbursements received for expenses incurred in moving back to the United States ordinarily are treated as U.S.-source income.[80]

Any deductions allocable to excluded foreign earned income, such as unreimbursed employee business expenses, are disallowed.[81] Certain deductions are considered unrelated to any specific item of gross income and are always deducted in full. These include medical expenses, charitable contributions, alimony payments, IRA contributions, real estate taxes and mortgage interest on a personal residence, and personal exemptions.[82]

---

[75] Code Sec. 911(b)(2).

[76] Code Sec. 911(b)(1)(A). For this purpose, U.S. possessions are considered part of the United States. Reg. § 1.911-2(g).

[77] Reg. § 1.911-3(e)(1).

[78] Code Sec. 911(b)(1)(B)(iv).

[79] Code Sec. 911(b)(1)(B)(i).

[80] Reg. § 1.911-3(e)(5)(i). An exception applies if, prior to moving abroad, there was a written agreement that the expatriate would be reimbursed for the expense of moving back to the United States, even if he or she were to leave the employer upon returning to the United States. In such cases, the reimbursement is treated as foreign-source income.

[81] Code Sec. 911(d)(6).

[82] Reg. § 1.911-6(a).

Housing Cost Allowance

An expatriate that qualifies for the foreign earned income exclusion also can claim an exclusion for the housing cost amount.[83] The housing cost amount equals the excess of eligible expenses incurred for the expatriate's foreign housing over a stipulated base amount ($9,865 in 1999), which is prorated for the number of qualifying days in the year.[84] Eligible housing expenses normally include rent, utilities (other than telephone charges), real and personal property insurance, certain occupancy taxes, nonrefundable security deposits, rental of furniture and accessories, household repairs, and residential parking. Housing expenses do not include the costs of purchasing or making improvements to a house, mortgage interest and real estate taxes related to a house that the taxpayer owns, purchased furniture, pay television subscriptions, or domestic help.[85]

> **Example 1.8:** During 1999, T satisfies the requirements for claiming a foreign earned income exclusion and has 300 qualifying days for the year. Therefore, T's base amount for 1999 is $8,108 [$9,865 base amount for 1999 × (300 days ÷ 365 days)]. T's eligible housing expenses include $15,000 of apartment rentals, $2,000 of utility expenses (not including telephone charges), $5,000 of rental expenses for furniture and accessories, and $1,500 of residential parking expenses. Thus, T's housing cost amount for 1999 is $15,392 [($15,000 + $2,000 + $5,000 + $1,500) − $8,108].

Electing the Exclusion

The election to claim the foreign earned income exclusion and housing cost amount is made by filing Form 2555, Foreign Earned Income Exclusion, and remains in effect until revoked by the taxpayer.[86] A taxpayer can revoke an exclusion election, but must then wait five years to reinstate the exclusion.[87] If significant uncertainties exist regarding whether to elect the exclusion, a taxpayer can file an original return without making the election, and then file an amended return at a later date electing the exclusion.[88] (Form 2555 is reproduced in the appendix to this chapter.)

¶ 105 A POLICY NOTE REGARDING THE CURRENT U.S. SYSTEM

The current U.S. jurisdictional system reflects a variety of tax policy objectives, including fairness, the need to collect tax revenues, economic neutrality, and enforcement constraints. The concept of fairness encompasses both horizontal equity and vertical equity. Horizon-

---

[83] Code Sec. 911(a)(2).
[84] Code Sec. 911(c)(1) and IRS Pub. No. 54 (1999).
[85] Reg. § 1.911-4(b). Special rules apply to the computation of a married couple's housing cost amount. Reg. § 1.911-5(a)(3).

[86] Reg. § 1.911-7(a)(1).
[87] Reg. § 1.911-7(b).
[88] Reg. § 1.911-7(a)(2)(i)(B).

tal equity requires similar treatment of taxpayers in similar economic situations, whereas vertical equity requires higher tax burdens for higher-income taxpayers. The U.S. government's use of a credit system to mitigate international double taxation generally enhances vertical equity. Under a territorial system, U.S. persons could split their total income between domestic and foreign sources. Under a credit system, however, U.S. persons must aggregate their worldwide income, and the United States taxes the total amount at graduated rates.

Whether the taxation of a U.S. person's worldwide income enhances or diminishes horizontal equity depends on how one interprets the concept of similarly situated. For example, one could argue that U.S. citizens residing abroad should pay less U.S. tax than citizens residing at home, on the grounds that the former benefit less from U.S. government expenditures. The Supreme Court addressed this issue in 1924 in the case of *G.W. Cook v. G.L. Tait*.[89] The Court ruled that the U.S. government could tax the Mexican-source income of a U.S. citizen who was a permanent resident of Mexico, on the grounds that government expenditures benefit U.S. citizens regardless of their residence or the source of their income. In other words, the basic rights and protections accorded all U.S. citizens, including the right to exit and reenter the United States at will (and thereby control the enjoyment of these benefits), are the primary determinants of whether individuals are similarly situated.

A second major tax policy objective is the collection of tax revenues to fund public services. The United States mitigates international double taxation by allowing U.S. persons to claim a credit for foreign income taxes imposed on their foreign-source income. The appeal of the credit system, as compared to a territorial system, is that it allows the United States to mitigate international double taxation without completely forgoing jurisdiction over the foreign-source income of U.S. persons. Double taxation is avoided by allowing the host country to claim primary jurisdiction over a U.S. person's foreign-source income. However, the United States does assert secondary jurisdiction, and therefore collects any residual U.S. tax on lightly taxed foreign-source income. Asserting secondary jurisdiction over foreign-source income increases U.S. tax collections and promotes fairness. Under a territorial system, U.S. persons could avoid U.S. taxes simply by shifting their income-producing assets to tax-haven countries that impose little or no income taxes.

A third basic tax policy objective is economic neutrality, or the effect of taxation on business and investment decisions. In terms of international trade, neutrality is an issue with respect to the location of

---

[89] 44 SCt 444 (1924).

production facilities and investment assets (capital export neutrality), as well as competition between domestic and foreign companies within the same country or market (capital import neutrality). Capital export neutrality exists if the decision to invest capital at home or abroad is unaffected by taxes. Therefore, capital export neutrality does not exist if, for example, tax rates are lower abroad, in which case there is a tax incentive to export capital. U.S. labor groups, in particular, are concerned that the tax laws do not give U.S. companies an incentive to move their manufacturing plants and other facilities overseas. Capital import neutrality exists if domestic and foreign companies competing within the same country or market all face the same total tax rate. Capital import neutrality is a major concern for U.S. companies attempting to compete in foreign markets.

The U.S. system exhibits elements of both capital export and capital import neutrality. For example, subjecting a U.S. company's worldwide income to taxation enhances capital export neutrality. On the other hand, U.S. companies that operate abroad through foreign subsidiaries can defer payment of any residual U.S. taxes until they repatriate those low-tax foreign earnings through a dividend distribution. During the 1950s and 1960s, capital export neutrality was the major U.S. tax policy goal, as U.S. multinational corporations dominated foreign competitors at home and abroad. However, as global competition has intensified during the last several decades, so have concerns about capital import neutrality.

The tensions created by the trade-offs between these two types of tax neutrality have created an on-going political debate. On one side are those U.S. lawmakers and constituency groups (e.g., organized labor organizations) that wish to emphasize capital export neutrality. These groups are concerned that too many high-paying U.S. manufacturing jobs are migrating offshore due, in part, to the tax savings offered by a number of low-tax foreign jurisdictions. These interests have resulted in recurring proposals, such as the "runaway plant" legislation proposed in 1996, to eliminate deferral. On the other side are those U.S. lawmakers and constituency groups (e.g., trade associations representing U.S. multinational corporations) that wish to emphasize capital import neutrality. These groups are concerned that U.S. businesses are at a competitive disadvantage in foreign markets, due to what they perceive to be the unusually harsh approach that U.S. lawmakers take in taxing foreign earnings.[90]

Another major policy issue in the international context is enforcement constraints. The United States can enforce a tax on a foreign

---

[90] For a comprehensive discussion of these issues, see *Foreign Income Project: International Tax Policy* *for the 21st Century* (National Foreign Trade Council, Inc., March 15, 1999).

person only if it can verify the correctness of the resulting tax liability and collect the tax if the taxpayer does not voluntarily pay it. As a practical matter, this is possible only when either the taxpayer or the taxable income is located within U.S. borders. The U.S. system for taxing foreigners reflects these constraints. For example, because withholding is the only sure way to collect taxes from passive offshore investors, the United States taxes the gross amount of a foreign person's U.S.-source nonbusiness income through flat rate withholding.

In sum, the current system for taxing international transactions, like the U.S. tax system generally, represents a compromise between the competing policy objectives of fairness, tax collections, economic neutrality, and enforcement constraints.

¶ 106   APPENDIX

Form **2555**	**Foreign Earned Income**	OMB No. 1545-0067
Department of the Treasury Internal Revenue Service	▶ See separate instructions. ▶ Attach to Form 1040.	19**99** Attachment Sequence No. **34**

For Use by U.S. Citizens and Resident Aliens Only

Name shown on Form 1040	Your social security number

Part I   **General Information**

1   Your foreign address (including country)   **2**   Your occupation

3   Employer's name ▶ ....

4a   Employer's U.S. address ▶ ....

  b   Employer's foreign address ▶ ....

5   Employer is (check   **a** ☐ A foreign entity   **b** ☐ A U.S. company   **c** ☐ Self
any that apply):   **d** ☐ A foreign affiliate of a U.S. company   **e** ☐ Other (specify) ▶ ....

6a   If, after 1981, you filed Form 2555 to claim either of the exclusions or Form 2555-EZ to claim the foreign earned income exclusion, enter the last year you filed the form. ▶ ....

  b   If you did not file Form 2555 or 2555-EZ after 1981 to claim either of the exclusions, check here ▶ ☐ and go to line 7 now.

  c   Have you ever revoked either of the exclusions?   .   .   .   .   ☐ Yes ☐ No

  d   If you answered "Yes," enter the type of exclusion and the tax year for which the revocation was effective. ▶ ....

7   Of what country are you a citizen/national? ▶ ....

8a   Did you maintain a separate foreign residence for your family because of adverse living conditions at your tax home? See **Second foreign household** on page 3 of the instructions   .   .   .   .   .   .   ☐ Yes ☐ No

  b   If "Yes," enter city and country of the separate foreign residence. Also, enter the number of days during your tax year that you maintained a second household at that address. ▶ ....

9   List your tax home(s) during your tax year and date(s) established. ▶ ....

Next, complete either Part II or Part III. If an item does not apply, enter "NA." If you do not give the information asked for, any exclusion or deduction you claim may be disallowed.

Part II   **Taxpayers Qualifying Under Bona Fide Residence Test** (See page 2 of the instructions.)

10   Date bona fide residence began ▶ ...., and ended ▶ ....

11   Kind of living quarters in foreign country ▶ **a** ☐ Purchased house   **b** ☐ Rented house or apartment   **c** ☐ Rented room
         d ☐ Quarters furnished by employer

12a   Did any of your family live with you abroad during any part of the tax year?   .   .   .   .   .   ☐ Yes ☐ No

  b   If "Yes," who and for what period? ▶ ....

13a   Have you submitted a statement to the authorities of the foreign country where you claim bona fide residence that you are not a resident of that country? (See instructions.)   .   .   .   .   .   .   ☐ Yes ☐ No

  b   Are you required to pay income tax to the country where you claim bona fide residence? (See instructions.)   ☐ Yes ☐ No
If you answered "Yes" to 13a and "No" to 13b, you do not qualify as a bona fide resident. Do not complete the rest of this part.

14   If you were present in the United States or its possessions during the tax year, complete columns **(a)–(d)** below. **Do not** include the income from column **(d)** in Part IV, but report it on Form 1040.

(a) Date arrived in U.S.	(b) Date left U.S.	(c) Number of days in U.S. on business	(d) Income earned in U.S. on business (attach computation)	(a) Date arrived in U.S.	(b) Date left U.S.	(c) Number of days in U.S. on business	(d) Income earned in U.S. on business (attach computation)

15a   List any contractual terms or other conditions relating to the length of your employment abroad. ▶ ....
....

  b   Enter the type of visa under which you entered the foreign country. ▶ ....

  c   Did your visa limit the length of your stay or employment in a foreign country? If "Yes," attach explanation   ☐ Yes ☐ No

  d   Did you maintain a home in the United States while living abroad?   .   .   .   .   .   .   ☐ Yes ☐ No

  e   If "Yes," enter address of your home, whether it was rented, the names of the occupants, and their relationship to you. ▶ ....

For Paperwork Reduction Act Notice, see page 4 of separate instructions.	Cat. No. 11900P	Form **2555** (1999)

Form 2555 (1999) Page **2**

Part III   **Taxpayers Qualifying Under Physical Presence Test** (See page 2 of the instructions.)

16   The physical presence test is based on the 12-month period from ▶ .... through ▶ ....
17   Enter your principal country of employment during your tax year. ▶ ....
18   If you traveled abroad during the 12-month period entered on line 16, complete columns **(a)–(f)** below. Exclude travel between foreign countries that did not involve travel on or over international waters, or in or over the United States, for 24 hours or more. If you have no travel to report during the period, enter "Physically present in a foreign country or countries for the entire 12-month period." **Do not** include the income from column **(f)** below in Part IV, but report it on Form 1040.

(a) Name of country (including U.S.)	(b) Date arrived	(c) Date left	(d) Full days present in country	(e) Number of days in U.S. on business	(f) Income earned in U.S. on business (attach computation)

Part IV   **All Taxpayers**

Note: *Enter on lines 19 through 23 all income, including noncash income, you earned and actually or constructively received during your 1999 tax year for services you performed in a foreign country. If any of the foreign earned income received this tax year was earned in a prior tax year, or will be earned in a later tax year (such as a bonus), see the instructions.* **Do not** *include income from line 14, column **(d)**, or line 18, column **(f)**. Report amounts in U.S. dollars, using the exchange rates in effect when you actually or constructively received the income.*

If you are a cash basis taxpayer, report on Form 1040 all income you received in 1999, no matter when you performed the service.

1999 Foreign Earned Income		Amount (in U.S. dollars)
19 Total wages, salaries, bonuses, commissions, etc.	**19**	
20 Allowable share of income for personal services performed (see instructions):		
a In a business (including farming) or profession	**20a**	
b In a partnership. List partnership's name and address and type of income. ▶	**20b**	
21 Noncash income (market value of property or facilities furnished by employer—attach statement showing how it was determined):		
a Home (lodging)	**21a**	
b Meals	**21b**	
c Car	**21c**	
d Other property or facilities. List type and amount. ▶	**21d**	
22 Allowances, reimbursements, or expenses paid on your behalf for services you performed:		
a Cost of living and overseas differential **22a**		
b Family **22b**		
c Education **22c**		
d Home leave **22d**		
e Quarters **22e**		
f For any other purpose. List type and amount. ▶ **22f**		
g Add lines 22a through 22f	**22g**	
23 Other foreign earned income. List type and amount. ▶	**23**	
24 Add lines 19 through 21d, line 22g, and line 23	**24**	
25 Total amount of meals and lodging included on line 24 that is excludable (see instructions)	**25**	
26 Subtract line 25 from line 24. Enter the result here and on line 27 on page 3. This is your **1999 foreign earned income** ▶	**26**	

Form **2555** (1999)

Part V   All Taxpayers

		27	
27	Enter the amount from line 26		

Are you claiming the housing exclusion or housing deduction?
☐ **Yes.** Complete Part VI.
☐ **No.** Go to Part VII.

Part VI   Taxpayers Claiming the Housing Exclusion AND/OR Deduction

28	Qualified housing expenses for the tax year (see instructions)	28	
29	Number of days in your qualifying period that fall within your 1999 tax year (see instructions) . . . . [29] **days**		
30	Multiply $27.03 by the number of days on line 29. If 365 is entered on line 29, enter $9,865.00 here.	30	
31	Subtract line 30 from line 28. If zero or less, do not complete the rest of this part or any of Part IX	31	
32	Enter employer-provided amounts (see instructions) . . . . . . [32]		
33	Divide line 32 by line 27. Enter the result as a decimal (rounded to at least three places), but do not enter more than "1.000"	33	× .
34	**Housing exclusion.** Multiply line 31 by line 33. Enter the result but do not enter more than the amount on line 32. Also, complete Part VIII . . . . ▶	34	

Note: *The housing deduction is figured in Part IX. If you choose to claim the foreign earned income exclusion, complete Parts VII and VIII before Part IX.*

Part VII   Taxpayers Claiming the Foreign Earned Income Exclusion

35	Maximum foreign earned income exclusion	35	$74,000	00
36	• If you completed Part VI, enter the number from line 29. • All others, enter the number of days in your qualifying period that fall within your 1999 tax year (see the instructions for line 29).	[36] **days**		
37	• If line 36 and the number of days in your 1999 tax year (usually 365) are the same, enter "1.000." • Otherwise, divide line 36 by the number of days in your 1999 tax year and enter the result as a decimal (rounded to at least three places).	37	× .	
38	Multiply line 35 by line 37	38		
39	Subtract line 34 from line 27	39		
40	**Foreign earned income exclusion.** Enter the **smaller** of line 38 or line 39. Also, complete Part VIII ▶	40		

Part VIII   Taxpayers Claiming the Housing Exclusion, Foreign Earned Income Exclusion, or Both

41	Add lines 34 and 40	41	
42	Deductions allowed in figuring your adjusted gross income (Form 1040, line 33) that are allocable to the excluded income. See instructions and attach computation	42	
43	Subtract line 42 from line 41. Enter the result here and in parentheses on **Form 1040, line 21.** Next to the amount enter "Form 2555." On Form 1040, subtract this amount from your income to arrive at total income on Form 1040, line 22 . . . . ▶	43	

Part IX   Taxpayers Claiming the Housing Deduction—Complete this part only if **(a)** line 31 is more than line 34 and **(b)** line 27 is more than line 41.

44	Subtract line 34 from line 31	44	
45	Subtract line 41 from line 27	45	
46	Enter the **smaller** of line 44 or line 45	46	

Note: *If line 45 is **more than** line 46 and you could not deduct all of your 1998 housing deduction because of the 1998 limit, use the worksheet on page 4 of the instructions to figure the amount to enter on line 47. Otherwise, go to line 48.*

47	Housing deduction carryover from 1998 (from worksheet on page 4 of the instructions) . . .	47	
48	**Housing deduction.** Add lines 46 and 47. Enter the total here and on Form 1040 to the left of line 32. Next to the amount on Form 1040, enter "Form 2555." Add it to the total adjustments reported on that line . . . . ▶	48	

¶ **106**

Chapter 2

Source-of-Income Rules

¶ 201   IMPORTANCE OF SOURCE RULES

U.S. Persons

The United States taxes U.S. persons on all of their income, from whatever source derived.[1] Therefore, the source of income generally has no effect on the computation of a U.S. person's taxable income. Sourcing can have a significant effect, however, on the computation of a U.S. person's foreign tax credit limitation, which equals the portion of the pre-credit U.S. tax that is attributable to foreign-source income (see Figure 2.1).[2] The limitation establishes a ceiling on the amount of foreign taxes that can offset U.S. taxes and is designed to prevent U.S. persons operating in high-tax foreign countries from offsetting those higher foreign taxes against the U.S. tax on domestic income.

FIGURE 2.1. FOREIGN TAX CREDIT LIMITATION

$$\text{Foreign tax credit limitation} = \text{Pre-credit U.S. tax} \times \frac{\text{Foreign-source taxable income}}{\text{Worldwide taxable income}}$$

The limitation is important to the extent it prevents taxpayers from crediting all of their foreign income taxes. When a U.S. person's creditable foreign taxes are less than the limitation, the cost of paying foreign income taxes is entirely offset by the U.S. tax savings associated

---

[1] Code Sec. 61(a).   [2] Code Sec. 904(a).

with the credit, and, therefore, foreign taxes do not represent an out-of-pocket tax cost for the U.S. person. In contrast, when a U.S. person's creditable foreign taxes exceed the limitation, the noncreditable foreign income taxes increase the U.S. person's total tax burden beyond what it would have been if only the United States had taxed the foreign-source income.[3] Therefore, the computation of the foreign tax credit limitation determines whether foreign taxes have an incremental effect on a U.S. person's worldwide tax costs.

Example 2.1: USAco, a domestic corporation, has taxable income of $100 (all numbers in thousands), all of which is attributable to a foreign branch operation. Assume the U.S. tax rate is 35%.

Case 1—Operating in a low-tax foreign country: If USAco's foreign branch is subject to foreign taxation at a 30% rate, USAco can claim a credit for the entire $30 of foreign taxes paid, as follows.

U.S. tax return		*Foreign tax return*	
Taxable income	$ 100	Taxable income	$ 100
Tax rate	× .35	Tax rate	× .30
Pre-credit tax	$ 35	Foreign tax	$ 30
Foreign tax credit	− 30		
U.S. tax	$ 5		

The total tax burden on USAco's foreign profits is $35 [$5 U.S. tax + $30 foreign tax]. Foreign taxes do not represent an incremental tax cost in this case. For example, if USAco were able to reduce its foreign tax from $30 to $29, the foreign tax savings would be completely offset by an increase in U.S. taxes from $5 to $6.

Case 2—Operating in a high-tax foreign country: If USAco's branch is subject to foreign taxation at a 40% rate, the foreign tax credit limitation (which equals the U.S. tax of $35 on USAco's foreign-source income) will prevent USAco from claiming a credit for $5 of the $40 of foreign taxes paid, as follows.

U.S. tax return		*Foreign tax return*	
Taxable income	$ 100	Taxable income	$ 100
Tax rate	× .35	Tax rate	× .40
Pre-credit tax	$ 35	Foreign tax	$ 40
Foreign tax credit	− 35		
U.S. tax	$ 0		

---

[3] Although creditable foreign taxes in excess of the limitation cannot be taken in the current year, they can be carried back up to two years and carried forward up to five years, and taken as a credit in a year in which the limitation exceeds the amount of creditable foreign taxes. Code Sec. 904(c).

Foreign taxation now increases the total tax burden on USAco's foreign profits from \$35 to \$40, resulting in a \$5 out-of-pocket tax cost.

Foreign taxes in excess of the foreign tax credit limitation are referred to as "excess credits." One strategy for eliminating excess credits is to increase the percentage of total taxable income that is classified as foreign-source for U.S. tax purposes. As a consequence, the rules for sourcing gross income and deductions play an important role in eliminating excess credits. For example, the title passage rule for sourcing income from inventory sales provides U.S. exporters with a significant opportunity for increasing their foreign-source income.[4] By arranging for the passage of title in the importing country, rather than in the United States, export sales will generate foreign-source income and thereby increase the taxpayer's foreign tax credit limitation. Recharacterizing deductions is an equally effective strategy for eliminating excess credits. A deduction reduces a taxpayer's pre-credit U.S. tax, regardless of how it is sourced. However, deductions allocated to foreign-source income also reduce the foreign tax credit limitation. In contrast, deductions allocated to U.S.-source income do not affect the foreign tax credit limitation and, therefore, provide a full U.S. tax benefit.

Foreign Persons

The source rules play a more prominent role in the taxation of foreign persons, since they effectively define the boundaries of U.S. taxation. The United States taxes the gross amount of a foreign person's U.S.-source nonbusiness income at a flat rate of 30%.[5] The United States also taxes foreign persons at graduated rates on the net amount of income effectively connected with the conduct of a U.S. trade or business.[6] Thus, the United States generally taxes the U.S.-source income of foreign persons and generally exempts their foreign-source income. The source of a foreign person's income also is an important issue for potential U.S. withholding agents since they are liable for any withholding taxes that they fail to withhold from a foreign person's U.S.-source nonbusiness income. (U.S. withholding taxes are discussed in Chapter 11.)

¶ 202   SOURCE RULES FOR GROSS INCOME

Introduction

The source rules for gross income are organized by categories of income, such as interest, dividends, personal services income, rentals,

---

[4] Reg. § 1.861-7(c).

[5] Code Secs. 871(a) and 881(a).

[6] Code Secs. 871(b) and 882(a).

royalties, and gains from the disposition of property.[7] Therefore, the first step in the sourcing process is to determine the applicable statutory category. This determination is sometimes ambiguous. For example, the same transaction may exhibit characteristics of both an installment sale and a lease. This distinction is important because a lease generates rental income, which is sourced on the basis of where the property is located, whereas an installment sale results in a gain on the sale as well as interest income, both of which are sourced under different rules. Thus, the same item of income may be allocated between U.S. and foreign sources differently, depending on how it is categorized.

> **Example 2.2:** T is an orchestra conductor. A U.S. record company hired T to conduct various songs at a recording session that took place in the United States. T was compensated based on a percentage of the sales of the recording, which is owned by the record company. Most of the record sales took place outside the United States. Under U.S. tax principles, personal services income is sourced on the basis of where the services were performed, whereas royalty income is sourced on the basis of where the intangible is used. Therefore, T's income is entirely U.S.-source income if it is classified as personal services income, but is mainly foreign-source income if it is classified as royalty income.[8]

In sum, an item of gross income cannot be sourced without first assigning the item to a statutory category, and the appropriate category may be ambiguous.

The best recent example of the importance of determining the applicable category of income are the final regulations issued in September 1998 regarding the classification of transactions involving computer programs. These regulations provide much needed guidance for classifying income from transfers of software. Under these regulations, a transaction involving the transfer of a computer program is classified as one of the following:

(i) a transfer of a copyright right in the computer program,

(ii) a transfer of a copy of the computer program (a copyrighted article),

(iii) the provision of services for the development or modification of the computer program, or

(iv) the provision of know-how relating to computer programming techniques.[9]

---

[7] Code Secs. 861 and 862.
[8] See, for example, *P. Boulez v. Comm'r,* 83 TC 584 (1984).

[9] Reg. § 1.861-18(b)(1).

For example, transactions involving mass-market software generally are classified as transfers of copyrighted articles, that is, a transfer of inventory.[10] Therefore, the source of income derived from the transfer of a copyrighted article is determined under the rules applicable to a sale of tangible personal property if the underlying license is perpetual, and a lease of tangible personal property if the use of the copyrighted article is limited in term.[11] The former is sourced under the title passage rule or the 50-50 method,[12] whereas the latter is sourced under a place of use rule.[13]

Once a taxpayer has determined the appropriate category of income, the next step is to apply the applicable source rule to classify the item of income as either U.S.- or foreign-source. In general, these rules for sourcing income are based on the location of the underlying income-producing property or activity. The general rules for sourcing gross income, which are described in detail in the following pages, are summarized in Table 2.1.

TABLE 2.1. GENERAL RULES FOR SOURCING GROSS INCOME

Type of income	U.S.-source income if:	Foreign-source income if:
Interest income	Debtor is a U.S. resident or a domestic corporation	Debtor is a foreign resident or a foreign corporation
Dividends	Payer is a domestic corporation	Payer is a foreign corporation
Personal services income	Services are performed in U.S.	Services are performed abroad
Rentals and royalties	Property is used in U.S.	Property is used abroad
Gain on sale of real property	Property is located in U.S.	Property is located abroad
Gain on sale of inventory purchased for resale	Title passes in U.S.	Title passes abroad
Gain on sale of inventory manufactured by taxpayer	Income is allocated between U.S. and foreign sources using either the independent factory price method or the 50-50 method	
Gain on sale of securities	Seller is a U.S. resident	Seller is a foreign resident
Gain on sale of depreciable property	Title passes in U.S.[a]	Title passes abroad[a]
Gain on sale of patents and other intangibles	Seller is a U.S. resident[b]	Seller is a foreign resident[b]

[a] Different rules apply to the portion of the gain attributable to prior-year depreciation deductions.
[b] Different rules apply if the intangible is sold for a contingent price, or if a portion of the gain is attributable to prior-year amortization deductions.

For purposes of sourcing income, the United States includes the 50 states and the District of Columbia, but not U.S. possessions.[14] However, for purposes of sourcing income from mines, oil and gas wells, and

---

[10] Reg. § 1.861-18(f)(2).
[11] Reg. § 1.861-18(h), Examples 1 and 2.
[12] Reg. § 1.861-7(c) and § 1.863-3.
[13] Code Secs. 861(a)(4) and 862(a)(4).
[14] Code Sec. 7701(a)(9).

other natural deposits, the United States also includes continental shelf areas.[15]

Interest Income

Interest income is U.S.-source income if the payer is a domestic corporation or U.S. resident, and foreign-source income if the payer is a foreign corporation or a nonresident.[16] U.S.-source interest also includes interest paid by the United States government or any agency or instrumentality thereof (not including U.S. possessions), one of the 50 states or any political subdivisions thereof, or the District of Columbia.[17] For this purpose, the following taxpayers are considered to be U.S. residents:

(i)   U.S. citizens or aliens who, at the time the interest is paid, are residents of the United States;

(ii) a domestic or foreign partnership which at any time during the taxable year was engaged in a U.S. trade or business; and

(iii) a trust or estate whose situs is in the United States.[18]

Factors other than the residence (or the place of incorporation) of the debtor, such as where the debt was incurred, or where the interest is paid, are irrelevant. Although this approach is relatively objective, it can produce dubious results.

> **Example 2.3:** USAco, a domestic corporation, is a retailer of women's apparel. Five years ago, USAco opened a retail store in London, which was structured as an unincorporated branch. USAco financed the store through a $10 million loan from a U.K. bank. The loan is being repaid out of the profits of the U.K. branch. Thus, the acquisition, use, and repayment of funds all occurred abroad. Nevertheless, under the residence-of-debtor source rule, the interest that USAco pays to the U.K. bank is U.S.-source income because USAco is a domestic corporation.

To address these types of situations, Congress enacted an exception that looks beyond the debtor's residence. This look-through rule applies to a domestic corporation or a resident alien individual who, during the preceding three taxable years, derived 80% or more of its gross income from the active conduct of a foreign business.[19] If the payer of interest meets the 80% test, all of the interest income is reclassified as foreign-

---

[15] Code Sec. 638.

[16] Code Secs. 861(a)(1) and 862(a)(1). For this purpose, interest income includes original issue discount, as well as any imputed interest. Reg. § 1.861-2(a)(4).

[17] Reg. § 1.861-2(a)(1).

[18] Reg. § 1.861-2(a)(2). Note that interest paid by a U.S. citizen residing abroad is treated as foreign-source income.

[19] Code Sec. 861(a)(1)(A) and (c)(1). This exception does not apply to partnerships, estates, trusts, or U.S. citizens.

source income, unless the recipient is a related person, in which case only that portion of the interest income equal to the payer's percentage of gross income from an active foreign business is reclassified as foreign-source income.[20]

> **Example 2.4:** The facts are the same as in Example 2.3, except now assume that USAco consistently derives 80% or more of its gross income from sales made at its U.K. store. Because USAco now meets the 80%-active-foreign-business test, all of the interest it pays to the unrelated U.K. bank is foreign-source income.

For purposes of the 80% test, dividend, interest, rental, and royalty income that a domestic corporation receives from a 50%-or-more-owned foreign subsidiary is classified as active foreign business income to the extent the income represents a distribution of earnings that the subsidiary derived from active foreign business activities.[21]

Other major exceptions to the general rules for sourcing interest income include the following:

(i)   Interest received from deposits made with a foreign branch of a domestic corporation or partnership engaged in the commercial banking business is treated as foreign-source income.[22]

(ii) Interest paid by a foreign corporation that is at least 50% owned by U.S. persons is U.S.-source income to the extent the interest payment is attributable to income that the foreign corporation derived from U.S. sources.[23] This exception applies only for purposes of computing the foreign tax credit limitation of a U.S. shareholder or other related person of the U.S.-owned foreign corporation, and is designed to prevent U.S. persons from artificially increasing their foreign tax credit limitation by routing U.S.-source income through a U.S.-owned foreign corporation.

(iii) Interest paid by a U.S. branch of a foreign corporation is treated as if it were paid by a domestic corporation,[24] which generally makes the interest U.S.-source income. This exception is part of the branch profits tax regime, which is a withholding-type tax imposed on a U.S. branch's dividend equivalent amount. The branch profits tax is discussed in Chapter 12.

---

[20] Code Sec. 861(c)(2).

[21] Code Sec. 861(c)(1)(B).

[22] Code Sec. 861(a)(1)(B)(i).

[23] Code Sec. 904(g)(3). This exception does not apply if less than 10% of the U.S.-owned foreign corpora-

tion's earnings are attributable to U.S.-source income. Code Sec. 904(g)(5).

[24] Code Sec. 884(f)(1)(A).

Dividend Income

Dividends are U.S.-source income if the payer is a domestic corporation and foreign-source income if the payer is a foreign corporation.[25] Unlike interest income, there is no look-through rule for determining whether a domestic corporation is distributing earnings that were derived predominantly from foreign sources.[26] However, there is a look-through rule that applies to a foreign corporation if, during the preceding three taxable years, 25% or more of its gross income was effectively connected with the conduct of a U.S. trade or business. If a foreign corporation meets the 25% test, the U.S. source-portion equals the amount of the dividend times the ratio of gross income that was effectively connected with a U.S. trade or business during the three-year test period to the foreign corporation's total gross income for that period.[27]

> **Example 2.5:** FORco, a foreign corporation, derived 40% of its gross income for the three preceding taxable years from a U.S. branch operation. Under the 25% look-through rule, 40% of any dividends that FORco pays are U.S.-source income. The remaining 60% is foreign-source income by reason of FORco's foreign corporation status.

One effect of this rule is to make foreign shareholders of such foreign corporations liable for U.S. withholding taxes on the U.S.-source portion of the dividends. U.S. withholding taxes are not due, however, if the foreign corporation is distributing earnings and profits from a taxable year in which it paid a branch profits tax.[28]

Other major exceptions to the general rule for sourcing dividend income include the following:

(i) Dividends paid by a foreign corporation that is at least 50% owned by U.S. persons are U.S.-source income to the extent the dividend is attributable to income that the foreign corporation derived from U.S. sources.[29] This exception applies only for purposes of computing the foreign tax credit limitation and is designed to prevent U.S. persons from artificially increasing their foreign tax credit limitation by routing U.S.-source income through a U.S.-owned foreign corporation.

(ii) A domestic corporation that claims a dividends-received deduction with respect to a portion of a dividend from a foreign

---

[25] Code Secs. 861(a)(2) and 862(a)(2).

[26] Nevertheless, a portion of the dividends that a foreign person receives from a domestic corporation is exempt from U.S. withholding tax if the payer meets an 80%-active-foreign-business test. Code Secs. 871(i)(2)(B) and 881(d).

[27] Code Sec. 861(a)(2)(B).

[28] Code Sec. 884(e)(3). The branch profits tax is discussed in Chapter 12.

[29] Code Sec. 904(g)(4). This exception does not apply if less than 10% of the U.S.-owned foreign corporation's earnings are attributable to U.S.-source income. Code Sec. 904(g)(5).

¶ 202

corporation must treat that portion of the dividend as U.S.-source income for purposes of computing the foreign tax credit limitation.[30]

(iii) Dividends paid by a domestic corporation that has made a possessions credit election are treated as foreign-source income.[31]

Personal Services Income

Compensation for personal services performed in the United States is U.S.-source income, and compensation for personal services performed abroad is foreign-source income.[32] Personal services income includes salaries, wages, fees, and commissions, including any payments that an employer receives as compensation for services performed by employees or other agents.

Under a *de minimis* rule, income of a nonresident alien that is attributable to U.S. services is recharacterized as foreign-source income if the following requirements are met:

(i)   the nonresident alien is present in the United States for 90 days or less during the taxable year,

(ii) the nonresident alien receives no more than $3,000 for his or her U.S. services, and

(iii) the nonresident alien works as an employee or under contract for either a foreign person who is not engaged in a U.S. trade or business or the foreign office of a U.S. person.[33]

This exception allows nonresident aliens to make short business trips to the United States free of U.S. taxes. Income tax treaties often contain more generous exemptions which allow for longer stays and increase or eliminate the limitation on earnings for business travelers from treaty countries (see Chapter 9).

Another exception applies to the compensation of nonresident aliens engaged in international transportation services. Under this exception, compensation for services performed by a nonresident alien in connection with the individual's temporary presence in the United States as a regular member of a foreign vessel engaged in transportation between the United States and a foreign country or U.S. possession

---

[30] Code Sec. 245(a)(9). A domestic corporation that owns 10% or more of a foreign corporation can claim a dividends-received deduction for a portion of the dividends paid by the foreign corporation out of post-1986 undistributed earnings attributable to either income effectively connected with the conduct of a U.S. trade or business or dividends received from a domestic subsidiary corporation. Code Sec. 245(a)(1). Code Sec. 861(a)(2)(B) further restricts, through a gross-up procedure, the portion of such dividends that can be treated as foreign-source income for purposes of the foreign tax credit limitation.

[31] Code Sec. 861(a)(2)(A). The possessions credit is discussed in Chapter 10.

[32] Code Secs. 861(a)(3) and 862(a)(3).

[33] Code Sec. 861(a)(3). A nonresident alien who meets these requirements also is considered not to be engaged in a U.S. trade or business. Code Sec. 864(b)(1).

is generally treated as foreign-source income that is exempt from U.S. tax.[34]

An allocation issue arises when a taxpayer is paid a lump-sum amount, such as an annual salary, for services performed both within and without the United States. In these situations, the lump-sum amount is apportioned between U.S.- and foreign-source income, typically on the basis of the relative number of days worked in the United States and abroad.[35]

> **Example 2.6:** T lived and worked in the United States throughout the current year, except for a five-week foreign business trip. T received an annual salary of $60,000 for a total of 250 working days, including the 25 days spent working abroad. The foreign-source component of T's $60,000 salary is $6,000 [$60,000 × (25 days ÷ 250 days)], and the remaining $54,000 is U.S.-source income.

When counting days of work, holidays, vacation days, and weekends are generally ignored, unless the taxpayer is on call during those days.[36]

The need to allocate compensation between U.S. and foreign sources also can arise with respect to pension income. Pension income has two basic components: employer contributions for services performed and interest on those contributions. The compensation component is sourced under the general rules for sourcing personal services income. Thus, the compensation component of pension income received by an individual for services performed both within and without the United States must be allocated between U.S.- and foreign-source income based on the ratio of employer contributions made while theretiree was working abroad to the total of all employer contributions made for that retiree.[37]

> **Example 2.7:** T receives an annual pension of $15,000 from a domestic trust, $5,000 of which is attributable to the earnings of the pension plan, and the remaining $10,000 to employer contributions. T's former employer contributed a total of $100,000 to the pension plan on T's behalf, $20,000 of which was contributed while T was on foreign assignments. Assuming the $5,000 of interest income is U.S. source, the foreign-source portion of T's annual pension is $2,000 [$10,000 × ($20,000 ÷ $100,000)].

The exercise of nonqualified stock options also gives rise to personal services income. If the taxpayer performed services both within and

---

[34] Code Sec. 861(a)(3). This exception does not apply for purposes of Code Sec. 79 (group-term life insurance), Code Sec. 105 (amounts received under accident and health plans), and Subchapter D (pertaining to deferred compensation, retirement plans, and other employee benefits).

[35] Reg. § 1.861-4(b)(1).
[36] Reg. § 1.861-4(b)(1)(ii), Example 1.
[37] Rev. Rul. 79-388, 1979-2 CB 270, and Rev. Rul. 79-389, 1979-2 CB 281. The interest component of pension income is sourced based on the residence of the payer. Code Secs. 861(a)(1) and 862(a)(2).

without the United States during the period beginning on the grant date and ending on the exercise date, the resulting compensation must be allocated between U.S.- and foreign-source income based on the relative number of months worked in the United States and abroad from the grant date to the exercise date.[38]

> **Example 2.8:** T is granted a stock option on January 1 of year 1. T exercises the option on June 30 of year 2, and recognizes $30,000 of income. T worked in the United States throughout year 1, but was on a foreign assignment throughout year 2. The foreign-source portion of T's option income is $10,000 [$30,000 × (6 months ÷ 18 months)].

Rental and Royalty Income

Rentals and royalties are U.S.-source income if the property is located or used in the United States and foreign-source income if the property is located or used abroad.[39] All other factors, such as where the property was produced or the place of contract, are ignored.

> **Example 2.9:** A California production company produces a motion picture at its Hollywood studio. The movie is licensed for use in, among other places, London, England. Royalties received for the presentation of the movie in London theaters are foreign-source income, even though the movie was produced entirely in the United States.

The source of royalty income depends not only on where the intangible is actually used, but also on whether the licensee is legally entitled touse, and legally protected in using, the intangible in that country.[40] For this purpose, an intangible includes any patent, copyright, secret process or formula, goodwill, trademark, trade brand, franchise, or other like property.[41]

The place of use of personal property may be both within and without the United States, in which case the taxpayer must apportion the rental income between U.S. and foreign sources. This apportionment may be done on the basis of time, mileage, or some other appropriate base.

> **Example 2.10:** The taxpayer leases testing equipment to a manufacturer for a flat fee. The lessee uses the equipment at manufacturing plants located both in the United States and abroad. Therefore, the lessor must apportion its rental income between

---

[38] Reg. § 1.911-3(e)(4).

[39] Code Secs. 861(a)(4) and 862(a)(4). Special source rules apply to rental income from railroad rolling stock, as well as rental income from the use of a vessel, aircraft, or shipping container. See Code Secs. 861(e) and 863(c), respectively.

[40] See, for example, Rev. Rul. 84-78, 1984-1 CB 173.

[41] Code Sec. 861(a)(4).

U.S. and foreign sources, probably on the basis of the relative amount of time the lessee uses the equipment at its U.S. and foreign plants.

Income from the Disposition of Property

Real property. A gain on the sale or exchange of a U.S. real property interest is U.S.-source income, whereas a gain on the sale or exchange of real property located abroad is foreign-source income.[42] All other factors, including where the selling activities took place, are ignored. For example, a gain on the sale of a U.S. office building to foreign investors is U.S.-source income, even if all of the related sale activities take place abroad.

A U.S. real property interest includes the following types of interests located within the United States or the U.S. Virgin Islands: land, buildings, other inherently permanent structures, mines, wells, and other natural deposits, growing crops and timber, and personal property associated with the use of real property (such as mining and farming equipment). U.S. real property interests also include shares of a corporation which is, or was, a U.S. real property holding corporation at any time during the five-year period preceding the disposition. A U.S. real property holding corporation is any corporation that holds U.S. real property with a market value equal to 50% or more of the market value of all the corporation's real property (U.S. and foreign) plus any other property used in a trade or business.[43]

Personal property—General rule. Personal property includes a wide variety of assets, including stocks and securities, inventories, machinery and equipment, and intangibles such as patents, trademarks, and copyrights. As a general rule, a gain on the sale of personal property is U.S.-source income if the taxpayer is a U.S. resident and foreign-source income if the taxpayer is a nonresident.[44] However, there are numerous exceptions to this residence-of-seller rule, including special source rules for depreciable property, intangibles, inventories, and stock of a foreign affiliate. As a consequence, the residence-of-seller source rule applies primarily to security sales.

Example 2.11: T, a citizen and resident of the Republic of Ireland, sells at a gain 100 shares of USAco, a U.S. utility company whose shares are traded on the New York Stock Exchange. Even though USAco is a domestic corporation that conducts business operations only within the United States, T's gain is nevertheless treated as foreign-source income because T is a nonresident.

---

[42] Code Secs. 861(a)(5) and 862(a)(5).

[43] Code Sec. 897(c) and Reg. § 1.897-1(b). The definition of U.S. real property interests is discussed in more detail in Chapter 11.

[44] Code Sec. 865(a). For this purpose, the term "sale" includes an exchange or any other disposition. Code Sec. 865(i)(2).

¶ 202

For purposes of this source rule, the following taxpayers are considered to be U.S. residents:

(i)   a domestic corporation,

(ii) a U.S. citizen or resident alien who does not have a tax home in a foreign country,

(iii) a nonresident alien who has a tax home in the United States, and

(iv) a trust or estate whose situs is in the United States.[45]

A nonresident is any person other than a U.S. resident.[46] An individual's tax home is his or her principal or regular place of business, provided that the individual is not treated as having a tax home in a foreign country during any period in which his or her abode is in the United States.[47]

One implication of these residency rules is that a gain realized by a U.S. citizen or resident alien who has a foreign tax home is treated as foreign-source income, which has the beneficial side effect of increasing the taxpayer's foreign tax credit limitation. However, if the taxpayer's gain is not subject to foreign tax at a rate of 10% or more, the gain is treated as U.S.-source income, despite the taxpayer's foreign tax home.[48] Another special rule applies to U.S. residents who maintain an office or other fixed base in a foreign country. If a sale is attributable to that foreign office, and the gain on the sale is subject to foreign tax at a rate of 10% or more, then the gain is treated as foreign-source income,despite the taxpayer's U.S. residency. This exception does not apply to sales of intangibles for a contingent price, inventory, depreciable personal property, goodwill, or stock of certain foreign affiliates.[49] For purposes of this exception, income is attributable to a foreign office if the office is a material factor in making the sale, and the office regularly engages in these types of sales activities.[50] A similar exception applies to nonresidents who maintain an office or other fixed base in the United States. If a sale is attributable to that U.S. office, the gain is treated as U.S.-source income, despite the taxpayer's foreign residency. This exception applies to all types of personal property, except for inventory that a taxpayer sells for use, disposition, or consumption outside the United States, where the taxpayer has a foreign office which materially participates in the sale.[51]

---

[45] Code Sec. 865(g)(1)(A). In the case of a sale of property by a partnership, the determination of residency generally is made at the partner level. Code Sec. 865(i)(5).

[46] Code Sec. 865(g)(1)(B).

[47] Code Sec. 911(d)(3) and Reg. § 1.911-2(b). An individual's abode is in the United States if that is where his or her economic, social, and personal ties are closest. See, for example, *J.T. Lemay v. Comm'r*, 837 F2d 681 (5th Cir. 1988), aff'g 53 TCM 862 (1987); and *Lansdown v. Comm'r*, 68 TCM 680 (1994).

[48] Code Sec. 865(g)(2).

[49] Code Sec. 865(e)(1).

[50] Code Secs. 865(e)(3) and 864(c)(5)(b).

[51] Code Sec. 865(e)(2).

Depreciable personal property. Depreciation deductions reduce a taxpayer's basis in the depreciable property and thereby increase the gain computed on the disposition of that property. The portion of the gain on the disposition of depreciable personal property that is attributable to prior depreciation deductions is treated as having the same source as the related deductions.[52] For example, if the prior depreciation deductions offset both U.S.- and foreign-source income in prior years, the depreciation recapture portion of the gain is generally allocated between U.S.- and foreign-source income in the same proportion as the prior deductions. When the total gain exceeds the prior depreciation deductions (i.e., the property has appreciated in value since its acquisition), that appreciation is sourced using the rules applicable to inventories.[53] This generally means the gain is sourced based upon where title to the property passes from seller to buyer.[54]

Example 2.12: During the current year, USAco (a domestic corporation) sold a machine to a Canadian company for $230,000, with title passing to the buyer upon delivery in Canada. USAco purchased the machine several years ago for $200,000, and took $120,000 of depreciation deductions on the machine, all of which was apportioned to U.S.-source income. Therefore, USAco's adjusted basis in the machine is $80,000 [$200,000 original cost − $120,000 of accumulated depreciation], and the total gain on the sale of the machine is $150,000 [$230,000 sales price − $80,000 adjusted basis]. The $120,000 depreciation recapture portion of the gain is U.S.-source income, whereas the $30,000 of appreciation is foreign-source income.

Intangibles. For purposes of the source-of-income rules, an intangible is any patent, copyright, secret process or formula, goodwill, trademark, trade brand, franchise, or other like property.[55] As with depreciable personal property, a gain on the disposition of an intangible may be attributable in whole or in part to prior amortization deductions. The portion of the gain which is attributable to prior amortization deductions is treated as having the same source as the related deductions, determined using the same tracing rule applicable to depreciation on tangible personal property.[56] Unlike tangible personal property, however, the inventory source rules do not apply to any

---

[52] Code Sec. 865(c)(1). In determining whether prior depreciation deductions were allocated to U.S.- or foreign-source income, a special rule applies to property used predominantly inside or outside the United States. All of the depreciation related to such property is deemed to have been allocated to either U.S.- or foreign-source income, depending on the location of the property's predominant use. Code Sec. 865(c)(3)(B). For an example, see Temp. Reg. § 1.865-1T(e), Example 1. This exception does not apply to property described in Code Sec. 168(g)(4).

[53] Code Sec. 865(c)(2).

[54] Code Sec. 865(b) and Reg. § 1.861-7(c). An exception applies if a foreign resident maintains an office or other fixed base in the United States, and the U.S. office is a material factor in making the sale and regularly engages in these types of sales activities. In such cases, the gain on the sale of depreciable property is treated as U.S.-source income. Code Sec. 865(e)(2) and (3).

[55] Code Sec. 865(d)(2).

[56] Code Sec. 865(d)(4)(A).

gain in excess of the depreciation recapture income.[57] Instead, any gain attributable to appreciation in the value of the intangible is sourced using the residence-of-seller rule, assuming the intangible is sold for a price that is not contingent on its productivity, use, or disposition.[58] If the intangible is sold for a price that is contingent on its productivity, use, or disposition, then the appreciation portion of the gain is sourced as if it were a royalty payment.[59] As discussed above, royalties are sourced based on the location of the actual use of, or the right to use, the underlying intangible.[60] A special rule also applies to a gain on the disposition of goodwill, which is treated as arising from sources within the country in which the goodwill was generated.[61]

Sale of stock of a foreign affiliate. Under the general rule, a U.S. resident treats a gain on the sale of stock as U.S.-source income.[62] However, if certain requirements are met, a U.S. resident can treat a gain on the sale of the stock of a foreign affiliate as foreign-source income, which has the beneficial side effect of increasing the taxpayer's foreign tax credit limitation (albeit in the passive basket). This exception applies if the following requirements are met:

(i)   the U.S. resident sells stock in an affiliate that is a foreign corporation,

(ii) the sale occurs in a foreign country in which the affiliate is engaged in the active conduct of a trade or business, and

(iii) the affiliate derived more than 50% of its gross income during the preceding three taxable years from the active conduct of a trade or business in such foreign country.[63]

Income from the Sale of Inventories

For purposes of the source-of-income rules, inventory includes personal property (and not real property) that is held by the taxpayer primarily for sale to customers in the ordinary course of business.[64] Developing an accurate, yet simple, source rule for income from the sale of inventories is a difficult task, given the complex nature of the underlying income-producing activities. For example, income from the sale of inventory by a wholesaler or retailer may be attributable to a number of geographically dispersed economic activities, such as

---

[57] Code Sec. 865(d)(4)(B).

[58] Code Sec. 865(d)(1)(A).

[59] Code Sec. 865(d)(1)(B).

[60] Code Secs. 861(a)(4) and 862(a)(4). Another special rule applies if a foreign resident maintains an office or other fixed base in the United States, and the U.S. office is a material factor in making the sale and regularly engages in these types of sales activities. In such cases, the gain on the sale of the intangible is treated as U.S.-source income. Code Sec. 865(e)(2) and (3).

[61] Code Sec. 865(d)(3).

[62] Code Sec. 865(a).

[63] Code Sec. 865(f). For this purpose, an affiliate is a member of the same affiliated group as defined in Code Sec. 1504(a), but without regard to Code Sec. 1504(b). Code Sec. 865(i)(4). In addition, for purposes of satisfying requirements (ii) and (iii), the U.S. resident can elect to treat the affiliate and all the corporations which are wholly owned, directly or indirectly, by the affiliate as one corporation.

[64] Code Secs. 865(i)(1) and 1221(1).

purchasing, marketing, and distribution. The problem of tracing inventory profits to the underlying income-producing activities is more severe for manufacturers. In addition to the functions outlined above for retailers and wholesalers, manufacturers also engage in research and development, production, and follow-up service activities. One way in which U.S. lawmakers have sought to address these complexities is to promulgate separate source rules for inventory purchased for resale, as opposed to inventory manufactured by the taxpayer.

Inventory purchased for resale. Gross income from the sale of inventory that the taxpayer purchased for resale is sourced on the basis of where the sale occurs.[65] Therefore, such income is U.S.-source income if the sale occurs within the United States, and foreign-source income if the sale occurs abroad. Other functions performed by a wholesaler or retailer, such as purchasing and distribution, are ignored. In addition, despite the multifaceted nature of selling activities, the place of sale is determined solely by where title to the goods passes from the seller to the buyer.[66]

> **Example 2.13:** USAco, a domestic corporation, is an independent broker that purchases used commercial aircraft from U.S. airlines for resale abroad. During the current year, USAco purchased 20 planes from a regional airline based in Texas and then resold the planes to a Spanish airline. The Spanish airline first learned about USAco's services at a trade show held in Las Vegas, Nevada. The sales agreement between USAco and the Spanish airline was negotiated and signed in Florida. Title to the airplanes passed in Spain upon delivery at the Madrid airport. Even though all of the selling activities, including solicitation, negotiation, and closing, took place within the United States, the entire profit from the sale of the airplanes is foreign-source income because title passed abroad.

Passing title at the destination point rather than at the shipping point generally is not of great economic consequence to a U.S. exporter, since it is a common business practice to insure shipments and obtain letters of credit from offshore customers. Therefore, the title passage rule provides U.S. exporters with a significant opportunity for increasing their foreign tax credit limitation. Foreign title passage has some potential disadvantages, however, such as the burden of satisfying local customs requirements and the possibility of creating nexus in certain developing countries.

An exception to the title passage rule prevents nonresidents from avoiding U.S. tax by passing title abroad on sales to U.S. customers.

---

[65] Code Secs. 861(a)(6) and 862(a)(6).

[66] Reg. §1.861-7(c). For U.S. export sales, title passes abroad if the goods are shipped F.O.B., place of destination, and in the United States if the goods are shipped F.O.B., place of shipment. For U.S. import sales, title passes abroad if the goods are shipped F.O.B., place of shipment, and in the United States if the goods are shipped F.O.B., place of destination.

This exception applies if a foreign resident maintains an office or other fixed base in the United States, and the U.S. office is a material factor in making the sale and regularly engages in these types of sales activities. Income from such sales is treated as U.S.-source income, unless the inventory is sold for use, disposition, or consumption outside the United States, and a foreign office of the taxpayer materially participates in the sale.[67]

Inventory manufactured by taxpayer. In contrast to the all-or-nothing approach of the title passage rule used to source income from the sale of inventory purchased for resale, income from the sale of inventory that the taxpayer produces is allocated between U.S. and foreign-source income.[68] Income from the sale of inventory produced in the United States and sold abroad (or vice-versa) is partitioned into its U.S. and foreign components using one of three methods: the 50-50 method, the independent factory price method, or the taxpayer's own books and records.[69] Taxpayers are generally required to use the 50-50 method.[70]

The 50-50 method is analogous to the apportionment formulas used to source a corporation's income for state income tax purposes. Under the 50-50 method, a U.S. manufacturer apportions 50% of the gross profit from export sales based on a sales factor, and the other 50% based on a property factor.[71] The sales factor equals the ratio of the gross amount of export sales that are classified as foreign (using the title passage rule) to the gross amount of all export sales.[72] The property factor equals the ratio of the average adjusted basis of the taxpayer's production assets located abroad to the average adjusted basis of the taxpayer's production assets everywhere. The average adjusted basis is computed by averaging the adjusted basis of production assets at the beginning and end of the taxable year. Production assets include tangible and intangible assets owned by the taxpayer and directly used to produce inventory sold abroad (e.g., a factory building, machinery and equipment, and patents). Production assets do not include accounts receivables, intangibles not related to the production of inventory (e.g., marketing intangibles, including trademarks and customer lists), transportation assets, warehouses, the inventory

---

[67] Code Sec. 865(e)(2) and (3). Another exception applies to income from the sale of unprocessed timber which is softwood and which was cut from an area within the United States. Such income is treated as U.S.-source income, regardless of where title passes. Code Sec. 865(b).

[68] Code Sec. 863(b). Production means an activity that creates, fabricates, manufactures, extracts, processes, cures, or ages inventory. Reg. § 1.863-3(c)(1)(i)(A).

[69] Reg. § 1.863-3(a)(1) and (b). Special rules apply to the sale of goods manufactured in the United States and sold in a U.S. possession (or vice versa). Reg. § § 1.863-3(f) and 1.863-3A(c).

[70] Reg. § 1.863-3(b)(1). These rules apply to taxable years beginning after December 30, 1996. However, taxpayers may apply these rules for taxable years beginning after July 11, 1995, and on or before December 30, 1996. For taxable years beginning before December 30, 1996, see Reg. § § 1.863-3A and 1.863-3AT. Reg. § 1.863-3(h).

[71] Reg. § 1.863-3(b)(1) and (c).

[72] Reg. § 1.863-3(c)(2).

¶ 202

itself, raw materials, or work-in-process. In addition, production assets do not include cash or other liquid assets (including working capital), investment assets, prepaid expenses, or stock of a subsidiary.[73]

If a U.S. manufacturer's foreign production assets are insignificant or nonexistent, and the taxpayer passes title abroad on all foreign sales, the 50-50 method will allocate roughly 50% of the taxpayer's gross profit from export sales to foreign-source income.[74]

> **Example 2.14:** USAco, a domestic corporation, manufactures computers at its U.S. plant at a cost of $1,200 per unit. USAco markets its computers in Mexico through a branch sales office located in Mexico City. During the year, USAco sold 1,000 computers through its Mexican branch at a price of $2,000 per unit. Therefore, USAco realized a gross profit of $800,000 [1,000 units × ($2,000 sales price − $1,200 cost of goods sold)] from its Mexican sales. USAco passed title abroad on all of its Mexican sales. USAco has no production assets located abroad, whereas the average value of its U.S. production assets is $5 million. Therefore, the sales factor apportions $400,000 of income to foreign sources [50% × $800,000 × ($2 million of foreign export sales ÷ $2 million of total export sales)], and the property factor apportions no income to foreign sources [50% × $800,000 × ($0 of foreign production assets ÷ $5 million of production assets everywhere)]. In sum, the foreign-source portion of USAco's export gross profit is $400,000, and the remaining $400,000 is U.S. source income.

After a taxpayer has apportioned the gross profit from export sales based on the sales and property factors, the taxpayer then apportions any related deductions between U.S. and foreign source income on a pro rata basis.[75]

If the taxpayer regularly sells part of its output to independent distributors such that an independent factory price can be fairly established, the taxpayer may elect to use the independent factory price method.[76] The 50-50 method generally will classify more of a U.S. manufacturer's export profits as foreign source income than will the independent factory price method. Therefore, it will typically not be advantageous to elect the independent factory price method. A tax-

---

[73] Reg. § 1.863-3(c)(1). Production assets used to produce inventory sold both domestically and abroad are included in the formula based on the ratio of export sales of the related inventory to sales everywhere of that inventory.

[74] The regulations are generally less favorable for exporters of natural resources, which must apply a special export terminal rule. Reg. § 1.863-1(b). This rule applies to sales outside the United States of products derived from the ownership or operation of any farm, mine, oil or gas well, other natural deposit, or timber within the United States. Reg. § 1.863-1(b)(1). However, any income from the sale of unprocessed timber which is softwood and was cut from an area within the United States is always treated as U.S. source income. Code Sec. 865(b).

[75] Reg. § 1.863-3(d). An exception applies to research and experimental expenditures.

[76] Reg. § 1.863-3(b)(2).

payer may also elect to use the books and records method, but only if the taxpayer receives advance permission from the IRS.[77]

Other Types of Income

Currency exchange gains and losses. Special source-of-income rules apply to a defined group of transactions referred to as "Section 988 transactions." Section 988 transactions include the following:

(i) dispositions of a nonfunctional currency, and

(ii) debt instruments, receivables and payables, and currency forward, futures, and option contracts, where the amount the taxpayer is entitled to receive, or required to pay, is denominated in (or determined by reference to) a nonfunctional currency.[78]

An example of a Section 988 transaction is a U.S. company that makes a sale on account to a foreign customer where the sales price is denominated in the customer's local currency.

Exchange gains and losses attributable to a Section 988 transaction are sourced by reference to the residence of the taxpayer or the qualified business unit of the taxpayer (e.g., a foreign branch or subsidiary) on whose books the underlying asset, liability, or item of income or expense is properly reflected.[79] For purposes of this source rule, a U.S. resident is any corporation, partnership, trust, or estate that is a U.S. person, as well as any individual who has a tax home in the United States.[80] An individual's tax home is his or her principal or regular place of business, provided that an individual is not treated as having a tax home in a foreign country during any period in which the taxpayer's abode is in the United States.[81] A foreign resident is any corporation, partnership, trust, or estate that is a foreign person, as well as any individual who has a tax home in a foreign country.[82] The residence of a qualified business unit of the taxpayer is the country in which the qualified business unit's principal place of business is located.[83]

A different source rule applies if the currency exchange gain or loss arises as a result of a branch remittance. If a foreign branch that has a functional currency other than the U.S. dollar remits its earnings to the

---

[77] Reg. § 1.863-3(b)(3).

[78] Code Sec. 988(c)(1).

[79] Code Sec. 988(a)(3)(A). However, any exchange gain or loss realized by a foreign person from the conduct of a U.S. trade or business is treated as U.S.-source income. Reg. § 1.988-4(c).

[80] Code Sec. 988(a)(3)(B)(i)(I) and (II).

[81] Code Sec. 911(d)(3) and Reg. § 1.911-2(b). An individual's abode is in the United States if that is where his or her economic, social, and personal ties

are closest (see, for example, *J.T. Lemay v. Comm'r*, 837 F2d 681 (5th Cir. 1988), *aff'g* 53 TCM 862 (1987)); and *Lansdown v. Comm'r*, 68 TCM 680 (1994). An individual who does not have a tax home is treated as a U.S. resident if the individual is a U.S. citizen or resident alien, and a foreign resident if the individual is not a U.S. citizen or resident alien. Code Sec. 988(a)(3)(B)(i).

[82] Code Sec. 988(a)(3)(B)(i)(I) and (III).

[83] Code Sec. 988(a)(3)(B)(ii).

U.S. home office, then the taxpayer must recognize a currency exchange gain or loss equal to the difference between the dollar value of the remittance and the taxpayer's basis in the distributed earnings.[84] In such cases, the resulting gain or loss has the same source as the income giving rise to the branch's distributed earnings.[85] In a similar vein, if a U.S. shareholder receives a distribution from a foreign corporation of earnings previously taxed as either a Subpart F inclusion or a qualified electing fund inclusion, the U.S. shareholder must recognize a currency exchange gain or loss equal to the difference between the dollar value of the distribution and the U.S. shareholder's basis in the distributed earnings.[86] Such gains have the same source as the associated Subpart F or qualified electing fund inclusion.[87]

See Chapter 8 for a more detailed discussion of currency exchange gains and losses.

Insurance underwriting income. Insurance income generally is sourced on the basis of where the insured risk is located. Therefore, premiums from issuing or reinsuring any insurance or annuity contract in connection with property located in the United States, a liability arising out of an activity located in the United States or in connection with the lives or health of residents of the United States, is treated as U.S.-source income.[88] Under an exception, U.S.-source insurance income also includes income from insuring risks located outside the United States if, as a result of an arrangement, another corporation receives a substantially equal amount of premiums for insuring risks located within the United States.[89] Any other type of underwriting income is treated as foreign-source income.[90]

International communications income. International communications income includes income derived from the transmission of communications or data from the United States to a foreign country or from a foreign country to the United States.[91] Examples include transmitting telephone calls or other data, images, or sounds by satellite or underwater cable. The source rule for international communications income varies depending on whether the taxpayer is a U.S. person or a foreign person. In the case of a U.S. person, 50% of international communications income is treated as U.S.-source income and the other 50% is treated as foreign-source income.[92] In contrast, a foreign person generally treats all international communications income as foreign-source income, unless that person maintains an office or other fixed place of business within the United States, in which case any income

---

[84] Prop. Reg. § 1.987-2.
[85] Code Sec. 987(3)(B).
[86] Code Sec. 986(c)(1).
[87] Code Sec. 986(c)(1).
[88] Code Sec. 861(a)(7)(A).

[89] Code Sec. 861(a)(7)(B).
[90] Code Sec. 862(a)(7).
[91] Code Sec. 863(e)(2).
[92] Code Sec. 863(e)(1)(A).

attributable to that fixed place of business is treated as U.S.-source income.[93]

Scholarships and fellowships. Scholarships and fellowships received by someone who is not required to perform services for the payer are sourced based upon the residence of the payer. Thus, an award is treated as U.S.- source income if it is made by a U.S. citizen or resident, a domestic corporation, the United States (or any instrumentality or agency thereof), one of the 50 states (or any political subdivision thereof), or the District of Columbia. On the other hand, awards made by a nonresident alien, a foreign corporation, a foreign government (or any instrumentality, agency, or political subdivision thereof), or an international agency, are treated as foreign-source income.[94]

Social security benefits. U.S. social security benefits are considered U.S.-source income,[95] regardless of whether the recipient spent his or her employment years working in the United States or abroad.

Space and ocean activities. Space and ocean activities include any activity conducted in space, any activity conducted on or under water not within the jurisdiction of a foreign country or the United States and any activity conducted in Antarctica.[96] Examples include fishing and mining activities undertaken on the high seas. Space and ocean activities are unique in the sense that they do not take place within the territory of any country. Thus, income from space and ocean activities is treated as U.S.-source income if derived by a U.S. person and as foreign-source income if derived by a foreign person.[97] Space and ocean activities do not include any activity that gives rise to transportation income or international communications income, or any activity connected with a mine, oil and gas well, or other natural deposit in a continental shelf area.[98]

Transportation income. Transportation income includes income derived from the use or lease of a vessel or aircraft (including any container used in connection with a vessel or aircraft) or from the performance of services directly related to the use of a vessel or aircraft.[99] Income from transportation that both begins and ends within the United States is treated as U.S.-source income.[100] If the transportation begins in the United States and ends abroad, or begins abroad and ends in the United States, then 50% of the resulting income is treated as U.S.-source income and the other 50% is treated as foreign-

---

[93] Code Sec. 863(e)(1)(B).

[94] Reg. § 1.863-1(d). An exception applies if a nonresident alien receives an award for study or research activities to be conducted outside the United States. Such grants are treated as foreign-source income, irrespective of the residence of the payer.

[95] Code Sec. 861(a)(8).

[96] Code Sec. 863(d)(2)(A).

[97] Code Sec. 863(d)(1).

[98] Code Sec. 863(d)(2)(B).

[99] Code Sec. 863(c)(3). Transportation income does not include income derived from transporting passengers or property between the United States and a foreign country by truck, rail, or bus, which is sourced under different rules (see Reg. § 1.863-4).

[100] Code Sec. 863(c)(1).

¶ 202

source income.[101] This rule generally does not apply to transportation income derived from personal services performed by the taxpayer.[102] Thus, flight and ship personnel source their compensation using the source rule for personal services income.

Distributive Share of Income from a Pass-Through Entity

In the case of partnerships, limited liability companies, and S corporations, the source of income usually is determined at the entity level, and that source characterization carries over to the partners, members, or shareholders in their distributive shares of income.[103] For example, a partner's distributive share of a partnership's foreign-source dividend income is foreign-source income to the partner. The same principle applies to trusts. Thus, distributions from a trust have the same character in the hands of the beneficiary as in the hands of the trust.[104] An exception applies to the sale of personal property by a partnership, in which case the applicable source rule is applied at the partner level rather than the partnership level.[105]

¶ 203   SOURCE RULES FOR DEDUCTIONS

Introduction

Sourcing a taxpayer's gross income will be sufficient in some situations. For example, there is no need to source the deductions of a foreign person whose only connection to the United States is as a passive investor deriving U.S.-source nonbusiness income, since such income is taxed on a gross basis through a flat rate withholding tax.[106] In other cases, however, the operative tax attribute is net taxable income, which necessitates the sourcing of items of both gross income and deduction. For example, a foreign corporation with a branch office in the United States is taxed on the net amount of income effectively connected with the conduct of that U.S. trade or business.[107] Similarly, a U.S. person's foreign tax credit limitation is based on the ratio of net taxable income from foreign sources to net taxable income from all sources.[108]

In computing taxable income from sources within (or without) the United States, the taxpayer is allowed deductions for expenses and losses directly related to either U.S.- or foreign-source gross income, as well as a ratable portion of expenses and losses that are not definitely related to any specific item of gross income.[109] The taxpayer makes

---

[101] Code Sec. 863(c)(2)(A). The source of transportation income may be of little or no consequence to a foreign person since both the Code and numerous tax treaties provide exemptions for income from the international operation of a vessel or aircraft. See, for example, Code Secs. 872(b) and 883(a).

[102] Code Sec. 863(c)(2)(B).

[103] Code Secs. 702(b) and 1366(b).

[104] Code Secs. 652(b) and 662(b).

[105] Code Sec. 865(i)(5).

[106] Code Secs. 871(a) and 881(a).

[107] Code Sec. 882(a).

[108] Code Sec. 904(a).

[109] Code Secs. 861(b) and 862(b).

these determinations through a two-step process referred to as "allocation and apportionment."

Allocation

The first step in sourcing a deduction is to allocate it to a related income-producing activity or class of gross income.[110] Examples ofpotential classes of gross income include compensation for services (including fees and commissions), gross income derived from business, gains derived from dealings in property, interest, rents, royalties, and dividends.[111] A deduction is related, and therefore allocable, to a class of gross income if it is incurred as a result of, or incident to, the activity or property from which the gross income is derived. Therefore, the allocation rules emphasize the factual relationship between a deduction and a class of gross income. The classes of gross income are not predetermined, but instead, are determined on the basis of the deductions to be allocated. Although most deductions are definitely related to a specific class of gross income, some deductions are related to all gross income.[112] Examples include overhead, general and administrative, and supervisory expenses. These deductions ordinarily are allocated to a class consisting of all of the taxpayer's gross income.[113]

Apportionment

The second step in sourcing a deduction is to apportion the deduction between U.S.- and foreign-source gross income.[114] This is accomplished by using an apportionment base that reflects, to a reasonably close extent, the factual relationship between the deduction and the gross income. Examples of potential apportionment bases include gross income, gross receipts or sales, units sold, cost of goods sold, profit contributions, expenses incurred, assets used, salaries paid, space utilized, and time spent. The effect of the resulting apportionment on the tax liability and the related record-keeping burden are both considered when determining whether or not the apportionment is sufficiently precise.[115]

Unfortunately, the relationship between deductions and U.S. and foreign operations often is ambiguous. For example, in concept, a U.S. exporter should apportion its marketing expenses between U.S. and foreign sources based upon the relative amounts of marketing resources expended to generate U.S., as opposed to foreign, sales. However, often it is unclear which, if any, of the conventional apportionment bases,

---

[110] Reg. § 1.861-8(a)(2).

[111] Reg. § 1.861-8(a)(3).

[112] Reg. § 1.861-8(b)(1) and (b)(2).

[113] Temp. Reg. § 1.861-8T(b)(3). If the taxpayer incurring the overhead-type expenses is a corporation that is a member of an affiliated group, the expense is

allocated and apportioned as if all members of the group were a single corporation. Code Sec. 864(e)(6) and Temp. Reg. § 1.861-14T.

[114] Reg. § 1.861-8(a)(2).

[115] Temp. Reg. § 1.861-8T(c)(1).

such as unit sales, gross sales, or gross margin, accurately reflects this relation. Moreover, if the mix of products sold in the United States differs from the mix of products sold abroad, the use of different apportionment bases will lead to different results. For example, if U.S. sales involve low-volume, high-margin products, while foreign sales involve high-volume, low-margin products, a smaller proportion ofmarketing expenses will be apportioned to foreign sources if gross profit, as opposed to gross sales, is used as an apportionment base.

> **Example 2.15:** USAco is a domestic corporation that sells its products both in the United States and abroad. During the current year, USAco had $10 million of sales and a gross profit of $5 million, and incurred $1 million of selling, general, and administrative (SG&A) expenses. USAco's $10 million of sales included $6 million of foreign sales and $4 million of domestic sales. On the other hand, because USAco's domestic sales generally involved higher-margin products than its foreign sales, USAco's gross profit of $5 million was split 50-50 between U.S. and foreign sources. Thus, if USAco uses gross profit as an apportionment base, it would apportion $500,000 of SG&A expenses to foreign-source income [50% × $1 million of SG&A expenses], as opposed to $600,000 if gross sales is used as an apportionment base [($6 million of foreign sales ÷ $10 million of total sales) × $1 million of SG&A expenses].

The selection of an apportionment base also is impacted by the type of records that the taxpayer maintains.

> **Example 2.16:** The facts are the same as in Example 2.15, except now assume that USAco's SG&A expenses of $1 million consist of the president's salary of $250,000, the sales manager's salary of $100,000, and other SG&A expenses of $650,000. Also assume that USAco's president and sales manager maintain time records which indicate that the president devoted 30% of her time to foreign operations and 70% to domestic operations, while the sales manager devoted 40% of her time to foreign operations and 60% to domestic operations. USAco should now apportion the salaries of the president and sales manager on the basis of time spent and apportion the other SG&A expenses on the basis of gross profit. Therefore, USAco apportions to foreign-source income $75,000 of the president's salary [30% × $250,000], $40,000 of the sales manager's salary [40% × $100,000], and $325,000 of the remaining SG&A expenses [50% × $650,000], for a total of $440,000 of SG&A expenses apportioned to foreign-source income.[116]

---

[116] Compare Reg. § 1.861-8(g), Examples (19) and (20).

Specialized Apportionment Rules

Interest expense. All income-producing activities require some degree of funding, and a taxpayer often has considerable flexibility as to the source and use of funds. For example, a multinational corporation could use the proceeds from a second mortgage on a U.S. factory toacquire an office building located abroad. Moreover, when money is borrowed for a specific purpose, such borrowing generally will free other funds for other purposes. Because money is fungible, interest expense is assumed to be related to all of the taxpayer's activities and property, regardless of the specific purpose of the borrowing. Thus, interest expense is allocated to all of the taxpayer's gross income.[117]

Interest expense is apportioned between U.S.- and foreign-source income using the relative value of U.S. and foreign assets as an apportionment base.[118] For example, if 20% of a taxpayer's assets are foreign in nature, then that taxpayer must apportion 20% of its interest expense to foreign-source income. For this purpose, an asset is characterized as U.S. or foreign based upon whether the asset produces U.S.- or foreign-source income.[119] For example, inventory is characterized as a foreign asset to the extent that inventory sales give rise to foreign-source income.[120] A taxpayer may elect to determine the value of its assets on the basis of either their tax book values or their fair market values.[121] Normally, the asset figures for a taxable year are the averages of the asset values (book or market) at the beginning and the end of the year.[122]

Numerous other special rules apply. For example, tax-exempt assets are not taken into account when computing a taxpayer's U.S. versus foreign assets.[123] In addition, for purposes of computing asset values, a taxpayer's basis in any nonaffiliated, 10%-or-more-owned corporation is adjusted for changes in that company's earnings and profits over time.[124] Another complication is a provision that requires a domestic corporation to specifically allocate certain interest expense deductions against foreign-source interest income derived from a controlled foreign corporation in computing its foreign tax credit limitation.[125]

Research and development expenditures. Congress has modified the rules for allocating and apportioning research and development

---

[117] Temp. Reg. § 1.861-9T(a). If the taxpayer is a corporation that is a member of an affiliated group, interest expense is allocated and apportioned as if all members of the group were a single corporation. Code Sec. 864(e)(1).

[118] Code Sec. 864(e)(2).

[119] Temp. Reg. § 1.861-9T(g)(3). The physical location of the asset is not relevant to this determination.

[120] Temp. Reg. § 1.861-12T(b).

[121] Temp. Reg. § 1.861-9T(g)(1)(ii).

[122] Temp. Reg. § 1.861-9T(g)(2)(i).

[123] Code Sec. 864(e)(3).

[124] Code Sec. 864(e)(4). See also Temp. Reg. §§ 1.861-9T and 1.861-11T through 1.861-13T for additional guidance regarding the allocation and apportionment of interest expense.

[125] Reg. § 1.861-10.

expenditures numerous times over the years. Under the current regime, research and development expenditures are apportioned between U.S.- and foreign-source income using the sales apportionment method or, if the taxpayer so elects, an optional gross income apportionment method.[126] Under the sales method, one-half of the research and development costs is allocated to the place at which the research and development activities were performed, and the remaining half of the costs is prorated between U.S. and foreign sources according to sales. Under the gross income method, one-fourth of the costs is allocated exclusively to the place at which the research and development activities were performed, and the remainder is apportioned according to gross income.

Losses from disposition of stock and other personal property. In January 1999, final and temporary regulations were issued regarding the source of losses from sales and other dispositions of stock and other personal property. The regulations are generally effective for losses recognized on or after January 1, 1999.[127] Losses from the sale or other disposition of stock and other personal property are generally sourced under the same rules that apply to gains from such property, that is, based on the residence of the seller.[128] For example, a loss from the sale of stocks and bonds issued by U.S. corporations are nevertheless classified as foreign source income if the seller resides outside the United States. However, as with the source rules governing gains from personal property, there is a wide range of exceptions to the general rule. Exceptions governing stock sales include a recapture rule with respect to dividends received within 24 months of the stock sale,[129] losses attributable to a foreign office,[130] stock of an S corporation[131] and stock of a real property holding company.[132] Exceptions governing sales of personal property other than stock include (i) inventory sales,[133] depreciable property,[134] foreign currency and certain financial instruments,[135] losses attributable to a foreign office[136] and trade receivables and certain interest equivalents.[137]

Other specialized rules. Additional guidance also is provided regarding the following types of deductions:

(i)   *Legal and accounting expenses*—Legal and accounting expenses incurred with respect to a specific property or activity (for example, to obtain a patent) are allocated to

---

[126] Reg. § 1.861-17.
[127] Reg. § 1.865-2(e) and Temp. Reg. § 1.865-1T(f). Under the prior regulations, losses from the disposition of stocks and other personal property (other than inventory) were sourced in the same manner as the gross income generated by the property.
[128] Reg. § 1.865-2 (stock) and Temp. Reg. § 1.865-1T (personal property).
[129] A de minimis exception applies when the dividend is less than 10% of the recognized loss. Reg. § 1.865-2(b)(1).

[130] Reg. § 1.865-2(a)(2).
[131] Reg. § 1.865-2(b)(3).
[132] Reg. § 1.865-2(a)(4).
[133] Temp. Reg. § 1.865-1T(c)(2).
[134] Temp. Reg. § 1.865-1T(b)(1).
[135] Temp. Reg. § 1.865-1T(c)(1).
[136] Temp. Reg. § 1.865-1T(a)(2).
[137] Temp. Reg. § 1.865-1T(c)(3).

the gross income produced by that property or activity (for example, royalties from the patent). On the other hand, the cost of general legal and accounting functions is allocated to all gross income and apportioned on the basis of gross income.[138]

(ii) *State income taxes*—State income taxes are allocated to the gross income on which the taxes were imposed and apportioned on the basis of gross income.[139]

(iii) *Net operating losses*—A net operating loss deduction allowed under Code Sec. 172 shall be allocated and apportioned in the same manner as the deductions giving rise to the net operating loss deduction.[140]

(iv) *Stewardship expenses*—Expenses associated with stewardship activities (e.g., activities undertaken by a parent corporation as an investor in a subsidiary) are allocated to the class of gross income that includes the dividends received from the subsidiary.[141]

(v) *Standard deduction*—The standard deduction is allocated to all of the individual taxpayer's gross income and apportioned on the basis of gross income.[142]

(vi) *Certain personal expenses*—An individual taxpayer's deductions for real estate taxes on a personal residence, medical expenses, charitable contributions, and alimony payments are allocated to all of the taxpayer's gross income and apportioned on the basis of gross income.[143]

(vii) *Personal exemption*—Personal exemption deductions are not taken into account for purposes of allocating and apportioning deductions.[144]

---

[138] Reg. § 1.861-8(e)(5).
[139] Reg. § 1.861-8(e)(6).
[140] Temp. Reg. § 1.861-8T(e)(1).
[141] Reg. § 1.861-8(e)(4).

[142] Code Secs. 861(b) and 862(b).
[143] Reg. § 1.861-8(e)(9).
[144] Reg. § 1.861-8(e)(11).

Chapter 3

Foreign Tax Credit

¶ 301   INTRODUCTION

The United States mitigates international double taxation by allowing U.S. persons a credit for any foreign income taxes paid on their foreign-source income. Chapter 3 explains how to compute the foreign tax credit, describes the role that the foreign tax credit limitation plays in this process, and introduces some basic planning strategies for maximizing the credit. Chapter 4 discusses the deemed paid foreign tax credit, which is the mechanism by which a domestic corporation can claim a credit for the foreign income taxes paid by a 10%-or-more-owned foreign corporation.

Computing the Foreign Tax Credit

The United States taxes U.S. persons on all of their income, regardless of its source.[1] This creates a double taxation problem with respect to a U.S. person's foreign-source income, since foreign countries

---

[1] Code Sec. 61(a).

usually tax all the income earned within their borders, including that derived by U.S. persons. If the United States did nothing to mitigate international double taxation, U.S. companies would be at a competitive disadvantage in overseas markets, since their total tax rate would exceed that of their foreign competitors by the amount of the U.S. tax burden on foreign-source income. The centerpiece of the U.S. system for mitigating international double taxation is the foreign tax credit.[2]

The computation of the foreign tax credit is a three-step process, as follows:

> *Step 1—Compute creditable foreign income taxes.* To be creditable, a foreign levy must be a tax, the predominant character of which is an income tax in the U.S. sense.[3]

> *Step 2—Compute the foreign tax credit limitation.* A key feature of the U.S. credit system is the foreign tax credit limitation, which restricts the credit to the portion of the pre-credit U.S. tax that is attributable to foreign-source income.[4] The purpose of the limitation is to confine the effects of the credit to mitigating double taxation of foreign-source income. The limitation accomplishes this by preventing U.S. persons operating in high-tax foreign countries from offsetting those higher foreign taxes against the U.S. taxes on U.S.-source income.

> *Step 3—Determine the lesser of creditable foreign income taxes (step 1) or the foreign tax credit limitation (step 2).* Creditable foreign taxes in excess of the limitation cannot be claimed as a credit in the current year. However, these excess credits can be carried back up to two years and carried forward up to five years, and taken as a credit in a year that the limitation exceeds creditable foreign taxes.[5]

Example 3.1: USAco, a domestic corporation, has $10 million of taxable income, including $3 million of foreign-source taxable income, on which USAco paid $1.5 million in foreign income taxes. Assume that the U.S. tax rate is 35%.

Step 1: Compute creditable foreign income taxes . . . . $1.5 million

Step 2: Compute the foreign tax credit limitation
  (A) Total taxable income . . . . $ 10 million
  (B) Pre-credit U.S. tax [35% × $10
      million] . . . . $3.5 million
  (C) Foreign-source taxable income . . . . . . $ 3 million
Limitation = [line B × (C ÷ A)]
      = [$3.5 million × ($3 million ÷ $10 million)] . . $ 1,050,000

Step 3: Credit equals the lesser of creditable taxes ($1.5 million) or the limitation ($1,050,000). . . . . $ 1,050,000

---

[2] Code Sec. 901(a).
[3] Reg. § 1.901-2(a)(1).

[4] Code Sec. 904(a).
[5] Code Sec. 904(c).

USAco can carry its excess credits of $450,000 [$1,500,000 − $1,050,000] back two years and forward five years.

Credit versus Deduction

Taxpayers have the option of deducting foreign income taxes in lieu of taking a credit.[6] A double tax benefit is not allowed, however, and a taxpayer cannot both deduct and claim a credit for the same foreign taxes.[7] Generally, a credit is more advantageous than a deduction because it reduces a person's tax dollar for dollar as opposed to a reduction in taxable income. For example, if a domestic corporation is subject to U.S. tax at a 35% rate, deducting $1 of foreign taxes saves only $0.35 in taxes, compared to $1 in tax savings from a credit.[8] When analyzing the relative benefits of a deduction versus a credit, taxpayers also should consider the impact of taking a deduction on their state income tax returns. No state allows a credit for foreign income taxes. Some states allow a deduction, however, but typically only if the corporation takes a deduction for federal income tax purposes. Therefore, an additional benefit of deducting foreign income taxes for federal income tax purposes is that, in certain states, the deduction also will reduce the taxpayer's state income tax liability.

The choice between a deduction and a credit applies to all foreign income taxes paid or accrued during the year.[9] In other words, it is not possible to claim a credit for a portion of the foreign taxes incurred in a taxable year and claim a deduction for the remaining foreign taxes. However, taxpayers can change their election from year to year. In addition, taxpayers can change their election any time before the expiration of the statute of limitations, which is 10 years in the case of a refund claim based on the foreign tax credit.[10] A taxpayer makes the annual election to claim a credit by including with its tax return Form 1118 (for domestic corporations) or Form 1116 (for individuals).[11]

Who Can Claim a Credit

Taxpayers entitled to claim a foreign tax credit primarily include U.S. citizens, resident aliens, and domestic corporations.[12] An affiliated group of corporations that files a consolidated return computes its foreign tax credit on a consolidated basis.[13] A U.S. citizen or resident alien who is a partner in a partnership or a beneficiary of an estate or trust also may claim a credit for his or her proportionate share of the

---

[6] Code Sec. 164(a).

[7] Code Sec. 275(a)(4)(A).

[8] A deduction may be more advantageous when, for example, a taxpayer has net operating losses for a sustained period of time. Neither a deduction nor a credit provides any current-year tax benefit in such situations, and there may be little chance that the foreign taxes will be creditable during one of the five carryforward years. On the other hand, deducting

foreign taxes would increase the taxpayer's net operating loss, which can be carried forward 20 years. Code Sec. 172(b)(1)(A).

[9] Reg. § 1.901-1(c).

[10] Reg. § 1.901-1(d) and Code Sec. 6511(d)(3)(A).

[11] Reg. § 1.905-2(a).

[12] Code Sec. 901(b)(1)–(3).

[13] Reg. § 1.1502-4(c).

creditable foreign taxes incurred by the partnership, estate, or trust.[14] A domestic corporation that is a partner in a partnership also is entitled to a credit for its share of the partnership's foreign taxes.[15] The rules applicable to partners in a partnership also apply to shareholders in an S corporation.[16]

In certain limited situations, nonresident alien individuals and foreign corporations can claim a foreign tax credit against the U.S. tax on their income effectively connected to the conduct of a U.S. trade or business.[17] See the discussion in Chapter 12.

¶ 302 CREDITABLE FOREIGN INCOME TAXES

Qualifying Foreign Levies

The foreign tax credit is intended to mitigate international double taxation of a U.S. person's foreign-source income. Therefore, the United States restricts the credit to foreign income taxes that duplicate the U.S. income tax against which the credit is taken. Specifically, to be creditable, a levy must satisfy the following two requirements:

(i)   the levy must be a "tax" paid to a foreign country or U.S. possession,

(ii) the predominant character of the tax must be that of an income tax in the U.S. sense.[18]

If a foreign levy satisfies the first requirement but not the second, it may still be creditable if the tax is imposed "in lieu of" an income tax.[19] Foreign taxes other than income taxes, such as sales and property taxes, are not creditable but generally are deductible.[20]

Tax requirement. A tax is a compulsory payment that a country imposes in order to raise funds for public purposes. Therefore, if a taxpayer receives a specific economic benefit in exchange for a foreign levy, the levy is not a tax.[21] Historically, the problem of distinguishing taxes from payments for specific economic benefits has been most difficult in the petroleum industry. In countries where the government owns the oil resources, the treasury is in a position to both collect taxes on an oil company's profits and receive royalties from those same companies. Thus, the government can designate as a tax what is actually a royalty, without affecting its total revenues. If the characterization of the payment as a tax is accepted for U.S. tax purposes, a U.S. oil company can claim a credit for what should be only a deductible royalty expense.

---

[14] Code Sec. 901(b)(5).
[15] Code Sec. 702(a)(6).
[16] Code Sec. 1373(a).
[17] Code Secs. 901(b)(4) and 906.

[18] Code Sec. 901(b) and Reg. § 1.901-2(a)(1).
[19] Code Sec. 903.
[20] Code Sec. 164(a).
[21] Reg. § 1.901-2(a)(2)(i).

To prevent this result, a foreign levy is not considered a tax to the extent the taxpayer receives a specific economic benefit in exchange for the levy. A person who is both a taxpayer and the recipient of a specific economic benefit is referred to as a dual-capacity taxpayer. Dual-capacity taxpayers have the burden of establishing what portion of a levy is a tax[22] and can use either a facts and circumstances approach or an elective safe-harbor method to satisfy their burden of proof.[23]

Income tax requirement. It generally is obvious whether a particular levy is a tax on income, as opposed to a tax on some other base. However, governments occasionally impose hybrid taxes that are difficult to classify, such as a tax on the gross value of minerals extracted from mining or a tax on the gross receipts from banking.[24] Such taxes are creditable only if their predominant character is that of an income tax in the U.S. sense.[25] In this regard, three aspects of U.S. income taxation are considered fundamental, and the foreign levy must exhibit each of these characteristics in order to be considered an income tax.[26]

    (i) *Realization test*—The tax must be imposed upon income that results from an exchange transaction or other event which would trigger a realization of income under U.S. principles.[27]

    (ii) *Gross receipts test*—The tax must be imposed either upon actual gross receipts or according to a formulary method that is not likely to produce an amount that is greater than fair market value.[28]

    (iii) *Net income test*—The tax base must permit the recovery of significant costs and expenses attributable to the taxpayer's gross income.[29]

Even if a tax satisfies all three requirements, it will still be denied income tax status if it is a soak-up tax.[30] A soak-up tax is a levy that a host country imposes only if the taxpayer can claim the tax as a credit on its home country tax return.[31] Soak-up taxes allow a country to collect taxes on inbound investments with the cost borne solely by the foreign investors' home country. Income tax status also is denied to any foreign levy that a foreign country uses to provide some type of subsidy to the taxpayer, a related person, or any party to a transaction to which the taxpayer is a party.[32]

Foreign withholding taxes. Creditable taxes also include any foreign taxes imposed "in lieu of" an income tax.[33] The most common

---

[22] Reg. § 1.901-2(a)(2)(i).

[23] Reg. § 1.901-2A(c) and (d).

[24] For an example, see *Texasgulf, Inc. v. United States*, No. 532-83T (Fed. Cl. Oct. 15, 1999).

[25] Reg. § 1.901-2(a)(1).

[26] Reg. § 1.901-2(a)(3)(i) and (b)(1).

[27] Reg. § 1.901-2(b)(2).

[28] Reg. § 1.901-2(b)(3).

[29] Reg. § 1.901-2(b)(4).

[30] Reg. § 1.901-2(a)(3)(ii).

[31] Reg. § 1.901-2(c)(1).

[32] Code Sec. 901(i) and Reg. § 1.901-2(e)(3).

[33] Code Sec. 903.

type of in-lieu-of tax is the flat rate withholding tax that countries routinely impose on the gross amount of interest, dividends, rents, and royalties derived by passive offshore investors. Withholding is required because it is the only sure way to collect taxes from passive offshore investors. In order to withhold, the withholding agent must be able to readily ascertain both the tax base and the applicable rate. This explains both the gross basis taxation and the use of a flat tax rate since it would be difficult for the withholding agent to determine the offshore investor's allocable expenses and appropriate tax bracket based on worldwide income. Flat rate withholding taxes are creditable as in-lieu-of taxes as long as the taxing country also imposes a general income tax.[34]

A taxpayer can not claim a tax credit for foreign withholding taxes paid with respect to a dividend unless a 16-day holding period for the dividend-paying stock (or a 46-day holding period for certain dividends on preferred stock) is satisfied. The 16-day holding period requirement must be met within the 30-day period beginning 15 days before the ex-dividend date. If the stock is held for 15 days or less during the 30-day period, the foreign tax credit for the withholding tax is disallowed. The holding period generally does not include any period during which the taxpayer is protected from risk of loss (e.g., by use of an option). In addition, regardless of the holding period, the taxpayer is not entitled to a credit to the extent that the dividend recipient is under an obligation, pursuant to a short sale or otherwise, to make related payments with respect to positions in substantially similar or related property. However, taxpayers that fail to meet the holding period requirement are allowed a deduction equal to the foreign tax credits disallowed. In addition, an exception to the holding period requirement is available to security dealers.[35] Congress enacted these provisions to curtail transactions designed to transfer foreign tax credits from persons unable to benefit from them to persons that can use the credits.[36]

Denial of credit for certain taxes. In an attempt to further U.S. foreign policy objectives, a credit is denied to any foreign income taxes paid to a country whose government the United States does not recognize, does not conduct diplomatic relations with, or has designated as a government that repeatedly supports acts of international terrorism.[37] Countries to which this provision has applied in the past or present include Afghanistan, Albania, Angola, Cambodia, Cuba, Iran, Iraq, Libya, North Korea, South Africa, Sudan, Syria, Vietnam, and the People's Democratic Republic of Yemen.[38]

---

[34] Reg. § 1.903-1(b)(3), Example 2.

[35] Code Sec. 901(k).

[36] See Notice 98-5, 1998-3 IRB 49; and *Compaq Computer Corporation v. Comm'r,* 113 TC No. 17 (1999).

[37] Code Sec. 901(j).

[38] Rev. Rul. 95-63, 1995-2 CB 85.

In addition, any taxpayer who participates in or cooperates with an international boycott must reduce its creditable foreign taxes by an international boycott factor.[39] Countries that may require participation in or cooperation with an international boycott include Bahrain, Iraq, Jordan, Kuwait, Lebanon, Libya, Oman, Qatar, Saudi Arabia, Syria, United Arab Emirates, and the People's Republic of Yemen.[40]

Accounting Method

Accrual-basis taxpayers compute the foreign tax credit on an accrual basis.[41] Under the accrual method, creditable foreign income taxes equal the taxpayer's foreign tax liability for the current year, regardless of when those taxes are actually paid. Normal accrual-basis accounting principles apply when determining the liability for the year. Thus, a foreign tax cannot be accrued unless all the events have occurred which determine the fact of the liability, and the amount of the liability can be determined with reasonable accuracy.[42]

Cash-basis taxpayers generally compute the credit on a cash basis.[43] Under the cash method, creditable foreign taxes equal the amount of foreign taxes paid during the year, regardless of whether the payment relates to the current year or some other taxable year. A tax payment is not creditable, however, to the extent that it is reasonably certain that the amount will be refunded in the future.[44]

Cash-basis taxpayers can elect to compute the credit on an accrual basis. Once made, this election applies for all subsequent years.[45] Allowing cash-basis taxpayers to account for foreign taxes on an accrual basis may provide a better matching of foreign income taxes to the associated foreign-source income. Matching is important because the foreign tax credit limitation for a given year is based on the amount of foreign-source income recognized in that year.

Currency Translation

Because foreign income taxes are paid in the local currency, taxpayers must translate foreign taxes into their U.S. dollar equivalents in order to compute the credit. For tax years beginning before 1998, foreign income taxes generally are translated into dollars using the spot rate, that is, the exchange rate for the date on which the taxes were paid. For tax years beginning on or after January 1, 1998, taxpayers that account for foreign taxes on an accrual basis generally may translate foreign income taxes accrued into U.S. dollars at the average

---

[39] Code Sec. 908.

[40] Notice 95-3, 1995-1 CB 290.

[41] Reg. § 1.905-1(a).

[42] Reg. § 1.446-1(c)(1)(ii). The economic performance requirement does not apply to an accrual for foreign taxes. Reg. § 1.461-4(g)(6)(iii)(B).

[43] Reg. § 1.905-1(a).

[44] Reg. § 1.901-2(e)(2)(i).

[45] Code Sec. 905(a).

exchange rate for the tax year to which the taxes relate.[46] See Chapter 8 for more details.

¶ 303   EXCESS VERSUS SHORT CREDIT POSITIONS

Purpose of Limitation

After a taxpayer has computed the amount of creditable foreign income taxes, the next step is to compute the foreign tax credit limitation. The limitation equals the portion of the pre-credit U.S. tax that is attributable to foreign-source income.[47] The purpose of the limitation is to confine the effects of the credit to mitigating double taxation of foreign-source income. The limitation accomplishes this by preventing U.S. persons operating in high-tax foreign countries from offsetting those higher foreign taxes against the U.S. tax on U.S.-source income.

Example 3.2: USAco is a domestic corporation. During the current year, USAco has $200 of U.S.-source taxable income and $100 of foreign-source taxable income (all numbers in thousands). Assume that the foreign tax rate is 45% and the U.S. tax rate is 35%.

Case 1—Credit is limited: If the foreign tax credit is limited to the U.S. tax on foreign-source income (i.e., 35% × $100 = $35), the total tax on USAco's $300 of worldwide income is $115, computed as follows:

U.S. tax return	
Taxable income	$300
U.S. tax rate	× .35
Pre-credit tax	$105
Foreign tax credit	− 35
U.S. tax	$ 70

Foreign tax return	
Taxable income	$100
Foreign tax rate	× .45
Foreign tax	$ 45

Case 2—No limitation: If there were no limitation on the foreign tax credit, the total tax on USAco's worldwide income would drop from $115 to $105, computed as follows:

U.S. tax return	
Taxable income	$300
U.S. tax rate	× .35
Pre-credit tax	$105
Foreign tax credit	− 45
U.S. tax	$ 60

Foreign tax return	
Taxable income	$100
Foreign tax rate	× .45
Foreign tax	$ 45

---

[46] Code Sec. 986(a).   [47] Code Sec. 904(a).

Without the limitation, the net U.S. tax on the $100 of foreign-source income is negative $10 [$35 pre-credit U.S. tax − $45 credit], which reduces the U.S. tax on USAco's domestic profits from $70 to $60.

Taxpayers compute their foreign tax credit limitation using the following formula.[48]

$$\text{Pre-credit U.S. tax} \times \frac{\text{Foreign-source taxable income}}{\text{Worldwide taxable income}}$$

Under a single foreign tax credit limitation, all foreign-source income, regardless of its character (e.g., active business versus passive investment) or country of origin (e.g., low-tax country versus high-tax country), is commingled to arrive at a single limitation. It also is possible to make more precise comparisons of the U.S. and foreign tax burdens on foreign-source income, including separate income limitations and separate country limitations. As discussed later in this chapter, taxpayers currently must compute separate limitations for each of the nine different categories of income.[49]

Exemption for Individuals with *De Minimis* Foreign Tax Credits

An individual with $300 or less of creditable foreign income taxes is exempt from the foreign tax credit limitation, provided he or she has no foreign-source income other than passive investment income. The $300 amount is increased to $600 in the case of married persons filing a joint return. The exemption is not automatic. To qualify, an individual must elect to take the exemption for the tax year. Congress enacted this rule to relieve the tax reporting burden (specifically, the need to complete Form 1116) in situations where the amount of foreign taxes paid and the corresponding credit was small. However, certain restrictions apply. An individual electing exemption from the foreign tax credit limitation may not carry over any excess foreign taxes paid or accrued to or from a tax year in which the election applies. Also, for purposes of the election, creditable foreign taxes are limited to those shown on a payee statement furnished to the taxpayer. Finally, the election is not available to estates or trusts.[50]

Importance of Relative Tax Rates

The relation of U.S. and foreign tax rates is a major determinant of whether a taxpayer is in an excess or short credit position. Taxpayers will be in a short credit position when the foreign tax rate is lower than the U.S. rate and in an excess credit position when the foreign tax rate

---

[48] Code Sec. 904(a).
[49] Code Sec. 904(d).

[50] Code Sec. 904(j).

is higher than the U.S. rate. Any other factors that impact the effective foreign tax rate, such as the use of different accounting methods or local country tax incentives, also will affect whether a taxpayer is in an excess or short credit position.

Example 3.3: USAco, a domestic corporation, has foreign-source taxable income of $100 and no U.S.-source taxable income (all numbers in thousands). Assume the U.S. tax rate is 35%.

Case 1—Foreign tax rate is 30%: If the foreign tax rate is 30%, USAco can claim a credit for the entire $30 of foreign taxes paid, as follows:

U.S. tax return		Foreign tax return	
Taxable income	$100	Taxable income	$100
U.S. tax rate	× .35	Foreign tax rate	× .30
Pre-credit tax	$ 35	Foreign tax	$ 30
Foreign tax credit	− 30		
U.S. tax	$ 5		

Case 2—Foreign tax rate is 40%: If the foreign tax rate is 40%, the foreign tax credit limitation (which equals the U.S. tax of $35 on USAco's $100 of foreign-source income) will prevent USAco from claiming a credit for $5 of the $40 of foreign taxes paid, as follows:

U.S. tax return		Foreign tax return	
Taxable income	$100	Taxable income	$100
U.S. tax rate	× .35	Foreign tax rate	× .40
Pre-credit tax	$ 35	Foreign tax	$ 40
Foreign tax credit	− 35		
U.S. tax	$ 0		

Planning Implications

The foreign tax credit limitation determines whether foreign taxes have an incremental effect on a U.S. person's total tax costs. When a taxpayer is in a short credit position (i.e., the taxpayer's creditable foreign taxes are less than the limitation), foreign taxes do not represent an out-of-pocket tax cost since the cost of paying those taxes is entirely offset by the U.S. tax savings associated with the credit. Therefore, tax planning focuses on reducing the residual U.S. tax due on foreign-source income. In contrast, when a taxpayer is in an excess credit position (i.e., creditable foreign taxes exceed the limitation), no U.S. tax is collected on foreign-source income because the credit fully offsets the pre-credit U.S. tax on that income. In addition, the non-creditable foreign income taxes increase the total tax burden on foreign-source income beyond what it would have been if only the United States had taxed that income.[51] Therefore, planning focuses on reducing those excess credits. As discussed in the next section, strategies for eliminating excess credits include foreign tax reduction planning, increasing the limitation, and cross-crediting.

¶ 304 STRATEGIES FOR ELIMINATING EXCESS CREDITS

Foreign Tax Reduction Planning

When a taxpayer is in a short credit position, any decrease in foreign tax costs is accompanied by an offsetting increase in the residual U.S. tax on foreign income. Therefore, foreign tax reduction planning has no effect on the taxpayer's total tax costs.[52] The circumstances are quite different, however, for U.S. persons in excess credit positions. Foreign taxes increase the total tax costs of such taxpayers by the amount of the excess credits. As a consequence, every dollar of foreign taxes saved reduces the taxpayer's total tax costs by a dollar, up to the amount of excess credits.

The techniques that a U.S. person can use to reduce foreign income taxes often are the same as those used to reduce income taxes in a purely domestic context. Examples include taking advantage of any special exemptions, deductions, or credits provided by local law, realizing income in a form that is taxed at a lower rate (such as a preferential rate for capital gains), deferring the recognition of gross income, and accelerating the recognition of deductions. Other foreign tax reduction planning strategies, including the use of debt financing, transfer pricing, and tax treaties, are discussed in Chapter 10.

Increasing the Limitation

A second basic strategy for reducing excess credits is to increase the foreign tax credit limitation by increasing the proportion of worldwide income that is classified as foreign-source income for U.S. tax purposes. As a consequence, the U.S. rules for sourcing gross income and deductions can play a decisive role in eliminating excess credits. For example, the title-passage rule for sourcing the income from inventory sales provides U.S. companies with a significant opportunity to increase foreign-source income. By arranging for the passage of title in

---

[51] Although creditable foreign taxes in excess of the limitation cannot be taken in the current year, they can be carried back up to two years and carried forward up to five years and taken as a credit in a year in which the limitation exceeds the amount of creditable foreign taxes. Code Sec. 904(c).

[52] However, foreign tax reduction planning does affect the allocation of tax revenues between the United States and other countries. Reducing foreign taxes reduces the foreign tax credit and, in turn, increases U.S. tax revenues.

the importing country rather than the United States, export sales will generate foreign-source income.

Recharacterizing deductions also is an effective strategy for eliminating excess credits. Deductions reduce a taxpayer's pre-credit U.S. tax, regardless of how they are sourced. However, if the deduction is allocated to foreign-source income, it also reduces the foreign tax credit limitation. Thus, a taxpayer in an excess credit position derives no net U.S. tax benefit from deductions allocated to foreign-source income. In contrast, deductions allocated to U.S.-source income do not affect the foreign tax credit limitation and therefore provide a full U.S. tax benefit. An example of how a taxpayer can recharacterize deductions is the use of alternative apportionment bases for sourcing selling, general, and administrative expenses which reduce the amount of these deductions allocated to foreign-source income.

As with any international tax planning strategy, reducing excess credits by resourcing gross income and deductions requires a careful analysis of both U.S. and foreign tax consequences. In particular, if a taxpayer takes an action that increases foreign-source income for both U.S. and foreign tax purposes, the resourced income may increase the taxpayer's foreign tax costs more than it increases the taxpayer's foreign tax credit limitation. If this happens, the net effect of the action may be an increase, rather than the desired decrease, in the taxpayer's excess credits. Therefore, the effectiveness of resourcing income as a strategy for eliminating excess credits depends critically on the existence of differences between the source-of-income rules used by the United States and other countries.

Example 3.4: USAco, a domestic corporation, has $2 million of U.S.-source taxable income and $4 million of foreign-source taxable income. Assuming the foreign tax rate is 50% and the U.S. rate is 35%, USAco has $600,000 of excess credits, computed as follows:

Foreign income taxes [$4 million × 50%] . . . . $2 million

Foreign tax credit limitation:
    (A) Total taxable income . . . . $ 6 million
    (B) Pre-credit U.S. tax [$6 million × 35%] $2.1 million
    (C) Foreign-source taxable income . . . . . . $ 4 million
Limitation = [line B × (C ÷ A)]
         = [$2.1 million × ($4 million ÷ $6 million)] . . . −$1.4 million

                                        $600,000

Excess foreign tax credits . . . .

Now assume that USAco can recharacterize $1 million of its U.S.-source income as foreign-source income, but only for U.S. tax purposes. Every dollar of resourced income increases USAco's limitation and has no effect on USAco's foreign taxes. The net effect is a reduction in USAco's excess credits from \$600,000 to \$250,000, computed as follows:

Foreign income taxes [\$4 million × 50%] . . . .   \$2 million

Foreign tax credit limitation:
    (A) Total taxable income . . . . \$ 6 million
    (B) Pre-credit U.S. tax
        [\$6 million × 35%] . . . . \$2.1 million
    (C) Foreign-source taxable income . . . . . \$ 5 million
Limitation = [line B × (C ÷ A)]
        = [\$2.1 million × (\$5 million ÷ \$6 million)] . . −\$1.75 million

Excess foreign tax credits \$250,000

On the other hand, if the resourcing of USAco's income for U.S. tax purposes also increases USAco's taxable income for foreign tax purposes, the \$1 million of resourced income will increase USAco's foreign taxes at a faster rate than it will increase its limitation. The net effect will be an increase in USAco's excess credits from \$600,000 to \$750,000, computed as follows.

Foreign income taxes [\$5 million × 50%] . . . .   \$2.5 million

Foreign tax credit limitation:
    (A) Total taxable income . . . . \$ 6 million
    (B) Pre-credit U.S. tax
        [\$6 million × 35%] . . . . \$2.1 million
    (C) Foreign-source taxable income . . . . . \$ 5 million
Limitation = [line B × (C ÷ A)]
        = [\$2.1 million × (\$5 million ÷ \$6 million)] . . −\$1.75 million

Excess foreign tax credits \$750,000

Cross-Crediting

A third basic strategy for eliminating excess credits is cross-crediting. This strategy is based on the fact that different items of foreign-source income have distinctly different effects on a taxpayer's excess credits. Foreign income that bears foreign taxes at a rate higher than the U.S. tax rate increases a taxpayer's excess credits, whereas foreign income that bears a low rate of foreign tax results in an excess limitation. Within a single foreign tax credit limitation, the excess limitation on lightly taxed foreign income is credited against the excess credits on heavily taxed foreign income. Through this process, known as "cross-crediting," the effects of individual items of heavily and lightly taxed foreign-source income are averaged. This averaging process produces an excess credit only when the average foreign tax rate on all of the items of income within a single limitation is higher than the U.S. rate.

Example 3.5: USAco, a domestic corporation, has $1 million of country X source income and no U.S.-source income. Assuming the U.S. tax rate is 35% and the country X rate is 40%, USAco has $50,000 of excess credits, computed as follows:

Foreign income taxes [$1 million × 40%] $400,000

Foreign tax credit limitation:
    (A) Total taxable income . . . . $1 million
    (B) Pre-credit U.S. tax [$1 million × 35%] . . . . $ 350,000
    (C) Foreign-source taxable income . . . . $1 million
Limitation = [line B × (C ÷ A)]
         = [$350,000 × ($1 million ÷ $1 million)] . . . . −$350,000

Excess foreign tax credits . . . . $ 50,000

Now assume that in addition to the $1 million of country X income, USAco also has $1 million of country Y income, which is subject to foreign tax at a 30% rate. If the country Y income is assigned to the same limitation as the country X income, cross-crediting will eliminate the $50,000 of excess credits, as follows:

Foreign income taxes [($1 million × 40%) +
    ($1 million × 30%)] $700,000

Foreign tax credit limitation:
    (A) Total taxable income
         [$1 million + $1 million] . . . . $2 million
    (B) Pre-credit U.S. tax [$2 million × 35%] . . . . $ 700,000
    (C) Foreign-source taxable income . . . . $2 million
Limitation = [line B × (C ÷ A)]
         = [$700,000 × ($2 million ÷ $2 million)] . . . . −$700,000

Excess foreign tax credits . . . .   None

USAco no longer has any excess credits because the average rate of foreign tax is now 35% (foreign taxes of $700,000 ÷ $2 million of foreign income), which is the same as the U.S. rate.

The third strategy for eliminating excess credits exploits the cross-crediting phenomenon. If a taxpayer can blend low-tax and high-tax foreign-source income within a single limitation, then the excess limitation on the low-tax income will soak up the excess credits on the high-tax income.

¶ 305   RESTRICTIONS ON CROSS-CREDITING

History

Cross-crediting is possible only to the extent the operative foreign tax credit limitation encompasses both low-tax and high-tax foreign-source income. Foreign income tax rates vary not only across countries, but also across different types of income within the same country. For example, countries often tax the local business profits of foreigners at a higher rate than the passive investment income derived by those same taxpayers. Therefore, restrictions on cross-crediting can be implemented by imposing either separate country or separate income limitations on the foreign tax credit.

Under a separate country limitation system, a separate limitation is computed for each foreign country. Separate country limitations prevent cross-crediting on income derived from different countries but still allow cross-crediting on low-tax and high-tax income derived from the same foreign country. Under a separate income limitation approach, a separate limitation is applied to each category of income designated by lawmakers. Cross-crediting is allowed between countries but not between different categories of income. For example, a separate limitation may be required for interest income. Interest income is a prime target for lawmakers wishing to restrict cross-crediting because interest income often bears little or no foreign taxes and because interest-producing assets are easily moved overseas.

Over the years, U.S. lawmakers have employed both separate country and separate income systems (see Table 3.1).

TABLE 3.1. U.S. RESTRICTIONS ON CROSS-CREDITING		
Time period	*Type of foreign tax credit limitation*	*Prohibited form of cross-crediting*
1918 to 1921	No limitation	n.a.
1922 to 1931	Overall limitation	None
1932 to 1975	Various types of separate country limitations	Between countries
1976 to 1986	Limited number of separate income limitations	Between categories of income
1987 to present	Nine separate income limitation categories [a]	Between categories of income

[a] Code Sec. 904(d).

Separate Income Limitations

The primary purpose of the current separate income limitation system is to prevent cross-crediting between lightly taxed passive foreign investment income and more heavily taxed active foreign business profits. Cross-crediting is still allowed, however, with respect to business profits derived from different foreign countries or investment income derived from different foreign countries. Congress enacted the current system in 1986 because it believed that little residual U.S. tax was being collected on foreign-source investment income, even though this income often bears little or no foreign tax. Congress attributed these negligible tax collections to the ability of U.S. multinational corporations to credit the excess foreign taxes on their foreign business profits against the residual U.S. tax on foreign-source investment income. Congress also believed that cross-crediting provided an undesirable tax incentive to shift investment capital overseas.

The formula for computing the separate income limitations is the same as that for computing the overall limitation, except that the numerator of the fraction is now separate category foreign taxable income, as follows:

$$\text{Pre-credit U.S. tax} \times \frac{\text{Separate category foreign-source taxable income}}{\text{Worldwide taxable income}}$$

The credit allowed with respect to each category of income is the lesser of that category's limitation or the foreign income taxes related to that category. A taxpayer's total credit for the year is the sum of the credits for each of the nine individual categories.

Under the current system, taxpayers must compute a separate limitation for each of the following nine categories of income: [53]

(i)   passive income,

(ii)   high withholding tax interest,

(iii)   financial services income,

(iv)   shipping income,

(v)   dividends from each noncontrolled section 902 corporation,

(vi)   certain dividends from a domestic international sales corporation or former domestic international sales corporation,

(vii)   a foreign sales corporation's taxable income attributable to foreign trade income,

(viii) certain distributions from a foreign sales corporation or former foreign sales corporation, and

(ix)   general limitation income (the residual category for income not assigned to one of the other income categories).

Example 3.6: USAco, a domestic corporation, has $12 million of U.S.-source taxable income, $8 million of foreign-source general limitation taxable income (on which USAco paid $3 million in foreign taxes), and $2 million of foreign-source passive taxable income (on which USAco paid $400,000 in foreign taxes). Assume

---

[53] Code Sec. 904(d)(1).

that the U.S. tax rate is 35%. Under a single overall limitation, all of USAco's foreign taxes are creditable, as follows:

Creditable foreign taxes [$3 million + $400,000] . . . . $3.4 million

Foreign tax credit limitation:
    (A) Total taxable income
        [$12 million + $8 million + $2 million] . $ 22 million
    (B) Pre-credit U.S. tax [$22 million × 35%] . $7.7 million
    (C) Foreign-source taxable income
        [$8 million + $2 million] . . . . $ 10 million
    Overall limitation = [line B × (C ÷ A)]
                = [$7.7 million × ($10 million ÷
                  $22 million)] . . . . $3.5 million

                                              $3.4 million
Foreign tax credit (equals creditable foreign taxes) . . . . ═══════════

In contrast, under the separate income limitations, USAco has $200,000 of excess credits within the general limitation category, computed as follows:

Pre-credit U.S. tax:
    (A) Total taxable income . . . . $ 22 million
    (B) Pre-credit U.S. tax [$22 million × 35%] . $7.7 million

Foreign tax credit:

General limitation income:
    (C) Foreign-source general limitation
        income . . . . $ 8 million
    Foreign taxes on general limitation income $ 3 million
    Limitation = [line B × (C ÷ A)]
            = [$7.7 million × ($8 million ÷ $22 million)]
            = $2.8 million
    Allowable credit [equals the limitation] . . . . $2.8 million

Passive income:
    (D) Foreign-source passive income . . . . $ 2 million
    Foreign taxes on passive income . . . . $ 400,000
    Limitation = [line B × (D ÷ A)]
            = [$7.7 million × ($2 million ÷ $22 million)]
            = $700,000
    Allowable credit [equals creditable taxes] . . . . $ 400,000

                                              $3.2 million
Total foreign tax credit . . . . ═══════════

According to the most recent IRS statistics, the principal types of income reported by U.S. corporations claiming a foreign tax credit for tax years ending in 1994 were general limitation income, which represented 70 percent of the total amount of foreign source taxable income reported for 1994, and financial services income, which accounted for 23 percent of the total amount of foreign source taxable income reported for 1994 (see Table 3.2).

TABLE 3.2. FOREIGN SOURCE INCOME REPORTED BY U.S. CORPORATIONS CLAIMING A FOREIGN TAX CREDIT FOR 1994

Separate income limitation category	*Amount (in millions)*
General limitation income	$ 71,456
Financial services income	22,937
Passive income	3,749
Dividends from 10/50 companies	1,790
Shipping income	666
High withholding tax interest	558
FSC distributions	161
DISC dividends	92
Other	112
Total foreign source taxable income	$101,521

Source: "Corporate Foreign Tax Credit, 1994," *IRS Statistics on Income Bulletin,* 1998.

General limitation income. General limitation income includes all income not described by one of the other eight categories of income. Because it is the residual category, there is no specific definition of the types of income that are allocated to this category. However, most of the income from active foreign business operations, including manufacturing, marketing, and services, falls into this category. Financial services income and shipping income are exceptions by virtue of the separate categories provided for these two types of business income.

Passive income. Passive income primarily includes the following items of gross income:

(i) dividends, interest, royalties, rents, and annuities,

(ii) net gains from the disposition of property that produces dividend, interest, rent, and royalty income (except for net gains from certain dealer sales and inventory sales), and

(iii) net gains from commodity and foreign currency transactions (except for net gains from active business, hedging, and section 988 transactions).[54]

Passive income also includes inclusions of undistributed foreign personal holding company income and certain inclusions of income from a passive foreign investment company that has made a qualified electing fund election.[55]

---

[54] Code Secs. 904(d)(2)(A)(i) and 954(c)(1).   [55] Code Sec. 904(d)(2)(A)(ii).

However, there are numerous exceptions to the general rules for passive income, including the following.

(i) *High-taxed income*—Passive income does not include any income that qualifies as high-taxed income.[56] In the case of a corporate taxpayer, income is high-taxed if, after allocating the corporation's expenses to the income, the creditable foreign taxes related to the income exceed the product of the amount of that income multiplied by 35% (the maximum U.S. corporate tax rate). Any high-taxed income is assigned to the general limitation category.[57] This exception removes from the passive income category any investment income that gives rise to excess credits and thereby prevents cross-crediting of low-tax and high-tax passive income.

(ii) *Controlled foreign corporation look-through rules*—A U.S. shareholder allocates payments received from a controlled foreign corporation, including dividends, interest, rents, and royalties, to the separate categories of income based on the character of the controlled foreign corporation's earnings.[58] These look-through rules are discussed in detail later in this chapter.

(iii) *Active rents and royalties*—Passive income does not include rents and royalties which are derived from the active conduct of a trade or business and which are received from unrelated persons.[59]

(iv) *Export financing interest*—Passive income does not include export financing interest.[60] Export financing interest is any interest (other than related-person factoring income) that is derived from financing the sale or other disposition of property for use or consumption outside the United States if the property was manufactured, produced, grown, or extracted in the United States by the taxpayer or a related person and if not more than 50% of the fair market value of the property is attributable to products imported into the United States.[61] Export financing interest is assigned to the general limitation category,[62] where it blends with the taxpayer's other foreign business profits.

(v) *Income described by another category*—Passive income does not include any income that is described by one of the other categories of income, such as high withholding tax interest,

---

[56] Code Sec. 904(d)(2)(A)(iii)(III).
[57] Code Sec. 904(d)(2)(F) and Reg. § 1.904-4(c)(1).
[58] Reg. § 1.904-4(b)(1)(i) and Code Sec. 904(d)(3).
[59] Reg. § 1.904-4(b)(2).

[60] Code Sec. 904(d)(2)(A)(iii)(II).
[61] Code Sec. 904(d)(2)(G) and Reg. § 1.904-4(h)(1).
[62] Reg. § 1.904-4(h)(2).

financial services income, dividends from a noncontrolled section 902 corporation, and certain dividends from a DISC or an FSC.[63]

High withholding tax interest. High withholding tax interest is defined as any interest (other than export financing interest) subject to a gross basis withholding tax at a rate of 5% or more.[64] Historically, many foreign countries, especially developing countries, have imposed high rates of withholding taxes on interest paid by local companies to U.S. banks and other offshore lenders. Congress perceived these taxes to be in the nature of soak-up taxes, since the U.S. lender could credit them against the excess limitation created by the lender's other low-tax, foreign-source interest income. The high withholding tax interest limitation prevents this type of cross-crediting.

Financial services income. Financial services income includes the following types of income derived by a financial services entity:

(i)   active financing income,

(ii) passive income (determined before the high-taxed income exception),

(iii) export financing interest that is subject to withholding tax at a rate of 5% or more, and

(iv) incidental income.[65]

An entity is considered a financial services entity during any taxable year in which 80% or more of its gross income for the year is active financing income, that is, income from the active conduct of a banking, insurance, financing, or similar business.[66] This category allows bona fide financial services entities to engage in cross-crediting with respect to all of their financial services income, including income from services, such as investment advisory, brokerage, fiduciary, investment banking, and trust services.

Shipping income. Shipping income primarily includes income derived from the following activities:

(i)   the use or lease of aircraft or vessels in foreign commerce,

(ii) the performance of services directly related to the use of any such aircraft or vessel,

(iii) the sale or other disposition of any such aircraft or vessel, and

---

[63] Code Sec. 902(d)(2)(A)(iii)(I) and Reg. § 1.904-4(b)(1)(i).

[64] Code Sec. 904(d)(2)(B) and Reg. § 1.904-4(d).

[65] Code Sec. 904(d)(2)(C)(i) and (ii), and Reg. § 1.904-4(e)(1). Excluded from the definition of financial services income are export financing interest that is subject to withholding tax at a rate of less than 5%,

high withholding tax interest (unless it is also export financing interest), and dividends from a noncontrolled section 902 corporation. Code Sec. 904(d)(2)(C)(iii) and Reg. § 1.904-4(e)(5).

[66] Reg. § 1.904-4(e)(3). See Reg. § 1.904-4(e)(2) for a detailed definition of active financing income.

(iv) certain space or ocean activities, such as fishing and mining activities undertaken on the high seas, as well as any activity conducted in Antarctica.[67]

Shipping income often bears little or no foreign tax. The shipping income category prevents U.S. persons from avoiding the residual U.S. tax on shipping income by blending shipping income with other high-tax foreign business profits within the general limitation.

Dividends from a noncontrolled section 902 corporation. A foreign corporation is a noncontrolled section 902 corporation (or "10/50 company") if a taxpayer owns between 10% and 50% of the foreign corporation's voting stock.[68] Dividends from each 10/50 company comprise a separate limitation category, and a taxpayer has as many 10/50 company limitations as there are 10/50 companies.[69] For example, a taxpayer that receives a dividend from four different 10/50 companies has four separate 10/50 company limitations, one for each 10/50 company. The existence of a separate limitation for each 10/50 company prevents a taxpayer from cross-crediting with respect to dividends from different 10/50 companies.

Congress created the separate 10/50 company limitations in 1986 for a couple of reasons. First, when U.S. shareholders do not hold a majority interest in a foreign corporation, that entity no longer resembles a foreign branch operation, which was a principal reason for enacting the look-through rule for controlled foreign corporations (discussed below). In addition, when a U.S. shareholder's ownership interest is less than 50%, it may not be feasible for the shareholder to obtain the information necessary to apply the look-through rule applicable to controlled foreign corporations. Without a look-through rule, it is uncertain whether the dividend is passive income (i.e., the 10/50 company's underlying earnings are derived from passive investments) or general limitation income (i.e., the 10/50 company's underlying earnings are derived from active business operations). Therefore, the separate 10/50 company limitations serve as a default category.

The foreign tax credit limitation regime for dividends from 10/50 companies is scheduled to be simplified for tax years beginning on or after January 1, 2003. Separate rules are applied, depending upon whether the dividends are paid from pre-2003 or post-2002 earnings and profits. In the case of dividends from 10/50 companies that are paid from earnings and profits accumulated in tax years beginning before 2003, a single limitation is applied to the dividends from all 10/50 companies, rather than separate limitations for each 10/50

[67] Code Secs. 904(d)(2)(D) and 954(f).

[68] Code Secs. 904(d)(2)(E)(i) and 902(a).

[69] Reg. § 1.904-4(g)(2)(i).

company as under prior law. However, if the 10/50 company in question is also a passive foreign investment company, then separate limitations are applied to dividends received from each such 10/50 company. A look-through rule applies to dividends paid by a 10/50 company from earnings and profits accumulated in tax years beginning after 2002. Under this rule, a dividend from a 10/50 company is treated as income in a foreign tax credit limitation category (e.g., the general limitation category) in proportion to the ratio of post-2002 earnings and profits attributable to income in that foreign tax credit limitation category to the total amount of post-2002 earnings and profits.[70]

Certain income related to FSCs and DISCs. The remaining three categories of income all relate to income of special export-oriented companies called foreign sales corporations (or "FSCs") and domestic international sales corporations (or "DISCs"). Congress enacted the DISC provisions in 1971 in an attempt to stimulate U.S. exports by providing a lower rate of U.S. tax on certain qualifying export sales. In 1984, Congress created FSCs, which have essentially replaced DISCs. Congress had a specific level of tax savings in mind when it enacted these export incentives, and it did not want to allow taxpayers to further reduce their U.S. taxes by engaging in cross-crediting with respect to the tax-favored export profits. The FSC and DISC separate income categories prevent taxpayers from blending low-tax income related to FSCs and DISCs with high-taxed general limitation income. Two of these separate income categories, dividends from a DISC or former DISC and distributions from an FSC or former FSC, apply to U.S. shareholders of FSCs and DISCs.[71] The third category, an FSC's taxable income attributable to foreign trade income, applies to the FSC itself.[72] The taxation of FSCs and DISCs is discussed in Chapter 7.

Look-Through Rules

Controlled foreign corporations. Under the general rules, the separate income limitations would yield significantly different results for domestic corporations operating abroad through foreign subsidiaries as opposed to foreign branches. For example, if a domestic corporation structures a foreign manufacturing operation as a branch, the related income and foreign taxes are assigned to the general limitation category. In contrast, if the domestic corporation were to structure the same manufacturing operation as a subsidiary, absent a look-through rule, the dividend distributions from that manufacturing subsidiary would be assigned to the passive income category. To better equate the

---

[70] Code Sec. 904(d)(2)(E) and (d)(4).   [72] Code Sec. 904(d)(1)(G).
[71] Code Sec. 904(d)(1)(F) and (H).

treatment of branches and subsidiaries, a U.S. shareholder allocates income derived from a controlled foreign corporation (or "CFC"), including dividends, interest, rents, and royalties, to the separate income categories based on the character of the controlled foreign corporation's earnings.

A foreign corporation is a controlled foreign corporation if, on any day during the foreign corporation's taxable year, U.S. shareholders own more than 50% of the combined voting power of all classes of stock, or 50% of the total value, of the foreign corporation.[73] Only U.S. shareholders are considered in applying the 50% test. A U.S. shareholder is any U.S. person owning at least 10% of the total combined voting power of all classes of voting stock of the foreign corporation.[74]

The specific look-through rule varies with the type of income derived from the CFC, as follows:

(i) *Dividends*—Dividends paid by a CFC to a taxpayer who is a U.S. shareholder of that CFC are prorated among the separate categories of income based on the ratio of the CFC's post-1986 undistributed earnings within each separate income category to the CFC's total post-1986 undistributed earnings.[75] For example, if a CFC has $1 million of earnings and profits, $900,000 of which is attributable to general limitation income and the other $100,000 to (non-Subpart F) financial services income, then 90% of a dividend distribution from the CFC is assigned to the general limitation category and the other 10% is assigned to the financial services income category.

(ii) *Rents and royalties*—Rent and royalty income derived from a CFC by a U.S. shareholder of that CFC is allocated among the separate categories of income based on the extent to which the related deduction (at the CFC level) is properly allocable to the CFC's income in that category.[76] For example, if the entire amount of a CFC's current-year taxable income is general limitation income, then any royalty paid to a U.S. shareholder is assigned to the general limitation category.

(iii) *Interest*—Interest income derived from a CFC by a U.S. shareholder of that CFC is assigned to the passive income category to the extent of the CFC's foreign personal holding

---

[73] Code Sec. 957(a).

[74] Code Sec. 951(b). All forms of ownership, including direct, indirect (i.e., beneficial ownership through intervening entities), and constructive (i.e., attribution of ownership by one related party to another), are considered in applying both the 10% shareholder and the 50% aggregate ownership tests. Code Sec. 958.

[75] Code Sec. 904(d)(3)(D) and Reg. § 1.904-5(c)(4)(i).

[76] Code Sec. 904(d)(3)(C) and Reg. § 1.904-5(c)(3).

company income.[77] Any interest income in excess of the CFC's foreign personal holding company income is apportioned among the separate income categories other than passive income.[78]

(iv) *Subpart F inclusion*—A Subpart F inclusion for an increase in a CFC's earnings invested in U.S. property is allocated among the separate categories of income using the same rule that applies to actual dividend distributions (see discussion above).[79] In contrast, a Subpart F inclusion for Subpart F income is allocated among the separate categories of income based on the nature of the CFC's current-year taxable income which gave rise to the Subpart F inclusion.[80] For example, if a CFC has $1 million of Subpart F income, including $850,000 of foreign base company shipping income and $150,000 of foreign personal holding company income, $850,000 of the Subpart F inclusion is assigned to the shipping income category and the other $150,000 is assigned to the passive income category.[81]

(v) *Passive foreign investment company inclusion*—If the taxpayer is a U.S. shareholder of a CFC that also is a passive foreign investment company that has made a qualified electing fund (or "QEF") election, then the same look-through rule that applies to Subpart F inclusions for Subpart F income also applies to a QEF inclusion from that CFC.[82] If the QEF is a 10/50 company rather than a CFC, the QEF inclusion is assigned to a separate 10/50 company limitation for that QEF.[83] If the QEF is neither a CFC nor a 10/50 company, the QEF inclusion is assigned to the passive income category.[84]

Partnerships. A partner's distributive share of partnership income is assigned to the partner's separate income limitations based on the character of the income at the partnership level.[85] For example, if a partnership has $800,000 of general limitation income and $200,000 of passive income, 80% of the partner's distributive share of the partnership's income is general limitation income and the other 20% is passive income. A look-through rule also applies, in certain circumstances, to payments of interest, rents, and royalties by a partnership to a part-

---

[77] Code Sec. 954(b)(5). See Chapter 6 for a definition of foreign personal holding company income.

[78] Code Sec. 904(d)(3)(C). See Reg. § 1.904-5(c)(2)(ii) regarding the applicable apportionment method.

[79] Code Sec. 904(d)(3)(G) and Reg. § 1.904-5(c)(4)(i).

[80] Code Sec. 904(d)(3)(B) and Reg. § 1.904-5(c)(1)(i).

[81] Reg. § 1.904-5(c)(1)(ii), Example (1).

[82] Code Sec. 904(d)(3)(I) and Reg. § 1.904-5(j).

[83] Code Sec. 904(d)(2)(E)(iii).

[84] Code Sec. 904(d)(2)(A)(ii).

[85] Reg. § 1.904-5(h)(1).

ner.[86] These look-through rules do not apply to a limited partner or corporate general partner that owns less than 10% of the value of the partnership. In such cases, the partner's distributive share of partnership income generally is treated as passive income, unless the partnership interest is held in the ordinary course of the partner's trade or business, in which case the general look-through rule applies.[87] The rules applicable to partners in a partnership also apply to shareholders in an S corporation.[88]

Allocating Foreign Income Taxes

In order to apply the separate category of income limitations, foreign income taxes also must be allocated among the nine income categories. Foreign income taxes are allocated to the category of income that includes the income upon which the foreign taxes were imposed.[89] For example, foreign withholding taxes imposed upon interest income included in the passive income category are assigned to the passive category, whereas withholding taxes imposed upon interest income included in the financial services income category are assigned to the financial services income category.

If the base upon which a foreign income tax is imposed includes income from more than one category, the taxpayer prorates the foreign taxes among the separate categories of income using the following formula: [90]

$$\text{Foreign income taxes related to more than one income category} \times \frac{\text{Net income subject to the foreign tax included in the separate income category}}{\text{Total net income subject to the foreign tax}}$$

Net income for this purpose is determined under the tax accounting rules of the foreign country to which the tax was paid or accrued, rather than under U.S. law.

Example 3.7: USAco, a domestic corporation, paid $300,000 of foreign income taxes on $1 million of foreign taxable income. The $1 million of foreign taxable income consists of $800,000 of general limitation income and $200,000 of shipping income. Therefore, for purposes of applying the separate income limitations, USAco allocates $240,000 of foreign taxes [$300,000 × ($800,000 ÷ $1,000,000)] to the general limitation category and the remaining $60,000 of foreign taxes [$300,000 × ($200,000 ÷ $1,000,000)] to the shipping income category.

---

[86] Reg. § 1.904-5(h)(1).
[87] Reg. § 1.904-5(h)(2). A gain on the sale of a partnership interest also is treated as passive income. Reg. § 1.904-5(h)(3).

[88] Code Sec. 1373(a).
[89] Reg. § 1.904-6(a)(1)(i).
[90] Reg. § 1.904-6(a)(1)(ii).

A problem arises when the foreign income tax base includes an item of income that is nontaxable for U.S. purposes. Under the general allocation rules, the income in question is not reflected in the numerators of any separate income category, and therefore the related foreign tax will not be allocated to any of the separate income categories. To prevent this result, a special rule assigns these foreign taxes to the general limitation category.[91] A similar problem arises when an item of income is subject to taxation in different years for U.S. and foreign tax purposes. For purposes of allocating the related foreign taxes, such income is deemed to be recognized for U.S. tax purposes in the same taxable year that it is recognized for foreign tax purposes.[92]

¶ 306 OTHER COMPLEXITIES OF THE LIMITATION

Capital Gains and Losses

Under general U.S. tax principles, capital gains and losses receive special treatment in the form of the netting of individual capital gains and losses, a maximum tax rate on a noncorporate taxpayer's net long-term capital gain,[93] and limited deductibility of a net capital loss.[94] This special treatment can distort the accuracy of the foreign tax credit limitation as an estimate of the U.S. tax burden on foreign-source income. To prevent these distortions, taxpayers with capital gains and losses must make various special adjustments to the limitation.

One potential distortion arises when a taxpayer nets a foreign-source capital gain against a U.S.-source capital loss in computing the net capital gain or loss for the year. Because capital losses are generally deductible only against capital gains, one U.S. tax benefit derived from the foreign-source capital gain is to soak up the U.S.-source capital loss. If the taxpayer also includes the foreign-source capital gain in the numerator of the foreign tax credit limitation, a second U.S. tax benefit may be realized in the form of additional foreign tax credits. To prevent this double tax benefit, a foreign-source capital gain is excluded from the numerator of the foreign tax credit limitation to the extent it offsets a U.S.-source capital loss.[95]

A second potential distortion arises when the tax rate applied to a taxpayer's net long-term capital gain is lower than the tax rate applied to the taxpayer's ordinary income. Under current tax law, there is no capital gain rate differential for corporations, but there is a rate differential for individuals. When a capital gain rate differential exists, the attribution of the pre-credit U.S. tax to foreign-source taxable

---

[91] Reg. § 1.904-6(a)(1)(iv).
[92] Reg. § 1.904-6(a)(1)(iv).
[93] Code Sec. 1(h).
[94] Code Sec. 1211.
[95] Code Sec. 904(b)(2)(A).

income for purposes of computing the foreign tax credit limitation will be based on the "average" rate of U.S. tax on both ordinary income and the net long-term capital gain. This is advantageous when the long-term capital gain is from foreign sources, since the average U.S. rate is greater than the actual U.S. tax burden on the foreign-source capital gain. This result is disadvantageous, however, when the long-term capital gain is from U.S. sources, since the average U.S. rate underestimates the actual U.S. tax burden on foreign-source income, which is all ordinary in nature.

To prevent these distortions, a taxpayer that has a capital gain rate differential must reduce the numerator of the foreign tax credit limitation fraction by a portion of any foreign-source capital gain net income.[96] The taxpayer also must reduce the denominator of the limitation by a portion of the overall capital gain net income.[97] The amount of these reductions is determined by the magnitude of the capital gain rate differential enjoyed by the taxpayer and is computed so as to remove the precise amount of bias in the unadjusted foreign tax credit limitation.

A capital gain rate differential also can create a distortion when a taxpayer in a net long-term capital gain position nets a foreign-source capital loss against a U.S.-source long-term capital gain. Under the general rules, the effect of the foreign-source capital loss on the foreign tax credit limitation is based on the average rate of U.S. tax on both ordinary income and the net long-term capital gain. This average rate overstates the U.S. tax benefit of the foreign-source capital loss, and therefore understates the U.S. tax burden on foreign-source taxable income. To prevent this result, a taxpayer that has a capital gain rate differential can increase the numerator of the foreign tax credit limitation fraction by a portion of the foreign-source capital loss.[98]

Impact of Losses

Under basic U.S. tax principles, a loss from one business activity ordinarily is deductible against income from any other business activity. This principle ignores two important distinctions that must be made when computing the foreign tax credit limitation: the distinction between U.S.- and foreign-source income, and the assignment of income to one of nine separate category of income limitations. As a consequence, for purposes of computing the taxpayer's foreign tax credit limitation, numerous special rules apply when a taxpayer's business activities give rise to a net loss.

---

[96] Code Sec. 904(b)(2)(B)(i).

[97] Code Sec. 904(b)(2)(B)(ii).

[98] Code Sec. 904(b)(2)(B)(iii).

Overall foreign losses. An overall foreign loss occurs when the taxpayer's foreign-source deductions exceed foreign-source gross income.[99] A taxpayer can receive a current year tax benefit from an overall foreign loss by using that loss to offset U.S.-source income. If this occurs, the U.S. tax burden on foreign-source income is, in effect, negative in the year of the overall foreign loss. Moreover, there is no guarantee that future U.S. tax collections on foreign-source income will compensate for this initial tax benefit. For example, the United States collects only the residual U.S. tax on foreign-source income, and there is no residual U.S. tax on foreign-source income that is taxed at a rate higher than the U.S. rate. Thus, an overall foreign loss presents the possibility of the best of both worlds: the immediate utilization of foreign losses to shelter U.S.-source income, and the availability of foreign tax credits in profitable years to shield foreign-source income from U.S. tax.

To prevent this result, a taxpayer that sustains an overall foreign loss must, in each succeeding tax year, recapture as U.S.-source income the lesser of the following two amounts:

(i) 50% (or a larger percentage if the taxpayer so elects) of its foreign-source taxable income for that succeeding year, or

(ii) the amount of the overall foreign loss that has not been previously recaptured.[100]

This recapture rule prevents a double U.S. tax benefit by denying the taxpayer foreign tax credits on foreign-source income earned in the succeeding tax years.

U.S.-source losses. A U.S.-source loss reduces the denominator of the foreign tax credit limitation (i.e., total taxable income) and also offsets foreign-source taxable income in one or more numerators of the separate income limitation categories. Taxpayers would prefer to allocate the U.S. loss to the separate income category that does not give rise to an excess credit. However, a neutral allocation rule requires taxpayers to allocate a U.S.-source loss among the separate income categories on a pro rata basis.[101]

Separate limitation losses. To apply the separate income limitation rules, a taxpayer must make a separate computation of foreign-source taxable income or loss for each of the nine separate limitation categories. When a computation results in a net loss in a separate limitation category, that loss is a separate limitation loss.[102] Separate

---

[99] Code Sec. 904(f)(2).

[100] Code Sec. 904(f)(1). A gain on the disposition of appreciated foreign business property also results in the recapture of an overall foreign loss. Code Sec. 904(f)(3).

[101] Code Sec. 904(f)(5)(D).

[102] Code Sec. 904(f)(5)(E)(iii).

limitation losses are subject to special ordering and recharacterization rules.

The first ordering rule is that a separate limitation loss (which, by definition, is a foreign-source loss) must be deducted against income in another separate limitation category (i.e., other foreign-source income) before it can be deducted against any U.S.-source income.[103] Taxpayers would prefer to offset their foreign losses against U.S.-source income first, and only then reduce the numerators of the other separate income limitations.

The second ordering rule is that a separate limitation loss is allocated among the other separate income categories on a pro rata basis.[104] The rationale for this rule is the same as that for U.S.-source losses, which is to prevent taxpayers from allocating the entire separate limitation loss to a separate income category that does not give rise to an excess credit.

To further maintain the integrity of the separate income limitations, in succeeding years, income earned in the category from which a separate limitation loss arose is recharacterized as income in the categories to which the loss deduction was allocated and deducted.[105] For example, if a loss from the general limitation category is used to offset income in the passive income category, then any general limitation income earned in succeeding tax years is recharacterized as passive income to the extent of the prior year loss deduction.[106]

Oil and Gas Activities

Special restrictions prevent oil and gas companies from using excess credits on oil and gas extraction income to soak up the residual U.S. tax on other types of income. Congress enacted these restrictions because it believed that high rates of foreign tax on extraction income may represent disguised royalties for the right to extract oil and gas resources from government-owned land. As discussed earlier in this chapter, one way in which lawmakers attempt to resolve this issue is by denying a credit to a foreign levy if the taxpayer receives a specific economic benefit in exchange for the payment.[107] In addition, a corporate taxpayer's creditable foreign oil and gas extraction taxes are limited to an amount equal to the taxpayer's foreign oil and gas extraction income (or "FOGEI") for the year, multiplied by 35% (the maximum U.S. corporate tax rate).[108] Foreign extraction taxes which

---

[103] Code Sec. 904(f)(5)(A).

[104] Code Sec. 904(f)(5)(B).

[105] Code Sec. 904(f)(5)(C).

[106] A gain from the disposition of appreciated foreign business property that is related to a separate limitation loss also is subject to recharacterization. Code Sec. 904(f)(5)(F).

[107] Reg. § 1.901-2(a)(2)(i).

[108] Code Sec. 907(a). Individual taxpayers are subject to a different limitation.

are disallowed because of this restriction can be carried back up to two years or forward up to five years and taken as a credit in a year in which the taxpayer has an excess limitation on FOGEI.[109]

A similar restriction applies to foreign taxes imposed on foreign oil-related income (or "FORI"). FORI primarily includes foreign-source income from refining, processing, transporting, distributing, or selling oil and gas or primary products derived from oil and gas.[110] If the foreign tax burden on FORI is materially greater over time than the rate of tax on income other than FOGEI or FORI, a foreign tax credit is disallowed for a portion of the taxes imposed on FORI.[111]

Special Source-of-Income Rules

As discussed in Chapter 2, there are several source-of-income rules which apply solely for purposes of computing the foreign tax credit limitation. For example, certain types of income derived from a foreign corporation that is at least 50% owned by U.S. persons are recharacterized as U.S.-source income to the extent the income is attributable to earnings that the foreign corporation derived from U.S. sources. This rule applies to interest, dividends, Subpart F inclusions, foreign personal holding company income, and income derived from a passive foreign investment corporation that has made a qualified electing fund election.[112] In addition, a domestic corporation that claims a dividends-received deduction with respect to a portion of a dividend from a foreign corporation must treat that portion of the dividend as U.S.-source income for purposes of computing the foreign tax credit limitation.[113] A third example is a provision which requires a domestic corporation to specifically allocate certain interest expense deductions against foreign-source interest income derived from a controlled foreign corporation in computing its foreign tax credit limitation.[114]

¶ 307 EXCESS CREDIT CARRYOVERS

Foreign taxes that exceed the limitation in a given taxable year can be carried back up to two years and forward up to five years and taken as a credit in a year that the limitation exceeds the amount of creditable foreign taxes.[115] This carryover process must take place, however, within the confines of the separate income categories. In other words, excess credits from one category of income can offset only past

---

[109] Code Sec. 907(f).

[110] Code Sec. 907(c)(2). Under a look-through rule, FORI also includes dividends and interest derived from a 10%-or-more-owned foreign corporation to the extent the interest or dividends are attributable to FORI. Code Sec. 907(c)(3).

[111] Code Sec. 907(b) and Reg. § 1.907(b)-1.

[112] Code Sec. 904(g)(1). This rule does not apply if less than 10% of the U.S.-owned foreign corporation's earnings are attributable to U.S.-source income. Code Sec. 904(g)(5).

[113] Code Sec. 245(a)(9).

[114] Reg. § 1.861-10.

[115] Code Sec. 904(c).

or future excess limitations on that same type of income.[116] Excess credits that are carried back or forward to another taxable year must be credited and cannot be deducted in the carryback or carryforward year.[117]

This carryover provision prevents U.S. persons from being denied a foreign tax credit solely because of changes in the effective rate of foreign taxation over time. Such fluctuations arise when a country changes its statutory tax rates, when income or expense is recognized at different times for U.S. and foreign tax purposes, or when a country enacts or eliminates tax preference items.

> **Example 3.8:** USAco, a domestic corporation, realizes $20 million of foreign-source gross income in both year 1 and year 2. Assume that the U.S. and foreign tax rates are both 35%. The only deduction allocable against this income is a $20 million expenditure that is deducted over two years for U.S. tax purposes, but just one year for foreign tax purposes. As a consequence, USAco's foreign taxes are $0 in year 1 and $7 million in year 2 [35% × $20 million of foreign taxable income]. In contrast, USAco's foreign-source taxable income for U.S. tax purposes is $10 million [$20 million of gross income − $10 million of deductions] in both year 1 and year 2. Therefore, USAco's foreign tax credit limitation is $3.5 million in each year [$10 million × 35%]. If there were no excess credit carryover provision, USAco could claim a credit (in year 2) for only $3.5 million of the $7 million in foreign taxes paid. With the carryover provisions, USAco can carry the excess credits from year 2 back to year 1 and credit them against the excess limitation of $3.5 million for that year.

¶ 308 COMPUTING THE ALTERNATIVE MINIMUM TAX FOREIGN TAX CREDIT

U.S. persons can use foreign tax credits to offset not only their regular income tax for the year, but also their alternative minimum tax (or "AMT"). A U.S. person is subject to the AMT if the taxpayer's tentative minimum tax exceeds the regular tax for the year.[118] A corporate taxpayer's tentative minimum tax equals 20% (in the case of noncorporate taxpayers, a two-tiered rate schedule of 26% and 28% applies) of the taxpayer's alternative minimum taxable income less an exemption amount, and reduced by the alternative minimum foreign tax credit.[119]

A taxpayer computes the AMT foreign tax credit in the same manner as the credit for regular tax purposes, with two major excep-

---

[116] Code Sec. 904(d)(1).
[117] Code Sec. 904(c).

[118] Code Sec. 55(a).
[119] Code Sec. 55(b)(1).

tions. The first exception relates to the foreign tax credit limitation. For regular tax purposes, the limitation equals the pre-credit U.S. tax multiplied by the ratio of foreign-source taxable income to total taxable income, with separate limitations computed for nine separate categories of income. For AMT purposes, the same basic formula and separate income categories apply, except that the pre-credit U.S. tax amount is now the tentative minimum tax (before any foreign tax credits) and the foreign-source and total taxable income amounts are computed on the basis of alternative minimum taxable income.[120] For example, the AMT limitation for the passive income category equals the pre-credit tentative minimum tax multiplied by the ratio of foreign-source passive alternative minimum taxable income to total alternative minimum taxable income.

The second exception is that the foreign tax credit for AMT purposes cannot exceed 90% of the taxpayer's tentative minimum tax.[121] Congress enacted this restriction to ensure that taxpayers would always owe some tax on their foreign-source alternative minimum taxable income. Any foreign tax credits disallowed by this rule can be carried over to another taxable year under the general provisions for foreign tax credit carryovers.[122]

Taxpayers may elect to use a simplified AMT foreign tax credit limitation when calculating their AMT foreign tax credit. The simplified limitation is the ratio of the taxpayer's foreign-source regular taxable income to the entire alternative minimum taxable income (AMTI). Because the simplified limitation uses foreign-source regular taxable income, rather than foreign-source AMTI, the taxpayer is not required to reallocate and reapportion deductions for AMTI purposes based on assets and income that reflect AMT adjustments (including depreciation). The AMT foreign tax credit limitation under the simplified method is computed using the following formula:[123]

$$\frac{\text{Foreign-source regular taxable income}}{\text{Worldwide AMTI}} \times \begin{pmatrix} [\text{Worldwide AMTI} - \text{AMT exemption}] \\ \times [\text{AMT rate}] \end{pmatrix}$$

The election may be made only in the taxpayer's first tax year beginning on or after January 1, 1998, for which the taxpayer claims an AMT foreign tax credit. The election applies to all subsequent tax years and can be revoked only with the consent of the IRS.[124]

---

[120] Code Sec. 59(a)(1).

[121] Code Sec. 59(a)(2)(A).

[122] Code Sec. 59(a)(2)(B).

[123] For purposes of the simplified limitation, foreign-source regular taxable income cannot exceed the taxpayer's entire AMTI.

[124] Code Sec. 59(a)(3)[sic 4].

¶ 309   FILING REQUIREMENTS

A corporation claiming a foreign tax credit must attach Form 1118, Foreign Tax Credit—Corporations, to its tax return, whereas an individual claiming a foreign tax credit must attach Form 1116, Foreign Tax Credit, to his or her tax return.[125] Taxpayers must complete a separate Form 1118 (or Form 1116) for each separate category of income limitation. (Forms 1116 and 1118 are reproduced in the appendix to this chapter.)

As with all other items on a tax return, a taxpayer must maintain appropriate documentation for the foreign tax credit. In this regard, foreign withholding taxes represent some unique problems, since they are not paid directly by the taxpayer. Indirect evidence, such as a letter from the foreign payer stating that the tax was withheld and paid, may not provide sufficient proof of payment to claim a credit. Instead, the taxpayer may be required to produce evidence that the foreign payer actually remitted the foreign withholding taxes to the foreign government.[126] Therefore, when possible, taxpayers should attempt to obtain a government receipt for any foreign withholding taxes.

Redeterminations

If an adjustment by a foreign tax authority results in an increase in the amount of foreign taxes paid (and, in turn, an increase in creditable foreign taxes), the taxpayer has 10 years from the date the return was originally filed to claim a refund of U.S. taxes.[127] On the other hand, if the redetermination results in a refund of foreign taxes, the taxpayer must file an amended tax return on which the taxpayer recomputes the U.S. tax liability for the year in which the foreign tax credit was originally claimed.[128] A failure to file an amended return can result in a penalty of up to 25% of the amount of the deficiency associated with the redetermination.[129]

A redetermination will also occur anytime that accrued foreign taxes remain unpaid for more than two years after the close of the tax year to which the taxes relate. If the foreign tax is paid within the two-year period, no redetermination is necessary even though the actual dollar value of the foreign tax paid may differ from the accrued amount due to currency fluctuations. Also, in lieu of redetermining foreign taxes for purposes of the indirect credit, under regulations to be

---

[125] Reg. § 1.905-2(a)(1).

[126] Reg. § 1.905-2(b)(3) and *Continental Illinois Corp. v. Comm'r,* 998 F2d 513 (7th Cir. 1993), *aff'g, rev'g, and rem'g* 61 TCM 1916 (1991).

[127] Code Sec. 6511(d)(3)(A).

[128] Temp. Reg. § 1.905-4T(b).

[129] Code Sec. 6689.

promulgated by the Treasury, adjustments may be made to the payor foreign corporation's pools of earnings and profits and foreign taxes.[130]

Redetermined taxes paid are generally translated into U.S. dollars using the exchange rate applicable on the date the foreign taxes are paid. This rule also applies to accrued taxes paid after the two-year period. Where foreign taxes are refunded or credited by the foreign government, the redetermined amount of taxes paid is translated into dollars using the exchange rate as of the date of the original payment of such taxes. For accrued taxes paid after the two-year period, if the taxpayer claimed a direct foreign tax credit, the payment is taken into account for the tax year to which the foreign tax relates. If an indirect credit was taken, foreign tax subsequently paid is taken into account in determining the taxpayer's foreign tax credit for the tax year in which the tax was paid.[131]

---

[130] Code Sec. 905(c).

[131] Code Sec. 905(c).

9

¶ 310 APPENDIX

Form **1116**	**Foreign Tax Credit**	OMB No. 1545-0121
Department of the Treasury Internal Revenue Service (99)	(Individual, Estate, Trust, or Nonresident Alien Individual) ▶ Attach to Form 1040, 1040NR, 1041, or 990-T. ▶ See separate instructions.	**1999** Attachment Sequence No. **19**

Name	Identifying number as shown on page 1 of your tax return

Use a separate Form 1116 for each category of income listed below. See **Categories of Income** on page 3 of the instructions. Check only one box on each Form 1116. Report all amounts in U.S. dollars except where specified in Part II below.

a ☐ Passive income
b ☐ High withholding tax interest
c ☐ Financial services income
d ☐ Shipping income
e ☐ Dividends from a DISC or former DISC
f ☐ Certain distributions from a foreign sales corporation (FSC) or former FSC
g ☐ Lump-sum distributions
h ☐ Section 901(j) income
i ☐ Income re-sourced by treaty
j ☐ General limitation income

k Resident of (name of country) ▶

Note: *If you paid taxes to only one foreign country or U.S. possession, use column A in Part I and line A in Part II. If you paid taxes to* ***more than one*** *foreign country or U.S. possession, use a separate column and line for each country or possession.*

Part I Taxable Income or Loss From Sources Outside the United States (for Category Checked Above)

		Foreign Country or U.S. Possession			Total
		A	B	C	(Add cols. A, B, and C.)
l	Enter the name of the foreign country or U.S. possession . . . . ▶				
1	Gross income from sources within country shown above and of the type checked above. See page 7 of the instructions:				**1**
	Deductions and losses (*Caution: See pages 7 through 9 of the instructions*):				
2	Expenses **definitely related** to the income on line 1 (attach statement)				
3	Pro rata share of other deductions **not definitely related:**				
a	Certain itemized deductions or standard deduction. See instructions				
b	Other deductions (attach statement)				
c	Add lines 3a and 3b				
d	Gross foreign source income. See instructions .				
e	Gross income from all sources. See instructions				
f	Divide line 3d by line 3e. See instructions . .				
g	Multiply line 3c by line 3f				
4	Pro rata share of interest expense. See instructions:				
a	Home mortgage interest (use worksheet on page 9 of the instructions)				
b	Other interest expense				
5	Losses from foreign sources				
6	Add lines 2, 3g, 4a, 4b, and 5				**6**
7	Subtract line 6 from line 1. Enter the result here and on line 14, page 2 . . . . ▶				**7**

Part II Foreign Taxes Paid or Accrued (See page 9 of the instructions.)

Country	Credit is claimed for taxes (you must check one) (m) ☐ Paid (n) ☐ Accrued	Foreign taxes paid or accrued								
		In foreign currency				In U.S. dollars				
		Taxes withheld at source on:			(s) Other foreign taxes paid or accrued	Taxes withheld at source on:			(w) Other foreign taxes paid or accrued	(x) Total foreign taxes paid or accrued (add cols. (t) through (w))
	(o) Date paid or accrued	(p) Dividends	(q) Rents and royalties	(r) Interest		(t) Dividends	(u) Rents and royalties	(v) Interest		
A										
B										
C										

8 Add lines A through C, column (x). Enter the total here and on line 9, page 2 . . . . ▶ **8**

For Paperwork Reduction Act Notice, see page 12 of the instructions.   Cat. No. 11440U   Form **1116** (1999)

Part III   **Figuring the Credit**

9	Enter amount from line 8. These are your total foreign taxes paid or accrued for the category of income checked above Part I	**9**
10	Carryback or carryover (attach detailed computation)	**10**
11	Add lines 9 and 10	**11**
12	Reduction in foreign taxes. See page 10 of the instructions . . .	**12**
13	Subtract line 12 from line 11. This is the total amount of foreign taxes available for credit	**13**
14	Enter amount from line 7. This is your taxable income or (loss) from sources outside the United States (before adjustments) for the category of income checked above Part I. See page 10 of the instructions . .	**14**
15	Adjustments to line 14. See page 10 of the instructions	**15**
16	Combine the amounts on lines 14 and 15. This is your net foreign source taxable income. (If the result is zero or less, you have no foreign tax credit for the category of income you checked above Part I. Skip lines 17 through 21.)	**16**
17	**Individuals:** Enter amount from Form 1040, line 37. If you are a nonresident alien, enter amount from Form 1040NR, line 36. **Estates and trusts:** Enter your taxable income without the deduction for your exemption	**17**
	Caution: *If you figured your tax using the special rates on capital gains, see page 12 of the instructions.*	
18	Divide line 16 by line 17. If line 16 is more than line 17, enter "1".	**18**
19	**Individuals:** Enter amount from Form 1040, line 40, **less** any amounts on Form 1040, lines 41 through 45, and any mortgage interest credit (from Form 8396) and District of Columbia first-time homebuyer credit (from Form 8859) on line 47. If you are a nonresident alien, enter amount from Form 1040NR, line 39, less any amount on Form 1040NR, lines 40, 41, 42, and any mortgage interest credit (from Form 8396) and District of Columbia first-time homebuyer credit (from Form 8859) on line 44. **Estates and trusts:** Enter amount from Form 1041, Schedule G, line 1c, or Form 990-T, lines 36 and 37 .	**19**
20	Multiply line 19 by line 18 (maximum amount of credit)	**20**
21	Enter the amount from line 13 or line 20, whichever is **smaller.** If this is the only Form 1116 you are completing, skip lines 22 through 29 and enter this amount on line 30. Otherwise, complete the appropriate line in Part IV. See page 12 of the instructions. . . . . ▶	**21**

Part IV   **Summary of Credits From Separate Parts III** (See page 12 of the instructions.)

22	Credit for taxes on passive income	**22**
23	Credit for taxes on high withholding tax interest	**23**
24	Credit for taxes on financial services income	**24**
25	Credit for taxes on shipping income	**25**
26	Credit for taxes on dividends from a DISC or former DISC and certain distributions from a FSC or former FSC	**26**
27	Credit for taxes on lump-sum distributions	**27**
28	Credit for taxes on income re-sourced by treaty	**28**
29	Credit for taxes on general limitation income	**29**
30	Add lines 22 through 29.	**30**
31	Reduction of credit for international boycott operations. See instructions for line 12 on page 10 . .	**31**
32	Subtract line 31 from line 30. This is your **foreign tax credit.** Enter here and on Form 1040, line 46; Form 1040NR, line 43; Form 1041, Schedule G, line 2a; or Form 990-T, line 39a. . . . . . ▶	**32**

Form **1116** (1999)

Form **1118**
(Rev. January 1999)
Internal Revenue Service
Department of the Treasury

Foreign Tax Credit—Corporations

▶ Attach to the corporation's tax return.

OMB No. 1545-0122

Name of corporation

Employer identification number

For calendar year ___, or other tax year beginning ___, and ending ___.

Complete this form for credit for taxes paid on the categories of income listed below. See page 2 of the instructions for descriptions. Also, see **Specific Instructions** on page 5.
Important: *Complete a **SEPARATE** Form 1118 for **each** applicable income category. Check only one box on each form.*

☐ Passive Income
☐ High Withholding Tax Interest
☐ Financial Services Income
☐ Shipping Income

☐ Dividends From a DISC or Former DISC
☐ Taxable Income Attributable To Foreign Trade Income
☐ Certain Distributions From a FSC or Former FSC
☐ Dividends From **Each** Noncontrolled Section 902 Corporation:
　Name of Foreign Corporation ▶

☐ General Limitation Income
☐ Section 901(j) Income: Name of Sanctioned Country ▶
☐ Income Re-sourced by Treaty: Name of Country ▶

Country of Incorporation ▶

Schedule A　**Income or (Loss) Before Adjustments** *(Report all amounts in U.S. dollars. See **Specific Instructions** on page 5.)*

Gross Income or (Loss) From Sources Outside the United States (*INCLUDE* Foreign Branch Gross Income here *and* on Schedule F)

1. Foreign Country or U.S. Possession (Enter two-letter code from page 11 of instructions. Use a separate line for each.) *	2. Deemed Dividends (see instructions)		3. Other Dividends		4. Interest	5. Gross Rents, Royalties, and License Fees	6. Gross Income From Performance of Services	7. Other (attach schedule)	8. Total (add columns 2(a) through 7)
	(a) Exclude gross-up	(b) Gross-up (sec. 78)	(a) Exclude gross-up	(b) Gross-up (sec. 78)					
A									
B									
C									
D									
E									
F									
G									
Totals (add lines A through G)									

* For section 863(b) income, use a single line and enter "863(b)."

Deductions (*INCLUDE* Foreign Branch Deductions here *and* on Schedule F)

9. Definitely Allocable Deductions					10. Apportioned Share of Deductions Not Definitely Allocable (enter amount from applicable line of Schedule H, Part II, column (d))	11. Total Deductions (add columns 9(e) and 10)	12. Total Income or (Loss) Before Adjustments (subtract column 11 from column 8)
Rental, Royalty, and Licensing Expenses		(c) Expenses Related to Gross Income From Performance of Services	(d) Other Definitely Allocable Deductions	(e) Total Definitely Allocable Deductions (add columns 9(a) through 9(d))			
(a) Depreciation, Depletion, and Amortization	(b) Other Expenses						
A							
B							
C							
D							
E							
F							
G							
Totals							

For Paperwork Reduction Act Notice, see page 1 of separate instructions.

Cat. No. 10900F

Form **1118** (Rev. 1-99)

Form 1118 (Rev. 1-99)   Page **2**

Schedule B   **Foreign Tax Credit** *(Report all foreign tax amounts in U.S. dollars.)*

Part I—Foreign Taxes Paid, Accrued, and Deemed Paid *(See page 5 of instructions.)*

1. Credit is Claimed for Taxes:		2. Foreign Taxes Paid or Accrued (attach schedule showing amounts in foreign currency and conversion rate(s) used)								3. Tax Deemed Paid (from Schedule C— Part I, column 10, Part II, column 8(b), and Part III, column 8)
		Tax Withheld at Source on:			Other Foreign Taxes Paid or Accrued on:					
☐ Paid ☐ Accrued		(a) Dividends	(b) Interest	(c) Rents, Royalties, and License Fees	(d) Section 863(b) Income	(e) Foreign Branch Income	(f) Services Income	(g) Other	(h) Total Foreign Taxes Paid or Accrued (add columns 2(a) through 2(g))	
Date Paid	Date Accrued									
A										
B										
C										
D										
E										
F										
G										
Totals (add lines A through G)										

Part II—Separate Credit Limitation *(Complete a separate Part II for each applicable category of income.)*

1   Total foreign taxes paid or accrued (total from Part I, column 2(h)) . . . .
2   Total taxes deemed paid (total from Part I, column 3) . . . .
3   Reductions of taxes paid, accrued, or deemed paid (enter total from Schedule G) . . . . . .
4   Total carryover of foreign taxes (attach schedule showing computation in detail—see page 6 of the instructions) .
5   Total foreign taxes (combine lines 1 through 4) . . . .
6   Enter the amount from the applicable column of Schedule J, Part I, line 11. (See instructions.) If Schedule J is **not** required to be completed, enter the result from the "Totals" line of column 12 of the applicable Schedule A . . . .
7a   Total taxable income from all sources (enter taxable income from the corporation's tax return) . . . .
b   Adjustments to line 7a. (See page 6 of instructions.) . . . .
c   Subtract line 7b from line 7a . . . .
8   Divide line 6 by line 7c. Enter the resulting fraction as a decimal. (See instructions.) If line 6 is greater than line 7c, enter **1** .
9   Total U.S. income tax against which credit is allowed (regular tax liability (see section 26(b)) minus possessions tax credit determined under section 936 or 30A) . . .
10   Credit limitation (multiply line 8 by line 9). (See page 6 of instructions.) . . . .
11   **Separate foreign tax credit** (enter the smaller of line 5 or line 10 here and on the appropriate line of Part III) .

Part III—Summary of Separate Credit Limitations (Enter amounts from Part I, line 11 for **each** applicable income category. **Do not** complete for section 901(j) income.)

1   Credit for taxes on passive income . . . .
2   Credit for taxes on high withholding tax interest. . . . .
3   Credit for taxes on financial services income. . . . .
4   Credit for taxes on shipping income. . . . .
5   Credit for taxes on dividends from each noncontrolled section 902 corporation (combine all such credits on this line)
6   Credit for taxes on dividends from a DISC or former DISC . . . .
7   Credit for taxes on taxable income attributable to foreign trade income . . . .
8   Credit for taxes on certain distributions from a FSC or former FSC . . . .
9   Credit for taxes on General Limitation income . . . .
10   Credit for taxes on income re-sourced by treaty (combine all such credits on this line) . . . . .
11   Total (add lines 1 through 10) . . . .
12   Reduction in credit for international boycott operations (see page 6 of instructions) . . . .
13   **Total foreign tax credit** (subtract line 12 from line 11). Enter here and on the appropriate line of the corporation's tax return.

¶ 310

Form 1118 (Rev. 1-99)

Page **3**

Schedule C | Tax Deemed Paid by Domestic Corporation Filing Return

Use this schedule to figure the tax deemed paid by the corporation with respect to dividends from a first-tier foreign corporation under section 902(a), and deemed inclusions of earnings from a first- or lower-tier foreign corporation under section 960(a). **Report all amounts in U.S. dollars unless otherwise specified.**

Part I—Dividends and Inclusions From Post-1986 Undistributed Earnings

1. Name of Foreign Corporation (identify DISCs and former DISCs)	2. Tax Year End (Yr-Mo) (see instructions)	3. Country of Incorporation (enter country code from page 11 of instructions)	4. Post-1986 Undistributed Earnings (in functional currency—attach schedule)	5. Opening Balance in Post-1986 Foreign Income Taxes	6. Foreign Taxes Paid and Deemed Paid for Tax Year Indicated		7. Post-1986 Foreign Income Taxes (add columns 5, 6(a), and 6(b))	8. Dividends and Deemed Inclusions		9. Divide Column 8(a) by Column 4	10. Tax Deemed Paid (multiply column 7 by column 9)
					(a) Taxes Paid	(b) Taxes Deemed Paid (from Schedule D, Part I—see instructions)		(a) Functional Currency	(b) U.S. Dollars		

Total (Add amounts in column 10. Include result here and on "Totals" line of Schedule B, Part I, column 3) ▲

Part II—Dividends Paid Out of Pre-1987 Accumulated Profits

1. Name of Foreign Corporation (identify DISCs and former DISCs)	2. Tax Year End (Yr-Mo) (see instructions)	3. Country of Incorporation (enter country code from page 11 of instructions)	4. Accumulated Profits for Tax Year Indicated (in functional currency computed under section 902) (attach schedule)	5. Foreign Taxes Paid and Deemed Paid on Earnings and Profits (E&P) for Tax Year Indicated (in functional currency) (see instructions)	6. Dividends Paid		7. Divide Column 6(a) by Column 4	8. Tax Deemed Paid (see instructions)	
					(a) Functional Currency	(b) U.S. Dollars		(a) Functional Currency	(b) U.S. Dollars

Total (Add amounts in column 8b. Include result here and on "Totals" line of Schedule B, Part I, column 3) ▲

Part III—Deemed Inclusions From Pre-1987 Earnings and Profits

1. Name of Foreign Corporation (identify DISCs and former DISCs)	2. Tax Year End (Yr-Mo) (see instructions)	3. Country of Incorporation (enter country code from page 11 of instructions)	4. E&P for Tax Year Indicated (in functional currency translated from U.S. dollars, computed under section 964) (attach schedule)	5. Foreign Taxes Paid and Deemed Paid for Tax Year Indicated (see instructions)	6. Deemed Inclusions		7. Divide Column 6(a) by Column 4	8. Tax Deemed Paid (multiply column 5 by column 7)
					(a) Functional Currency	(b) U.S. Dollars		

Total (Add amounts in column 8. Enter the result here and include on "Totals" line of Schedule B, Part I, column 3) ▲

¶ 310

Form 1118 (Rev. 1-99)   Page **4**

Schedule D | **Tax Deemed Paid by First- and Second-Tier Foreign Corporations under Section 902(b)**

Use Part I to compute the tax deemed paid by a first-tier foreign corporation with respect to dividends from a second-tier foreign corporation. Use Part II to compute the tax deemed paid by a second-tier foreign corporation with respect to dividends from a third-tier foreign corporation. **Report all amounts in U.S. dollars unless otherwise specified.**

Part I—Tax Deemed Paid by First-Tier Foreign Corporations

Section A—Dividends Paid Out of Post-1986 Undistributed Earnings (Include the column 10 results in Schedule C, Part I, column 6(b).)

1. Name of Second-Tier Foreign Corporation and Its Related First-Tier Foreign Corporation	2. Tax Year End (Yr-Mo) (see instructions)	3. Country of Incorporation (enter country code from page 11 of instructions)	4. Post-1986 Undistributed Earnings (in functional currency)—attach schedule)	5. Opening Balance in Post-1986 Foreign Income Taxes	6. Foreign Taxes Paid and Deemed Paid for Tax Year Indicated		7. Post-1986 Foreign Income Taxes (add columns 5, 6(a), and 6(b))	8. Dividends Paid (in functional currency)		9. Divide Column 8(a) by Column 4	10. Tax Deemed Paid (multiply column 7 by column 9)
					(a) Taxes Paid	(b) Taxes Deemed Paid (see instructions)		(a) of Second-tier Corporation	(b) of First-tier Corporation		

Section B—Dividends Paid Out of Pre-1987 Accumulated Profits (Include the column 8(b) results in Schedule C, Part I, column 6(b).)

1. Name of Second-Tier Foreign Corporation and Its Related First-Tier Foreign Corporation	2. Tax Year End (Yr-Mo) (see instructions)	3. Country of Incorporation (enter country code from page 11 of instructions)	4. Accumulated Profits for Tax Year Indicated (in functional currency)—attach schedule	5. Opening Balance in Post-1986 Foreign Income Taxes	6. Foreign Taxes Paid and Deemed Paid for Tax Year Indicated (in functional currency—see instructions)	7. Foreign Taxes Paid and Deemed Paid for Tax Year Indicated	8. Dividends Paid (in functional currency)		9. Divide Column 6(a) by Column 4	10. Tax Deemed Paid (multiply column 7 by column 9)
					(a) Taxes Paid		(a) of Second-tier Corporation	(b) Functional Currency of Second-tier Corporation		(b) U.S. Dollars

Part II—Tax Deemed Paid by Second-Tier Foreign Corporations

Section A—Dividends Paid Out of Post-1986 Undistributed Earnings (Include the column 10 results in Section A, column 6(b), of Part I above.)

1. Name of Third-Tier Foreign Corporation and Its Related Second-Tier Foreign Corporation	2. Tax Year End (Yr-Mo) (see instructions)	3. Country of Incorporation (enter country code from page 11 of instructions)	4. Post-1986 Undistributed Earnings (in functional currency)—attach schedule	5. Opening Balance in Post-1986 Foreign Income Taxes	6. Foreign Taxes Paid and Deemed Paid for Tax Year Indicated		7. Post-1986 Foreign Income Taxes (add columns 5, 6(a), and 6(b))	8. Dividends Paid (in functional currency)		9. Divide Column 8(a) by Column 4	10. Tax Deemed Paid (multiply column 7 by column 9)
					(a) Taxes Paid	(b) Taxes Deemed Paid (from Schedule E, Part I, column 10)		(a) of Third-tier Corporation	(b) of Second-tier Corporation		

Section B—Dividends Paid Out of Pre-1987 Accumulated Profits (Include the column 8(b) results in Section A, column 6(b), of Part I above.)

1. Name of Third-Tier Foreign Corporation and Its Related Second-Tier Foreign Corporation	2. Tax Year End (Yr-Mo) (see instructions)	3. Country of Incorporation (enter country code from page 11 of instructions)	4. Accumulated Profits for Tax Year Indicated (in functional currency)—attach schedule	5. Foreign Taxes Paid and Deemed Paid for Tax Year Indicated (in functional currency)—see instructions	6. Dividends Paid (in functional currency)		7. Divide Column 6(a) by Column 4	8. Tax Deemed Paid (see instructions)
					(a) of Third-tier Corporation	(b) of Second-tier Corporation		(a) in functional Currency of Third-tier Corporation	(b) U.S. Dollars

Form 1118 (Rev. 1-99)
Page **5**

Schedule E Tax Deemed Paid by Certain Third-, Fourth-, and Fifth-Tier Foreign Corporations Under Section 902(b)

Use this schedule to report taxes deemed paid with respect to dividends paid with respect to dividends paid from eligible post-1986 undistributed earnings of fourth-, fifth- and sixth-tier controlled foreign corporations. **Report all amounts in U.S. dollars unless otherwise specified.**

Part I—Tax Deemed Paid by Third-Tier Foreign Corporations (Include the column 10 results in Schedule D, Part II, Section A, column 6(b).)

1. Name of Fourth-Tier Foreign Corporation and Its Related Third-Tier Foreign Corporation	2. Country of Incorporation (enter country code from page 11 of instructions)	3. Tax Year End (Yr-Mo) (see instructions)	4. Post-1986 Undistributed Earnings (in functional currency—attach schedule)	5. Opening Balance in Post-1986 Foreign Income Taxes	6. Foreign Taxes Paid and Deemed Paid for Tax Year Indicated		7. Post-1986 Foreign Income Taxes (add columns 5, 6(a), and 6(b))	8. Dividends Paid (in functional currency)		9. Divide Column 8(a) by Column 4	10. Tax Deemed Paid (multiply column 7 by column 9)
					(a) Taxes Paid	(b) Taxes Deemed Paid (from Part II, column 10)		(a) Of Fourth-tier CFC	(b) Of Third-tier CFC		

Part II—Tax Deemed Paid by Fourth-Tier Foreign Corporations (Include the column 10 results in column 6(b) of Part I above.)

1. Name of Fifth-Tier Foreign Corporation and Its Related Fourth-Tier Foreign Corporation	2. Country of Incorporation (enter country code from page 11 of instructions)	3. Tax Year End (Yr-Mo) (see instructions)	4. Post-1986 Undistributed Earnings (in functional currency—attach schedule)	5. Opening Balance in Post-1986 Foreign Income Taxes	6. Foreign Taxes Paid and Deemed Paid for Tax Year Indicated		7. Post-1986 Foreign Income Taxes (add columns 5, 6(a), and 6(b))	8. Dividends Paid (in functional currency)		9. Divide Column 8(a) by Column 4	10. Tax Deemed Paid (multiply column 7 by column 9)
					(a) Taxes Paid	(b) Taxes Deemed Paid (from Part III, column 10)		(a) Of Fifth-tier CFC	(b) Of Fourth-tier CFC		

Part III—Tax Deemed Paid by Fifth-Tier Foreign Corporations (Include the column 10 results in column 6(b) of Part II above.)

1. Name of Sixth-Tier Foreign Corporation and Its Related Fifth-Tier Foreign Corporation	2. Country of Incorporation (enter country code from page 11 of instructions)	3. Tax Year End (Yr-Mo) (see instructions)	4. Post-1986 Undistributed Earnings (in functional currency—attach schedule)	5. Opening Balance in Post-1986 Foreign Income Taxes	6. Foreign Taxes Paid For Tax Year Indicated	7. Post-1986 Foreign Income Taxes (add columns 5 and 6)	8. Dividends Paid (in functional currency)		9. Divide Column 8(a) by Column 4	10. Tax Deemed Paid (multiply column 7 by column 9)
							(a) Of Sixth-tier CFC	(b) Of Fifth-tier CFC		

¶ 310

Form 1118 (Rev. 1-99)   Page **6**

Schedule F   Gross Income and Definitely Allocable Deductions for Foreign Branches

1. Name of Foreign Country or U.S. Possession (Use a separate line for each.)	2. Gross Income	3. Definitely Allocable Deductions
A		
B		
C		
D		
E		
F		
G		
H		

Totals (add lines A through H)* ▲

* **Note:** The Schedule F totals are not carried over to any other Form 1118 Schedule. (These totals were already included in Schedule A.) However, the IRS requires the corporation to complete Schedule F under the authority of section 905(b).

Schedule G   Reductions of Taxes Paid, Accrued, or Deemed Paid

A	Reduction of Taxes Under Section 901(e)—Attach separate schedule
B	Reduction of Oil and Gas Extraction Taxes—Enter amount from Schedule I, Part II, line 6
C	Reduction of Taxes Due to International Boycott Provisions—Enter appropriate portion of Schedule C (Form 5713), line 2b. **Important:** Enter only "specifically attributable taxes" here.
D	Reduction of Taxes for Section 6038(c) Penalty—Attach separate schedule
E	Other Reductions of Taxes—Attach schedule(s)
	Total (add lines A through E). Enter here and on Schedule B, Part II, line 3 . . . . ▲

¶ 310

Form 1118 (Rev. 1-99)

Page 7

Schedule H Apportionment of Deductions Not Definitely Allocable *(Complete Only Once)*

Part I—Research and Development Deductions

	Product line #1 (SIC Code:	(a) Sales Method — Product line #2 (SIC Code:			(b) Gross Income Method—Check method used: (See page 9 of instructions.) ☐ Option 1 ☐ Option 2			(c) Total R&D Deductions Not Definitely Allocable (enter all amounts from column (a)(v) or all amounts from column (b)(vii))
	(i) Gross Sales	(ii) R&D Deductions	(iii) Gross Sales	(iv) R&D Deductions	(v) Total R&D Deductions Under Sales Method (add columns (ii) and (iv))	(vi) Gross income	(vii) Total R&D Deductions Under Gross Income Method	
1 Totals (see page 8 of instructions)								
2 Total to be apportioned								
3 Apportionment among statutory groupings:								
a General limitation income								
b Passive income								
c High withholding tax interest								
d Financial services income								
e Shipping income								
f Dividends from noncontrolled section 902 corp.*								
g Taxable income attributable to foreign trade income								
h Section 901(j) income*								
i Income re-sourced by treaty*								
4 Total foreign (add lines 3a through 3i)								

Part II—Interest Deductions, All Other Deductions, and Total Deductions

	(a) Average Value of Assets—Check method used: ☐ Tax book value ☐ Fair market value		(b) Interest Deductions		(c) All Other Deductions Not Definitely Allocable	(d) Totals (add the corresponding amounts from column (c), Part I; columns (b)(iii) and (b)(iv), Part II; and column (c), Part II). Enter each amount from lines 3a through 3k below in column 10 of the corresponding Schedule A.
	(i) Nonfinancial Corporations	(ii) Financial Corporations	(iii) Nonfinancial Corporations	(iv) Financial Corporations		
1a Totals (see page 9 of instructions)						
b Amounts specifically allocable under Temp. Regs. 1.861-10T(e)						
c Other specific allocations under Temp. Regs. 1.861-10T						
d Assets excluded from apportionment formula						
2 Total to be apportioned (subtract lines 1b, 1c, and 1d from line 1a)						
3 Apportionment among statutory groupings:						
a General limitation income						
b Passive income						
c High withholding tax interest						
d Financial services income						
e Shipping income						
f Dividends from noncontrolled section 902 corporation*						
g Taxable income attributable to foreign trade income						
h Certain distributions from a FSC or former FSC						
i Dividends from a DISC or former DISC						
j Section 901(j) income*						
k Income re-sourced by treaty*						
4 Total foreign (add lines 3a through 3k)						

*Important: See *Computer-Generated Schedule H* in instructions.

*See page 9 of instructions.

¶310

Chapter 4

Deemed Paid Foreign Tax Credit

¶ 401 TAXATION OF DIVIDEND REPATRIATIONS—OVERVIEW

Gross Income

A domestic corporation generally cannot claim a dividends-received deduction for a dividend from a foreign corporation, even if that foreign corporation is a wholly owned subsidiary.[1] Thus, a domestic corporation generally must include the entire amount of such dividends in U.S. taxable income. A dividends-received deduction is not allowed because the domestic parent corporation's receipt of a dividend from a foreign corporation is normally the U.S. Treasury's first opportunity to tax the underlying foreign-source earnings. In contrast, a dividends-received deduction is allowed for dividends received from domestic corporations, based on the premise that the United States has already taxed the underlying earnings at the subsidiary corporation level, and therefore those earnings should not be taxed again at the parent corporation level.

An exception applies if a domestic corporation owns 10% or more of a foreign corporation, and that foreign corporation distributes a dividend out of post-1986 undistributed earnings that are attributable to either income effectively connected with the conduct of a U.S. trade or

---

[1] Code Sec. 243(a).

business or dividends received from a domestic subsidiary corporation.[2] The domestic corporation can claim a dividends-received deduction in this situation because the dividends represent a distribution of earnings that have already been taxed by the United States. Another exception applies to dividends received from a foreign sales corporation (or "FSC"). As part of the special tax regime for FSCs, a domestic corporation can claim a 100% dividends-received deduction for a dividend paid out of an FSC's foreign trade income, and an 80% or 70% dividends-received deduction for a dividend paid out of other earnings of the FSC which the United States has already taxed as income effectively connected with the conduct of a U.S. trade or business.[3]

Direct Foreign Tax Credit

Most foreign countries impose flat rate withholding taxes on the gross amount of dividends paid by a locally organized corporation to a U.S. shareholder. Tax treaties usually reduce the statutory withholding tax rate to 15% or less, and the treaty withholding rate often is lower for controlling shareholders (e.g., a shareholder owning 10% or more of the payer's stock) than for noncontrolling shareholders.

A U.S. person can claim a direct foreign tax credit for any foreign withholding taxes it pays on a dividend from a foreign corporation.[4] However, a credit generally is not allowed for any foreign withholding taxes imposed on an FSC's distribution of foreign trade income, since the domestic shareholder is already allowed a 100% dividends-received deduction for such distributions.[5] A similar prohibition applies to any foreign withholding taxes related to the U.S.-source portion of a dividend from a foreign corporation for which the taxpayer has claimed a dividends-received deduction.[6]

Taxpayers cannot claim a credit for foreign income taxes deemed paid with respect to a dividend unless a 16-day holding period for the dividend-paying stock (or a 46-day holding period for certain dividends on preferred stock) is satisfied with respect to each corporation in the chain of corporations for which the deemed paid credit is claimed. The 16-day holding period requirement must be met within the 30-day period beginning 15 days before the ex-dividend date. If the stock is held for 15 days or less during the 30-day period, the foreign tax credit for the deemed paid tax is disallowed. The holding period generally does not include any period during which the taxpayer is protected from risk of loss (e.g., by use of an option). In addition, regardless of the holding

---

[2] Code Sec. 245(a). See also Code Sec. 245(b).

[3] Code Sec. 245(c). FSCs are discussed in detail in Chapter 7.

[4] Reg. § 1.903-1(b)(3), Example (2).

[5] Code Sec. 901(h). An exception applies to any foreign withholding taxes imposed on an FSC's distri-

bution of non-foreign trade income, which are creditable. Temp. Reg. § 1.921-3T(d)(2)(iii).

[6] Code Sec. 245(a)(8).

period, the taxpayer is not entitled to a credit to the extent that the dividend recipient is under an obligation, pursuant to a short sale or otherwise, to make related payments with respect to positions in substantially similar or related property. An exception to the holding period requirement is available to security dealers.[7] Congress enacted these provisions to curtail transactions designed to transfer foreign tax credits from persons unable to benefit from them to persons that can use the credits.

Deemed Paid Foreign Tax Credit

In addition to the direct credit for foreign withholding taxes, a domestic corporation also can claim a deemed paid foreign tax credit if it owns 10% or more of the voting stock of the foreign corporation from which it receives a dividend distribution.[8] The term "deemed paid" is a reference to how the foreign income taxes paid by a foreign corporation are made available as a credit to the domestic corporation. Specifically, the domestic corporation is deemed to have paid the foreign corporation's foreign income taxes upon receipt of a dividend from that subsidiary.

> **Example 4.1:** USAco, a domestic corporation, owns 100% of FORco, a foreign corporation. During its first year of operations, FORco derives $1 million of foreign-source taxable income, pays $250,000 of foreign income taxes, and distributes its $750,000 of after-tax earnings to USAco as a dividend. The $750,000 dividend is subject to foreign withholding taxes at a 5% rate. USAco can claim a direct foreign tax credit for the foreign withholding taxes of $37,500 [$750,000 dividend × 5% withholding rate]. In addition, because USAco owns 10% or more of FORco and received a dividend distribution from FORco during the year, it also can claim a deemed paid credit for the $250,000 of foreign income taxes related to the earnings distribution.

Congress enacted the deemed paid credit to protect domestic corporations with foreign subsidiaries against double taxation, as well as to better equate the tax treatment of U.S. companies with foreign subsidiaries to those with foreign branches. A domestic corporation operating abroad through a branch can claim a direct foreign tax credit for the foreign taxes it pays directly on its foreign earnings.[9] In contrast, a domestic corporation operating abroad through a foreign subsidiary cannot claim a direct credit because the foreign subsidiary, not the domestic parent, is the entity paying the foreign taxes. Allowing domestic corporations to claim a credit for the foreign taxes paid by their foreign subsidiaries allows U.S. companies to make legal form

---

[7] Code Sec. 901(k).
[8] Code Sec. 902(a).

[9] Code Sec. 901(a).

decisions on the basis of general business considerations rather than U.S. tax consequences.

Gross-Up for Deemed Paid Foreign Taxes

Because a dividend represents a distribution from after-tax earnings, the amount of income that a domestic corporation recognizes upon receiving a dividend from a foreign corporation is net of all the foreign income taxes paid by that foreign corporation. In effect, the domestic corporation is allowed a deduction for the foreign corporation's income taxes when computing the gross income from a dividend. To prevent a double tax benefit in the form of both an implicit deduction and a deemed paid credit with respect to the same foreign taxes, a domestic corporation must gross up its dividend income by the amount of the deemed paid credit.[10] This gross-up requirement prevents the double tax benefit by eliminating the implicit deduction.

> **Example 4.2:** USAco, a domestic corporation, owns 100% of ASIAco, a foreign corporation. During its first year of operations, ASIAco derives $10 million of foreign-source taxable income, pays $2 million of foreign income taxes, and distributes its $8 million of after-tax earnings to USAco as a dividend. Assume the dividend is not subject to foreign withholding taxes and that the U.S. tax rate is 35%.
>
> Because USAco owns 10% or more of ASIAco and received a dividend distribution from ASIAco during the year, it can claim a deemed paid credit for the $2 million of foreign income taxes related to the earnings that were distributed. After the gross-up, USAco has a pre-credit U.S. tax of $3.5 million [35% × ($8 million dividend + $2 million gross-up)], $2 million of deemed paid credits, and a residual U.S. tax of $1.5 million. Thus, the total tax on the $10 million of repatriated foreign earnings is $3.5 million [$2 million of foreign taxes + $1.5 million of U.S. taxes], which indicates that ASIAco's earnings are being taxed only once at the higher U.S. rate of 35%. In other words, the deemed paid credit in conjunction with the gross-up has its intended effect, which is to prevent international double taxation.
>
> Without the gross-up, however, the residual U.S. tax on ASIAco's repatriated earnings would drop from $1.5 million to $800,000 [(35% U.S. rate × $8 million dividend) − $2 million deemed paid credit]. The $700,000 reduction in the residual U.S. tax reflects the U.S. tax benefit of an implicit deduction for ASIAco's $2 million of

---

[10] Code Sec. 78. The gross-up requirement does not apply if the taxpayer is denied a deemed paid credit by virtue of not satisfying the holding period requirement of Code Sec. 901(k).

foreign income taxes that arises because USAco included only ASIAco's after-tax earnings in U.S. taxable income.

¶ 402 WHO CAN CLAIM A DEEMED PAID CREDIT

Only a domestic corporation can claim a deemed paid foreign tax credit. A domestic corporation can claim a deemed paid foreign tax credit only if it owns 10% or more of the voting stock of a foreign corporation and receives a dividend distribution from that foreign corporation.[11]

U.S. persons other than a domestic corporation, such as a U.S. citizen or resident alien, are not eligible for the deemed paid credit. This includes an S corporation since, for purposes of the deemed paid credit, an S corporation is treated as a partnership.[12] An S corporation's shareholders, who by statute must be individuals, estates, or trusts, also cannot claim a deemed paid credit. Thus, an S corporation may wish to structure its foreign operations as a branch or a partnership rather than a foreign corporation, in which case the S corporation's shareholders can claim a direct credit for the foreign income taxes incurred by the foreign branch or partnership.[13]

Credit Derived from Second- and Third-Tier Foreign Corporations

A domestic corporation that operates abroad through multiple layers of foreign corporations also can obtain deemed paid credits for taxes paid by second- and third-tier foreign corporations (and, under conditions discussed below, fourth-, fifth- and sixth-tier foreign corporations). This is possible because, for purposes of computing the deemed paid credit, a first-tier foreign corporation's foreign income taxes include not only the foreign income taxes it actually paid, but also any foreign income taxes it is deemed to have paid by reason of receiving a dividend from a qualifying lower-tier foreign corporation.[14]

Foreign income taxes paid by a second-tier foreign corporation pass up to a first-tier foreign corporation if the following requirements are satisfied:

(i)   the domestic corporation owns 10% or more of the voting stock of the first-tier foreign corporation,

---

[11] Code Sec. 902(a). Members of an affiliated group may not aggregate their ownership interests for purposes of satisfying the 10% ownership requirement. *First Chicago NBD Corp.,* 135 F3d 457 (7th Cir. 1998), aff'g 96 TC 421 (1991). However, a domestic corporation that is a general partner of a domestic general partnership can claim a deemed paid credit for its distributive share of foreign taxes paid by a foreign corporation owned by the partnership, as long as the corporate partner indirectly owns 10% or more of the foreign corporation. Code Sec. 702(a) and Rev. Rul. 71-141, 1971-1 CB 211.

[12] Code. Sec. 1373(a).

[13] Code Sec. 901.

[14] Code Sec. 902(c)(4).

(ii) the first-tier foreign corporation owns 10% or more of the voting stock of the second-tier corporation,

(iii) the domestic corporation indirectly owns at least 5% of the second-tier foreign corporation, determined by multiplying the percentage ownership at the two levels, and

(iv) the first-tier foreign corporation receives a dividend from the second-tier foreign corporation.[15]

Likewise, foreign income taxes paid by a third-tier foreign corporation pass up to a second-tier foreign corporation if the following requirements are satisfied:

(i)   the domestic corporation owns 10% or more of the voting stock of the first-tier foreign corporation,

(ii) the first-tier foreign corporation owns 10% or more of the voting stock of the second-tier corporation,

(iii) the second-tier foreign corporation owns 10% or more of the voting stock of the third-tier corporation,

(iv) the domestic corporation indirectly owns at least 5% of the third-tier foreign corporation, determined by multiplying the percentage ownership at the three levels, and

(v)   the second-tier foreign corporation receives a dividend from the third-tier foreign corporation.[16]

Credit Derived from Fourth- Through Sixth-Tier Foreign Corporations

The deemed paid credit also extends to taxes paid or accrued by fourth-, fifth-, and sixth-tier foreign corporations. To qualify, the corporation in question must be a controlled foreign corporation (CFC), the U.S. corporation claiming the credit must be a U.S. shareholder, and the product of the percentage ownership of voting stock at each level from the U.S. corporation down must equal at least five percent. The deemed paid credit is extended to lower tiers only with respect to taxes paid or incurred in tax years during which the payor is a CFC.[17] A foreign corporation is a CFC if, on any day during the foreign corporation's tax year, U.S. shareholders own more than 50% of the combined voting power of all classes of stock, or 50% of the total value, of the foreign corporation.[18] Only U.S. shareholders are considered in applying the 50% test. A U.S. shareholder is any U.S. person owning at least 10% of the total combined voting power of all classes of voting stock of the foreign corporation.[19]

---

[15] Code Sec. 902(b).
[16] Code Sec. 902(b).
[17] Code Sec. 902(b).

[18] Code Sec. 957(a).
[19] Code Sec. 951(b).

¶ 403   COMPUTING THE DEEMED PAID CREDIT

Tracing Foreign Taxes to Dividend Distributions

Pooling rule. A major administrative challenge in computing the deemed paid credit is determining the amount of foreign income taxes that are pulled out by a foreign corporation's dividend distribution. In theory, a dividend represents a distribution of corporate earnings from one or more specific taxable years. Associated with each year's earnings are the foreign income taxes for that year. The practical problem is determining the taxable year(s) from which the earnings distribution emanates. If a foreign corporation distributes all of its after-tax earnings each year, then the tracing problem is relatively easy to solve. The foreign income taxes related to each year's dividend are simply the foreign income taxes paid for that taxable year. However, if a foreign corporation does not distribute all of its earnings each year, a tracing problem arises.

One possible approach to solving this problem is to assume that dividend distributions pull out a foreign corporation's undistributed earnings and the related foreign income taxes in chronological order (a first-in, first-out rule), or in reverse chronological order (a last-in, first-out rule). A third approach is to pool a foreign corporation's undistributed earnings and foreign income taxes, and then assume that a dividend distribution pulls out deemed paid taxes equal to the pool of foreign income taxes multiplied by the ratio of the dividend to the pool of undistributed earnings. If the effective foreign tax rate varies over time, the amount of deemed paid foreign taxes associated with a dividend will vary with which approach is taken.

Example 4.3: USAco, a domestic corporation, owns 100% of EURco, a foreign corporation. EURco's earnings, foreign income taxes, and dividend distributions for its first two years of operations are as follows.

Year	Pre-tax earnings	Foreign income taxes	Effective foreign rate	After-tax earnings	Dividend distributions
Year 1	$10 million	$2 million	20%	$8 million	$0
Year 2	$10 million	$4 million	40%	$6 million	$3 million

Because the foreign tax rate on EURco's earnings increased from 20% in year 1 to 40% in year 2, the last-in, first-out method will pull out more foreign taxes than the pooling method, as discussed below.

Last-in, first-out method: Under a last-in, first-out tracing rule, the $3 million dividend represents a distribution of 50% of EURco's year 2 after-tax earnings of $6 million, and therefore the dividend pulls out foreign income taxes of $2 million [50% × $4 million of year 2 foreign income taxes].

Pooling method: Prior to the dividend, EURco has undistributed earnings of $14 million [$8 million + $6 million] and foreign income taxes of $6 million [$2 million + $4 million]. Therefore, under a pooling approach, the $3 million dividend pulls out foreign income taxes of roughly $1,285,714 [$6 million of foreign income taxes × ($3 million dividend ÷ $14 million of undistributed earnings)].

A pooling approach is required for post-1986 dividends, whereby a domestic corporation that receives a dividend from a 10% or more owned foreign corporation is deemed to have paid the following portion of the foreign corporation's foreign income taxes:[20]

$$\text{Foreign corporation's post-1986 foreign income taxes} \times \frac{\text{Dividend }^{21}}{\text{Foreign corporation's post-1986 undistributed earnings}}$$

Example 4.4: USAco, a domestic corporation, owns 100% of AFRIco, a foreign corporation. During its first year of operations, AFRIco derives $10 million of foreign-source taxable income, pays $4 million of foreign income taxes, and distributes a $3 million dividend to USAco. The $3 million dividend carries with it deemed paid taxes of $2 million [$4 million of post-1986 foreign income taxes × ($3 million dividend ÷ $6 million of post-1986 undistributed earnings)].

If a dividend exceeds the amount of post-1986 undistributed earnings (i.e., the dividend represents a distribution of pre-1987 earnings), then the tracing rule in effect prior to 1987 is used.[22] Prior to 1987, a last-in, first-out rule was used, whereby pre-1987 annual earnings were layered in chronological order and a dividend pulled out a layer of earnings (and, in turn, a layer of foreign income taxes) in reverse chronological order.[23] The portion of a dividend traced to a pre-1987 year's accumulated profits pulls out deemed paid taxes equal to the foreign income taxes for that year multiplied by the ratio of the dividend from that year's accumulated profits to the total accumulated profits for that year.

Congress enacted the pooling method in 1986, in part, because it believed that U.S. companies were manipulating the preexisting rule to maximize their deemed paid credits. Under a last-in, first-out rule, there is an advantage to bunching a foreign corporation's taxable income and, in turn, its foreign income taxes into particular years, and then having the foreign corporation distribute its earnings in those high-tax years. This technique causes deemed paid taxes to flow through to the domestic parent corporation at a higher rate than the

---

[20] Code Sec. 902(a).

[21] The dividend amount in the numerator does not include the Code Sec. 78 gross-up income.

[22] Code Sec. 902(c)(6).

[23] Code Sec. 902(c)(1), before amendment in 1986.

long-run effective rate of foreign taxation. In contrast, under the pooling method, the amount of foreign taxes pulled out by a dividend more accurately reflects the long-run effective rate of foreign taxation.

Post-1986 undistributed earnings. Post-1986 undistributed earnings is computed as of the close of the foreign corporation's taxable year in which it distributes the dividend, and equals the cumulative amount of the foreign corporation's undistributed earnings and profits for taxable years beginning after December 31, 1986. Post-1986 undistributed earnings is reduced by actual dividend distributions from prior taxable years, as well as any prior year inclusions of the foreign corporation's earnings in a shareholder's income (e.g., income inclusions under Subpart F, the passive foreign investment company provisions, or the foreign personal holding company regime). However, post-1986 undistributed earnings is not reduced by the dividend distribution or any other inclusions in a shareholder's income for the current taxable year.[24]

The computation of post-1986 undistributed earnings is based on the foreign corporation's earnings and profits, as opposed to its taxable income. Roughly speaking, a foreign corporation's earnings and profits equals its taxable income, plus or minus various adjustments designed to make earnings and profits a better measure of the corporation's economic income. Examples of the required adjustments include adding back tax-exempt income, adding back the excess of accelerated depreciation over straight-line depreciation, and subtracting income taxes.[25] In all cases, a foreign corporation's earnings and profits are determined according to substantially the same U.S. tax accounting principles that apply to domestic corporations.[26] As a consequence, financial statements prepared under a foreign corporation's local country accounting principles will have to be adjusted to make them consistent with U.S. accounting principles.[27]

Post-1986 foreign income taxes. Post-1986 foreign income taxes equal the cumulative amount of a foreign corporation's foreign income taxes for taxable years beginning after December 31, 1986 (including the foreign income taxes for the year of the dividend), reduced by the amount of foreign income taxes related to prior-year dividend distributions or other inclusions of the foreign corporation's earnings in a shareholder's income (e.g., income inclusions under Subpart F, the passive foreign investment company provisions, or the foreign personal

---

[24] Code Sec. 902(c)(1) and Reg. § 1.902-1(a)(9).

[25] Code Sec. 312.

[26] Code Sec. 964(a).

[27] See Reg. § 1.964-1(a) for the applicable computation procedures.

holding company regime), regardless of whether those other shareholders were eligible to claim a deemed paid credit.[28]

The term "foreign income taxes" has the same meaning for purposes of the deemed paid credit as it does for purposes of the direct foreign tax credit.[29] Thus, to be creditable, a levy paid by a foreign corporation must meet two basic requirements. First, the levy must be a tax (as opposed to a payment in exchange for a specific economic benefit) that is paid to a foreign country or U.S. possession. Second, the predominant character of the tax must be that of an income tax in the U.S. sense.[30] If a foreign levy satisfies the first requirement but not the second, it may still be creditable if the tax is imposed in lieu of an income tax.[31] Foreign income taxes also include any taxes that a foreign corporation is deemed to have paid by reason of receiving a dividend from a second- or third-tier foreign corporation.[32]

Currency translation. Foreign corporations usually conduct a significant part of their activities in an economic environment in which a foreign currency is used and usually keep their books and records in a foreign currency. This creates a currency translation problem for a domestic corporation, which must translate the tax attributes of the foreign corporation into U.S. dollars. The currency translation rules for dividend distributions from a foreign corporation, including the computation of the deemed paid credit, are discussed in Chapter 8.

Lower-tier foreign corporations. If certain requirements are met, a domestic corporation that operates abroad through multiple layers of foreign corporations can obtain deemed paid credits for taxes paid by second- through sixth-tier foreign corporations. The mechanism by which foreign income taxes pass up from a lower-tier foreign corporation to a higher-tier foreign corporation is almost identical to that by which foreign income taxes pass up from a first-tier foreign corporation to a domestic corporation.[33] For example, when a domestic corporation receives a dividend from a first-tier foreign corporation, and in the same taxable year the first-tier foreign corporation receives a dividend from a second-tier foreign corporation, then the domestic corporation computes its deemed paid foreign taxes by starting with the lowest-tier

---

[28] Code Sec. 902(c)(2) and Reg. § 1.902-1(a)(8). However, a domestic corporation generally cannot claim a deemed paid credit for any foreign income taxes related to a distribution of an FSC's foreign trade income, since the domestic corporation is already allowed a 100% dividends-received deduction for such distributions. Code Sec. 901(h). A similar prohibition applies to any foreign taxes related to the U.S.-source portion of a dividend from a foreign corporation for which a domestic corporation claims a dividends-received deduction. Code Sec. 245(a)(8). On the other hand, a domestic corporation can claim a deemed paid credit for foreign income taxes related to

an FSC's non-foreign trade income. Temp. Reg. § 1.921-3T(d)(2)(ii).

[29] Code Sec. 902(c)(4)(A) and Reg. § 1.902-1(a)(7).

[30] Code Sec. 901(b) and Reg. § 1.901-2(a)(1).

[31] Code Sec. 903.

[32] Code Sec. 902(c)(4)(B).

[33] Code Sec. 902(b)(1). One difference is that the first-tier foreign corporation does not recognize any gross-up income for deemed paid taxes, since the gross-up requirement applies only to a domestic corporation that claims a credit against its U.S. taxes. Code Sec. 78.

corporation and working up.[34] The same types of procedures allow the foreign income taxes paid by a third-tier foreign corporation to pass up to a second-tier foreign corporation, and so on for fourth-, fifth-, and sixth-tier foreign corporations.[35]

> **Example 4.5:** USAco (a domestic corporation) owns 100% of F1, and F1 owns 100% of F2. F1 and F2 are both foreign corporations. At end of the current year, the undistributed earnings and foreign income taxes of F1 and F2 are as follows:

	F1	*F2*
Post-1986 undistributed earnings	$18 million	$6 million
Post-1986 foreign income taxes	$ 4 million	$3 million

> During the current year, F2 distributed a $2 million dividend to F1, and F1 distributed a $2 million dividend to USAco. The $2 million dividend from F2 pulls out $1 million of deemed paid taxes for F1 [$3 million of post-1986 foreign income taxes × ($2 million dividend ÷ $6 million of post-1986 undistributed earnings)]. After taking into account the $2 million dividend from F1, F2's post-1986 undistributed earnings are $20 million [$18 million + $2 million], and (assuming F1's dividend is exempt from local taxation) its post-1986 foreign income taxes are $5 million [$4 million + $1 million]. As a consequence, USAco's receipt of a $2 million dividend from F1 pulls out deemed paid taxes of $500,000 [$5 million of post-1986 foreign income taxes × ($2 million dividend ÷ $20 million of post-1986 undistributed earnings)], and USAco must recognize dividend income of $2.5 million [$2 million dividend + $500,000 gross-up].

Foreign Tax Credit Limitation

Under the separate category of income limitations, a taxpayer must compute a separate foreign tax credit limitation for each of the following nine categories of income:[36]

(i)   passive income,

(ii)   high withholding tax interest,

(iii)   financial services income,

(iv)   shipping income,

(v)   dividends from each noncontrolled section 902 corporation,

(vi)   certain dividends from a domestic international sales corporation or former domestic international sales corporation,

(vii)   a foreign sales corporation's taxable income attributable to foreign trade income,

---

[34] Reg. § 1.902-1(c)(1)(i).

[35] Code Sec. 902(b)(2) and Reg. § 1.902-1(c)(1)(i).

[36] Code Sec. 904(d)(1).

(viii) certain distributions from a foreign sales corporation or former foreign sales corporation, and

(ix) general limitation income (the residual category for income not assigned to one of the other income categories).

The manner in which a domestic corporation allocates a foreign corporation's dividend distributions and deemed paid foreign taxes to the separate categories of income depends on whether the foreign corporation is a controlled foreign corporation or a noncontrolled section 902 corporation.

CFC look-through rule. A look-through rule applies to dividends received from a controlled foreign corporation (or "CFC"). A foreign corporation is a CFC if, on any day during the foreign corporation's taxable year, U.S. shareholders own more than 50% of the combined voting power of all classes of stock, or 50% of the total value, of the foreign corporation.[37] Only U.S. shareholders are considered in applying the 50% test. A U.S. shareholder is any U.S. person owning at least 10% of the total combined voting power of all classes of voting stock of the foreign corporation.[38]

If it were not for the CFC look-through rule, the separate category of income limitations would yield significantly different results for domestic corporations operating abroad through foreign subsidiaries as opposed to foreign branches. For example, if a domestic corporation structures a foreign manufacturing operation as a branch, the related income and foreign taxes are assigned to the general limitation category. In contrast, if a domestic corporation were to structure the same foreign manufacturing operation as a subsidiary, absent a look-through rule, dividend distributions from that foreign manufacturing subsidiary would be assigned to the passive income category.

To better equate the treatment of foreign branch and subsidiary operations, dividends paid by a CFC to a taxpayer who is a U.S. shareholder are prorated among the separate categories of income based on the ratio of the CFC's post-1986 undistributed earnings within each separate income category to the CFC's total post-1986 undistributed earnings.[39] For example, if a CFC has $1 million of earnings and profits, $900,000 of which is attributable to general limitation income and the other $100,000 to (non-Subpart F) financial services income, then 90% of a dividend distribution from the CFC is assigned to the general limitation category and the other 10% is assigned to the financial services income category. The amount of deemed paid foreign

---

[37] Code Sec. 957(a).

[38] Code Sec. 951(b). All forms of ownership, including direct, indirect (i.e., beneficial ownership through intervening entities), and constructive (i.e., attribution of ownership from one related party to another),

are considered in applying both the 10% shareholder and the 50% aggregate ownership tests. Code Sec. 958.

[39] Code Sec. 904(d)(3)(D) and Reg. § 1.904-5(c)(4)(i).

taxes related to a dividend attributable to a specific category of income is then determined using the following formula:[40]

$$\text{Post-1986 foreign income taxes of CFC attributable to the separate category of income}^{41} \times \frac{\text{Portion of dividend attributable to the separate category of income}}{\text{Post-1986 undistributed earnings of CFC attributable to the separate category of income}}$$

To make these computations, a domestic corporation must maintain (for each CFC in which it is a shareholder) separate pools of post-1986 undistributed earnings and post-1986 foreign income taxes for each category of income.

> **Example 4.6:** USAco, a domestic corporation, owns 100% of FORco, a foreign corporation. At end of the current year, FORco's pools of post-1986 undistributed earnings and post-1986 foreign income taxes are as follows:

	Post-1986 undistributed earnings	Post-1986 foreign income taxes
General limitation income	$ 8 million	$7 million
Financial services income (non-Subpart F)	$ 4 million	$1 million
Total income	$12 million	$8 million

During the current year, FORco distributed a $6 million dividend to USAco. Under the CFC look-through rule, $4 million of this amount [$6 million × ($8 million ÷ $12 million)] is assigned to the general limitation category, and the other $2 million [$6 million × ($4 million ÷ $12 million)] is assigned to the financial services income category. Thus, FORco's $6 million dividend pulls out deemed paid taxes of $3.5 million in the general limitation category [$7 million of post-1986 foreign income taxes × ($4 million dividend ÷ $8 million of post-1986 undistributed earnings)], and $500,000 in the financial services category [$1 million of post-1986 foreign income taxes × ($2 million dividend ÷ $4 million of post-1986 undistributed earnings)].

Dividends from noncontrolled section 902 corporations. A foreign corporation is a noncontrolled section 902 corporation (or "10/50 company") if the taxpayer owns between 10% and 50% of the foreign corporation's voting stock.[42] A 10/50 company is a foreign corporation that meets the 10% ownership requirement for claiming a

---

[40] Reg. § 1.902-1(d)(2)(i).

[41] Foreign income taxes are allocated to the category of income that includes the income upon which the foreign taxes were imposed. Reg. § 1.904-6(a)(1)(i). If the base upon which a foreign income tax is imposed includes income from more than one category, the taxpayer prorates the foreign taxes among the separate categories of income based on the relative amount of foreign taxable income within each category. Reg. § 1.904-6(a)(1)(ii).

[42] Code Secs. 904(d)(2)(E)(i) and 902(a).

deemed paid credit, but does not meet the more than 50% ownership requirement for CFC status. Therefore, the CFC look-through rule does not apply. Instead, each 10/50 company comprises a separate limitation category, and a taxpayer has as many 10/50 company limitations as there are 10/50 companies.[43] For example, a domestic corporation that receives a dividend from four different 10/50 companies has four separate 10/50 company limitations, one for each 10/50 company. The existence of a separate limitation for each 10/50 company prevents a taxpayer from cross-crediting with respect to dividends from different 10/50 companies.

> **Example 4.7:** USAco, a domestic corporation, owns 20% of F1 and 30% of F2. F1 and F2 are both foreign corporations. During the current year, F1 pays USAco a $100,000 dividend (which pulls out $30,000 of deemed paid taxes), and F2 pays USAco a $5 million dividend (which pulls out $2 million of deemed paid taxes). Neither dividend is subject to foreign withholding taxes. For purposes of the foreign tax credit limitation, the dividend from F1 is assigned to its own separate 10/50 company limitation. Within that limitation, there is foreign-source dividend income of $130,000 [$100,000 dividend + $30,000 gross-up], and deemed paid foreign taxes of $30,000. The dividend from F2 also is assigned to its own separate 10/50 company limitation. Within that separate limitation, there is foreign-source dividend income of $7 million [$5 million dividend + $2 million gross-up], and deemed paid foreign taxes of $2 million.

Congress created the separate 10/50 company limitations in 1986 for a couple of reasons. First, when U.S. shareholders do not hold a majority interest in a foreign corporation, that entity no longer resembles a foreign branch operation, which was a principal reason for enacting the CFC look-through rule. In addition, when a U.S. shareholder's ownership interest is less than 50%, it may not be feasible for the shareholder to obtain the information necessary to apply the look-through rule applicable to CFCs. Without a look-through rule, it is uncertain whether the dividend is passive income (i.e., the 10/50 company's underlying earnings are derived from passive investments) or general limitation income (i.e., the 10/50 company's underlying earnings are derived from active business operations). Therefore, the separate 10/50 company limitations serve as a default category.

The foreign tax credit limitation regime for dividends from 10/50 companies is scheduled to be simplified for tax years beginning on or after January 1, 2003. Separate rules are applied, depending upon whether the dividends are paid from pre-2003 or post-2002 earnings

---

[43] Reg. § 1.904-4(g)(2)(i).

and profits. In the case of dividends from 10/50 companies that are paid from earnings and profits accumulated in tax years beginning before January 1, 2003, a single limitation is applied to the dividends from all 10/50 companies, rather than separate limitations for each 10/50 company as under prior law. However, if the 10/50 company in question is also a passive foreign investment company, then separate limitations are applied to dividends received from each such 10/50 company. A look-through rule applies to dividends paid by a 10/50 company from earnings and profits accumulated in tax years beginning after December 31, 2002. Under this rule, a dividend from a 10/50 company is treated as income in a foreign tax credit limitation category (e.g., the general limitation category) in proportion to the ratio of post-2002 earnings and profits attributable to income in that foreign tax credit limitation category to the total amount of post-2002 earnings and profits.[44]

Lower-tier foreign corporations. If certain requirements are met, a domestic corporation that operates abroad through multiple layers of foreign corporations can obtain deemed paid credits for taxes paid by second- through sixth-tier foreign corporations. For purposes of the foreign tax credit limitation in a pre-2003 tax year, if the first-tier foreign corporation is a 10/50 company, then the status of a lower-tier foreign corporation is irrelevant since a U.S. shareholder assigns dividends from 10/50 companies (including one that owns 10% or more of a lower-tier foreign corporation) to a special 10/50 company limitation.

On the other hand, if the first-tier foreign corporation is a CFC, then the status of the lower-tier foreign corporations will affect the characterization of the domestic corporation's dividend income for limitation purposes. For example, if a first-tier CFC distributes a dividend to its domestic parent corporation, and that dividend is attributable in part to dividends that the CFC received from a second-tier 10/50 company, then the domestic parent must assign that portion of its dividend income to the special 10/50 company limitation.[45] If both the first- and second-tier foreign corporations are CFCs, then the CFC look-through applies at both the first- and second-tier foreign corporation levels. As a consequence, the domestic parent corporation would assign the portion of its dividend income that is attributable to the earnings and profits of the second-tier CFC to the separate categories of income based upon the underlying character of the second-tier CFC's earnings and profits. The same principles apply for purposes of characterizing dividend income attributable to the earnings and profits of a third- or lower-tier foreign corporation.

---

[44] Code Sec. 904(d)(2)(E) and (d)(4).   [45] Reg. § 1.904-5(f)(2).

Special source-of-income rules. As discussed in Chapter 2, there are some special source-of-income rules which apply to dividends received from a foreign corporation. For example, for purposes of computing the foreign tax credit limitation, a dividend received from a foreign corporation that is at least 50% owned by U.S. persons is recharacterized as U.S.-source income to the extent the dividend is attributable to earnings that the foreign corporation derived from U.S. sources.[46] In addition, a domestic corporation that claims a dividends-received deduction with respect to a portion of a dividend from a foreign corporation must treat that portion of the dividend as U.S.-source income for purposes of computing the foreign tax credit limitation.[47]

Deemed Paid Credits for Subpart F and QEF Inclusions

Subpart F requires a U.S. shareholder of a CFC to recognize a deemed dividend equal to its pro rata share of the CFC's Subpart F income, plus any increase in the CFC's earnings invested in U.S. property.[48] In the case of a domestic corporation that owns 10% or more of the CFC's voting stock, a Subpart F inclusion carries with it a deemed paid foreign tax credit that is conceptually identical to the deemed paid credit that is allowed with respect to actual dividend distributions.[49] Domestic corporations that own 10% or more of the voting stock of a passive foreign investment company that has made a qualified electing fund election also can claim a deemed paid credit with respect to the qualified electing fund income inclusion.[50] The taxation of Subpart F and qualified electing fund inclusions, including the computation of the related deemed paid foreign tax credit, is discussed in Chapter 6.

¶ 404   FILING REQUIREMENTS

A domestic corporation claiming a deemed paid foreign tax credit generally must satisfy the same filing and documentation requirements that apply to the direct credit.[51] Therefore, a domestic corporation claims a deemed paid credit by attaching Form 1118, Foreign Tax Credit—Corporations, to its tax return.[52] A separate Form 1118 must be completed for each separate category of income limitation. (Form 1118 is reproduced in the appendix to Chapter 3.)

¶ 405   PLANNING FOR DIVIDEND REPATRIATIONS

The decision to repatriate earnings from a foreign subsidiary may be influenced by a variety of factors, such as the cash needs of the

---

[46] Code Sec. 904(g)(1)(C). This rule does not apply if less than 10% of the U.S.-owned foreign corporation's earnings are attributable to U.S.-source income. Code Sec. 904(g)(5).

[47] Code Sec. 245(a)(9).

[48] Code Sec. 951(a)(1).

[49] Code Sec. 960(a)(1).

[50] Code Sec. 1293(f)(1).

[51] Reg. § 1.902-1(e).

[52] Reg. § 1.905-2(a)(1).

domestic parent corporation, the preferences of foreign managers, financial reporting considerations, local company laws requiring the maintenance of reserves, as well as U.S. and foreign tax consequences. As discussed below, the precepts of U.S. tax planning for dividend repatriations include cross-crediting, avoiding the 10/50 company limitation, minimizing foreign withholding taxes, and considering alternative methods of repatriating earnings.

Cross-Crediting

The U.S. tax consequences of a dividend repatriation depend critically on whether the foreign corporation is operating in a low- or high-tax foreign jurisdiction. No U.S. tax is due on a dividend from a foreign corporation operating in a high-tax foreign jurisdiction, since the available foreign tax credits more than offset the pre-credit U.S. tax. Therefore, planning focuses on reducing these excess credits. In contrast, a dividend from a foreign corporation operating in a low-tax foreign jurisdiction results in a residual U.S. tax. In such situations, planning focuses on reducing that residual U.S. tax. For example, through cross-crediting, the excess credits on dividends from high-tax foreign subsidiaries can be used to soak up the residual U.S. tax due on dividends from low-tax foreign subsidiaries. The CFC look-through rule makes cross-crediting possible with respect to dividends from CFCs located in low- and high-tax foreign jurisdictions, as long as the underlying earnings of the CFC are assigned to the same category of income limitation (e.g., the general limitation category).

Example 4.8: USAco is a domestic corporation that owns 100% of both LOWco and HIGHco, two foreign corporations. At end of the current year, LOWco's and HIGHco's pools of undistributed earnings and foreign income taxes are as follows:

	LOWco	HIGHco
Post-1986 undistributed earnings in general limitation category	$8 million	$6 million
Post-1986 foreign income taxes in general limitation category	$2 million	$9 million

Assume the U.S. tax rate is 35%, and that any dividends that LOWco or HIGHco distribute to USAco are not subject to foreign withholding taxes.

Case 1—Repatriate earnings from low-tax subsidiary: Assume LOWco distributed a $4 million dividend to USAco. The dividend would pull out $1 million of deemed paid taxes [$2 million of post-1986 foreign income taxes × ($4 million dividend ÷ $8 million of post-1986 undistributed earnings)]. With the gross-up, USAco would have dividend income of $5 million [$4 million dividend + $1 million gross-up]. Under the CFC look-through rule, the entire amount of this dividend and the related foreign income taxes would be assigned to the general limitation category. Therefore, within USAco's general limitation, there would be a limitation of $1.75 million [35% U.S. rate × $5 million], deemed paid taxes of $1 million, and a residual U.S. tax of $750,000 [$1.75 million − $1 million].

Case 2—Repatriate earnings from both low- and high-tax subsidiaries: Every dollar of dividends from HIGHco increases the deemed paid taxes within USAco's general limitation by $1.50 [$9 million of post-1986 foreign income taxes × ($1 dividend ÷ $6 million of post-1986 undistributed earnings)] and also increases USAco's general limitation by $0.875 [35% U.S. tax rate × ($1.00 dividend + $1.50 gross-up)]. The net effect is an excess credit of $0.625 for every dollar of dividends [$1.50 of additional deemed paid taxes − $0.875 of additional limitation]. Therefore, USAco can completely eliminate the $750,000 residual U.S. tax on LOWco's $4 million dividend by having HIGHco distribute a dividend of $1.2 million [$750,000 ÷ $0.625]. A $1.2 million dividend from HIGHco would pull out $1.8 million of deemed paid taxes [$9 million of post-1986 foreign income taxes × ($1.2 million dividend ÷ $6 million of post-1986 undistributed earnings)] and increase USAco's general limitation by $1,050,000 [35% U.S. tax rate × ($1.2 million dividend + $1.8 million gross-up)], for a net excess credit of $750,000.

Avoiding the 10/50 Company Limitation

There is a separate foreign tax credit limitation for 10/50 companies. Therefore, excess credits on dividends from a 10/50 company cannot be used to offset the residual U.S. tax on dividends from a CFC that is assigned to a different category of income limitation (e.g., the general limitation category). One strategy for avoiding this restriction is for the taxpayer to acquire more than 50% of the 10/50 company's stock (by vote or value), which would make the foreign corporation a CFC, and thereby allow for the use of the CFC look-through rule. For example, if a domestic corporation has entered into a 50-50 foreign joint venture structured as a foreign corporation, it can satisfy the more than 50% of value test for CFC status by having that foreign corporation issue it some nonvoting preferred stock. Another possible solution would be for the domestic corporation to acquire one or more shares of its joint venture partner, since indirect ownership is taken into account for purposes of the more than 50% ownership test.

A second basic strategy for avoiding the 10/50 company limitation is to structure a 10/50 company as an entity that is considered a partnership for U.S. tax purposes. Partnership status allows for the use of the look-through rule applicable to partnerships.[53] In addition, through the use of hybrid entities (which are discussed in Chapter 10), a taxpayer may be able to obtain partnership treatment for U.S. tax purposes, without giving up limited liability in the host country.

Minimizing Foreign Withholding Taxes

Most foreign countries impose flat rate withholding taxes on the gross amount of dividends paid by a locally organized corporation to its U.S. shareholders. Foreign withholding taxes can exacerbate the excess credit problem created by dividends from foreign subsidiaries operating in high-tax foreign jurisdictions. However, tax treaties usually reduce the statutory withholding rate on dividends to 15% or less. Moreover, the treaty withholding rate often is lower for controlling shareholders (e.g., a shareholder owning 10% or more of the payer's stock) than for noncontrolling shareholders. Therefore, a U.S. parent corporation may be able to use tax treaties to reduce foreign withholding taxes by, for example, owning foreign operating subsidiaries through a foreign holding company located in a country with a favorable treaty network.

Alternatives to Dividend Repatriations

It may be advantageous for a domestic corporation to repatriate the earnings of a foreign corporation through interest, rental, and royalty payments, rather than dividend distributions. A foreign corporation usually can claim a foreign tax deduction for interest, rents, and royalties paid to its domestic parent, whereas dividend distributions typically are not deductible. On the other hand, only a dividend distribution can provide the domestic parent corporation with a deemed paid credit. Nevertheless, if the foreign corporation is operating in a high-tax foreign jurisdiction, the benefits of a deduction at the foreign subsidiary level may exceed the costs of losing the deemed paid credit at the domestic parent level.

> **Example 4.9:** USAco, a domestic corporation, owns 100% of ASIAco, a foreign corporation. During its first year of operations, ASIAco's taxable income is $10 million, assuming no deductible interest payments are made to USAco. Further assume that the foreign income tax rate is 45%, the U.S. rate is 35%, and that no foreign withholding taxes are imposed on any dividend distributions or interest payments that ASIAco makes to USAco.
>
> *Case 1—Repatriate earnings through dividend:* If USAco repatriated all of ASIAco's after-tax earnings through a dividend, the foreign tax on those earnings would be $4.5 million [$10 million of

---

[53] Reg. § 1.904-5(h)(1). For example, a U.S. partner's distributive share of a foreign partnership's active business income is assigned to the general limitation rather than a separate 10/50 company limitation.

taxable income × 45% foreign tax rate]. USAco would receive a $5.5 million dividend distribution, which would pull out $4.5 million of deemed paid foreign taxes [$4.5 million of post-1986 foreign income taxes × ($5.5 million dividend ÷ $5.5 million of post-1986 undistributed earnings)]. With the gross-up, USAco would have dividend income of $10 million [$5.5 million dividend + $4.5 million gross-up], and its pre-credit U.S. tax would be $3.5 million [$10 million × 35% U.S. tax rate]. There would be no residual U.S. tax due on the dividend income since USAco's deemed paid credits would offset the entire pre-credit U.S. tax. In sum, if USAco repatriates ASIAco's earnings through a dividend distribution, the total tax on those earnings would equal the foreign tax of $4.5 million.

Case 2—Repatriate earnings through interest payments: USAco may be able to reduce the total tax burden on ASIAco's earnings by repatriating those earnings through deductible interest payments, as opposed to dividend distributions. As an extreme example, if USAco financed ASIAco in a way that provided ASIAco with $10 million of deductible interest payments, that interest expense would reduce ASIAco's taxable income to $0. On the other hand, USAco would owe a $3.5 million residual U.S. tax on the interest payments it received from ASIAco [$10 million of interest income × 35% U.S. rate]. Nevertheless, the total tax on ASIAco's repatriated earnings would equal the U.S. tax of $3.5 million, which is $1 million less than the total tax if ASIAco's earnings are repatriated through a dividend distribution.

The tax implications of using debt financing for a foreign subsidiary are discussed in more detail in Chapter 10.

Chapter 5

Transfer Pricing

¶ 501 WHAT IS TRANSFER PRICING?

The operating units of a multinational corporation usually engage in a variety of intercompany transactions. For example, a U.S. manufacturer may market its products abroad through foreign marketing subsidiaries. The same U.S. parent corporation also may provide managerial, technical, and administrative services for its subsidiaries. Another common arrangement is for a U.S. parent corporation to license its manufacturing and marketing intangibles to its foreign subsidiaries for exploitation abroad. A "transfer price" must be computed for these controlled transactions in order to satisfy various financial reporting, tax, and other regulatory requirements. Although transfer prices do not affect the combined income of a controlled group of corporations, they do affect how that income is allocated among the group members.

Example 5.1: USAco, a domestic corporation, manufactures small engines for sale both in the United States and abroad. Foreign sales are made through FORco, a wholly owned foreign corporation. USAco's engines cost $600 to manufacture and $100 to market, and sell for $1,000 abroad. Regardless of the transfer price used for sales by USAco to FORco, the combined income from a foreign sale is $300 per engine [$1,000 final sales price − $600 manufacturing cost − $100 selling expense]. However, transfer prices do affect the allocation of that combined profit between USAco and FORco.

At one extreme, a transfer price of $600 would allocate the combined profit of $300 entirely to FORco, as follows.

Transaction	Effect on USAco	Effect on FORco
Manufacture engine	Production cost = $600	
Controlled sale	Sales revenue = $600	Cost of sales = $600
Foreign selling activities		Selling expense = $100
Sale to foreign customer		Sales revenue = $1,000
	Net profit = $0	Net profit = $300

At the other extreme, a transfer price of $900 would allocate the combined profit of $300 entirely to USAco, as follows.

Transaction	Effect on USAco	Effect on FORco
Manufacture engine	Production cost = $600	
Controlled sale	Sales revenue = $900	Cost of sales = $900
Foreign selling activities		Selling expense = $100
Sale to foreign customer		Sales revenue = $1,000
	Net profit = $300	Net profit = $0

For income tax purposes, multinational corporations must allocate their worldwide profits among the various countries in which they operate. The ideal allocation would permit each country to tax an appropriate portion of the taxpayer's total profit, while avoiding taxation of the same income by more than one country. The mechanism for allocating a multinational's worldwide profits between its U.S. and foreign affiliates is the transfer prices used for intercompany transactions. When tax rates vary across countries, transfer pricing can have a significant effect on the taxpayer's total tax costs.

For example, the foreign tax credit limitation prevents U.S. companies operating in high-tax foreign jurisdictions from claiming a credit for those excess foreign taxes. These noncreditable foreign taxes increase the worldwide tax rate on foreign earnings above the U.S. corporate rate of 35%.[1] A domestic corporation may be able to avoid

---

[1] See discussion of excess foreign tax credits in Chapter 3.

¶501

these higher foreign taxes by altering its transfer prices so as to shift income out of these high-tax jurisdictions. For example, a U.S. manufacturer may be able to reduce a foreign marketing subsidiary's share of worldwide profits by using higher prices for controlled inventory sales.

> **Example 5.2:** The facts are the same as in Example 5.1. Assume that the U.S. tax rate is 35% and the applicable foreign tax rate is 45%. Given this rate differential, the USAco group can reduce its worldwide taxes by using higher transfer prices for its controlled sale. For example, if a transfer price of $600 is used for a sale by USAco to FORco, the $300 gross profit is allocated entirely to FORco, and the total tax on that profit equals the foreign tax of $135 [$300 of income × 45% foreign tax rate]. If a transfer price of $900 is used for the controlled sale, the $300 gross profit is allocated entirely to USAco, and the total tax on that profit equals the U.S. tax of $105 [$300 of income × 35% U.S. tax rate].

Transfer pricing also is a relevant issue for U.S. companies with operations in low-tax foreign jurisdictions. In these situations, a U.S. parent corporation has an incentive to shift income to its low-tax foreign subsidiary by, for example, using lower transfer prices on controlled inventory sales. Although shifting income to a low-tax foreign subsidiary does not permanently avoid the residual U.S. tax on those low-taxed foreign earnings, it does defer that tax until the foreign subsidiary repatriates those earnings through a dividend distribution.

¶ 502   TRANSFER PRICING METHODS

Basic Principles

The purpose of Code Sec. 482 is to ensure that taxpayers report and pay tax on their actual share of income arising from controlled transactions.[2] To this end, the Regulations under Code Sec. 482 adopt an arm's-length or market value standard for evaluating the appropriateness of a transfer price. Under this standard, a taxpayer should realize the same amount of income from a controlled transaction as an uncontrolled party would have realized from a similar transaction under similar circumstances.[3]

To arrive at an arm's-length result, the taxpayer must select and apply the method that provides the most reliable estimate of an arm's-length price.[4] Thus, the primary focus in selecting a transfer pricing method is the reliability of the result, not its theoretical accuracy. The reliability of a pricing method is determined by the degree of comparability between the controlled and uncontrolled transactions, as well as

---

[2] Reg. § 1.482-1(a)(1).   [4] Reg. § 1.482-1(c)(1).
[3] Reg. § 1.482-1(b)(1).

the quality of the data and the assumptions used in the analysis.[5] The principal factors to consider in assessing the comparability of controlled and uncontrolled transactions include the following:[6]

- Functions performed—The functional analysis identifies and compares the economically significant activities undertaken. These activities would include, for example, research and development, manufacturing or production, marketing and distribution, transportation and warehousing, and administrative functions. The theory behind this part of the regulations is that a party performing more functions should receive more of the income.[7]

- Contractual terms—Significant contractual terms could affect the results of two transactions. For example, the quantity of items purchased or sold, the form of consideration (paid in local or foreign currency), the scope of any warranties, the rights to updates or modifications, the duration of the contract, the extent of any collateral transactions between the parties, and the extension of any credit or payment terms may have an economic effect on the transaction.

- Risks assumed—This analysis requires a comparison of the significant risks that could affect the prices to be charged. For example, risk associated with the success or failure of research and development activities, finances (such as fluctuations in foreign currency and interest rates), credit and collection, product liability, and market fluctuation.

- Economic conditions and markets—This comparability factor focuses on the economic conditions that could affect the prices to be charged. This includes the similarity of geographic markets, the level of the market (e.g., wholesale or retail), the extent of competition in each market, the economic conditions of the particular industry, and the alternatives realistically available to either party.

- Nature of the property or services transferred in the transaction—As discussed more later in this chapter, the comparability of property sold or services provided is more relevant to the transaction-based methods than the profit-based methods.

Example 5.3: USAco, a U.S. subsidiary of ASIAco, a Japanese parent corporation, purchases televisions from its Japanese parent that USAco markets in the U.S. If it were to use one of the

---

[5] Reg. § 1.482-1(c)(2).
[6] Reg. § 1.482-1(d)(1).
[7] Preamble to the Intercompany Transfer Pricing Regulations Under Section 482; 59 F.R. 34971; T.D. 8552.

transaction-based methods, USAco must compare prices charged for televisions, or at the very least, consumer electronic products. However, if the taxpayer chooses a profit-based method, such as the comparable profits method, USAco must merely find companies comparable to itself with respect to the type of functions performed and the risks assumed.

Adjustments must be made for any material differences between the controlled and uncontrolled transactions, assuming the effect of the difference can be ascertained with enough accuracy to improve the reliability of the results.[8]

As a practical matter, comparable transactions often are not readily available for the types of transactions entered into by affiliates of a vertically integrated multinational corporation. For example, inventory sales between affiliated companies often involve component parts and semifinished goods that are unique and are not sold in public markets. As a consequence, the appropriate arm's-length price is ambiguous. The only significant exceptions are publicly traded fungible goods such as oil, lumber, and agricultural products, for which information regarding market prices is readily available.

The concept of the arm's-length range helps taxpayers deal with this uncertainty. Under this provision, a taxpayer may use two or more comparable uncontrolled transactions (of similar comparability and reliability) to establish an arm's-length range of prices. If the taxpayer's transfer prices lie within the range, the IRS will not make an adjustment.[9] If the taxpayer's transfer prices lie outside the arm's-length range, then the IRS will make an adjustment using either the mean or the median of the range as the benchmark price.[10] Taxpayers also are allowed, under certain circumstances, to satisfy the arm's-length requirement by showing that the average result for a multiple-year period is comparable to that of uncontrolled transactions for the same period.[11] The use of multiple-year data helps reduce the effects of short-term variations in prices, such as the effects of an industry business cycle, that are unrelated to transfer pricing.

Loans and Advances

Controlled entities generally must charge each other an arm's-length rate of interest on any intercompany loans or advances.[12] There is an exception, however, for intercompany trade receivables, which are

---

[8] Reg. § 1.482-1(d)(2).

[9] Reg. § 1.482-1(e)(1) and (e)(2)(i). All comparable uncontrolled transactions are included in the range if adjustments can be made for all of the material differences between the controlled and uncontrolled transactions. If adjustments cannot be made for all material differences, then the range is limited by statistical techniques, such as restricting the range to those comparable uncontrolled transactions which fall within the 25th and 75th percentiles of the range. Reg. § 1.482-1(e)(2)(iii).

[10] Reg. § 1.482-1(e)(3).

[11] Reg. § 1.482-1(f)(2)(iii).

[12] Reg. § 1.482-2(a)(1)(i).

debts that arise in the ordinary course of business and are not evidenced by a written agreement requiring the payment of interest.[13] If the controlled borrower is located outside the United States, it is not necessary to charge interest on a intercompany trade receivable until the first day of the fourth month following the month in which the receivable arises.[14] If the controlled borrower is located within the United States, the interest-free period extends to the first day of the third month following the month in which the receivable arises.[15] This exception reflects the common business practice of not charging interest on trade receivables.

> **Example 5.4:** USAco, a domestic corporation, owns 100% of ASIAco, a foreign corporation. On November 1, ASIAco purchases $1 million of inventory on account from USAco. The $1 million debt, on which ASIAco pays no interest, is still outstanding on December 31, which is the end of USAco's taxable year. Since the $1 million intercompany trade receivable was outstanding for only two months, USAco does not have to recognize any interest income.

Longer interest-free periods are possible if the controlled lender ordinarily allows unrelated parties a longer interest-free period,[16] or if a controlled borrower purchased the goods for resale in a foreign country and the average collection period for its sales is longer than the interest-free period.[17]

Intercompany debt other than a trade receivable generally must bear an arm's-length interest charge.[18] To determine the arm's-length rate, the taxpayer must consider all relevant factors, including the amount and duration of the loan, the security involved, the credit standing of the borrower, and the interest rate prevailing at the situs of the lender for comparable loans between uncontrolled parties.[19] If an arm's-length rate is not readily determinable, the taxpayer can still protect itself against an IRS adjustment by satisfying the requirements of a safe-harbor provision. Under this safe harbor, an interest rate is deemed to be an arm's-length rate if it is between 100% and 130% of the applicable federal rate.[20] The applicable federal rate is the average interest rate (redetermined monthly) on obligations of the federal government with maturities similar to the term on the intercompany loan.[21]

> **Example 5.5:** USAco, a domestic corporation, owns 100% of EURco, a foreign corporation. During the current year, USAco borrows $1 million from EURco. The loan is denominated in U.S.

---

[13] Reg. § 1.482-2(a)(1)(iii)(A).
[14] Reg. § 1.482-2(a)(1)(iii)(C).
[15] Reg. § 1.482-2(a)(1)(iii)(B).
[16] Reg. § 1.482-2(a)(1)(iii)(D).
[17] Reg. § 1.482-2(a)(1)(iii)(E).

[18] Reg. § 1.482-2(a)(1)(i).
[19] Reg. § 1.482-2(a)(2)(i).
[20] Reg. § 1.482-2(a)(2)(iii)(B).
[21] Code Sec. 1274(d).

dollars and has a three-year term. At the time of the loan, the applicable federal rate for a three-year obligation is 8%. Under the safe-harbor provision, an interest rate of between 8% (100% of the applicable federal rate) and 10.4% (130% of the applicable federal rate) is automatically acceptable to the IRS. A rate lower than 8% or higher than 10.4% also can be used if the taxpayer can establish that it is an arm's-length rate, taking into account all of the relevant facts and circumstances.

The safe harbor is not available if the intercompany debt is denominated in a foreign currency,[22] or if the controlled lender is in the business of making loans to unrelated parties.[23]

A special rule applies if the controlled lender obtains the funds used to make the intercompany loan at the situs of the controlled borrower. In such cases, the controlled lender is treated as a mere conduit for the loan entered into with the unrelated lender. Thus, the arm's-length rate on such pass-through loans is assumed to be equal to the rate paid by the controlled lender on the original loan, increased by any associated borrowing costs, unless the taxpayer can establish that a different rate is more appropriate under the general rules.[24]

Example 5.6: USAco, a domestic corporation, owns 100% of GERco, a German corporation. During the current year, USAco borrows $10 million from a German bank at a 10% rate, and then relends the funds to GERco. The arm's-length rate on the intercompany loan is deemed to be equal to 10% plus any borrowing costs incurred by USAco in securing the original loan. A rate other than 10% also can be used if USAco can establish that such a rate is arm's length, taking into account all of the relevant facts and circumstances.

Performance of Services

An arm's-length fee generally must be charged if one controlled entity performs services for the benefit of, or on behalf of, another controlled entity.[25] However, under a safe-harbor provision, a charge equal to the direct and indirect costs incurred by the controlled entity in providing the service is deemed to be an arm's-length charge.[26] This safe harbor reflects the reality that intercompany services sometimes are provided for reasons of convenience, rather than profit.

Example 5.7: USAco, a domestic corporation, produces food products at its U.S. plant for sale domestically and abroad. USAco markets its products abroad through FORco, a wholly owned

---

[22] Reg. § 1.482-2(a)(2)(iii)(E).
[23] Reg. § 1.482-2(a)(2)(iii)(D).
[24] Reg. § 1.482-2(a)(2)(ii).

[25] Reg. § 1.482-2(b)(1).
[26] Reg. § 1.482-2(b)(3)–(b)(5).

foreign marketing subsidiary. During the current year, USAco performs some payroll services for FORco as a convenience for FORco's management. The costs associated with these services include $10,000 of salaries plus an overhead allocation of $3,000. Under the safe-harbor rule, $13,000 is deemed to be an arm's-length charge for these services. A charge other than $13,000 also is allowable if USAco can establish that such a charge is arm's length, taking into account all of the relevant facts and circumstances.

The safe harbor is not available if the services are an integral part of the business activity of either the service provider or the service recipient.[27] For example, if in Example 5.6, the domestic parent was in the business of providing payroll services, it would have to charge its affiliate the same amount that it charges its unrelated customers for payroll services. A service is an integral part of the business activities of the service provider or recipient in the following situations:

(i) the service provider or recipient is engaged in the business of rendering similar services to unrelated parties,

(ii) a principal activity of the service provider is providing such services to related parties,

(iii) the service provider is peculiarly capable of rendering the service and such services are a principal element in the operations of the recipient, or

(iv) the recipient receives a substantial amount of services from affiliates during the year.[28]

Another exception applies to services that are ancillary and subsidiary to a controlled transfer of tangible or intangible property. Consistent with the common business practice of including installation and start-up services in the associated sale or rental price, it is not necessary to provide a separate charge for ancillary and subsidiary services.[29]

Example 5.8: USAco, a domestic corporation, owns 100% of AFRIco, a foreign corporation. During the current year, USAco sells some manufacturing equipment to AFRIco. An engineer employed by USAco travels abroad to install the equipment. Although AFRIco must pay an arm's-length price for the equipment, a separate charge need not be made for the installation services. On the other hand, if the engineer also supervises AFRIco's manufacturing operation after the equipment has been effectively integrated into AFRIco's manufacturing operations, then AFRIco

---

[27] Reg. § 1.482-2(b)(7).
[28] Reg. § 1.482-2(b)(7)(i)–(iv).

[29] Reg. § 1.482-2(b)(8).

must pay USAco for these follow-on services since they are not ancillary and subsidiary to the sale.

An exception also applies to services performed by a parent corporation for one of its subsidiaries, where the parent's services merely duplicate those performed by the subsidiary. The parent need not charge the subsidiary for these services if they are undertaken for the parent's benefit in overseeing its investment rather than for the subsidiary's benefit.[30]

> **Example 5.9:** The financial staff of a foreign subsidiary prepares a report regarding the subsidiary's financing needs. An executive from the U.S. parent corporation's home office reviews the report. The parent need not charge the subsidiary for this service because it merely duplicates those performed by the subsidiary itself. On the other hand, if the foreign subsidiary did not have a financial staff, and the home office executive performed the original analysis rather than merely reviewing it, a charge would have to be made.[31]

Use of Tangible Property

Intercompany leases of tangible property generally must bear an arm's-length rental charge.[32] The arm's-length rental is the amount that would have been charged for the use of the same or similar property in a transaction between unrelated parties under similar circumstances. All relevant factors must be considered in determining the arm's-length rental, including the period and location of the property's use, the owner's investment in the property, the owner's maintenance expenses, and the type and condition of the property.[33]

A special rule applies if the controlled lessor first leased the property from an unrelated person and then subleased it to the controlled lessee. In such cases, the controlled lessor is treated as a mere conduit for the lease it entered into with the unrelated lessor. Thus, the arm's-length rental for such pass-through leases is deemed to be equal to the rental paid by the controlled lessor on the original lease, increased by any associated rental costs (e.g., maintenance, repairs, utilities, and managerial expenses).[34] This rule does not apply if either the controlled lessor or controlled lessee is regularly engaged in the business of leasing the type of property in question to unrelated persons, or if the taxpayer establishes a more appropriate rental rate under the general rules.[35]

---

[30] Reg. § 1.482-2(b)(2)(ii).

[31] Compare Reg. § 1.482-2(b)(2)(ii), Examples 1 and 2.

[32] Reg. § 1.482-2(c)(1).

[33] Reg. § 1.482-2(c)(2)(i).

[34] Reg. § 1.482-2(c)(2)(iii)(A).

[35] Reg. § 1.482-2(c)(2)(iii)(B).

Transfers of Tangible Property

Introduction. There are five specified methods for estimating an arm's-length charge for transfers of tangible property:

   (i)   the comparable uncontrolled price method,

   (ii) the resale price method,

   (iii) the cost plus method,

   (iv) the comparable profits method, and

   (v) the profit split method.[36]

The taxpayer must select and apply the method that provides the most reliable estimate of an arm's-length price.[37] In addition to the five specified methods, the taxpayer also has the option of using an unspecified method. However, an unspecified method can be used only if it provides the most reliable estimate of an arm's-length price.[38]

When the transfer involves tangible property with embedded intangibles, such as a controlled sale of inventory where the related seller attaches its trademark to the goods, it is not necessary to develop separate arm's-length charges for the intangible if the purchaser does not acquire the right to exploit the intangible other than in connection with the resale of the property. However, the embedded intangible must be taken into account for purposes of determining the arm's-length price for the sale of the related tangible property.[39]

Comparable uncontrolled price method. Under the comparable uncontrolled price method, the arm's-length price is the price charged for comparable goods in transactions between uncontrolled parties, adjusted for any material differences that exist between the controlled and uncontrolled transactions.[40] The comparable uncontrolled price method ordinarily is the most reliable method for estimating an arm's-length price if there are only minor differences between the controlled and uncontrolled transactions for which appropriate adjustments can be made.[41]

Example 5.10: USAco, a domestic corporation, owns 100% of MEXco, a Mexican corporation. USAco manufactures telecommunications equipment at a cost of $500 per unit and sells the equipment to unrelated foreign distributors at a price of $750 per unit. USAco also sells the equipment to MEXco, which then resells the goods to unrelated foreign customers for $850 each. The conditions of USAco's sales to MEXco are essentially equivalent to those of the sales made to unrelated foreign distributors. Because information is available regarding comparable uncontrolled sales,

---

[36] Reg. § 1.482-3(a).
[37] Reg. § 1.482-1(c)(1).
[38] Reg. § 1.482-3(e)(1).

[39] Reg. § 1.482-3(f).
[40] Reg. § 1.482-3(b)(1) and (b)(2)(ii)(B).
[41] Reg. § 1.482-3(b)(2)(ii)(A).

USAco and MEXco should use the comparable uncontrolled price method. Under this method, the estimate of the arm's-length price is $750.

In assessing the comparability of controlled and uncontrolled transactions for purposes of the comparable uncontrolled price method, the most important factor is product similarity. Other significant factors include the similarity of contractual terms and economic conditions.[42] Because information regarding comparable uncontrolled transactions is usually not available, the comparable uncontrolled price method is usually difficult to apply in practice.

Resale price method. The type of transaction envisioned by the resale price method is a controlled sale of finished goods followed by the related distributor's resale of the goods to unrelated customers.[43] Under this method, the arm's-length price is the resale price charged by the related distributor, reduced by the arm's-length gross profit margin for such resales, and adjusted for any material differences that exist between the controlled and uncontrolled transactions. The gross profit margin realized by independent distributors on similar uncontrolled sales provides an estimate of the arm's-length gross profit, which is expressed as a percentage of the resale price.[44]

Example 5.11: USAco, a domestic corporation, owns 100% of CANco, a Canadian corporation. USAco manufactures medical equipment at a cost of $1,000 per unit and sells the equipment to CANco, which resells the goods (without any further processing) to unrelated foreign customers for $1,500 each. Independent foreign distributors typically earn commissions of 10% (expressed as a percentage of the resale price) on the purchase and resale of products comparable to those produced by USAco. Under the resale price method, the estimate of the arm's-length price is $1,350 [$1,500 − (10% × $1,500)].

In assessing the comparability of controlled and uncontrolled transactions for purposes of the resale price method, product similarity is less important than under the comparable uncontrolled price method, while the similarity of the functions performed, risks borne, and contractual terms agreed to is relatively more important.[45] Consistency between the accounting methods used to compute the gross profit for the controlled and uncontrolled transactions also is important.[46]

Cost plus method. The type of controlled transaction envisioned by the cost plus method is the manufacture, assembly, or other production of goods that are sold to related parties.[47] Under the cost plus

---

[42] Reg. § 1.482-3(b)(2)(ii)(A).
[43] Reg. § 1.482-3(c)(1).
[44] Reg. § 1.482-3(c)(2) and (c)(3)(ii)(C).

[45] Reg. § 1.482-3(c)(3)(ii)(A) and (B).
[46] Reg. § 1.482-3(c)(3)(iii)(B).
[47] Reg. § 1.482-3(d)(1).

method, the arm's-length price is the manufacturing cost incurred by the related manufacturer, increased by the arm's-length gross profit markup for such manufacturers, and adjusted for any material differences that exist between the controlled and uncontrolled transactions. The gross profit realized by independent manufacturers on similar uncontrolled sales provides an estimate of the arm's-length gross profit markup, which is expressed as a percentage of the manufacturing costs.[48]

> **Example 5.12:** USAco, a domestic corporation, owns 100% of FORco, a foreign corporation. FORco manufactures power tools at a cost of $60 each and sells them to USAco. USAco attaches its trade name to the power tools (which has a significant effect on their resale price) and resells them to unrelated customers in the United States for $100 each. Independent foreign manufacturers producing similar power tools typically earn a gross profit markup of 20%. Under the cost plus method, the estimate of the arm's-length price is $72 [$60 + (20% × $60)].

As with the resale price method, in assessing the comparability of controlled and uncontrolled transactions for purposes of the cost plus method, product similarity is less important than under the comparable uncontrolled price method, while the similarity of the functions performed, risks borne, and contractual terms agreed to is relatively more important.[49] Consistency between the accounting methods used to compute the gross profit markup for the controlled and uncontrolled transactions also is important.[50]

Comparable profits method. The comparable profits method looks to the profits of uncontrolled entities, rather than the prices used in uncontrolled transactions, to determine an arm's-length allocation of profit between two related corporations. Under this method, the profitability of comparable uncontrolled entities is used as a benchmark for determining an arm's-length net profit for one of the controlled parties (the "tested party"), and then a transfer price is established which leaves the tested party with that amount of net profit.[51]

The methodology for developing an arm's-length profit involves the following six steps:

(1) *Determine the tested party*—The tested party should be the participant in the controlled transactions for which the most reliable data regarding comparable uncontrolled parties can be located. This is likely to be the least complex of the controlled parties, and the controlled party that does not own

---

[48] Reg. § 1.482-3(d)(2) and (d)(3)(ii)(C).
[49] Reg. § 1.482-3(d)(3)(ii)(A) and (B).
[50] Reg. § 1.482-3(d)(3)(iii)(B).
[51] Reg. § 1.482-5(b)(1).

valuable intangible property or unique assets that distinguish it from potential uncontrolled comparables.[52]

(2) *Obtain financial data regarding comparable uncontrolled parties*—The key factors in assessing the comparability of the tested party to uncontrolled parties are the resources employed and the risks assumed. Because resources and risks usually are directly related to functions performed, it also is important to consider the functions performed in determining the degree of comparability between the tested party and an uncontrolled party.[53] Another important factor is the consistency between the accounting methods used by the controlled and uncontrolled parties to compute their operating profits.[54] Adjustments must be made for any differences between the tested party and the comparable uncontrolled parties that would materially affect the profitability measures used.[55]

(3) *Select a profit level indicator*—Examples of the profitability measures that can be used include the ratio of operating profit to operating assets, the ratio of operating profit to sales, and the ratio of gross profit to operating expenses. To enhance the reliability of a profitability measure, the taxpayer should perform a multiyear analysis which generally should encompass at least the taxable year under review and the two preceding years.[56]

(4) *Develop an arm's-length range of comparable operating profits*—To construct an arm's-length range of comparable operating profits, the selected profitability measure (e.g., the ratio of operating profits to operating assets) is applied to the tested party's most narrowly identifiable business activity for which data incorporating the controlled transaction is available (e.g., the operating assets used in the manufacture and sale of inventory).[57]

(5) *Determine if an adjustment must be made*—An adjustment is required if the tested party's reported profit lies outside the arm's-length range of comparable operating profits developed in step 4.[58]

(6) *Adjust the transfer price used for the controlled transaction*—If the tested party's reported profit lies outside the arm's-length range, an adjustment is made equal to the difference

---

[52] Reg. § 1.482-5(b)(2)(i).
[53] Reg. § 1.482-5(c)(2)(ii).
[54] Reg. § 1.482-5(c)(3)(ii).
[55] Reg. § 1.482-5(c)(2)(iv).
[56] Reg. § 1.482-5(b)(4). However, any required adjustments are made on a year-by-year basis. Reg. § 1.482-5(e), Example 2.

[57] Reg. § 1.482-5(b)(1).
[58] Reg. § 1.482-5(b)(1).

between the tested party's reported profit and the benchmark arm's-length profit,[59] such as the mean or the median of the arm's-length range of comparable operating profits.[60]

Example 5.13: [61] EURco, a foreign corporation, owns 100% of USAco, a domestic corporation. EURco manufactures consumer products for worldwide distribution. USAco imports EURco's finished goods for resale in the United States. USAco's average financial results for the last three years are as follows:

Sales	$50 million
Cost of goods sold	<$40 million>
Operating expenses	<$ 9 million>
Operating profit	**$ 1 million**

USAco is selected as the tested party because it engages in activities that are less complex than those of EURco. An analysis of five comparable uncontrolled U.S. distributors indicates that the ratio of operating profits to sales is the most appropriate profitability measure. After adjustments have been made to account for material differences between USAco and the uncontrolled distributors, the average ratio of operating profit to sales for each uncontrolled distributor is as follows: 3%, 4%, 5%, 5%, and 7%.

Applying these percentages to USAco's sales of $50 million yields the following arm's-length range of comparable operating profits: $1.5 million, $2 million, $2.5 million, $2.5 million, and $3.5 million. The data is not sufficiently complete to conclude that all of the material differences between USAco and the uncontrolled distributors have been identified. Therefore, the interquartile range of comparable operating profits is used for purposes of testing USAco's profits. This range includes $2 million, $2.5 million, and $2.5 million.

Because USAco's reported operating profit of $1 million lies outside the arm's-length range, an adjustment is required. The median of the interquartile range of comparable operating profits (i.e., $2.5 million) is determined to be the arm's-length profit for USAco. Therefore, the transfer prices that USAco pays EURco for its inventory are reduced by $1.5 million, which equals the difference between USAco's reported profit of $1 million and the arm's-length profit of $2.5 million. This adjustment increases USAco's U.S. taxable income by $1.5 million per year, with a corresponding decrease in EURco's taxable income.

Profit split method. The profit split method is the most complicated of the specified pricing methods for transfers of tangible prop-

---

[59] Reg. § 1.482-5(b)(1).
[60] Reg. § 1.482-1(e)(3).

[61] This example is based on Reg. § 1.482-5(e), Example 2.

erty, and therefore is difficult to apply in practice. The profit split method evaluates whether the allocation of the combined operating profit attributable to a controlled transaction is arm's length by reference to the relative value of each controlled taxpayer's contribution to that combined profit.[62] The relative value of each controlled taxpayer's contribution is determined using either the comparable profit split method or the residual profit split method.

Under the comparable profit split method, the allocation of the combined operating profit between two controlled taxpayers is based on how uncontrolled taxpayers engaged in similar activities under similar circumstances allocate their joint profits.[63] Under the residual profit split method, the comparable profits method is used to estimate and allocate an arm's-length profit for the routine contributions made by each controlled taxpayer. Routine contributions ordinarily include contributions of tangible property and services. The residual profit not allocated on the basis of routine functions is then allocated between the two controlled taxpayers on the basis of the relative value of the intangible property contributed by each party.[64]

Ceiling on transfer price for imported goods. There is a statutory ceiling on the transfer prices used for property imported into the United States in a transaction between controlled parties. Examples of such transactions include a U.S. parent corporation purchasing goods from a foreign manufacturing subsidiary, or a U.S. marketing subsidiary purchasing goods from its foreign parent corporation. In such cases, the transfer price used by the controlled purchaser for income tax purposes (which becomes the controlled purchaser's cost basis for computing the gain on resale) cannot exceed the value amount taken into account for purposes of determining custom duties.[65] This ceiling is designed to prevent taxpayers from simultaneously avoiding U.S. custom duties and U.S. income taxes by using a low transfer price for custom purposes and a high price for income tax purposes.

Transfer or Use of Intangibles

Introduction. For transfer pricing purposes, an "intangible" includes any of the following items:

  (i)   patents, inventions, formulae, processes, designs, patterns, or know-how,

  (ii) copyrights and literary, musical, or artistic compositions,

  (iii) trademarks, trade names, or brand names,

  (iv) franchises, licenses, or contracts,

---

[62] Reg. § 1.482-6(a).
[63] Reg. § 1.482-6(c)(2).
[64] Reg. § 1.482-6(c)(3).
[65] Code Sec. 1059A.

(v) methods, programs, systems, procedures, campaigns, surveys, studies, forecasts, estimates, customer lists, or technical data, and

(vi) other similar items.[66]

The owner of an intangible for tax purposes ordinarily is the taxpayer who owns the legally protected right to exploit that intangible.[67] However, if an intangible is not legally protected, it may be unclear which of the controlled parties is the owner of the intangible. In such cases, the controlled party that bore the largest portion of the direct and indirect costs of developing the intangible ordinarily is treated as the owner for tax purposes.[68]

There are three specified methods for estimating an arm's-length charge for transfers of intangibles:

(i)   the comparable uncontrolled transaction method,

(ii) the comparable profits method, and

(iii) the profit split method.[69]

The taxpayer must select and apply the method which provides the most reliable estimate of an arm's length price.[70] In addition to the three specified methods, the taxpayer also has the option of using an unspecified method. However, an unspecified method can be used only if it provides the most reliable estimate of an arm's-length price.[71]

Comparable uncontrolled transaction method. The comparable uncontrolled transaction method is equivalent to the comparable uncontrolled price method used for transfers of tangible property. Thus, under the comparable uncontrolled transaction method, the arm's-length charge for the transfer of an intangible is the amount charged for comparable intangibles in transactions between uncontrolled parties, adjusted for any material differences that exist between the controlled and uncontrolled transactions.[72] In order for the intangibles involved in the uncontrolled transaction to be considered comparable to the intangible involved in the controlled transaction, both intangibles must be used in connection with similar products or processes within the same general industry or market and must have similar profit potential.[73] The comparable uncontrolled transaction method ordinarily is the most reliable method for estimating an arm's-length price if there are only minor differences between the controlled and uncontrolled transactions for which appropriate adjustments can

---

[66] Reg. § 1.482-4(b).

[67] Reg. § 1.482-4(f)(3)(ii)(A).

[68] Reg. § 1.482-4(f)(3)(ii)(B). If any other controlled party contributed to the development of the intangible, the owner must allocate an arm's-length compensation to that party. Reg. § 1.482-4(f)(3)(iii).

[69] Reg. § 1.482-4(a).

[70] Reg. § 1.482-1(c)(1).

[71] Reg. § 1.482-4(d)(1).

[72] Reg. § 1.482-4(c)(1).

[73] Reg. § 1.482-4(c)(2)(iii)(B)(1).

be made.[74] Because information regarding comparable uncontrolled transactions is usually not available regarding intangible assets such as patents and trademarks, the comparable uncontrolled transaction method usually is difficult to apply in practice.

Comparable profits method. The same comparable profits method used to determine arm's-length prices for transfers of tangible property also can be used to determine arm's-length sales prices or royalty rates for transfers of intangible property.

Example 5.14: [75] USAco, a domestic corporation, owns 100% of the stock of ASIAco, a foreign corporation. ASIAco manufactures one of USAco's patented technologies under a licensing agreement. ASIAco then sells its entire output of this product at an arm's-length price to USAco, which markets the product in the United States. ASIAco's average financial results for the last three years are as follows:

Sales	$20 million
Cost of goods sold	<$12 million>
Royalty paid to USAco (5% of sales)	<$ 1 million>
Operating expenses	<$ 2 million>
Operating profit	$ 5 million
Operating assets	$25 million

ASIAco is selected as the tested party because it engages in relatively routine manufacturing activities, whereas USAco engages in a variety of complex activities using unique and valuable intangibles. Because ASIAco is engaged in manufacturing, the ratio of operating profits to operating assets is the most appropriate profitability measure. After adjustments have been made to account for material differences between ASIAco and a sample of five uncontrolled foreign manufacturers for which data is available, the average ratio of operating profit to operating assets for each uncontrolled distributor is as follows: 8%, 10%, 15%, 15%, and 18%.

Applying these percentages to ASIAco's operating assets yields the following arm's-length range of comparable operating profits for ASIAco: $2 million, $2.5 million, $3.75 million, $3.75 million, and $4.5 million. The data is not sufficiently complete to conclude that all of the material differences between ASIAco and the uncontrolled manufacturers have been identified. Therefore, the interquartile range of comparable operating profits is used for purposes of testing ASIAco's profits. This range includes $2.5 million, $3.75 million, and $3.75 million.

---

[74] Reg. § 1.482-4(c)(2)(ii).

[75] This example is based on Reg. § 1.482-5(e), Example 4.

Because ASIAco's reported operating profit of $5 million lies outside the arm's-length range, an adjustment is required. The median of the interquartile range of comparable operating profits (i.e., $3.75 million) is determined to be the arm's-length profit for ASIAco. Therefore, the royalty that ASIAco pays USAco is increased by $1.25 million, which equals the difference between ASIAco's reported profit of $5 million and the arm's-length profit of $3.75 million. This adjustment increases USAco's U.S. taxable income by $1.25 million per year, with a corresponding decrease in ASIAco's taxable income.

Profit split method. See the discussion of the profit split method under "Transfers of Tangible Property," above.

Commensurate with income requirement. Many U.S. companies have moved operations to foreign countries offering low-cost labor, low tax rates, less government regulation, and new markets. These companies typically have manufacturing and marketing intangibles that they can transfer to their foreign subsidiaries. For example, a foreign manufacturing subsidiary might manufacture a good under a license from its domestic parent corporation and then sell its entire output to the parent at a markup. If the foreign subsidiary is located in a low-tax foreign jurisdiction, the domestic parent will defer U.S. taxes to the extent the intercompany royalty rate understates the economic value of the intangible. It is often very difficult to determine the appropriate arm's-length royalty rate because information regarding comparable uncontrolled transactions is usually not available regarding intangible assets such as patents and trademarks.

In response to these problems, in 1986 Congress enacted a requirement that transfer prices for sales or licenses of intangibles must be "commensurate with the income attributable to the intangible." [76] In other words, transfer prices must reflect the actual profit experience realized subsequent to the outbound transfer. To meet this requirement, the original sales price or royalty rate must be adjusted annually to reflect any unanticipated changes in the income actually generated by the intangible.[77] For example, if a new patent leads to a product that turns out to be far more successful than was expected at the time the patent was licensed, the taxpayer must increase the intercompany royalty payments to reflect that unanticipated profitability. A determination in an earlier year that the royalty was arm's length does not preclude the IRS from making an adjustment in a subsequent year.[78]

---

[76] Code Sec. 482.

[77] Reg. § 1.482-4(f)(2)(i).

[78] Reg. § 1.482-4(f)(2)(i).

The need to make periodic adjustments places a significant administrative burden on taxpayers. This burden is mitigated somewhat by the following exceptions:

(i) *De minimis exception*—Periodic adjustments are not required if the total profits actually realized by the controlled transferee from the use of the intangible are between 80% and 120% of the profits that were foreseeable when the agreement was entered into, and there have been no substantial changes in the functions performed by the transferee since the agreement was executed, except for changes required by unforeseeable events. Other requirements include the existence of a written royalty agreement, and the preparation of contemporaneous supporting documentation.[79] In addition, if the requirements of the *de minimis* exception are met for each of five consecutive taxable years, then no further periodic adjustments are required under any conditions.[80]

(ii) *Extraordinary event exception*—Even if the total profits actually realized by the controlled transferee from the use of the intangible are less than 80% or more than 120% of the profits that were foreseeable when the agreement was entered into, the taxpayer need not make periodic adjustments if the unexpected variation in profits is due to extraordinary events that could not have been reasonably anticipated and are beyond the taxpayer's control. In order to use this exception, all of the requirements of the *de minimis* exception, other than the 80%–120% test, also must be met.[81]

(iii) *Same intangible exception*—No periodic adjustments are required if the following requirements are met: (i) the same intangible was transferred to an uncontrolled taxpayer under circumstances similar to those of the controlled transaction, (ii) the uncontrolled transaction serves as the basis for the application of the comparable uncontrolled transaction method, and (iii) an arm's-length charge is made in the first taxable year of the transfer.[82]

Cost-sharing arrangements. One way for controlled parties to avoid the administrative burden and uncertainties associated with transfer pricing for intangibles is to enter into a cost-sharing arrangement. For example, a U.S. parent corporation and a foreign subsidiary may agree to equally share the costs of developing a new product. Under such an agreement, the parent might own the rights to manufac-

---

[79] Reg. § 1.482-4(f)(2)(ii)(C)). A slightly different set of requirements applies if the arm's-length amount was determined under the comparable uncontrolled transaction method. Reg. § 1.482-4(f)(2)(ii)(B).

[80] Reg. § 1.482-4(f)(2)(ii)(E).

[81] Reg. § 1.482-4(f)(2)(ii)(D).

[82] Reg. § 1.482-4(f)(2)(ii)(A).

ture and market the new product in the United States, while the subsidiary might own the rights to manufacture and market the new product abroad. The advantage of a cost-sharing arrangement is that the foreign subsidiary's ownership of the foreign rights to the intangible negates the need to have that subsidiary pay a royalty to its U.S. parent. A bona fide cost-sharing arrangement must allocate research and development costs in proportion to the profits earned by each controlled party from the intangible, and each controlled party must bear a portion of the costs incurred at each stage of the development of both successful and unsuccessful intangibles.[83]

Correlative Adjustments and Setoffs

When the IRS increases the taxable income of a related party through a transfer pricing adjustment, it will also reduce the income of the related party for U.S. purposes.

> **Example 5.15:** USAco sells machinery to FORco, its foreign subsidiary. The IRS makes a transfer pricing adjustment, increasing the income of USAco on the sale of machinery by $1 million. The IRS will also decrease the income of FORco by $1 million, which will reduce FORco's earnings and profits and affect the foreign tax credit computation. Accordingly, the IRS may permit USAco to establish an account receivable so that FORco's payment of cash in the amount of the adjustment will not result in additional income.

The IRS will generally permit a taxpayer to offset a negative transfer pricing adjustment with a favorable transfer pricing adjustment provided that the adjustments are for the same two related parties.

> **Example 5.16:** USAco sells machinery to FORco, its foreign subsidiary. The IRS makes a transfer pricing adjustment, increasing the income of USAco on the sale of machinery by $1 million. If the IRS also determines that USAco should have paid FORco an additional $600,000 for services, the adjustments are offset for a net adjustment of $400,000. If, however, the IRS makes the adjustment for USAco's sales of machinery to FORco and a negative transfer pricing adjustment for the services received from ASIAco (another of USAco's foreign subsidiaries), USAco would not be able to offset the adjustments.

¶ 503   INFORMATION REPORTING REQUIREMENTS

In order to effectively audit the transfer prices used by a U.S. subsidiary of a foreign corporation, the IRS often must examine the books and records of the foreign parent corporation. Historically, for-

---

[83] Reg. § 1.482-7.

eign parties have resisted making their records available to the IRS or have not maintained records sufficient to determine arm's-length transfer prices. In response, Congress enacted the requirement that each year certain reporting corporations must file Form 5472, Information Return of a 25% Foreign-Owned U.S. Corporation or a Foreign Corporation Engaged in a U.S. Trade or Business, and maintain certain books and records.[84] A domestic corporation is a reporting corporation if, at any time during the taxable year, 25% or more of its stock, by vote or value, is owned directly or indirectly by one foreign person. A foreign corporation is a reporting corporation if, at any time during the taxable year, it is engaged in a U.S. trade or business, and 25% or more of its stock, by vote or value, is owned directly or indirectly by one foreign person.[85] In filing a Form 5472, the reporting corporation must provide information regarding its foreign shareholders, certain other related parties, and the dollar amounts of transactions that it entered into during the year with foreign related parties.[86] A separate Form 5472 is filed for each foreign or domestic related party with which the reporting corporation engaged in reportable transactions during the year.[87] The practical importance of Form 5472 is that the IRS often uses this form as a starting point for conducting a transfer pricing examination.[88] (Form 5472 is reproduced in the appendix to Chapter 12.)

In addition to filing Form 5472, a reporting corporation also must maintain permanent books and records sufficient to establish the correctness of the reporting corporation's U.S. tax liability, with an emphasis on transactions with related parties.[89] Certain reporting corporations are exempted from these special record maintenance requirements, but still must file Form 5472. These include reporting corporations whose U.S. gross receipts are less than $10 million,[90] and reporting corporations whose annual payments to and from foreign related persons with respect to related party transactions are not more than $5 million and are less than 10% of the reporting corporation's U.S. gross income.[91] Any reporting corporation that fails to either file Form 5472 or maintain the requisite records may be subject to an annual penalty of $10,000.[92]

Information reporting also is required with respect to the foreign subsidiaries of domestic corporations.[93] Specifically, each year a U.S. person who owns more than 50% or more of the stock, by vote or value, of a foreign corporation must file a Form 5471, Information Return of

---

[84] See generally, Code Secs. 6038A and 6038C.

[85] Reg. § 1.6038A-1(c).

[86] Reg. § 1.6038A-2(b).

[87] Reg. § 1.6038A-2(a).

[88] See Internal Revenue Manual Audit Guidelines for Transfer Pricing Cases, dated June 14, 1994, 522.1(2).

[89] Reg. § 1.6038A-3(a)(1).

[90] Reg. § 1.6038A-1(h).

[91] Reg. § 1.6038A-1(i).

[92] Reg. § 1.6038A-4(a).

[93] See generally, Code Sec. 6038.

U.S. Persons With Respect to Certain Foreign Corporations.[94] In the Form 5471, the U.S. shareholder must provide a wide variety of information regarding the controlled foreign corporation, including the dollar amounts of transactions it entered into with related parties.[95] Any U.S. person who fails to furnish the required information may be subject to an annual penalty of $10,000, as well as a reduction in the taxpayer's foreign tax credit.[96] As with Form 5472, the practical importance of Form 5471 is that the IRS often uses this form as a starting point for conducting a transfer pricing examination.[97] (Form 5471 is reproduced in the appendix to Chapter 6.)

¶ 504   TRANSACTIONAL AND NET ADJUSTMENT PENALTIES

In an attempt to promote more voluntary compliance with the arm's-length standard, Congress has enacted two special transfer pricing penalties: the transactional penalty and the net adjustment penalty.[98] Both penalties equal 20% of the tax underpayment related to a transfer pricing adjustment made by the IRS.[99] The transactional penalty applies if the transfer price used by the taxpayer is 200% or more (or 50% or less) of the amount determined under Code Sec. 482 to be the correct amount.[100] The net adjustment penalty applies if the net increase in taxable income for a taxable year as a result of Code Sec. 482 adjustments exceeds the lesser of $5 million or 10% of the taxpayer's gross receipts.[101] Both penalties increase to 40% of the related tax underpayment if the transfer price used by the taxpayer is 400% or more (or 25% or less) of the amount determined under Code Sec. 482 to be the correct amount, or if the net adjustment to taxable income exceeds the lesser of $20 million or 20% of the taxpayer's gross receipts.[102]

The transactional and net adjustment penalties apply automatically whenever an IRS adjustment exceeds the numerical thresholds. The only way to avoid the penalty in such cases is to satisfy certain safe-harbor requirements. In the case of the transactional penalty, the penalty is waived only if the taxpayer can demonstrate that it had reasonable cause and acted in good faith.[103] In the case of the net adjustment penalty, the reasonable cause and good faith requirements can be met only if the taxpayer can demonstrate, through contemporaneous documentation provided to the IRS within 30 days of a request, that it acted reasonably in selecting and applying a transfer pricing

---

[94] Reg. § 1.6038-2(a) and (b).

[95] Reg. § 1.6038-2(f).

[96] Code Sec. 6038(b) and (c).

[97] See Internal Revenue Manual Audit Guidelines for Transfer Pricing Cases, dated June 14, 1994, 522.1(2).

[98] For a comprehensive discussion of the difficulties that the IRS has faced in administrating Code Sec.

482, see "Report on the Application and Administration of Section 482" IRS Pub. 3218 (1999).

[99] Code Sec. 6662(a) and (b)(3).

[100] Code Sec. 6662(e)(1)(B)(i).

[101] Code Sec. 6662(e)(1)(B)(ii) and (e)(3)(A).

[102] Code Sec. 6662(h).

[103] Reg. § 1.6662-6(b)(3) and Reg. § 1.6664-4(a).

method.[104] These added requirements for avoiding the net adjustment penalty are designed to force taxpayers to develop and have waiting for the IRS all of the documentation that the IRS ordinarily would need to review in a transfer pricing examination. In addition to providing protection against the transfer pricing penalty, the documentation may also persuade the IRS that a transfer pricing adjustment is not necessary.

A taxpayer cannot reasonably conclude that a specified method it selected provided the most reliable measure of an arm's-length result unless it has made a reasonable effort to evaluate the potential application of the other specified methods.[105] If the taxpayer used an unspecified method, the taxpayer must demonstrate that none of the specified methods would provide a result that clearly reflected income, and that the unspecified method is likely to clearly reflect income.[106]

Preparing Transfer Pricing Documentation

The principal supporting documents that a taxpayer normally must include in its contemporaneous documentation are as follows:

(i)   an overview of the taxpayer's business, including an analysis of the economic and legal factors that affect the pricing of its property and services,

(ii)   a description of the organizational structure (including an organization chart) covering all related parties engaged in potentially relevant transactions,

(iii)   any documentation explicitly required by the Regulations under Code Sec. 482,

(iv)   a description of the pricing method selected and an explanation of why that method was selected,

(v)   a description of the alternative methods that were considered and an explanation of why they were not selected,

(vi)   a description of the controlled transactions and any internal data used to analyze those transactions,

(vii)   a description of the comparables used, how comparability was evaluated, and what adjustments were made,

(viii) an explanation of the economic analyses and projections relied upon in developing the pricing method, and

---

[104] Code Sec. 6662(e)(3)(B)(i). Documentation is considered contemporaneous if it is in existence at the time the tax return is filed. Reg. § 1.6662-6(d)(2)(iii)(A). For taxable years beginning after April 21, 1993, the contemporaneous documentation requirements must be met in order to avoid the net adjustment penalty. However, contemporaneous documentation is not mandatory in order to avoid a penalty for taxable years beginning before April 22, 1993. Rev. Proc. 94-33, 1994-1 CB 628.

[105] Reg. § 1.6662-6(d)(2)(ii).

[106] Reg. § 1.6662-6(d)(3)(ii).

(ix)   a general index of the principal and background documents along with a description of the recordkeeping system used for cataloging and accessing those documents.[107]

Information Gathering

The information gathering stage is usually the most time-consuming aspect of preparing transfer pricing documentation. The taxpayer will typically have to interview operational personnel on both sides of the intercompany transaction. In addition, it will also have to obtain relevant financial information, including internal cost accounting and profit margin analysis for the transactions at issue and the latest four years' financial statements. The taxpayer will have to identify unrelated party transactions, which may be between either two unrelated parties or one of the related parties and an unrelated party.

> **Example 5.17:** USAco sells cheese to FORco, its foreign subsidiary, and wants to apply the CUP method to determine the appropriate transfer price. USAco has to interview the appropriate personnel to determine the price USAco charges unrelated parties in comparable cheese sales. In addition, USAco also needs to identify, to the extent available, the price charged on comparable sales of cheese by other cheese wholesalers.

The culmination of the information gathering process is the preparation of a functional analysis. This functional analysis reviews the functions performed and risks assumed by the respective parties, focusing on competition, the market, and other economic factors that may help to determine arm's-length pricing.

Identification of the Best Method

The regulations require the taxpayer to apply the "best method" to its intercompany transactions. This requires choosing one of the methods prescribed in the regulations and supporting its applicability. At the same time, the taxpayer must explain why the other prescribed methods are not applicable. The taxpayer must review accurate and reliable data for application of the method; the degree of comparability between controlled and uncontrolled transactions or companies to which the methods are applied; and the number, magnitude, and accuracy of adjustments required to apply the method.[108]

Economic Analysis

The taxpayer should retain an economist to analyze the transactional data and obtain information concerning comparable companies from reliable databases.

---

[107] Reg. § 1.6662-6(d)(2)(iii)(B).   [108] Reg. § 1.482-1(d)(2).

Example 5.18: USAco, a U.S. subsidiary of ASIAco, a Singapore parent corporation, purchases software from its parent that USAco markets and sells in the U.S. USAco wants to apply the comparable profits method to determine the appropriate transfer price. USAco must find companies comparable to itself with respect to the type of functions performed and the risks assumed. As a result, the economist will have to search for potentially comparable companies based, for example, on disclosures required by the Securities and Exchange Commission, such as Form 10-K.

The economic analysis may further compare the financial results of the tested party to the financial results of the comparable transactions or companies. In addition to assuring functional comparability, an economist may also examine financial ratios such as return on costs, return on sales, and return on assets. Where appropriate, an economist may make adjustments for differences in relevant factors such as the relative levels of inventory, receivables, and payables.

Transfer Pricing in Other Countries

The U.S. transfer pricing rules are generally more detailed and stricter than those in other countries. As a result, many of the United States' trading partners have become concerned that multi-nationals were reporting more income from intercompany transactions in the U.S. and less in the other country. Because of this concern, many of these countries have specifically adopted transfer pricing rules and many others have adopted the guidelines issued by the Organization for Economic Corporation and Development.[109] A methodology and transfer price that the IRS may accept, may not, however, be acceptable to a foreign country's taxing authority. Many foreign countries have a preference for the transaction-based methods (i.e., comparable uncontrolled price method, resale price method, and cost plus method) as opposed to the profit-based methods (comparable profits method and profit split methods).[110]

Example 5.19: USAco, a U.S. subsidiary of CANco, a Canadian parent corporation, purchases oil from its parent that USAco markets and sells in the U.S. USAco properly applies the comparable profits method to justify to the IRS the transfer price of $100 a barrel. The Canada Customs and Revenue Agency audits CANco, disregards USAco's comparable profits method analysis, and applies a profit split method to support an adjustment to CANco, increasing the transfer price to $120 a barrel.

---

[109] Organization for Economic Corporation and Development, *Transfer Pricing Guidelines for Multinational Enterprises and Tax Administration.*

[110] Culbertson, Robert E., "A Rose By Any Other Name: Smelling the Flowers at the OECD's (Last) Resort," *Tax Notes International,* August 4, 1995; Revenue Canada Information Circular 87-2.

Although contemporaneous documentation provides protection in most developed countries from a transfer pricing penalty, the documentation in these foreign countries is not as rigorous as the U.S.' requirement. For example, only Australia,[111] Japan,[112] and the Netherlands [113] require that documentation explain why the taxpayer rejected the alternative methods.

¶ 505   DEVELOPING A TRANSFER PRICING STRATEGY

In the current environment, transfer pricing strategy is driven, to a great extent, by the need to develop an effective defense against the transactional and net adjustment penalties.[114] The first step in developing a defense against these penalties is to assess the amount of risk associated with the taxpayer's current position. One major determinant of risk is the aggregate dollar value of controlled transactions between U.S. and foreign affiliates. Another major determinant of risk is the relative profitability of U.S. and foreign operations, in particular, the percentage of the taxpayer's worldwide profits that is allocated to low-tax foreign jurisdictions.

As a practical matter, the transactional penalty is likely to arise only if the taxpayer provides for no transfer price.[115] In contrast, any large corporation with a significant volume of cross-border transactions could conceivably exceed the $5 million net adjustment threshold. For example, a company with $100 million of cross-border controlled transactions is potentially subject to the 20% penalty if its transfer prices are off by just 5%.

The only sure way to guard against the net adjustment penalty is to demonstrate, through contemporaneous documentation provided to the IRS within 30 days of a request, that the taxpayer acted reasonably in selecting and applying a transfer pricing method. As a consequence, the keys to avoiding the net adjustment penalty are the use of transfer prices which are supported by sufficient documentation and allocating to each affiliate a reasonable profit which reflects the economic realities of the parties' contractual relations. In this regard, reliance on a transfer pricing study done by a professional qualified to conduct such an analysis, such as an attorney, accountant, or economist, is a relevant factor in determining whether the taxpayer selected and applied a transfer pricing method in a reasonable manner.[116] Therefore, a formal transfer pricing study, whether prepared internally

---

[111] Division 13 of Part III, Income Tax Assessment Act; Final Ruling TR 97/05.

[112] STML—Enforcement Order 39-12, STML—Circular 66-4-1-66-4-9.

[113] Article 7 of the Income Tax Act.

[114] In *DHL Corp. v. Comm'r*, 76 TCM 1122 (1998), the Tax Court upheld the IRS's assertion of accuracy-related penalties under Code Sec. 6662.

[115] For example, if a domestic parent corporation transfers an intangible to a foreign subsidiary and does not provide for any royalty payments, then any price adjustment will exceed the 200% threshold.

[116] Reg. § 1.6662-6(d)(2)(ii)(D).

by the taxpayer's employees or externally through the use of outside consultants, is an important factor in establishing defensible transfer pricing positions.

An alternative strategy for avoiding the transactional and net adjustment penalties is to obtain an advance pricing agreement (or "APA"). Under the APA procedure, the IRS reviews and agrees to the taxpayer's transfer pricing method before the taxpayer implements it.[117] An APA spells out the factual nature of the related party transactions, an appropriate pricing method, and the expected range of results from applying the agreed-upon method to the transactions. If the agreed-upon methodology is applied faithfully by the taxpayer, the IRS will not adjust the taxpayer's transfer prices in any future audits. Thus, the advantages of an APA include the certainty of results for the taxpayer, as well as the possibility of reduced record keeping because the taxpayer knows in advance what information the IRS considers to be relevant. The disadvantages include the cost of developing the documentation needed to obtain an APA (including the opinions of independent experts), as well as the up-front disclosure of information to the IRS. Disclosure may be only a timing issue, however, for large multinational corporations which the IRS routinely audits. Although taxpayers may have some concern that they are disclosing information about their company to potential competitors, the 1999 Act prohibited disclosure of the written APAs and any background documents from disclosure.[118] Taxpayers that have traditionally benefited the most from APAs include large multinational corporations, companies with bad audit histories, conservative companies concerned about penalties, and U.S. subsidiaries of foreign multinational corporations. These businesses typically have significant transfer pricing exposure.

The IRS has recently provided streamlined procedures for small taxpayers, which the IRS defines as those whose intercompany transactions are under $50 million.[119] These streamlined procedures provide for an APA within 6 months of filing, meetings in local districts instead of the national office in Washington, and permitting a taxpayer's transfer pricing documentation to serve as pre-filing materials.

---

[117] Rev. Proc. 96-53, 1996-2 CB 34. See Notice 98-65, 1998-52 IRB 10 regarding simplified procedures applicable to small business taxpayers.

[118] Code Secs. 6103 and 6110.
[119] Notice 98-10, I.R.B. 1998-6, 9.

Chapter 6

Anti-avoidance Provisions Governing Foreign Corporations

¶ 601   SUBPART F

Background

The United States generally does not tax foreign business profits earned through a foreign subsidiary until the subsidiary repatriates those earnings through a dividend. This policy, known as "deferral," allows U.S. companies to compete in foreign markets on a tax parity with their foreign competitors. In addition to promoting the competitiveness of U.S. companies abroad, however, deferral also creates an opportunity for avoiding U.S. taxes on inventory trading profits and other income which can be easily shifted to a foreign base company. Various foreign countries, such as the Cayman Islands, Hong Kong, the Republic of Ireland, Puerto Rico, and Singapore, offer tax holidays or low tax rates to attract foreign investment. A U.S. multinational can shift income to a base company organized in these tax-haven countries by, for example, selling goods to the base company at an artificially low price. The base company can then resell the goods at a higher price to a marketing affiliate located in another country for resale to the ultimate foreign customer. The spread between the two transfer prices shifts the profit on the export sale from the countries in which manufacturing and marketing actually take place to a tax-haven country.

Example 6.1: USAco is a domestic corporation that manufactures electric generators for sale both in the United States and Germany. German sales are made through GERco, a wholly owned German marketing subsidiary. USAco's generators cost $600 to manufacture and $100 to market, and they sell for $1,000 in Germany. Therefore, the combined income from a German sale is $300 per generator [$1,000 final sales price − $600 manufacturing cost − $100 selling expense]. USAco also has a wholly owned Cayman Island subsidiary, CAYco, which performs no significant functions with respect to the manufacture or sale of USAco's generators. Assume that the U.S. tax rate is 35%, that the German rate is 45%, and that the Cayman Islands does not have a corporate income tax.

Case 1—Do not route sale through base company: If a German sale is not routed through CAYco, and the transfer price used for USAco's sale to GERco is, say, $800, the $300 of profits will be allocated as follows:

Transaction	Effect on USAco	Effect on CAYco	Effect on GERco
Manufacture good	Cost of sales = $600		
Intercompany sale	Sales = $800		Cost of sales = $800
Selling activities			Expense = $100
Final sale			Sales = $1,000
	Net profit = $200	Net profit = $0	Net profit = $100

The total tax on the $300 profit equals $115 [($200 × 35% U.S. tax rate) + ($100 × 45% German tax rate)].

Case 2—Route sale through base company: Now assume that the German sale is routed through CAYco, that a $700 transfer price is used for USAco's sale to CAYco, and that an $800 transfer price is used for CAYco's sale to GERco. The $300 of profits is now allocated as follows:

Transaction	Effect on USAco	Effect on CAYco	Effect on GERco
Manufacture good	Cost of sales = $600		
Intercompany sale	Sales = $700	Cost of sales = $700	
Intercompany sale		Sales = $800	Cost of sales = $800
Selling activities			Expense = $100
Final sale			Sales = $1,000
	Net profit = $100	Net profit = $100	Net profit = $100

The total tax on the $300 profit now equals $80 [($100 × 35% U.S. tax rate) + ($100 × 0% Cayman Island tax rate) + ($100 × 45% German tax rate)]. Thus, ignoring Code Sec. 482 and Subpart F, USAco can reduce the total tax burden on its German sales by routing those sales through a Cayman Island base company.

One weapon that the IRS can use to attack such schemes is Code Sec. 482, which gives the IRS the authority to allocate income among domestic and foreign affiliates whenever an allocation is necessary to clearly reflect the income of each party. The arm's-length standard of Code Sec. 482 has proven difficult to administer, however, due to a lack of information regarding comparable uncontrolled transactions. As a result, in 1962 Congress enacted Subpart F, which automatically denies deferral to certain types of tainted income earned through a foreign corporation.[1]

Subpart F Inclusions

Subpart F requires every person who is a U.S. shareholder of a controlled foreign corporation (or "CFC"), and who owns stock in such corporation on the last day of the CFC's taxable year, to include in gross income a deemed dividend equal to the shareholder's pro rata share of the CFC's tainted earnings.[2] The principal types of tainted earnings include:

(i) Subpart F income, and

(ii) earnings invested in U.S. property.[3]

---

[1] The term "Subpart F" refers to the part of the Internal Revenue Code where the applicable statutes, i.e., Code Secs. 951–964, are found.

[2] Code Sec. 951(a)(1). This requirement applies only if the foreign corporation was classified as a CFC for an uninterrupted period of 30 days or more during the taxable year.

[3] Code Sec. 951(a)(1). Two other categories of CFC earnings subject to Subpart F are (i) previously excluded Subpart F income withdrawn from investments in less developed countries (see Code Sec. 955 as in effect prior to the enactment of the Tax Reduction Act of 1975 (P.L. 94-12)) and (ii) previously excluded Subpart F income withdrawn from foreign

A U.S. shareholder's pro rata share is the amount that the shareholder would have received if, on the last day of its taxable year, the CFC had actually distributed pro rata to all of its shareholders a dividend equal to the Subpart F inclusion.[4] For this purpose, both direct ownership of the CFC's stock and indirect ownership through foreign entities are considered.[5]

> **Example 6.2:** USAco, a domestic corporation, owns 100% of the stock of FORco, a foreign corporation. During the current year, FORco derived $10 million of Subpart F income in the form of passive interest income, paid $1 million in foreign income taxes (for an effective foreign rate of 10%), and distributed no dividends. USAco is not allowed to defer the residual U.S. tax due on FORco's earnings but instead must recognize a deemed dividend equal to FORco's $9 million of net Subpart F income.

Definition of a CFC

Subpart F applies only to a CFC. A foreign corporation is a CFC if, on any day during the foreign corporation's taxable year, U.S. shareholders own more than 50% of the combined voting power of all classes of stock, or more than 50% of the total value, of the foreign corporation.[6] Only U.S. shareholders are considered in applying the 50% test. A U.S. shareholder is any U.S. person owning at least 10% of the total combined voting power of all classes of voting stock of the foreign corporation.[7] All forms of ownership, including direct, indirect (i.e., beneficial ownership through intervening entities), and constructive (i.e., attribution of ownership from one related party to another), are considered in applying both the 10% shareholder and the 50% aggregate ownership tests.[8] As a consequence, determining a foreign corporation's CFC status can be complex, and the results may be unexpected.

> **Example 6.3:** USAco, a domestic corporation, owns 50% of the stock of F1, a foreign corporation. Unrelated foreign persons own the remaining 50% of F1. USAco also owns 10% of the stock of F2, a foreign corporation. F1 owns 51% of F2, and unrelated foreign persons own the remaining 39%. F1 is not a CFC because USAco, F1's only U.S. shareholder, does not own more than 50% of the stock. USAco also is a U.S. shareholder of F2 because it owns 10% of F2 directly. Under the constructive ownership rules, F1 is treated as constructively owning 100% of F2 because it owns more

---

(Footnote Continued)

base company shipping operations (see Code Sec. 955).

[4] Code Sec. 951(a)(2). The shareholder's pro rata amount may be reduced if the foreign corporation was a CFC for only part of the year or if the U.S. shareholder acquired the CFC's stock during the year.

[5] Code Sec. 958(a).

[6] Code Sec. 957(a). The taxable year of a CFC generally must conform to that of its majority U.S. shareholder. Code Sec. 898.

[7] Code Sec. 951(b).

[8] Code Sec. 958.

than 50% of F2.[9] Thus, USAco is treated as owning 60% of F2, 10% directly and 50% through F1 [50% of 100%]. As a consequence, F2 is a CFC.

In theory, it is possible to avoid CFC status by spreading ownership of a foreign corporation among 11 U.S. persons, each owning only 9.09% of the company. However, because indirect and constructive ownership are considered in applying the 10% shareholder test,[10] the 11 U.S. persons would have to be unrelated to one another, by both family and business connections, in order to avoid U.S. shareholder status. In addition, even if the ownership of a foreign corporation can be structured so as to avoid CFC status, the foreign corporation may still qualify as a passive foreign investment company or a foreign personal holding company. Therefore, planning designed to take advantage of the deferral privilege requires a careful analysis of all of the anti-deferral provisions.

Subpart F Income—Overview

Subpart F income includes the following five categories of tainted income derived by a CFC: [11]

(i) insurance income,

(ii) foreign base company income,

(iii) a portion of international boycott income,[12]

(iv) the sum of any illegal bribes or kickbacks paid by or on behalf of the CFC to a government employee or official, and

(v) income derived from certain disfavored foreign countries.[13]

The amount of a CFC's Subpart F income for any taxable year cannot exceed the CFC's current-year earnings and profits before any reductions for current-year dividend distributions.[14] Insurance income and foreign base company income, which are the two most prevalent types of Subpart F income, are discussed in detail below.

---

[9] Code Sec. 958(b)(2).

[10] Code Sec. 958.

[11] Code Sec. 952(a).

[12] International boycott income is determined under Code Sec. 999. Countries which may require participation in or cooperation with an international boycott include Bahrain, Iraq, Jordan, Kuwait, Lebanon, Libya, Oman, Qatar, Saudi Arabia, Syria, United Arab Emirates, and the Republic of Yemen. Notice 95-3, 1995-1 CB 290.

[13] These include foreign countries whose governments the United States does not recognize, does not conduct diplomatic relations with, or has designated as a government which repeatedly supports acts of international terrorism. Code Sec. 901(j). Countries to which this provision has applied in the past or present include Afghanistan, Albania, Angola, Cambodia, Cuba, Iran, Iraq, Libya, North Korea, South Africa, Sudan, Syria, Vietnam, and People's Democratic Republic of Yemen. Rev. Rul. 95-63, 1995-2 CB 85.

[14] Code Sec. 952(c)(1)(A) and Reg. § 1.952-1(c)(1). Under certain conditions, prior-year deficits also can be used to reduce the amount of Subpart F income. Code Sec. 952(c)(1)(B) and (C).

Insurance Income

Premiums and other income from insurance activities represent the type of portable income that can be readily shifted to a foreign corporation in order to avoid U.S. taxation. Prior to the enactment of Subpart F, a domestic corporation could exploit the portability of insurance income by establishing an offshore insurance company. For example, a U.S. insurance company that had issued policies insuring U.S. risks (e.g., a casualty policy on a U.S. office building) might form a subsidiary in a low-tax jurisdiction and reinsure that U.S. risk with that foreign subsidiary. Assuming there was a bona fide shifting of risks, the U.S. parent could deduct the premiums paid to the subsidiary against its U.S. taxable income. In addition, assuming the foreign subsidiary had no office or other taxable presence in the United States, the premium income was not subject to U.S. taxation. The net effect was the avoidance of U.S. taxes on the premium income routed through the foreign subsidiary.

To negate the tax benefits of such arrangements, Subpart F income includes any income attributable to issuing or reinsuring any insurance or annuity contract in connection with a risk located outside the CFC's country of incorporation. The location of a risk is determined by where the insured property or activity is located or by where the insured individual resides.[15] Income from insuring risks located within the CFC's country of incorporation also qualifies as Subpart F income if, as a result of an arrangement, another corporation receives a substantially equal amount of premiums for insuring risks located outside the CFC's country of incorporation.[16] The taxable amount of insurance income equals the gross amount of such income, less any deductions properly allocable to such income.[17]

More stringent rules apply to related-person insurance income. Related-person insurance income includes any income attributable to issuing or reinsuring any insurance or annuity contract that directly or indirectly covers a U.S. shareholder or a person related to a U.S. shareholder.[18] For this purpose, a U.S. shareholder is defined as any U.S. person who owns any stock of the foreign corporation, and a CFC is defined as any foreign corporation that is 25% or more owned by such U.S. shareholders.[19] Under this rule, any U.S. person who owns stock of such a CFC is taxed on his or her pro rata share of related-person insurance income.[20]

---

[15] Code Sec. 953(a)(1)(A).

[16] Code Sec. 953(a)(1)(B).

[17] Code Sec. 953(b)(3).

[18] Code Sec. 953(c)(2).

[19] Code Sec. 953(c)(1).

[20] Code Sec. 953(c)(1)(C). Code Sec. 953(c)(3) provides several exceptions to the related-person insurance rules.

Foreign Base Company Income

Subpart F income also includes foreign base company income, which consists of the following five categories of income derived by a CFC:

(i)   foreign personal holding company income,

(ii) foreign base company sales income,

(iii) foreign base company services income,

(iv) foreign base company shipping income, and

(v)   foreign base company oil-related income.[21]

The taxable amount of foreign base company income equals the gross amount of such income, less any deductions (including foreign income taxes) properly allocable to such income.[22]

Foreign personal holding company income. Foreign personal holding company income primarily includes:

(i)   dividends, interest, royalties, rents, and annuities,

(ii) net gains from the disposition of property that produces dividend, interest, rent, and royalty income (except for net gains from certain dealer sales and inventory sales), and

(iii) net gains from commodity and foreign currency transactions (excluding net gains from active business and hedging transactions).[23]

However, foreign personal holding company income does not include (i) rents and royalties which are derived from the active conduct of a trade or business and which are received from unrelated persons,[24] (ii) export financing interest derived from the conduct of a banking business,[25] (iii) dividends and interest received from related parties incorporated in the same country as the CFC,[26] and (iv) rents and royalties received from related parties for the use of property in the CFC's country of incorporation.[27] The Taxpayer Relief Act of 1997 and the Tax and Trade Relief Extension Act of 1998 provided temporary exceptions from foreign personal holding company income for certain income that is derived from the active conduct of a banking, financing, insurance or similar business. These exceptions are applicable only for taxable years of a CFC beginning in 1998 or 1999.[28]

---

[21] Code Sec. 954(a).

[22] Code Sec. 954(b)(5). Any interest paid by a CFC to a U.S. shareholder must first be allocated to the CFC's foreign personal holding company income which is passive income for foreign tax credit limitation purposes.

[23] Code Sec. 954(c)(1). See Reg. § 1.954-2(g)(2) regarding the excludable commodity and foreign currency transactions.

[24] Code Sec. 954(c)(2)(A).

[25] Code Sec. 954(c)(2)(B).

[26] Code Sec. 954(c)(3)(A)(i).

[27] Code Sec. 954(c)(3)(A)(ii).

[28] Code Sec. 954(h).

Foreign base company sales income. Foreign base company sales income includes any gross profit, commissions, fees, or other income derived from the sale of personal property which meets the following requirements:

(i) the CFC buys the goods from or sells them to a related person,

(ii) the property is manufactured, produced, grown, or extracted outside the CFC's country of incorporation, and

(iii) the property is sold for use, consumption, or disposition outside the CFC's country of incorporation.[29]

Therefore, if a good is neither manufactured nor sold for use in the CFC's country of incorporation, then it is assumed that the CFC is not a bona fide foreign manufacturing or marketing subsidiary, but rather a base company organized to avoid tax.

> **Example 6.4:** USAco, a domestic corporation, manufactures consumer products for sale both in the United States and Norway. Norwegian sales are made through NORco, a wholly owned Norwegian marketing subsidiary. USAco also has a wholly owned Belgian subsidiary, BELco, which performs no real functions with respect to the manufacture or sale of USAco's products. The gross profit realized by NORco on the resale of goods to Norwegian customers is not foreign base company sales income because the goods are sold for use in NORco's country of incorporation. In contrast, if a sale to a Norwegian customer is routed through BELco, the gross profit realized by BELco is foreign base company sales income because the good was neither manufactured nor sold for use in Belgium.

A CFC is considered to have manufactured a good if it substantially transforms the good. Examples of substantial transformation include converting wood pulp to paper, steel rods to screws and bolts, and fresh fish to canned fish.[30] Manufacturing also occurs if component parts are purchased and combined, but only if the transformation is substantial in nature and generally considered to constitute manufacturing. Whether or not the substantial transformation test is met depends on the facts and circumstances of each case. However, under a safe-harbor rule, manufacturing is deemed to occur if the CFC's conversion costs (i.e., direct labor and overhead) account for 20% or more of the total cost of the goods sold. In no event, however, is packaging, repackaging, labeling, or minor assembly considered manufacturing.[31]

---

[29] Code Sec. 954(d)(1). Foreign base company sales income also includes any income derived from the sale of unprocessed timber which is softwood and which was cut from an area in the United States and any income derived from the milling of such timber outside the United States. Code Sec. 954(d)(4).

[30] Reg. § 1.954-3(a)(4)(ii).

[31] Reg. § 1.954-3(a)(4)(iii); *Bausch & Lomb, Inc. v. Comm'r,* 71 TCM 2031 (1996); and *Dave Fischbein Manufacturing Company v. Comm'r,* 59 TC 338 (1972).

Example 6.5: USAco, a domestic corporation, owns 100% of the stock of CANco, a Canadian corporation. CANco sells industrial engines for use outside of its country of incorporation. CANco performs some machining and assembly operations with respect to the engines it sells, but purchases the component parts for these engines from related and unrelated suppliers. On a per-engine basis, CANco's direct material costs are $30,000 and its conversion costs (direct labor and overhead) are $10,000. Although it is unclear whether CANco meets the substantial transformation test, it does meet the safe-harbor test since conversion costs are 25% of the total costs of goods sold [$10,000 ÷ ($10,000 + $30,000)]. As a result, CANco's gross profit from the sale of engines is not foreign base company sales income.[32]

Foreign base company services income. Foreign base company services income includes any compensation, commissions, fees, or other income derived from the performance of technical, managerial, engineering, architectural, scientific, skilled, industrial, commercial, and like services, where the CFC performs the services for or on behalf of a related person and the services are performed outside the CFC's country of incorporation.[33] This provision denies deferral to a foreign service subsidiary that is separated from its manufacturing and marketing affiliates and that is organized in another country.

Example 6.6: USAco, a domestic corporation, owns 100% of GERco, a German corporation. USAco is in the business of manufacturing drill presses for industrial use. During the year, USAco sells drill presses to both French and German customers. A condition of these sales is that USAco will install and provide maintenance services with respect to the drill presses. GERco performs these services on USAco's behalf in both France and Germany. The fees that GERco receives for services performed in Germany are not foreign base company services income. In contrast, the fees that GERco receives for services performed in France are foreign base company services income.

Foreign base company shipping income. Foreign base company shipping income includes income derived from the following activities:

(i)   the use or lease of aircraft or vessels in foreign commerce,

(ii) the performance of services directly related to the use of any such aircraft or vessel,

(iii) the sale or other disposition of any such aircraft or vessel, and

---

[32] Compare Reg. § 1.954-3(a)(4)(iii), Example (1).

[33] Code Sec. 954(e)(1). An exception applies to services which are directly related to the sale of property which was manufactured, produced, grown, or extracted by the CFC, and the services are performed before the time of the sale. Code Sec. 954(e)(2).

(iv) certain space or ocean activities, such as fishing and mining activities undertaken on the high seas, and any activity conducted in Antarctica.[34]

In addition, under a look-through rule, foreign base company shipping income also includes dividends and interest derived from a 10%-or-more-owned foreign corporation and any gains from the disposition of stock in such corporations, but only to the extent such dividends, interest, or gains are attributable to foreign base company shipping income.[35]

Foreign base company oil-related income. Foreign base company oil-related income includes foreign-source income derived from refining, processing, transporting, distributing, or selling oil and gas or primary products derived from oil and gas. However, it does not include oil-related income derived from sources within a foreign country in which such oil or gas is either extracted or used. Under a look-through rule, foreign base company oil-related income also includes dividends and interest derived from a 10%-or-more-owned foreign corporation to the extent such dividends or interest are attributable to foreign base company oil-related income.[36]

Special Exclusions and Inclusions

There are several exceptions to the general rules for computing Subpart F income. First, if any part of a CFC's Subpart F income is U.S.-source income that is effectively connected to the conduct of a U.S. trade or business, such income is excluded from Subpart F income. This exception does not apply, however, to any effectively connected income that is exempt from U.S. taxation (or that is subject to a reduced rate of tax) by reason of a tax treaty, nor does it apply to any U.S.-source nonbusiness income, even if that income was subject to U.S. withholding taxes.[37]

The second exception is a *de minimis* rule, under which no part of a CFC's income is treated as insurance or foreign base company income if the sum of the CFC's gross insurance and gross foreign base company income for the taxable year (before any deductions) is less than both $1 million and 5% of the CFC's total gross income for the year.[38]

---

[34] Code Sec. 954(f). There is no requirement that the income arise from transactions involving related parties.

[35] Code Sec. 954(f).

[36] Code Secs. 954(g)(1) and 907(c)(2) and (3). An exception applies to foreign corporations which are not "large oil producers," as defined in Code Sec. 954(g)(2).

[37] Code Sec. 952(b) and Reg. § 1.952-1(b)(2). There is no reason to tax effectively connected income to the U.S. shareholder since it has already been subjected to net-basis U.S. taxation at the regular graduated rates at the CFC level. Code Sec. 882(a).

[38] Code Sec. 954(b)(3)(A). This exception also does not apply to any U.S.-source portfolio interest derived by a CFC from an unrelated U.S. person. Code Sec. 881(c)(5)(A)(i).

Example 6.7: During the current year, ASIAco (a CFC) has gross income of $30 million, including $800,000 of interest income and $29.2 million of gross income from the sale of inventory that ASIAco manufactured at a factory located within its country of incorporation. Under the general rules, the $800,000 of interest income would be treated as foreign base company income. Under the *de minimis* rule, however, none of ASIAco's income is foreign base company income because $800,000 is less than both $1 million and 5% of ASIAco's gross income.

The third exception is a *de maximis* rule, under which all of a CFC's gross income is treated as Subpart F income if the sum of the CFC's gross insurance income and gross foreign base company income for the taxable year (before any deductions) exceeds 70% of the CFC's total gross income for the year.[39]

Example 6.8: During the current year, AFRIco (a CFC) has gross income of $20 million, including $16 million of interest income and $4 million of gross income from the sale of inventory that AFRIco manufactured at a factory located within its country of incorporation. Foreign base company income ordinarily would include only the $16 million of interest income. Under the full-inclusion rule, however, AFRIco's entire $20 million of gross income is Subpart F income since the $16 million of gross foreign base company income exceeds 70% of AFRIco's total gross income.

The final exception is an elective high-tax rule, under which a U.S. shareholder can elect to exclude from Subpart F income any insurance or foreign base company income that is subject to foreign income tax at an effective rate exceeding 90% of the maximum U.S. corporate rate.[40] The effective rate of foreign tax on an item of foreign income equals the amount of foreign income taxes paid or accrued with respect to that income divided by the net amount of that income, as determined under U.S. tax principles.[41] The high-tax exception reflects the reality that there is little or no residual U.S. tax for the U.S. Treasury to collect when the foreign tax rate exceeds 90% of the U.S. rate. At present, this exception is available whenever the effective foreign rate exceeds 31.5% (90% × 35%).

Example 6.9: USAco, a domestic corporation, owns 100% of the stock of EURco, a foreign corporation. EURco purchases goods manufactured by USAco at its U.S. factory and then resells them to foreign customers located outside EURco's country of incorporation. Under local tax law, EURco's taxable income from inventory sales is $10 million, on which EURco pays $3 million in foreign

---

[39] Code Sec. 954(b)(3)(B).

[40] Code Sec. 954(b)(4). The high-tax exception does not apply to foreign base company oil-related income.

[41] Reg. § 1.954-1(d)(2).

income taxes. Under U.S. tax principles, EURco's taxable income is only $8 million due to a difference in tax accounting rules. The $8 million of taxable income is foreign base company sales income because the goods were neither manufactured nor sold for use within EURco's country of incorporation. However, USAco can elect to exclude the $8 million of taxable income from Subpart F income because the effective rate of foreign income tax on that income of 37.5% [$3 million of foreign income taxes ÷ $8 million of net foreign base company sales income] exceeds 90% of the maximum U.S. corporate rate of 35%.

Earnings Invested in U.S. Property

A CFC's investment in U.S. property often is substantially equivalent to distributing a dividend to its U.S. shareholders. For example, a loan made by a CFC to a U.S. shareholder makes funds available for the shareholder's use in the same manner as a dividend distribution. The advantage of disguising a dividend as a loan used to be that, under the general rules, a loan did not trigger a shareholder-level tax on the CFC's earnings. Congress closed this loophole in 1962 by enacting a provision which automatically recharacterizes investments made by a CFC in U.S. property as constructive dividends. Under this provision, a U.S. shareholder must include in gross income the excess of the shareholder's pro rata share of the CFC's current-year investment in U.S. property over investments in U.S. property taxed to the shareholder in prior tax years, but only to the extent the CFC has undistributed earnings which have not yet been taxed to U.S. shareholders.[42]

The amount of a CFC's earnings invested in U.S. property is the quarterly average of the adjusted basis of U.S. property held (directly or indirectly) by the CFC, reduced by any liabilities to which the property is subject.[43] To determine the quarterly average, the taxpayer determines the amount of a CFC's investment in U.S. property at the end of each quarter, totals the quarterly amounts, and divides by four.

> **Example 6.10:** During the current year, FORco (a CFC) has no earnings invested in U.S. property at the end of either the first or the second quarter, $5 million invested in U.S. property at the end of the third quarter, and $11 million invested in U.S. property at the end of the fourth quarter. FORco's average quarterly investment in U.S. property for the year is $4 million [($0 + $0 + $5 million + $11 million) ÷ 4].

The definition of U.S. property for this purpose is an attempt to distinguish U.S. investments that are equivalent to a dividend distribu-

---

[42] Code Secs. 951(a)(1)(B) and 956(a).   [43] Code Sec. 956(a).

tion from U.S. investments that are part of the CFC's normal business operations. The principal types of U.S. property are as follows:

(i) *Debt obligations*—U.S. property includes an obligation of a U.S. person, such as a loan to a U.S. shareholder,[44] including any pledge or guarantee by a CFC of a U.S. person's obligation.[45] There are exceptions for obligations of unrelated domestic corporations,[46] obligations of the United States and deposits with a U.S. bank,[47] obligations that arise from regular business transactions to the extent such amounts are ordinary and necessary,[48] and certain deposits of cash or securities made or received by a securities or commodities dealer.[49]

(ii) *Certain receivables*—U.S. property includes trade or service receivables acquired, directly or indirectly, from a related U.S. person where the obligor is a U.S. person.[50]

(iii) *Stock*—U.S. property includes stock of a U.S. shareholder or other related domestic corporation but not stock of unrelated domestic corporations.[51]

(iv) *Tangible property*—U.S. property includes any tangible property located in the United States, such as a U.S. manufacturing facility.[52] There are exceptions for property that is purchased in the United States for export to or use in foreign countries,[53] as well as aircraft, railroad rolling stock, vessels, motor vehicles, and transport containers used predominantly outside the United States.[54]

(v) *Intangibles*—U.S. property includes any right to use in the United States a patent, copyright, invention, model, design, secret formula or process, or any similar property right.[55]

Example 6.11: CANco is a wholly owned Canadian subsidiary of USAco, a domestic corporation. During the year, USAco obtains a $2 million loan from a U.S. bank. At the bank's request, the loan agreement contains a provision whereby the loan is guaranteed by all of USAco's affiliates, including CANco. CANco's guarantee of USAco's loan from the U.S. bank may inadvertently trigger an investment in U.S. property.

In addition to the inclusions for Subpart F income and earnings invested in U.S. property, for tax years of CFCs beginning on or before December 31, 1996, a U.S. shareholder was also required to include in gross income the excess of the shareholder's pro-rata share of the CFC's

---

[44] Code Sec. 956(c)(1)(C).
[45] Code Sec. 956(d).
[46] Code Sec. 956(c)(2)(F).
[47] Code Sec. 956(c)(2)(A).
[48] Code Sec. 956(c)(2)(C).
[49] Code Sec. 956(c)(2)(J).

[50] Code Sec. 956(c)(3).
[51] Code Sec. 956(c)(1)(B) and (2)(F).
[52] Code Sec. 956(c)(1)(A).
[53] Code Sec. 956(c)(2)(B).
[54] Code Sec. 956(c)(2)(D).
[55] Code Sec. 956(c)(1)(D).

current year excess passive assets over excess passive assets taxed to the U.S. shareholder in prior years, but only to the extent the CFC had undistributed earnings which have not yet been taxed to its U.S. shareholders.[56] Excess passive assets equals the excess of a CFC's passive assets over 25% of the CFC's total assets. Passive assets are assets which produce passive income, as defined for purposes of the passive foreign investment company rules. The excess passive assets provisions were enacted in 1993 and apply only to earnings accumulated in taxable years beginning after September 30, 1993. The law was intended to eliminate the deferral privilege for active business profits that a CFC reinvested in passive foreign investments, rather than repatriating to its U.S. shareholders. However, the law also created an unintended incentive to reinvest profits in active foreign, as opposed to domestic, business operations. Therefore, in 1996 Congress repealed the excess passive assets provisions, effective for taxable years of CFCs beginning after December 31, 1996.

Deemed Paid Foreign Tax Credit

Consistent with the notion that a Subpart F inclusion represents a deemed dividend, a domestic corporation which directly owns 10% or more of a CFC's voting stock can claim a deemed paid credit for the CFC's foreign income taxes in the same year that the shareholder is taxed on the CFC's earnings.[57] The deemed paid credit that is allowed with respect to a Subpart F inclusion generally is identical to the deemed paid credit that is allowed with respect to actual dividend distributions.[58]

> **Example 6.12:** USAco, a domestic corporation, owns 100% of the stock of ASIAco, a foreign corporation. During its first year of existence, ASIAco had $20 million of Subpart F income, paid $2 million in foreign income taxes, and distributed no dividends. Because ASIAco is a CFC, USAco must include in gross income a deemed dividend equal to its share of ASIAco's net Subpart F income, which is $18 million [$20 million of Subpart F income − $2 million of foreign income taxes]. The deemed dividend of Subpart F income carries with it a deemed paid credit of $2 million [ASIAco's post-1986 foreign income taxes of $2 million × ($18 million Subpart F inclusion ÷ $18 million of post-1986 undistributed earnings)]. With the gross-up, USAco has a $20 million Subpart F inclusion and $2 million of deemed paid foreign tax credits.

---

[56] Code Sec. 951(a)(1)(C) and 956A, prior to their repeal by P.L. 104-188 (August 20, 1996).

[57] Code Sec. 960(a)(1). A U.S. shareholder who is an individual can elect to have a Subpart F inclusion taxed as if the taxpayer were a domestic corporation, in which case the individual can claim a deemed paid credit. Code Sec. 962.

[58] Reg. § § 1.960-1–1.960-7. An exception is the hopscotch rule, which is discussed later in this chapter.

For foreign tax credit limitation purposes, a Subpart F inclusion is allocated among the separate categories of income under one of two CFC look-through rules. A Subpart F inclusion for an increase in a CFC's earnings invested in U.S. property is prorated among the separate income categories based on the ratio of the CFC's post-1986 undistributed earnings within each separate income category to the CFC's total post-1986 undistributed earnings.[59]

> **Example 6.13:** USAco, a domestic corporation, owns 100% of the stock of MEXco, a Mexican corporation. As of the end of the current year, MEXco has $100 million of post-1986 undistributed earnings, including $90 million of earnings attributable to general limitation income and $10 million attributable to non-Subpart F financial services income. During the current year, MEXco made a $1 million loan to USAco, which resulted in an increase in MEXco's earnings invested in U.S. property of $1 million. Under the CFC look-through rule, $900,000 of this amount [$1 million × ($90 million ÷ $100 million)] is assigned to the general limitation category, and the other $100,000 [$1 million × ($10 million ÷ $100 million)] is assigned to the financial services income category.

A Subpart F inclusion for Subpart F income is allocated among the separate categories of income based on the nature of the CFC's current year taxable income which gave rise to the Subpart F inclusion.[60]

> **Example 6.14:** USAco, a domestic corporation, owns 100% of the stock of EURco, a foreign corporation. During the current year, EURco has $1 million of Subpart F income which is taxed to USAco, including $850,000 of foreign base company shipping income and $150,000 of foreign personal holding company income. Under the CFC look-through rule, $850,000 of this amount is assigned to the shipping income category and the other $150,000 is assigned to the passive income category.[61]

Mechanisms to Prevent Double Taxation

To avoid taxing the same earnings twice, the current taxation of a CFC's undistributed earnings to its U.S. shareholders must be coordinated with the taxation of actual dividend distributions made by the CFC, as well as the taxation of dispositions of the CFC's stock.

Distributions of previously taxed income. A U.S. shareholder can exclude from income distributions of a CFC's earnings that were previously taxed to the U.S. shareholder by reason of a Subpart F inclusion.[62] For this purpose, an actual distribution of earnings and

---

[59] Code Sec. 904(d)(3)(D) and Reg. § 1.904-5(c)(4)(i).
[60] Code Sec. 904(d)(3)(B) and Reg. § 1.904-5(c)(1)(i).

[61] Compare Reg. § 1.904-5(c)(1)(ii), Example (1).

[62] Code Sec. 959(a). In addition, a distribution of previously taxed income by a lower-tier CFC is not

profits is traced first to the CFC's previously taxed income, and the remaining portion of the actual distribution, if any, is then traced to the CFC's other earnings and profits.[63] A U.S. shareholder cannot claim a deemed paid credit with respect to a distribution of previously taxed income to the extent a credit was already taken for those taxes in the year of the Subpart F inclusion.[64] However, the U.S. shareholder can increase its foreign tax credit limitation by the lesser of (i) the amount of excess limitation, if any, created in the prior year by the Subpart F inclusion, or (ii) the amount of foreign withholding taxes imposed on the distribution of previously taxed income.[65] This adjustment is designed to prevent a U.S. shareholder from being unfairly denied a credit for any foreign withholding taxes imposed on an actual dividend distribution simply because, for U.S. tax purposes, the dividend income was recognized in a prior year.

> **Example 6.15:** USAco, a domestic corporation, owns 100% of the stock of AFRIco, a foreign corporation which was organized in year 1. During year 1, AFRIco had $10 million of foreign personal holding company income, paid $2 million in foreign income taxes, and distributed no dividends. In year 2, AFRIco had no earnings and profits, paid no foreign income taxes, and distributed an $8 million dividend. The dividend was subject to $800,000 of foreign withholding taxes. The U.S. tax consequences of AFRIco's activities are as follows.
>
> *Year 1.* Because AFRIco is a CFC, USAco must include in gross income a deemed dividend equal to its share of AFRIco's net Subpart F income, which is $8 million [$10 million of Subpart F income − $2 million of foreign income taxes]. The deemed dividend of Subpart F income carries with it a deemed paid credit of $2 million [AFRIco's post-1986 foreign income taxes of $2 million × ($8 million Subpart F inclusion ÷ $8 million of post-1986 undistributed earnings)]. With the gross-up, USAco has $10 million of foreign-source passive limitation income and a pre-credit U.S. tax of $3.5 million (assuming a 35% U.S. rate). Thus, the residual U.S. tax on AFRIco's Subpart F income is $1.5 million [$3.5 million pre-credit U.S. tax − $2 million credit].
>
> *Year 2.* USAco can exclude the $8 million dividend from U.S. taxation because it represents a distribution of previously taxed

---

(Footnote Continued)

included in the income of a higher-tier CFC. Code Sec. 959(b).

[63] Code Sec. 959(c). More specifically, actual dividend distributions are traced first to income previously taxed as earnings invested in U.S. property. The remaining portion of the actual distribution, if any, is traced next to income previously taxed as Subpart F income and then to any other earnings and profits.

Only that portion of a distribution traced to other earnings and profits constitutes a taxable dividend to the U.S. shareholder.

[64] Code Sec. 960(a)(2).

[65] Code Sec. 960(b)(1). A U.S. shareholder keeps track of these excess limitation amounts by establishing an excess limitation account in the year of the Subpart F inclusion. Code Sec. 960(b)(2).

Subpart F income. In addition, USAco cannot claim a deemed paid credit because it claimed a credit for AFRIco's income taxes in year 1. However, USAco can claim a direct credit for the $800,000 of foreign withholding taxes. USAco's foreign tax credit limitation equals the lesser of the excess limitation from year 1 of $1.5 million or the $800,000 of withholding taxes imposed on the distribution of previously taxed income, and therefore USAco can claim a credit for the full amount of withholding taxes.

Increase in basis of CFC's stock. A U.S. shareholder increases its basis in the stock of a CFC by the amount of a Subpart F inclusion.[66] This adjustment prevents double taxation of any proceeds from the sale or exchange of a CFC's stock that are attributable to earnings and profits that were already taxed to the U.S. shareholder as a Subpart F inclusion. For similar reasons, a U.S. shareholder reduces its basis in the stock of a CFC when it receives a distribution of previously taxed earnings.[67]

Example 6.16: In January of year 1, USAco (a domestic corporation) organizes FORco, a wholly owned foreign corporation, and contributes $10 million of cash to FORco in exchange for 100% of its stock. During year 1, FORco derives $2 million of Subpart F income (net of foreign income taxes and other allocable deductions), which is taxed to USAco in year 1 as a deemed dividend. In January of year 2, USAco completely liquidates FORco and receives a $12 million liquidating distribution. If no adjustments are made to USAco's basis in FORco's stock, USAco would realize a $2 million gain on the receipt of the liquidating distribution [$12 million amount realized − $10 million original basis]. In effect, FORco's year 1 Subpart F income of $2 million would be subject to U.S. taxation for a second time. However, USAco is allowed to increase its basis in FORco's stock by the $2 million of previously taxed Subpart F income, and therefore USAco recognizes no gain on the receipt of the liquidating distribution.

Use of Hopscotch Rule in Foreign Tax Credit Planning

Although Congress enacted Subpart F to prevent abuses of the deferral privilege, a U.S. shareholder can use aspects of Subpart F to its advantage in foreign tax credit planning. For example, if a U.S. shareholder repatriates the earnings of a second- or third-tier CFC up the chain through a series of actual dividend distributions, the lower-tier CFC's earnings will be blended with those of the higher-tier foreign corporations in the chain, which can alter the effective foreign tax rate on the repatriated earnings. In contrast, a Subpart F inclusion occurs

---

[66] Code Sec. 961(a). [67] Code Sec. 961(b).

as if the lower-tier CFC distributes its earnings directly to the U.S. shareholders, which avoids the diluting effect of distributing earnings up through a chain of foreign corporations.[68] Through the use of this "hopscotch" rule, a U.S. shareholder in an excess credit position can repatriate low-tax foreign earnings directly from a lower-tier CFC located in a low-tax foreign jurisdiction. Likewise, a U.S. shareholder in a short credit position can use the hopscotch rule to repatriate high-tax foreign earnings directly from a lower-tier CFC located in a high-tax foreign jurisdiction.[69]

> **Example 6.17:** USAco, a domestic corporation, owns 100% of the stock of F1, and F1 owns 100% of the stock of F2. F1 and F2 are both foreign corporations that derive only general limitation income. At the end of the current year, the undistributed earnings and foreign income taxes of F1 and F2 are as follows:

	F1	*F2*
Post-1986 undistributed earnings	$4 million	$8 million
Post-1986 foreign income taxes	$6 million	$2 million
Effective foreign tax rate	60%	20%

USAco has excess foreign tax credits in the general limitation category and would like to repatriate $4 million of F2's low-tax foreign earnings (which have an effective foreign rate of 20%) in order to soak up those excess credits.

Strategy 1—Dividend distribution up the chain of ownership: One strategy for repatriating F2's earnings is to have F2 distribute a dividend up through F1. A $4 million dividend from F2 would pull out $1 million of deemed paid taxes for F1 [$2 million of post-1986 foreign income taxes × ($4 million dividend ÷ $8 million of post-1986 undistributed earnings)]. After taking into account the $4 million dividend from F2, F1's post-1986 undistributed earnings are $8 million [$4 million + $4 million], and F1's post-1986 foreign income taxes are $7 million [$6 million + $1 million], assuming that neither F1's nor F2's home country taxed the dividend distribution. As a consequence, USAco's receipt of a $4 million dividend from F1 pulls out deemed paid taxes of $3.5 million [$7 million of post-1986 foreign income taxes × ($4 million dividend ÷ $8 million of post-1986 undistributed earnings)] and increases USAco's general limitation by $2,625,000 [35% U.S. rate × ($4 million dividend + $3.5 million gross-up)]. Thus, the net effect of a dividend distribution up the chain of ownership is an increase in USAco's excess credits of $875,000 [$3,500,000 increase in credits − $2,625,000 increase in limitation], as opposed to the desired reduction in excess credits.

---

[68] Reg. § 1.960-1(c)(4), Example (3).   [69] See discussion of cross-crediting in Chapter 4.

Strategy 2—Investment in U.S. property: An alternative strategy for repatriating F2's earnings is to have F2 make a $4 million loan to USAco that qualifies as an investment in U.S. property for purposes of Subpart F. As a result of the hopscotch rule, a $4 million deemed dividend from F2 increases USAco's deemed paid taxes by $1 million [$2 million of post-1986 foreign income taxes × ($4 million dividend ÷ $8 million of post-1986 undistributed earnings)] and increases USAco's general limitation by $1.75 million [U.S. rate of 35% × ($4 million deemed dividend + $1 million gross-up)]. The net effect is a residual U.S. tax of $750,000 [$1.75 million pre-credit tax − $1 million credit], which USAco can use to soak up $750,000 of excess credits.

Another potential advantage of repatriating a CFC's earnings through an investment in U.S. property is that it avoids any foreign withholding taxes that might be due on an actual dividend distribution to U.S. shareholders.

Currency Translation

CFCs usually conduct a significant part of their activities in an economic environment in which a foreign currency is used, and they usually keep their books and records in a foreign currency. This creates a currency translation problem for U.S. shareholders, who must translate a CFC's tax attributes into U.S. dollars. The currency translation rules for Subpart F inclusions are discussed in Chapter 8.

Earnings and Profits

The concept of earnings and profits plays a central role in the determination of the amount and character of a U.S. shareholder's Subpart F inclusions, as well as the related deemed paid foreign tax credits. Roughly speaking, a CFC's earnings and profits equal its taxable income, plus or minus various adjustments designed to make earnings and profits a better measure of the corporation's economic income. Examples of the required adjustments include adding back tax-exempt income, adding back the excess of accelerated depreciation over straight-line depreciation, and subtracting income taxes.[70] A CFC's earnings and profits are determined according to substantially the same U.S. tax accounting principles that apply to domestic corporations.[71] As a consequence, financial statements prepared under a CFC's local country accounting principles will have to be adjusted to make them consistent with U.S. accounting principles.[72]

---

[70] Code Sec. 312.
[71] Code Sec. 964(a).

[72] See Reg. § 1.964-1(a) for the applicable computation procedures.

Information Reporting for CFCs

In order to provide the IRS with the information necessary to ensure compliance with Subpart F, each year a U.S. person who owns more than 50% or more of the stock, by vote or value, of a foreign corporation must file a Form 5471, Information Return of U.S. Persons With Respect to Certain Foreign Corporations.[73] Other persons who must file a Form 5471 include (i) U.S. persons who acquire a 10% ownership interest, acquire an additional 10% ownership interest, or dispose of stock holdings to reduce their ownership in the foreign corporation to less than 10%[74] and (ii) U.S. citizens and residents who are officers or directors of a foreign corporation in which a U.S. person acquires a 10% ownership interest or an additional 10% interest.[75]

In Form 5471, the reporting agent must provide the following information regarding the CFC: [76]

(i)   stock ownership, including current year acquisitions and dispositions,

(ii)   U.S. shareholders,

(iii)   GAAP income statement and balance sheet,

(iv)   foreign income taxes,

(v)   current and accumulated earnings and profits, including any actual dividend distributions during the year,

(vi)   the U.S. shareholder's pro rata share of Subpart F income and any increase in earnings invested in U.S. property, and

(vii)   transactions between the CFC and shareholders or other related persons.

A Form 5471 ordinarily is filed by attaching it to the U.S. person's regular federal income tax return.[77] Any U.S. person who fails to furnish the required information may be subject to an annual penalty of $10,000, as well as a reduction in the taxpayer's foreign tax credit.[78] Form 5471 is reproduced in the appendix to this chapter.

¶ 602   FOREIGN PERSONAL HOLDING COMPANIES

Prior to 1937, wealthy U.S. citizens and residents could defer U.S. tax on investment income by transferring their investment assets to a wholly owned corporation incorporated in a tax haven country. Even if the foreign corporation invested its funds within the United States, significant U.S. tax savings could be realized since U.S. withholding tax rates have historically been lower than the regular graduated rates. Congress closed this loophole in 1937 by enacting the foreign personal

---

[73] Reg. § 1.6038-2(a) and (b).
[74] Reg. § 1.6046-1(c)(1).
[75] Reg. § 1.6046-1(a)(2)(i) and Code Sec. 6046(a).

[76] Reg. § 1.6038-2(f) and (g).
[77] Reg. § 1.6038-2(i).
[78] Reg. § 1.6038-2(k).

holding company regime,[79] which represented Congress's first major attack on deferral-based tax avoidance schemes. Under current law, however, the importance of the foreign personal holding company regime is diminished by Subpart F. This is because when Subpart F and the foreign personal holding company rules apply to the same item of income, the item is included in the U.S. shareholder's income under Subpart F.[80]

A foreign corporation is a foreign personal holding company if it satisfies the following requirements:

(i) at least 60% of the foreign corporation's gross income for the taxable year is foreign personal holding company income, and

(ii) at any time during the foreign corporation's taxable year, five or fewer U.S. citizens or resident aliens own (directly or indirectly) more than 50% of the stock, by vote or value, of the foreign corporation.[81]

Foreign personal holding company income includes primarily dividends, interest, royalties, annuities, rents, certain gains from transactions involving securities and commodities, income from trusts and estates, and income from certain personal services contracts.[82]

U.S. persons who own shares in a foreign personal holding company on the last day of the corporation's taxable year must include in their gross incomes a deemed dividend equal to their pro rata shares of the foreign corporation's undistributed foreign personal holding company income.[83] This requirement applies not only to the group of five or fewer U.S. citizens or residents responsible for establishing foreign personal holding company status, but also to all other U.S. persons who are shareholders of the foreign personal holding company.[84] Undistributed foreign personal holding company income equals the foreign corporation's taxable income, with certain adjustments, minus a dividends-paid deduction.[85] Thus, U.S. shareholders are taxed currently on both the passive investment income and any active business profits of the foreign personal holding company.

Each U.S. citizen or resident who is an officer, director, or 10% shareholder of a foreign personal holding company is responsible for the annual filing of at least one Form 5471, Information Return of U.S. Persons With Respect to Certain Foreign Corporations.[86] (Form 5471 is reproduced in the appendix to this chapter.)

---

[79] Code Secs. 551–558.

[80] Code Sec. 951(d).

[81] Code Secs. 552(a) and 554(a).

[82] Code Sec. 553(a).

[83] Code Sec. 551(a) and (b).

[84] Reg. § 1.551-2(a).

[85] Code Sec. 556(a).

[86] Reg. § 1.6035-1(a).

¶ 603 FOREIGN INVESTMENT AND PASSIVE FOREIGN INVESTMENT COMPANIES

Background

U.S. investors in domestic mutual funds are taxed currently on the fund's investment income because a domestic fund must distribute at least 90% of its income each year in order to avoid U.S. taxation at the corporate level.[87] In contrast, investors in foreign mutual funds have historically been able to avoid current U.S. taxation. The fund itself avoided U.S. tax because it was a foreign corporation that derived only foreign-source income. The U.S. investors avoided U.S. tax because the fund paid no dividends. These funds are able to avoid the foreign personal holding company and CFC taints because the ownership of the fund was dispersed among a large number of U.S. and foreign investors, each owning a relatively small percentage of the fund. Another significant tax benefit of these funds was that when U.S. investors eventually did realize the fund's earnings through the sale of the fund's stock, they were able to effectively convert the fund's ordinary income (dividends and interest) into capital gains.

Foreign Investment Companies

In 1962, Congress closed the capital gain aspect of this loophole by enacting the foreign investment company regime.[88] Under this regime, a U.S. person's gain on the sale or exchange of stock in a foreign investment company is recharacterized as ordinary income to the extent of the taxpayer's ratable share of the foreign corporation's post-1962 earnings and profits that were accumulated while the taxpayer owned the stock.[89] A foreign investment company is any foreign corporation that is either:

(i) registered under the Investment Company Act of 1940 as either a management company or a unit investment trust (irrespective of the degree of U.S. ownership), or

(ii) engaged primarily in the business of investing or trading in securities or commodities, but only if 50% or more of the foreign corporation's stock (by vote or value) is owned directly or indirectly by U.S. persons.[90]

The enactment in 1986 of the passive foreign investment company rules substantially diminished the importance of the foreign investment company provisions. This is because foreign investment companies

---

[87] Code Secs. 851 and 852.

[88] Code Secs. 1246 and 1247.

[89] Code Sec. 1246(a).

[90] Code Sec. 1246(b).

ordinarily also qualify as passive foreign investment companies, and the passive foreign investment company rules take precedence.[91]

Passive Foreign Investment Companies

The enactment in 1986 of the passive foreign investment company (or "PFIC") regime significantly expanded the reach of U.S. taxing authorities with respect to passive investment income earned by U.S. persons through foreign corporations.[92] Congress enacted the PFIC provisions to deal with perceived abuses by U.S. investors in foreign mutual funds. However, the PFIC rules apply to any foreign corporation which meets either the PFIC income test or assets test, regardless of whether U.S. shareholders individually or in the aggregate have a significant ownership stake in the company. The lack of a U.S. control requirement represents a major policy shift from earlier anti-deferral provisions (i.e., Subpart F, foreign personal holding companies, and foreign investment companies), which generally apply only to foreign corporations with controlling U.S. shareholders.

Definition of a PFIC. A foreign corporation is a PFIC if it meets either an income test or an asset test.[93] Under the income test, a foreign corporation is a PFIC if 75% or more of the corporation's gross income for the taxable year is passive income.[94] Passive income is foreign personal holding company income (as defined for purposes of Subpart F),[95] with certain adjustments. The adjustments include exclusions for income derived from the active conduct of a banking, insurance, or securities business, as well as any interest, dividends, rents, and royalties received from a related person to the extent such income is properly allocable to nonpassive income of the related person.[96] In addition, to prevent foreign holding companies of operating subsidiaries from being treated as PFICs, a foreign corporation that owns directly or indirectly at least 25% (by value) of the stock of another corporation is treated as if it earned a proportionate share of that corporation's income.[97]

Under the assets test, a foreign corporation is a PFIC if the average market value of the corporation's passive assets during the taxable year is 50% or more of the corporation's total assets. However, a foreign corporation that is a CFC, as well as any other foreign corporation that so elects, bases the assets test on the adjusted basis of its assets, rather than their market values.[98] Passive assets are assets

---

[91] Code Sec. 1298(b)(7).

[92] Code Secs. 1291–1298.

[93] Code Sec. 1297(a). Exceptions to the income test and asset test apply to a foreign corporation's first taxable year and to a year in which a foreign corporation experiences a change in business. Code Sec. 1298(b)(2) and (3).

[94] Code Sec. 1297(a)(1).

[95] Code Sec. 1297(b)(1) by reference to Code Sec. 954(c).

[96] Code Sec. 1297(b)(2).

[97] Code Sec. 1297(c)(2).

[98] Code Sec. 1297(a).

which produce passive income (as defined for purposes of the PFIC income test), with certain adjustments. For example, a CFC can increase its total assets by the amount of research or experimental expenditures incurred by the CFC during the current and preceding two taxable years, and by an amount equal to 300% of the payments made by the CFC for certain licensed intangibles used by the CFC in the active conduct of a trade or business.[99] In addition, a foreign corporation is treated as the owner of any tangible personal property with respect to which it is a lessee under a lease with a term of 12 or more months.[100] Finally, as with the income test, a foreign corporation that owns directly or indirectly at least 25% (by value) of the stock of another corporation is treated as if it owned directly a proportionate share of that corporation's assets.[101]

For tax years of U.S. persons beginning on or after January 1, 1998, the assets of all PFICs that are publicly traded are measured using a special fair market value computation. Thus, a publicly traded foreign corporation is a PFIC if the fair market value of its passive income-producing assets equals or exceeds 50% of the sum of the market value of its outstanding stock plus its liabilities.[102]

Taxation of a PFIC. A PFIC's undistributed earnings are subject to U.S. taxation under one of two methods, each of which is designed to eliminate the benefits of deferral. Under the qualified electing fund (or "QEF") method, shareholders who can obtain the necessary information can elect to be taxed currently on their pro rata share of the PFIC's earnings and profits. The income inclusion is treated as ordinary income to the extent of the taxpayer's pro rata share of the QEF's ordinary income, and capital gains to the extent of the taxpayer's pro rata share of the QEF's net capital gain.[103] A taxpayer's pro rata share is the amount that the taxpayer would have received if, on each day of the QEF's taxable year, it had actually distributed to each of its shareholders a pro rata share of that day's ratable share of the QEF's ordinary earnings and net capital gains for the year.[104] To prevent double taxation of the QEF's earnings, any actual distributions made by a QEF out of its previously taxed earnings and profits are tax-free to the U.S. investor.[105] In addition, a U.S. investor increases its basis in

---

[99] Code Sec. 1298(e). This provision does not apply if the licenser is a related foreign person.

[100] Code Sec. 1298(d). This provision does not apply if the lessor is a related person.

[101] Code Sec. 1297(c)(1).

[102] Code Sec. 1297(e)[sic (f)].

[103] Code Secs. 1293(a) and 1295(a). When the QEF method and Subpart F apply to the same income, the item is included in the U.S. shareholder's gross income under Subpart F. Code Sec. 951(f). Likewise, when the QEF method and foreign personal holding company regimes apply to the same income, the item is included in the taxpayer's gross income under the foreign personal holding company rules. Code Sec. 551(g).

[104] Code Sec. 1293(b).

[105] Code Sec. 1293(c).

¶ 603

the QEF's stock for any income inclusions and reduces its basis in the stock when it receives a distribution of previously taxed income.[106]

A U.S. investor who does not make a QEF election is taxed under a special excess distributions regime. Under this regime, the taxpayer is allowed to defer taxation of the PFIC's undistributed income until the PFIC makes an excess distribution. An excess distribution includes the following:

(i)   a gain realized on the sale of PFIC stock,[107] and

(ii) any actual distribution made by the PFIC, but only to the extent the total actual distributions received by the taxpayer for the year exceeds 125% of the average actual distribution received by the taxpayer in the preceding three taxable years (or, if shorter, the taxpayer's holding period before the current taxable year).[108]

The amount of an excess distribution is treated as if it had been realized pro rata over the holding period for the PFIC's stock, and, therefore, the tax due on an excess distribution is the sum of the deferred yearly tax amounts (computed using the highest tax rate in effect in the years the income was accumulated), plus interest.[109] Thus, the excess distribution method eliminates the benefits of deferral by assessing an interest charge on the deferred yearly tax amounts. Any actual distributions that fall below the 125% threshold are treated as dividends (assuming they represent a distribution of earnings and profits), which are taxable in the year of receipt and are not subject to the special interest charge.[110] Taxpayers can claim a direct foreign tax credit with respect to any withholding taxes imposed on a distribution by a PFIC, and a domestic corporation owning 10% or more of the PFIC's voting stock also can claim a deemed paid credit.[111]

PFICs that are also CFCs. A corporation that otherwise would be a PFIC will not be treated as such with respect to certain shareholders if the corporation is also a CFC. As a result, shareholders who are taxed currently on their pro rata shares of Subpart F income of a CFC are not subject to a PFIC income inclusion with respect to the same stock. This rule change was prompted by the undue complexity created by the overlap of the PFIC and CFC rules under prior law. However, in the case of a PFIC that has not made a QEF election, stock held by a 10% U.S. shareholder in a CFC will continue to be treated as PFIC

---

[106] Code Sec. 1293(d). Domestic corporations owning 10% or more of the QEF's voting stock can claim a deemed paid foreign tax credit with respect to a QEF income inclusion. Code Sec. 1293(f)(1).

[107] Code Sec. 1291(a)(2).

[108] Code Sec. 1291(b)(1) and (2)(A). Any amounts currently or previously included in the U.S. investor's gross income by reason of Subpart F or the foreign personal holding company regime are not treated as excess distributions. Prop. Reg. § 1.1291-2(b)(2). In addition, it is not possible to have an excess distribution in the year that the taxpayer first acquires shares in the PFIC. Code Sec. 1291(b)(2)(B).

[109] Code Sec. 1291(a)(1) and (c).

[110] Prop. Reg. § 1.1291-2(e)(1).

[111] Code Sec. 1291(g) and Prop. Reg. § 1.1291-5.

stock unless the shareholder elects to pay tax and an interest charge with respect to the stock's unrealized appreciation or the corporation's accumulated earnings.[112]

Mark-to-market election for marketable PFIC stock. A U.S. shareholder of a PFIC may make a mark-to-market election with respect to the stock of the PFIC if such stock is marketable. Under this election, any excess of the fair market value of the PFIC stock at the close of the tax year over the shareholder's adjusted basis in the stock is included in the shareholder's income. The shareholder may deduct any excess of the adjusted basis of the PFIC stock over its fair market value at the close of the tax year. However, deductions are limited to the net mark-to-market gains on the stock that the shareholder included in income in prior years, or so-called "unreversed inclusions." Any income or loss recognized under the mark-to-market election is treated as ordinary in nature. In addition, a shareholder's adjusted basis of PFIC stock is increased by the income recognized under the mark-to-market election and decreased by the deductions allowed under the election.[113] The mark-to-market election was enacted to extend the current income inclusion method to PFIC shareholders who could not obtain the information from the PFIC necessary to making a QEF election, and therefore were forced to use the complex and burdensome interest-charge method.

Information reporting for PFIC U.S. shareholders. A U.S. person must file annually, with its federal income tax return for the year, a separate Form 8621, Return by a Shareholder of a Passive Foreign Investment Company or Qualified Electing Fund, for each PFIC for which the taxpayer was a shareholder during the taxable year. (Form 8621 is reproduced in the appendix to this chapter.)

¶ 604   GAIN FROM THE SALE OR EXCHANGE OF A CFC'S STOCK

A gain on the sale or exchange of stock normally is capital in nature.[114] However, an exception applies if, at any time during the five-year period ending on the date of the sale or exchange, the taxpayer was a U.S. shareholder of the foreign corporation at which time the foreign corporation was a CFC. In such cases, the U.S. person must treat the gain on the sale or exchange of the foreign corporation's stock as a dividend to the extent of the shareholder's pro rata share of the corporation's post-1962 earnings and profits that were accumulated while the shareholder owned the stock and the corporation was a CFC.[115] Any gain in excess of the deemed dividend is still accorded

---

[112] Code Sec. 1297(e).
[113] Code Sec. 1296.
[114] Code Sec. 1221.

[115] Code Sec. 1248(a). In the case of U.S. shareholders who are individuals, the tax attributable to the deemed dividend inclusion cannot exceed the tax that

capital gain treatment. For purposes of this provision, earnings and profits does not include certain amounts already subjected to U.S. tax, including prior-year Subpart F inclusions, income effectively connected with the conduct of a U.S. trade or business, and an inclusion from a PFIC that has made a QEF election.[116]

Congress enacted this provision in 1962 to ensure that the U.S. Treasury collects the "full U.S. tax" when a U.S. shareholder repatriates a CFC's foreign earnings. Before 1963, a U.S. shareholder that operated abroad through a CFC could defer U.S. taxes on the CFC's earnings, and then repatriate those earnings through the sale of the CFC's stock (rather than a dividend distribution), in which case the CFC's earnings were subject to U.S. tax at a lower capital gains rate. The requirement that U.S. shareholders treat part or all of the gain on the sale of a CFC's stock as a dividend ensures that the United States is allowed to tax the CFC's accumulated earnings at ordinary income rates.

At present, there is a capital gains rate differential for noncorporate taxpayers, but not for corporate taxpayers. Nevertheless, the recharacterization of a gain as a dividend remains an important feature of the law for domestic corporations that own 10% or more of the voting stock of the foreign corporation because a deemed dividend carries with it deemed paid foreign tax credits.[117] Thus, this anti-abuse provision can work to a domestic corporation's advantage by allowing it to claim deemed paid foreign tax credits which can be used to offset the tax on the disposition of a CFC's stock.

> **Example 6.18:** ASIAco is a wholly owned manufacturing subsidiary of USAco, a domestic corporation. USAco has been ASIAco's sole shareholder since ASIAco was organized several years ago. At the end of the current year, USAco sells all of ASIAco's stock to an unrelated foreign buyer for $15 million. At that time, ASIAco had $3 million of post-1986 undistributed earnings and $1 million of post-1986 foreign income taxes. USAco's basis in ASIAco's stock was $10 million immediately prior to the sale. Assume USAco's capital gain on the sale of ASIAco's stock is not subject to foreign taxation and that the U.S. corporate tax rate is 35%.
>
> USAco realizes a gain on the sale of ASIAco's stock of $5 million [$15 million amount realized − $10 million basis in ASIAco's stock]. The deemed dividend portion of the gain equals ASIAco's undistributed earnings of $3 million, and the remaining $2 million is treated as a capital gain. The $3 million dividend carries with it

---

(Footnote Continued)

would have been due if the foreign corporation had been a domestic corporation. Code Sec. 1248(b).

[116] Code Sec. 1248(d).
[117] Reg. § 1.1248-1(d).

$1 million of deemed paid foreign taxes. Thus, with the gross-up, ASIAco has $4 million of foreign-source dividend income. Assume the $2 million capital gain also is foreign-source income.[118] Therefore, the pre-credit U.S. tax on the stock sale is $2.1 million [35% U.S. tax rate × ($4 million dividend + $2 million capital gain)], the credit is $1 million, and USAco has a residual U.S. tax of $1.1 million. In contrast, if the entire $5 million gain had been treated as a capital gain, the residual U.S. tax would have been $1.75 million [35% U.S. tax rate × $5 million capital gain].

¶ 605   OUTBOUND TRANSFERS TO FOREIGN CORPORATIONS

Outbound Toll Charge

In response to changing business conditions, U.S. companies routinely organize new subsidiaries and divide, merge, and liquidate existing subsidiaries. These routine corporate adjustments generally are tax-free transactions, based on the principle that the transactions involve a change in the form of the parent corporation's investment, not the parent corporation's ultimate control of the investment. For example, in a wholly domestic context, if a domestic corporation transfers appreciated property to a newly organized subsidiary in exchange for all of the stock of that subsidiary, the gain realized on that exchange is not recognized immediately, but is instead postponed by having the transferee take a carryover basis in the property received.[119] However, if the transferee is a foreign corporation, then the ultimate disposition of the appreciated property may occur outside U.S. taxing jurisdiction. As a consequence, transfers of appreciated property to a foreign corporation may represent the U.S. Treasury's last opportunity for taxing the appreciation.

> **Example 6.19:** During the current year, USAco (a domestic corporation) organizes EURco, a marketing subsidiary incorporated in a foreign country. USAco then transfers inventory, which has a basis of $1 million and a market value of $3 million, to EURco in exchange for all of EURco's stock. Immediately thereafter, EURco sells the inventory to local customers for $3 million. Ignoring Code Sec. 367, USAco's outbound transfer to EURco is not subject to U.S. tax because it is part of a tax-free incorporation transaction. EURco's gain on the sale of the inventory also is not subject to U.S. taxation since the United States does not tax the foreign-source income of foreign corporations. In sum, the $2 million gain is not subject to U.S. tax at either the foreign corporation or U.S. shareholder level.

---

[118] Code Sec. 865(f).   [119] Code Secs. 351(a) and 362.

In 1932, Congress closed this loophole by enacting Code Sec. 367, which requires a U.S. person transferring appreciated property to a foreign corporation to recognize a gain on the transfer. This result is achieved by denying the foreign corporation its corporate status,[120] in which case the general rules for taxable exchanges apply.[121]

> **Example 6.20:** The facts are the same as in Example 6.19, except now take into account the effects of Code Sec. 367(a). USAco's transfer of inventory to EURco in exchange for all of EURco's stock is treated as a taxable exchange. As a result, USAco recognizes a $2 million gain, which represents the excess of the value of stock received ($3 million) over USAco's basis in the inventory given ($1 million).

The outbound toll charge applies only for purposes of recognizing gains, and, thus, transfers of property that produce losses are still accorded nonrecognition treatment, assuming the transaction satisfies the requirements of the applicable corporate nonrecognition provision.[122] The character and source of the gain produced by the outbound toll charge is determined as if the transferor had sold the property to the transferee in a taxable transaction.[123] For example, if the outbound transfer involves inventory which the taxpayer purchased for resale, any resulting gain would be sourced under the title passage rule applicable to inventory sales in general.[124] In a similar vein, the U.S. transferor must recapture and recognize as ordinary income any depreciation deductions claimed on depreciable property that was used in the United States.[125] Finally, the U.S. transferor's basis in any stock received in an outbound transfer equals the transferor's basis in the property transferred, increased by the amount of the gain recognized on the transfer.[126]

The types of corporate transactions governed by the outbound toll charge provisions include:

(i) *Incorporations*—A U.S. person's contribution of property to a foreign corporation in exchange for stock of the foreign corporation, where, immediately after the exchange, the U.S. person controls the foreign corporation.[127]

---

[120] Code Sec. 367(a)(1).

[121] Code Sec. 1001.

[122] Temp. Reg. § 1.367(a)-1T(b)(3)(ii).

[123] Temp. Reg. § 1.367(a)-1T(b)(4)(i)(A).

[124] Reg. § 1.861-7(c).

[125] Temp. Reg. § 1.367(a)-4T(b). The U.S. portion of depreciable property used both within and without the United States is determined based on the ratio of the number of months the property was used in the United States to the total number of months the property was used.

[126] Temp. Reg. § 1.367(a)-1T(a)(4)(i)(B) and (ii), Example.

[127] Code Sec. 367(a)(1), which denies the nonrecognition treatment otherwise provided by Code Sec. 351. Code Sec. 367(c)(2) extends this treatment to contributions to capital.

(ii) *Reorganizations*—A U.S. person's transfer of stock, securities, or property to a foreign corporation as part of a corporate reorganization.[128]

(iii) *Liquidations*—A domestic subsidiary corporation's distribution of assets in complete liquidation to its foreign parent corporation.[129]

However, there are several major exceptions to the basic outbound toll charge, including:

(i) *Active foreign business use exception*—The outbound toll charge does not apply to certain types of property transferred to a foreign corporation for use by that corporation in the active conduct of a trade or business located outside the United States.[130]

(ii) *Branch loss recapture rule*—A U.S. person must recognize a gain on the incorporation of a foreign branch to the extent that person has previously deducted branch losses against its other taxable income.[131]

(iii) *Deemed royalty regime for intangible property*—An outbound transfer of intangible property is treated as a sale in return for a series of payments which are received annually over the useful life of the intangible and which are contingent upon the productivity, use, or disposition of the intangible.[132]

(iv) *Transfers of stocks and securities*—Outbound transfers of stocks and securities are subject to special rules.[133]

These exceptions are discussed in the following sections.

Active Foreign Business Use Exception

The outbound toll charge does not apply to property transferred to a foreign corporation if the following requirements are satisfied:

(i) the foreign corporation actively conducts a trade or business;

(ii) the trade or business is conducted outside the United States; and

(iii) the foreign corporation uses the property in that trade or business.[134]

---

[128] Code Sec. 367(a)(1) and (e)(1), which deny the nonrecognition treatment otherwise provided by Code Secs. 354, 355, 356, and 361.

[129] Code Sec. 367(e)(2), which denies the nonrecognition treatment otherwise provided by Code Secs. 332 and 337.

[130] Code Sec. 367(a)(3)(A).

[131] Code Sec. 367(a)(3)(C).

[132] Code Sec. 367(d).

[133] Code Sec. 367(a)(2) and Reg. § 1.367(a)-3.

[134] Code Sec. 367(a)(3)(A). To qualify for this exception, the transferor also must attach Form 926, Return by Transferor of Property to a Foreign Corporation, Foreign Estate or Trust, or Foreign Partnership, to its regular tax return for the year of the transfer. Temp. Reg. § 1.367(a)-2T(a)(2) and Reg. § 1.6038B-1.

In these situations, the policy of allowing companies to make routine corporate adjustments unaffected by taxes is considered more important than the policy of taxing all appreciated property being transferred out of U.S. taxing jurisdiction. The depreciation recapture rule discussed above still applies, however, and therefore the U.S. transferor still must recapture and recognize as ordinary income any depreciation deductions claimed on depreciable property that was used in the United States.[135]

Whether a particular transfer satisfies the requirements of the active foreign business use exception is a question of fact.[136] In general, the active conduct of a trade or business requirement is satisfied only if the officers and employees of the transferee, or the officers and employees of related entities if supervised and paid by the transferee, carry out substantial managerial and operational activities.[137] To satisfy the requirement that the business be conducted outside the United States, the primary managerial and operational activities of the trade or business must be conducted abroad, and immediately after the transfer, substantially all of the transferred assets must be located abroad.[138]

Special rules apply to property that the foreign transferee will lease,[139] property that is expected to be sold in the reasonably foreseeable future other than in the ordinary course of business,[140] working interests in oil and gas property,[141] and compulsory transfers.[142] In addition, certain assets are ineligible for the active foreign business use exception, based on the presumption that a primary motive behind their transfer is the avoidance of U.S. taxes. These tainted assets include the following:

(i) inventories, including raw materials and supplies, work-in-process, and finished goods,[143]

(ii) installment obligations, accounts receivable, and similar property,[144]

(iii) foreign currency or other property denominated in foreign currency, such as an installment obligation, forward contract, or account receivable,[145]

(iv) intangible property,[146] and

---

[135] Temp. Reg. § 1.367(a)-4T(b).

[136] Temp. Reg. § 1.367(a)-2T(b)(1).

[137] Temp. Reg. § 1.367(a)-2T(b)(3).

[138] Temp. Reg. § 1.367(a)-2T(b)(4).

[139] Temp. Reg. § 1.367(a)-4T(c).

[140] Temp. Reg. § 1.367(a)-4T(d).

[141] Temp. Reg. § 1.367(a)-4T(e).

[142] Temp. Reg. § 1.367(a)-4T(f).

[143] Code Sec. 367(a)(3)(B)(i) and Temp. Reg. § 1.367(a)-5T(b).

[144] Code Sec. 367(a)(3)(B)(ii).

[145] Code Sec. 367(a)(3)(B)(iii) and Temp. Reg. § 1.367(a)-5T(d). An exception applies to an obligation that is denominated in the currency of the transferee's country of incorporation and that was acquired in the ordinary course of the business of the transferor that will be carried on by the transferee.

[146] Code Sec. 367(a)(3)(B)(iv).

(v) property which the transferor is leasing at the time of the transfer, with certain exceptions.[147]

For these purposes, intangible property includes any patent, invention, formula, process, design, pattern, know-how, copyright, literary, musical, or artistic composition, trademark, trade name, brand name, franchise, license, contract, method, program, system, procedure, campaign, survey, study, forecast, estimate, customer list, technical data, or other similar item.[148] Foreign goodwill and going concern value are specifically excluded, however, and therefore can qualify for the active business use exception.[149]

> **Example 6.21:** During the current year, USAco (a domestic corporation) organizes MEXco, a manufacturing subsidiary incorporated in Mexico. USAco then transfers inventory and some machinery and equipment to MEXco in exchange for all of MEXco's stock. At the time of the transfer, the adjusted basis and the market value of the transferred property was as follows:
>
> | | Adjusted basis | Market value |
> |---|---|---|
> | Inventory | $ 5 million | $ 7 million |
> | Machinery and equipment | $10 million | $15 million |
>
> The machinery and equipment were purchased two years ago for $14 million, and USAco took $4 million of depreciation deductions on the machinery prior to the transfer. The machinery was used solely in USAco's U.S. factory.
>
> Assuming MEXco's foreign manufacturing operation satisfies the active foreign business requirements, the outbound transfer does not trigger U.S. taxation of the $1 million of appreciation in the value of the machinery and equipment [$15 million market value − $14 million original cost]. However, because USAco previously used the machinery and equipment in its U.S. factory, USAco must recognize $4 million of depreciation recapture income. The inventory is a tainted asset, and therefore USAco must recognize $2 million of gross income [$7 million market value − $5 million basis] on its transfer. In sum, USAco must recognize $6 million of income on the incorporation of MEXco.

Branch Loss Recapture Rule

A major exception to the active foreign business use exception is the branch loss recapture rule. Under this provision, a U.S. person must recognize a gain on the incorporation of a foreign branch to the extent it has previously deducted branch losses against its other taxable

---

[147] Code Sec. 367(a)(3)(B)(v) and Temp. Reg. §§ 1.367(a)-5T(f) and 1.367(a)-4T(c).

[148] Code Sec. 936(h)(3)(B).

[149] Temp. Reg. §§ 1.367(a)-5T(e) and 1.367(d)-1T(b).

income. The recapture income is treated as foreign-source income that has the same character as the related branch losses.[150]

Example 6.22: Two years ago, USAco (a domestic corporation) established a foreign branch. During its first two years of operations, the branch produced $5 million of losses, which USAco deducted against its other taxable income. If USAco were to incorporate the branch, it would have to recognize $5 million of branch loss recapture income.

It is not necessary to recapture pre-incorporation losses to the extent those losses are either offset by items of branch income or did not provide the taxpayer with a U.S. tax benefit. Thus, the pre-incorporation losses are reduced by the following amounts:

(i)   any taxable income of the branch recognized prior to incorporation,[151]

(ii) the amount of any U.S.-source income that the taxpayer had to recognize in the current or a prior taxable year by reason of the overall foreign loss recapture provisions of the foreign tax credit limitation,[152]

(iii) any gain recognized on the transfer of the branch's appreciated property to the newly organized foreign corporation,[153]

(iv) any branch losses that were part of an expired net operating loss or capital loss carryforward,[154] and

(v)   the taxable income equivalent amount of any foreign tax credit carryforwards that expired by reason of the foreign tax credit limitation.[155]

After taking into account these reductions, the remaining branch loss recapture income is further limited to the amount of gain that the taxpayer would have recognized on a taxable sale of the transferred property if each item was sold separately and without offsetting individual losses against individual gains.[156]

Deemed Royalty Regime for Intangible Property

The market value of patents, trademarks, and other intangibles often is highly uncertain, due to the inherent uniqueness of these assets. This uncertainty significantly weakens the deterrent effect of a one-

---

[150] Code Sec. 367(a)(3)(C).

[151] Temp. Reg. § 1.367(a)-6T(e)(2).

[152] Temp. Reg. § 1.367(a)-6T(e)(3) and (e)(5). See Code Sec. 904(f)(3) regarding the computation of the foreign loss recapture amount. See also the discussion of overall foreign losses in Chapter 3.

[153] Temp. Reg. § 1.367(a)-6T(e)(4). Special rules apply for purposes of computing the creditable gain with respect to intangible property. Temp. Reg. § 1.367(d)-1T(g)(3).

[154] Temp. Reg. § 1.367(a)-6T(d)(2) and (d)(3).

[155] Temp. Reg. § 1.367(a)-6T(d)(4).

[156] Temp. Reg. §§ 1.367(a)-6T(c)(2) and 1.367(a)-1T(b)(3)(i). Any gain realized on the transfer of foreign goodwill and going concern value is taken into account for purposes of computing this limitation. Temp. Reg. § 1.367(a)-6T(c)(3).

time toll charge imposed at the time of the transfer, since new technologies and products can turn out to be far more successful than originally anticipated. As a consequence, in 1984, Congress enacted a special deemed royalty regime for intangibles, under which an outbound transfer of an intangible is treated as a sale in return for a series of royalty payments which are received annually over the useful life of the intangible and which are contingent upon the productivity, use, or disposition of the intangible.[157] The royalty income is treated as foreign-source to the extent that an actual payment made by the foreign corporation under a license or sale agreement with the transferor would be treated as foreign-source income.[158]

Example 6.23: USAco (a domestic corporation) organizes ASIAco, a manufacturing subsidiary incorporated in a foreign country. USAco then transfers a patent to ASIAco in exchange for all of ASIAco's stock. USAco had a zero basis in the patent because it had deducted the related research and development expenditures as incurred.[159] Ignoring Code Sec. 367, USAco's outbound transfer to ASIAco is not subject to U.S. tax because it is part of a tax-free incorporation transaction.[160] However, Code Sec. 367(d) recharacterizes the transaction as a sale in return for royalty payments received annually over the life of the patent.

Based on the assumption that the value of the intangible is attributable to research and development activities undertaken in the United States, for transfers made and royalties deemed received on or before August 5, 1997, the deemed royalties were treated as income derived from U.S. sources.[161]

The deemed royalty regime applies to a U.S. person's contribution of intangible property to a foreign corporation in exchange for stock of the foreign corporation, where immediately after the exchange the U.S. person controls the foreign corporation.[162] The deemed royalty regime also applies to a U.S. person's transfer of intangible property to a foreign corporation as part of a corporate reorganization.[163] However, it does not apply to a domestic subsidiary corporation's distribution of intangible property in complete liquidation to its foreign parent corporation.[164] In addition, a limited exception to the deemed royalty regime is available for transfers of operating intangibles (e.g., long-term purchase or supply contracts, surveys, studies, and customer lists),

---

[157] Code Sec. 367(d).

[158] Code Sec. 367(d)(2)(C).

[159] Code Sec. 174.

[160] Code Sec. 351(a).

[161] Code Sec. 367(d)(2)(C), prior to amendment by the Taxpayer Relief Act of 1997 (August 5, 1997).

[162] Code Sec. 367(d)(1), which denies the nonrecognition treatment otherwise provided by Code Sec. 351.

[163] Code Sec. 367(d)(1), which denies the nonrecognition treatment otherwise provided by Code Sec. 361.

[164] However, such transfers generally are subject to the outbound toll charge that governs tangible property. Temp. Reg. § 1.367(a)-5T(e).

certain compulsory transfers, and certain transfers made to a foreign joint venture. Under this exception, the U.S. transferor can elect to recognize in the year of the transfer U.S.-source ordinary income equal to the excess of the intangible's market value over its adjusted basis.[165]

For purposes of the deemed royalty regime, intangible property includes any patent, invention, formula, process, design, pattern, know-how, copyright, literary, musical, or artistic composition, trademark, trade name, brand name, franchise, license, contract, method, program, system, procedure, campaign, survey, study, forecast, estimate, customer list, technical data, or other similar item.[166] However, foreign goodwill and going concern value are specifically exempted from the deemed royalty requirement[167] and thus can be transferred to a foreign corporation tax-free as long as the requirements of the active business use exception are satisfied.

The deemed royalty must be an arm's-length amount, computed in accordance with the provisions of Code Sec. 482 and the Regulations thereunder.[168] The deemed royalty amount also must be "commensurate with the income attributable to the intangible."[169] In other words, the royalty amounts must reflect the actual profit experience realized subsequent to the outbound transfer. To meet this requirement, the royalty amount must be adjusted annually to reflect any unanticipated changes in the income actually generated by the intangible.[170] For example, if a new patent leads to a product that turns out to be far more successful than was expected at the time the patent was transferred, the taxpayer must increase the amount of the deemed royalties to reflect that unanticipated profitability. If subsequent to the transfer, the foreign transferee disposes of the intangible to an unrelated person, the U.S. transferor must recognize a gain equal to the excess of the intangible's market value on the date of the subsequent disposition over its adjusted basis on the date of the initial transfer.[171]

To prevent double taxation of the foreign transferee's income, the transferee reduces its earnings and profits by the amount of deemed royalties included in the income of the U.S. transferor. In addition, the U.S. transferor can treat the deemed royalty as an expense properly allocable to the transferee's gross Subpart F income.[172] The U.S. trans-

---

[165] Temp. Reg. §§ 1.367(d)-1T(g)(2) and 1.367(a)-1T(d)(5)(ii).

[166] Code Secs. 367(d)(1) and 936(h)(3)(B).

[167] Temp. Reg. § 1.367(d)-1T(b). A copyright, literary, musical, or artistic composition transferred by the taxpayer whose personal efforts created the property also is exempted from the deemed royalty requirement. Temp. Reg. §§ 1.367(d)-1T(b) and 1.367(a)-5T(b)(2).

[168] Temp. Reg. § 1.367(d)-1T(c)(1). See Chapter 5 for a discussion of transfer pricing methods for intangible property.

[169] Code Sec. 367(d)(2)(A).

[170] Reg. § 1.482-4(f)(2)(i).

[171] Temp. Reg. § 1.367(d)-1T(f). Special rules also apply if, subsequent to the initial transfer of the intangible, the U.S. transferor disposes of the stock of the foreign transferee before the intangible's useful life expires. Temp. Reg. § 1.367(d)-1T(d) and (e).

[172] Temp. Reg. § 1.367(d)-1T(c)(2)(ii).

feror also can establish an account receivable for the hypothetical royalty, in which case any royalties actually paid by the foreign transferee with respect to the intangible are treated as a tax-free payment on account.[173]

In light of the deemed royalty regime, a taxpayer may find it advantageous to structure the transfer of intangible property to a foreign corporation as an actual license rather than as a contribution to capital. One advantage of an actual license is that the foreign transferee ordinarily can deduct actual royalty payments for foreign tax purposes, whereas deemed royalties generally are not deductible. For transfers made and royalties received on or before August 5, 1997, a second advantage for a taxpayer in an excess foreign tax credit position is that an actual license for the use of intangible property outside the United States gives rise to foreign-source income,[174] whereas a deemed royalty was treated as U.S.-source income.[175] One potential disadvantage of an actual licensing agreement is that the royalty payments may be subject to foreign withholding taxes, although tax treaties often reduce the withholding rate to 10% or less. In addition, under an actual license, the U.S. transferor still must adjust its royalty income annually to reflect any unanticipated changes in the income actually generated by the intangible.[176]

The Taxpayer Relief Act of 1997 eliminated one of the disadvantages of contributing intangible property to a foreign corporation, as opposed to structuring the transaction as an actual royalty agreement. Prior to the amendments made by this Act (which are effective for transfers made and royalties deemed received after August 5, 1997), deemed royalties were characterized as U.S.-source income, and therefore did not improve the taxpayer's foreign tax credit limitation position. However, for transfers made and royalties deemed received after August 5, 1997, deemed royalties are treated as foreign-source to the extent that an actual payment made by the foreign corporation under a license or sale agreement with the transferor would be treated as foreign-source income.[177] The 1997 Act also gives the IRS regulatory authority to extend the deemed royalty treatment to the transfer of intangible property to a partnership. Accordingly, to the extent provided by regulations, such a transfer will be treated as a sale that

---

[173] Temp. Reg. § 1.367(d)-1T(g)(1)(i). If no actual payments are made by the last day of the third taxable year following the year in which the account was established, the account receivable is recharacterized as a contribution to the capital of the foreign transferee, which increases the U.S. transferor's basis in the stock of that foreign corporation. Temp. Reg. § 1.367(d)-1T(g)(1)(ii).

[174] Code Sec. 862(a)(4). An outright sale of the intangible to a buyer that uses the intangible outside

the United States would yield the same results (i.e., foreign-source royalty income), as long as the sales price is contingent on the productivity, use, or disposition of the intangible. Code Sec. 865(d)(1)(B).

[175] Code Sec. 367(d)(2)(C), prior to amendment by the Taxpayer Relief Act of 1997 (August 5, 1997).

[176] Reg. § 1.482-4(f)(2)(i).

[177] Code Sec. 367(d)(2)(C).

generates deemed annual payments from the partnership to the transferor.[178] Such payments are considered to be ordinary income, must be established on an arm's length basis, and must be commensurate with the annual income attributable to the intangible.

Liquidation of a Domestic Subsidiary into Its Foreign Parent

Under general U.S. tax principles, the complete liquidation of a corporation is a taxable transaction for both the corporation distributing the assets and the shareholders receiving those assets.[179] An exception applies to the liquidation of an 80% or more owned subsidiary corporation into its parent corporation, which is tax-free to both parties.[180] This exception is based, in part, on the premise that any appreciated property not taxed at the time of the liquidation will be subject to corporate-level U.S. taxation when the surviving parent corporation disposes of the property. However, if a domestic subsidiary is liquidating into its foreign parent, the liquidating distribution may represent the U.S. Treasury's last opportunity for taxing appreciation that occurred within U.S. taxing jurisdiction. As a consequence, the domestic subsidiary must recognize a gain equal to the excess of the distributed property's market value over its adjusted basis.[181]

Various rules mitigate the effects of the outbound toll charge imposed on the complete liquidation of a domestic subsidiary corporation. First, to the extent the liquidating subsidiary must recognize gains on property that has appreciated in value, it also may recognize offsetting losses on property that has declined in value.[182] Second, the basis of the property distributed to the foreign parent corporation equals the basis of the property in the hands of the domestic subsidiary, increased by the amount of net gain, if any, recognized by the liquidating subsidiary.[183] Finally, the toll charge does not apply to property that remains within U.S. taxing jurisdiction even though it is now held by a foreign corporation. This exception covers U.S. real property interests, other than stock in a former U.S. real property holding corporation.[184] It also covers property used by the foreign corporation

---

[178] Code Sec. 367(d)(3).

[179] The corporation recognizes a gain equal to the excess of the market value of the property distributed over its basis in that property (Code Sec. 336(a)), and the shareholders recognize a gain equal to the excess of the market value of the property received over their basis in the corporation's stock (Code Sec. 331(a)).

[180] Code Secs. 332 and 337.

[181] Code Sec. 367(e)(2) and Temp. Reg. § 1.367(e)-2T(b)(1)(i). Code Sec. 367(a)(1) does not apply to such liquidations. Temp. Reg. § 1.367(e)-2T(a)(2).

[182] Temp. Reg. § 1.367(e)-2T(b)(1)(ii). However, losses cannot be recognized on property that the distributing corporation acquired in a nontaxable exchange within five years before the date of liquidation.

[183] Temp. Reg. § 1.367(e)-2T(b)(3)(i).

[184] Temp. Reg. § 1.367(e)-2T(b)(2)(ii). A foreign person's gain on the disposition of a U.S. real property interest is taxed in the same manner as income effectively connected with the conduct of a U.S. trade or business. Code Sec. 897(a)(1).

in the conduct of a U.S. trade or business, but only if the following requirements are satisfied:

(i) the distributee foreign corporation is not a CFC,

(ii) the foreign corporation continues to use the property in the conduct of a U.S. trade or business for 10 years after the distribution (or, in the case of inventory, until it is disposed of), and

(iii) the distributing and distributee corporations file a gain recognition agreement under which an amended tax return must be filed, and back taxes plus interest paid, if requirement (ii) is not satisfied.[185]

Information Reporting

To help the IRS better police outbound transfers, a U.S. person who transfers property to a foreign corporation must attach Form 926, Return by Transferor of Property to a Foreign Corporation, Foreign Estate or Trust, or Foreign Partnership, to their regular tax return for the year of the transfer.[186] (Form 926 is reproduced in the appendix to this chapter.) This reporting requirement applies to outbound transfers of both tangible and intangible property. The penalty for a failure of a U.S. person to properly report a transfer to a foreign corporation equals 10% of the fair market value of the property transferred. However, the penalty does not apply if the transferor can show that the failure to comply was due to reasonable cause and not to willful neglect. Moreover, the total penalty cannot exceed $100,000 unless the failure is due to intentional disregard of the reporting requirements.[187]

¶606 SPECIAL RULES FOR NONCORPORATE FOREIGN ENTITIES

Outbound Toll Charges

A separate toll charge regime applies to outbound transfers of property made to noncorporate foreign entities prior to August 5, 1997. Under former Code Sec. 1491 (repealed in 1997), a 35% excise tax was imposed on the excess of the transferred property's market value over the sum of its adjusted basis plus the amount of gain recognized by the U.S. person on the transfer. The excise tax applied to transfers of property by a U.S. person to a foreign corporation (as paid-in surplus or as a contribution to capital), foreign estate or trust, or foreign partnership.[188]

---

[185] Temp. Reg. § 1.367(e)-2T(b)(2)(i). This exception does not apply to intangible property described in Code Sec. 936(h)(3)(B).

[186] Reg. § 1.6038B-1(b)(1) and (2).

[187] Code Sec. 6038B(c) and Reg. § 1.6038B-1(f).

[188] The excise tax did not apply in the following situations:

(i) the transferee is a tax-exempt organization,

Electing to treat the transfer as a taxable sale had the advantage of providing the foreign transferee with a stepped-up basis in the transferred property, and also raised the possibility of a tax rate lower than 35% for a taxpayer that is either in a lower tax bracket or can take advantage of a lower capital gains rate. The 35% excise tax was due at the time of the transfer, as was the filing of a Form 926, Return by Transferor of Property to a Foreign Corporation, Foreign Estate or Trust, or Foreign Partnership, to report the transfer.[189]

The 35% excise tax on transfers of property by a U.S. person to a foreign corporation does not apply to transfers made on or after August 5, 1997. Thus, Code Sec. 1491 is repealed for such transfers, and all capital contributions and transfers of paid-in surplus to foreign corporations are now subject only to the provisions of Code. Sec. 367, including any regulations promulgated under new Code Sec. 367(f). In addition, in lieu of the Code Sec. 1491 excise tax on transfers of property to foreign partnerships, the Treasury Department is empowered to write regulations denying the normal nonrecognition treatment of Code Sec. 721 on partnership contributions by a U.S. partner in circumstances where gain inherent in the property contributed ultimately will be recognized by a foreign person.[190] In the case of foreign trusts and estates, any transfer of property by a U.S. person to a foreign trust or estate made on or after August 5, 1997, is taxable, except to the extent provided by regulations. Such a transfer is treated as a sale or exchange of the property for its fair market value. The U.S. transferor must recognize gain equal to the excess of the property's fair market value over its adjusted basis in the hands of the transferor. The gain recognition rule does not apply if the U.S transferor is considered to be the owner of the trust under the grantor trust rules.[191]

Information Reporting for Foreign Partnerships

The Taxpayer Relief Act of 1997 added new information reporting requirements for foreign partnerships controlled by U.S. persons. These requirements are similar to the information reporting rules that have applied to CFCs since 1962. Under these provisions, a U.S. partner that controls a foreign partnership must file an annual information return.[192] A U.S. partner is considered to be in control of a foreign

---

(Footnote Continued)

(ii) the transfer is either governed by the outbound toll charge of Code Sec. 367 (in which case the transfer may already be treated as a taxable sale), or the taxpayer elects the application of principles similar to those of Code Sec. 367, or

(iii) the taxpayer elects to treat the transfer as a taxable sale, in which case the taxpayer recognizes a gain equal to the excess of the market value of the transferred property over its adjusted basis.

Code Secs. 1491 through 1494, repealed by the Taxpayer Relief Act of 1997 (August 5, 1997).

[189] Reg. § 1.1494-1(a).

[190] Code Sec. 721(c).

[191] Code Sec. 684(a).

[192] Code Sec. 6038(a).

partnership if the partner holds, directly or indirectly, a greater than 50% interest in the capital, profits, or, to the extent provided in the regulations, deductions or losses of the partnership.[193] Where there is no single controlling partner, but the partnership is controlled by a number of U.S. persons each holding at least a 10% interest in the partnership, similar reporting is required of one or more of the 10% U.S. partners.[194] The penalty for failure to comply with these reporting obligations is $10,000, and may also include a reduction in the taxpayer's foreign tax credit.[195] In addition to the requirements for U.S. persons that "hold" interests in a controlled foreign partnership, U.S. persons that "acquire" or "dispose" of such interests are also subject to reporting requirements.[196] Moreover, the 1997 Act also added new reporting requirements for U.S. persons who transfer property to a foreign partnership.[197] This reporting requirement applies only if the U.S. person transferor owns, directly or indirectly, at least a 10% interest in the partnership, or if the market value of the property transferred to the foreign partnership during a 12-month period exceeds $100,000.[198] As with the new reporting requirements for controlled foreign partnerships, the reporting of contributions to foreign partnerships parallels the reporting of similar transfers to foreign corporations. The penalty for a failure to report a contribution to a foreign partnership is equal to 10% of the fair market value of the property transferred, as well as gain recognition as if the property had been sold.[199]

In September 1998, the IRS issued proposed regulations implementing the reporting requirements for U.S. persons that hold interests in controlled foreign partnerships,[200] U.S. persons that acquire or dispose of an interest in a controlled foreign partnership,[201] and U.S. persons that transfer property to a foreign partnership.[202] In these regulations, the IRS indicates that it is developing a comprehensive form (Form 8865) that taxpayers can use to satisfy all three sets of reporting requirements. These regulations are generally effective for transfers made on or after January 1, 1998.[203] The other reporting requirements regarding foreign partnerships will not be effective until final regulations are issued.

---

[193] Code Sec. 6038(e)(3).

[194] Code Sec. 6038(a)(5).

[195] Code Sec. 6038(b) and (c).

[196] Code Sec. 6046A.

[197] Code Sec. 6038B(a)(1)(B).

[198] Code Sec. 6038B(b)(1).

[199] Code Sec. 6038B(c). However, the penalty does not apply if the transferor can show that the failure to comply was due to reasonable cause and not to willful neglect. Moreover, the total penalty cannot exceed $100,000 unless the failure is due to intentional disregard of the reporting requirements.

[200] Prop. Reg. § 1.6038-3.

[201] Prop. Reg. § 1.6046A-1.

[202] Prop. Reg. § 1.6038B-2.

[203] Reg. § 1.6038B-2, and Notice 98-17, 1998-11 IRB 6.

¶ 607   INBOUND TRANSFERS FROM A FOREIGN CORPORATION

Liquidation of a Foreign Subsidiary into Its Domestic Parent

Under general U.S. tax principles, the complete liquidation of a corporation is a taxable transaction for both the corporation distributing the assets and the shareholders receiving those assets.[204] An exception applies to the liquidation of an 80% or more owned subsidiary corporation into its parent corporation, which is tax-free to both parties.[205] This exception is based, in part, on the premise that the United States has already taxed the distributed earnings when they were derived by the subsidiary corporation. This assumption does not hold true, however, with respect to the foreign earnings of a foreign corporation. As a consequence, an inbound liquidating distribution of a foreign subsidiary may represent the U.S. Treasury's first and last opportunity for subjecting those earnings to the corporate-level U.S. tax.

> **Example 6.24:** Several years ago, USAco (a domestic corporation) organized AFRIco, a wholly owned subsidiary incorporated in a foreign country. Since its inception, AFRIco has derived $50 million of earnings and profits from foreign manufacturing activities. None of these foreign-source earnings have been taxed to USAco as a Subpart F inclusion, nor have any of AFRIco's earnings been distributed to USAco as a dividend. Thus, AFRIco's earnings have not yet been subjected to U.S. taxation at either the foreign subsidiary or domestic parent corporation level. At the end of the current year, AFRIco distributes all of its assets to USAco in complete liquidation. Ignoring Code Sec. 367, AFRIco's inbound repatriating liquidation is not subject to U.S. tax because it is part of a tax-free parent-subsidiary liquidation. As a consequence, the $50 million of earnings derived by AFRIco and then transferred to USAco would escape U.S. tax at both the foreign subsidiary and domestic parent corporation levels.

To prevent this result, a domestic parent corporation that receives a liquidating distribution from an 80% or more owned foreign subsidiary corporation must include in income all of the subsidiary's earnings and profits attributable to the parent's ownership interest in the liquidating subsidiary.[206] Any gain in excess of the foreign subsidiary's earnings and profits is accorded tax-free treatment.[207] The inclusion in income of a foreign subsidiary's earnings and profits is treated as a cash

---

[204] The corporation recognizes a gain equal to the excess of the market value of the property distributed over its basis in that property (Code Sec. 336(a)), and the shareholders recognize a gain equal to the excess of the market value of the property received over their basis in the corporation's stock (Code Sec. 331(a)).

[205] Code Secs. 332 and 337.

[206] Code Sec. 367(b) and Reg. § 7.367(b)-5(b). See Reg. § 1.367(b)-2(f) for a definition of earnings and profits for this purpose.

[207] Reg. § 7.367(b)-5(b) and Code Sec. 332.

dividend,[208] and therefore the domestic parent corporation can claim a deemed paid foreign tax credit for the foreign income taxes related to those earnings and profits.[209] However, the domestic parent corporation does not get a step-up in basis for the dividend income recognized on the liquidation but instead takes a carryover basis in the property received in liquidation.[210]

If the domestic parent corporation fails to include the foreign subsidiary's earnings and profits in income, the domestic parent must recognize the entire gain on the liquidating exchange.[211] Such gains are characterized as a dividend to the extent of the U.S. shareholder's pro rata share of the liquidating corporation's post-1962 earnings and profits that were accumulated while the shareholder owned the stock and the corporation was a CFC.[212] This deemed dividend also carries with it a deemed paid foreign tax credit.[213] Any gain in excess of the deemed dividend is accorded capital gain treatment. However, despite gain recognition, the domestic parent still must take a carryover basis in the distributed assets.[214]

> **Example 6.25:** Several years ago, USAco (a domestic corporation) organized FORco, a wholly owned subsidiary incorporated in a foreign country. At the end of the current year, FORco distributes all of its assets, which have a market value of $7 million, to USAco as part of a complete liquidation. On the date of the liquidation, FORco had $3 million of accumulated earnings and profits, and $1 million of foreign income taxes that have not yet been deemed paid by USAco. Assume that USAco's basis in FORco's stock was $2 million immediately prior to the liquidation and that the U.S. corporate tax rate is 35%.
>
> USAco's gain on the receipt of the liquidating distribution is $5 million [$7 million amount realized − $2 million basis in FORco's stock]. If USAco recognizes a dividend equal to FORco's accumulated earnings and profits of $3 million, the remaining gain of $2 million will qualify for tax-free treatment. Moreover, the $3 million dividend income will carry with it $1 million of deemed paid foreign taxes. Thus, the pre-credit U.S. tax on the liquidation is $1.4 million [35% U.S. tax rate × ($3 million deemed dividend + $1 million gross-up)], the deemed paid credit is $1 million, and USAco has a residual U.S. tax of $400,000. If USAco fails to

---

[208] Reg. § 7.367(b)-3(b).

[209] Reg. § 7.367(b)-3(f) and Code Sec. 902(a).

[210] Reg. § 7.367(b)-5(b) and Code Sec. 334(b).

[211] Reg. § 7.367(b)-5(b). Gain recognition is triggered by denying the foreign corporation its corporate status, in which case the general rules for taxable exchanges apply (see Code Sec. 1001).

[212] Code Sec. 1248(a). For this purpose, earnings and profits do not include certain amounts already

subject to U.S. tax, including prior-year Subpart F inclusions, income effectively connected with the conduct of a U.S. trade or business, and an inclusion from a PFIC that has made a QEF election. Code Sec. 1248(d).

[213] Reg. § 1.1248-1(d).

[214] Reg. § 7.367(b)-5(b) and Code Sec. 334(b).

include a \$3 million dividend in income, the entire \$5 million gain is taxable. In either case, USAco will take a carryover basis in the assets distributed.

Other Inbound and Foreign-to-Foreign Transfers

Provisions similar to those governing inbound repatriating liquidations of foreign subsidiaries also govern a variety of other exchanges involving inbound transfers of property made by foreign corporations, as well as transfers of property from one foreign corporation to another foreign corporation.[215] The principal purpose of these provisions is to preserve the ability of the United States to tax, either currently or at some future date, the earnings and profits of a foreign corporation attributable to stock owned by U.S. shareholders. Examples of the types of transfers governed by this regime include:

(i)   a foreign corporation's contribution of property to a domestic corporation in exchange for stock of the domestic corporation, where immediately after the exchange the foreign corporation controls the domestic corporation,

(ii) a foreign corporation's transfer of stock, securities, or property to a domestic corporation as part of a corporate reorganization,

(iii) a foreign corporation's transfer of property to another foreign corporation, in exchange for stock of the controlled transferee, where the transferee is a not a CFC, or where a U.S. shareholder of the transferor foreign corporation will not be a U.S. shareholder in the transferee foreign corporation, and

(iv) a corporate reorganization involving only foreign corporations, where a U.S. shareholder receives stock in a noncontrolled foreign corporation or stock of a CFC in which the U.S. person is not a U.S. shareholder.

---

[215] Code Sec. 367(b), and Reg. §§ 7.367(b)-2–7.367(b)-13. See also Prop. Reg. §§ 1.367(b)-1–1.367(b)-6.

¶ 608   APPENDIX

Form **926**	**Return by a U.S. Transferor of Property**	
(Rev. October 1998)	**to a Foreign Corporation**	OMB No. 1545-0026
Department of the Treasury Internal Revenue Service	**(under section 367)**	

Part I   U.S. Transferor Information (see instructions)

Name of transferor	Identification number (see instructions)
Number, street, and room or suite no. (If a P.O. box, see instructions.)	
City or town, state, and ZIP code	

1   The following questions apply only if the transferor is a corporation:

a If the transfer was a section 361(a) or (b) transfer, was the transferor controlled (under section 368(c)) by 5 or fewer domestic corporations? . . . . ☐ Yes ☐ No

b Did the transferor remain in existence after the transfer? . . . . ☐ Yes ☐ No
If not, list the controlling shareholder(s) and their identification number(s):

Controlling shareholder	Identification number

c If the transferor was a member of an affiliated group filing a consolidated return, was it the parent corporation? . . . . ☐ Yes ☐ No
If not, list the name and employer identification number (EIN) of the parent corporation:

Name of parent corporation	EIN of parent corporation

2   If the transferor was a partner in a partnership that was the actual transferor (but is not treated as such under section 367), list the name and EIN of the transferor's partnership:

Name of partnership	EIN of partnership

Part II   Transferee Foreign Corporation Information (see instructions)

3 Name of transferee (foreign corporation)	4 Identification number, if any
5 Address (including country)	
6 Place of organization or creation	7 Foreign law characterization (see instructions)

8   Is the transferee foreign corporation a controlled foreign corporation? . . . . ☐ Yes ☐ No

For Paperwork Reduction Act Notice, see separate instructions.   Cat No. 16982D   Form **926** (Rev. 10-98)

Form 926 (Rev. 10-98) Page **2**

| **Part III** | Information Regarding **Transfer of Property** (see instructions) |

| 9 Date of transfer | 10 Type of nonrecognition transaction (see instructions) |

11 Description of property transferred:

12 Did this transfer result from a change in the classification of the transferee to that of a foreign corporation? ☐ **Yes** ☐ **No**

13 Was the transferor required to recognize income under Temporary Regulations sections 1.367(a)-4T through 1.367(a)-6T (e.g., for tainted property, depreciation recapture, branch loss recapture, etc.)? . . ☐ **Yes** ☐ **No**

14a Was intangible property (within the meaning of section 936(h)(3)(B)) transferred pursuant to the transaction? . . . . ☐ **Yes** ☐ **No**

b If yes, describe the nature of the rights to the intangible property that was transferred in the transfer:

Please Sign Here

Under penalties of perjury, I declare that I have examined this return, including accompanying schedules and statements, and to the best of my knowledge and belief it is true, correct, and complete. Declaration of preparer (other than taxpayer) is based on all information of which preparer has any knowledge.

▶ _____ | _____ | ▶ _____
Signature | Date | Title

Paid Preparer's Use Only

Preparer's signature ▶	Date	Check if self-employed ▶ ☐	Preparer's social security no.
Firm's name (or yours if self-employed), and address ▶		EIN ▶	
		ZIP code ▶	

¶ 608

| Form **5471**
(Rev. January 1999)
Department of the Treasury
Internal Revenue Service | **Information Return of U.S. Persons With Respect To Certain Foreign Corporations**
▶ See separate instructions.
Information furnished for the foreign corporation's annual accounting period (tax year required by section 898) (see instructions) beginning _____ , and ending _____ , | OMB No. 1545-0704
File In Duplicate
(see **When and Where To File** in the instructions) |

Name of person filing this return	**A** Identifying number

Number, street, and room or suite no. (or P.O. box number if mail is not delivered to street address)	**B** Category of filer (See page 2 of the instructions. Check applicable box(es)): (1) ☐ (2) ☐ (3) ☐ (4) ☐ (5) ☐

City or town, state, and ZIP code	**C** Enter the total percentage of voting stock of the foreign corporation you owned at the end of its annual accounting period .... %

Filer's tax year beginning _____ , and ending _____ .

D Person(s) on whose behalf this information return is filed:

(1) Name	**(2)** Address	**(3)** Identifying number	**(4)** Check applicable box(es)		
			Shareholder	Officer	Director

Important: *Fill in all applicable lines and schedules. All information* **MUST** *be in the English language. All amounts* **MUST** *be stated in U.S. dollars unless otherwise indicated.*
Enter the foreign corporation's functional currency ▶

1a Name and address of foreign corporation	**b** Employer identification number, if any
	c Country under whose laws incorporated

d Date of incorporation	**e** Principal place of business	**f** Principal business activity code number **(NEW)**	**g** Principal business activity

2 Provide the following information for the foreign corporation's accounting period stated above.

a Name, address, and identifying number of branch office or agent (if any) in the United States	**b** If a U.S. income tax return was filed, please show:	
	(i) Taxable income or (loss)	*(ii)* U.S. income tax paid (after all credits)

c Name and address of foreign corporation's statutory or resident agent in country of incorporation	**d** Name and address (including corporate department, if applicable) of person (or persons) with custody of the books and records of the foreign corporation, and the location of such books and records, if different

---

Schedule A **Stock of the Foreign Corporation**

Part I—ALL Classes of Stock

(a) Description of each class of stock	**(b)** Number of shares issued and outstanding	
	(i) Beginning of annual accounting period	*(ii)* End of annual accounting period

Part II—Additional Information for PREFERRED Stock
(To be completed **only** by Category (1) filers for foreign personal holding companies)

(a) Description of each class of PREFERRED stock (**Note:** *This description should match the corresponding description entered in Part I, column (a).*)	**(b)** Par value in functional currency	**(c)** Rate of dividend	**(d)** Indicate whether the stock is cumulative or noncumulative

For Paperwork Reduction Act Notice, see page 1 of the separate instructions.   Cat. No. 49958V   Form **5471** (Rev. 1-99)

Form 5471 (Rev. 1-99)

Page **2**

Schedule B   U.S. Shareholders of Foreign Corporation (See page 4 of the instructions.)

(a) Name, address, and identifying number of shareholder	(b) Description of each class of stock held by shareholder (**Note:** *This description should match the corresponding description entered in Schedule A, Part I, column (a).*)	(c) Number of shares held at beginning of annual accounting period	(d) Number of shares held at end of annual accounting period	(e) Pro rata share of subpart F income (enter as a percentage)

Schedule C   Income Statement (See page 4 of the instructions.)

Important: *Report all information in functional currency in accordance with U.S. GAAP. Also, report each amount in U.S. dollars translated from functional currency (using GAAP translation rules). However, if the functional currency is the U.S. dollar, complete only the U.S. Dollars column. See instructions for special rules for DASTM corporations.*

			Functional Currency	U.S. Dollars
Income	1a	Gross receipts or sales	1a		
	b	Returns and allowances	1b		
	c	Subtract line 1b from line 1a	1c		
	2	Cost of goods sold	2		
	3	Gross profit (subtract line 2 from line 1c)	3		
	4	Dividends	4		
	5	Interest	5		
	6	Gross rents, royalties, and license fees	6		
	7	Net gain or (loss) on sale of capital assets	7		
	8	Other income (attach schedule)	8		
	9	Total income (add lines 3 through 8)	9		
Deductions	10	Compensation not deducted elsewhere	10		
	11	Rents, royalties, and license fees	11		
	12	Interest	12		
	13	Depreciation not deducted elsewhere	13		
	14	Depletion	14		
	15	Taxes (exclude provision for income, war profits, and excess profits taxes)	15		
	16	Other deductions (attach schedule—exclude provision for income, war profits, and excess profits taxes)	16		
	17	Total deductions (add lines 10 through 16)	17		
Net Income	18	Net income or (loss) before extraordinary items, prior period adjustments, and the provision for income, war profits, and excess profits taxes (subtract line 17 from line 9)	18		
	19	Extraordinary items and prior period adjustments (see instructions)	19		
	20	Provision for income, war profits, and excess profits taxes (see instructions)	20		
	21	Current year net income or (loss) per books (line 18 plus line 19 minus line 20)	21		

¶ 608

Form 5471 (Rev. 1-99)   Page **3**

Schedule E	Income, War Profits, and Excess Profits Taxes Paid or Accrued (See page 4 of instructions.)			
	(a)	Amount of tax		
	Name of country or U.S. possession	(b) In foreign currency	(c) Conversion rate	(d) In U.S. dollars
1	U.S.			
2				
3				
4				
5				
6				
7				
8	Total . . . . ▶			

Schedule F	Balance Sheet

Important: *Report all amounts in U.S. dollars prepared and translated in accordance with U.S. GAAP. See instructions for an exception for DASTM corporations.*

Assets		(a) Beginning of annual accounting period	(b) End of annual accounting period
1	Cash	1		
2a	Trade notes and accounts receivable	2a		
b	Less allowance for bad debts	2b	( )( )
3	Inventories	3		
4	Other current assets (attach schedule)	4		
5	Loans to stockholders and other related persons	5		
6	Investment in subsidiaries (attach schedule).	6		
7	Other investments (attach schedule)	7		
8a	Buildings and other depreciable assets	8a		
b	Less accumulated depreciation	8b	( )( )
9a	Depletable assets	9a		
b	Less accumulated depletion	9b	( )( )
10	Land (net of any amortization)	10		
11	Intangible assets:			
a	Goodwill.	11a		
b	Organization costs	11b		
c	Patents, trademarks, and other intangible assets	11c		
d	Less accumulated amortization for lines 11a, b, and c	11d	( )( )
12	Other assets (attach schedule)	12		
13	Total assets	13		

Liabilities and Stockholders' Equity			
14	Accounts payable	14		
15	Other current liabilities (attach schedule)	15		
16	Loans from stockholders and other related persons	16		
17	Other liabilities (attach schedule)	17		
18	Capital stock:			
a	Preferred stock	18a		
b	Common stock	18b		
19	Paid-in or capital surplus (attach reconciliation).	19		
20	Retained earnings	20		
21	Less cost of treasury stock	21	( )( )
22	Total liabilities and stockholders' equity	22		

Does the foreign corporation have an interest in a partnership or trust? . . . . ☐ Yes ☐ No

¶ 608

Form 5471 (Rev. 1-99)   Page **4**

Schedule H   **Current Earnings and Profits** (See page 5 of the instructions.)

Important: *Enter the amounts on lines 1 through 5c in functional currency.*

		Net Additions	Net Subtractions	
1	Current year net income or (loss) per foreign books of account			1
2	Net adjustments made to line 1 to determine current earnings and profits according to U.S. financial and tax accounting standards (see instructions):			
a	Capital gains or losses			
b	Depreciation and amortization			
c	Depletion			
d	Investment or incentive allowance			
e	Charges to statutory reserves			
f	Inventory adjustments			
g	Taxes			
h	Other (attach schedule)			
3	Total net additions			
4	Total net subtractions			
5a	Current earnings and profits (line 1 plus line 3 minus line 4)			5a
b	DASTM gain or (loss) for foreign corporations that use DASTM (see instructions)			5b
c	Combine lines 5a and 5b			5c
d	Current earnings and profits in U.S. dollars (line 5c translated at the appropriate exchange rate as defined in section 989(b) and the related regulations (see instructions)			5d

Enter exchange rate used for line 5d ▶

Schedule I   **Summary of Shareholder's Income From Foreign Corporation** (See page 5 of the instructions.)

1	Subpart F income (line 40b, Worksheet A in the instructions)	1
2	Earnings invested in U.S. property (line 17, Worksheet B in the instructions)	2
3	Previously excluded subpart F income withdrawn from qualified investments (line 6b, Worksheet C in the instructions)	3
4	Previously excluded export trade income withdrawn from investment in export trade assets (line 7b, Worksheet D in the instructions)	4
5	Factoring income	5
6	Total of lines 1 through 5. Enter here and on your income tax return	6
7	Dividends received (translated at spot rate on payment date under section 989(b)(1))	7
8	Exchange gain or (loss) on a distribution of previously taxed income	8

                                                                  Yes No

● Was any income of the foreign corporation blocked? . . . . ☐ ☐
● Did any such income become unblocked during the tax year (see section 964(b))? . . . . ☐ ☐

If the answer to either question is "Yes," attach an explanation.

SCHEDULE J
(Form 5471)
(Rev. January 1999)
Department of the Treasury
Internal Revenue Service

Accumulated Earnings and Profits (E&P) of Controlled Foreign Corporation

▶ Attach to Form 5471.

OMB No. 1545-0704

Name of person filing Form 5471

Identifying number

Name of foreign corporation

Important. Enter amounts in functional currency.	(a) Post-1986 Undistributed Earnings (post-86 section 959(c)(3) balance)	(b) Pre-1987 E&P Not Previously Taxed (pre-87 section 959(c)(3) balance)	(c) Previously Taxed E&P (see instructions) (sections 959(c)(1) and (2) balances)			(d) Total Section 964(a) E&P (combine columns (a), (b), and (c))
			(i) Earnings Invested in U.S. Property	(ii) Earnings Invested in Excess Passive Assets	(iii) Subpart F Income	
1 Balance at beginning of year						
2a Current year E&P						
b Current year deficit in E&P						
3 Total current and accumulated E&P not previously taxed (line 1 plus line 2a, minus line 2b)						
4 Amounts included under section 951(a) or reclassified under section 959(c) in current year						
5a Actual distributions or reclassifications of previously taxed E&P						
b Actual distributions of nonpreviously taxed E&P						
6a Balance of previously taxed E&P at end of year (line 1 plus line 4, minus line 5a)						
b Balance of E&P not previously taxed at end of year (line 3 minus line 4, minus line 5b)						
7 Balance at end of year. (Enter amount from line 6a or line 6b, whichever is applicable.)						

For Paperwork Reduction Act Notice, see page 1 of the separate Instructions for Form 5471.   Cat. No. 21111K   Schedule J (Form 5471) (Rev. 1-99)

¶ 608

SCHEDULE M
(Form 5471)
(Rev. January 1999)
Department of the Treasury
Internal Revenue Service

**Transactions Between Controlled Foreign Corporation
and Shareholders or Other Related Persons**

OMB No. 1545-0704

▶ **Attach to Form 5471.**

Name of person filing Form 5471	Identifying number

Name of foreign corporation

Important: *Complete a separate Schedule M for each controlled foreign corporation. Enter the totals (in U.S. dollars) for each type of transaction that occurred during the annual accounting period between the foreign corporation and the persons listed in columns (b) through (f). Translate all amounts from functional currency to U.S. dollars using the appropriate exchange rate for the tax year of the foreign corporation. See page 9 of the instructions.*

Enter the relevant functional currency and the exchange rate used throughout this schedule ▶

(a) Transactions of foreign corporation	(b) U.S. person filing this return	(c) Any domestic corporation or partnership controlled by U.S. person filing this return	(d) Any other foreign corporation or partnership controlled by U.S. person filing this return	(e) 10% or more U.S. shareholder of controlled foreign corporation (other than the U.S. person filing this return)	(f) 10% or more U.S. shareholder of any corporation controlling the foreign corporation
1 Sales of stock in trade (inventory)					
2 Sales of property rights (patents, trademarks, etc.) . .					
3 Compensation received for technical, managerial, engineering, construction, or like services. .					
4 Commissions received . . .					
5 Rents, royalties, and license fees received					
6 Dividends received (exclude deemed distributions under subpart F and distributions of previously taxed income) . .					
7 Interest received					
8 Premiums received for insurance or reinsurance					
9 Add lines 1 through 8 . . .					
10 Purchases of stock in trade (inventory)					
11 Purchases of tangible property other than stock in trade . .					
12 Purchases of property rights (patents, trademarks, etc.) . .					
13 Compensation paid for technical, managerial, engineering, construction, or like services .					
14 Commissions paid					
15 Rents, royalties, and license fees paid					
16 Dividends paid					
17 Interest paid					
18 Add lines 10 through 17 . .					
19 Amounts borrowed (enter the maximum loan balance during the year) — see instructions .					
20 Amounts loaned (enter the maximum loan balance during the year) — see instructions .					

For Paperwork Reduction Act Notice, see page 1 of the Instructions for Form 5471.   Cat. No. 49963O   Schedule M (Form 5471) (Rev. 1-99)

SCHEDULE N (Form 5471) (Rev. January 1999) Department of the Treasury Internal Revenue Service	**Return of Officers, Directors, and 10% or More** **Shareholders of a Foreign Personal Holding Company** ▶ Attach to Form 5471.	OMB No. 1545-0704

Name of person filing Form 5471	Identifying number

Name of foreign corporation

Important: All amounts must be stated in U.S. dollars translated from functional currency. See page 10 of the instructions for the relevant exchange rate.

Enter the relevant functional currency and the exchange rate used throughout this schedule ▶

Part I   Shareholder Information

Section A—Outstanding Securities Convertible Into Stock of the Corporation or Options Granted by the Corporation

Description of securities (attach a complete, detailed statement of conversion privileges)	Interest rate (%)	Face value	
		Beginning of year	End of year

Section B—List of Holders of Convertible Securities or Options Granted by the Corporation

Name and address of each holder of convertible securities or options (designate nonresident aliens)	Class of securities	Securities held				Explanation and date of any change in holdings of securities during the year
		Beginning of year		End of year		
		Number	Face value	Number	Face value	

Part II   Income Information

Section A—Computation of Undistributed Foreign Personal Holding Company Income

1	Gross income as defined in section 555 (attach schedule)	**1**	
2	Deductions allowable under section 161 (attach schedule)	**2**	
3	Taxable income or (loss) (subtract line 2 from line 1)	**3**	
4	Adjustments to taxable income or (loss) (see instructions):		
a	Taxes (see instructions)	**4a**	
b	Charitable contributions	**4b**	
c	Special deductions disallowed	**4c**	
d	Net operating loss	**4d**	
e	Expenses and depreciation applicable to property of the taxpayer	**4e**	
f	Taxes and contributions to pension trusts	**4f**	
g	Total adjustments (combine lines 4a through 4f)	**4g**	
5	Combine line 3 and line 4g	**5**	
6	Deduction for dividends paid during the tax year. Enter the amount from Section B, line 12	**6**	
7	Subtract line 6 from line 5	**7**	
8	Deduction allowed under section 563(c) for dividends paid after close of tax year (see instructions). Attach designation required by Rev. Proc. 90-26, 1990-1 C.B. 512	**8**	
9	Undistributed foreign personal holding company income (subtract line 8 from line 7) . .	**9**	

Section B—Deduction for Dividends Paid During Tax Year (see instructions)

		Date paid		Amount
10	Taxable dividends paid during tax year:			
a	Cash		**10a**	
b	Property other than cash or the corporation's own securities (indicate nature of property)		**10b**	
c	Obligations of the corporation (bonds, notes, scrip, etc.) . . .		**10c**	
11	Consent dividends (attach schedule)		**11**	
12	Deduction for dividends paid during tax year (add lines 10a through 11). Enter here and on line 6 above		**12**	

For Paperwork Reduction Act Notice, see page 1 of the Instructions for Form 5471.   Cat. No. 61925Q   **Schedule N (Form 5471)** (Rev. 1-99)

¶ 608

SCHEDULE O	Organization or Reorganization of Foreign	
(Form 5471)	**Corporation, and Acquisitions and**	
(Rev. January 1999)	**Dispositions of its Stock**	OMB No. 1545-0704
Department of the Treasury Internal Revenue Service	▶ Attach to Form 5471.	

Name of person filing Form 5471	Identifying number

Name of foreign corporation

Important: *Complete a **separate** Schedule O for each foreign corporation for which information must be reported.*

Part I   **To Be Completed by U.S. Officers and Directors** (See instructions.)

(a) Name of shareholder for whom acquisition information is reported	(b) Address of shareholder	(c) Identifying number of shareholder	(d) Date of original 10% acquisition	(e) Date of additional 10% acquisition

Part II   **To Be Completed by U.S. Shareholders**

    Note: *If this return is required because one or more shareholders became U.S. persons, attach a list showing the names of such persons and the date each became a U.S. person.*

Section A—General Shareholder Information

(a) Name, address, and identifying number of shareholder(s) filing this schedule	(b) For shareholder's latest U.S. income tax return filed, indicate:			(c) Date (if any) shareholder last filed information return under section 6046 for the foreign corporation
	(1) Type of return (enter form number)	(2) Date return filed	(3) Internal Revenue Service Center where filed	

Section B—U.S. Persons Who Are Officers or Directors of the Foreign Corporation

(a) Name of U.S. officer or director	(b) Address	(c) Social security number	(d) Check appropriate box(es)	
			Officer	Director

Section C—Acquisition of Stock

(a) Name of shareholder(s) filing this schedule	(b) Class of stock acquired	(c) Date of acquisition	(d) Method of acquisition	(e) Number of shares acquired		
				(1) Directly	(2) Indirectly	(3) Constructively

For Paperwork Reduction Act Notice, see page 1 of the Instructions for Form 5471.   Cat. No. 61200O   **Schedule O (Form 5471)** (Rev. 1-99)

(f) Amount paid or value given	**(g)** Name and address of person from whom shares were acquired

Section D—Disposition of Stock

(a) Name of shareholder disposing of stock	**(b)** Class of stock	**(c)** Date of disposition	**(d)** Method of disposition	**(e)** Number of shares disposed of		
				(1) Directly	**(2)** Indirectly	**(3)** Constructively

(f) Amount received	**(g)** Name and address of person to whom disposition of stock was made

Section E—Organization or Reorganization of Foreign Corporation

(a) Name and address of transferor	**(b)** Identifying number (if any)	**(c)** Date of transfer

(d) Assets transferred to foreign corporation			**(e)** Description of assets transferred by, or notes or securities issued by, foreign corporation
(1) Description of assets	**(2)** Fair market value	**(3)** Adjusted basis (if transferor was U.S. person)	

Section F—Additional Information

(a) If the foreign corporation or a predecessor U.S. corporation filed (or joined with a consolidated group in filing) a U.S. income tax return for any of the last 3 years, attach a statement indicating the year for which a return was filed (and, if applicable, the name of the corporation filing the consolidated return), the taxable income or loss, and the U.S. income tax paid (after all credits).

(b) List the date of any reorganization of the foreign corporation that occurred during the last 4 years while any U.S. person held 10% or more in value or vote (5% or more in value for transactions that occurred prior to January 1, 1998) (directly or indirectly) of the corporation's stock ▶

(c) If the foreign corporation is a member of a group that make up a chain of ownership, attach a chart, for each unit of which a shareholder owns 10% or more in value or vote (5% or more in value for transactions that occurred prior to January 1, 1998) of the outstanding stock. The chart must indicate the corporation's position in the chain of ownership and the percentages of stock ownership (see page 12 of the instructions for an example).

Form **8621** (Rev. February 1999) Department of the Treasury Internal Revenue Service	**Return by a Shareholder of a Passive Foreign Investment Company or Qualified Electing Fund** ▶ See separate instructions.	OMB No. 1545-1002 Attachment Sequence No. **69**

Name of shareholder	Identifying number (see page 3 of instructions)

Number, street, and room or suite no. (If a P.O. box, see page 3 of instructions.)	Your tax year: calendar year .... or other tax year beginning and ending

City or town, state, and ZIP code or country	

Check type of shareholder filing the return: ☐ Individual ☐ Corporation ☐ Partnership ☐ S Corporation ☐ Nongrantor Trust ☐ Estate

Name of passive foreign investment company (PFIC) or qualified electing fund (QEF)	Employer identification number (if any)

Address (Enter number, street, city or town, and country.)	Tax year of company or fund: calendar year .... or other tax year beginning .... and ending ....

Part I   Elections (See instructions.)

A ☐ I, a shareholder of a PFIC, elect to treat the PFIC as a QEF. (Section 1295.) *Complete lines 1a through 2c of Part II.*

B ☐ I, a shareholder on the first day of a PFIC's first tax year, elect to recognize gain on the deemed sale of my interest in the PFIC. (Section 1291(d)(2)(A).) *Enter gain or loss on line 10f of Part IV.*

C ☐ I, a shareholder on the first day of a PFIC's first tax year as a QEF that is a controlled foreign corporation (CFC), elect to treat an amount equal to my share of the post-1986 earnings and profits of the CFC as an excess distribution. (Section 1291(d)(2)(B).) *Enter this amount on line 10e.*

D ☐ I, a shareholder of a QEF, elect to extend the time for payment of tax on the undistributed earnings and profits of the QEF until this election is terminated. (Section 1294.) *Complete lines 3a through 4c of Part II to calculate the tax that may be deferred.*
     Note: *If any portion of line 1a or line 2a of Part II is includible under section 551 or 951, you may* **not** *make this election. Also, see sections 1294(c) and 1294(f) and the related regulations for events that terminate this election.*

E ☐ I, a shareholder of a former PFIC, elect to treat as an excess distribution the gain recognized on the deemed sale of my interest in the PFIC, or, if I qualify, my share of the PFIC's post-1986 earnings and profits deemed distributed, on the last day of its last tax year as a PFIC under section 1297(a). (Section 1298(b)(1).) *Enter excess distribution on line 10e or 10f of Part IV.*

F ☐ I, a shareholder of a PFIC, elect to mark-to-market the stock of that PFIC, which stock is marketable within the meaning of section 1296(e). (Section 1296.) *Complete Part III.*

Part II   Income From a Qualified Electing Fund (QEF). All QEF shareholders complete lines 1a through 2c. If you are making Election D, also complete lines 3a through 4c. (See page 3 of instructions.)

1a Enter your pro rata share of the ordinary earnings of the QEF .	**1a**		
b Enter the portion of line 1a that is included in income under section 551 or 951 or that may be excluded under section 1293(g)	**1b**		
c Subtract line 1b from line 1a. Enter this amount on your tax return as dividend income . . .		**1c**	
2a Enter your pro rata share of the total net capital gain of the QEF	**2a**		
b Enter the portion of line 2a that is included in income under section 551 or 951 or that may be excluded under section 1293(g)	**2b**		
c Subtract line 2b from line 2a. This amount is a net long-term capital gain. Enter this amount in Part II of the Schedule D used for your income tax return. (See page 5 of instructions.) . .		**2c**	
3a Add lines 1c and 2c		**3a**	
b Enter the total amount of cash and the fair market value of other property distributed or deemed distributed to you during the tax year of the QEF. (See page 5 of instructions.)	**3b**		
c Enter the portion of line 3a to the extent not already included in line 3b that is attributable to shares in the QEF that you disposed of, pledged, or otherwise transferred during the tax year . . .	**3c**		
d Add lines 3b and 3c		**3d**	
e Subtract line 3d from line 3a, and enter the difference (if zero or less, enter amount in brackets)		**3e**	
Important: *If line 3e is greater than zero, and no portion of line 1a or 2a is includible in income under section 551 or 951, you may make Election D with respect to the amount on line 3e.*			
4a Enter the total tax for total taxable income for the tax year . .	**4a**		
b Enter the total tax for the tax year determined without regard to the amount entered on line 3e	**4b**		
c Subtract line 4b from line 4a. **This is the deferred tax, the time for payment of which is extended by making Election D. See instructions.**		**4c**	

For Paperwork Reduction Act Notice, see page 7 of separate instructions.   Cat. No. 64174H   Form **8621** (Rev. 2-99)

Form 8621 (Rev. 2-99)   Page **2**

| **Part III** | **Income or (Loss) From Mark-to-Market Election** (See page 5 of instructions.) |

5 Enter the fair market value of your PFIC stock at the end of the tax year . . . . | **5** |
6 Enter your adjusted basis in the stock at the end of the tax year . . . . | **6** |
7 **Excess.** Subtract line 6 from line 5. If a gain, **stop here.** Include this amount as ordinary income on your tax return. If a loss, go to line 8 . . . . | **7** |
8 Enter any unreversed inclusions (as defined in section 1296(d)) . . . . | **8** |
9 Enter the smaller of line 7 or line 8. Include this amount as an ordinary loss on your tax return | **9** |

| **Part IV** | **Distributions and Disposition of Stock in a Section 1291 Fund** (See page 6 of instructions.) |

Complete a separate Part IV for each excess distribution.

10a Enter your total distributions from the PFIC during the current tax year. If the holding period of the PFIC stock began in the current tax year, this amount is dividend income to the extent there are accumulated earnings and profits . . . . | **10a** |

b Enter the total distributions (reduced by the portions of such distributions that were excess distributions but not included in income under section 1291(a)(1)(B)) made by the company for each of the 3 years preceding the current tax year (or if shorter, the portion of the shareholder's holding period before the current tax year). . . . . | **10b** |

c Divide line 10b by 3. (See instructions if the number of preceding tax years is less than 3.) . | **10c** |

d Multiply line 10c by 125%. Enter the lesser of line 10a or line 10d as a dividend on your income tax return | **10d** |

e Subtract line 10d from line 10a. This amount, if more than zero, is the total excess distribution. If zero or less and you did not dispose of stock during the tax year, **do not** complete the rest of Part IV. See instructions if you received more than one distribution during the current tax year . . . | **10e** |

f Enter gain or loss from the disposition of stock of a section 1291 fund or former section 1291 fund. If a gain, complete line 11. If a loss, show it in brackets and **do not** complete line 11 . | **10f** |

11a On an attached statement for each distribution and disposition, show your holding period for each share of stock or block of shares held. Allocate the excess distribution to each day in your holding period. Add all amounts that are allocated to days in each tax year.

b Enter the total of the amounts determined in line 11a that are allocable to the current tax year and tax years before the foreign corporation became a PFIC (pre-PFIC tax years). Enter these amounts on your income tax return as other income . . . . | **11b** |

c Enter the aggregate increases in tax (before credits) for each tax year in your holding period (other than the current tax year and pre-PFIC years). (See instructions.) . . . . | **11c** |

d Foreign tax credit. (See instructions.) . . . . | **11d** |

e Subtract line 11d from line 11c. Enter this amount on your income tax return as "additional tax." (See instructions.) . . . . | **11e** |

f Determine interest on each net increase in tax determined on line 11e using the rates and methods of section 6621. Enter the aggregate amount of interest here. (See instructions.). . | **11f** |

| **Part V** | **Status of Prior Year Section 1294 Elections and Termination of Section 1294 Elections** |

Complete a separate column for each outstanding election. Complete lines 9 and 10 only if there is a partial termination of the section 1294 election.

		(i)	(ii)	(iii)	(iv)	(v)	(vi)
1	Tax year of outstanding election						
2	Undistributed earnings to which the election relates						
3	Deferred tax						
4	Interest accrued on deferred tax (line 3) as of the filing date						
5	Event terminating election						
6	Earnings distributed or deemed distributed during the tax year						
7	Deferred tax due with this return						
8	Accrued interest due with this return.						
9	Deferred tax outstanding after partial termination of election						
10	Interest accrued after partial termination of election . .						

¶ 608

Chapter 7

Foreign Sales Corporations

¶ 701   INTRODUCTION

What Is an FSC?

In 1971, Congress enacted the domestic international sales corporation (or "DISC") provisions in an attempt to stimulate U.S. exports. Under these provisions, a U.S. exporter could defer the U.S. tax on a portion of its export profits by allocating those profits to a special type of domestic subsidiary known as a DISC. During the late 1970s and early 1980s, many of our major trading partners complained that the DISC provisions were an illegal export subsidy in violation of the General Agreement on Tariffs and Trade (or "GATT"). Congress settled the controversy in 1984 by largely terminating DISCs and enacting the foreign sales corporation (or "FSC") provisions.[1] A vestige of the DISC provisions, called an "interest-charge DISC," remains in the law, however.[2] Interest-charge DISCs are discussed at the end of this chapter.

The FSC provisions respond to the GATT controversy by requiring U.S. exporters to establish a foreign corporation that performs certain activities abroad in order to obtain preferential tax treatment. An FSC

---

[1] Code Secs. 921–927.   [2] Code Secs. 991–997.

operates as either a "buy-sell FSC," which purchases the U.S. parent's products for resale abroad, or a "commission FSC," which acts as a commission agent with respect to the parent's export sales. Thus, an FSC is a foreign subsidiary that conducts certain well-defined foreign management and marketing activities. The magnitude of these activities is typically negligible, however, and, therefore, the FSC need not significantly disrupt the exporter's normal business operations.

The GATT controversy regarding the legality of this export incentive erupted again when in 1997 the European Union filed a formal complaint with the World Trade Organization (WTO), asserting that the FSC regime (like the DISC regime that preceded it) was an illegal export subsidy in violation of GATT. In October 1999, the WTO released its final report on the European Union's complaint, ruling that the FSC regime was an illegal export subsidy, and calling for its elimination by October 1, 2000. At the time of this writing, U.S. lawmakers have not yet decided how to respond to this latest GATT controversy.

A domestic corporation that establishes an FSC allocates a portion of its qualified export profits to the FSC through either intercompany sales or the payment of a commission. A prespecified portion of the FSC's profits are exempt from U.S. tax. In addition, a domestic corporation can generally repatriate the FSC's exempt income free of U.S. tax. The net effect of this arrangement is that a portion of a domestic corporation's export profits are permanently excluded from U.S. tax at both the FSC and U.S. shareholder levels. The amount of the exclusion usually is 15% of the net income from qualifying export sales.

In addition to the regular FSC, Congress also created the "small FSC" to make it easier for smaller U.S. exporters to obtain the tax benefits of an FSC. Small FSCs are subject to fewer qualification requirements, but are limited in terms of the amount of export sales for which the FSC exclusion is available.

Who Should Use an FSC?

Only domestic corporations are entitled to a special dividends-received deduction for dividends distributions from an FSC.[3] As a consequence, individuals generally will not own an FSC since the lack of a dividends-received deduction effectively denies the taxpayer the FSC benefit. The same is true for partnerships, S corporations, limited liability companies, and other conduit entities whose shareholders or owners are individuals. Not all domestic corporations will find it cost-effective to operate an FSC, however. For reasons discussed later in this

---

[3] Code Sec. 245(c)(1)(A).

chapter, domestic corporations that are most likely to benefit from an FSC are those which exhibit the following characteristics:

(i)   have a high volume of export sales,

(ii) enjoy a high profit margin on their export sales,

(iii) produce their products in the United States,

(iv) are not in a net operating loss position, and

(v)   do not have a binding foreign tax credit limitation in the general limitation category.

Domestic corporations that are less likely to benefit from an FSC are those that:

(i)   have a low volume of export sales,

(ii) have a low profit margin on their export sales,

(iii) have a high percentage of import content in their product,

(iv) are in a net operating loss position for U.S. tax purposes, and

(v)   have excess foreign tax credits in the general limitation basket.

¶ 702   TAX BENEFITS OF AN FSC

Qualified Exports Sales

Foreign trading gross receipts. Only foreign trade income qualifies for the FSC exclusion.[4] Foreign trade income means the gross income of the FSC attributable to foreign trading gross receipts.[5] An FSC has foreign trading gross receipts only if the FSC meets certain foreign management and foreign economic processes requirements that are discussed later in this chapter.[6] Assuming these requirements are met, foreign trading gross receipts primarily include gross receipts from:

(i)   the sale, exchange, or other disposition of export property,

(ii) the lease or rental of export property for use by the lessee outside the United States,

(iii) services that are related and subsidiary to the sale, exchange, lease, rental, or other disposition of export property (e.g., warranty, repair, maintenance, and installation services), and

(iv) engineering and architectural services for construction projects located (or proposed for location) outside the United States.[7]

---

[4] Code Sec. 921(a).

[5] Code Sec. 923(b). Foreign trade income is the FSC's gross profit from inventory sales, in the case of a buy-sell FSC, or its commission income, in the case of a commission FSC. Temp. Reg. § 1.923-1T(a).

[6] Code Sec. 924(b)(1).

[7] Code Sec. 924(a) and Temp. Reg. § 1.924(a)-1T(a)–(f). In the case of a commission FSC, gross receipts means the gross receipts of the FSC's

Therefore, gross receipts for most services do not qualify as foreign trading gross receipts. The only exceptions are those outlined in (iii) and (iv) above.

Certain items are specifically excluded from foreign trading gross receipts, including gross receipts from:

(i)   export property or services that are for ultimate use in the United States,

(ii) export property or services that are for use by the United States, or any instrumentality thereof, and such use is required by law or regulation,

(iii) a transaction that is accomplished by a subsidy granted by the United States or any instrumentality thereof,

(iv) another FSC which is a member of the same controlled group as the FSC, and

(v)   investment income or carrying charges.[8]

For this purpose, investment income primarily includes dividends, interest, royalties, certain rents, and gains from certain security and commodity transactions.[9] Carrying charges include any stated or unstated interest charges.[10]

Export property. A sale or lease must involve export property in order to qualify as foreign trading gross receipts. Export property is property that satisfies the following three requirements:

(i)   *U.S. manufactured test*—The property must be manufactured, produced, grown, or extracted in the United States by a person other than an FSC.[11]

(ii) *Foreign content test*—Not more than 50% of the fair market value of the property may be attributable to articles imported into the United States.[12]

(iii) *Foreign destination test*—The property must be held primarily for sale, lease, or rental in the ordinary course of business for direct use, consumption, or disposition outside the United States.[13] This destination test is satisfied only if the ultimate

---

(Footnote Continued)

related supplier (e.g., its U.S. parent corporation) on which the commissions arose. Code Sec. 927(b)(2).

[8] Code Sec. 924(f) and Temp. Reg. § 1.924(a)-1T(g).

[9] Code Sec. 927(c).

[10] Unstated interest is present if any part of the sales proceeds (or service or rental payment) is paid after the end of the normal payment period, which generally is 60 days. Reg. § 1.927(d)-1(a).

[11] Code Sec. 927(a)(1)(A). Property which is first produced in the United States, but is then sent outside the United States for further manufacturing

or processing, is considered to be produced in the United States only if the property is reimported into the United States for further manufacturing or processing prior to the final export sale. Temp. Reg. § 1.927(a)-1T(c). The definition of the United States for this purpose includes Puerto Rico. Code Sec. 927(d)(3).

[12] Code Sec. 927(a)(1)(C) and Temp. Reg. § 1.927(a)-1T(e). For this purpose, the fair market value of any article imported into the United States is its appraised value for custom purposes.

[13] Code Sec. 927(a)(1)(B).

delivery point for the property is a point located outside the United States.[14] The type of person purchasing the good (U.S. or foreign) is irrelevant. For example, if a U.S. manufacturer sells goods to a U.S.-based retailer which then resells the goods at retail outlets located abroad, the original sale by the U.S. manufacturer satisfies the foreign destination test.[15] Therefore, to the extent it is administratively feasible, taxpayers should not overlook sales to U.S. companies where the ultimate use or disposition of the property is outside the United States.

The following items are specifically excluded from the definition of export property:

(i) patents, inventions, models, designs, formulas, processes, copyrights, goodwill, trademarks, trade brands, franchises, and other like property, but not including copyrighted films, tapes, records, or similar reproductions for commercial or home use, and copyrighted articles, such as a book or mass market computer software, that are exported without the right to reproduce it for external use (however, see exception for computer software, below);[16]

(ii) oil or gas, or any primary products derived thereof, such as crude oil, motor fuel, lubricating oils, and natural gas;[17]

(iii) any unprocessed timber which is a softwood;[18]

(iv) products determined to be in short supply, and products the export of which has been officially prohibited or curtailed to protect the domestic economy;[19] and

(v) property leased or rented by an FSC for use by an affiliated corporation.[20]

In an effort to extend the FSC tax benefit to software companies, in the Taxpayer Relief Act of 1997, Congress amended the law such that computer software could be treated as export property, even if the sale or license agreement permits reproduction of the software abroad.[21] This provision applies to gross receipts attributable to periods after December 31, 1997, in tax years ending after such date. According to the Conference Report to the 1997 Act, in the case of multi-year licenses, the FSC benefit is available for gross receipts attributable to the period of the license after December 31, 1997. Moreover, in administering the new rule, the House Report to the 1997 Act indicates

---

[14] Temp. Reg. § 1.927(a)-1T(d)(1)(i) and (d)(2).

[15] Temp. Reg. § 1.927(a)-1T(d)(4)(iv).

[16] Code Sec. 927(a)(2)(B) and Temp. Reg. § 1.927(a)-1T(f)(3).

[17] Code Sec. 927(a)(2)(C) and Temp. Reg. § 1.927(a)-1T(g).

[18] Code Sec. 927(a)(2)(E).

[19] Code Sec. 927(a)(2)(D), (a)(3) and Temp. Reg. § 1.927(a)-1T(h) and (i).

[20] Code Sec. 927(a)(2)(A) and Temp. Reg. § 1.927(a)-1T(f)(2).

[21] Code Sec. 927(a)(2)(B).

that the term "software" is to be interpreted broadly in order to accommodate future technological changes and preserve the FSC benefit now extended by the Act to computer software transactions with rights to reproduce software. In addition, the House Report specifically stated that no inference should be drawn from this provision as to whether, prior to the effective date of the Act, computer software licensed for reproduction abroad could qualify as export property.

Allocating Profits to an FSC

The mechanism for allocating export profits to an FSC is the intercompany sales price, in the case of a buy-sell FSC, or the commission, in the case of a commission FSC. A U.S. exporter determines the amount of taxable income allocable to an FSC using one of following three transfer pricing methods:

(i)   1.83% of gross receipts method,

(ii) 23% of combined taxable income method, or

(iii) Code Sec. 482 method.

The taxpayer is free to use the method that allocates the greatest amount of income to the FSC.

Under the 1.83% of gross receipts method, the taxable income allocable to the FSC equals 1.83% of the foreign trading gross receipts derived from export sales made by the FSC or the FSC's related supplier.[22] An FSC's related supplier usually is its U.S. parent corporation.[23]

> **Example 7.1:** USAco, a domestic corporation, owns and operates a commission FSC. USAco makes an export sale which generates $10,000 of foreign trading gross receipts. Under the 1.83% of gross receipts method, the amount of taxable income allocable to the FSC with respect to this sale is $183 [1.83% × $10,000].

The amount of income allocable to an FSC under the 1.83% of gross receipts method cannot exceed two times the amount allowed under the 23% of combined taxable income method.[24]

Under the 23% of combined taxable income method, the taxable income allocable to the FSC equals 23% of the combined taxable income that the FSC and its related supplier derive from foreign trading gross receipts.[25]

---

[22] Code Sec. 925(a)(1).

[23] More generally, a related supplier is a related party which directly supplies to an FSC any property or services which the FSC disposes of in a transaction producing foreign trading gross receipts, or a related party which uses the FSC as a commission agent in the disposition of any property or services producing foreign trading gross receipts. An FSC may have different related suppliers with respect to different transactions. Temp. Reg. § 1.927(d)-2T(a).

[24] Code Sec. 925(d).

[25] Code Sec. 925(a)(2).

Example 7.2: USAco, a domestic corporation, owns and operates an FSC. The combined taxable income of USAco and the FSC from an export sale is $1,000. Under the 23% of combined taxable income method, the amount of taxable income allocable to the FSC with respect to this sale is $230 [23% × $1,000].

Combined taxable income equals the excess of foreign trading gross receipts over the total costs of the FSC and the related supplier, which include deductions that are definitely related to export sales (e.g., cost of goods sold) and a ratable portion of any deductions that are not definitely related to any specific class of gross income (e.g., interest expense).[26]

Under the Code Sec. 482 method, the taxable income allocable to the FSC equals an amount based on the use of arm's-length transfer prices for transactions between the FSC and the related supplier.[27] As discussed in Chapter 5, under an arm's-length transfer pricing approach, the amount of taxable income allocable to an FSC is determined by the functions performed and the risks assumed by the FSC with respect to export sales. The more functions an FSC performs and the greater the risks it assumes, the more income it should earn. In most cases, however, an FSC's activities with respect to export sales are negligible. Therefore, under the Code Sec. 482 method, generally only a small amount of taxable income is allocable to the FSC. It is for this reason that Congress enacted the 1.83% of gross receipts and 23% of combined taxable income methods (the so-called "administrative pricing methods"), which make it possible for a U.S. exporter to allocate a significant portion of its export profits to an FSC.

Example 7.3: USAco, a domestic corporation, makes an export sale that generates $1 million of foreign trading gross receipts. USAco's FSC does not perform any significant functions with respect to the export sale. The combined taxable income of USAco and the FSC from this export sale is $100,000. The amount of taxable income allocable to the FSC is $23,000 [23% × $100,000] under the 23% of combined taxable income method, $18,300 [1.83% × $1 million] under the 1.83% of gross receipts method, and a insignificant amount under the Code Sec. 482 method. Therefore, USAco uses the 23% of combined taxable income method and allocates $23,000 of taxable income to the FSC. The remaining $77,000 [$100,000 − $23,000] of taxable income from the export sale is taxed to USAco.

The FSC transfer pricing methods are all designed to effect an allocation of "net" taxable income to the FSC. Therefore, if the FSC

---

[26] Temp. Reg. § 1.925(a)-1T(c)(6).   [27] Code Sec. 925(a)(3).

incurs expenses related to an export sale, the intercompany sales price or commission is grossed-up by the amount of these expenses. For example, if the FSC transfer pricing methods indicate that $100,000 of net income is allocable to a commission FSC that incurs $15,000 of expenses, the U.S. exporter allocates to the FSC a commission of $115,000 in order to give it a net profit of $100,000.

The 23% of combined taxable income method allocates more income to the FSC than the 1.83% of gross receipts method whenever the profit margin on export sales exceeds 7.96% (23% of a 7.96% profit margin is 1.83%). Consequently, the 1.83% of gross receipts method is aimed at high-volume, low-margin taxpayers, such as companies in agricultural and other commodity-type industries.

Techniques for increasing the amount of taxable income allocated to the FSC, including the use of special marginal costing rules and transaction grouping, are discussed later in this chapter.

Taxation of an FSC

A portion of an FSC's foreign trade income is exempt from U.S. tax.[28] The exempt portion varies with whether the FSC's U.S. shareholder is a corporate or noncorporate taxpayer, and whether the taxpayer uses the administrative pricing rules or the Code Sec. 482 method to compute the FSC's income. The typical arrangement is a corporate shareholder that uses the administrative pricing rules to compute the FSC's income. In this situation, the exempt portion of an FSC's foreign trade income is 15/23 (65.22%).[29] The other 8/23 (34.78%) of foreign trade income is treated as U.S.-source income effectively connected with a U.S. trade or business conducted through a permanent establishment.[30] This means that the FSC's nonexempt foreign trade income is subject to current year U.S. tax at the regular U.S. corporate tax rates.

> **Example 7.4:** The facts are the same as in Example 7.3. Of the $23,000 of taxable income allocated to the FSC, $15,000 [15/23 × $23,000] is exempt from U.S. tax, and the remaining $8,000 [8/23 × $23,000] is subject to U.S. tax at the regular corporate tax rates.

---

[28] Code Sec. 921(a).

[29] The exempt portion is 30% for corporate shareholders that use the Code Sec. 482 pricing rules, 16/23 for noncorporate shareholders that use the administrative pricing rules, and 32% for noncorporate shareholders that use the Code Sec. 482 pricing rules. Code Secs. 923(a) and 291(a)(4). Special rules apply to sales of agricultural or horticultural products by a cooperative and sales of military property. Code Sec. 923(a)(4) and (5), and Temp. Reg. § 1.923-1T(b)(2) and (3).

[30] Code Sec. 921(d). This characterization rule does not apply if the taxpayer uses the Code Sec. 482 method to compute the FSC's income, in which case the income's source (U.S. versus foreign) and character (whether or not it is effectively connected with the conduct of a U.S. trade or business) are determined under the general rules for taxing foreign corporations. Temp. Reg. § 1.921-3T(a)(2)(iii).

In sum, $85,000 of USAco's $100,000 in combined taxable income from the export sale is subject to U.S. taxation ($77,000 taxed to USAco and $8,000 taxed to the FSC), and the remaining $15,000 is exempt from U.S. tax at both the FSC and U.S. shareholder levels.

Any carrying charges or investment income received by an FSC also is deemed to be income effectively connected with a U.S. trade or business conducted through a permanent establishment.[31] The taxation of any other income of the FSC is determined under the general rules for determining the source and character of a foreign corporation's income.[32]

In computing an FSC's U.S. taxable income, the FSC's deductions are first allocated and apportioned between the FSC's foreign trade income and non-foreign trade income. Any deductions allocated and apportioned to foreign trade income are then allocated on a proportionate basis between exempt and nonexempt foreign trade income.[33] These rules force taxpayers to allocate some of the FSC's expenses against its exempt foreign trade income, which is important since any deductions allocated to exempt income provide no U.S. tax savings.

The FSC's U.S. tax liability is determined by applying the applicable corporate tax rate to the net amount of nonexempt foreign trade income, plus any investment income, carrying charges, and other taxable income. An FSC that is structured as an 80% or more owned subsidiary of a domestic corporation (which is the typical structure), must share the corporate low-tax brackets of 15%, 25%, and 34% with the other members of its controlled group.[34]

An FSC can claim neither a credit nor a deduction for any foreign taxes paid on foreign trade income.[35] Therefore, U.S. exporters generally incorporate their FSCs in countries that impose little or no tax on the FSC (including no withholding taxes on dividends paid by the FSC to its U.S. shareholders). Otherwise, the U.S. tax benefits of the FSC may be partially or wholly offset by foreign tax costs. Popular FSC locations have historically included the U.S. Virgin Islands, Guam, and Barbados.

In terms of administrative requirements, an FSC must report its income and compute its tax on Form 1120-FSC, U.S. Income Tax Return of an FSC. (Form 1120-FSC is reproduced in the appendix to this chapter.) The taxable year of an FSC must be the same as that of

---

[31] Code Sec. 921(d). The source of such income is determined under the general source of income rules. Temp. Reg. § 1.921-3T(a)(2)(iv).

[32] Temp. Reg. § 1.921-3T(a)(2)(v).

[33] Code Sec. 921(b) and Temp. Reg. § 1.921-3T(b).

[34] Temp. Reg. § 1.921-3T(j). See also Form 1120-FSC, Schedule J.

[35] Code Secs. 275(a)(4)(B) and 906(b)(5). On the other hand, the general rules for claiming a deduction or a foreign tax credit apply to any foreign income taxes related to an FSC's investment income, carrying charges, and other income. See Code Secs. 164(a) and 906, and Temp. Reg. § 1.921-3T(d)(2)(i).

its principal shareholder.[36] In addition, an FSC that expects its U.S. tax liability for the year to be at least $500 must make quarterly estimated tax payments.[37]

Taxation of U.S. Shareholders

General rules. As discussed in the previous section, a portion of an FSC's foreign trade income (generally 15/23) is exempt from U.S. tax. This exemption would only be temporary, however, if the United States were to tax the FSC's U.S. shareholders on dividend distributions received from the FSC. Therefore, Congress enacted a special dividends-received deduction to make the FSC exemption a permanent exclusion. Under this provision, a domestic corporation can claim a 100% dividends-received deduction for the receipt of a distribution by an FSC of earnings and profits attributable to either exempt or nonexempt foreign trade income.[38] A domestic corporation also can claim an 80% or 70% dividends-received deduction for a dividend paid out of other earnings of the FSC which the United States has already taxed as income effectively connected with the conduct of a U.S. trade or business.[39]

A dividends-received deduction is available only to a domestic corporation. Therefore, any U.S. citizen or resident alien who owns an FSC directly, or indirectly through an interest in a partnership, S corporation, limited liability company, or other conduit entity, is subject to U.S. tax on the full amount of any dividends received from the FSC. This shareholder-level U.S. tax substantially eliminates the benefit of using an FSC (as opposed to direct export sales) for noncorporate taxpayers. As a consequence, typically only domestic corporations establish an FSC.

Because a domestic corporation can claim a 100% dividends-received deduction with respect to a distribution of foreign trade income, it cannot also claim a deemed paid foreign tax credit for the foreign income taxes related to those earnings and profits. The same prohibition applies to the direct foreign tax credit for any foreign withholding taxes imposed on distributions of foreign trade income.[40] However, direct and deemed paid foreign tax credits are available with respect to distributions of earnings and profits attributable to the FSC's non-foreign trade income.[41]

---

[36] Code Sec. 441(h)(1).

[37] Temp. Reg. § 1.921-3T(f) and Code Sec. 6655.

[38] Code Sec. 245(c)(1)(A).

[39] Code Sec. 245(c)(1)(B). Reg. § 1.926(a)-1(b)(1) provides an ordering rule for tracing an FSC's dividend distributions to different types of earnings and profits.

[40] Code Sec. 901(h).

[41] Temp. Reg. § 1.921-3T(d)(2)(ii) and (iii).

FSC dividends may increase a shareholder's alternative minimum tax liability, however, since 15/23 of the FSC dividend amount is added back as an adjusted current earnings adjustment.[42]

Taxpayers in excess credit positions. There is a downside to having an FSC if the related supplier has excess foreign tax credits in the general limitation category. An FSC can exacerbate this excess credit problem by reducing the amount of low-tax foreign-source export profits assigned to the general limitation category. This occurs for two reasons. First, when a U.S. shareholder repatriates export profits that were allocated to the FSC, the dividend is assigned to a separate limitation category for distributions from an FSC.[43] This separate limitation category prevents taxpayers from blending export profits routed through an FSC (which tend to be subject to little or no foreign taxes) with any high-taxed foreign business profits assigned to the general limitation basket. Second, a special sourcing rule applies to the U.S. exporter's foreign trading gross receipts which are not allocated to the FSC. Generally, a U.S. manufacturer sources its export profits using the 50-50 method.[44] Assuming the taxpayer's foreign assets are insignificant and it passes title abroad on export sales, the 50-50 method characterizes roughly 50% of the manufacturer's export profits as foreign-source income. However, if the taxpayer operates an FSC, the foreign-source portion of the combined taxable income of the FSC and its related supplier is limited to 25%.[45] This reduction in foreign-source income also can exacerbate a U.S. exporter's excess credit problem.

Comprehensive Example

USAco, a domestic corporation, manufactures products at its U.S. factory for sale in the United States and abroad. During the current year, USAco's foreign trading gross receipts were $4 million, and the related cost of goods sold was $3 million. USAco has a commission FSC that is responsible for certain foreign marketing activities. The FSC hires USAco to perform these activities on its behalf, and reimburses USAco for its costs. USAco's selling expenses related to export sales were $195,000, which includes $15,000 of expenses for activities performed as the FSC's agent. USAco also has $40,000 of administrative expenses and $60,000 of interest expense allocable to export sales. In addition to the $15,000 paid to USAco, the FSC incurs $5,000 of administrative expenses during the year.

---

[42] Reg. § 1.56(g)-1(d)(2).

[43] Code Sec. 904(d)(1)(H).

[44] Reg. § 1.863-3(b)(1).

[45] Code Sec. 927(e)(1); Rev. Rul. 89-93, 1989-2 CB 133; and Reg. § 1.927(e)-1.

The maximum amount of taxable allocable to the FSC under the 23% of combined taxable income and 1.83% of gross receipts methods is $161,000, computed as follows.

23% of combined taxable income method

Foreign trading gross receipts	$	4,000,000
Cost of goods sold	−	3,000,000
Combined gross profit	$	1,000,000
USAco's allocable selling expenses ($195,000 − $15,000 reimbursement from the FSC)	−	180,000
USAco's allocable interest expense	−	60,000
USAco's allocable administrative expenses	−	40,000
FSC's selling expenses	−	15,000
FSC's administrative expenses	−	5,000
Combined taxable income	$	700,000
Percentage allocable to FSC	×	23%
Profit allocable to FSC	$	161,000

1.83% of gross receipts method

Export sales	$	4,000,000
Percentage allocable to FSC	×	1.83%
Profit allocable to FSC	$	73,200

USAco pays the FSC a commission equal to the maximum profit allocable to the FSC, grossed-up by the selling and administrative expenses incurred by the FSC, as follows.

FSC commission

Profit allocated to FSC	$	161,000
Gross-up for FSC's expenses [$15,000 + $5,000]	+	20,000
Commission	$	181,000

After taking into account the FSC's commission income and its selling and administrative expenses, the FSC is deemed to have income effectively connected with a U.S. trade or business equal to $56,000, computed as follows:

FSC's U.S. taxable income

Commission income	$	181,000
Selling expenses	−	15,000
Administrative expenses	−	5,000
FSC's income		161,000
Taxable portion	×	8/23
FSC's taxable income	$	56,000

After taking into account the commission paid to the FSC, USAco's taxable income from export sales is $539,000, computed as follows:

USAco's U.S. taxable income

Export sales	$ 4,000,000
Cost of goods sold	− 3,000,000
Gross profit on export sales....................	$ 1,000,000
Allocable selling expenses ($195,000 − $15,000 reimbursement from the FSC)	− 180,000
Allocable interest expenses	− 60,000
Allocable administrative expenses	− 40,000
Commission paid to FSC......................	− 181,000
USAco's taxable income	$ 539,000

In sum, $595,000 of the $700,000 in combined taxable income from export sales is subject to U.S. taxation, $539,000 to USAco and $56,000 to the FSC. The remaining $105,000 of combined taxable income (or 15% of the total export profits of $700,000) is exempt from U.S. taxation. Assuming a 35% U.S. corporate tax rate, the FSC saves USAco $36,075 in taxes [35% × $105,000].

The following table summarizes the accounting for the transactions entered into by USAco and its FSC.

Transaction	Effect on USAco	Effect on FSC	Net effect
Export sales	$4,000,000	n.a.	$4,000,000
Cost of goods sold	<$3,000,000>	n.a.	<$3,000,000>
USAco's selling expenses	<$ 195,000>	n.a.	<$ 195,000>
USAco's administrative expenses	<$ 60,000>	n.a.	<$ 60,000>
USAco's interest expense	<$ 40,000>	n.a.	<$ 40,000>
FSC reimburses USAco for selling expenses	$ 15,000	<$ 15,000>	None
FSC commission	<$ 181,000>	$ 181,000	None
FSC's administrative expenses	n.a.	<$ 5,000>	<$ 5,000>
Net profit	$ 539,000	$ 161,000	$ 700,000

¶ 702

¶ 703   ADMINISTRATIVE REQUIREMENTS

Background

There are numerous administrative requirements for organizing and operating an FSC. These requirements are designed to locate the presence and management of the FSC outside the United States and to ensure that some sales activities take place outside the United States. Congress enacted the FSC administrative requirements to give an FSC the minimal amount of substance needed to convince our trading partners that an FSC is not an illegal export subsidy in violation of GATT. Nevertheless, operating an FSC need not significantly disrupt the exporter's normal business operations. In addition, because of the rather novel nature of the administrative requirements, U.S. exporters often hire an FSC management company to ensure that these requirements are satisfied.

Definition of an FSC

Whether an entity qualifies as an FSC is determined on a year-to-year basis. To be considered an FSC, an entity must satisfy the following 10 requirements:

(i)   the FSC must be a corporation;[46]

(ii)   the FSC must be organized under the laws of a qualified foreign country or an eligible U.S. possession.[47] Popular FSC locations have historically included the U.S. Virgin Islands, Guam, and Barbados;

(iii)   the FSC must not have more than 25 shareholders at any time during the year;[48]

(iv)   the FSC must not have any preferred stock outstanding at any time during the year;[49]

(v)   the FSC must maintain an office located outside the United States at all times during the taxable year. The office need not be located in the FSC's country of incorporation;[50]

(vi)   the FSC must maintain a set of permanent books of account, including invoices, at its foreign office;[51]

(vii)   the FSC must maintain at a location within the United States records sufficient to substantiate the income, de-

---

[46] Code Sec. 922(a) and Reg. § 1.922-1(c).

[47] Code Sec. 922(a)(1)(A) and Reg. § 1.922-1(d) and (e). Notice 84-15, 1984-2 CB 474, provides a list of qualifying countries.

[48] Code Sec. 922(a)(1)(B) and Reg. § 1.922-1(f).

[49] Code Sec. 922(a)(1)(C) and Reg. § 1.922-1(g).

[50] Code Sec. 922(a)(1)(D)(i) and Reg. § 1.922-1(h). In the case of a newly organized FSC, 30 days may elapse between the first day for which the FSC election is effective and the time an office is established.

[51] Code Sec. 922(a)(1)(D)(ii) and Reg. § 1.922-1(i).

ductions, and other U.S. income tax attributes of the
FSC;[52]

(viii)   at all times during the taxable year, the FSC must have at
least one director who is not a U.S. resident;[53]

(ix)   the FSC cannot be a member of a controlled group which,
at any time during the taxable year, had as another
member a DISC; and [54]

(x)   the FSC must make a timely election to be treated as an
FSC.[55] The election is made by filing Form 8279, Election
to be Treated as an FSC or as a Small FSC.[56] (Form 8279
is reproduced in the appendix to this chapter.)

Foreign Management Requirements

The FSC benefit is available only for a taxable year in which the
FSC is managed from outside the United States.[57] To meet this test, the
FSC must satisfy all of the following requirements for the taxable year:

(i)   all board of directors and shareholder meetings of the FSC
take place outside the United States,

(ii)   at all times during the taxable year, the FSC maintains its
principal bank account in either a foreign country which
meets certain exchange of information requirements or in an
eligible U.S. possession, and

(iii)   the FSC disburses all its dividends, legal and accounting fees,
and the salaries of its officers and directors out of its foreign
bank account(s).[58]

FSCs typically employ FSC management companies to satisfy these
requirements.[59]

Foreign Economic Processes Requirements

The FSC benefit is available with respect to a particular transaction only if the economic processes with respect to that transaction take
place outside the United States.[60] To meet this requirement, the FSC
must satisfy a sales participation test and a foreign direct costs test.
Both tests are imposed on a transaction-by-transaction basis.[61] How-

---

[52] Code Secs. 922(a)(1)(D)(iii) and 6001.

[53] Code Sec. 922(a)(1)(E) and Reg. § 1.922-1(j). The nonresident director can be a U.S. citizen.

[54] Code Sec. 922(a)(1)(F). This rule prevents a tax-payer from obtaining the benefits of both an FSC and an interest-charge DISC within the same taxable year.

[55] Code Sec. 922(a)(2).

[56] Temp. Reg. § 1.921-1T(b)(1). Assuming the election is being made for a new corporation's first taxa-ble year, the election must be made within 90 days

after the beginning of that taxable year. In the case of an election for any other taxable year, the election must be made during the 90-day period preceding the first day of that taxable year.

[57] Code Sec. 924(b)(1)(A).

[58] Code Sec. 924(c).

[59] For more details regarding the foreign manage-ment requirements, see Reg. § 1.924(c)-1.

[60] Code Sec. 924(b)(1)(B).

[61] Code Sec. 924(d)(1).

ever, special grouping rules make it easier to satisfy this requirement by permitting taxpayers to qualify all of the transactions within a group by qualifying only a limited number of transactions within that group. Transactions can be grouped on the basis of contracts, customers, products, or product lines.[62]

Under the sales participation test, the FSC must participate outside the United States in at least one of three selling activities with respect to the transaction: solicitation (other than advertising), negotiation, or the making of the sales contract.[63] An FSC can hire its related supplier or an unrelated service provider to perform these functions as the FSC's agent.[64] Having the FSC participate in solicitation is a popular choice because it tends to be the least disruptive to the U.S. exporter's normal foreign marketing activities.[65]

Under the foreign direct costs test, the FSC must incur outside the United States 50% or more of the total direct costs associated with the transaction.[66] For this purpose, direct costs include the costs of the following five activities: [67]

(i)   advertising and sales promotion,

(ii) processing customer orders and arranging for delivery of the export property,

(iii) transporting export products to the customer,

(iv) determining and transmitting a final invoice or statement of account and the receipt of payment, and

(v)   assuming credit risk.

An FSC also can satisfy the foreign direct costs test by incurring 85% or more of the direct costs in each of two activities.[68] The 85% option allows taxpayers to track only two categories of costs, rather than five. As with the sales participation test, an FSC can hire another person to perform these functions as the FSC's agent.[69]

The foreign economic processes requirements also impact whether a taxpayer can use the administrative pricing rules to allocate profits to an FSC. Specifically, in order to use the administrative pricing rules, an FSC must perform all three activities prescribed by the sales participation test and incur costs in all five categories under the foreign direct costs test.[70] For this purpose, however, the FSC need not perform the requisite activities outside the United States, and the FSC can hire another person to perform the activities as the FSC's agent.[71]

---

[62] Code Sec. 927(d)(2)(B) and Reg. § 1.924(d)-1(c)(5) and (e).
[63] Code Sec. 924(d)(1)(A).
[64] Reg. § 1.924(d)-1(b)(1).
[65] For a definition of solicitation, see Reg. § 1.924(d)-1(c)(2).
[66] Code Sec. 924(d)(1)(B).
[67] Code Sec. 924(e).
[68] Code Sec. 924(d)(2).
[69] Reg. § 1.924(d)-1(b)(1).
[70] Code Sec. 925(c).
[71] Temp. Reg. § 1.925(a)-1T(b)(2)(ii).

Special Rules for Small Businesses

When enacting the FSC legislation, Congress realized that the foreign management and economic processes requirements might make FSCs impractical for smaller exporters. As a consequence, Congress created the "small FSC." The advantage of a small FSC is that it can earn foreign trading gross receipts without meeting the foreign management and foreign economic processes requirements.[72] The disadvantage of a small FSC is that no more than $5 million of foreign trading gross receipts can be taken into account each year in determining exempt foreign trade income. However, the taxpayer may include in the $5 million its most profitable export sales.[73] Any foreign trading gross receipts of a small FSC in excess of $5 million are taxed as nonexempt foreign trade income.[74]

A small FSC must meet the 10 definitional requirements for FSC status discussed earlier in this chapter.[75] This includes making a timely election to be treated as a small FSC.[76] In order to use the administrative pricing rules, a small FSC also must meet the same foreign economic processes requirements as a regular FSC.[77]

Another way to reduce the administrative cost of operating an FSC is for a group of up to 25 exporters to operate a "shared FSC."[78] A shared FSC can be a regular FSC or a small FSC. A properly structured shared FSC retains the confidentiality of each exporter's financial records and customer lists, and does not entangle one exporter's operations with those of other group members. Instead, each shareholder in the shared FSC maintains a separate account for its transactions and operates its export business completely separate from the other group members.

¶ 704 MAXIMIZING THE FSC BENEFIT

Transaction-by-Transaction Pricing

Taxpayers can make an annual election to compute the FSC profit on the basis of products, product line groupings, or a transaction-by-transaction basis.[79] Transactional pricing allows a taxpayer to simultaneously use the 23% of combined taxable income method for high-margin sales (i.e., those with profit margins greater than 7.96%), the 1.83% of gross receipts method for low-margin sales, and eliminate export sales made at a loss from the computation.

---

[72] Code Sec. 924(b)(2)(A).

[73] Code Sec. 924(b)(2)(B)(i) and (ii). It is not possible to circumvent the $5 million limitation by creating multiple small FSCs. Code Sec. 924(b)(2)(B)(iii).

[74] Temp. Reg. § 1.924(a)-1T(j).

[75] Code Sec. 922(a)(1).

[76] Code Sec. 922(b)(1).

[77] Reg. § 1.921-2(b), Question 4.

[78] Code Secs. 927(g) and 922(a)(1)(B).

[79] Code Sec. 927(d)(2)(B) and Temp. Reg. § 1.925(a)-1T(c)(8)(i).

Example 7.5: USAco, a domestic corporation, owns and operates a commission FSC. USAco exports domestically produced red and white wines. The annual gross receipts and combined taxable income from these export sales are as follows:

	Gross receipts	Combined taxable income	Profit margin
Red wine	$ 500,000	$100,000	20%
White wine	$ 500,000	$ 20,000	4%
Total export sales .	$1,000,000	$120,000	12%

Through product grouping, USAco can use the 23% of combined taxable income method for sales of red wine, which allocates $23,000 [23% × $100,000] of taxable income to the FSC. At the same time, USAco can use the 1.83% of gross receipts method for sales of white wine, which allocates $9,150 [1.83% × $500,000] of taxable income to the FSC. The total amount of taxable income allocated to the FSC is $32,150 [$23,000 + $9,150].

Taxpayers have considerable flexibility in grouping. A taxpayer's product or product line groupings will be accepted if they conform to recognized trade or industry usage, or the two-digit major groups (or inferior classifications) of Standard Industrial Classification codes.[80] The taxpayer's groupings for purposes of computing combined taxable income can be different from those used for purposes of satisfying the foreign economic processes requirements.[81] In addition, within the same taxable year, a taxpayer can use grouping for one product line and the transaction-by-transaction method for another product line.[82] The availability of specialized software designed to optimize the FSC profit generated by transactional pricing (as well as marginal costing and expense allocations, as discussed below) has greatly enhanced the ability of companies to take advantage of these planning techniques.[83]

Marginal Costing

A second technique for increasing the benefits of an FSC is marginal costing.[84] Under the general rule, combined taxable income of an FSC and its related supplier equals the excess of the foreign trading gross receipts over the total direct and indirect costs of the FSC and its

---

[80] Temp. Reg. § 1.925(a)-1T(c)(8)(ii). Special grouping rules apply in the case of military property and agricultural and horticultural products sold by a cooperative. Temp. Reg. § 1.925(a)-1T(c)(8)(iv) and (v).

[81] Temp. Reg. § 1.925(a)-1T(c)(8)(viii).

[82] Temp. Reg. § 1.925(a)-1T(c)(8)(iii).

[83] In March 1998, the Treasury issued Temp. Treas. Reg. § 1.925(a)-1T in an attempt to limit planning in this area. These regulations prohibit taxpayers from changing their grouping method via an amended return for tax years beginning after December 31, 1997. As a result, FSC grouping positions cannot be changed after the due date (including extensions) of the original tax return for such years, and taxpayers must maximize their FSC benefits on their originally filed tax returns. These regulations also impose a deadline for taxpayers to file amended returns claiming re-determined FSC benefits for tax years beginning prior to January 1, 1998 (see Notice 99-24, 1999-20 IRB 74).

[84] Code Sec. 925(b)(2) and Temp. Reg. § 1.925(b)-1T(a).

related supplier.[85] If the taxpayer elects marginal costing, however, only marginal costs are taken into account in computing combined taxable income. Therefore, marginal costing allows a taxpayer to increase combined taxable income by the amount of the fixed costs related to export sales. In the case of a manufacturer, marginal costs include only the direct material and direct labor costs. In the case of a wholesaler or retailer, marginal costs include only the cost of inventory purchased for resale. All other costs, such as selling, general, and administrative expenses, and interest expense, are ignored for purposes of computing combined taxable income.[86] The only requirement for the use of marginal costing is that the amount of combined taxable income under marginal costing is greater than that under a full costing approach.[87]

There are two limitations on the benefits of marginal costing. First, an overall profit percentage limitation restricts the combined taxable income of an FSC and its related supplier to an amount equal to full costing combined taxable income from all sales (domestic and foreign) multiplied by the ratio of foreign trading gross receipts to total gross receipts (domestic and foreign).[88] Because of this limitation, marginal costing is advantageous only when export sales are less profitable than domestic sales. In addition, a no-loss rule restricts the amount of income that can be allocated to an FSC to the amount of full costing combined taxable income.[89] This rule prevents a U.S. exporter from allocating more income to the FSC than the total income from the export sale.

> **Example 7.6:** USAco, a domestic corporation, owns and operates a commission FSC. During the current year, USAco's results from operations are as follows:
>
> | | Export sales | U.S. sales | Total sales |
> |---|---|---|---|
> | Sales . . . . | $ 10 million | $15 million | $25 million |
> | Direct material and labor . . | − 6 million | − 7 million | − 13 million |
> | Marginal costing income . . . | $ 4 million | $ 8 million | $12 million |
> | Indirect expenses . . . . | − 3 million | − 3 million | − 6 million |
> | Full costing income . . . . | $ 1 million | $ 5 million | $ 6 million |
>
> The marginal costing profit margin on export sales of 40% [$4 million ÷ $10 million] exceeds the overall profit percentage of 24% [$6 million ÷ $25 million]. Therefore, the overall profit limitation restricts combined taxable income to $2.4 million [24% × $10

---

[85] Temp. Reg. § 1.925(a)-1T(c)(6).

[86] Temp. Reg. § 1.925(b)-1T(b)(1). Reg. § 1.471-11(b)(2)(i) describes what expenses are included in direct material and labor costs.

[87] Temp. Reg. § 1.925(b)-1T(a) and (c)(1). When computing marginal costing combined taxable income, taxpayers generally can use the same transaction grouping procedures available when computing full costing combined taxable income. Temp. Reg. § 1.925(b)-1T(b)(3).

[88] Temp. Reg. § 1.925(b)-1T(b)(2) and (c)(2).

[89] Temp. Reg. § 1.925(b)-1T(b)(4).

million of export sales]. Marginal costing is still preferable to a full costing approach, however, since the latter produces only $1 million of combined taxable income. Thus, USAco can allocate $552,000 [23% × $2.4 million] of income to the FSC. The no-loss rule does not apply, since even after allocating $552,000 of income to the FSC, USAco still recognizes $448,000 [$1 million − $552,000] of income from export sales.

Expense Allocations

A third technique for increasing the benefits of an FSC is expense allocations. As discussed above, combined taxable income equals the excess of foreign trading gross receipts over the total costs of the FSC and the related supplier, which includes deductions that are definitely related to export sales (e.g., cost of goods sold), and a ratable portion of any deductions that are not definitely related to any specific class of gross income (e.g., interest expense and selling, general and administrative expenses).[90] Therefore, a taxpayer can increase combined taxable income, and, in turn, the amount of profit allocated to the FSC, by developing defensible apportionment bases that allocate fewer deductions against foreign trading gross receipts.[91]

Noncorporate Taxpayers

Only a domestic corporation can claim a dividends-received deduction for dividend distributions received from an FSC.[92] In contrast, any U.S. citizen or resident alien who owns an FSC directly, or indirectly through an interest in a conduit entity, such as a partnership or S corporation, is subject to U.S. tax on the full amount of any dividends received from an FSC. This shareholder-level U.S. tax substantially eliminates the benefit of using an FSC, as opposed to direct export sales, for noncorporate taxpayers. As a consequence, typically only domestic corporations establish an FSC.

One potential strategy for dealing with the lack of a dividends-received deduction is for an individual taxpayer to own an FSC through an individual retirement account (or "IRA").[93]

Example 7.7: T is a U.S. citizen who owns 100% of the stock of an S corporation. During the current year, T establishes and contributes $2,000 to an IRA. The trustee of the IRA then establishes an FSC and has the IRA contribute the $2,000 to the FSC in return for all of the FSC's stock. The FSC then enters into a commission

---

[90] Treas. Reg. § 1.925(a)-1T(c)(6).

[91] For examples in the context of research and development expenditures, see *St. Jude Medical, Inc. v. Comm'r*, 34 F3d 1394 (8th Cir. 1994), and *Boeing Company v. U.S.*, 98-2 USTC ¶ 50,722 (DCt WA 1998).

[92] Code Sec. 245(c).

[93] The Tax Court has ruled that this is not a prohibited transaction under Code Sec. 4975 (see *J.H. Swanson v. Comm'r*, 106 TC 76 (1996)).

agreement with T's S corporation to receive an allocation each year of the maximum amount of taxable income allowable under the administrative pricing rules. The FSC distributes all of its earnings and profits each year as a dividend to the IRA.

The commission paid by the S corporation to the FSC is fully deductible, while the FSC pays tax on only 7/23 (30.43%) of its commission income.[94] Therefore, fully 69.57% of the export profits allocable to the FSC are tax-free at both the S corporation and the FSC level. In addition, the IRA pays no tax on the dividends it receives from the FSC. However, the export profits funneled through the FSC to the IRA will be taxed when T makes a withdrawal from the IRA.[95] Therefore, the tax benefits of owning an FSC through an IRA is in the nature of a deferral, not a permanent exclusion. The use of a Roth IRA could result in a permanent exclusion. The benefits of this arrangement also are limited by other factors, such as the possibility of higher tax rates in the future and the penalties on premature withdrawals from an IRA.[96]

¶ 705 INTEREST-CHARGE DISCS

DISC vs. FSC

As originally enacted in 1971, DISCs allowed U.S. exporters to defer the U.S. tax on a portion of their export profit. In 1984, Congress responded to complaints from other countries that DISCs were an illegal export subsidy by effectively terminating DISCs and enacting the FSC provisions. A vestige of the DISC provisions, called an interest-charge DISC, still remains in the law, however.[97] The major differences between an interest-charge DISC and an FSC are as follows:

(i) *Type of corporation*—An FSC is a foreign corporation, whereas an interest-charge DISC is a domestic corporation.[98]

(ii) *Qualification requirements*—An interest-charge DISC need not meet the foreign management and foreign economic processes requirements applicable to FSCs. However, interest-charge DISCs must meet certain export gross receipts and export assets requirements.[99]

(iii) *Nature of tax preference*—An FSC allows a U.S. exporter to permanently exclude a portion of its export profits (typically, 15%) from U.S. tax. In contrast, an interest-charge DISC allows a taxpayer to merely defer U.S. taxes on export profits.

---

[94] The exempt portion of an FSC's foreign trade income is 16/23 for noncorporate shareholders that use the administrative pricing rules. Code Sec. 923(a)(3).

[95] Code Sec. 408(d)(1).

[96] Code Sec. 72(t).

[97] Code Secs. 991–997.

[98] Code Sec. 992(a)(1).

[99] Code Sec. 992(a)(1)(A) and (B).

(iv) *Interest charge on U.S. tax savings*—Shareholders of an interest-charge DISC must pay an interest charge on the tax that would have been due if not for the deferral.[100] There is no interest charge on the tax benefits of an FSC.

(v) *Maximum amount of qualifying export sales*—In the case of a regular FSC, there is no limit on the amount of export sales that can qualify for the FSC benefit. In contrast, no more than $10 million of a taxpayer's export gross receipts can qualify each year for the benefits of an interest-charge DISC.[101]

In essence, an interest-charge DISC is a means by which a U.S. exporter can borrow funds from the U.S. Treasury. In contrast, an FSC allows an exporter to permanently exclude a portion of its export profits from U.S. tax. Because the FSC benefit is usually greater, FSCs are more common than interest-charge DISCs.

Taxation of a DISC and Its Shareholders

An interest-charge DISC is a domestic corporation that is not subject to the regular U.S. corporate income tax.[102] Although the interest-charge DISC itself is not a taxable entity, the DISC's U.S. shareholders are subject to tax on deemed dividend distributions from the DISC.[103] These deemed distributions do not include income derived from the first $10 million of the DISC's qualified export receipts each year.[104] Thus, an interest-charge DISC allows a U.S. shareholder to defer paying U.S. tax on the income derived from up to $10 million of qualified export receipts each year. The taxpayer generally may include in the $10 million its most profitable export sales.[105]

The U.S. shareholder must pay an interest charge on its DISC-related deferred tax liability, which equals the difference between the shareholder's tax for the taxable year computed first with, and then without, the accumulated DISC income of the shareholder that has been deferred over the years.[106] Therefore, a shareholder must continue to pay interest on deferred DISC income until that income is distributed or deemed distributed by the DISC. The interest rate is the current market rate for 52-week Treasury bills.[107] It is adjusted annually and applies for the fiscal year ending September 30. The rates for the last several years are as follows:

---

[100] Code Sec. 995(f).

[101] Code Sec. 995(b)(1)(E).

[102] Code Sec. 991.

[103] Code Sec. 995(a) and (b).

[104] Code Sec. 995(b)(1)(E). It is not possible to circumvent the $10 million limitation by creating multiple interest-charge DISCs. Code Sec. 995(b)(4)(B).

[105] Prop. Reg. § 1.995-8(b).

[106] Code Sec. 995(f)(2).

[107] Code Sec. 995(f)(4).

Year ending September 30	Interest rate
1990	8.02% [108]
1991	6.42% [109]
1992	4.23% [110]
1993	3.47% [111]
1994	4.55% [112]
1995	6.30% [113]
1996	5.51% [114]
1997	5.68% [115]
1998	5.34% [116]

The interest charge is treated as interest paid on an underpayment of tax,[117] which means that the payment is not deductible by noncorporate taxpayers.[118] This diminishes the benefits of operating an interest-charge DISC for any U.S. citizen or resident alien who owns a DISC either directly, or indirectly through an interest in a partnership, S corporation, limited liability company, or other conduit entity. Interest-charge DISC shareholders compute the interest charge on Form 8404, Computation of Interest Charge on DISC-Related Deferred Tax Liability, and the interest is due on the same date as the shareholder's regular tax return, without any extensions.[119] No estimated tax payments are required with respect to the interest charge.[120] (Form 8404 is reproduced in the appendix to this chapter.)

---

[108] Rev. Rul. 90-96, 1990-2 CB 188.
[109] Rev. Rul. 91-59, 1991-2 CB 347.
[110] Rev. Rul. 92-98, 1992-2 CB 201.
[111] Rev. Rul. 93-77, 1993-2 CB 253.
[112] Rev. Rul. 94-68, 1994-2 CB 177.
[113] Rev. Rul. 95-77, 1995-2 CB 122.
[114] Rev. Rul. 96-55, 1996-2 CB 57.

[115] Rev. Rul. 97-49, IRB 1997-48, 4.
[116] Rev. Rul. 98-55, IRB 1998-47, 5.
[117] Code Sec. 995(f)(6).
[118] Code Sec. 163(h)(2)(E).
[119] Prop. Reg. § 1.995(f)-1(j)(3)(i).
[120] Prop. Reg. § 1.995(f)-1(a)(2)(iii).

¶ 706   APPENDIX

Form **1120-FSC**	**U.S. Income Tax Return of a Foreign Sales Corporation**	OMB No. 1545-0935
Department of the Treasury Internal Revenue Service	For calendar year 1999 or other tax year beginning .... , 1999, and ending .... , ... ▶ See separate instructions. Please type or print.	**1999**

A Foreign country or U.S. possession of incorporation (See p. 8 of the instrs.)	Name	**C** Employer identification number
		D Date incorporated
B Check type of election made: ☐ FSC ☐ Small FSC Enter the effective date of the election:	Number, street, and room or suite no. (See page 7 of the instructions.)	**E** Total assets (See page 8 of the instructions.)
	City or town, state, and ZIP code	$

F Check applicable boxes: **(1)** ☐ Initial return **(2)** ☐ Final return **(3)** ☐ Change of address **(4)** ☐ Amended return

FSC Information

1 Principal shareholder. Complete for the shareholder that was the principal shareholder at the beginning of the FSC's tax year. If two or more shareholders own equal amounts of stock, complete for the shareholder that has the same tax year as the FSC. (See page 8 of the instructions.)

a Name		**b** Identification number
c Address (number, street, and room or suite no., city or town, state, ZIP code, or country)		**d** Total assets (corporations only) $
e Percentage of voting stock of the principal shareholder %	**f** Tax year ends (month and year) **g** Service Center where tax return is filed	**h** Foreign owner? (check one) ☐ Yes ☐ No

2 Parent-subsidiary controlled group. Is the FSC a subsidiary in a parent-subsidiary controlled group? . . . . ▶ ☐ Yes   ☐ No

If "Yes," and the principal shareholder (described in **1** above) is not the common parent of the group, complete lines 2a through 2g below for the common parent. (See page 8 of the instructions.)

a Name of common parent		**b** Identification number
c Address (number, street, and room or suite no., city or town, state, ZIP code, or country)		**d** Total assets (consolidated, if applicable) $
e Percentage of voting stock of the common parent %	**f** Tax year ends (month and year)	**g** Service Center where tax return is filed

3 Administrative pricing rules

a Check the applicable box(es) to show the pricing rule(s) used to determine taxable income on transactions resulting in foreign trading gross receipts.

(1) ☐ 1.83% of foreign trading gross receipts   **(2)** ☐ 23% of combined taxable income   **(3)** ☐ Marginal costing

(4) ☐ Section 482 method   **(5)** ☐ Transactions at arm's length with unrelated supplier(s)

b If the FSC and the related supplier(s) meet the payment rules of Temporary Regulations section 1.925(a)-1T(b)(2)(ii) and elect to use the administrative pricing rules, check here . . . . ▶ ☐

Tax and Payments (See page 8 of instructions.)

1	**Total tax** (Schedule J, line 8)		**1**	
2	**Payments:**			
a	1998 overpayment credited to 1999 .	**2a**		
b	1999 estimated tax payments . . .	**2b**		
c	Less 1999 refund applied for on Form 4466	**2c** ( ) d Bal ▶	**2d**	
e	Tax deposited with Form 7004		**2e**	
f	Credit for Federal tax paid on fuels (attach Form 4136)		**2f**	
g	U.S. income tax paid or withheld at source (attach Form 1042-S) . .		**2g**	
h	Add lines 2d through 2g		**2h**	
3	Estimated tax penalty. Check if Form 2220 is attached . . . . ▶ ☐		**3**	
4	**Tax due.** If line 2h is smaller than the total of lines 1 and 3, enter amount owed		**4**	
5	**Overpayment.** If line 2h is larger than the total of lines 1 and 3, enter amount overpaid		**5**	
6	Enter amount of line 5 you want: **Credited to 2000 estimated tax** ▶ Refunded ▶		**6**	

Sign Here	Under penalties of perjury, I declare that I have examined this return, including accompanying schedules and statements, and to the best of my knowledge and belief, it is true, correct, and complete. Declaration of preparer (other than taxpayer) is based on all information of which preparer has any knowledge.
	▶ Signature of officer Date ▶ Title

Paid Preparer's Use Only	Preparer's signature ▶	Date	Check if self-employed ▶ ☐	Preparer's SSN or PTIN
	Firm's name (or yours if self-employed) and address ▶		EIN ▶	
			ZIP code ▶	

For Paperwork Reduction Act Notice, see page 1 of separate instructions.   Cat. No. 11531K   Form **1120-FSC** (1999)

Schedule A	Cost of Goods Sold Related to Foreign Trading Gross Receipts (See page 8 of the instructions.)		
		(a) Using administrative pricing rules	(b) Not using administrative pricing rules
1	Inventory at beginning of year	1		
2	Purchases	2		
3	Cost of labor	3		
4	Additional section 263A costs (attach schedule)	4		
5	Other costs (attach schedule)	5		
6	**Total.** Add lines 1 through 5	6		
7	Inventory at end of year	7		
8	**Cost of goods sold.** Subtract line 7 from line 6. Enter here and on line 7 of Schedule B. Small FSCs, see instructions for Schedule A.	8		

9a Check all methods used for valuing closing inventory: **(1)** ☐ Cost as described in Regulations section 1.471-3

  (2) ☐ Lower of cost or market as described in Regulations section 1.471-4

  (3) ☐ Other (Specify method used and attach explanation.) ▶ ....

b Check if there was a writedown of subnormal goods as described in Regulations section 1.471-2(c) . . . . . . ▶ ☐

c Check if the LIFO inventory method was adopted this tax year for any goods. (If checked, attach Form 970.) . . . ▶ ☐

d If the LIFO inventory method was used for this tax year, enter percentage (or amounts) of closing inventory computed under LIFO . . . . | 9d | |

e If property is produced or acquired for resale, do the rules of section 263A apply to the FSC? . . . . ☐ Yes ☐ No

f Was there any change in determining quantities, cost, or valuations between opening and closing inventory? If "Yes," attach explanation . . . . ☐ Yes ☐ No

Additional Information (See page 9 of the instructions.) **Note:** *Small FSCs, complete lines 1 through 7f only.*

		Yes	No
1	See the instructions on page 16 and enter the FSC's: **a** Business activity code no. ▶		
b	Business activity ▶ .... **c** Product or service ▶		
2	Enter the amount of tax-exempt interest received or accrued during the tax year ▶ |$		
3	At any time during the tax year was the FSC engaged in a trade or business in the United States?		
4	Is the FSC a foreign personal holding company or a personal holding company? (See page 9 of the instructions.)		
5	If the FSC has an NOL for the tax year and is electing to forego the carryback period, check here . . . ▶ ☐		
6	Enter the available NOL carryover from prior tax years. (Do not reduce it by any deduction in Schedule B, Part II, line 19a.) . . . . ▶ |$			
7	**FSC qualification rules** (See page 2 of the instructions.):		
a	Enter the largest number of FSC shareholders at any time during the tax year ▶		
b	Did the FSC have any preferred stock outstanding at any time during the tax year?		
c	During the tax year, did the FSC maintain an office in a qualifying foreign country or U.S. possession in which a complete set of books and records was maintained? (See page 2 of the instructions.)		
d	During the tax year did the FSC maintain the records required under section 6001 at a location within the U.S.?		
e	At all times during the tax year, did the FSC have at least one non-U.S. resident on its board of directors? . .		
f	**Small FSCs only:** Check the applicable box if during the tax year the small FSC was a member of a controlled group of corporations that included a ☐ DISC or a ☐ FSC.		
g	Check the applicable box if during the tax year the FSC was a member of a controlled group of corporations that included a ☐ DISC or a ☐ small FSC.		
8	**Foreign management rules** (**does not** apply to small FSCs):		
a	Did all formally convened meetings of the board of directors and of the shareholders occur outside the U.S.? .		
b	**(1)** Were all cash dividends, legal and accounting fees, salaries of officers, and salaries or fees of members of the board of directors disbursed from bank accounts maintained outside the United States? (If "Yes," these accounts are considered to be the FSC's principal bank accounts.)		
	(2) At all times during the tax year, did the FSC maintain its principal bank accounts in a qualifying foreign country or U.S. possession? (See page 3 of the instructions).		
	Name of bank(s) ▶ .... Account number(s) ▶		

9 Foreign economic process rules (**does not** apply to small FSCs):

a Check the applicable box if the FSC is electing to group transactions from its sales activities (Regulations section 1.924(d)-1(c)(5)):

  ☐ Customer grouping ☐ Contract grouping ☐ Product or product line grouping ☐ Product or product line subgroupings

b Check the applicable box(es) to indicate how the FSC met the foreign direct costs requirement: (See page 3 of the instructions.)

  ☐ The FSC (or any person under contract with the FSC) met the 50% test of section 924(d)(1).

  ☐ The FSC (or any person under contract with the FSC) met the alternative 85% test of section 924(d)(2). Check to indicate the subparagraph of section 924(e) for which this alternative test was met: (e)(1) ☐ (e)(2) ☐ (e)(3) ☐ (e)(4) ☐ (e)(5) ☐

c If box (e)(5) on line 9b is checked, enter which of the five methods in Regulations section 1.924(e)-1(e)(1) (i) through (v) describes how the FSC bears the economic risk of nonpayment ▶ ....

d Check the applicable box if the FSC is electing to group its foreign direct costs on one of the following (Regulations section 1.924(d)-1(e)): ☐ Customer grouping ☐ Contract grouping ☐ Product or product line grouping

Schedule B | Taxable Income or (Loss) (See page 9 of the instructions.)

Part I—Net Income Attributable to Nonexempt Foreign Trade Income

		(a) Using administrative pricing rules	(b) Not using administrative pricing rules
1	Sale, exchange, or other disposition of export property. (Enter 50% of military property sales. Include the other 50% on Schedule F, line 1.) . . **1**		
2	Lease or rental of export property for use outside the United States . . **2**		
3	Services related and subsidiary to:		
a	Sale, exchange, or other disposition of export property. (Enter 50% of services related to the sale or other disposition of military property. Include the other 50% on Schedule F, line 1.). **3a**		
b	Lease or rental of export property **3b**		
4	Engineering or architectural services for construction projects outside the U.S. **4**		
5	Managerial services for an unrelated FSC or IC-DISC **5**		
6a	**Total foreign trading gross receipts.** Add lines 1 through 5 . . . . . **6a**		
	Small FSCs: Complete lines 6b through 6h.		
b	Small FSC limitation (section 924(b)(2)(B)) **6b** \$5,000,000 00		
c	Controlled group member's share of line 6b . . . **6c**		
d	Enter 1. (Short tax year: Divide the number of days in the short tax year by the number of days in the full tax year. Enter as a decimal less than 1.00000.) . . **6d**		
e	Multiply line 6b or line 6c (whichever applies) by line 6d **6e**		
f	Total of line 6a, columns (a) and (b) **6f**		
	Note: *See the instructions for line 6f if commission income is included on line 6a.*		
g	Enter the smaller of line 6e or line 6f. **Note:** *If line 6f exceeds line 6e, enter the excess on line 7 of Schedule F* **6g**		
h	Allocate the amount from line 6g to columns (a) and (b) (see instructions) **6h**		
7	Cost of goods sold (Schedule A, line 8). (Small FSCs, enter only the part of cost of goods sold from the receipts on line 6h above. See instructions for Schedule A on page 8.) **7**		
8	**Foreign trade income.** Subtract line 7 from line 6a or line 6h (whichever applies) **8**		
9a	Exemption percentage from Schedule E, line 3d . . . . **9a** %		
b	Exemption percentage from Schedule E, line 2d **9b**		%
10	**Exempt foreign trade income.** Multiply line 8 (column (a)) by line 9a and line 8 (column (b)) by line 9b **10**		
11	**Nonexempt foreign trade income.** Subtract line 10 from line 8 . . . **11**		
12	Deductions attributable to nonexempt foreign trade income. Enter amount from Schedule G, line 18 . . . . **12**		
13	Net income attributable to nonexempt foreign trade income. Subtract line 12 from line 11 . . . . **13**		
14	Net income attributable to nonexempt foreign trade income from Schedule F, line 6 . . . . **14**		
15	**Total net income attributable to nonexempt foreign trade income.** Add lines 13 and 14 . . . . **15**		

Part II—Taxable Income or (Loss)

16	Taxable income from foreign trade income. Enter total of line 15, columns (a) and (b), minus any nontaxable income included in line 15, column (b). Attach a schedule that shows the computation of the taxable and nontaxable income included in line 15, column (b)	**16**
17	Taxable nonforeign trade income from Schedule F, line 19	**17**
18	Taxable income or (loss) before net operating loss deduction and dividends-received deduction. Add lines 16 and 17.	**18**
19a	Net operating loss deduction (attach schedule) **19a**	
b	Dividends-received deduction (attach schedule) **19b**	
c	Add lines 19a and 19b.	**19c**
20	**Taxable income or (loss).** Subtract line 19c from line 18. (See instructions for Schedule J on page 13 to figure the tax on this income.)	**20**

Form 1120-FSC (1999)   Page **4**

Exemption Percentages Used in Figuring Exempt Foreign Trade Income (See page 10 of the instructions.)

Note: *Enter .30000 on line 2d and .65217 on line 3d if all shareholders of the FSC are C corporations. Skip all other lines.*
Enter .32000 on line 2d and .69565 on line 3d if all shareholders of the FSC are other than C corporations. Skip all other lines.

1	Percentage (round to at least five decimal places) of voting stock owned by shareholders that are C corporations	**1**	
2	Exemption percentage for foreign trade income determined by not using the administrative pricing rules:		
a	Difference between section 923(a)(2) and section 291(a)(4)(A) percentage	**2a**	.02000
b	Section 923(a)(2) percentage	**2b**	.32000
c	Multiply line 1 by line 2a	**2c**	
d	**Exemption percentage.** Subtract line 2c from line 2b. Enter here and on Schedule B, line 9b, and on Schedule G, line 16b	**2d**	
3	Exemption percentage for foreign trade income determined using administrative pricing rules:		
a	Difference between section 923(a)(3) fraction and section 291(a)(4)(B) fraction (16/23 – 15/23 = 1/23) shown as a decimal	**3a**	.04348
b	Section 923(a)(3) fraction (16/23) shown as a decimal	**3b**	.69565
c	Multiply line 1 by line 3a	**3c**	
d	**Exemption percentage.** Subtract line 3c from line 3b. Enter here and on Schedule B, line 9a, and on Schedule G, line 16a	**3d**	

Net Income From Nonexempt Foreign Trade Income and Taxable Nonforeign Trade Income (See page 10 of the instructions.)

Part I—Net Income From Nonexempt Foreign Trade Income

			(a) Using administrative pricing rules	(b) Not using administrative pricing rules
1	Enter 50% of total receipts from the sale, exchange, or other disposition of military property and related services	**1**		
2	International boycott income	**2**		
3	Illegal bribes and other payments	**3**		
4	**Total.** Add lines 1, 2, and 3	**4**		
5	Cost of goods sold and other costs related to above income (attach schedule)	**5**		
6	**Net income from nonexempt foreign trade income.** Subtract line 5 from line 4. Enter here and on Schedule B, line 14, columns (a) and (b) . . .	**6**		

Part II—Taxable Nonforeign Trade Income

7	**Small FSCs:** If line 6f, Schedule B, is greater than line 6e, Schedule B, enter the excess here .	**7**	
8	Interest	**8**	
9	Dividends (attach schedule—see page 11 of the instructions)	**9**	
10	Carrying charges	**10**	
11	Royalties	**11**	
12	Other investment income	**12**	
13	Receipts excluded under section 924(f) on the basis of use, subsidized receipts, and receipts from related parties	**13**	
14	Income from excluded property under sections 927(a)(2) and (3)	**14**	
15	Income from transactions that did not meet the **Foreign economic process rules** (see page 3 of the instructions). (See **Foreign Trading Gross Receipts** on page 3 of the instructions.) . .	**15**	
16	Other income	**16**	
17	**Total.** Add lines 7 through 16	**17**	
18	Enter deductions allocated or apportioned to line 17 income. (Attach schedule. Small FSCs also include the cost of goods sold deduction attributable to the amount entered on line 7 above) .	**18**	
19	**Taxable nonforeign trade income.** Subtract line 18 from line 17. Enter here and on Schedule B, line 17	**19**	

Schedule G Deductions Attributable to Foreign Trade Income Other Than Foreign Trade Income Reported on Schedule F (See instructions on pages 12 and 13 for limitations before completing lines 1 through 14.)

			(a) Using administrative pricing rules		(b) Not using administrative pricing rules	
1	Foreign direct costs described in section 924(e):					
a	Advertising and sales promotion	1a				
b	Certain processing and arranging costs	1b				
c	Certain transportation costs	1c				
d	Certain determination and transmittal costs.	1d				
e	Assumption of credit risk	1e				
f	**Total foreign direct costs.** Add lines 1a through 1e	1f				
2	Advertising	2				
3	Interest	3				
4	Depreciation from Form 4562 (less any depreciation claimed elsewhere on this return) (attach Form 4562)	4				
5	Salaries and wages.	5				
6	Rents	6				
7	Sales commissions	7				
8	Warehousing	8				
9	Freight	9				
10	Compensation of officers	10				
11	Bad debts	11				
12	Pension, profit-sharing, etc., plans	12				
13	Employee benefit programs	13				
14	Other deductions (attach list)	14				
15	**Total deductions.** Add lines 1f through 14	15				
16a	Exemption percentage from Schedule E, line 3d	16a		%		
b	Exemption percentage from Schedule E, line 2d	16b				%
17	Deductions attributable to exempt foreign trade income. Multiply line 15, column (a) by line 16a and enter the result in column (a), and multiply line 15, column (b) by line 16b and enter the result in column (b)	17				
18	**Deductions attributable to nonexempt foreign trade income other than foreign trade income reported on Schedule F.** Subtract line 17 from line 15. Enter here and in Schedule B, line 12, columns (a) and (b)	18				

Schedule J Tax Computation (See page 13 of the instructions.)

1 Check if the FSC is a member of a controlled group (see section 927(d)(4)) ▶ ☐

Important: Members of a controlled group, see page 13 of the instructions.

2a If the box on line 1 is checked, enter the FSC's share of the $50,000, $25,000, and $9,925,000 taxable income brackets (in that order):

(1) $ _____ (2) $ _____ (3) $ _____

b Enter the FSC's share of:
(1) Additional 5% tax (not more than $11,750) . . . . $ ____
(2) Additional 3% tax (not more than $100,000) . . . . $ ____

3	Income tax. Check this box if the FSC is a qualified personal service corporation as defined in section 448(d)(2). (See page 14 of the instructions.) ▶ ☐	3	
4	Foreign tax credit (attach Form 1118)	4	
5	Subtract line 4 from line 3	5	
6	Personal holding company tax (attach Schedule PH (Form 1120))	6	
7	Alternative minimum tax (attach Form 4626)	7	
8	**Total tax.** Add lines 5 through 7. Enter here and on line 1, page 1	8	

Form 1120-FSC (1999)   Page **6**

Schedule L **Balance Sheets per Books**	Beginning of tax year		End of tax year	
Assets	(a)	(b)	(c)	(d)
1 Cash				
2a Trade notes and accounts receivable .				
b Commissions receivable				
c Less allowance for bad debts	( )		( )	
3 Inventories				
4 U.S. government obligations				
5 Tax-exempt securities (See page 14 of the instructions.)				
6 Other current assets (attach schedule) .				
7 Loans to shareholders				
8 Mortgage and real estate loans . . .				
9 Other investments (attach schedule) . .				
10a Buildings and other depreciable assets .				
b Less accumulated depreciation . . .	( )		( )	
11a Depletable assets				
b Less accumulated depletion . . .	( )		( )	
12 Land (net of any amortization)				
13a Intangible assets (amortizable only) . .				
b Less accumulated amortization . . .	( )		( )	
14 Other assets (attach schedule) . . .				
15 Total assets				
Liabilities and Shareholders' Equity				
16 Accounts payable				
17 Mtges., notes, bonds payable in less than 1 year				
18 Transfer prices payable				
19 Other current liabilities (attach schedule).				
20 Loans from shareholders				
21 Mtges., notes, bonds payable in 1 year or more .				
22 Other liabilities (attach schedule) . . .				
23 Capital stock				
24 Additional paid-in capital				
25 Retained earnings—Appropriated (attach schedule)				
26 Retained earnings—Unappropriated . .				
27 Adjustments to shareholders' equity (attach schedule).				
28 Less cost of treasury stock		( )		( )
29 Total liabilities and shareholders' equity .				

Schedule M-1   **Reconciliation of Income (Loss) per Books With Income per Return** (See page 15 of the instructions.)

1 Net income (loss) per books		7 Income recorded on books this year not included on this return (itemize):		
2 Federal income tax				
3 Excess of capital losses over capital gains .		a Tax-exempt interest $		
4 Income subject to tax not recorded on books this year (itemize):		b Exempt foreign trade income . . . $		
5 Expenses recorded on books this year not deducted on this return (itemize):		8 Deductions on this return not charged against book income this year (itemize):		
a Depreciation . . . $		Depreciation . . . $		
b Deductions attributable to exempt foreign trade income $		. . . .		
c Travel and entertainment $		9 Add lines 7 and 8		
		10 Taxable income (line 18, Schedule B)—		
6 Add lines 1 through 5		line 6 less line 9		

Schedule M-2   **Analysis of Unappropriated Retained Earnings per Books (Line 26, Schedule L)**

1 Balance at beginning of year		5 Distributions: a Cash		
2 Net income (loss) per books		b Stock		
3 Other increases (itemize):		c Property		
		6 Other decreases (itemize):		
		7 Add lines 5 and 6		
4 Add lines 1, 2, and 3		8 Balance at end of year (line 4 less line 7)		

SCHEDULE P (Form 1120-FSC)	**Transfer Price or Commission**	OMB No. 1545-0935
Department of the Treasury Internal Revenue Service	For amount reported on line .... , Schedule .... , Form 1120-FSC. ► See separate instructions. Please type or print. ► Attach Schedule P to Form 1120-FSC.	19**99**

Name as shown on Form 1120-FSC

Employer identification number

A Product or product line (see back of schedule and instructions)

C Principal business activity code (if applicable) (see back of schedule and instructions)

B Basis of reporting (see instructions):
1. Transaction-by-transaction:
   a. Aggregate . . . . ☐
   b. Tabular schedule . . . . ☐
2. Group of transactions . . . . ☐

Part I   FSC Profit

Section A—Combined Taxable Income (see instructions)

Full Costing

1	Foreign trading gross receipts from transaction between FSC or related supplier and third party		**1**	
2	Costs and expenses allocable to foreign trading gross receipts from transaction:			
a	Cost of goods sold attributable to property if sold, or depreciation attributable to property if leased	**2a**		
b	Related supplier's expenses allocable to foreign trading gross receipts (see instructions)	**2b**		
c	FSC's expenses allocable to foreign trading gross receipts	**2c**		
d	Add lines 2a through 2c.		**2d**	
3	**Combined taxable income.** Subtract line 2d from line 1. If zero or less, enter -0-		**3**	

Marginal Costing

4	Foreign trading gross receipts from resale by FSC, or sale by related supplier, to third party		**4**	
5	Costs and expenses allocable to foreign trading gross receipts from sale:			
a	Cost of direct material attributable to property sold	**5a**		
b	Cost of direct labor attributable to property sold	**5b**		
c	Add lines 5a and 5b		**5c**	
6	Subtract line 5c from line 4. If zero or less, skip lines 7 through 11 and enter -0- on line 12		**6**	
7	Gross receipts of related supplier and FSC or controlled group from foreign and domestic sales of the product or product line		**7**	
8	Costs and expenses of related supplier and FSC or controlled group allocable to gross income from sales:			
a	Cost of goods sold attributable to property sold	**8a**		
b	Expenses allocable to gross income	**8b**		
c	Add lines 8a and 8b		**8c**	
9	Subtract line 8c from line 7. If zero or less, skip lines 10 and 11 and enter -0- on line 12		**9**	
10	Overall profit percentage. Divide line 9 by line 7. Check if the controlled group optional method is used . ► ☐		**10**	%
11	Overall profit percentage limitation. Multiply line 4 by line 10		**11**	
12	**Combined taxable income.** Enter the smaller of line 6 or line 11		**12**	

Section B—23% of Combined Taxable Income Method (see instructions)

13	Multiply line 3 or line 12 (as elected by related supplier) by 23%.	**13**	
14	**FSC profit.** Enter amount from line 13. If marginal costing is used, enter the smaller of line 3 or line 13 . . .	**14**	

Section C—1.83% of Foreign Trading Gross Receipts Method (see instructions)

15	Multiply line 1 by 1.83%.	**15**	
16	Multiply line 3 or line 12 (as elected by related supplier) by 46%	**16**	
17	**FSC profit.** Enter the smallest of line 3, line 15, or line 16	**17**	

Part II   Transfer Price From Related Supplier to FSC

18	Enter amount from line 1 or line 4, whichever is applicable		**18**	
19a	FSC profit. Enter amount from line 14 or line 17, whichever is applicable	**19a**		
b	FSC expenses allocable to foreign trading gross receipts from transaction . . .	**19b**		
c	Add lines 19a and 19b		**19c**	
20	**Transfer price from related supplier to FSC.** Subtract line 19c from line 18 (see instructions)		**20**	

Part III   FSC Commission From Related Supplier

21	FSC profit. Enter amount from line 14 or line 17, whichever is applicable	**21**	
22	FSC expenses allocable to foreign trading gross receipts from transaction.	**22**	
23	**FSC commission from related supplier.** Add lines 21 and 22 (see instructions)	**23**	

For Paperwork Reduction Act Notice, see page 1 of the Instructions for Form 1120-FSC.   Cat. No. 11537Y   **Schedule P (Form 1120-FSC) 1999**

Schedule P (Form 1120-FSC) Codes for Principal Business Activity

This list of Principal Business Activity codes and corresponding product or product lines is designed to classify enterprises by the type of activity in which they are engaged. Though the principal business activity codes are similar in format and structure to the Standard Industrial Classification (SIC) Codes, they should not be used as SIC codes.

Items A and C.—If using the list below to report the product or product line for which Schedule P is completed, enter on item A of Schedule P, the principal business activity. Enter on item C the corresponding four-digit code.

Agriculture, Forestry, and Fishing
Code
- 0400 Agricultural production.
- 0600 Agricultural services (except veterinarians), forestry, fishing, hunting, and trapping.

Mining
Metal mining:
- 1010 Iron ores.
- 1070 Copper, lead and zinc, gold and silver ores.
- 1098 Other metal mining.
- 1150 Coal mining.

Oil and gas extraction:
- 1330 Crude petroleum, natural gas, and natural gas liquids.
- 1380 Oil and gas field services.

Nonmetallic minerals, except fuels:
- 1430 Dimension, crushed and broken stone; sand and gravel.
- 1498 Other nonmetallic minerals, except fuels.

Construction
General building contractors and operative builders:
- 1510 General building contractors.
- 1531 Operative builders.
- 1600 Heavy construction contractors.

Special trade contractors:
- 1711 Plumbing, heating, and air conditioning.
- 1731 Electrical work.
- 1798 Other special trade contractors.

Manufacturing
Food and kindred products:
- 2010 Meat products.
- 2020 Dairy products.
- 2030 Preserved fruits and vegetables.
- 2040 Grain mill products.
- 2050 Bakery products.
- 2060 Sugar and confectionary products.
- 2081 Malt liquors and malt.
- 2088 Alcoholic beverages, except malt liquors and malt.
- 2089 Bottled soft drinks, and flavorings.
- 2096 Other food and kindred products.
- 2100 Tobacco manufacturers.

Textile mill products:
- 2228 Weaving mills and textile finishing.
- 2250 Knitting mills.
- 2298 Other textile mill products.

Apparel and other textile products:
- 2315 Men's and boys' clothing.
- 2345 Women's and children's clothing.
- 2388 Other apparel and accessories.
- 2390 Miscellaneous fabricated textile products.

Lumber and wood products:
- 2415 Logging, sawmills, and planing mills.
- 2430 Millwork, plywood, and related products.
- 2498 Other wood products, including wood buildings and mobile homes.
- 2500 Furniture and fixtures.

Paper and allied products:
- 2625 Pulp, paper, and board mills.
- 2699 Other paper products.

Printing and publishing:
- 2710 Newspapers.
- 2720 Periodicals.
- 2735 Books, greeting cards, and miscellaneous publishing.
- 2799 Commercial and other printing, and printing trade services.

Code
Chemicals and allied products:
- 2815 Industrial chemicals, plastics materials and synthetics.
- 2830 Drugs.
- 2840 Soap, cleaners, and toilet goods.
- 2850 Paints and allied products.
- 2898 Agricultural and other chemical products.

Petroleum refining and related industries (including those integrated with extraction):
- 2910 Petroleum refining (including integrated).
- 2998 Other petroleum and coal products.

Rubber and misc. plastics products:
- 3050 Rubber products; plastics footwear, hose and belting.
- 3070 Miscellaneous plastics products.

Leather and leather products:
- 3140 Footwear, except rubber.
- 3198 Other leather and leather products.

Stone, clay, and glass products:
- 3225 Glass products.
- 3240 Cement, hydraulic.
- 3270 Concrete, gypsum, and plaster products.
- 3298 Other nonmetallic mineral products.

Primary metal industries:
- 3370 Ferrous metal industries; misc. primary metal products.
- 3380 Nonferrous metal industries.

Fabricated metal products:
- 3410 Metal cans and shipping containers.
- 3428 Cutlery, hand tools, and hardware; screw machine products, bolts, and similar products.
- 3430 Plumbing and heating, except electric and warm air.
- 3440 Fabricated structural metal products.
- 3460 Metal forgings and stampings.
- 3470 Coating, engraving, and allied services.
- 3480 Ordnance and accessories, except vehicles and guided missiles.
- 3490 Misc. fabricated metal products.

Machinery, except electrical:
- 3520 Farm machinery.
- 3530 Construction and related machinery.
- 3540 Metalworking machinery.
- 3550 Special industry machinery.
- 3560 General industrial machinery.
- 3570 Office, computing, and accounting machines.
- 3598 Other machinery except electrical.

Electrical and electronic equipment:
- 3630 Household appliances.
- 3665 Radio, television, and communication equipment.
- 3670 Electronic components and accessories.
- 3698 Other electrical equipment.

Transportation equipment, except motor vehicles:
- 3710 Motor vehicles and equipment
- 3725 Aircraft, guided missiles and parts.
- 3730 Ship and boat building and repairing.
- 3798 Other transportation equipment, except motor vehicles.

Instruments and related products:
- 3815 Scientific instruments and measuring devices; watches and clocks.
- 3845 Optical, medical, and ophthalmic goods.
- 3860 Photographic equipment and supplies.
- 3998 **Other manufacturing products.**

Transportation and Public Utilities
Code
Transportation:
- 4000 Railroad transportation.
- 4100 Local and interurban passenger transit.
- 4200 Trucking and warehousing.
- 4400 Water transportation.
- 4500 Transportation by air.
- 4600 Pipe lines, except natural gas.
- 4700 Miscellaneous transportation services.

Communication:
- 4825 Telephone, telegraph, and other communication services.
- 4830 Radio and television broadcasting.

Electric, gas, and sanitary services:
- 4910 Electric services.
- 4920 Gas production and distribution.
- 4930 Combination utility services.
- 4990 Water supply and other sanitary services.

Wholesale Trade
Durable:
- 5008 Machinery, equipment, and supplies.
- 5010 Motor vehicles and automotive equipment.
- 5020 Furniture and home furnishings.
- 5030 Lumber and construction materials.
- 5040 Sporting, recreational, photographic, and hobby goods, toys and supplies.
- 5050 Metals and minerals, except petroleum and scrap.
- 5060 Electrical goods.
- 5070 Hardware, plumbing and heating equipment and supplies.
- 5098 Other durable goods.

Nondurable:
- 5110 Paper and paper products.
- 5129 Drugs, drug proprietaries, and druggists' sundries.
- 5130 Apparel, piece goods, and notions.
- 5140 Groceries and related products.
- 5150 Farm-product raw materials.
- 5160 Chemicals and allied products.
- 5170 Petroleum and petroleum products.
- 5180 Alcoholic beverages.
- 5190 Miscellaneous nondurable goods.

Retail Trade
Building materials, garden supplies, and mobile home dealers:
- 5220 Building materials dealers.
- 5251 Hardware stores.
- 5265 Garden supplies and mobile home dealers.
- 5300 **General merchandise stores.**

Food stores:
- 5410 Grocery stores.
- 5490 Other food stores.

Automotive dealers and service stations:
- 5515 Motor vehicle dealers.
- 5541 Gasoline service stations.
- 5598 Other automotive dealers.
- 5600 Apparel and accessory stores.
- 5700 Furniture and home furnishings stores.
- 5800 Eating and drinking places.

Miscellaneous retail stores:
- 5912 Drug stores and proprietary stores.
- 5921 Liquor stores.
- 5995 Other retail stores.

Finance, Insurance, and Real Estate
Code
Banking:
- 6030 Mutual savings banks.
- 6060 Bank holding companies.
- 6090 Banks, except mutual savings banks and bank holding companies.

Credit agencies other than banks:
- 6120 Savings and loan associations.
- 6140 Personal credit institutions.
- 6150 Business credit institutions.
- 6199 Other credit agencies.

Security, commodity brokers and services:
- 6210 Security brokers, dealers, and flotation companies.
- 6299 Commodity contracts brokers and dealers; security and commodity exchanges; and allied services.

Insurance:
- 6355 Life insurance.
- 6356 Mutual insurance, except life or marine and certain fire or flood insurance companies.
- 6359 Other insurance companies.
- 6411 Insurance agents, brokers, and service.

Real estate:
- 6511 Real estate operators and lessors of buildings.
- 6516 Lessors of mining, oil, and similar property.
- 6518 Lessors of railroad property and other real property.
- 6530 Condominium management and cooperative housing associations.
- 6550 Subdividers and developers.
- 6599 Other real estate.
- 6749 **Holding and investment companies except bank holding companies.**

Services
- 7000 **Hotels and other lodging places.**
- 7200 **Personal services.**

Business services:
- 7310 Advertising.
- 7389 Business services, except advertising.

Auto repair; miscellaneous repair services:
- 7500 Auto repair and services.
- 7600 Miscellaneous repair services.

Amusement and recreation services:
- 7812 Motion picture production, distribution, and services.
- 7830 Motion picture theaters.
- 7900 Amusement and recreation services, except motion pictures.

Other services:
- 8015 Offices of physicians, including osteopathic physicians.
- 8021 Offices of dentists.
- 8040 Offices of other health practitioners.
- 8050 Nursing and personal care facilities.
- 8060 Hospitals.
- 8071 Medical laboratories.
- 8099 Other medical services.
- 8111 Legal services.
- 8200 Educational services.
- 8300 Social services.
- 8600 Membership organizations.
- 8911 Architectural and engineering services.
- 8930 Accounting, auditing, and bookkeeping.
- 8980 Miscellaneous services (including veterinarians).

Form **1120-IC-DISC**	**Interest Charge Domestic International Sales Corporation Return**	OMB No. 1545-0938
Department of the Treasury Internal Revenue Service	► See separate instructions. (Please type or print.)	19**99**

For calendar year 1999, or other tax year beginning _____ , 1999, and ending _____

A Date of IC-DISC election	Name	**C** Employer identification number
	Number, street, and room or suite no. (or P.O. box if mail is not delivered to street address)	**D** Date incorporated
B Business activity code no. (See page 15 of instructions.)	City or town, state, and ZIP code	**E** Enter total assets from line 3, column (b), Schedule L (See instructions, page 6.) $

F Check applicable box(es): (1) ☐ Initial return (2) ☐ Final return (3) ☐ Change in address (4) ☐ Amended return

G(1) Did any corporation, individual, partnership, trust, or estate own, directly or indirectly, 50% or more of the IC-DISC's voting stock at the end of the IC-DISC's tax year? (See section 267(c) for rules of attribution.) . . If "Yes," complete the following schedule. (See instructions, page 6, if foreign owner.)   Yes ☐ No ☐

Name	Identifying number	Address	Voting stock owned	Total assets (corporations only)	Foreign owner Yes	No
			%			
			%			

(2) Enter the following for any corporation listed in G(1) that will report the IC-DISC's income:

Tax year of first corporation	IRS Service Center where return will be filed
Tax year of second corporation	IRS Service Center where return will be filed

H(1) Check the appropriate box(es) to indicate any intercompany pricing rules that were applied to 25% or more of total receipts (line 1 below):

☐ 50-50 combined taxable income method ☐ 4% gross receipts method ☐ Section 482 method ("arm's length pricing")

(2) Check here ☐ if the marginal costing rules under section 994(b)(2) were applied in figuring the combined taxable income for any transactions.

All Computations Must Reflect Intercompany Pricing Rules If Used (Section 994)
See separate Schedule P (Form 1120-IC-DISC).

Taxable Income

1	Gross income. Enter amount from Schedule B, line 4, column (e)	**1**	
2	Cost of goods sold from Schedule A, line 8	**2**	
3	Total income. Subtract line 2 from line 1	**3**	
4	Deductions. Enter amount from Schedule E, line 3	**4**	
5	Taxable income before net operating loss deduction and dividends-received deduction. Subtract line 4 from line 3	**5**	
6a	Net operating loss deduction (attach schedule)	**6a**	
b	Dividends-received deduction from Schedule C, line 9	**6b**	
c	Add lines 6a and 6b.	**6c**	
7	**Taxable income.** Subtract line 6c from line 5	**7**	
8	Refundable credit for Federal tax paid on fuels (attach Form 4136)	**8**	

Sign Here

Under penalties of perjury, I declare that I have examined this return, including accompanying schedules and statements, and to the best of my knowledge and belief, it is true, correct, and complete. Declaration of preparer (other than taxpayer) is based on all information of which preparer has any knowledge.

► Signature of officer	Date	► Title

Paid Preparer's Use Only	Preparer's signature ►	Date	Check if self-employed ► ☐	Preparer's SSN or PTIN
	Firm's name (or yours if self-employed) and address ►		EIN ► ZIP code ►	

For Paperwork Reduction Act Notice, see page 1 of the instructions.   Cat. No. 11473P   Form **1120-IC-DISC** (1999)

¶ 706

Form 1120-IC-DISC (1999)   Page **2**

| **Schedule A** | **Cost of Goods Sold** (See instructions starting on page 7.) |

If the intercompany pricing rules of section 994 are used, reflect ACTUAL purchases from a related supplier at the transfer price determined under such rules. See separate Schedule P (Form 1120-IC-DISC).

1	Inventory at beginning of the year.	**1**
2	Purchases	**2**
3	Cost of labor.	**3**
4	Additional section 263A costs (attach schedule)	**4**
5	Other costs (attach schedule)	**5**
6	**Total.** Add lines 1 through 5	**6**
7	Inventory at end of the year.	**7**
8	**Cost of goods sold.** Subtract line 7 from line 6. Enter here and on line 2, page 1	**8**

9a Check all methods used for valuing closing inventory: *(i)* ☐ Cost as described in Regulations section 1.471-3

     (ii) ☐ Lower of cost or market as described in Regulations section 1.471-4

     (iii) ☐ Other (Specify method used and attach explanation.) ▶...

b Check if there was a writedown of "subnormal" goods as described in Regulations section 1.471-2(c). . . . . ▶ ☐

c Check if the LIFO inventory method was adopted this tax year for any goods. (If checked, attach Form 970.) . . ▶ ☐

d If the LIFO inventory method was used for this tax year, enter percentage (or amounts) of closing inventory computed under LIFO . . . . | **9d** |

e Was there any change in determining quantities, costs, or valuations between the opening and closing inventory? (If "Yes," attach explanation.) ☐ Yes ☐ No

f If property is produced or acquired for resale, do the rules of section 263A apply to the corporation? . . . ☐ Yes ☐ No

| **Schedule B** | **Gross Income** (See instructions starting on page 7.) |

(a) Type of receipts	Commission sales		(d) Other receipts	(e) Total (add columns (c) and (d))
	(b) Gross receipts	(c) Commission		
1 Qualified export receipts from sale of export property—				
a To unrelated purchasers:				
(i) Direct foreign sales				
(ii) Foreign sales through a related foreign entity				
(iii) Persons in the United States (other than an unrelated IC-DISC)				
(iv) An unrelated IC-DISC				
b To related purchasers:				
(i) Direct foreign sales				
(ii) Persons in the United States				
c Total				
2 Other qualified export receipts:				
a Leasing or renting of export property.				
b Services related and subsidiary to a qualified export sale or lease				
c Engineering and architectural services				
d Export management services				
e Qualified dividends (Schedule C, line 15)				
f Interest on producer's loans				
g Other interest (attach schedule)				
h Capital gain net income (attach Schedule D (Form 1120)).				
i Net gain or (loss) from Part II, Form 4797 (attach Form 4797).				
j Other (attach schedule)				
k Total				
3 Nonqualified gross receipts:				
a Ultimate use in United States				
b Exports subsidized by the U.S. Government				
c Certain direct or indirect sales or leases for use by the U.S. Government				
d Sales to other IC-DISCs in the same controlled group				
e Nonqualified dividends (line 16, Schedule C)				
f Other (attach schedule)				
g Total				
4 Total. Add lines 1c, 2k, 3g, column (e). Enter here and on line 1, page 1				

Form **1120-IC-DISC** (1999)

Schedule C Dividends and Special Deductions (See instructions starting on page 8.)

		(a) Dividends received	(b) %	(c) Special deductions: ((a) × (b))
1	Dividends from less-than-20%-owned domestic corporations that are subject to the 70% deduction (other than debt-financed stock)		70	
2	Dividends from 20%-or-more-owned domestic corporations that are subject to the 80% deduction (other than debt-financed stock)		80	
3	Dividends on debt-financed stock of domestic and foreign corporations (section 246A)		see instructions	
4	Dividends on certain preferred stock of less-than-20%-owned public utilities		42	
5	Dividends on certain preferred stock of 20%-or-more-owned public utilities		48	
6	Dividends from less-than-20%-owned foreign corporations and certain FSCs that are subject to the 70% deduction		70	
7	Dividends from 20%-or-more-owned foreign corporations and certain FSCs that are subject to the 80% deduction		80	
8	Dividends from wholly owned foreign subsidiaries subject to the 100% deduction (section 245(b))		100	
9	**Total.** Add lines 1 through 8. For limitations, see page 9 of instructions .			
10	Other dividends from foreign corporations not included on lines 3, 6, 7, and 8.			
11	Income from controlled foreign corporations under subpart F (attach Forms 5471)			
12	IC-DISC and former DISC dividends not included on lines 1, 2, or 3 (section 246(d))			
13	Other dividends			
14	**Total dividends.** Add lines 1 through 13, column (a)			
15	Qualified dividends. Enter here and on Schedule B, line 2e, column (d). .			
16	Nonqualified dividends. Subtract line 15 from line 14. Enter here and on Schedule B, line 3e, column (d)			

Schedule E Deductions (Before completing, see **Limitations on Deductions**, starting on page 9 of instructions.)

1	Export promotion expenses:		
a	Market studies	1a	
b	Advertising	1b	
c	Depreciation (attach Form 4562).	1c	
d	Salaries and wages	1d	
e	Rents.	1e	
f	Sales commissions	1f	
g	Warehousing	1g	
h	Freight (excluding insurance)	1h	
i	Compensation of officers	1i	
j	Repairs and maintenance	1j	
k	Pension, profit-sharing, etc., plans	1k	
l	Employee benefit programs	1l	
m	Other (list):		
	....	1m	
n	**Total.** Add lines 1a through 1m	1n	
2	Other expenses not deducted on line 1:		
a	Bad debts	2a	
b	Taxes and licenses	2b	
c	Interest	2c	
d	Contributions (not over 10% of line 7, page 1, adjusted per instructions on page 11)	2d	
e	Freight	2e	
f	Freight insurance	2f	
g	Other (list):		
	....	2g	
h	**Total.** Add lines 2a through 2g	2h	
3	**Total deductions.** Add lines 1n and 2h. Enter here and on line 4, page 1	3	

Form 1120-IC-DISC (1999)   Page **4**

Schedule J   Deemed and Actual Distributions and Deferred DISC Income for the Tax Year

Part I.—Deemed Distributions Under Section 995(b)(1) (See instructions starting on page 12.)

1	Gross interest derived during the tax year from producer's loans (section 995(b)(1)(A))	1	
2	Gain recognized on the sale or exchange of section 995(b)(1)(B) property (attach schedule)	2	
3	Gain recognized on the sale or exchange of section 995(b)(1)(C) property (attach schedule)	3	
4	50% of taxable income attributable to military property (section 995(b)(1)(D)) (attach schedule)	4	
5	Taxable income from line 7, Part II, below	5	
6	Taxable income of the IC-DISC (from line 7, page 1)	6	
7	Add lines 1 through 5	7	
8	Subtract line 7 from line 6	8	
9	If you have shareholders that are C corporations, enter one-seventeenth of line 8 (.0588235 times line 8)	9	
10	International boycott income (see instructions)	10	
11	Illegal bribes and other payments	11	

Note: *Separate computations for lines 12–23 are required for shareholders that are C corporations and shareholders that are not C corporations. Complete lines 12, 14, 15, 17a, 18, 20, and 22 for shareholders that are not C corporations. Complete lines 13, 14, 16, 17b, 19, 21, and 23 for shareholders that are C corporations.*

12	Add lines 7, 10, and 11	12	
13	Add lines 7, 9, 10, and 11	13	
14	Earnings and profits for the tax year (attach schedule)	14	
15	Enter the smaller of line 12 or 14	15	
16	Enter the smaller of line 13 or 14	16	
17	Foreign investment attributable to producer's loans (attach schedule):		
a	Computation of amount for shareholders other than C corporations	17a	
b	Computation of amount for shareholders that are C corporations	17b	
18	Add lines 15 and 17a	18	
19	Add lines 16 and 17b	19	
20	Enter percentage of stock owned by shareholders other than C corporations	20	%
21	Enter percentage of stock owned by shareholders that are C corporations	21	%
22	Multiply line 18 by line 20 (Allocate to shareholders other than C corporations)	22	
23	Multiply line 19 by line 21 (Allocate to C corporation shareholders)	23	
24	**Total deemed distributions under section 995(b)(1) for all shareholders.** Add lines 22 and 23	24	

Part II.—Section 995(b)(1)(E) Taxable Income (See instructions starting on page 12.)

1	Total qualified export receipts (see instructions)	1	
2	Statutory maximum	2	$10,000,000
3	Controlled group member's portion of the statutory maximum	3	
4	Enter smaller of **(a)** 1 or **(b)** number of days in tax year divided by 365 (see instructions)	4	
5	Proration. Multiply line 2 or 3, whichever is applicable, by line 4	5	
6	Excess qualified export receipts. Subtract line 5 from line 1. (If line 5 exceeds line 1, enter -0- here and on line 7 below.)	6	
7	Taxable income attributable to line 6 receipts. Enter here and on line 5 of Part I above	7	

Part III.—Deemed Distributions Under Section 995(b)(2) (See instructions on page 13.)

1	Annual installment of distribution attributable to revocation of election in an earlier year	1	
2	Annual installment of distribution attributable to not qualifying as a DISC or IC-DISC in an earlier year	2	
3	**Total deemed distributions under section 995(b)(2).** Add lines 1 and 2	3	

Part IV.—Actual Distributions (See instructions on page 13.)

1	Distributions to meet qualification requirements under section 992(c) (attach computation)	1	
2	Other actual distributions	2	
3	**Total.** Add lines 1 and 2	3	
4	Amount on line 3 treated as distributed from:		
a	Previously taxed income	4a	
b	Accumulated IC-DISC income (including IC-DISC income of the current year)	4b	
c	Other earnings and profits	4c	
d	Other	4d	

Part V.—Deferred DISC Income Under Section 995(f)(3) (See instructions on page 13.)

1	Accumulated IC-DISC income (for periods after 1984) at end of computation year	1	
2	Distributions-in-excess-of-income for the tax year following the computation year to which line 1 applies	2	
3	Deferred DISC income under section 995(f)(3). Subtract line 2 from line 1	3	

Form **1120-IC-DISC** (1999)

¶ 706

Form 1120-IC-DISC (1999)   Page **5**

Schedule L	**Balance Sheets per Books**	**(a)** Beginning of tax year	**(b)** End of tax year
	1 Qualified assets:		
	a Working capital (cash and necessary temporary investments)		
	b Funds awaiting investment (cash in U.S. banks in excess of working capital needs to acquire other qualified export assets)		
	c Export-Import Bank obligations		
	d Trade receivables (accounts and notes receivable)		
	Less allowance for bad debts	( )	( )
Assets	**e** Export property (net) (including inventory and qualified property held for lease)		
	f Producer's loans		
	g Investment in related foreign export corporations		
	h Depreciable assets		
	Less accumulated depreciation.	( )	( )
	i Other (attach schedule)		
	2 Nonqualified assets (net) (list):		
	3 **Total assets.** Combine lines 1a through 2		
	4 Accounts payable		
	5 Other current liabilities (attach schedule)		
	6 Mortgages, notes, bonds payable in 1 year or more		
Liabilities and Shareholders' Equity	**7** Other liabilities (attach schedule)		
	8 Capital stock		
	9 Additional paid-in capital		
	10 Other earnings and profits		
	11 Previously taxed income (section 996(f)(2))		
	12 Accumulated pre-1985 DISC income (see instructions on page 13) . . .		
	13 Accumulated IC-DISC income (see instructions on page 13)		
	14 Less cost of treasury stock	( )	( )
	15 Total liabilities and shareholders' equity		

Schedule M-1	**Reconciliation of Income per Books With Income per Return**		
1 Net income (loss) per books . . .		**6** Income recorded on books this year not included on this return (itemize):	
2 Excess of capital losses over capital gains			
3 Taxable income not recorded on books this year (itemize):			
4 Expenses recorded on books this year and not deducted on this return (itemize):		**7** Deductions on this return not charged against book income this year (itemize):	
		8 Add lines 6 and 7	
5 Add lines 1 through 4		**9** Income (line 5, page 1)—line 5 less line 8	

Schedule M-2	**Analysis of Other Earnings and Profits (Line 10, Schedule L)**		
1 Balance at beginning of year . . .		**5** Distributions to qualify under section 992(c).	
2 Increases (itemize):		**6** Other decreases (itemize):	
3 Add lines 1 and 2		**7** Add lines 4 through 6	
4 Deficit in earnings and profits . . .		**8** Balance at end of year (line 3 less line 7).	

Schedule M-3	**Analysis of Previously Taxed Income (Line 11, Schedule L)**		
1 Balance at beginning of year . . .		**5** Deficit in earnings and profits	
2 Deemed distributions under section 995(b).		**6** Distributions to qualify under section 992(c).	
3 Other increases (itemize):		**7** Other decreases (itemize):	
		8 Add lines 5 through 7	
4 Add lines 1 through 3		**9** Balance at end of year (line 4 less line 8).	

Schedule M-4	**Analysis of Accumulated IC-DISC Income (Line 13, Schedule L)**		
1 Balance at beginning of year . . .		**6** Distributions to qualify under section 992(c).	
2 Increases (itemize):		**7** Distributions upon disqualification (sec. 995(b)(2))	
		8 Other decreases (itemize):	
3 Add lines 1 and 2			
4 Deficit in earnings and profits . . .		**9** Add lines 4 through 8	
5 Redemptions under section 996(d) .		**10** Balance at end of year (line 3 less line 9).	

Form **1120-IC-DISC** (1999)

¶ **706**

Form 1120-IC-DISC (1999)   Page **6**

| Schedule N | **Export Gross Receipts of the IC-DISC and Related U.S. Persons** (See instructions starting on page 13.) |

1 See page 16 of the instructions and enter the product code and percentage of total export gross receipts for **(a)** the largest and **(b)** 2nd largest product or service sold or provided by the IC-DISC:

(a) Code	Percentage of total	%	(b) Code	Percentage of total	%

2 Export gross receipts for 1999

(a) Export gross receipts of the IC-DISC	Export gross receipts of related U.S. persons	
	(b) Related IC-DISCs	(c) All other related U.S. persons

3 If item 2(b) or 2(c) is completed, complete the following (if more space is needed, attach a schedule following the format below):

(a) Related U.S. Persons, Except IC-DISCs, in Your Controlled Group

Name	Address	Identifying number

(b) IC-DISCs in Your Controlled Group

Name	Address	Identifying number

| Schedule O | **Other Information** (See instructions on page 14.) | | Yes | No |

1 See page 15 of the instructions and enter the main—
a Business activity ▶.................................... **b** Product or service ▶...............................
2 Was the corporation a U.S. shareholder of any controlled foreign corporation?. . . . .
(See sections 951 and 957.) If "Yes," attach Form 5471 for each corporation.
3a Did 95% or more of the IC-DISC's gross receipts for the tax year consist of qualified export receipts (defined in section 993(a))?. . . . .
  b Did the adjusted basis of IC-DISC's qualified export assets (as defined in section 993(b)) at end of tax year equal or exceed 95% of the sum of the adjusted basis of all the IC-DISC's assets at end of tax year?. . . . . .
  c If **a** or **b** is "No," did the IC-DISC make a pro rata distribution of property as defined in section 992(c)? . . .
4 Did the IC-DISC have more than one class of stock at any time during the tax year? . . . .
5 Was the par or stated value of the IC-DISC's stock at least $2,500 on each day of the tax year (for a new corporation, this means on the last day for making an election to be an IC-DISC and for each later day)? . . .
6 Did the IC-DISC keep separate books and records? . . . .
7 At any time during calendar year 1999, did the IC-DISC have an interest in or a signature or other authority over a financial account (such as a bank account, securities account, or other financial account) in a foreign country? If "Yes," the IC-DISC may have to file Form TD F 90-22.1. See page 14 of the instructions.
If "Yes," enter name of foreign country ▶ ....
8 During the tax year, did the IC-DISC receive a distribution from, or was it the grantor of, or transferor to, a foreign trust? If "Yes," see page 14 of the instructions for other forms the IC-DISC may have to file . . . . . .
9a Does the IC-DISC or any member of the IC-DISC's controlled group (as defined in section 993(a)(3)) have operations in or related to any country (or with the government, a company, or a national of that country) associated with carrying out the boycott of Israel that is on the list kept by the Secretary of the Treasury under section 999(a)(3)?. . . . .
  b Did the IC-DISC or any member of the controlled group of which the IC-DISC is a member have operations in any unlisted country that the IC-DISC knows or has reason to know requires participation in or cooperation with an international boycott against Israel?. . . . .
  c Did the IC-DISC or any member of the controlled group of which the IC-DISC is a member have operations in any country that the IC-DISC knows or has reason to know requires participation in or cooperation with an international boycott other than the boycott of Israel?. . . . .
If the answer to any of the questions in 9 is "Yes," see instructions and **Form 5713**, International Boycott Report.

10 Enter the amount of tax-exempt interest income received or accrued during the tax year ▶ $

Form **1120-IC-DISC** (1999)

| Form **4876-A** (Rev. July 1998) Department of the Treasury Internal Revenue Service | **Election To Be Treated as an Interest Charge DISC** | OMB No. 1545-0190 |

Part I   The corporation named below elects to be treated as an interest charge domestic international sales corporation (IC-DISC) for income tax purposes. All of the corporation's shareholders must consent to this election.

Name of corporation	**A** Employer identification number
Number, street, and room or suite no. (or P.O. box if mail is not delivered to street address)	**B** Principal business classification (see instructions)
City or town, state, and ZIP code	**D** Name of person who may be called for information: (optional)

C Tax year of IC-DISC: Must use tax year of shareholder (or shareholder group) with the highest percentage of voting power (see instructions). Enter ending month and day ▶

E Election is to take effect for the tax year beginning (month, day, year)   **F** Date corporation began doing business   Telephone number: ( )

G Name and address (including ZIP code) of each shareholder (or expected shareholder) at the beginning of the tax year the election takes effect and when the election is filed.	**H** Number of shares of stock held on— (Complete both columns for each shareholder.)		**I** Identifying number (see instructions)
	First day of year of election	Date consent is made	
1			
2			
3			
4			
5			
6			
7			
8			
9			
10			
Total. Enter total shares for all shareholders (include shares of shareholders listed on any attachments)			

Under penalties of perjury, I declare that the corporation named above has authorized me to make this election for the corporation to be treated as an IC-DISC and that the statements made are to the best of my knowledge and belief true, correct, and complete.

Signature and Title of Officer ▶   Date ,

Part II   **Shareholders' Consent Statement. Part II may be used instead of attachments. For this election to be valid, each shareholder must sign and date below or attach a separate consent to this form (see instructions).**

We, the undersigned shareholders, consent to the election of the corporation named above to be treated as an IC-DISC. Our consent is irrevocable and is binding upon all transferees of our shares in this corporation.

Signature of shareholder and date. (If consent involves transferred shares, attach a schedule showing the name and address of the holder of the shares at the beginning of the tax year and the number of shares for which the consent is made.)

1	6
2	7
3	8
4	9
5	10

For Paperwork Reduction Act Notice, see instructions on back.   Cat. No. 62075X   Form **4876-A** (Rev. 7-98)

¶ **706**

General Instructions

Section references are to the Internal Revenue Code unless otherwise noted.

Purpose of Form

A corporation files Form 4876-A to elect to be treated as an interest charge domestic international sales corporation (IC-DISC).

Once the election is made, it remains in effect until terminated or revoked. It applies to each shareholder who owns stock in the corporation while the election is in effect.

What Is an IC-DISC?

An IC-DISC is a U.S. corporation that meets certain conditions regarding its organization and international sales and that elects to be treated as an IC-DISC. The corporation must be organized under the laws of a state or the District of Columbia and meet the following tests:

● At least 95% of its gross receipts during the tax year are qualified export receipts.

● At the end of the tax year, the adjusted basis of its qualified export assets is at least 95% of the sum of the adjusted basis of all its assets.

● It has one class of stock, and its outstanding stock has a par value of at least $2,500 on each day of the tax year (or, for a new corporation, on the last day to elect IC-DISC status for the year and on each later day).

● It keeps separate books and records.

● Its tax year must conform to the tax year of the shareholder (or shareholder group) who has the highest percentage of voting power. If two or more shareholders (or shareholder groups) have the same highest percentage of voting power, the IC-DISC's tax year may be the same as that of any such shareholder (or group). See section 441(h) and its regulations for more information.

● Its election to be treated as an IC-DISC is in effect.

See section 992 and its regulations for details. Also see section 993 and its regulations for definitions of qualified export receipts and qualified export assets.

Ineligible organizations. S corporations, certain financial institutions, and other corporations listed in section 992(d) are not eligible for IC-DISC treatment.

When To File

If it is the corporation's first tax year, complete and file Form 4876-A within 90 days after the beginning of the tax year. For any tax year that is not the corporation's first tax year, the election must be made during the 90-day period immediately preceding the first day of that tax year.

For the election to be valid, all the corporation's shareholders, as of the first day of the tax year the election is to take effect, must consent to it.

Where To File

File Form 4876-A with the IRS Service Center where the corporation will file its annual return, **Form 1120-IC-DISC,** Interest Charge Domestic International Sales Corporation Return.

Specific Instructions

Part I

Address. Include the suite, room, or other unit number after the street address. If the Post Office does not deliver mail to the street address and the corporation has a P.O. Box, show the box number instead of the street address.

Item B—Principal business classification. Use the list of Codes for Principal Business Activity in the Instructions for Form 1120-IC-DISC to enter the corporation's business code number, principal business activity, and principal product or service.

Item C—Tax year change. If a corporation electing to be an IC-DISC has to change its tax year to meet the tax year requirements of section 441(h), the corporation does not need IRS consent to make the change. A tax year change by a shareholder or a subsequent change by the corporation to meet the tax year requirements of section 441(h) may require IRS consent. See section 442 and the regulations under sections 441, 442, and 921 for more information.

Column I—Identifying number. The identifying number for an individual is the social security number. For all others, it is the employer identification number.

Signature. Form 4876-A must be signed by the president, vice president, treasurer, assistant treasurer, chief accounting officer, or other officer (such as tax officer) authorized to sign for the corporation.

Part II

Shareholders' Consent Statement. An election for IC-DISC treatment will be valid only if all shareholders sign either the consent statement in Part II or a separate statement as described below. Several shareholders may combine their consents in one statement.

If a husband and wife jointly own the stock or the income from it, both must sign the consent. If tenants in common, joint tenants, or tenants by the entirety own the stock, each person must sign. The legal guardian should sign for a minor; if none has been appointed, the natural guardian should sign.

The executor or administrator should sign for an estate, and the trustee should sign for a trust. If the estate or trust has more than one executor, administrator, or trustee, any of them who is authorized to file the returns may sign the consent. For a corporation or partnership, an officer or partner who is authorized to sign the other returns may sign the consent for the IC-DISC election.

A foreign person's consent may be signed by any individual who would be authorized to sign if the person were a U.S. person.

Extension. Normally, the consents must be attached to Form 4876-A. If you establish reasonable cause for not filing a consent on time, you may file the consent within an extended period granted by an Internal Revenue Service Center. File the consents with the same service center where you filed Form 4876-A.

If shares are transferred before a consent is filed, the transferee shareholder may consent to the IC-DISC election as long as the transfer occurs and the consent is filed within the first 90 days of the tax year. The service center may grant an extension beyond that date. If the transfer takes place

more than 90 days after the tax year began, an extension can be granted only if the transferor was eligible for one.

Separate statement. Any shareholder who does not sign the consent in Part II of Form 4876-A must sign a separate consent statement for the election to be valid. The statement must say: "I, (shareholder's name), a shareholder of (corporation's name) consent to the election of (corporation's name) to be treated as an IC-DISC. The consent so made by me is irrevocable and is binding on all transferees of my shares in (corporation's name)."

In addition, the statement must show **(a)** the names, addresses, and identification numbers of both the corporation and the shareholder; **(b)** the number of shares the shareholder owned (or expects to own) at the beginning of the tax year the election takes effect; and **(c)** the number of shares the shareholder owns when making the consent.

For transferred stock, also show the name and address of the person who held the shares at the beginning of the tax year and the number of shares to which this consent applies.

Supplemental Form 4876-A. If, between the date the election is filed and the date it takes effect, the corporation issues more shares of stock or the share ownership changes, it must file a supplemental Form 4876-A, with "SUPPLEMENTAL" written across the top of the form. The form must be filed within the first 90 days of the tax year the election takes effect.

On the supplemental form, include all the information from the earlier form except for the list of owners contained in Parts I and II. Report only the owners of the new or additional shares in Part I, and in Part II obtain their consents only. Each new shareholder or holder of additional shares must consent to the IC-DISC election for the Supplemental Form 4876-A to be valid.

Form **8279**
(Rev. July 1998)
Department of the Treasury
Internal Revenue Service

Election To Be Treated as a FSC or as a Small FSC

Under section 927(f)(1) of the Internal Revenue Code

OMB No. 1545-0884

▶ **Election under section 927(f)(1).** Check the applicable box to show that the corporation elects to be treated as a
☐ Foreign sales corporation (FSC), or a ☐ Small foreign sales corporation (small FSC).

Name of corporation	**A** Employer identification number (see instructions)
Address **in** the United States (number, street, and room or suite no.) (See instructions.)	**B** Principal business classifications (see instructions)
City or town, state, and ZIP code	(1) Business activity code no. _____ (2) Business activity _____ (3) Product or service _____
Address **outside** the United States (number, street, and room or suite no.) (See instructions.)	**C** Country in which the FSC or small FSC was created or organized
City or town, and country	**D** Number of common stock shares issued and outstanding

E Name and address of a member of the Board of Directors who is not a resident of the United States

F Tax year of FSC (see instructions for **Who may elect**). Enter ending month and day of the tax year ▶	**G** Election to take effect for the tax year beginning (month, day, and year)	**H** Date corporation began doing business

I Name and address (including ZIP code) of each shareholder (or expected shareholder) (1) at the beginning of the tax year the election takes effect, and (2) when the election is filed.	**J** Shareholders' Consent Statement— We, the undersigned shareholders, consent to the corporation's election to be treated as a FSC (or small FSC) under section 927(f)(1). Our consent is irrevocable and is binding upon all transferees of our shares in this corporation.* (See instructions.)	**K** Number of common stock shares held on—(Complete both columns for each shareholder.)		**L** Shareholder's identification number (see instructions)
		First day of year of election	Date election is filed	
1				
2				
3				
4				
5				
6				
7				
8				
9				
10				

*For this election to be valid, the consent of each shareholder must be given in item J above or on a separate consent statement attached to this form. (See **Separate consent statement** in the instructions for required content if the statement is needed.)

Signature. Under penalties of perjury, I declare that the corporation named above has authorized me to make this election under section 927(f)(1) for the corporation to be treated as a FSC or small FSC and that the statements made are to the best of my knowledge and belief true, correct, and complete. I also certify that the corporation meets all required tests under **Who may elect** (in the instructions).

Signature of officer ▶ _____ Title ▶ _____ Date ▶ _____

For Paperwork Reduction Act Notice, see instructions on back.   Cat. No. 62018C   Form **8279** (Rev. 7-98)

¶ 706

General Instructions

Section references are to the Internal Revenue Code unless otherwise noted.

Purpose of form. Form 8279 is used by a corporation to make the election to be treated as a foreign sales corporation (FSC) **or** as a small FSC.

Once the election is made, it remains in effect until terminated or revoked. The election applies to each shareholder who owns stock in the corporation while the election is in effect.

Who may elect. A corporation may make the election if it meets **all** of the following tests:

1. It is a corporation created or organized under the laws of any qualifying foreign country or a U.S. possession (other than Puerto Rico). The foreign country must meet the requirements of section 927(e)(3).

2. It does not have more than 25 shareholders.

3. It does not have preferred stock.

4. It maintains an office in a qualifying foreign country or U.S. possession (other than Puerto Rico) and maintains a set of permanent books of account (including invoices) for the corporation at that office. It must also maintain books and records that sufficiently establish the amount of gross income, deductions, credits, or other matters required to be shown on the FSC's (or small FSC's) income tax return, at a location in the United States as required by section 6001.

5. It has at least one director who is not a resident of the United States.

6. It is not a member of a controlled group of corporations that has a domestic international sales corporation (DISC) as a member.

7. Its tax year is the tax year of the principal shareholder (or group of shareholders with the same tax year) with the highest percentage of voting power or, if two or more shareholders (or groups) hold the same highest percentage of voting power, it is the tax year of any such shareholder (or group). See section 441(h).

IRS consent is not necessary if the electing corporation has to change its tax year to conform to the tax year of the principal shareholder. However, IRS consent may be required for a tax year change by the principal shareholder or a subsequent change by the corporation to meet the tax year requirement of section 441(h). See section 442 and the regulations under sections 441, 442, and 921.

8. Each person who is a shareholder on the first day of the first tax year for which the election is effective consents to the corporation's FSC (or small FSC) election.

After a valid election is made, the corporation must meet tests **2** through **7** above for its entire tax year to qualify as a FSC (or small FSC) for that year. See sections 922 through 927 for additional information.

Where to file. File Form 8279 with the Internal Revenue Service Center, Philadelphia, PA 19255.

When to file. A corporation generally files Form 8279 during the 90-day period immediately preceding the beginning of the corporation's tax year. However, for the corporation's first tax year, the election is made at any time during the 90-day period after the beginning of the tax year. An election may be terminated by revocation after the first tax year for which the election is effective. A revocation made during the first 90-day period of the tax year is effective for the tax year in which it is made and all subsequent tax years. If the revocation is made after the 90-day period, it is effective for all tax years following the one in which the revocation was made. For details, see Regulations section 1.927(f)-1(b).

Specific Instructions

Address in the United States. Enter the address where the books and records required under section 6001 are maintained. Include the suite, room, or other unit number after the street address. If the Post Office does not deliver mail to the street address and the corporation has a P.O. box, show the box number instead of the street address.

Address outside the United States. Enter the address where the permanent books of account are maintained.

Item A. Employer identification number (EIN). Show the corporation's correct EIN. If the corporation does not have an EIN, it should apply for one on **Form SS-4,** Application for Employer Identification Number. Form SS-4 can be obtained at most IRS or Social Security Administration (SSA) offices. If the corporation has not received its EIN by the time the election is due, write "Applied for" in the space for the EIN.

Item B. Principal business classifications. See the Form 1120-FSC Codes for Principal Business Activity in the Instructions for Form 1120-FSC for what to enter in item B, lines **(1), (2),** and **(3).**

Item J. Shareholders' consent statement. An election to be a FSC (or a small FSC) is valid only if all persons who are shareholders on the first day the election goes into effect sign the consent statement in item **J** and provide the other information requested in items **I, K,** and **L** of Form 8279 or sign a separate consent statement as described below. When stock of the corporation is owned by a husband and wife as community property (or the income from that stock is community property), both husband and wife must sign the consent. Each tenant in common, joint tenant, and tenant by the entirety must sign the consent for each person who has a community interest in the stock or in the income from the stock. A legal guardian must sign for a minor. However, if a legal guardian has not been appointed, the natural guardian must sign.

The executor or administrator must sign for an estate, and the trustee must sign for a trust. If the estate or trust has more than one executor, administrator, or trustee, any such person who is authorized to file the return of the estate or trust may sign the consent. An officer of a corporation who is authorized to sign the corporation's tax return must sign the consent.

Separate consent statement. Any shareholder who does not sign the consent statement in item **J** of Form 8279 must sign a separate consent statement for the election to be valid. The statement must read: "I, (shareholder's name), a shareholder of (corporation's name), consent to the election of (corporation's name) to be treated as a FSC (or small FSC) under section 927(f)(1) of the Internal Revenue Code. The consent made by me is irrevocable and is binding upon all transferees of my stock in (corporation's name)."

In addition, the statement must show the name, address, and identifying number of the corporation and for every shareholder the information requested for items **I, K,** and **L** of Form 8279. For transferred stock, also show the name and address of the person who held the shares at the beginning of the tax year and the number of shares to which this consent applies.

Extension of time to file or shareholders' consent statements. The corporation may request an extension of time to file Form 8279 or the shareholders' consent statements. Under Regulations section 301.9100-1, the corporation may submit a ruling request to file Form 8279 after the 90-day period (see **When to file** above). The ruling request is subject to payment of a user fee; see Rev. Proc. 98-1 (or its successor), 1998-1 I.R.B. 7. In general, the filing will be considered as timely filed under Regulations section 301.9100-3 provided the corporation establishes that in failing to file Form 8279 timely it acted reasonably and in good faith, and that granting the extension will not prejudice the interests of the Government. The corporation may also request an extension to file shareholder consent statements if the corporation previously filed a Form 8279 that would have been valid if **(a)** all of the shareholder consent statements had been filed with the form, or **(b)** a shareholder who received transferred shares failed to file a consent statement within the required 90-day period.

Transfers of stock after Form 8279 is filed. If shares of the corporation's stock are transferred before or during the first tax year the election is to take effect but the transferor has not filed a consent

statement, the recipient of the transferred shares may consent to the election by filing a separate consent statement (see instructions above for the required format) in 90 days after the beginning of the tax year the election is to take effect. If the recipient does not file the consent within the 90-day period, an extension of time to file the consent may be granted by the IRS. See **Extension of time to file or shareholders' consent statements** above. If the transfer occurs more than 90 days after the beginning of the tax year the election is to take effect, an extension of time to file the consent may be granted by the IRS if it is determined that an extension of time to file would have been granted to the transferor if the transfer had not occurred.

If shares of the corporation's stock are transferred before the beginning of the tax year the election is to take effect, and the transferor filed a consent statement, the recipient of the transferred shares must consent to the election for the election to be valid. The consent must be filed within 90 days after the beginning of the tax year the election is to take effect. If the recipient does not file the consent in the 90-day period, an extension of time to file the consent may be granted by the IRS. See **Extension of time to file or shareholders' consent statements** above.

Item L. Shareholder's identification number. The identification number for an individual is the social security number. For all others, it is their employer identification number.

Supplemental Form 8279. If the corporation issues more stock or the ownership of its stock changes after the election is filed but before the beginning of the tax year for which the election is made, the corporation must file a supplemental Form 8279, and write "SUPPLEMENTAL" across the top of the form. The supplemental form must be filed in the first 90 days of the tax year the election takes effect.

Complete items **I** through **L** of the supplemental form only for shareholders acquiring additional stock and new shareholders. Each additional or new shareholder must consent to this election for the supplemental Form 8279 to be valid. Attach a copy of the Form 8279 filed.

Signature. Form 8279 must be signed by the president, vice president, treasurer, assistant treasurer, chief accounting officer, or other officer (such as tax officer) who is authorized to sign for the corporation.

Paperwork Reduction Act Notice

We ask for the information on this form to carry out the Internal Revenue laws of the United States. You are required to give us the information. We need it to ensure that you are complying with these laws and to allow us to figure and collect the right amount of tax.

You are not required to provide the information requested on a form that is subject to the Paperwork Reduction Act unless the form displays a valid OMB control number. Books or records relating to a form or its instructions must be retained as long as their contents may become material in the administration of any Internal Revenue law. Generally, tax returns and return information are confidential, as required by Code section 6103.

The time needed to complete and file this form will vary depending on individual circumstances. The estimated average time is:

Recordkeeping . . . . 4 hr., 32 min.

Learning about the law
or the form . . . . 1 hr., 47 min.

Preparing and sending
the form to the IRS . . . . . 1 hr., 56 min.

If you have comments concerning the accuracy of these time estimates or suggestions for making this form simpler, we would be happy to hear from you. You can write to the Tax Forms Committee, Western Area Distribution Center, Rancho Cordova, CA 95743-0001. **DO NOT** send Form 8279 to this address. Instead, see **Where to file** above.

Form **8404**	Interest Charge on DISC-Related		
(Rev. December 1999)	Deferred Tax Liability		OMB No. 1545-0939
Department of the Treasury Internal Revenue Service	▶ Do not attach this form to your tax return; file it separately.		

A Check applicable box to show type of taxpayer:	Name	**B** Shareholder's identifying number
☐ Corporation	Address of shareholder (number, street, room, suite, or P.O. box number)	
☐ Individual		**C** IC-DISC's identifying number
☐ Trust or Decedent's estate	City, state, and ZIP code	

D Shareholder's tax year for which interest charge is required to be paid (see instructions) **E** Name of IC-DISC for which identifying number in item C is reported:

1	Taxable income or loss on tax return (actual or estimated)	1	
2	Deferred DISC income from line 10, Part III, Schedule K (Form 1120-IC-DISC)	2	
3	Section 995(f)(2) adjustments to line 1 income or loss (see instructions)	3	
4	Combine lines 1, 2, and 3. If zero or a loss, don't file this form	4	
5	Tax liability on line 4 amount (see instructions)	5	
6	Tax liability per return (actual or estimated) (see instructions)	6	
7	DISC-related deferred tax liability. Subtract line 6 from line 5.	7	
8	Base period T-bill rate factor (see instructions)	8	
9	**Interest charge due.** Multiply line 7 by line 8. (See instruction on **Paying the Interest Charge.**)	9	

Please Sign Here

Under penalties of perjury, I declare that I have examined this return, including accompanying schedules and statements, and to the best of my knowledge and belief, it is true, correct, and complete. Declaration of preparer (other than taxpayer) is based on all information of which preparer has any knowledge.

▶ Signature and Title (if any) ▶ Date

Paid Preparer's Use Only

Preparer's signature ▶	Date	Check if self-employed ▶ ☐	Preparer's SSN or PTIN
Firm's name (or yours if self-employed) and address ▶		EIN ▶	
		ZIP code ▶	

General Instructions

See Paperwork Reduction Act Notice on page 2. For Privacy Act Notice, individual filers should see the Instructions for Form 1040.

Section references are to the Internal Revenue Code unless otherwise noted.

Purpose of Form. Shareholders of Interest Charge Domestic International Sales Corporations (IC-DISCs) use Form 8404 to figure and report their interest on DISC-related deferred tax liability.

Who Must File. You must file Form 8404 if: (a) you are a shareholder of an IC-DISC; (b) the IC-DISC reports deferred DISC income to you on line 10, Part III of **Schedule K (Form 1120-IC-DISC);** and (c) the addition of this income would result in increased taxable income if it were included on your tax return for the tax year.

When To File. File Form 8404 at the time you are required to file your Federal income tax return (excluding extensions) for your tax year that ends with or in which the IC-DISC's tax year ends.

For example, you are a fiscal year corporation with a July 1, 1999, to June 30, 2000, tax year and you are a shareholder in an IC-DISC with a July 1, 1999, to June 30, 2000, tax year that reports deferred DISC income to you for its year ending June 30, 2000. Because your tax year ends with the IC-DISC's tax year, you are required to file Form 8404 on September 15, 2000 (2½ months after your tax year ends).

Where To File. File Form 8404 with the Internal Revenue Service Center where you are required to file your Federal income tax return. File the form in a separate envelope than that of your income tax return. Keep a copy for your records.

Paying the Interest Charge. You must pay the interest charge shown on line 9 by the date your Federal income tax for the tax year is required to be paid. For individuals, the interest is due on the 15th day of the 4th month following the close of the tax year. For corporations, the interest is due on the 15th day of the 3rd month following the close of the tax year.

Attach a check or money order made payable to "United States Treasury" for the full amount of the interest charge. **Do not** combine the interest charge with any other tax or interest due. Write your identification number and "Form 8404—Interest Due" on your payment. Do not use **Form 8109,** Federal Tax Deposit Coupon.

If the interest charge is not paid by the due date, interest, compounded daily, at the rate specified under section 6621, will be imposed on the amount of unpaid interest from the due date until the date the interest is paid. Payment of estimated tax is not required for the interest charge. See proposed Regulations section 1.995(f)-1(j)(3) for other details.

Amended Form 8404. You are required to file an amended Form 8404 only if the amount of the DISC-related deferred tax liability (line 7) changes as a result of audit adjustments, changes you make by the filing of an amended return, or if estimates were used on your original Form 8404 and changes were made to these estimates when you filed your tax return. See proposed Regulations section 1.995(f)-1(j)(4) for details.

Specific Instructions

A. Type of Taxpayer. Check the applicable box to indicate your status as a taxpayer.

Shareholders that are partnerships, S corporations, estates or trusts, see proposed Regulations section 1.995(f)-1(h) for special rules. Under these rules, only trusts and estates complete Form 8404 and check the applicable box in item A. Partnerships and S corporations distribute their share of deferred DISC income to partners and shareholders and the partners and shareholders complete Form 8404.

Name and Address. Enter the name and address as shown on your tax return from which the income or loss on line 1 of Form 8404 is obtained. If the return is a joint return, also enter your spouse's name as shown on Form 1040.

B. Identifying Number. Individuals must enter their social security number. Other filers must enter their employer identification number. See section 6109.

C. IC-DISC's Identifying Number. Enter the identifying number of the IC-DISC from the Schedule K (Form 1120-IC-DISC) on which line 2 deferred DISC income was reported to you. If income is reported to you from more than one IC-DISC, enter each IC-DISC's identifying number in item C, each IC-DISC's name in item E, and report the combined income on line 2.

Cat. No. 62423Z Form **8404** (Rev. 12-99)

D. Tax Year. Enter in item D the calendar year or the beginning and ending dates of the tax year shown on your tax return for which the interest charge is figured.

Special Computation Rules

Carrybacks. The determination of the shareholder's DISC-related deferred tax liability on lines 1 through 7 shall be made without taking into account any net operating loss (NOL) or capital loss carryback; or credit carryback to the tax year.

Carryovers. The determination of the shareholder's tax liability (line 5) for the tax year is made by disregarding any loss, deduction, or credit to the extent that such loss, deduction, or credit may be carried (either back or forward) by the shareholder to any other tax year.

Note: *If the tax year is the last tax year to which the amount of carryforward (of loss, deduction, or credit) may be carried, the line 3 adjustments and line 5 tax shall be figured with regard to the full amount of such carryforward.*

For example, a shareholder had a NOL carryover to 2000 of $12,000; $10,000 income to which $10,000 of the NOL can be applied; $2,000 allowable NOL carryover to 2001; and $5,000 deferred DISC income for 2000. In this case, the allowed NOL is $10,000. **Note:** *If 2000 were the last tax year to which the $12,000 NOL could be carried, the full $12,000 NOL would be allowed for purposes of figuring line 5 tax liability. The additional $2,000 loss would be entered on line 3.*

Other Adjustments. In figuring line 3 adjustments, take into account any income and expense adjustments that do not result in amounts that may be carried back or forward to other tax years. For example, in the case of an IC-DISC shareholder who is an individual, the amount of medical expenses allowable as a deduction under section 213 must be redetermined for purposes of line 3 adjustments. However, the amount allowable as a charitable deduction under section 170 is not redetermined because this adjustment could result in a carryback or carryover.

See proposed Regulations sections 1.995(f)-1(d)(1) through (8) for other details regarding these and other special computation rules.

Line-by-Line Instructions

Line 1. Enter on line 1 the taxable income or loss from your Federal income tax return for your tax year that ends with or in which the IC-DISC's tax year ends. If you have not yet filed your tax return, estimate your income or loss based on all information available to you.

Line 2. Enter the deferred DISC income from line 10, Part III of Schedule K (Form 1120-IC-DISC), for the IC-DISC tax year that ends with or within your tax year. If

you are a shareholder in more than one IC-DISC that reports deferred DISC income to you, report on line 2 the sum of all deferred DISC income reported to you for the year.

Line 3. Enter the net amount of all section 995(f)(2) adjustments to taxable income. See **Special Computation Rules,** above, for details on the income (loss) and expense adjustments to be made. If more than one adjustment is involved, attach a schedule listing each item and show the computation of the net amount.

Line 4. Combine amounts on lines 1, 2, and 3. If the line 4 amount is zero or a loss, you do not have to file Form 8404.

Lines 5 and 6. The tax liability on lines 5 and 6 (with and without the deferred DISC income) means the amount of tax imposed on the IC-DISC shareholder for the tax year by Chapter 1 of the Internal Revenue Code (other than taxes listed below) reduced by allowable credits (other than credits listed below).

See **Special Computation Rules** on carrybacks and carryovers that may affect the line 5 computation.

The following taxes are **not** taken into account:

- Alternative minimum tax (individuals, corporations, estates, or trusts).

- Any other provisions described in section 26(b)(2) (relating to certain other taxes treated as not imposed by Chapter 1).

The following credits are **not** taken into account:

- Section 31 (taxes withheld on wages).
- Section 32 (earned income credit).
- Section 34 (fuels credit).

For individuals or corporations, figure the line 6 tax liability from **Form 1040,** U.S. Individual Income Tax Return, or **Form 1120,** U.S. Corporation Income Tax Return. (For other filers, enter amounts from corresponding lines of other income tax returns.) If you have not yet filed your return, estimate the line 6 tax liability based on all information available to you.

For 1999, for individuals and corporations, figure the line 6 tax liability using the items shown below as reported on the corresponding lines of Forms 1040 and 1120. (For tax years beginning before or after 1999, figure the line 6 tax liability by matching the item descriptions to the lines of Forms 1040 and 1120 for that year.)

	1999 Form 1040 Line	1999 Form 1120 Line
Tax less nonrefundable credits (adjusted for prior year minimum tax credit (Form 8801 or 8827)) . .	49	6, Sch. J
Plus: (1) Advance earned income credit payments . .	54	......
(2) Recapture taxes except Form 8828 .	56	8, Sch. J
Less: Credit for tax paid on undistributed capital gains (Form 2439)	63	32f, pg.1

Line 8. The base period T-bill rate is defined in section 995(f)(4). The base period T-bill rate is compounded daily based on the number of days in the shareholder's tax year to determine the base period T-bill rate factor.

The base period T-bill rate for the one-year period ending September 30, 1999, is 4.80%. The 4.80% compounded daily for a 365-day tax year produces a base period T-bill factor of .049167344. This factor is entered on line 8 of Form 8404 that shareholders prepare for their 365-day tax years beginning in 1999. Factors used for shareholders' 1999 tax years of less or more than 365 days are published in Revenue Ruling 99-52, 1999-50 I.R.B. 652. It also includes citations for base period T-bill rates for tax years beginning before 1999.

The base period T-bill rate and factors for tax years beginning in 2000 will be published as a new revenue ruling in late 2000.

Line 9. Multiply line 7 by the factor on line 8. See **Paying the Interest Charge** on page 1 for details on when and how to pay the interest.

For corporations (other than S corporations), the annual interest charge **is** deductible as an interest expense for the tax year it is paid or accrued. See proposed Regulations section 1.995(f)-1(j)(2) for details on the tax year of deductibility. **For other filers, this interest is not deductible.**

Paperwork Reduction Act Notice. We ask for the information on this form to carry out the Internal Revenue laws of the United States. You are required to give us the information. We need it to ensure that you are complying with these laws and to allow us to figure and collect the right amount of interest.

You are not required to provide the information requested on a form that is subject to the Paperwork Reduction Act unless the form displays a valid OMB control number. Books or records relating to a form or its instructions must be retained as long as their contents may become material in the administration of any Internal Revenue law. Generally, tax returns and return information are confidential, as required by section 6103.

The time needed to complete and file this form will vary depending on individual circumstances. The estimated average time is: **Recordkeeping,** 4 hr., 4 min.; **Learning about the law or the form,** 2 hr., 17 min.; and **Preparing, copying, and sending the form to the IRS,** 2 hr., 27 min.

If you have comments concerning the accuracy of these time estimates or suggestions for making this form simpler, we would be happy to hear from you. You can write to the Tax Forms Committee, Western Area Distribution Center, Rancho Cordova, CA 95743-0001. DO NOT send the form to this office. Instead, see **Where To File** on page 1.

Chapter 8

Foreign Currency Translation and Transactions

¶ 801 INTRODUCTION

The foreign branches and subsidiaries of U.S. companies often conduct business and maintain their books and records in the currency of the host country. This creates a currency translation problem for the domestic parent corporation, which must restate into U.S. dollars the results from its foreign operations. Tax attributes that require translation include the taxable income or loss of a foreign branch, earnings remittances from a foreign branch, actual and deemed distributions from a foreign corporation, and foreign income taxes. Foreign currency translation would be the only issue if currency exchange rates did not fluctuate. However, the U.S. dollar floats freely against other currencies, and this results in currency exchange gains and losses on assets and liabilities denominated in other currencies. Translational exchange gains and losses arise when a foreign branch or subsidiary that has a functional currency other than the U.S. dollar repatriates earnings that were previously taxed to the U.S. parent, and the exchange rate has changed since the parent included those earnings in U.S. taxable income. Transactional exchange gains and losses arise when, for example, a U.S. company enters into a transaction denominated in a foreign currency, and the exchange rate fluctuates between the time the transaction is entered into and the time it is closed out. Foreign currency translation, including the tax treatment of translational exchange gains and losses, is discussed in the section entitled "Foreign Currency Translation." Transactional exchange gains and losses are discussed in the section entitled "Foreign Currency Transactions."

¶ 802   FOREIGN CURRENCY TRANSLATION

Qualified Business Unit

A taxpayer generally must make all of its U.S. tax determinations in its functional currency.[1] A taxpayer's functional currency is the U.S. dollar, except for a qualified business unit (or "QBU") that conducts a significant part of its activities in an economic environment in which a foreign currency is used and maintains its books and records in that foreign currency.[2] A corporation is always considered to be a QBU.[3] In addition, a branch of a corporation can qualify as a QBU if the branch is a separate and clearly identified unit of a trade or business of the corporation for which separate books and records are maintained.[4]

Whether a branch operation constitutes a separate trade or business of the corporation is a question of fact. For this purpose, a trade or business is a specific unified group of activities that constitutes an independent economic activity carried on for profit. This group of activities ordinarily must include every operation which is part of the process by which an enterprise earns a profit, including the collection of income and the payment of expenses. It is not necessary that the trade or business carried out by the branch be of a different type than that carried out by other QBUs of the taxpayer. For example, a sales branch that is located in a different geographic market than the home office sales operation can constitute a separate trade or business. However, activities that are merely ancillary to a trade or business of the corporation do not constitute a separate trade or business.[5]

Example 8.1:[6] USAco, a domestic corporation, manufactures goods for sale both in the United States and abroad. USAco sells goods in the United Kingdom through a branch office located in London. The London office has its own employees who solicit and process orders. USAco maintains separate books and records for all of the transactions entered into by the London office. USAco qualifies as a QBU because of its corporate status. The branch sales office in London also qualifies as a separate QBU because its sales operation constitutes a separate trade or business for which USAco maintains separate books and records.

---

[1] Code Sec. 985(a).

[2] Code Sec. 985(b)(1).

[3] Reg. § 1.989(a)-1(b)(2)(i).

[4] Code Sec. 989(a) and Reg. § 1.989(a)-1(b)(2)(ii). A separate set of books and records generally includes books of original entry and ledger accounts, both general and subsidiary. Reg. § 1.989(a)-1(d).

[5] Reg. § 1.989(a)-1(c). An activity of a foreign person which produces income effectively connected with the conduct of a U.S. trade or business is always treated as a separate QBU. Reg. § 1.989(a)-1(b)(3).

[6] Compare Reg. § 1.989(a)-1(e), Example 1.

Example 8.2:[7] USAco, a domestic corporation, incorporates a wholly owned subsidiary in Switzerland to market its products in Europe. In addition to its sales operation located in Switzerland, the Swiss subsidiary has branch sales offices in France and Germany that are responsible for all marketing operations in those countries. Each branch has its own employees, solicits and processes orders, and maintains a separate set of books and records. USAco and the Swiss subsidiary are both QBUs because of their corporate status. The French and German branches also are QBUs of the Swiss subsidiary because each sales operation constitutes a separate trade or business for which separate books and records are maintained.

Unlike a corporation, an individual is not a QBU.[8] Moreover, activities of an individual conducted as an employee do not constitute a QBU.[9] However, activities of an individual conducted as a sole proprietor do constitute a QBU if they satisfy the separate trade or business and separate books and records requirements discussed above.[10] Like a corporation, a partnership, trust, or estate is always considered to be a QBU of the partner or beneficiary, regardless of the scope of the entity's activities, or whether it keeps separate books and records.[11] In addition, an activity of a partnership, trust, or estate also can qualify as a separate QBU if it satisfies the separate trade or business and separate books and records requirements.[12]

Functional Currency

A QBU's functional currency is the U.S. dollar, unless the QBU conducts a significant part of its activities in an economic environment in which a foreign currency is used and maintains its books and records in that foreign currency.[13] For this purpose, a QBU is presumed to keep its books and records in the currency of the economic environment in which a significant part of its activities are conducted.[14] The taxpayer must consider all of the facts and circumstances in identifying the relevant economic environment, including the currency of the country in which the QBU is a resident, as well as the currencies in which the QBU realizes its cash flows, generates its revenues, incurs its expenses, borrows and lends, sells its products, and makes its pricing and other financial decisions.[15] If a QBU has more than one currency that

---

[7] Compare Reg. § 1.989(a)-1(e), Example 2.

[8] Reg. § 1.989(a)-1(b)(2)(i).

[9] Reg. § 1.989(a)-1(c).

[10] Reg. § 1.989(a)-1(b)(2)(ii).

[11] Reg. § 1.989(a)-1(b)(2)(i).

[12] Reg. § 1.989(a)-1(b)(2)(ii).

[13] Code Sec. 985(b)(1) and Reg. § 1.985-1(c)(1). Activities of a foreign person which produce income effectively connected with the conduct of a U.S. trade or business are always treated as a separate QBU, with the U.S. dollar as its functional currency. Reg. § 1.985-1(b)(1)(v). Special rules also apply to a foreign corporation with two or more QBUs that do not have the same functional currency. Reg. § 1.985-1(d).

[14] Reg. § 1.985-1(c)(3).

[15] Reg. § 1.985-1(c)(2)(i). Other relevant factors include the duration of the qualified business unit's

satisfies these requirements, then the QBU may choose any of those currencies as its functional currency.[16]

Special rules apply to any QBU that would otherwise be required to use a hyperinflationary currency as its functional currency. Such QBUs must use the U.S. dollar as their functional currency, and must compute their taxable income (and earnings and profits) using the dollar approximate separate transactions method.[17] A hyperinflationary currency is defined as the currency of a foreign country in which there is a cumulative compounded rate of inflation of at least 100% during the 36-month period immediately before the start of the current taxable year.[18] Hyperinflationary currency creates significant problems with the conventional methods for translating the results of a foreign operation into U.S. dollars. For example, in a hyperinflationary environment, these methods do not provide an accurate comparison of current-year inflated revenues to the costs of prior-year investments in property, plant, and equipment. The dollar approximate separate transactions method attempts to mitigate these problems by translating the QBU's taxable income (and earnings and profits) on at least a monthly basis,[19] and by annually recognizing certain unrealized exchange gains and losses.[20]

The adoption of a functional currency is treated as a method of accounting. As a consequence, the functional currency used in the year of adoption must be used for all subsequent taxable years unless permission to change is granted by the Commissioner.[21] Permission to change functional currencies generally is not granted unless significant changes in the facts and circumstances of the QBU's economic environment occur. The QBU's functional currency for U.S. financial reporting purposes is a relevant factor in this regard.[22]

Foreign Income Taxes

For taxable years beginning prior to December 31, 1997, foreign income taxes were translated into dollars at the spot rate, that is, the exchange rate for the date on which the taxes were paid.[23] Therefore, an estimated tax payment was translated at the spot rate for the date on which the estimated tax payment is made, and withholding taxes

---

(Footnote Continued)

business operations and the significance or volume of the qualified business unit's independent activities.

[16] Reg. § 1.985-1(c)(4).

[17] Reg. §§ 1.985-1(b)(2)(ii)(A) and 1.985-3. There are exceptions for noncontrolled foreign corporations and certain QBU branches of foreign corporations. Reg. § 1.985-1(b)(2)(ii)(B).

[18] Reg. § 1.985-1(b)(2)(ii)(D).

[19] Reg. § 1.985-3(b)(3) and (c)(7). The conventional approach is to translate taxable income on an annual basis.

[20] Reg. § 1.985-3(b)(4) and (d)(1).

[21] Reg. § 1.985-4(a).

[22] Reg. § 1.985-4(b). If a QBU is granted permission to change its functional currency, adjustments may be required. Reg. § 1.985-5.

[23] Code Sec. 986(a)(1)(A), prior to amendment by the Taxpayer Relief Act of 1997 (August 5, 1997).

were translated at the spot rate for the date on which the tax is withheld.

For tax years beginning on or after January 1, 1998, taxpayers that account for foreign taxes on an accrual basis generally may translate foreign income taxes accrued into U.S. dollars at the average exchange rate for the tax year to which the taxes relate. However, this rule does not apply to (i) foreign taxes actually paid more than two years from the close of such tax year, (ii) foreign taxes paid in a tax year prior to the year to which they relate, and (iii) taxes paid in an inflationary currency. All foreign taxes not eligible for translation at the yearly average exchange rate must be translated using the exchange rate on the date of payment. In addition, any adjustment to the amount of the taxes is translated using the exchange rate at the time the adjustment is paid to the foreign country. In the case of any refund or credit of foreign taxes, taxpayers must use the exchange rate in effect at the time when the original payment of the foreign taxes is made. However, the IRS has the authority to issue regulations that would allow these foreign tax payments to be translated into U.S. dollar amounts using an average exchange rate for a specified period.[24]

> **Example 8.3:** USAco is an accrual-basis, calendar-year domestic corporation that has a branch in a foreign country where the franc (F) is the local currency. During the current year, USAco remits F2 million of foreign income taxes on June 30, and F3 million of foreign income taxes on September 30. When closing its books for the year, USAco estimates that it owes an additional F1 million of foreign income taxes for the year. The franc was worth $0.10 on June 30, $0.12 on September 30, $0.13 on December 31, and had an average value during the year of $0.11. Therefore, USAco's creditable taxes are $660,000, computed as follows:
>
> | | | |
> |---|---|---|
> | June 30 | $220,000 | [F2 million × $0.11] |
> | September 30 | $330,000 | [F3 million × $0.11] |
> | December 31 | $110,000 | [F1 million × $0.11] |
> | Total | $660,000 | |

Foreign Branches

If a foreign branch is a QBU that has a functional currency other than the dollar, the taxpayer first computes the branch's taxable income for the year in the branch's functional currency, and then translates the net income amount into dollars using the average exchange rate for the branch's taxable year.[25] The average exchange rate

---

[24] Code Sec. 986(a).
[25] Code Secs. 987 and 989(b)(4). See also Prop. Reg. § 1.987-1(b)(1).

means the simple average of the daily exchange rates, excluding week-ends, holidays, and any other nonbusiness days for the taxable year.[26]

This method of translating a foreign branch's taxable income into U.S. dollars ignores the currency exchange gains and losses that arise when the foreign currency in which the branch's assets and liabilities are denominated strengthens or weakens against the U.S. dollar. These currency exchange gains and losses are recognized, however, when the branch remits its earnings to the U.S. home office.[27] The currency exchange gain and loss recognized upon an earnings remittance from a branch equals the difference between:

(i)   the dollar value of the remittance as determined using the spot rate for the date of the remittance, and

(ii) the taxpayer's basis in the distributed earnings as determined by the dollar amount at which the taxpayer previously in-cluded the earnings in U.S. taxable income.[28]

For purposes of determining the taxpayer's basis in a remittance, the remittance is treated as being paid pro rata out of the branch's post-1986 accumulated earnings, which are maintained in the branch's functional currency.[29] The resulting gain or loss is treated as ordinary income which has the same source as the income giving rise to the branch's post-1986 accumulated earnings.[30]

> **Example 8.4:** USAco is a domestic corporation with the dollar as its functional currency. USAco establishes a foreign sales branch, which qualifies as a QBU with the franc (F) as its functional currency. The branch's tax attributes for its first two years of operations are as follows:

	Year 1	Year 2
Taxable income	F8 million	None
Foreign income taxes	F3 million	None
Remittance to USAco (paid December 31) . .	None	F2 million

> The franc had an average daily value during year 1 of $0.12, and was worth $0.15 on December 31 of year 2. Therefore, the F3 million of foreign income taxes paid in year 1 translates into $360,000 [F3 million × $0.12], and the F8 million of branch income in year 1 translates into $960,000 [F3 million of foreign income

---

[26] Reg. § 1.989(b)-1. For taxable years beginning prior to December 31, 1997, an exception applies if the taxpayer claims a foreign tax credit for foreign taxes imposed on branch income. In such cases, an amount of branch income equal to the related foreign income taxes (i.e., the tax equivalent amount) is translated into U.S. dollars at the same rate used to translate the foreign income taxes. Prop. Reg. § 1.987-1(b)(3).

[27] Code Sec. 987(3) and Prop. Reg. § 1.987-2(a). The incorporation or other termination of a branch

also triggers recognition of a currency exchange gain or loss. Prop. Reg. § 1.987-3.

[28] Prop. Reg. § 1.987-2(d)(1).

[29] Code Sec. 987(3)(A) and Prop. Reg. § 1.987-2(d)(2). Foreign income taxes for which the taxpayer claimed a foreign tax credit reduce the branch's post-1986 accumulated earnings pool, as well as the taxpayer's U.S. dollar basis in that pool of earnings. Prop. Reg. § 1.987-1(b)(3)(iii).

[30] Code Sec. 987(3)(B).

taxes $\times$ \$0.12]. The branch remittance in year 2 triggers the recognition of a currency exchange gain produced as a result of the franc strengthening against the dollar. The gain equals \$60,000, which represents the excess of the remittance's value of \$300,000 [F2 million $\times$ \$0.15] over USAco's basis in the distributed earnings of \$240,000 [(F2 million $\div$ {F8 million of taxable income $-$ F3 million of foreign income taxes}) $\times$ (\$960,000 of taxable income $-$ \$360,000 of foreign income taxes)].

Foreign Corporations

Dividend distributions. The translation rules for computing the U.S. tax attributes of a dividend distribution from a foreign corporation are as follows:

(i) *Dividend*—If a foreign corporation pays a dividend in a foreign currency, the U.S. taxpayer translates the dividend income into dollars using the spot rate for the date on which the dividend was included in the taxpayer's income.[31]

(ii) *Foreign withholding taxes*—Any foreign withholding taxes imposed on a dividend from a foreign corporation are translated into dollars using the spot rate or the average exchange rate, whichever is applicable (see Foreign Income Taxes, above).[32]

(iii) *Deemed paid foreign tax credit*—For purposes of computing the deemed paid credit, the foreign corporation's dividend distribution and post-1986 undistributed earnings are not translated into U.S. dollars, but are instead maintained in the foreign corporation's functional currency.[33] On the other hand, foreign taxes included in the pool of post-1986 foreign income taxes are translated into dollars using the spot rate or the average exchange rate, whichever is applicable (see Foreign Income Taxes, above).[34]

Example 8.5: USAco, a domestic corporation, owns 100% of the stock of EURco. EURco is a calendar year, foreign corporation with the franc (F) as its functional currency. During its first year of operations, EURco derives F10 million of taxable income, pays F4 million in foreign income taxes, and distributes a F3 million dividend to USAco on December 31. The franc was worth \$0.15 on December 31 and had an average daily value during the year of \$0.14. Therefore, the F3 million dividend translates into \$450,000 [F3 million $\times$ \$0.15], and EURco's post-1986 foreign income taxes are \$560,000 [F4 million $\times$ \$0.14]. EURco's post-1986 undistributed earnings are F6 million [F10 million of taxable income $-$ F4

---

[31] Code Secs. 986(b)(2) and 989(b)(1).
[32] Code Sec. 986(a).

[33] Code Sec. 986(b)(1).
[34] Code Sec. 986(a).

million of foreign income taxes]. Thus, EURco's dividend pulls out deemed paid taxes of $280,000 [$560,000 of post-1986 foreign income taxes × (F3 million dividend ÷ F6 million of post-1986 undistributed earnings)], and USAco must recognize dividend income of $730,000 [$450,000 dividend + $280,000 gross-up].

Subpart F inclusions. The translation rules for computing the tax attributes of a U.S. shareholder's Subpart F inclusion from a controlled foreign corporation (or "CFC") are as follows:

(i) *Subpart F inclusion*—The appropriate exchange rate for computing an income inclusion under Subpart F varies with the type of inclusion. An inclusion of Subpart F income is translated into dollars using the average exchange rate for the CFC's taxable year, whereas inclusions for investments in U.S. property are computed using the spot rate for the last day of the CFC's taxable year.[35] The average exchange rate means the simple average of the daily exchange rates, excluding weekends, holidays, and any other nonbusiness days for the taxable year.[36]

(ii) *Deemed paid foreign tax credit*—For purposes of computing the deemed paid credit, the CFC's Subpart F inclusion and post-1986 undistributed earnings are not translated into U.S. dollars, but are instead maintained in the CFC's functional currency.[37] On other hand, foreign taxes included in the pool of post-1986 foreign income taxes are translated into dollars using the spot rate or the average exchange rate, whichever is applicable (see Foreign Income Taxes, above).[38]

(iii) *Distributions of previously taxed income*—For purposes of tracing actual dividend distributions to previously taxed income, the taxpayer measures the CFC's earnings in its functional currency.[39] In addition, upon the receipt of a distribution of previously taxed income, the U.S. shareholder must recognize a currency exchange gain or loss equal to the difference between:

(a) the dollar value of the distribution as determined using the spot rate for the date of the distribution, and

(b) the U.S. shareholder's basis in the distribution as determined by the dollar amount at which the taxpayer previously included the earnings in U.S. taxable income.[40]

---

[35] Code Secs. 986(b)(2) and 989(b).

[36] Reg. § 1.989(b)-1.

[37] Code Sec. 986(b)(1).

[38] Code Sec. 986(a).

[39] Code Sec. 986(b)(1).

[40] Code Sec. 986(c)(1).

Such gains are treated as ordinary income which has the same source as the associated Subpart F inclusion.[41]

Example 8.6: USAco, a domestic corporation, owns 100% of the stock of FORco, which was organized in year 1. FORco is a calendar year, foreign corporation with the mark (M) as its functional currency. FORco's tax attributes for its first two years of operations are as follows:

	Year 1	Year 2
Taxable income	M50 million	None
Foreign income taxes	M10 million	None
Net Subpart F income	M20 million	None
Investments in U.S. property	M5 million	None
Actual dividend distributions (paid December 31)	None	M4 million

The mark had an average value of $1.10 during year 1, and was worth $1.20 on December 31 of year 1, and $1.40 on December 31 of year 2. USAco's Subpart F inclusion for year 1 is $28 million [(M20 million of Subpart F income × $1.10) + (M5 million investment in U.S. property × $1.20)]. With respect to the deemed paid credit, FORco has post-1986 foreign income taxes of $11 million [M10 million × $1.10] and post-1986 undistributed earnings of M40 million [M50 million of taxable income − M10 million of foreign income taxes]. Therefore, USAco's deemed paid taxes are $6,875,000 [$11 million of post-1986 foreign income taxes × (M25 million Subpart F inclusion ÷ M40 million of post-1986 undistributed earnings)].

USAco can exclude from income the M4 million dividend received in year 2 because it is traced to FORco's previously taxed income from year 1. For this purpose, USAco measures FORco's earnings in marks and traces the distribution to FORco's M5 million investment of earnings in U.S. property from year 1.[42] However, the dividend does trigger the recognition of a currency exchange gain produced as a result of the mark strengthening against the dollar. The gain equals $800,000, which represents the excess of the distribution's value of $5.6 million [M4 million dividend × $1.40] over USAco's basis in the previously taxed earnings of $4.8 million [M4 million × $1.20].

Passive foreign investment company inclusions. A U.S. person translates his or her pro rata share of the undistributed earnings and profits of a qualified electing fund (or "QEF") into dollars using the average exchange rate for the QEF's taxable year.[43] The average exchange rate means the simple average of the daily exchange rates,

---

[41] Code Sec. 986(c)(1).
[42] Code Sec. 959(c).

[43] Code Secs. 986(b)(2) and 989(b)(3).

¶ 802

excluding weekends, holidays, and any other nonbusiness days for the taxable year.[44] For purposes of tracing subsequent actual dividend distributions to the QEF's previously taxed income, the taxpayer measures the QEF's earnings in its functional currency.[45] In addition, a U.S. person who receives a distribution of a QEF's previously taxed income must recognize a currency exchange gain or loss equal to the difference between:

(i)   the dollar value of the actual distribution as determined using the spot rate for the date of the distribution, and

(ii) the taxpayer's basis in the distribution as determined by the dollar amount at which the taxpayer previously included the earnings in U.S. taxable income.[46]

Such gains are treated as ordinary income which has the same source as the associated QEF inclusion.[47]

Foreign personal holding company inclusions. A U.S. person translates his or her pro rata share of a foreign personal holding company's undistributed foreign personal holding company income into dollars using the average exchange rate for the foreign personal holding company's taxable year.[48] The average exchange rate means the simple average of the daily exchange rates, excluding weekends, holidays, and any other nonbusiness days for the taxable year.[49]

¶ 803   FOREIGN CURRENCY TRANSACTIONS

Applicable Transactions

Special rules apply for purposes of determining the amount, timing, character, and source of currency exchange gains and losses associated with Code Sec. 988 transactions. Code Sec. 988 transactions include the following:

(i)   dispositions of a nonfunctional currency, and

(ii) the following three categories of transactions where the amount the taxpayer is entitled to receive, or required to pay, is denominated in (or determined by reference to) a nonfunctional currency:

(a) *Debt instruments*—This includes transactions where the taxpayer lends or borrows funds through the use of a bond, debenture, note, certificate, or other evidence of indebtedness.

(b) *Receivables and payables*—This includes transactions where the taxpayer accrues an item of income or expense

---

[44] Reg. § 1.989(b)-1.
[45] Code Sec. 986(b)(1).
[46] Code Sec. 986(c)(1).

[47] Code Sec. 986(c)(1).
[48] Code Secs. 986(b)(2) and 989(b)(3).
[49] Reg. § 1.989(b)-1.

which will be received or paid at a future date, including a payable or receivable relating to a capital expenditure.

(c) *Forward, futures, and option contracts*—This includes transactions where the taxpayer enters into or acquires a forward contract, futures contract, option, warrant, or similar financial instrument.[50]

However, Code Sec. 988 transactions do not include regulated futures contracts and nonequity options,[51] any transaction entered into by an individual unless the transaction is related to a business or investment activity,[52] and certain transactions between or among a taxpayer and/or QBUs of that taxpayer.[53]

The entire amount of gain or loss arising from a disposition of a nonfunctional currency is treated as an exchange gain or loss.[54] The same is true of any gain or loss arising from a currency forward, futures, or option contract.[55] In contrast, a gain or loss arising from a transaction involving a debt instrument, receivable, or payable is treated as an exchange gain or loss only to the extent it is attributable to a change in exchange rates that occurs between the transaction's booking date and the payment date.[56] For this purpose, the payment date is the date on which payment is made or received,[57] whereas the booking date is the date on which funds are borrowed or lent in the case of a debt instrument [58] or the date on which the item is accrued in the case of a receivable or payable.[59]

A special rule applies to simplify the accounting for trade receivables and trade payables. If an average exchange rate is consistent with the taxpayer's financial accounting, the taxpayer can elect to use it, based on intervals of one quarter year or less, to both accrue and record the receipt and payment of amounts in satisfaction of trade receivables and payables that are denominated in a nonfunctional currency. For example, a taxpayer may use the average exchange rate for the month of January to accrue all payables and receivables incurred during January. The same average rate also would be used to record all payments made and amounts received in satisfaction of payables and receivables during January.[60]

---

[50] Code Sec. 988(c)(1)(A), (B), and (C), and Reg. § 1.988-1(a)(1) and (a)(2). A forward contract is an agreement to buy or sell a given amount of foreign currency on a future date at a specified exchange rate. A futures contract is an agreement to buy or sell foreign currency that is traded on a futures exchange. A currency option gives the holder the right to buy or sell a given amount of currency at a specified exchange rate prior to the contract's expiration date.

[51] Code Sec. 988(c)(1)(D)(i) and Reg. § 1.988-1(a)(7)(i).

[52] Code Sec. 988(e) and Reg. § 1.988-1(a)(9).

[53] Reg. § 1.988-1(a)(10).

[54] Code Sec. 988(c)(1)(C)(i)(II).

[55] Code Sec. 988(b)(3).

[56] Code Sec. 988(b)(1) and (2).

[57] Code Sec. 988(c)(3).

[58] Code Sec. 988(c)(2)(A).

[59] Code Sec. 988(c)(2)(B).

[60] Reg. § 1.988-1(d)(3). A taxpayer cannot change the use of a convention without the consent of the Commissioner once it has been adopted.

Tax Consequences

Amount and timing of exchange gains and losses. The taxation of exchange gains and losses is based on the premise that, for U.S. tax purposes, only U.S. dollars are money. As a consequence, currencies other than the U.S. dollar are treated as "property" that has a tax basis independent of its specific denomination. One implication of this approach is that exchange gains and losses arising from a Code Sec. 988 transaction involving debt instruments, receivables, or payables generally are accounted for separately from the gain or loss on the underlying transaction.[61] For example, if a domestic corporation with the U.S. dollar as its functional currency makes a sale on account which is denominated in a foreign currency, the gross profit from the sale is recognized separately from any exchange gain or loss on the receivable denominated in the foreign currency.

> **Example 8.7:** USAco is an accrual-basis, domestic corporation with the U.S. dollar as its functional currency. On January 1, USAco makes an export sale denominated in marks (M). The sales price is M2,000. The foreign customer remits the M2,000 on April 1, and USAco converts the M2,000 marks into U.S. dollars on April 10. The mark was worth $1.50 on January 1, $1.45 on April 1, and $1.43 on April 10. Therefore, on January 1, USAco recognizes sales revenues of $3,000 [M2,000 × $1.50]. In addition, because the mark weakened against the dollar between the booking date (January 1) and the payment date (April 1), USAco realizes an exchange loss upon the collection of the receivable. The loss is $100, which represents the difference between the value of the marks received in payment of $2,900 [M2,000 × $1.45] and USAco's basis in the related account receivable of $3,000 [M2,000 × $1.50].[62] USAco also must recognize an exchange loss upon converting the marks into dollars. The loss is $40, which represents the difference between the amount realized from the sale of the marks of $2,860 [M2,000 × $1.43] and USAco's basis in the marks of $2,900 [M2,000 × $1.45].[63]

Character and source of exchange gains and losses. Exchange gains and losses attributable to a Code Sec. 988 transaction are treated as ordinary income or loss[64] and are sourced by reference to the residence of the taxpayer or the QBU of the taxpayer on whose books the underlying asset, liability, or item of income or expense is properly

---

[61] Code Sec. 988(a)(1)(A) and Reg. § 1.988-1(e). However, the exchange gain or loss realized on transactions involving debt instruments is limited to the total gain or loss realized on the transaction. Reg. § 1.988-2(b)(8).

[62] Reg. § 1.988-2(c)(2).

[63] Reg. § 1.988-2(a)(2)(i).

[64] Code Sec. 988(a)(1)(A). However, a taxpayer can elect to characterize exchange gains or losses on certain identified currency forward, futures, or option contracts as capital gains or losses. Code Sec. 988(a)(1)(B) and Reg. § 1.988-3(b).

reflected.[65] For purposes of this source rule, a U.S. resident is any corporation, partnership, trust, or estate that is a U.S person, as well as any individual who has a tax home in the United States.[66] An individual's tax home is his or her regular or principal place of business, provided that an individual is not treated as having a tax home in a foreign country during any period in which the taxpayer's abode is in the United States.[67] A foreign resident is any corporation, partnership, trust, or estate that is a foreign person, as well as any individual who has a tax home in a foreign country.[68] The residence of any QBU of the taxpayer (e.g., a branch of a domestic corporation) is the country in which the QBU's principal place of business is located.[69]

For purposes of the foreign tax credit limitation, net gains from foreign currency transactions generally are assigned to the passive income category.[70] An exception applies to qualified business and hedging transactions,[71] which are assigned to the general limitation category.

Hedging Transactions

A taxpayer can reduce or eliminate the currency exchange risk component of a transaction through the use of a variety of financial instruments, such as currency forward, futures and options contracts.

> **Example 8.8:** On February 1, USAco, a domestic corporation, agrees to pay a Mexican supplier 600,000 pesos for the delivery of some raw materials on July 1. Also on February 1, USAco hedges against the currency exchange risk associated with this purchase agreement by entering into a currency forward agreement with a bank to buy 600,000 pesos for $100,000 on July 1. The forward contract effectively eliminates the currency exchange risk component of the purchase agreement by fixing the purchase price of the raw materials in U.S. dollars at $100,000.

Because there is no currency exchange risk associated with a fully hedged transaction, in certain circumstances a taxpayer is allowed to integrate the accounting for the hedge with the accounting for the underlying hedged transaction. This approach reflects the reality that a fully hedged transaction is, in substance, a transaction denominated in the hedge security (in Example 8.8, the U.S. dollar).

---

[65] Code Sec. 988(a)(3)(A). However, any exchange gain or loss realized by a foreign person from the conduct of a U.S. trade or business is treated as U.S. source income. Reg. § 1.988-4(c).

[66] Code Sec. 988(a)(3)(B)(i)(I) and (II).

[67] Code Sec. 911(d)(3) and Reg. § 1.911-2(b). An individual's abode is in the United States if that is where his or her economic, social, and personal ties are closest (see, for example, *J.T. Lemay v. Comm'r*, 837 F2d 681 (5th Cir. 1988), *aff'g* 53 TCM 862

(1987)); and *Lansdown v. Comm'r*, 68 TCM 680 (1994). An individual who does not have a tax home is treated as a U.S. resident if such individual is a U.S. citizen or resident alien and as a foreign resident if such individual is not a U.S. citizen or resident alien. Code Sec. 988(a)(3)(B)(i).

[68] Code Sec. 988(a)(3)(B)(i)(I) and (III).

[69] Code Sec. 988(a)(3)(B)(ii).

[70] Code Secs. 904(d)(2)(A)(i) and 954(c)(1)(D).

[71] Reg. § 1.954-2(g)(2).

A hedge and hedged transaction qualify for integration treatment only if they meet the definitional requirements of a Code Sec. 988 hedging transaction.[72] If these requirements are met, the taxpayer can ignore the nonfunctional currency aspect of the transaction and account for the transaction as if it were denominated in the hedge currency, in which case no exchange gain or loss is recognized. Code Sec. 988 includes the following three categories of hedging transactions:

(i) *Hedged debt instruments*—This includes hedges associated with transactions in which the taxpayer lends or borrows funds through the use of a bond, debenture, note, certificate, or other evidence of indebtedness (but not accounts payable, accounts receivable, or similar items of income and expense).[73]

(ii) *Hedged executory contracts for goods and services*—This includes hedges involving executory contracts to pay or receive nonfunctional currency in the future with respect to the sale or purchase of property or services in the ordinary course of the taxpayer's business.[74]

(iii) *Hedge of the period between the trade and settlement dates on the purchase or sale of a publicly traded stock or security.*[75]

Example 8.9:[76] USAco is an accrual-basis, calendar year domestic corporation with the dollar as its functional currency. On June 1 of the current year, USAco enters into a contract with a Swiss steel manufacturer to buy steel for 200,000 Swiss francs (SF) for delivery and payment on November 1. USAco hedges against the currency exchange risk associated with this purchase agreement by purchasing SF195,000 on June 1 and depositing them in a separate bank account. The account bears interest such that by November 1 the SF195,000 have grown to SF200,000. On November 1, USAco withdraws SF200,000 from the bank account and makes payment in exchange for delivery of the steel. Assume the Swiss franc was worth $0.80 on June 1 and $0.85 on November 1, and had an average daily value of $0.82 between June 1 and November 1. The contract to purchase the steel and the simultaneous purchase of Swiss francs are part of a single economic transaction. In recognition of this fact, the tax laws allow USAco to treat them as an integrated transaction if USAco satisfies certain requirements (e.g., USAco identifies the transaction as a hedged executory contract and deposits the Swiss francs in a separate account).[77] Under this approach, USAco treats the $156,000 paid under the hedge

---

[72] Code Sec. 988(d).
[73] Reg. § 1.988-5(a).
[74] Reg. § 1.988-5(b).
[75] Reg. § 1.988-5(c). Prop. Reg. § 1.988-5(d) also provides integration treatment for hedged qualified

payments, which include declared but unpaid dividends and unaccrued rent or royalty payments.

[76] Compare Reg. § 1.988-5(b)(4), Example 6 (v).

[77] Reg. § 1.988-5(b).

[SF195,000 × $0.80] as an amount paid directly for the steel, and recognizes no gain or loss for the exchange rate fluctuation between June 1 and November 1. USAco treats the SF5,000 of interest as part of the hedge, and also reports it as gross income.[78] Using the average exchange rate for the interest accrual period to translate the interest into dollars,[79] USAco recognizes interest income of $4,100 [SF5,000 × $0.82]. Because the interest is part of the hedge, USAco recognizes no exchange gain or loss when the interest is used to purchase the steel. USAco's basis in the steel is $160,100 [$156,000 + $4,100].

Euro Conversion

Effective January 1, 1999, eleven of the fifteen members of the European Union began the process of adopting a common currency called the "euro." The eleven countries that are converting to the euro include Austria, Belgium, Finland, France, Germany, Ireland, Italy, Luxembourg, the Netherlands, Portugal and Spain. For the time being, the United Kingdom has chosen not to adopt the euro. Under the European Union's current timetable, the euro became a legal currency in the eleven participating countries in 1999. From 1999 to 2001 (the exact dates vary from country to country), certain types of borrowings can be denominated in euros and businesses can conduct wholesale-level transactions in euros. However, retail and other cash transactions will be conducted only in "legacy currencies" (francs, lire, marks, etc.). By July 2002, euro notes will be circulated and the legacy currencies will no longer be legal tender.

The introduction of the euro raises a number of federal income tax issues, including (i) whether the conversion of a legacy-denominated financial instrument into a euro-denominated instrument is considered a realization event for purposes of Code Sec. 1001, and (ii) whether the euro conversion is treated as a change in functional currency for a qualified business unit. In July 1998, the IRS issued temporary and proposed regulations that provide guidance regarding conversions from legacy currencies to the euro. The regulations indicate that a euro conversion will not be considered a realization event for U.S. tax purposes,[80] and generally (but not always) allow for deferral with respect to any gains triggered by the euro conversion until such time as an actual realization event occurs.[81] Therefore, these regulations generally minimize the tax consequences associated with the euro conversion.

---

[78] Reg. § 1.988-5(b)(2)(iii)(E).

[79] Reg. § 1.988-2(b)(1).

[80] Temp. Reg. § 1.1001-5T.

[81] Temp. Reg. § 1.985-8T.

Foreign Currency Transactions for Personal Use

For tax years beginning on or after January 1, 1998, exchange gains of an individual from the disposition of foreign currency in a personal transaction is not taxable, provided that the gain realized does not exceed $200. Note that the threshold is $200 per transaction, as opposed to cumulative gains of $200 per year. This simplification measure is intended to eliminate the need to compute and report gains arising from exchanges of currency that are small in amount and that are associated with personal and business travel, as well as other nonbusiness activities. The term "personal transaction" refers to any transaction other than one with respect to which properly allocable expenses are deductible as trade or business expenses under Code. Sec. 162 (other than travel expenses in connection with a business trip) or investment expenses under Code Sec. 212. Thus, transaction entered into in connection with a business trip are personal transactions under this provision. Exchange gains in excess of $200 will continue to be taxed as before, and exchange losses are unaffected by this provision.[82]

---

[82] Code Sec. 988(e).

Chapter 9

Tax Treaties

¶ 901 INTRODUCTION

The major purpose of an income tax treaty is to mitigate international double taxation through tax reductions or exemptions on certain types of income derived by residents of one treaty country from sources within the other treaty country. Because tax treaties often substantially modify U.S. and foreign tax consequences, the relevant treaty must be considered in order to fully analyze the taxation of any outbound or inbound transaction.

The United States currently has income tax treaties with over 40 countries, including all of our major trading partners. Table 9.1 presents the list of foreign countries with which an income tax treaty is currently in force.

TABLE 9.1. COUNTRIES WITH WHICH THE UNITED STATES HAS INCOME TAX TREATIES IN FORCE[a]

Australia	Hungary	Pakistan
Austria	Iceland	Philippines
Barbados	India	Poland
Belgium	Indonesia	Portugal
Canada	Ireland	Romania
China, Peoples	Israel	Russia
Republic of[b]	Italy	Slovak Republic
Commonwealth of	Jamaica	South Africa
Independent States[c]	Japan	Spain
Cyprus	Kazakstan	Sweden
Czech Republic	Korea	Switzerland
Denmark	Luxembourg	Thailand
Egypt	Mexico	Trinidad and Tobago
Finland	Morocco	Tunisia
France	Netherlands	Turkey
Germany	New Zealand	United Kingdom
Greece	Norway	

[a] Taken from Table 3 of IRS Pub. No. 515 (1999), which is reproduced in its entirety in the appendix to this chapter.

[b] Does not apply to Hong Kong.

[c] The members of the Commonwealth of Independent States include: Armenia, Azerbaijan, Belarus, Georgia, Kyrgyzstan, Moldova, Tajikistan, Turkmenistan, Ukraine, and Uzbekistan.

There are several basic treaty provisions, such as permanent establishment provisions and reduced withholding tax rates, that are common to most of the income tax treaties to which the United States is a party. In many cases, these provisions are patterned after or similar to the United States Model Income Tax Convention of September 20, 1996 (hereinafter the "U.S. Model Treaty"), which reflects the traditional baseline negotiating position of the United States in establishing income tax treaties with other countries. Because the U.S. Model Treaty reflects the general pattern of most treaties, it is used as the reference point for the following discussion of typical treaty provisions. Keep in mind, however, that each tax treaty is separately negotiated and therefore is unique. As a consequence, to determine the impact of treaty provisions in any specific situation, one must consult the applicable treaty.

In most foreign countries, a treaty provision will supercede the foreign country's domestic law. The term "treaty override" describes legislation that conflicts with an earlier enacted treaty. In the U.S., the supremacy clause of the U.S. Constitution treats treaties and federal legislation equally. Consequently, if a treaty provision conflicts with legislation, whichever is later enacted will prevail.[1]

---

[1] *Reid v. Covert*, 354 U.S. 1, 18 (1956). See also Code Sec. 894(a) and 7852(d).

¶ 902 COMMON TREATY PROVISIONS

Definition of Resident

The tax exemptions and reductions that treaties provide are available only to a resident of one of the treaty countries. Under the U.S. Model Treaty, a resident is any person who, under a country's internal laws, is subject to taxation by reason of domicile, residence, citizenship, place of management, place of incorporation, or other criterion of a similar nature.[2] In other words, a resident is someone who a country taxes by virtue of a personal relationship, such as citizenship or residence, as opposed to taxation on the basis of the source of income. Whether a person is a resident of a particular country for treaty purposes is determined by reference to the internal tax laws of the specific country.

Because each country has its own unique definition of residency, a person may qualify as a resident in more than one country. For example, an alien who qualifies as a U.S. resident under U.S. tax principles may simultaneously qualify as a resident of a foreign country under its definition of residency. To resolve this issue, the United States has included tie-breaker provisions in many of its income tax treaties. Tie-breaker rules are hierarchical in nature, such that a subordinate rule is considered only if the superordinate rule fails to resolve the issue. For example, Article 4(2) of the U.S. Model Treaty provides the following tie-breaker rules for individuals:

(i) The taxpayer is a resident of the country in which he or she has available a permanent home.

(ii) If the taxpayer has a permanent home available in both countries, the taxpayer is a resident of the country in which his or her personal and economic relations are closer (center of vital interests).

(iii) If the country in which the taxpayer's center of vital interests cannot be determined, or if the taxpayer does not have a permanent home available to him or her in either state, the taxpayer is a resident of the country in which he or she has a habitual abode.

(iv) If the taxpayer has a habitual abode in both countries or in neither country, the taxpayer is a resident of the country in which he or she is a citizen.

(v) If the taxpayer is a citizen of both countries or of neither country, the competent authorities of the two countries will settle the matter by mutual agreement.

---

[2] Article 4(1) of the U.S. Model Treaty.

Tie-breaker rules also are provided for corporations and other types of entities.[3]

There is an exception to the principle that residence determines the availability of treaty benefits. Under so-called savings clause provisions, a treaty country saves the right to tax its own citizens as though the treaty did not exist.[4] For example, under Article 11(1) of the income tax treaty between the United States and the United Kingdom, interest received by U.K. residents is exempt from U.S. taxation. However, under Article 1(3) of that treaty, the United States reserves the right to tax the payee if a U.K. resident also is a U.S. citizen. As a consequence, the treaty does not impede the right of the United States to tax the worldwide income of U.S. citizens.

Business Profits and Permanent Establishments

A central tax issue for any company exporting its goods or services is whether it is subject to taxation by the importing country. Most countries assert jurisdiction over all of the income derived from sources within their borders, regardless of the citizenship or residence of the person receiving that income. Such an extreme approach has its limits, however. For example, if the exporter's marketing activities within the importing country are *de minimis* (e.g., a company salesperson makes a few sales calls), the administrative costs of collecting the tax on those activities may exceed the related tax revenues. Moreover, a policy of imposing unreasonable compliance costs on foreign companies may inhibit a country's ability to benefit from international trade. These concerns have led countries to include permanent establishment provisions in their income tax treaties.

Under a permanent establishment provision, the business profits of a resident of one treaty country are exempt from taxation by the other treaty country unless those profits are attributable to a permanent establishment located within the host country.[5] A permanent establishment includes a fixed place of business, such as a place of management, a branch, an office, a factory, a workshop, or a mine, well, quarry, or other place of natural resource extraction.[6] A fixed base of business does not constitute a permanent establishment if that fixed place of business is used solely for auxiliary functions (e.g., purchasing, storing, displaying, or delivering inventory) or for activities of a preparatory nature (e.g., collecting information about potential customers).[7] A building or

---

[3] Article 4(3) and (4) of the U.S. Model Treaty.

[4] Article 1(3) of the U.S. Model Treaty.

[5] Article 7(1) of the U.S. Model Treaty. A special exemption applies to the business profits of taxpayers that operate or rent ships, aircraft, or containers used in international traffic. Under Article 8 of the U.S. Model Treaty, such income generally is taxable only by the taxpayer's home country.

[6] Article 5(1) and (2) of the U.S. Model Treaty.

[7] Article 5(4) of the U.S. Model Treaty.

construction site is a permanent establishment only if it continues for more than 12 months.[8]

A permanent establishment also exists if employees or other dependent agents habitually exercise in the host country an authority to conclude sales contracts in the taxpayer's name.[9] As a consequence, an exporter that sends executives or salespeople abroad to enter into contracts may create a permanent establishment even if those employees operate out of hotels, as opposed to a formal sales office. Employees who limit their activities to auxiliary or preparatory functions, such as collecting information about potential customers, with sales concluded in the home country, will not create a permanent establishment. Marketing products abroad solely through independent brokers or distributors also does not create a permanent establishment, regardless of whether these independent agents conclude sales contracts in the exporter's name.[10] In addition, the presence within the importing country of a locally incorporated subsidiary does not create a permanent establishment for a parent company incorporated in another country.[11]

> **Example 9.1:** USAco, a domestic corporation, markets its products abroad by mailing catalogs to potential foreign customers, who then mail orders back to USAco's home office in the United States. Under the U.S. Model Treaty, the mere solicitation of orders through the mail does not constitute a permanent establishment. Therefore, USAco's export profits are not subject to foreign taxation.

> **Example 9.2:** The facts are the same as in Example 9.1, except now assume that USAco decides to expand its foreign marketing activities by leasing retail store space in a major foreign city in order to display its goods and keep an inventory from which to fill foreign orders. Under the U.S. Model Treaty, USAco's business profits would still not be subject to foreign taxation as long as USAco does not conclude any sales through its foreign office. Technically, this may be possible. However, as a practical matter, significant foreign sales would make it burdensome to conclude sales in this manner. Once USAco's employees start concluding sales at the foreign office, USAco would have a permanent establishment in the importing country.

If a resident of one treaty country has a permanent establishment in the other treaty country, the importing country may tax the taxpayer's business profits, but only to the extent those business profits are attributable to the permanent establishment.[12] The portion of an

---

[8] Article 5(3) of the U.S. Model Treaty.
[9] Article 5(5) of the U.S. Model Treaty.
[10] Article 5(6) of the U.S. Model Treaty.

[11] Article 5(7) of the U.S. Model Treaty.
[12] Article 7(1) of the U.S. Model Treaty.

exporter's business profits that is attributable to a permanent establishment is computed based on the fiction that the permanent establishment is a distinct and independent enterprise dealing at arm's
length with the home office.[13] Therefore, the more functions performed
and the greater the risks assumed by the permanent establishment, the
more profit it should earn. In making this determination, the taxpayer
can allocate all direct costs, such as the cost of goods sold abroad,
against the permanent establishment's income. The taxpayer also can
make a reasonable allocation of indirect expenses, such as general and
administrative expenses, research and development expenses, and interest expense, against the permanent establishment's income.[14]

Personal Services Income

Treaty provisions covering personal services compensation are similar to the permanent establishment clauses covering business profits
generally, in that they create a higher threshold of activity for host
country taxation. Generally, when an employee or other dependent
agent who is a resident of one treaty country derives income from
services performed in the other treaty country, that income is usually
taxable by the host country.[15] However, such income is exempt from
taxation by the host country if the following requirements are satisfied:

(i) the dependent agent is present in the host country for 183
days or less,

(ii) the agent's compensation is paid by, or on behalf of, an
employer which is not a resident of the host country, and

(iii) the compensation is not borne by a permanent establishment
or a fixed base which the employer has in the host country.[16]

Most tax treaties also contain a separate independent services
provision that governs the taxation of personal services income derived
by self-employed professionals, such as accountants, doctors, engineers,
and lawyers. Such income is exempt from host country taxation unless
the services are performed in the host country and the income is
attributable to an office or other fixed base of business that is located in
the host country and is regularly available to the taxpayer for purposes
of performing the services.[17] This provision allows self-employed professionals to provide services abroad without local taxation as long as they
do not maintain an office or other fixed base of business within the host
country.

Income tax treaties also usually contain special rules regarding
specific types of compensation for personal services. For example,

---

[13] Article 7(2) of the U.S. Model Treaty.
[14] Article 7(3) of the U.S. Model Treaty.
[15] Article 15(1) of the U.S. Model Treaty.
[16] Article 15(2) of the U.S. Model Treaty.
[17] Article 14 of the U.S. Model Treaty.

under the U.S. Model Treaty, there are special provisions governing pensions, annuities, alimony, and child support,[18] as well as income derived by crew members of ships and aircraft operated in international traffic,[19] entertainers and athletes,[20] government workers,[21] and students and trainees.[22] A summary of the treaty provisions governing compensation for personal services can be found in the appendix to this chapter.

Dividends, Interest, and Royalties

Like the United States, most foreign countries impose flat rate withholding taxes on dividend, interest, and royalty income derived by offshore investors from sources within the country's borders. As an example, the U.S. statutory withholding tax rate is 30% for both nonresident alien individuals and foreign corporations.[23] However, most tax treaties provide for reduced withholding tax rates, as long as the dividend, interest, or royalty income is not attributable to a permanent establishment of the taxpayer that is located within the host country. Tax treaties usually reduce the withholding tax rate on dividends to 15% or less. Moreover, the rate often is lower for controlling shareholders (e.g., a shareholder owning 10% or more of the payer's stock) than for noncontrolling shareholders. Under the U.S. Model Treaty, the withholding rate on dividends is 5% for taxpayers owning 10% or more of the corporation distributing the dividend, and 15% for all other shareholders.[24] Table 9.2 presents the dividend withholding tax rates for our major trading partners.

TABLE 9.2. TREATY WITHHOLDING TAX RATES ON DIVIDENDS PAID BY U.S. CORPORATION [a]

Payee's country of residence	*Type of shareholder*	
	Controlling	*Noncontrolling*
Canada	5%	15%
China	10%	10%
France	5%	15%
Germany	5%	15%
Italy	5%	15%
Japan	10%	15%
Mexico	5%	15%
United Kingdom	5%	15%

[a] Taken from Table 1 of IRS Pub. No. 515 (1999), which is reproduced in its entirety in the appendix to this chapter.

Tax treaties also usually reduce the withholding tax rate on interest to 15% or less. Under the U.S. Model Treaty, interest is exempt

---

[18] Article 18 of the U.S. Model Treaty.
[19] Article 15(3) of the U.S. Model Treaty.
[20] Article 17 of the U.S. Model Treaty.
[21] Article 19 of the U.S. Model Treaty.

[22] Article 20 of the U.S. Model Treaty.
[23] Code Secs. 871(a) and 881(a).
[24] Article 10(2) of the U.S. Model Treaty.

from withholding tax.[25] Table 9.3 presents the interest withholding tax rates for our major trading partners.

TABLE 9.3. TREATY WITHHOLDING TAX RATES ON INTEREST PAID BY U.S. PERSON [a]

Payee's country of residence	Treaty withholding rate
Canada	.10%
China	.10%
France	.0%
Germany	.0%
Italy	.15%
Japan	.10%
Mexico	15%[b]
United Kingdom	.0%

[a] Taken from Table 1 of IRS Pub. No. 515 (1999), which is reproduced in its entirety in the appendix to this chapter.

[b] A 10% rate applies to interest on bank loans and on bonds or other securities traded on certain securities markets.

Most tax treaties also provide for lower withholding tax rates on royalties. Typically, the rate is 10% or less, and in some treaties varies with whether the payment is an industrial royalty (e.g., a payment for the use of a patent, trade secret, or formula), a motion picture or television royalty, or some other type of royalty, such as a payment for the use of a copyright on a book. Under the U.S. Model Treaty, all royalties are exempt from withholding.[26] A royalty is any payment for the use of, or the right to use, the following:

(i) any copyright of literary, artistic, or scientific work (but not including motion pictures, or films or tapes used for television or radio broadcasting),

(ii) any patent, trademark, design, model, plan, secret formula or process, or other like right or property,

(iii) any information concerning industrial, commercial, or scientific experience, or

(iv) any gains derived from the disposition of any right or property described in (i) through (iii), where the proceeds are contingent upon the future productivity, use, or disposition of that property.[27]

Table 9.4 presents the royalty withholding tax rates for our major trading partners.

---

[25] Article 11(1) of the U.S. Model Treaty. When interest is paid by one related party to another, the treaty exemption applies only to an arm's-length amount of interest. Article 11(5) of the U.S. Model Treaty.

[26] Article 12(1) of the U.S. Model Treaty. When a royalty is paid by one related party to another, the treaty exemption applies only to the arm's-length royalty amount. Article 12(4) of the U.S. Model Treaty.

[27] Article 12(2) of the U.S. Model Treaty.

**TABLE 9.4. TREATY WITHHOLDING TAX
RATES ON ROYALTIES PAID BY U.S. PERSON** [a]

	Type of royalty		
Payee's country of residence	Industrial	Motion picture and television	Other
Canada	0%	10%	0%
China	10%	10%	10%
France	5%	0%	0%
Germany	0%	0%	0%
Italy	10%	8%	5%
Japan	10%	10%	10%
Mexico	10%	10%	10%
United Kingdom	0%	0%	0%

[a] Taken from Table 1 of IRS Pub. No. 515 (1999), which is reproduced in its entirety in the appendix to this chapter.

A full listing of the treaty withholding rates for dividends, interest, and royalties can be found in the appendix to this chapter.

Gains from the Disposition of Property

Under the U.S. Model Treaty, gains from the disposition of property, such as capital gains on the sale of stocks and securities, generally are taxable only by the country in which the seller resides.[28] An exception applies to gains arising from the disposition of real property, including gains from the disposition of shares of a corporation that has significant real property holding, and gains from the disposition of interests in a partnership, trust, or estate to the extent attributable to real property situated in a contracting state.[29] An exception also applies to gains arising from the disposition of personal property, such as inventory, that are attributable to a fixed base or permanent establishment.[30] Under these exceptions, the gain can be taxed by the country in which the real property, fixed base, or permanent establishment is located.

Income from Real Property

Tax treaties typically do not provide tax exemptions or reductions for income from real property. Therefore, both the home and the host country maintain the right to tax real property income, which includes income from agriculture and forestry.[31] This rule applies to rental income,[32] as well as gains from the sale of real property.[33] If the real property income of a resident of one treaty country is taxed by the other treaty country, that taxpayer can elect to have its income taxed on a net basis at the normal graduated rates applicable to business profits, rather than having its income taxed on a gross basis through

---

[28] Article 13(6) of the U.S. Model Treaty.
[29] Article 13(1) and (2) of the U.S. Model Treaty.
[30] Article 13(3) of the U.S. Model Treaty.

[31] Article 6(1) of the U.S. Model Treaty.
[32] Article 6(3) of the U.S. Model Treaty.
[33] Article 13(1) and (2) of the U.S. Model Treaty.

flat rate withholding taxes.[34] This election allows a taxpayer who owns rental property to offset the gross rental income with the related rental expenses, such as depreciation, interest, insurance, and maintenance expenses.

Associated Enterprises Provisions

An associated enterprise treaty provision allows the U.S. and its treaty partners to allocate profits between two related businesses, as if their financial relations were those of unrelated businesses. Treating related businesses as independent businesses resembles the arm's-length standard used to allocate income pursuant to Code Sec. 482.

> **Example 9.3:** USAco sells copper tubing to FORco, a wholly owned country X subsidiary, at a price of $100 per tube. USAco sells the same tubing to independent foreign distributors at a price of $120 per tube. The U.S. and country X have entered a treaty with an associated enterprises provision similar to the U.S. Model Treaty.[35] As a result, the IRS can make a transfer pricing adjustment, increasing the price on tube sold from USAco to FORco to $120 per tube.

Anti-treaty Shopping Provisions

Because tax treaties provide lower withholding tax rates on dividend, interest, and royalty income, a multinational corporation may be able to reduce its foreign withholding taxes by owning its subsidiaries through strategically located holding companies. This practice is known as "treaty shopping."

> **Example 9.4:** USAco is a domestic corporation with a subsidiary in country X. The treaty between the United States and X provides a 15% withholding rate for dividends paid to a controlling shareholder. In contrast, the withholding rate on dividends is 5% under the treaty between the United States and country Z, and 0% under the treaty between countries Z and X. Therefore, USAco may be able to reduce the withholding tax rate on earnings repatriated from its country X subsidiary from 15% to 5% by interposing a Z holding company between itself and the X subsidiary.

> **Example 9.5:** FORco is a country B corporation with a subsidiary in the United States. Country B does not have an income tax treaty with the United States. Therefore, the U.S. withholding tax rate on any dividends received by FORco from its U.S. subsidiary

---

[34] Article 6(5) of the U.S. Model Treaty. Code Secs. 871(d) and 882(d) allow nonresident aliens and foreign corporations to make similar elections with respect to their U.S. real property interests.

[35] Article 9 of the U.S. Model Treaty.

is 30%. In contrast, the withholding tax rate on dividends is 0% under the treaty between the United States and country C, and 10% under the treaty between countries C and B. Therefore, FORco may be able to reduce the withholding tax rate on dividend distributions from its U.S. subsidiary from 30% to 10% by interposing a country C holding company between itself and the U.S. subsidiary.

Because of the extensive treaty network of the Netherlands, a Dutch holding company has historically been a popular choice for multinational corporations attempting to avoid withholding taxes through treaty shopping. However, the current treaty between the United States and the Netherlands contains an anti-treaty shopping provision which restricts the ability of taxpayers to engage in treaty shopping. Article 22 of the U.S. Model Treaty contains a similar provision designed to deter treaty shopping.

In treaties entered into prior to the 1990s, there are traditionally two tests that a corporation had to pass to receive treaty benefits. First, the corporation had to be 50 percent owned by residents of either country. Second, no more than 50 percent of any deductible payment could have gone to a resident of a country other than the two treaty countries. The limitations of benefits provision in the U.S.-Netherlands treaty is typical. For a company to receive the benefits of the treaty, the company must pass one of the following tests:

(i)   The company must have over 50 percent U.S. or Netherlands ownership, not be a conduit company (specially defined in the treaty), and be publicly traded on a recognized stock exchange in either country;

(ii)   A Netherlands company must be 30 percent Netherlands-owned and 70 percent owned by either U.S. or European Union residents, and no more than 50 percent of deductible payments go to non-Netherlands or non-U.S. residents;

(iii) The company is engaged in the active conduct of a trade or business in either country and either (a) derives substantial income from the trade or business in the resident state or (b) earns income outside the resident state that is incidental to the trade or business in the resident state;

(iv)   The company has, in either the Netherlands or the U.S., its headquarters, which the treaty subjectively defines as providing a substantial portion of overall supervision;

(v)   The company has shares held by European Union residents that reside in a country that has a comprehensive tax treaty with the U.S. that provides equal or greater withholding benefits; or

(vi) The Competent Authority of either the U.S. or the Netherlands decides to offer the treaty benefits.

Although the U.S. Model Treaty does not have as much detail in its limitation of benefits provisions as the Netherlands treaty, a review of recently negotiated treaties and protocols indicates that a Netherlands-type limitation of benefits provision will continue in the future.[36]

In addition to the anti-treaty shopping provisions contained in some treaties, the IRS has sought to disallow treaty benefits obtained through the use of intermediary entities by invoking the judicial doctrine of substance over form. The seminal case in this area is *Aiken Industries, Inc. v. Comm'r*,[37] in which the IRS successfully denied treaty benefits that the taxpayer attempted to obtain through the use of a back-to-back loan arrangement. In addition, Code Sec. 7701(l) gives the IRS the authority to disregard the existence of an intermediary or conduit entity with respect to treaty shopping that results in the avoidance of U.S. taxes. A multi-party financing arrangement is subject to recharacterization if a related intermediate entity participates in a back-to-back loan arrangement as part of a plan to avoid U.S. withholding taxes. These rules also apply to certain unrelated intermediaries, back-to-back leases, and licenses, but do not extend to equity investments or debt guarantees.[38]

The availability of reduced U.S. withholding tax under an income tax treaty for payments to hybrid entities was further limited by the Taxpayer Relief Act of 1997. Specifically, a foreign person is not entitled to a reduced rate of withholding tax under a tax treaty on an item of income derived through a partnership (or other fiscally transparent entity) if all of the following apply: (i) the income item is not treated by the treaty partner as an item of income to such foreign person, (ii) the foreign country does not impose tax on a distribution of the item by the U.S. entity to the foreign person, and (iii) the treaty does not contain a provision addressing the applicability of the treaty in the case of an item of income derived through a partnership.[39]

Non-Discrimination Provisions

The non-discrimination treaty provisions are designed to prevent the U.S. from taxing a foreign taxpayer at a greater rate than a U.S. taxpayer. Article 24 of the U.S. Model Treaty specifically prevents the following types of tax discrimination:

---

[36] See, for example, the limitation of benefits treaty provisions in the U.S.-Irish treaty of 1998 and the U.S.-Denmark treaty of 1999.

[37] 56 TC 925 (1971). See also *Northern Ind. Pub. Serv. Co. v. Comm'r*, 105 TC 341 (1995), *aff'd* 115 F3d 506 (7th Cir., 1997).

[38] Reg. § 1.881-3.

[39] Code Sec. 894(c) and Temp. Reg. § 1.894-1T.

- Paragraph 1, which prohibits tax discrimination against foreign nationals, specifies that the U.S. cannot tax a foreign national more burdensomely than U.S. nationals;

- Paragraph 2, which prohibits tax discrimination against domestically located branches of foreign corporations, specifies that the U.S. cannot tax a permanent establishment of a foreign corporation more burdensomely than a U.S. establishment carrying on the same activities (the term "same activities" refers to the same type of industry);

- Paragraph 3, which prohibits tax discrimination with respect to deductions for interest and royalty payments, allows discrimination only if the discriminatory treatment satisfies the associated enterprises provisions.

- Paragraph 4, which prohibits tax discrimination with respect to capital ownership, prevents the U.S. from taxing a U.S. corporation owned by foreign investors more burdensomely than it taxes a similarly situated U.S. corporation owned by U.S. shareholders.

Example 9.6: FORco, a country Y parent corporation, owns all of the stock of USsub. USsub competes in the U.S. steel market with USAco, a domestic corporation wholly owned by U.S. citizens. In order to protect the U.S. steel industry, Congress enacts legislation increasing the rate of income tax on all steel wholesalers that are foreign-owned from 35% to 45%. Subsequently, the U.S. and country Y enter into a treaty that contains an anti-discrimination provision similar to the U.S. Model Treaty, which includes a paragraph prohibiting tax discrimination based on capital ownership. As a result, USsub is exempt from the 45% rate, and will pay tax at the same 35% rate as USAco.

Competent Authorities and Exchanges of Information

Tax treaties provide a procedure by which a resident of a treaty country can request assistance from the competent authority of that country in obtaining relief from actions of one or both treaty countries which the taxpayer believes are inconsistent with the treaty.[40] The competent authority is the governmental office that administers tax treaties. For example, if one or both treaty countries makes an adjustment to the intercompany transfer prices used by affiliated companies located within their respective countries, it is possible that both countries will tax the same stream of income. In such cases, the taxpayer may wish to seek relief from double taxation by petitioning the appropriate competent authority. Assuming the taxpayer's objections are

---

[40] Article 25(1) and (2) of the U.S. Model Treaty.

justified, the competent authority is empowered to resolve the case by mutual agreement with the competent authority of the other treaty country. Other situations in which the taxpayer may wish to seek competent authority assistance include conflicts regarding the proper characterization of an item of income, the application of a source-of-income rule, or the meaning of a term.[41]

In addition to the mutual agreement procedures outlined above, tax treaties also provide for exchanges of information regarding taxpayers as a mechanism for enhancing compliance with respect to international transactions. Under the U.S. Model Treaty, the competent authorities of the two treaty countries shall exchange such information as is necessary for enforcing provisions of the tax treaty, as well as the internal laws of the two countries concerning taxes covered by the treaty.[42] For example, the two treaty countries might share information regarding a taxpayer that both countries are auditing. Another example is an exchange of computerized lists of residents of one treaty country deriving dividend, interest, or royalty income from sources within the other treaty country.

¶ 903 DISCLOSURE OF TREATY-BASED RETURN POSITIONS

Any taxpayer, U.S. or foreign, that claims the benefits of a treaty by taking a tax return position that is in conflict with the Internal Revenue Code must disclose the position.[43] A tax return position is considered to be in conflict with the Code, and therefore treaty-based, if the U.S. tax liability under the treaty is different from the tax liability that would have to be reported in the absence of a treaty.[44] This reporting requirement is waived in various situations. Examples include certain foreign persons who claim a lower treaty withholding tax rate on U.S.-source nonbusiness income, and foreign persons who claim treaty relief for certain other types of personal services income.[45] A taxpayer reports treaty-based positions either by attaching a statement to its return or by using Form 8833.[46] If a taxpayer fails to report a treaty-based return position, each such failure is subject to a penalty of $1,000, or a penalty of $10,000 in the case of a Subchapter C corporation.[47]

Specific Disclosure Requirements

The regulations require disclosure of reduced withholding taxes on payments to related persons. Examples include interest, dividend,

---

[41] Article 25(3) of the U.S. Model Treaty. The procedures for requesting assistance from U.S. competent authorities are found in Rev. Proc. 96-13, 1996-1 CB 18.

[42] Article 26(1) of the U.S. Model Treaty.

[43] Code Sec. 6114.

[44] Reg. § 301.6114-1(a)(2)(i).

[45] Reg. § 301.6114-1(c).

[46] Reg. § 301.6114-1(d) and Announcement 93-63, 1993-16 IRB 11.

[47] Code Sec. 6712.

rents, and royalties that a U.S. person pays to a related foreign person who is entitled to reduced rates to a withholding tax under a treaty. The related foreign recipient must file a return disclosing these treaty benefits claimed only if the payment was not properly reported to the IRS on Form 1042S.[48]

Example 9.7: USsub is a U.S. subsidiary of FORco, its country Z parent. FORco provides services in the U.S. that are exempt from withholding under Code Sec. 1442 because of the tax treaty between the U.S. and country Z. However, USsub fails to report the payment to the IRS on a Form 1042S. As a result, FORco must file a Form 1120F with the IRS that reports the payment, but does not show any tax due.

Foreign persons claiming exemption from U.S. tax because their trade or business does not constitute a permanent establishment under a treaty also must disclose that position.

Example 9.8: FORco sells zinc to customers in the United States. FORco's only U.S. presence is a warehouse from which it ships zinc to U.S. customers. Without a tax treaty, FORco's sales in the U.S. combined with a U.S. warehouse would constitute carrying on a trade or business in the U.S. that would be subject to U.S. income tax. However, FORco is a resident of a country that has a treaty with the U.S., under which a permanent establishment does not include a warehouse. Although FORco is not subject to tax in the U.S. under the treaty, FORco will still have to file a return disclosing the treaty position.

A foreign corporation operating in the U.S. through a branch may be subject to the Code Sec. 884 branch profits tax. Some treaties provide exemptions or reduce these branch taxes. Any foreign corporation claiming such an exemption or reduction must disclose this position.

Example 9.9: FORco, a country X corporation, sells paper to customers in the U.S. through its U.S. branch, which constitutes a permanent establishment under the tax treaty between the U.S. and country X. The treaty reduces the branch profits tax from 30% to 5%. FORco must disclose the reduced branch profits tax on its Form 1120F.

Finally, to the extent that a treaty may alter the sourcing of an item of income, a taxpayer must disclose this alteration.

Example 9.10: FORco, a country Y corporation sells U.S. real estate at a gain. Code Sec. 861(a)(5) treats the gain as U.S. source

---

[48] A CFC of which the U.S. payer is a 10 percent U.S. shareholder, a foreign corporation controlled U.S. payer, or a 25 percent foreign shareholder of the U.S. payer, or a foreign related party. This rule applies even though the foreign recipient may not otherwise have to file a U.S. income tax return.

income. However, the recently enacted tax treaty between the U.S. and country Y, unlike the U.S. Model Treaty, sources gains on real estate based on the residence of the seller. As a result, FORco sources the gain as foreign source, but must file a Form 1120F disclosing this position.

Waiver of Disclosure Requirements[49]

In contrast to payments to related parties, payments of interest, dividends, rents or royalties by a U.S. person to an unrelated party are not subject to disclosure. As a result, the unrelated foreign recipient will not incur any filing obligation unless engaged in a trade or business within the United States.

The disclosure requirements also do not apply to a U.S. withholding agent. These withholding agents already have reporting obligations in that they must file Forms 1042 and 1042S and do not have any further obligations with respect to reduced withholding pursuant to a treaty.

No reporting is required when the treaty benefit is based on residency in a treaty partner country due to the tie-breaker rules in the treaty. For example, suppose an individual is considered a resident of the U.S. under the green card test, and a resident of a treaty partner due to that treaty partner's internal laws. If, pursuant to the tie-breaker provisions in that treaty, the individual is classified a resident of the treaty partner, he or she does not have to file a U.S. return.

The regulations also do not require reporting of treaty benefits for income derived from dependent personal services, pensions, annuities, social security and other pension benefits.

Finally, for any other treaty benefit not specifically described in the regulations, the recipient must disclose that benefit to the IRS.

The regulations meticulously describe the form of the disclosure. The disclosure statement typically requires six items: (1) the name and employer identification number of both the recipient and payer of the income at issue; (2) the type of treaty benefited item and its amount; (3) the facts and an explanation supporting the return position taken; (4) the specific treaty provisions on which the taxpayer bases its claim; (5) the Internal Revenue Code provision exempted or reduced; and (6) an explanation of any applicable limitations on benefits provisions. The penalty for failure to disclose is $10,000 for corporate taxpayers and $1,000 for noncorporate taxpayers.

Nonresident aliens and foreign corporations may occasionally desire to make a protective tax return filing to avoid any penalties and to

---

[49] Reg. § 301.6114-1(c).

ensure that the statute of limitations begins to run. This would occur in a situation where it is uncertain whether the foreign corporation has a filing requirement.

Example 9.11: FORco, a country Z corporation, is engaged in the conduct of a U.S. trade or business. Under the tax treaty between the U.S. and country Z, only permanent establishments are subject to tax in a host country. FORco is uncertain whether its conduct of a U.S. trade or business constitutes a permanent establishment. Due to this uncertainty, the regulations allow the timely filing of a protective return containing only identifying information and a statement invoking the protective procedure, but is otherwise blank. If the IRS later determines that the taxpayer must file a complete tax return, the foreign corporation would still be entitled to applicable deductions on its return.

[¶ 904]

United States Model Income Tax Convention of September 20, 1996

CONVENTION BETWEEN THE UNITED STATES OF AMERICA AND .... FOR THE AVOIDANCE OF DOUBLE TAXATION AND THE PREVENTION OF FISCAL EVASION WITH RESPECT TO TAXES ON INCOME

The United States of America and ...., desiring to conclude a Convention for the avoidance of double taxation and the prevention of fiscal evasion with respect to taxes on income, have agreed as follows:

Article 1—General Scope

1. This Convention shall apply only to persons who are residents of one or both of the Contracting States, except as otherwise provided in the Convention.

2. The Convention shall not restrict in any manner any benefit now or hereafter accorded:

(a) by the laws of either Contracting State; or

(b) by any other agreement between the Contracting States.

3. Notwithstanding the provisions of subparagraph 2(b):

(a) the provisions of Article 26 (Mutual Agreement Procedure) of this Convention exclusively shall apply to any dispute concerning whether a measure is within the scope of this Convention, and the procedures under this Convention exclusively shall apply to that dispute; and

(b) unless the competent authorities determine that a taxation measure is not within the scope of this Convention, the nondiscrimination obligations of this Convention exclusively shall apply with respect to that measure, except for such national treatment or most-favored-nation obligations as may apply to trade in goods under the General Agreement on Tariffs and Trade. No national treatment or most-favored-nation obligation under any other agreement shall apply with respect to that measure.

(c) For the purpose of this paragraph, a "measure" is a law, regulation, rule, procedure, decision, administrative action, or any similar provision or action.

¶ 904

4. Notwithstanding any provision of the Convention except paragraph 5 of this Article, a Contracting State may tax its residents (as determined under Article 4 (Residence)), and by reason of citizenship may tax its citizens, as if the Convention had not come into effect. For this purpose, the term "citizen" shall include a former citizen or long-term resident whose loss of such status had as one of its principal purposes the avoidance of tax (as defined under the laws of the Contracting State of which the person was a citizen or long-term resident), but only for a period of 10 years following such loss.

5. The provisions of paragraph 4 shall not affect:

(a) the benefits conferred by a Contracting State under paragraph 2 of Article 9 (Associated Enterprises), paragraphs 2 and 5 of Article 18 (Pensions, Social Security, Annuities, Alimony, and Child Support), and Articles 23 (Relief From Double Taxation), 24 (Non-Discrimination), and 25 (Mutual Agreement Procedure); and

(b) the benefits conferred by a Contracting State under paragraph 6 of Article 18 (Pensions, Social Security, Annuities, Alimony, and Child Support), Articles 19 (Government Service), 20 (Students and Trainees), and 27 (Diplomatic Agents and Consular Officers), upon individuals who are neither citizens of, nor have been admitted for permanent residence in, that State.

Article 2—Taxes Covered

1. The existing taxes to which this Convention shall apply are:

(a) in the United States: the Federal income taxes imposed by the Internal Revenue Code (but excluding social security taxes), and the Federal excise taxes imposed with respect to private foundations.

(b) in ....

2. The Convention shall apply also to any identical or substantially similar taxes that are imposed after the date of signature of the Convention in addition to, or in place of, the existing taxes. The competent authorities of the Contracting States shall notify each other of any significant changes that have been made in their respective taxation laws or other laws affecting their obligations under the Convention, and of any official published material concerning the application of the Convention, including explanations, regulations, rulings, or judicial decisions.

Article 3—General Definitions

1. For the purposes of this Convention, unless the context otherwise requires:

(a) the term "person" includes an individual, an estate, a trust, a partnership, a company, and any other body of persons;

(b) the term "company" means any body corporate or any entity that is treated as a body corporate for tax purposes according to the laws of the state in which it is organized;

(c) the terms "enterprise of a Contracting State" and "enterprise of the other Contracting State" mean respectively an enterprise carried on by a resident of a Contracting State, and an enterprise carried on by a resident of the other Contracting State; the terms also include an enterprise carried on by a resident of a Contracting State through an entity that is treated as fiscally transparent in that Contracting State;

(d) the term "international traffic" means any transport by a ship or aircraft, except when such transport is solely between places in a Contracting State;

(e) the term "competent authority" means:

(i) in the United States: the Secretary of the Treasury or his delegate; and

(ii) in ....;

(f) the term "United States" means the United States of America, and includes the states thereof and the District of Columbia; such term also includes the territorial sea thereof and the sea bed and subsoil of the submarine areas adjacent to that territorial sea, over which the United States exercises sovereign rights in accordance with international law; the term, however, does not include Puerto Rico, the Virgin Islands, Guam or any other United States possession or territory;

(g) the term .... means ....;

(h) the term "national" of a Contracting State, means:

(i) any individual possessing the nationality or citizenship of that State; and

(ii) any legal person, partnership or association deriving its status as such from the laws in force in that State;

(i) the term "qualified governmental entity" means:

(i) any person or body of persons that constitutes a governing body of a Contracting State, or of a political subdivision or local authority of a Contracting State;

(ii) a person that is wholly owned, directly or indirectly, by a Contracting State or a political subdivision or local authority of a Contracting State, provided (a) it is organized under the laws of the Contracting State, (b) its earnings are credited to its own account with no portion of its income inuring to the benefit of any private person, and (c) its assets vest in the Contracting State, political subdivision or local authority upon dissolution; and

(iii) a pension trust or fund of a person described in subparagraph (i) or (ii) that is constituted and operated exclusively to administer or provide pension benefits described in Article 19; provided that an entity described in subparagraph (ii) or (iii) does not carry on commercial activities.

2. As regards the application of the Convention at any time by a Contracting State any term not defined therein shall, unless the context otherwise requires, or the competent authorities agree to a common meaning pursuant to the provisions of Article 25 (Mutual Agreement Procedure), have the meaning which it has at that time under the law of that State for the purposes of the taxes to which the Convention applies, any meaning under the applicable tax laws of that State prevailing over a meaning given to the term under other laws of that State.

Article 4—Residence

1. Except as provided in this paragraph, for the purposes of this Convention, the term "resident of a Contracting State" means any person who, under the laws of that State, is liable to tax therein by reason of his domicile, residence, citizenship, place of management, place of incorporation, or any other criterion of a similar nature.

(a) The term "resident of a Contracting State" does not include any person who is liable to tax in that State in respect only of income from sources in that State or of profits attributable to a permanent establishment in that State.

(b) A legal person organized under the laws of a Contracting State and that is generally exempt from tax in that State and is established and maintained in that State either:

(i) exclusively for a religious, charitable, educational, scientific, or other similar purpose; or

(ii) to provide pensions or other similar benefits to employees pursuant to a plan is to be treated for purposes of this paragraph as a resident of that Contracting State.

(c) A qualified governmental entity is to be treated as a resident of the Contracting State where it is established.

(d) An item of income, profit or gain derived through an entity that is fiscally transparent under the laws of either Contracting State shall be considered to be derived by a resident of a State to the extent that the item is treated for purposes of the taxation law of such Contracting State as the income, profit or gain of a resident.

2. Where by reason of the provisions of paragraph 1, an individual is a resident of both Contracting States, then his status shall be determined as follows:

(a) he shall be deemed to be a resident of the State in which he has a permanent home available to him; if he has a permanent home available to him in both States, he shall be deemed to be a resident of the State with which his personal and economic relations are closer (center of vital interests);

(b) if the State in which he has his center of vital interests cannot be determined, or if he does not have a permanent home available to him in either State, he shall be deemed to be a resident of the State in which he has an habitual abode;

(c) if he has an habitual abode in both States or in neither of them, he shall be deemed to be a resident of the State of which he is a national;

(d) if he is a national of both States or of neither of them, the competent authorities of the Contracting States shall endeavor to settle the question by mutual agreement.

3. Where by reason of the provisions of paragraph 1 a company is a resident of both Contracting States, then if it is created under the laws of one of the Contracting States or a political subdivision thereof, it shall be deemed to be a resident of that State.

4. Where by reason of the provisions of paragraph 1 a person other than an individual or a company is a resident of both Contracting States, the competent authorities of the Contracting States shall endeavor to settle the question by mutual agreement and determine the mode of application of the Convention to such person.

Article 5—Permanent Establishment

1. For the purposes of this Convention, the term "permanent establishment" means a fixed place of business through which the business of an enterprise is wholly or partly carried on.

2. The term "permanent establishment" includes especially:

(a) a place of management;

(b) a branch;

(c) an office;

(d) a factory;

(e) a workshop; and

(f) a mine, an oil or gas well, a quarry, or any other place of extraction of natural resources.

3. A building site or construction or installation project, or an installation or drilling rig or ship used for the exploration of natural resources, constitutes a permanent establishment only if it lasts or the activity continues for more than twelve months.

4. Notwithstanding the preceding provisions of this Article, the term "permanent establishment" shall be deemed not to include:

(a) the use of facilities solely for the purpose of storage, display or delivery of goods or merchandise belonging to the enterprise;

(b) the maintenance of a stock of goods or merchandise belonging to the enterprise solely for the purpose of storage, display or delivery;

(c) the maintenance of a stock of goods or merchandise belonging to the enterprise solely for the purpose of processing by another enterprise;

(d) the maintenance of a fixed place of business solely for the purpose of purchasing goods or merchandise, or of collecting information, for the enterprise;

(e) the maintenance of a fixed place of business solely for the purpose of carrying on, for the enterprise, any other activity of a preparatory or auxiliary character;

(f) the maintenance of a fixed place of business solely for any combination of the activities mentioned in subparagraphs (a) through (e).

5. Notwithstanding the provisions of paragraphs 1 and 2, where a person—other than an agent of an independent status to whom paragraph 6 applies—is acting on behalf of an enterprise and has and habitually exercises in a Contracting State an authority to conclude contracts that are binding on the enterprise, that enterprise shall be deemed to have a permanent establishment in that State in respect of any activities that the person undertakes for the enterprise, unless the activities of such person are limited to those mentioned in paragraph 4 that, if exercised through a fixed place of business, would not make this fixed place of business a permanent establishment under the provisions of that paragraph.

6. An enterprise shall not be deemed to have a permanent establishment in a Contracting State merely because it carries on business in

that State through a broker, general commission agent, or any other agent of an independent status, provided that such persons are acting in the ordinary course of their business as independent agents.

7. The fact that a company that is a resident of a Contracting State controls or is controlled by a company that is a resident of the other Contracting State, or that carries on business in that other State (whether through a permanent establishment or otherwise), shall not constitute either company a permanent establishment of the other.

Article 6—Income from Real Property (Immovable Property)

1. Income derived by a resident of a Contracting State from real property (immovable property), including income from agriculture or forestry, situated in the other Contracting State may be taxed in that other State.

2. The term "real property (immovable property)" shall have the meaning which it has under the law of the Contracting State in which the property in question is situated.

3. The provisions of paragraph 1 shall apply to income derived from the direct use, letting, or use in any other form of real property.

4. The provisions of paragraphs 1 and 3 shall also apply to the income from real property of an enterprise and to income from real property used for the performance of independent personal services.

5. A resident of a Contracting State who is liable to tax in the other Contracting State on income from real property situated in the other Contracting State may elect for any taxable year to compute the tax on such income on a net basis as if such income were business profits attributable to a permanent establishment in such other State. Any such election shall be binding for the taxable year of the election and all subsequent taxable years unless the competent authority of the Contracting State in which the property is situated agrees to terminate the election.

Article 7—Business Profits

1. The business profits of an enterprise of a Contracting State shall be taxable only in that State unless the enterprise carries on business in the other Contracting State through a permanent establishment situated therein. If the enterprise carries on business as aforesaid, the business profits of the enterprise may be taxed in the other State but only so much of them as are attributable to that permanent establishment.

2. Subject to the provisions of paragraph 3, where an enterprise of a Contracting State carries on business in the other Contracting State

through a permanent establishment situated therein, there shall in each Contracting State be attributed to that permanent establishment the business profits that it might be expected to make if it were a distinct and independent enterprise engaged in the same or similar activities under the same or similar conditions. For this purpose, the business profits to be attributed to the permanent establishment shall include only the profits derived from the assets or activities of the permanent establishment.

3. In determining the business profits of a permanent establishment, there shall be allowed as deductions expenses that are incurred for the purposes of the permanent establishment, including a reasonable allocation of executive and general administrative expenses, research and development expenses, interest, and other expenses incurred for the purposes of the enterprise as a whole (or the part thereof which includes the permanent establishment), whether incurred in the State in which the permanent establishment is situated or elsewhere.

4. No business profits shall be attributed to a permanent establishment by reason of the mere purchase by that permanent establishment of goods or merchandise for the enterprise.

5. For the purposes of the preceding paragraphs, the profits to be attributed to the permanent establishment shall be determined by the same method of accounting year by year unless there is good and sufficient reason to the contrary.

6. Where business profits include items of income that are dealt with separately in other Articles of the Convention, then the provisions of those Articles shall not be affected by the provisions of this Article.

7. For the purposes of the Convention, the term "business profits" means income from any trade or business, including income derived by an enterprise from the performance of personal services, and from the rental of tangible personal property.

8. In applying paragraphs 1 and 2 of Article 7 (Business Profits), paragraph 6 of Article 10 (Dividends), paragraph 3 of Article 11 (Interest), paragraph 3 of Article 12 (Royalties), paragraph 3 of Article 13 (Gains), Article 14 (Independent Personal Services) and paragraph 2 of Article 21 (Other Income), any income or gain attributable to a permanent establishment or fixed base during its existence is taxable in the Contracting State where such permanent establishment or fixed base is situated even if the payments are deferred until such permanent establishment or fixed base has ceased to exist.

Article 8—Shipping and Air Transport

1. Profits of an enterprise of a Contracting State from the operation of ships or aircraft in international traffic shall be taxable only in that State.

2. For the purposes of this Article, profits from the operation of ships or aircraft include profits derived from the rental of ships or aircraft on a full (time or voyage) basis. They also include profits from the rental of ships or aircraft on a bareboat basis if such ships or aircraft are operated in international traffic by the lessee, or if the rental income is incidental to profits from the operation of ships or aircraft in international traffic. Profits derived by an enterprise from the inland transport of property or passengers within either Contracting State, shall be treated as profits from the operation of ships or aircraft in international traffic if such transport is undertaken as part of international traffic.

3. Profits of an enterprise of a Contracting State from the use, maintenance, or rental of containers (including trailers, barges, and related equipment for the transport of containers) used in international traffic shall be taxable only in that State.

4. The provisions of paragraphs 1 and 3 shall also apply to profits from participation in a pool, a joint business, or an international operating agency.

Article 9—Associated Enterprises

1. Where:

(a) an enterprise of a Contracting State participates directly or indirectly in the management, control or capital of an enterprise of the other Contracting State; or

(b) the same persons participate directly or indirectly in the management, control, or capital of an enterprise of a Contracting State and an enterprise of the other Contracting State, and in either case conditions are made or imposed between the two enterprises in their commercial or financial relations that differ from those that would be made between independent enterprises, then, any profits that, but for those conditions, would have accrued to one of the enterprises, but by reason of those conditions have not so accrued, may be included in the profits of that enterprise and taxed accordingly.

2. Where a Contracting State includes in the profits of an enterprise of that State, and taxes accordingly, profits on which an enterprise of the other Contracting State has been charged to tax in that other State, and the other Contracting State agrees that the profits so

included are profits that would have accrued to the enterprise of the first-mentioned State if the conditions made between the two enterprises had been those that would have been made between independent enterprises, then that other State shall make an appropriate adjustment to the amount of the tax charged therein on those profits. In determining such adjustment, due regard shall be paid to the other provisions of this Convention and the competent authorities of the Contracting States shall if necessary consult each other.

Article 10—Dividends

1. Dividends paid by a resident of a Contracting State to a resident of the other Contracting State may be taxed in that other State.

2. However, such dividends may also be taxed in the Contracting State of which the payor is a resident and according to the laws of that State, but if the dividends are beneficially owned by a resident of the other Contracting State, except as otherwise provided, the tax so charged shall not exceed:

   (a) 5 percent of the gross amount of the dividends if the beneficial owner is a company that owns directly at least 10 percent of the voting stock of the company paying the dividends;

   (b) 15 percent of the gross amount of the dividends in all other cases. This paragraph shall not affect the taxation of the company in respect of the profits out of which the dividends are paid.

3. Subparagraph (a) of paragraph 2 shall not apply in the case of dividends paid by a United States person that is a Regulated Investment Company or a Real Estate Investment Trust (REIT). In the case of a United States person that is a REIT, subparagraph (b) of paragraph 2 also shall not apply, unless the dividend is beneficially owned by an individual holding a less than 10-percent interest in the REIT.

4. Notwithstanding paragraph 2, dividends may not be taxed in the Contracting State of which the payor is a resident if the beneficial owner of the dividends is a resident of the other Contracting State that is a qualified governmental entity that does not control the payor of the dividend.

5. For purposes of the Convention, the term "dividends" means income from shares or other rights, not being debt-claims, participating in profits, as well as income that is subjected to the same taxation treatment as income from shares under the laws of the State of which the payor is a resident.

6. The provisions of paragraphs 1 and 2 shall not apply if the beneficial owner of the dividends, being a resident of a Contracting State, carries on business in the other Contracting State, of which the

payor is a resident, through a permanent establishment situated therein, or performs in that other State independent personal services from a fixed base situated therein, and the dividends are attributable to such permanent establishment or fixed base. In such case the provisions of Article 7 (Business Profits) or Article 14 (Independent Personal Services), as the case may be, shall apply.

7. A Contracting State may not impose any tax on dividends paid by a resident of the other State, except insofar as the dividends are paid to a resident of the first-mentioned State or the dividends are attributable to a permanent establishment or a fixed base situated in that State, nor may it impose tax on a corporation's undistributed profits, except as provided in paragraph 8, even if the dividends paid or the undistributed profits consist wholly or partly of profits or income arising in that State.

8. A corporation that is a resident of one of the States and that has a permanent establishment in the other State or that is subject to tax in the other State on a net basis on its income that may be taxed in the other State under Article 6 (Income from Real Property (Immoveable Property)) or under paragraph 1 of Article 13 (Gains) may be subject in that other State to a tax in addition to the tax allowable under the other provisions of this Convention. Such tax, however, may be imposed on only the portion of the business profits of the corporation attributable to the permanent establishment and the portion of the income referred to in the preceding sentence that is subject to tax under Article 6 (Income from Real Property (Immoveable Property)) or under paragraph 1 of Article 13 (Gains) that, in the case of the United States, represents the dividend equivalent amount of such profits or income and, in the case of ...., is an amount that is analogous to the dividend equivalent amount.

9. The tax referred to in paragraph 8 may not be imposed at a rate in excess of the rate specified in paragraph 2(a).

Article 11—Interest

1. Interest arising in a Contracting State and beneficially owned by a resident of the other Contracting State may be taxed only in that other State.

2. The term "interest" as used in this Convention means income from debt-claims of every kind, whether or not secured by mortgage, and whether or not carrying a right to participate in the debtor's profits, and in particular, income from government securities and income from bonds or debentures, including premiums or prizes attaching to such securities, bonds or debentures, and all other income that is subjected to the same taxation treatment as income from money lent

by the taxation law of the Contracting State in which the income arises. Income dealt with in Article 10 (Dividends) and penalty charges for late payment shall not be regarded as interest for the purposes of this Convention.

3. The provisions of paragraph 1 shall not apply if the beneficial owner of the interest, being a resident of a Contracting State, carries on business in the other Contracting State, in which the interest arises, through a permanent establishment situated therein, or performs in that other State independent personal services from a fixed base situated therein, and the interest is attributable to such permanent establishment or fixed base. In such case the provisions of Article 7 (Business Profits) or Article 14 (Independent Personal Services), as the case may be, shall apply.

4. Where, by reason of a special relationship between the payer and the beneficial owner or between both of them and some other person, the amount of the interest, having regard to the debt-claim for which it is paid, exceeds the amount which would have been agreed upon by the payer and the beneficial owner in the absence of such relationship, the provisions of this Article shall apply only to the last-mentioned amount. In such case the excess part of the payments shall remain taxable according to the laws of each State, due regard being had to the other provisions of this Convention.

5. Notwithstanding the provisions of paragraph 1:

(a) interest paid by a resident of a Contracting State and that is determined with reference to receipts, sales, income, profits or other cash flow of the debtor or a related person, to any change in the value of any property of the debtor or a related person or to any dividend, partnership distribution or similar payment made by the debtor to a related person, and paid to a resident of the other State also may be taxed in the Contracting State in which it arises, and according to the laws of that State, but if the beneficial owner is a resident of the other Contracting State, the gross amount of the interest may be taxed at a rate not exceeding the rate prescribed in subparagraph (b) of paragraph 2 of Article 10 (Dividends); and

(b) Interest that is an excess inclusion with respect to a residual interest in a real estate mortgage investment conduit may be taxed by each State in accordance with its domestic law.

Article 12—Royalties

1. Royalties arising in a Contracting State and beneficially owned by a resident of the other Contracting State may be taxed only in that other State.

2. The term "royalties" as used in this Convention means:

(a) any consideration for the use of, or the right to use, any copyright of literary, artistic, scientific or other work (including computer software, cinematographic films, audio or video tapes or disks, and other means of image or sound reproduction), any patent, trademark, design or model, plan, secret formula or process, or other like right or property, or for information concerning industrial, commercial, or scientific experience; and

(b) gain derived from the alienation of any property described in subparagraph (a), provided that such gain is contingent on the productivity, use, or disposition of the property.

3. The provisions of paragraph 1 shall not apply if the beneficial owner of the royalties, being a resident of a Contracting State, carries on business in the other Contracting State through a permanent establishment situated therein, or performs in that other State independent personal services from a fixed base situated therein, and the royalties are attributable to such permanent establishment or fixed base. In such case the provisions of Article 7 (Business Profits) or Article 14 (Independent Personal Services), as the case may be, shall apply.

4. Where, by reason of a special relationship between the payer and the beneficial owner or between both of them and some other person, the amount of the royalties, having regard to the use, right, or information for which they are paid, exceeds the amount which would have been agreed upon by the payer and the beneficial owner in the absence of such relationship, the provisions of this Article shall apply only to the last-mentioned amount. In such case the excess part of the payments shall remain taxable according to the laws of each Contracting State, due regard being had to the other provisions of the Convention.

Article 13—Gains

1. Gains derived by a resident of a Contracting State that are attributable to the alienation of real property situated in the other Contracting State may be taxed in that other State.

2. For the purposes of this Convention the term "real property situated in the other Contracting State" shall include:

(a) real property referred to in Article 6 (Income from Real Property (Immovable Property));

(b) a United States real property interest; and

(c) an equivalent interest in real property situated in ....

3. Gains from the alienation of personal property that are attributable to a permanent establishment that an enterprise of a Contracting

State has in the other Contracting State, or that are attributable to a fixed base that is available to a resident of a Contracting State in the other Contracting State for the purpose of performing independent personal services, and gains from the alienation of such a permanent establishment (alone or with the whole enterprise) or of such a fixed base, may be taxed in that other State.

4. Gains derived by an enterprise of a Contracting State from the alienation of ships, aircraft, or containers operated or used in international traffic or personal property pertaining to the operation or use of such ships, aircraft, or containers shall be taxable only in that State.

5. Gains from the alienation of any property other than property referred to in paragraphs 1 through 4 shall be taxable only in the Contracting State of which the alienator is a resident.

Article 14—Independent Personal Services

1. Income derived by an individual who is a resident of a Contracting State in respect of the performance of personal services of an independent character shall be taxable only in that State, unless the individual has a fixed base regularly available to him in the other Contracting State for the purpose of performing his activities. If he has such a fixed base, the income attributable to the fixed base that is derived in respect of services performed in that other State also may be taxed by that other State.

2. For purposes of paragraph 1, the income that is taxable in the other Contracting State shall be determined under the principles of paragraph 3 of Article 7.

Article 15—Dependent Personal Services

1. Subject to the provisions of Articles 16 (Directors' Fees), 18 (Pensions, Social Security, Annuities, Alimony, and Child Support) and 19 (Government Service), salaries, wages, and other remuneration derived by a resident of a Contracting State in respect of an employment shall be taxable only in that State unless the employment is exercised in the other Contracting State. If the employment is so exercised, such remuneration as is derived therefrom may be taxed in that other State.

2. Notwithstanding the provisions of paragraph 1, remuneration derived by a resident of a Contracting State in respect of an employment exercised in the other Contracting State shall be taxable only in the first-mentioned State if:

(a) the recipient is present in the other State for a period or periods not exceeding in the aggregate 183 days in any twelve month period commencing or ending in the taxable year concerned;

(b) the remuneration is paid by, or on behalf of, an employer who is not a resident of the other State; and

(c) the remuneration is not borne by a permanent establishment or a fixed base which the employer has in the other State.

3. Notwithstanding the preceding provisions of this Article, remuneration described in paragraph 1 that is derived by a resident of a Contracting State in respect of an employment as a member of the regular complement of a ship or aircraft operated in international traffic shall be taxable only in that State.

Article 16—Directors' Fees

Directors' fees and other compensation derived by a resident of a Contracting State for services rendered in the other Contracting State in his capacity as a member of the board of directors of a company that is a resident of the other Contracting State may be taxed in that other Contracting State.

Article 17—Artistes and Sportsmen

1. Income derived by a resident of a Contracting State as an entertainer, such as a theater, motion picture, radio, or television artiste, or a musician, or as a sportsman, from his personal activities as such exercised in the other Contracting State, which income would be exempt from tax in that other Contracting State under the provisions of Articles 14 (Independent Personal Services) and 15 (Dependent Personal Services) may be taxed in that other State, except where the amount of the gross receipts derived by such entertainer or sportsman, including expenses reimbursed to him or borne on his behalf, from such activities does not exceed twenty thousand United States dollars ($20,000) or its equivalent in .... for the taxable year concerned.

2. Where income in respect of activities exercised by an entertainer or a sportsman in his capacity as such accrues not to the entertainer or sportsman himself but to another person, that income, notwithstanding the provisions of Articles 7 (Business Profits) and 14 (Independent Personal Services), may be taxed in the Contracting State in which the activities of the entertainer or sportsman are exercised, unless it is established that neither the entertainer or sportsman nor persons related thereto participate directly or indirectly in the profits of that other person in any manner, including the receipt of deferred remuneration, bonuses, fees, dividends, partnership distributions, or other distributions.

¶ 904

Article 18—Pensions, Social Security, Annuities, Alimony, and Child Support

1. Subject to the provisions of Article 19 (Government Service), pension distributions and other similar remuneration beneficially owned by a resident of a Contracting State, whether paid periodically or as a single sum, shall be taxable only in that State, but only to the extent not included in taxable income in the other Contracting State prior to the distribution.

2. Notwithstanding the provisions of paragraph 1, payments made by a Contracting State under provisions of the social security or similar legislation of that State to a resident of the other Contracting State or to a citizen of the United States shall be taxable only in the first-mentioned State.

3. Annuities derived and beneficially owned by an individual resident of a Contracting State shall be taxable only in that State. The term "annuities" as used in this paragraph means a stated sum paid periodically at stated times during a specified number of years, under an obligation to make the payments in return for adequate and full consideration (other than services rendered).

4. Alimony paid by a resident of a Contracting State, and deductible therein, to a resident of the other Contracting State shall be taxable only in that other State. The term "alimony" as used in this paragraph means periodic payments made pursuant to a written separation agreement or a decree of divorce, separate maintenance, or compulsory support, which payments are taxable to the recipient under the laws of the State of which he is a resident.

5. Periodic payments, not dealt with in paragraph 4, for the support of a child made pursuant to a written separation agreement or a decree of divorce, separate maintenance, or compulsory support, paid by a resident of a Contracting State to a resident of the other Contracting State, shall be exempt from tax in both Contracting States.

6. For purposes of this Convention, where an individual who is a participant in a pension plan that is established and recognized under the legislation of one of the Contracting States performs personal services in the other Contracting State:

(a) Contributions paid by or on behalf of the individual to the plan during the period that he performs such services in the other State shall be deductible (or excludible) in computing his taxable income in that State. Any benefits accrued under the plan or payments made to the plan by or on behalf of his employer during that period shall not be treated as part of the employee's taxable income and shall be allowed as a deduction in computing the profits of his employer in that other State.

(b) Income earned but not distributed by the plan shall not be taxable in the other State until such time and to the extent that a distribution is made from the plan.

(c) Distributions from the plan to the individual shall not be subject to taxation in the other Contracting State if the individual contributes such amounts to a similar plan established in the other State within a time period and in accordance with any other requirements imposed under the laws of the other State.

(d) The provisions of this paragraph shall not apply unless:

(i) contributions by or on behalf of the individual to the plan (or to another similar plan for which this plan was substituted) were made before he arrived in the other State; and

(ii) the competent authority of the other State has agreed that the pension plan generally corresponds to a pension plan recognized for tax purposes by that State.

The benefits granted under this paragraph shall not exceed the benefits that would be allowed by the other State to its residents for contributions to, or benefits otherwise accrued under a pension plan recognized for tax purposes by that State.

Article 19—Government Service

1. Notwithstanding the provisions of Articles 14 (Independent Personal Services), 15 (Dependent Personal Services), 16 (Director's Fees) and 17 (Artistes and Sportsmen):

(a) Salaries, wages and other remuneration, other than a pension, paid from the public funds of a Contracting State or a political subdivision or a local authority thereof to an individual in respect of services rendered to that State or subdivision or authority in the discharge of functions of a governmental nature shall, subject to the provisions of subparagraph (b), be taxable only in that State;

(b) such remuneration, however, shall be taxable only in the other Contracting State if the services are rendered in that State and the individual is a resident of that State who:

(i) is a national of that State; or

(ii) did not become a resident of that State solely for the purpose of rendering the services.

2. Notwithstanding the provisions of paragraph 1 of Article 18 (Pensions, Social Security, Annuities, Alimony, and Child Support):

(a) any pension paid from the public funds of a Contracting State or a political subdivision or a local authority thereof to an individual in respect of services rendered to that State or subdivision or authority in the discharge of functions of a governmental nature shall, subject to the provisions of subparagraph (b), be taxable only in that State;

(b) such pension, however, shall be taxable only in the other Contracting State if the individual is a resident of, and a national of, that State.

Article 20—Students and Trainees

Payments received by a student, apprentice, or business trainee who is, or was immediately before visiting a Contracting State, a resident of the other Contracting State, and who is present in the first-mentioned State for the purpose of his full-time education at an accredited educational institution, or for his full-time training, shall not be taxed in that State, provided that such payments arise outside that State, and are for the purpose of his maintenance, education or training. The exemption from tax provided by this Article shall apply to an apprentice or business trainee only for a period of time not exceeding one year from the date he first arrives in the first-mentioned Contracting State for the purpose of his training.

Article 21—Other Income

1. Items of income beneficially owned by a resident of a Contracting State, wherever arising, not dealt with in the foregoing Articles of this Convention shall be taxable only in that State.

2. The provisions of paragraph 1 shall not apply to income, other than income from real property as defined in paragraph 2 of Article 6 (Income from Real Property (Immovable Property)), if the beneficial owner of the income, being a resident of a Contracting State, carries on business in the other Contracting State through a permanent establishment situated therein, or performs in that other State independent personal services from a fixed base situated therein, and the income is attributable to such permanent establishment or fixed base. In such case the provisions of Article 7 (Business Profits) or Article 14 (Independent Personal Services), as the case may be, shall apply.

Article 22—Limitation on Benefits

1. A resident of a Contracting State shall be entitled to benefits otherwise accorded to residents of a Contracting State by this Convention only to the extent provided in this Article.

2. A resident of a Contracting State shall be entitled to all the benefits of this Convention if the resident is:

(a) an individual;

(b) a qualified governmental entity;

(c) a company, if

(i) all the shares in the class or classes of shares representing more than 50 percent of the voting power and value of the company are regularly traded on a recognized stock exchange, or

(ii) at least 50 percent of each class of shares in the company is owned directly or indirectly by companies entitled to benefits under clause (i), provided that in the case of indirect ownership, each intermediate owner is a person entitled to benefits of the Convention under this paragraph;

(d) described in subparagraph 1(b)(i) of Article 4 (Residence);

(e) described in subparagraph 1(b)(ii) of Article 4 (Residence), provided that more than 50 percent of the person's beneficiaries, members or participants are individuals resident in either Contracting State; or

(f) a person other than an individual, if:

(i) On at least half the days of the taxable year persons described in subparagraphs (a), (b), (c), (d) or (e) own, directly or indirectly (through a chain of ownership in which each person is entitled to benefits of the Convention under this paragraph), at least 50 percent of each class of shares or other beneficial interests in the person, and

(ii) less than 50 percent of the person's gross income for the taxable year is paid or accrued, directly or indirectly, to persons who are not residents of either Contracting State (unless the payment is attributable to a permanent establishment situated in either State), in the form of payments that are deductible for income tax purposes in the person's State of residence.

3.

(a) A resident of a Contracting State not otherwise entitled to benefits shall be entitled to the benefits of this Convention with respect to an item of income derived from the other State, if:

(i) the resident is engaged in the active conduct of a trade or business in the first-mentioned State,

(ii) the income is connected with or incidental to the trade or business, and

(iii) the trade or business is substantial in relation to the activity in the other State generating the income.

(b) For purposes of this paragraph, the business of making or managing investments will not be considered an active trade or business unless the activity is banking, insurance or securities activity conducted by a bank, insurance company or registered securities dealer.

(c) Whether a trade or business is substantial for purposes of this paragraph will be determined based on all the facts and circumstances. In any case, however, a trade or business will be deemed substantial if, for the preceding taxable year, or for the average of the three preceding taxable years, the asset value, the gross income, and the payroll expense that are related to the trade or business in the first-mentioned State equal at least 7.5 percent of the resident's (and any related parties') proportionate share of the asset value, gross income and payroll expense, respectively, that are related to the activity that generated the income in the other State, and the average of the three ratios exceeds 10 percent.

(d) Income is derived in connection with a trade or business if the activity in the other State generating the income is a line of business that forms a part of or is complementary to the trade or business. Income is incidental to a trade or business if it facilitates the conduct of the trade or business in the other State.

4. A resident of a Contracting State not otherwise entitled to benefits may be granted benefits of the Convention if the competent authority of the State from which benefits are claimed so determines.

5. For purposes of this Article the term "recognized stock exchange" means:

(a) the NASDAQ System owned by the National Association of Securities Dealers, Inc. and any stock exchange registered with the U.S. Securities and Exchange Commission as a national securities exchange under the U.S. Securities Exchange Act of 1934; and

(b) [stock exchanges of the other Contracting State].

Article 23—Relief from Double Taxation

1. In accordance with the provisions and subject to the limitations of the law of the United States (as it may be amended from time to time without changing the general principle hereof), the United States shall allow to a resident or citizen of the United States as a credit against the United States tax on income

(a) the income tax paid or accrued to .... by or on behalf of such citizen or resident; and

(b) in the case of a United States company owning at least 10 percent of the voting stock of a company that is a resident of .... and from which the United States company receives dividends, the income tax paid or accrued to .... by or on behalf of the payor with respect to the profits out of which the dividends are paid. For the purposes of this paragraph, the taxes referred to in paragraphs 1(b) and 2 of Article 2 (Taxes Covered) shall be considered income taxes.

2. In accordance with the provisions and subject to the limitations of the law of .... (as it may be amended from time to time without changing the general principle hereof), ... shall allow to a resident or citizen of .... as a credit against the .... tax on income

(a) the income tax paid or accrued to the United States by or on behalf of such resident of citizen; and

(b) in the case of a .... company owning at least 10 percent of the voting stock of a company that is a resident of the United States and from which the .... company receives dividends, the income tax paid or accrued to the United States by or on behalf of the payor with respect to the profits out of which the dividends are paid.

For the purposes of this paragraph, the taxes referred to in paragraphs 1(a) and 2 of Article 2 (Taxes Covered) shall be considered income taxes.

3. Where a United States citizen is a resident of ....

(a) with respect to items of income that under the provisions of this Convention are exempt from United States tax or that are subject to a reduced rate of United States tax when derived by a resident of .... who is not a United States citizen, ... shall allow as a credit against .... tax, only the tax paid, if any, that the United States may impose under the provisions of this Convention, other than taxes that may be imposed solely by reason of citizenship under the saving clause of paragraph 4 of Article 1 (General Scope);

(b) for purposes of computing United States tax on those items of income referred to in subparagraph (a), the United States shall allow as a credit against United States tax the income tax paid to .... after the credit referred to in subparagraph (a); the credit so allowed shall not reduce the portion of the United States tax that is creditable against the .... tax in accordance with subparagraph (a); and

(c) for the exclusive purpose of relieving double taxation in the United States under subparagraph (b), items of income referred to in subparagraph (a) shall be deemed to arise in .... to the extent necessary to avoid double taxation of such income under subparagraph (b).

Article 24—Non-Discrimination

1. Nationals of a Contracting State shall not be subjected in the other Contracting State to any taxation or any requirement connected therewith that is more burdensome than the taxation and connected requirements to which nationals of that other State in the same circumstances, particularly with respect to taxation on worldwide income, are or may be subjected. This provision shall also apply to persons who are not residents of one or both of the Contracting States.

2. The taxation on a permanent establishment or fixed base that a resident or enterprise of a Contracting State has in the other Contracting State shall not be less favorably levied in that other State than the taxation levied on enterprises or residents of that other State carrying on the same activities. The provisions of this paragraph shall not be construed as obliging a Contracting State to grant to residents of the other Contracting State any personal allowances, reliefs, and reductions for taxation purposes on account of civil status or family responsibilities that it grants to its own residents.

3. Except where the provisions of paragraph 1 of Article 9 (Associated Enterprises), paragraph 4 of Article 11 (Interest), or paragraph 4 of Article 12 (Royalties) apply, interest, royalties, and other disbursements paid by a resident of a Contracting State to a resident of the other Contracting State shall, for the purpose of determining the taxable profits of the first-mentioned resident, be deductible under the same conditions as if they had been paid to a resident of the first-mentioned State. Similarly, any debts of a resident of a Contracting State to a resident of the other Contracting State shall, for the purpose of determining the taxable capital of the first-mentioned resident, be deductible under the same conditions as if they had been contracted to a resident of the first-mentioned State.

4. Enterprises of a Contracting State, the capital of which is wholly or partly owned or controlled, directly or indirectly, by one or more residents of the other Contracting State, shall not be subjected in the first-mentioned State to any taxation or any requirement connected therewith that is more burdensome than the taxation and connected requirements to which other similar enterprises of the first-mentioned State are or may be subjected.

5. Nothing in this Article shall be construed as preventing either Contracting State from imposing a tax as described in paragraph 8 of Article 10 (Dividends).

6. The provisions of this Article shall, notwithstanding the provisions of Article 2 (Taxes Covered), apply to taxes of every kind and description imposed by a Contracting State or a political subdivision or local authority thereof.

Article 25—Mutual Agreement Procedure

1. Where a person considers that the actions of one or both of the Contracting States result or will result for him in taxation not in accordance with the provisions of this Convention, he may, irrespective of the remedies provided by the domestic law of those States, and the time limits prescribed in such laws for presenting claims for refund, present his case to the competent authority of either Contracting State.

2. The competent authority shall endeavor, if the objection appears to it to be justified and if it is not itself able to arrive at a satisfactory solution, to resolve the case by mutual agreement with the competent authority of the other Contracting State, with a view to the avoidance of taxation which is not in accordance with the Convention. Any agreement reached shall be implemented notwithstanding any time limits or other procedural limitations in the domestic law of the Contracting States. Assessment and collection procedures shall be suspended during the pendency of any mutual agreement proceeding.

3. The competent authorities of the Contracting States shall endeavor to resolve by mutual agreement any difficulties or doubts arising as to the interpretation or application of the Convention. In particular the competent authorities of the Contracting States may agree:

(a) to the same attribution of income, deductions, credits, or allowances of an enterprise of a Contracting State to its permanent establishment situated in the other Contracting State;

(b) to the same allocation of income, deductions, credits, or allowances between persons;

(c) to the same characterization of particular items of income, including the same characterization of income that is assimilated to income from shares by the taxation law of one of the Contracting States and that is treated as a different class of income in the other State;

(d) to the same characterization of persons;

(e) to the same application of source rules with respect to particular items of income;

(f) to a common meaning of a term;

(g) to advance pricing arrangements; and

(h) to the application of the provisions of domestic law regarding penalties, fines, and interest in a manner consistent with the purposes of the Convention.

They may also consult together for the elimination of double taxation in cases not provided for in the Convention.

4. The competent authorities also may agree to increases in any specific dollar amounts referred to in the Convention to reflect economic or monetary developments.

5. The competent authorities of the Contracting States may communicate with each other directly for the purpose of reaching an agreement in the sense of the preceding paragraphs.

Article 26—Exchange of Information and Administrative Assistance

1. The competent authorities of the Contracting States shall exchange such information as is relevant for carrying out the provisions of this Convention or of the domestic laws of the Contracting States concerning taxes covered by the Convention insofar as the taxation thereunder is not contrary to the Convention, including information relating to the assessment or collection of, the enforcement or prosecution in respect of, or the determination of appeals in relation to, the taxes covered by the Convention. The exchange of information is not restricted by Article 1 (General Scope). Any information received by a Contracting State shall be treated as secret in the same manner as information obtained under the domestic laws of that State and shall be disclosed only to persons or authorities (including courts and administrative bodies) involved in the assessment, collection, or administration of, the enforcement or prosecution in respect of, or the determination of appeals in relation to, the taxes covered by the Convention or the oversight of the above. Such persons or authorities shall use the information only for such purposes. They may disclose the information in public court proceedings or in judicial decisions.

2. In no case shall the provisions of paragraph 1 be construed so as to impose on a Contracting State the obligation:

(a) to carry out administrative measures at variance with the laws and administrative practice of that or of the other Contracting State;

(b) to supply information that is not obtainable under the laws or in the normal course of the administration of that or of the other Contracting State;

(c) to supply information that would disclose any trade, business, industrial, commercial, or professional secret or trade process, or information the disclosure of which would be contrary to public policy (order public).

3. Notwithstanding paragraph 2, the competent authority of the requested State shall have the authority to obtain and provide information held by financial institutions, nominees or persons acting in an agency or fiduciary capacity, or respecting interests in a person, including bearer shares, regardless of any laws or practices of the requested State that might otherwise preclude the obtaining of such information. If information is requested by a Contracting State in accordance with this Article, the other Contracting State shall obtain that information in the same manner and to the same extent as if the tax of the first-mentioned State were the tax of that other State and were being imposed by that other State, notwithstanding that the other State may not, at that time, need such information for purposes of its own tax. If specifically requested by the competent authority of a Contracting State, the competent authority of the other Contracting State shall provide information under this Article in the form of depositions of witnesses and authenticated copies of unedited original documents (including books, papers, statements, records, accounts, and writings), to the same extent such depositions and documents can be obtained under the laws and administrative practices of that other State with respect to its own taxes.

4. Each of the Contracting States shall endeavor to collect on behalf of the other Contracting State such amounts as may be necessary to ensure that relief granted by the Convention from taxation imposed by that other State does not inure to the benefit of persons not entitled thereto. This paragraph shall not impose upon either of the Contracting States the obligation to carry out administrative measures that would be contrary to its sovereignty, security, or public policy.

5. For the purposes of this Article, the Convention shall apply, notwithstanding the provisions of Article 2 (Taxes Covered), to taxes of every kind imposed by a Contracting State.

6. The competent authority of the requested State shall allow representatives of the applicant State to enter the requested State to interview individuals and examine books and records with the consent of the persons subject to examination.

Article 27—Diplomatic Agents and Consular Officers

Nothing in this Convention shall affect the fiscal privileges of diplomatic agents or consular officers under the general rules of international law or under the provisions of special agreements.

Article 28—Entry into Force

1. This Convention shall be subject to ratification in accordance with the applicable procedures of each Contracting State. Each Contracting State shall notify the other as soon as its procedures have been complied with.

2. The Convention shall enter into force on the date of the receipt of the later of such notifications, and its provisions shall have effect:

(a) in respect of taxes withheld at source, for amounts paid or credited on or after the first day of the second month next following the date on which the Convention enters into force;

(b) in respect of other taxes, for taxable periods beginning on or after the first day of January next following the date on which the Convention enters into force.

Article 29—Termination

1. This Convention shall remain in force until terminated by a Contracting State. Either Contracting State may terminate the Convention by giving notice of termination to the other Contracting State through diplomatic channels. In such event, the Convention shall cease to have effect:

(a) in respect of taxes withheld at source, for amounts paid or credited after the expiration of the 6 month period beginning on the date on which notice of termination was given; and

(b) in respect of other taxes, for taxable periods beginning on or after the expiration of the 6 month period beginning on the date on which notice of termination was given.

IN WITNESS WHEREOF, the undersigned, being duly authorized thereto by their respective Governments, have signed this Convention.

DONE at .... in duplicate, in the English and .... languages, both texts being equally authentic, this .... day of (month), 19 ....

FOR THE GOVERNMENT OF THE UNITED STATES OF AMERICA:

FOR THE GOVERNMENT OF ....:

¶905 APPENDIX

Table 1. Withholding Tax Rates on Income Other Than Personal Service Income Under Chapter 3, Internal Revenue Code, and Income Tax Treaties- For Withholding in 2000

Country of residence of payee (Name)	Code	1 Interest paid by U.S. obligors General	2 Interest on real property mortgages	3 Interest paid to controlling foreign corporations	6 Dividends — U.S. Corporations General	7 Dividends — U.S. subsidiaries to foreign parent corporations	9 Capital Gains	10 Industrial Royalties	11 Motion Pictures and Television	12 Copyright royalties — Other	13 Real Property Income and Natural Resources Royalties	14 Pensions and Annuities
Australia	AS	g10	g10	g10	g15	g15	30	g10	g10	g10	30	g0
Austria	AU	ga g0	ga ad g0	g ad 0	g a 15	g a 5	g0	g0	g10	g0	30	0
Barbados	BB	g5	g5	g5	g a m 15	b g 5	g0	g5	g5	g5	30	g0
Belgium	BE	g15	g15	g15	g15	b 5	g0	g0	g0	g0	30	g0
Canada	CA	g10	g ae 10	g10	g ae 15	g ae 5	r30	g ae 10	g10	g0	30	15
China, People's Republic of / Commonwealth of Independent States	CH	g10	g10	g10	g10	g10	30	g a 10	g10	g10	30	g0
Cyprus	CY	r0	30	30	30	30	r0	0	0	0	30	30
Czech Republic	EZ	g10	g ad 10	g10	g a m 15	b g 5	r0	g10	g0	g0	30	g0
Denmark	DA	r0	r0	r0	r15	b 5	30	r0	r0	r0	30	r0
Egypt	EG	h15	30	g0	h15	b g 5	r0	g5	r0	g15	30	d0
Finland	FI	g0	g0	g0	g a 15	b g 5	r0	g5	g0	g0	30	d0
France	FR	g0	g ae g0	g0	g a m 15	b g 5	r0	g5	g ac 0	g0	30	j d0
Germany	GM	g0	r0	g0	g a m 15	b g a 5	r0	r0	g ac 0	g0	30	d0
Greece	GR	r0	r0	30	30	30	30	r0	30	r0	30	r0
Hungary	HU	g0	g0	g0	g15	b g 5	g0	g0	g0	g0	30	d0
Iceland	IC	g0	g0	g0	g a m 15	b g 5	r0	g5	30	g15	30	d0
India	IN	g a 15	g a 15	g15	g a m 25	b g ah 15	30	g a ah 10	30	g15	30	d 15
Indonesia	ID	g10	g10	g10	g15	b g 10	30	g a 10	g10	g10	30	d0
Ireland	EI	g0	r0	g0	g a 15	b g 5	g0	g0	g0	g0	30	d0
Israel	IS	j ag 17½	j ae aj 17½	j ae aj 17½	ag aj 25	b ae ag 12½	g0	ag g 15	ag g 10	ag g 10	r30	r0
Italy	IT	g15	g15	g15	g15	b g 5	g0	g g 10	g g 8	g g 5	30	d0
Jamaica	JM	g12½	g12½	g12½	g15	b g 10	g0	g10	g10	g10	30	d0
Japan	JA	g10	g10	g10	g a m 15	b g 10	g0	g10	g10	g10	30	d0
Kazakhstan	KZ	g10	g ae 10	g10	g af 15	b g 5	g0	g10	g10	g10	30	d 15
Korea, Rep. of	KS	g12	g12	g12	g15	b g 10	g0	g15	g10	g10	30	d0
Luxembourg	LU	r0	30	r0	g15	b g 5	30	r0	r0	r0	30	d0
Mexico	MX	g am 15	g am 15	g15	g am 15	b g 5	g0	g10	g10	g10	30	d0
Morocco	MO	g15	g15	g15	g15	b g 10	30	g10	g10	g10	30	u 15
Netherlands	NL	g0	g0	g0	g a m 15	b g 5	0	g0	g ac 0	g0	30	d0
New Zealand	NZ	g10	g10	g10	g15	g15	g0	g10	g10	g10	30	d0
Norway	NO	g0	g0	g0	g15	g15	g0	g0	r0	r0	30	d0
Pakistan	PK	30	30	30	30	b 15	30	r0	30	r0	30	d0
Philippines	RP	g15	g15	g15	g25	b g 20	g0	g15	g15	g15	30	g30

Table 1. Withholding Tax Rates on Income Other Than Personal Service Income Under Chapter 3, Internal Revenue Code, and Income Tax Treaties- For Withholding in 2000

| Income code number | | 1 | 2 | 3 | Dividends paid by | | 9 | 10 | Copyright royalties [dd] | | 13 | 14 |
| Country of residence of payee | | | | | 6 | 7 | | | 11 | 12 | | |
Name	Code	Interest paid by U.S. obligors, General [dd]	Interest on real property mortgages [dd]	Interest paid to controlling foreign corporations [dd]	U.S. Corporations General [dd]	U.S. subsidiaries to foreign parent corporations [dd]	Capital Gains [a, dd]	Industrial Royalties [dd]	Motion Pictures and Television	Other	Real Property Income and Natural Resources Royalties [d]	Pensions and Annuities [c]
Poland	PL	0	0	0	g15	b,g5	0	g10	g10	g10	30	30
Portugal	PO	h10	h,dd10	h10	h,w15	h,w5	0	h10	h10	h10	30	d,f0
Romania	RO	dd10	10	g10	g10	g10	0	g15	g10	g10	30	d,f0
Russia	RS	0	0	0	g,dd10	b,g,dd5	0	0	0	0	30	d0
Slovak Republic	LO	dd0	g,dd0	g0	g,dd15	b,g,dd5	0	g10	0	0	30	d0
South Africa	SF	g0	g,dd0	g0	g,dd15	g,dd5	0	g,dd0	g,dd0	0	30	d,f5
Spain	SP	g10	g10	g10	g,dd15	b,g,dd10	0	g,dd8	g,dd8	0	30	0
Sweden	SW	0	h,dd0	0	h,dd15	b,h,dd5	0	0	0	0	30	0
Switzerland	SZ	g,i15	g,i,p0	g,p0	g,dd15	g,dd5	0	g,dd0	0	g,i15	30	d,f0
Thailand	TH	30	30	30	30	g,dd10	30	g,dd8	g5	g15	30	0
Trinidad & Tobago	TD	30	30	30	s20	30	30	g15	30	30	30	d,f0
Tunisia	TS	15	g15	g15	s,w14	b,g,w14	0	g,i10	g,i15	g,i15	30	0
Turkey	TU	g,m,z15	g,m,z15	g,m,z15	g,w20	g,w15	0	g,i5	g,i10	g,i10	30	d,f0
United Kingdom	UK	0	0	0	g15	b,g5	30	0	0	0	30	30
Other countries		30	30	30	30	30	30	30	30	30	30	30

aa This is the rate is 5% for royalties for the use of, or the right to use, industrial, commercial, and scientific equipment. The rate for royalties for information concerning industrial, commercial and scientific know-how is subject to the rate in column 12, but use Income Code 10 for reporting purposes.

bb Exemption applies to U.S. Government (federal, state, or local) pensions only if the individual is both a resident and national of France and is not a U.S. national.

cc The exemption does not apply to cinematographic films, or works on film, tape, or other means of reproduction for use in radio or television broadcasting.

dd Under some treaties, the reduced rates of withholding may not apply to a foreign corporation unless a minimum percentage of its owners are citizens or residents of the United States or the treaty country.

ee Exemption or reduced rate does not apply to an excess inclusion for a residual interest in a real estate mortgage investment conduit (REMIC).

ff The rate in column 6 applies to dividends paid by a regulated investment company (RIC). Dividends paid by a real estate investment trust (REIT) are subject to a 30% rate.

gg Under the treaty the exemption or reduction in rate does not apply if the recipient has a permanent establishment in the U.S. and the income is effectively connected with this permanent establishment. Instead, tax is not withheld at source and the provisions of Article 8 (Business Profits) apply. Additionally, even if interest income is not effectively connected with a U.S. permanent establishment, the recipient may choose to treat net interest income as industrial or commercial profits subject to Article 8 of the treaty.

hh The rate is 4.9% for interest derived from (1) loans granted by banks and insurance companies and (2) bonds or securities that are regularly and substantially traded on a recognized securities market. The rate is 10% for interest not described in the preceding sentence and paid (i) by banks or (ii) by the buyer of machinery and equipment to the seller due to a sale on credit.

ii The exemption does not apply if (1) the recipient was a U.S. resident during the 5-year period before the date of payment, (2) the amount was paid for employment performed in the United States, and (3) the amount is not a periodic payment, or is a lump-sum payment in lieu of a right to receive an annuity.

jj The rate is 15% for contingent interest that does not qualify as portfolio interest. Generally, this is interest based on receipts, sales, income, or changes in the value of property.

a No U.S. tax is imposed on a percentage of any dividend paid by a U.S. corporation that received at least 80% of its gross income from an active foreign business for the 3-year period before the dividend is declared. (See sections 871(i)(2)(B) and 881(d) of the Internal Revenue Code.)

b The reduced rate applies to dividends paid by a subsidiary to a foreign parent corporation that has the required percentage of stock ownership. In some cases, the income of the subsidiary must meet certain requirements (e.g. a certain percentage of its total income must consist of income other than dividends and interest). In the case of Italy, the reduced rate is 10% if the foreign corporation owns 10% to 50% of the voting stock (for a 12-month period) of the company paying the dividends.

c The exemption or reduction in rate applies only if the recipient is subject to tax on this income in the country of residence. Otherwise a 30% rate applies.

d Exemption does not apply to U.S. Government (federal, state, or local) pensions and annuities; a 30% rate applies to these pensions and annuities. U.S. government pensions paid to an individual who is both a resident and national of China, Finland, Hungary, India, Ireland, Mexico, The Netherlands, Portugal, Russia, South Africa, Spain, Switzerland, Thailand, Turkey, or the United Kingdom are exempt from U.S. tax. U.S. government pensions paid to an individual who is both a resident and citizen of Kazakstan, New Zealand, or Sweden are exempt from U.S. tax.

e No withholding is required on capital gains other than those listed earlier under Capital Gains, even if the gain is subject to U.S. tax.

f Includes alimony.

g The exemption or reduction in rate does not apply if the recipient has a permanent establishment in the United States and the property giving rise to the income is effectively connected with this permanent establishment. In the case of Australia, Austria, Barbados, Canada, China, Cyprus, the Czech Republic, Finland, France, Germany, Hungary, India, Indonesia, Ireland, Italy, Jamaica, Kazakstan, Mexico, the Netherlands, New Zealand, Philippines, Portugal, Russia, the Slovak Republic, South Africa, Spain, Sweden, Switzerland, Thailand, Tunisia, Turkey, and the United Kingdom, the exemption or reduction in rate also does not apply if the property giving rise to the income is effectively connected with a fixed base in the United States from which the recipient performs independent personal services (professional services for royalties paid to a Philippines resident). Even with the treaty, if the income is not effectively connected with a trade or business in the United States by the recipient, the recipient will be considered as not having a permanent establishment in the United States under IRC section 894(b).

h The exemption or reduction in rate does not apply if the recipient is engaged in a trade or business in the United States through a permanent establishment that is in the United States. However, if the income is not effectively connected with a trade or business in the United States by the recipient, the recipient will be considered as not having a permanent establishment in the United States for the purpose of applying the reduced treaty rate to that item of income. IRC section 894(b).

i The rate is 5% for royalties on the use of any copyright of literary, artistic, or scientific work, including software.

j Exemption is not available when paid from a fund, under an employees' pension or annuity plan, if contributions to it are deductible under U.S. tax laws in determining taxable income of the employer.

k Exemption from or reduction in rate of tax does not apply to income of holding companies entitled to special tax benefits under the laws of Luxembourg.

l Annuities that were purchased while the annuitant was not a resident of the United States are not taxable in the United States. The reduced rate applies if the distribution is not subject to a penalty for early withdrawal.

m Contingent interest that does not qualify as portfolio interest is treated as a dividend and is subject to the rates under income codes 6 and 7, as appropriate.

n The exemption applies only to interest on credits, loans, and other indebtedness connected with the financing of trade between the United States and C.I.S. member countries. It does not include interest from the conduct of a general banking business.

o The exemption applies only to gains from the sale or other disposition of property acquired by gift or inheritance.

p The exemption does not apply if the recipient was a resident of the United States when the pension was earned or when the annuity was purchased.

q Annuities paid in return for other than the recipient's personal services are exempt.

r Generally, if the property was owned by the Canadian resident on September 26, 1980, not as part of the business property of a permanent establishment of fixed base in the U.S., the taxable gain is limited to the appreciation after 1984. Capital gains on personal property not belonging to a permanent establishment or fixed base of the taxpayer in the U.S. are exempt.

s The reduced rate for royalties with respect to tangible personal property is 7%.

t Does not apply to annuities.

u Withholding at a special rate may be required on the disposition of U.S. real property interests. See U.S. Real Property Interest earlier in this publication.

v Tax imposed on 70% of gross royalties for rentals of industrial or scientific equipment.

w The rate in column 6 applies to dividends paid by a regulated investment company (RIC) or a real estate investment trust (REIT). However, that rate applies to dividends paid by a REIT only if the beneficial owner of the dividends is an individual holding less than a 10% interest (25% in the case of the Netherlands, Portugal, Spain, Thailand, and Tunisia) in the REIT.

x Royalties not taxed at the 5% or 8% rate are taxed at a 10% rate, unless footnote (g) applies.

y The exemption does not apply to contingent interest that does not qualify as portfolio interest. Generally, this is interest based on receipts, sales, income, or changes in the value of property.

z The rate is 10% if the interest is paid on a loan granted by a bank or similar financial institution. For Thailand, the 10% rate also applies to interest from an arm's length sale on credit of equipment, merchandise, or services.

Table 2. Compensation for Personal Services Performed in United States Exempt from Withholding and U.S. Income Tax Under Income Tax Treaties

Country (1)	Code[1] (2)	Category of Personal Services — Purpose (3)	Maximum Presence in U.S. (4)	Required Employer or Payer (5)	Maximum Amount of Compensation (6)	Treaty Article Citation (7)
Australia	16	Independent personal services[7,22]	183 days	Any contractor	No limit	14
	20	Public entertainment[1]	183 days	Any contractor	$10,000	17
	17	Dependent personal services[17]	183 days	Any foreign resident	No limit	15
	20	Public entertainment	183 days	Any foreign resident	$10,000	17
	19	Studying and training: Remittances or allowances[11]	No limit	Any foreign resident	No limit	20
Austria	15	Scholarship or fellowship grant[1]	No limit	Any U.S. or foreign resident[5]	No limit	XIII(3)
	16	Independent personal services[22]	183 days	Austrian resident contractor	No limit	X
			183 days	Other foreign or U.S. resident contractor	$3,000	X
	17	Dependent personal services	183 days	Austrian resident	No limit	X
			2 years	Other foreign or U.S. resident	$3,000	X
	18	Teaching	2 years	U.S. educational institution	No limit	XII
	19	Studying and training: Remittances or allowances	No limit	Any foreign resident	No limit[3]	XIII(1) & (2)
		Compensation while gaining experience[2]	1 year	Austrian resident	$10,000[3]	XIII(4)
Barbados	16	Independent personal services[7,22]	89 days	Any foreign contractor	No limit	14
	20	Public entertainment[22]	89 days	Any U.S. contractor	$5,000 p.a.	14
			No limit	Any contractor	$250 per day[6] or $4,000 p.a.	
	17	Dependent personal services[8,17]	183 days	Any foreign resident	$5,000 p.a.	17
	20	Public entertainment	No limit	Any U.S. or foreign resident	$250 per day[6] or $4,000 p.a.	17
	19	Studying and training[23]: Remittances or allowances[11]	No limit	Any foreign resident	No limit	20
Belgium	15	Scholarship or fellowship grant[15]	5 years	Any U.S. or foreign resident[5]	No limit	21(1)
	16	Independent personal services[7,22]	182 days	Any contractor	No limit	14(2)(a)(b)
	20	Public entertainment[17]	90 days	Any contractor	$3,000	14(2)(c)
	17	Dependent personal services[17]	182 days	Belgian resident	No limit	15
	19	Studying and training:	2 years	U.S. educational institution	No limit	20
		Remittances or allowances	5 years	Any U.S. or foreign resident	No limit	21(1)
		Compensation during training	5 years	Other foreign or U.S. resident	$2,000 p.a.	21(1)
		Compensation while gaining experience[2]	12 consec. mo.	Belgian resident	$5,000	21(2)(b)
		Compensation under U.S. Government program	12 consec. mo.	Belgian resident	$5,000	21(2)(a)
			1 year	U.S. Government or its contractor	$10,000	21(3)
Canada	16	Independent personal services[7,22]	No limit	Any contractor	No limit	XIV
	17	Dependent personal services	No limit	Any U.S. or foreign resident	$10,000[13]	XV
			183 days	Any foreign resident	No limit[13]	XV
	19	Studying and training: Remittances or allowances[11]	No limit	Any foreign resident	No limit	XX
China, People's Rep. of	15	Scholarship or fellowship grant[15]	No limit	Any U.S. or foreign resident[5]	No limit	20(b)
	16	Independent personal services[7,22]	183 days	Any contractor	No limit	13
	20	Public entertainment[25]	No limit	Any contractor	No limit	16
	17	Dependent personal services[8,17]	183 days	Any foreign resident	No limit	14
	18	Teaching[3]	3 years	U.S. educational or research institute	No limit	19
	19	Studying and training: Remittances or allowances	No limit	Any foreign resident	No limit	20(a)
		Compensation during training or while gaining experience	No limit	Any U.S. or foreign resident	$5,000 p.a.	20(c)

¶ 905

Table 2. *(Continued)*

Country (1)	Code[1] (2)	Category of Personal Services — Purpose (3)	Maximum Presence in U.S. (4)	Required Employer or Payer (5)	Maximum Amount of Compensation (6)	Treaty Article Citation (7)
Commonwealth of Independent States	15	Scholarship or fellowship grant	5 years	Any U.S. or foreign resident	Limited[19]	VI(1)
	16	Independent personal services[22]	183 days	Any U.S. or foreign contractor	No limit	VI(2)
	17	Dependent personal services	183 days	Any U.S. or foreign resident	No limit	VI(2)
	18	Teaching[4,20]	2 years	U.S. educational or scientific institution	No limit	VI(1)
	19	Studying and training:				
		Remittances or allowances	5 years	Any U.S. or foreign resident.	Limited	VI(1)
		Compensation while gaining experience	1 year	C.I.S. resident.	No limit[21]	VI(1)
		Compensation under U.S. Government program	1 year	Any U.S. or foreign resident	No limit	VI(1)
Cyprus	15	Scholarship or fellowship grant[15]	Generally, 5 years	Any U.S. or foreign resident[5]	No limit	21(1)
	16	Independent personal services[22]	182 days	Any contractor	No limit	17
	20	Public entertainment[22]	No limit	Any contractor	$500 per day or $5,000 p.a.	19(1)
	17	Dependent personal services[17]	182 days	Any foreign resident	No limit	18
		Directors' fees	No limit	U.S. corporation	No limit[24]	20
	20	Public entertainment	No limit	Any U.S. or foreign resident.	$500 per day or $5,000 p.a.	19(1)
	19	Studying and training:				
		Remittances or allowances	Generally, 5 years	Any foreign resident	No limit	21(1)
		Compensation during training	Generally, 5 years		$2,000 p.a.	21(1)
		Compensation while gaining experience[2]	1 year	Cyprus resident	$7,500	21(2)
		Compensation under U.S. Government program	1 year	U.S. Government or its contractor	$10,000	21(3)
Czech Republic	15	Scholarship or fellowship grant[15]	5 years	Any U.S. or foreign resident[5]	No limit	21(1)
	16	Independent personal services[1,22]	183 days	Any contractor	No limit	14
	20	Public entertainment[5]	183 days	Any foreign resident	$20,000 p.a.[30]	18
	17	Dependent personal services[8,17]	183 days	Any foreign resident	No limit	15
		Public entertainment[35]	183 days	Any foreign resident	$20,000 p.a.[30]	18
	18	Teaching[18]	2 years	Any U.S. educational or research institution	No limit	21(5)
	19	Studying and training:				
		Remittances or allowances	5 years	Any foreign resident	No limit	21(1)
		Compensation during training	5 years	Any U.S. or foreign resident	$5,000 p.a.	21(1)
		Compensation while gaining experience[2]	12 consec. mos.	Czech resident	$8,000	21(2)
		Compensation under U.S. Government program	1 year	U.S. Government	$10,000	21(3)
Denmark	16	Independent personal services[22]	180 days	Danish resident contractor	No limit	XI
			90 days	Other foreign or U.S. resident contractor	$3,000	XI
	17	Dependent personal services	180 days	Danish resident	No limit	XI
			90 days	Other foreign or U.S. resident	$3,000	XI
	18	Teaching	2 years	U.S. educational institution	No limit	XIV
	19	Studying and training: Remittances or allowances	No limit	Any foreign resident	No limit	XIII

Table 2. (Continued)

Country (1)	Code[1] (2)	Category of Personal Services — Purpose (3)	Maximum Presence in U.S. (4)	Required Employer or Payer (5)	Maximum Amount of Compensation (6)	Treaty Article Citation (7)
Egypt	15	Scholarship or fellowship grant[15]	Generally, 5 years	Any U.S. or foreign resident[5]	No limit	23(1)
	16	Independent personal services[22]	89 days	Any foreign contractor	No limit	15
	20	Public entertainment[22]	No limit	Any contractor	$400 per day	17
	17	Dependent personal services[16,17]	89 days	Egyptian resident	No limit	16
	20	Public entertainment	No limit	Any U.S. or foreign resident	$400 per day	17
	18	Teaching[4]	2 years	U.S. educational institution	No limit	22
	19	Studying and training: Remittances or allowances	Generally, 5 years	Any foreign resident	No limit	22(1)
		Compensation during training	Generally, 5 years	Any or any foreign resident	$3,000 p.a.	22(1)
		Compensation while gaining experience[2]	12 consec. mos.	Egyptian resident	$7,500	23(2)
		Compensation while under U.S. Government program	1 year	U.S. Government or its contractor	$10,000	23(3)
Finland	16	Independent personal services[7,22]	No limit	Any contractor	No limit	14
	20	Public entertainment[17]	No limit	Any contractor	$20,000 p.a.[25]	17
	17	Dependent personal services	183 days	Any foreign resident	No limit	15
	20	Public entertainment	No limit	Any U.S. or foreign resident	$20,000 p.a.[25]	17
	19	Studying and training: Remittances or allowances[11]	No limit	Any foreign resident	No limit	20
France	15	Scholarship or fellowship grant[15]	5 years[43]	Any U.S. or foreign resident[5]	No limit	21(1)
	16	Independent personal services[22]	No limit	Any contractor	No limit	14
	20	Public entertainment	No limit	Any contractor	$10,000[30]	17
	17	Dependent personal services[8,17]	183 days	Any foreign resident	No limit	15
	20	Public entertainment	No limit	Any U.S. or foreign resident	$10,000[30]	17
	18	Teaching[4]	2 years[43]	U.S. educational or research institution	No limit	20
	19	Studying and training: Remittances or allowances	5 years[43]	Any foreign resident	No limit	21(1)
		Compensation during study or training	12 consec. mos.	French resident	$8,000	21(2)
		Compensation while gaining experience[2]	5 years[43]	Other foreign or U.S. resident	$5,000 p.a.	21(1)
			12 consec. mos.	French resident	$8,000	21(2)
Germany	15	Scholarship or fellowship grant[15,A,22]	No limit	Any U.S. or foreign resident[5]	No limit	20(3)
	16	Independent personal services[22]	No limit	Any contractor	No limit	14
	20	Public entertainment	No limit	Any contractor	$20,000 p.a.[30]	17
	17	Dependent personal services[8,17]	183 days	Any foreign resident	No limit	15
	20	Public entertainment	No limit	Any U.S. or foreign resident	$20,000 p.a.[30]	17
	18	Teaching[4]	2 years	U.S. educational or research institution	No limit	20(1)
	19	Studying and training: Remittances or allowances[11]	No limit	Any foreign resident	No limit	20(2)
		Compensation during study or training	4 years	Any U.S. or foreign resident	No limit	20(4)
		Compensation while gaining experience[2]	1 year	Any German enterprise or foreign organization or institution	$10,000[28]	20(5)
Greece	16	Independent personal services[27]	183 days	Greek resident contractor	No limit	X
	17	Dependent personal services	183 days	Other foreign or U.S. resident contractor	$10,000	X
			183 days	Greek resident	$10,000	X
	18	Teaching	183 days	Other foreign or U.S. resident	$10,000	XII
	19	Studying and training: Remittances or allowances	3 years	U.S. educational institution	No limit	XIII
			No limit	Any foreign resident	No limit	
Hungary	16	Independent personal services[7,22]	183 days	Any contractor	No limit	13
	17	Dependent personal services[8]	183 days	Any foreign resident	No limit	14
	18	Teaching[23]	2 years	U.S. educational institution	No limit	17
	19	Studying and training: Remittances or allowances[11]	No limit	Any foreign resident	No limit	18(1)

¶ 905

Table 2. *(Continued)*

Country (1)	Category of Personal Services		Maximum Presence in U.S. (4)	Required Employer or Payer (5)	Maximum Amount of Compensation (6)	Treaty Article Citation (7)
	Code[1] (2)	Purpose (3)				
Iceland	15	Scholarship and fellowship grant[15]	5 years	Any U.S. or foreign resident[5]	No limit	22(1)
	16	Independent personal services[22]	182 days	Any contractor	No limit	18
	20	Public entertainment	90 days	Any resident contractor	$100 per day	18
	17	Dependent personal services[17]	182 days	Iceland resident[18]	No limit	19
	18	Teaching[4]	2 years	U.S. educational institution	No limit	21
	19	Studying and training:				
		Remittances or allowances	5 years	Any foreign resident	No limit	22(1)
		Compensation during training	5 years	U.S. or any foreign resident	$2,000 p.a.	22(1)
		Compensation while gaining experience[2]	12 consec. mo.	Iceland resident	$5,000	22(2)
		Compensation under U.S. Government program	1 year	U.S. Government or its contractor	$10,000	22(3)
India	16	Independent personal services[7,8,22]	89 days	Any contractor	No limit	15
	20	Public entertainment[22]	89 days	Any contractor	$1,500 p.a.[26]	18
	17	Dependent personal services[8,17]	183 days	Any foreign resident	No limit	16
	20	Public entertainment[17]	183 days	Any foreign resident	$1,500 p.a.[26]	18
	18	Teaching[4]	2 years	U.S. educational institution	No limit	22
	19	Studying and training:				
		Remittances or allowances[27]	No limit	Any foreign resident[27]	No limit	21(1)
Indonesia	15	Scholarship or fellowship grant[15]	5 years	Any U.S. or foreign resident[5]	No limit	19(1)
	16	Independent personal services[22]	119 days	Any contractor	No limit	15
	20	Public entertainment	No limit	Any contractor	$2,000 p.a.[25]	17
	17	Dependent personal services[17]	119 days	Any foreign resident	No limit	16
	20	Public entertainment	No limit	Any U.S. or foreign resident	$2,000 p.a.[25]	17
	18	Teaching	2 years	U.S. educational institution	No limit	20
	19	Studying and training:				
		Remittances or allowances	5 years	Any foreign resident	No limit	19(1)
		Compensation during training	5 years	Any foreign or U.S. resident	$2,000 p.a.	19(1)
		Compensation while gaining experience	12 consec. mo.	Any U.S. or foreign resident	$7,500	19(2)
Ireland	16	Independent personal services[22]	183 days	Irish resident contractor	No limit	XI
	17	Dependent personal services	183 days	Irish resident	No limit	X
	18	Teaching	2 years	U.S. educational institution	No limit	XVIII
	19	Studying and training:				
		Remittances or allowances[11]	No limit	Irish resident	No limit	XIX
Israel	15	Scholarship or fellowship grant	5 years	Any U.S. or foreign resident[5]	No limit	24(1)
	16	Independent personal services[22]	182 days	Any contractor	No limit	16
	20	Public entertainment[22]	No limit	Any contractor	$400 per day[37]	18
	17	Dependent personal services	182 days	Israeli resident[16,17,18]	No limit	17
	20	Public entertainment	No limit	Any U.S. or foreign resident	$400 per day[37]	18
	18	Teaching[39]	2 years	U.S. educational institution	No limit	23
	19	Studying and training:				
		Remittances or allowances	5 years	Any foreign resident	No limit	24(1)
		Compensation during study or training	5 years	Any U.S. or foreign resident	$3,000 p.a.	24(1)
		Compensation while gaining experience[2]	5 years	Israeli resident	$7,500	24(2)
		Compensation under U.S. Government program	1 year	U.S. Government or its contractor	$10,000	24(3)

Page 32

Table 2. *(Continued)*

Country (1)	Code (2)	Category of Personal Services — Purpose (3)	Maximum Presence in U.S. (4)	Required Employer or Payer (5)	Maximum Amount of Compensation (6)	Treaty Article Citation (7)
Italy	16	Independent personal services[18,22]	183 days	Any contractor	No limit	14
	20	Public entertainment[3]	90 days	Any contractor	$12,000 p.a.[25]	17(1)
	17	Dependent personal services[4,17]	183 days	Any foreign resident	No limit	15
	20	Public entertainment	90 days	Any U.S. or foreign resident	$12,000 p.a.[25]	17(1)
	18	Teaching	2 years	U.S. educational institution	No limit	20
	19	Studying and training: Remittances or allowances	No limit	Any foreign resident	No limit	21
Jamaica	16	Independent personal services[7,22]	89 days	Any foreign contractor	No limit	14
	20	Public entertainment[22]	89 days	Any U.S. contractor	$400 per day or $5,000 p.a.[6]	14
	17	Dependent personal services[17]	183 days	Any foreign resident	$5,000 p.a.	18
	20	Public entertainment	No limit	Any U.S. or foreign resident	$400 per day or $5,000 p.a.[6]	15
	18	Directors' fees	No limit	U.S. resident	$400 per day[5]	18
		Teaching[21]	2 years	U.S. educational institution	No limit	16
	19	Studying and training: Remittances or allowances[11]	No limit	Any foreign resident	No limit	22
		Compensation during study	12 consec. mo	Jamaican resident	$7,500 p.a.	21(1)
		Compensation while gaining experience[7]	12 consec. mo	Jamaican resident	$7,500 p.a.	21(2)
Japan	15	Scholarship or fellowship grant[15]	5 years	Any U.S. or foreign resident[5]	No limit	20(1)
	16	Independent personal services[22]	183 days	Any contractor	No limit	17
	20	Public entertainment[22]	90 days	Any contractor	No limit	17
	17	Dependent personal services[17,18,19]	183 days	Japanese resident	No limit	18
	18	Teaching[4]	2 years	U.S. educational institution	No limit	19
	19	Studying and training: Remittances or allowances	5 years	Any foreign resident	No limit	20(1)
		Compensation during training	5 years	U.S. or any foreign resident	$2,000 p.a.[6]	20(1)
		Compensation while gaining experience[7]	12 consec. mo	Japanese resident	$5,000[7]	20(2)
		Compensation under U.S. Government program	1 year	U.S. Government or its contractor	$10,000[6]	20(3)
Kazakhstan	15	Scholarship or fellowship grant[16,43]	5 years[31]	Any U.S. or foreign resident[5]	No limit	19
	17	Independent personal services[31]	183 days	Any contractor	No limit	19
		Dependent personal services[31]	183 days	Any foreign resident	No limit	15
	19	Studying and training[4]	5 years	Any foreign resident	No limit	19
		Remittances or allowances			No limit	
Korea, Rep. of	15	Scholarship or fellowship grant[15]	5 years	Any U.S. or foreign resident[5]	No limit	21(1)
	17	Independent personal services[22]	182 days	Any contractor[14]	$3,000 p.a.	18
		Dependent personal services[22]	182 days	Korean resident[14]	$3,000 p.a.	19
	18	Teaching	2 years	U.S. educational institution	No limit	20
	19	Studying and training: Remittances or allowances	5 years	Any foreign resident	No limit	21(1)
		Compensation during training	5 years	Any foreign or U.S. resident	$2,000 p.a.	21(1)
		Compensation while gaining experience[7]	1 year	Korean resident	$5,000	21(2)
		Compensation under U.S. Government program	1 year	U.S. Government or its contractor	$10,000	21(3)

Table 2. (Continued)

Country (1)	Code[1] (2)	Category of Personal Services — Purpose (3)	Maximum Presence in U.S. (4)	Required Employer or Payer (5)	Maximum Amount of Compensation (6)	Treaty Article Citation (7)
Luxembourg	15	Scholarship or fellowship grant[7]	No limit	Any foreign resident[5]	No limit	XIV(1)
	16	Independent personal services[2]	180 days	Luxembourg resident[40]	No limit	XII
	17	Dependent personal services[8]	180 days	Any U.S. or foreign resident	$3,000	XII
			180 days	Luxembourg resident[40]	No limit	XII
	18	Teaching[9]	2 years	U.S. educational institution	No limit	XIII
	19	Studying and training:				
		Remittances or allowances	No limit	Any foreign resident	No limit	XIV(1)
		Compensation during training	1 year	Any foreign resident	No limit	XIV(1)
		Compensation while gaining experience[2]	1 year	Any foreign resident	$5,000	XIV(2)
		Compensation under U.S. Government program	1 year	U.S. Government, its contractor, or a foreign resident.	$10,000	XIV(3)
Mexico	16	Independent personal services[7,22]	183 days	Any contractor	No limit	14
	20	Public entertainment[22]	No limit	Any contractor	$3,000 p.a.[30]	18
	17	Dependent personal services[8,17]	183 days	Any foreign resident	No limit	15
	20	Public entertainment	No limit	Any U.S. or foreign resident	$3,000 p.a.[30]	18
	19	Studying and training:				
		Remittances and allowances	No limit	Any foreign resident	No limit	21
Morrocco	15	Scholarship or fellowship grant[15]	No limit	Any U.S. or foreign resident[5]	No limit	18
	16	Independent personal services[22]	182 days	Any contractor[13]	$5,000	14
	17	Dependent personal services[17,18]	182 days	Moroccan resident[13]	No limit	15
	19	Studying and training:[5]				
		Remittances or allowances	5 years	Any foreign resident	No limit	18
		Compensation during training	5 years	U.S. or any foreign resident	$2,000 p.a.	18
Netherlands	15	Scholarship or fellowship grant[15,33]	3 years	Any U.S. or foreign resident[5]	No limit	22(2)
	16	Independent personal services[22]	No limit	Any contractor	$10,000 p.a.[30]	15
	20	Public entertainment[8,17]	No limit	Any contractor	No limit	18
	17	Dependent personal services[22]	183 days	Any foreign resident	$10,000 p.a.[30]	16
	20	Public entertainment	183 days	Any foreign resident	No limit	18
	18	Teaching[4,34]	2 years	U.S. educational institution	No limit	21(1)
	19	Studying and training:[33]				
		Remittances or allowances	No limit	Any foreign resident	No limit	22(1)
		Compensation while gaining experience	No limit	Any U.S. or foreign resident	$2,000 p.a.	22(1)
		Compensation while recipient of scholarship or fellowship grant	3 years	Any U.S. or foreign resident	$2,000 p.a.[36]	22(2)
New Zealand	16	Independent personal services[7,22]	183 days	Any contractor	No limit	14
	20	Public entertainment[22]	183 days	Any contractor	$10,000[25]	17
	17	Dependent personal services[17]	183 days	Any foreign resident	No limit	15
	20	Public entertainment[1]	183 days	Any foreign resident	$10,000[25]	17
	19	Studying and training:				
		Remittances or allowances[11]	No limit	Any foreign resident	No limit	20

Page 34

¶905

Table 2. *(Continued)*

Country (1)	Code[1] (2)	Category of Personal Services — Purpose (3)	Maximum Presence in U.S. (4)	Required Employer or Payer (5)	Maximum Amount of Compensation (6)	Treaty Article Citation (7)
Norway	15	Scholarship or fellowship grant[15]	5 years	Any U.S. or foreign resident[5]	No limit	16(1)
	16	Independent personal services[22]	182 days	Any resident contractor	No limit	13
	20	Public entertainment[22]	90 days	Any resident contractor	$10,000 p.a.	13
	17	Dependent personal services[18]	182 days	Norwegian resident[4]	No limit	14
	18	Teaching[4]	2 years	U.S. educational institution	No limit	15
	19	Studying and training:				
		Remittances or allowances	5 years	Any foreign resident	No limit	16(1)
		Compensation during training	5 years	U.S. or any foreign resident	$2,000 p.a.	16(1)
		Compensation while gaining experience[2]	12 consec. mo.	Norwegian resident	$5,000	16(2)
		Compensation under U.S. Government program	1 year	U.S. Government or its contractor	$10,000	16(3)
Pakistan	15	Scholarship or fellowship grant[15]	No limit	Pakistani nonprofit organization	No limit	XIII(1)
	16	Independent personal services[16,22]	183 days	Pakistani resident contractor	No limit	XI
	17	Dependent personal services[16]	183 days	Pakistani resident	No limit	XI
	18	Teaching	2 years	U.S. educational institution	No limit	XII
	19	Studying and training:				
		Remittances or allowances	No limit	Any foreign resident	No limit	XIII(1)
		Compensation during training	No limit	U.S. or any foreign resident	$5,000 p.a.	XIII(1)
		Compensation while gaining experience[2]	1 year	Pakistani resident	$6,000	XIII(2)
		Compensation under U.S. Government program	No limit	U.S. Government, its contractor, or any foreign resident employer	$10,000	XIII(3)
Philippines	15	Scholarship or fellowship grant[15]	5 years	Any U.S. or foreign resident[5]	No limit	22(1)
	16	Independent personal services[22]	89 days	Any foreign contractor	No limit	15
	20	Public entertainment[22]	89 days	Any U.S. contractor	$100 per day or $3,000 p.a.	15
			No limit	Any contractor	No limit	17
	17	Dependent personal services[17]	89 days	Any Philippines resident[18]	No limit	16
	20	Public entertainment	No limit	Any U.S. or foreign resident	$100 per day or $3,000 p.a.	17
	18	Teaching[4,38]	2 years	U.S. educational institution	No limit	21, 22(4)
	19	Studying and training:				
		Remittances or allowances	5 years	Any foreign resident	No limit	22(1)
		Compensation during study	5 years	Any U.S. or foreign resident	$3,000 p.a.	22(1)
		Compensation while gaining experience[2]	12 consec. mo.	Philippines resident	$7,500 p.a.	22(2)
		Compensation under U.S. Government program	1 year	U.S. Government or its contractor	$10,000 p.a.	22(3)
Poland	15	Scholarship or fellowship grant[15]	5 years	Any U.S. or foreign resident[5]	No limit	18(1)
	16	Independent personal services[22]	182 days	Any contractor	No limit	15
	17	Dependent personal services[22]	182 days	Any foreign resident	No limit	16
	18	Teaching[4]	2 years	U.S. educational institution	No limit	17
	19	Studying and training:				
		Remittances or allowances	5 years	Any foreign resident	No limit	18(1)
		Compensation during training	5 years	U.S. or any foreign resident	$2,000 p.a.	18(1)
		Compensation while gaining experience[2]	1 year	Polish resident	$5,000	18(2)
		Compensation under U.S. Government program	1 year	U.S. Government or its contractor	$10,000	18(3)

Table 2. *(Continued)*

Country (1)	Code[1] (2)	Category of Personal Services — Purpose (3)	Maximum Presence in U.S. (4)	Required Employer or Payer (5)	Maximum Amount of Compensation (6)	Treaty Article Citation (7)
Portugal	15	Scholarship or fellowship grant[15,22]	5 years	Any U.S. or foreign resident[5]	No limit	23(1)
	16	Independent personal services[22]	182 days	Any contractor	No limit	15
	20	Public entertainment[22]	No limit	Any contractor	$10,000 p.a.[30]	19
	17	Dependent personal services[8,17]	183 days	Any foreign resident	No limit	16
	20	Public entertainment	No limit	Any U.S. or foreign resident	$10,000 p.a.[30]	19
	18	Teaching[4,42]	2 years	U.S. educational or research institution	No limit	22
	19	Studying and training:[4]				
		Remittances or allowances	5 years	Any foreign resident	No limit	23(1)
		Compensation during training	5 years	Any foreign or U.S. resident	$5,000 p.a.	23(1)
		Compensation while gaining experience[2]	12 consec. mos.	Portuguese resident	$8,000	23(2)
			12 consec. mos.	Portuguese resident	$8,000	23(2)
Romania	15	Scholarship or fellowship grant[15]	5 years	Any U.S. or foreign resident[5]	No limit	20(1)
	16	Independent personal services[22]	182 days	Any contractor	No limit	14
	20	Public entertainment	90 days	Any contractor	$3,000	14
	17	Dependent personal services[17]	182 days	Romanian resident	No limit	15
	20	Public entertainment	89 days	Romanian resident	$2,999.99	15
	18	Teaching[4]	2 years	U.S. educational institution	No limit	19
	19	Studying and training:				
		Remittances or allowances	5 years	Any foreign resident	No limit	20(1)
		Compensation during training	5 years	U.S. or any foreign resident	$2,000 p.a.	20(1)
		Compensation while gaining experience[2]	1 year	Romanian resident	$5,000	20(2)
		Compensation while under U.S. Government program	1 year	U.S. Government or its contractor	$10,000	20(3)
Russia	15	Scholarship or fellowship grant[15,41]	5 years[31]	Any U.S. or foreign resident[5]	No limit	18
	16	Independent personal services[22]	183 days	Any contractor	No limit	13
	17	Dependent personal services[8,17,32]	183 days	Any foreign resident	No limit	14
	19	Studying and training:				
		Remittances and allowances	5 years[31]	Any foreign resident	No limit	18
Slovak Republic	15	Scholarship or fellowship grant[15]	5 years	Any U.S. or foreign resident[5]	No limit	21(1)
	16	Independent personal services[22]	183 days	Any contractor	No limit	14
	20	Public entertainment	183 days	Any contractor	$20,000 p.a.[30]	18
	17	Dependent personal services[8,17]	183 days	Any foreign resident	No limit	15
	20	Public entertainment	183 days	Any foreign resident	$20,000 p.a.[30]	18
	18	Teaching[35]	2 years	U.S. educational or research institution	No limit	21(5)
	19	Studying and training:				
		Remittances and allowances	5 years	Any foreign resident	No limit	21(1)
		Compensation during training	5 years	Any U.S. or foreign resident	$5,000 p.a.	21(1)
		Compensation while gaining experience[2]	12 consec. mos.	Slovak resident	$8,000	21(2)
		Compensation under U.S. Government program	1 year	U.S. Government	$10,000	21(3)
Spain	15	Scholarship or fellowship grant[15,22]	5 years	Any U.S. or foreign resident[5]	No limit	22(1)
	16	Independent personal services[22]	No limit	Any contractor	No limit	15
	20	Public entertainment[22]	No limit	Any contractor	$10,000 p.a.[30]	19
	17	Dependent personal services[17]	183 days	Any foreign resident	No limit	16
	20	Public entertainment	No limit	Any U.S. or foreign resident	$10,000 p.a.[30]	19
	19	Studying and training:[4]				
		Remittances or allowances	5 years	Any foreign resident	No limit	22(1)
		Compensation while gaining experience[2]	5 years	Any U.S. or foreign resident	$5,000 p.a.	22(1)
			12 consec. mo.	Spanish resident	$8,000	22(2)

Table 2. *(Continued)*

Country (1)	Code (2)	Category of Personal Services — Purpose (3)	Maximum Presence in U.S. (4)	Required Employer or Payer (5)	Maximum Amount of Compensation (6)	Treaty Article Citation (7)
Sweden	16	Independent personal services[3]	No limit	Any contractor	No limit	14
	20	Public entertainment	No limit	Any contractor	$6,000[5]	18
	17	Dependent personal services[4,17]	183 days	Any foreign resident	No limit	15
	20	Public entertainment	No limit	Any U.S. or foreign resident	$6,000[25]	18
	19	Studying and training: Remittances or allowances[11]	No limit	Any foreign resident	No limit	21
Switzerland	16	Independent personal services[3]	No limit	Any contractor	No limit	14
	20	Public entertainment[2]	No limit	Any contractor	$10,000[25]	17
	17	Dependent personal services[4,17]	183 days	Any foreign resident	No limit	15
	20	Public entertainment[22]	No limit	Any U.S. or foreign resident	$10,000[25]	17
	19	Studying and training[11]: Remittances or allowances	No limit	Any foreign resident	No limit	20
Thailand	15	Scholarship or fellowship grant[1]	5 years	Any U.S. or foreign resident[5]	No limit	22(1)
	16	Independent personal services[22]	89 days	Any U.S. resident	$10,000	15
	20	Public entertainment[22]	89 days	Any foreign contractor	No limit[49]	15
			No limit	Any contractor	$100 per day or $3,000 p.a.[48]	
	17	Dependent personal services[17,47]	183 days	Any foreign resident	No limit	19
	20	Public entertainment	No limit	Any U.S. or foreign resident	$100 per day or $3,000 p.a.[48]	16
	18	Teaching or research[4,38]	2 years	Any U.S. or foreign resident	No limit	19
	19	Studying and training: Remittances or allowances	5 years	Any foreign resident	No limit	23
		Compensation during training	5 years	Any U.S. or foreign resident	$3,000 p.a.	22(1)
		Compensation while gaining experience	12 consec. mos.	Thai resident[2]	$7,500	22(2)
		Compensation while under U.S. Government program	1 year	U.S. Government	$10,000[36]	22(3)
Trinidad and Tobago	15	Scholarship or fellowship grant[1,14]	5 years	Any U.S. or foreign resident[5]	No limit	19(1)
	16	Independent personal services[1,22]	183 days	Any foreign resident contractor	No limit	17
	17	Dependent personal services[14]	183 days	Any U.S. contractor	$3,000[8]	17
			183 days	Any foreign resident	$3,000[8]	17
	18	Teaching[4]	2 years	Any U.S. resident	No limit	18
				U.S. educational institution or U.S. Government		
	19	Studying and training: Remittances or allowances	5 years	Any foreign resident	No limit	19(1)
		Compensation during training	5 years	U.S. or any foreign resident	$2,000 p.a.[6]	19(1)
		Compensation during professional training	5 years	U.S. or any foreign resident	$5,000 p.a.[6]	19(1)
		Compensation while gaining experience	1 year	Trinidad—Tobago resident	$5,000[6]	19(2)
		Compensation under U.S. Government program	1 year	U.S. Government or its contractor	$10,000[6]	19(3)
Tunisia	15	Scholarship or fellowship grant[11,15]	5 years	Any U.S. or foreign resident[5]	No limit	20
	16	Independent personal services[22]	183 days	U.S. resident contractor	$7,500 p.a.[25]	14
	20	Public entertainment[3]	No limit	Any contractor	$7,500 p.a.[25]	17
	17	Dependent personal services[17]	183 days	Any contractor	No limit	15
	20	Public entertainment	No limit	Any U.S. or foreign resident	$7,500 p.a.[25]	17
	19	Studying and training: Remittances or allowances[11]	5 years	Any foreign resident	No limit	20
		Compensation during training	5 years	Any U.S. or foreign resident	$4,000 p.a.	20
Turkey	16	Independent personal services[3]	No limit	Any contractor	No limit	14
	20	Public entertainment[22,50]	No limit	Any contractor	$3,000[46]	17
	17	Dependent personal services[12,17]	183 days	Any foreign resident	$3,000[46]	15
	20	Public entertainment[22]	No limit	Any U.S. or foreign resident.	$3,000[46]	17
	18	Teaching or research[11]	2 years	Any U.S. or foreign resident.	No limit	20(2)
	19	Studying and training[11]: Remittances or allowances	No limit	Any foreign resident	No limit	20(1)

Table 2. *(Continued)*

Country (1)	Category of Personal Services		Maximum Presence in U.S. (4)	Required Employer or Payer (5)	Maximum Amount of Compensation (6)	Treaty Article Citation (7)
	Code[1] (2)	Purpose (3)				
United Kingdom	16	Independent personal services[7,22]	183 days	Any contractor	No limit[13]	14
	17	Dependent personal services[17]	183 days	Any foreign resident	No limit[13]	15
	18	Teaching[4]	2 years	U.S. educational institution	No limit	20
	19	Studying and training: Remittances or allowances[11]	No limit	Any foreign resident	No limit	21

¶ 905

[1] Refers to income code numbers described in this publication and to be reported on Forms 1042-S. Personal services must be performed by a nonresident alien individual who is a resident of the specified treaty country.

[2] Applies only if training or experience is received from a person other than the alien's employer.

[3] Annual compensation for services wherever performed.

[4] Does not apply to compensation for research work primarily for private benefit.

[5] Grant must be from a nonprofit organization. In many cases, the exemption applies to amounts from either the U.S. or foreign government. In the case of Indonesia and the Netherlands, the exemption also applies if the amount is awarded under a technical assistance program entered into by the United States or foreign government, or its political subdivisions or local authorities.

[6] Reimbursed expenses are not taken into account in figuring any maximum compensation to which the exemption applies. For Japan and Trinidad and Tobago, only reimbursed travel expenses are disregarded in figuring maximum compensation.

[7] Exemption does not apply to the extent income is attributable to the recipient's fixed U.S. base. For residents of Japan, this fixed base must be maintained in the U.S. for more than 183 days during the tax year for the exemption not to apply; for residents of Belgium, Iceland, Korea, and Norway, the fixed base must be maintained for more than 182 days; for residents of Morocco, the fixed base must be maintained for more than 89 days.

[8] Does not apply to fees of a foreign director of a U.S. corporation.

[9] Does not apply to compensation for research work for other than the U.S. educational institution involved.

[10] Applies to public entertainment in accordance with U.S. reservation rejecting exclusion contained in Art. X(4) of the Switzerland treaty.

[11] Applies only to full-time student or trainee.

[12] Fees paid to a resident of Turkey for services performed in the United States as a director of a U.S. corporation are subject to U.S. tax.

[13] Does not apply to compensation paid to public entertainers (actors, artists, musicians, athletes, etc.). For Canadian and U.K. residents public entertainers, the exemption does not apply if the gross receipts (including reimbursements) are more than $15,000 in any year.

[14] Does not apply to compensation paid to public entertainers in excess of $100 a day.

[15] Does not apply to payments from the National Institutes of Health under its Visiting Associate Program and Visiting Scientist Program.

[16] Exemption applies only if the compensation is subject to tax in the country of residence.

[17] The exemption does not apply if the employee's compensation is borne by a permanent establishment or in some cases a fixed base that the employer has in the United States.

[18] The exemption applies if the employer is a permanent establishment in the treaty country but is not a resident of the treaty country.

[19] This exemption does not apply in certain cases if the employee is a substantial owner of that employer and the employer is engaged in certain defined activities.

[20] The exemption is also extended to journalists and correspondents who are temporarily in the U.S. for periods not exceeding 2 years and who receive compensation from abroad.

[21] Also exempt are amounts of up to $10,000 received from U.S. sources to provide ordinary living expenses. For students, the amount will be less than $10,000, determined on a case-by-case basis.

[22] Withholding at 30% may be required because the factors on which the treaty exemption is based may not be determinable until after the close of the tax year. However, see *Withholding agreements*, and *Final payment exemption*, under *Pay for independent personal services*, and *Central Withholding Agreements*, under *Artists and Athletes*, discussed in this publication.

[23] A student or trainee may choose to be treated as a U.S. resident for tax purposes. If the choice is made, it may not be revoked without the consent of the U.S. competent authority.

[24] Does not apply to amounts received in excess of reasonable fees payable to all directors of the company for attending meetings in the United States.

[25] Exemption does not apply if gross receipts (including reimbursements) exceed this amount during the year (or during any 12-month period for Sweden).

[26] Exemption does not apply if net income exceeds this amount.

[27] Exemption does not apply to payments borne by a permanent establishment in the United States or paid by a U.S. citizen or resident or the federal, state, or local government.

[28] Exemption does not apply if compensation exceeds this amount.

[29] The exemption applies only to income from activities performed under special cultural exchange programs agreed to by the U.S. and Chinese governments.

[30] Exemption does not apply if gross receipts (or compensation for Portugal) including reimbursements, exceed this amount during the year. Income is fully exempt if visit to the United States is substantially supported by public funds of the treaty country or its political subdivisions or local authorities.

[31] The 5-year limit pertains only to training or research.

[32] Compensation from employment directly connected with a place of business that is not a permanent establishment is exempt if the alien is present in the United States for a period not exceeding 12 consecutive months. Compensation for technical services directly connected with the application of a right or property giving rise to a royalty is exempt if the services are provided as part of a contract granting the use of the right or property.

[33] Exemption does not apply if, during the immediately preceding period, the individual claimed the benefits of Article 21.

[34] Exemption does not apply if, during the immediately preceding period, the individual claimed the benefits of Article 22.

[35] Exemption does not apply if the individual either (a) claimed the benefit of Article 21(5) previously, or (b) during the immediately preceding period, claimed the benefit of Article 21(1), (2), or (3).

[36] Exemption applies only to compensation for personal services performed in connection with, or incidental to, the individual's study, research, or training.

[37] If the compensation exceeds $400 per day, the entertainer may be taxed on the full amount. If the individual receives a fixed amount for more than one performance, the amount is prorated over the number of days the individual performs the services (including rehearsals).

[38] Exemption does not apply if during the immediately preceding period, the individual derived any benefits of Article 22(1).

[39] Exemption does not apply if during the immediately preceding period, the individual derived any benefits of Article 24(1).

[40] The exemption also applies if the income is borne by an employer that is a permanent establishment of a U.S. enterprise in Luxembourg.

[41] Applies to grants, allowances, and other similar payments received for studying or doing research.

[42] Exemption does not apply if the individual either (a) previously claimed the benefit of this Article, or (b) during the immediately preceding period, claimed the benefit of Article 23. The benefits under Articles 22 and 23 cannot be claimed at the same time.

[43] The combined period of benefits under Articles 20 and 21(1) cannot exceed 5 years.

[44] The exemption does not apply if the individual previously claimed the benefit of this Article.

[45] The time limit pertains only to an apprentice or business trainee.

[46] Exemption does not apply if gross receipts exceed this amount.

[47] Fees paid to a resident of Thailand for services as a director of a U.S. corporation are subject to U.S. tax, unless the services are performed in Thailand.

[48] Exemption does not apply if gross receipts exceed this amount. Income is fully exempt if visit to the United States is substantially supported by public funds of the treaty country or its political subdivisions or local authorities.

[49] A $10,000 limit applies if the expense is borne by a permanent establishment or a fixed base in the United States.

[50] This provision does not apply if these activities are substantially supported by a nonprofit organization of the treaty country or by public funds of the treaty country or its political subdivisions or local authorities.

¶ 905

Table 3. List of Tax Treaties

Country	Official Text Symbol[1]	General Effective Date	Citation	Applicable Treasury Explanations or Treasury Decision (T.D.)
Australia	TIAS 10773	Dec. 1, 1983	1986-2 C.B. 220	1986-2 C.B. 246.
Austria	TIAS	Jan. 1, 1999		
Barbados	TIAS 11090	Jan. 1, 1984	1991-2 C.B. 436	1991-2 C.B. 466
Protocol	TIAS	Jan. 1, 1994		
Belgium	TIAS 7463	Jan. 1, 1971	1973-1 C.B. 619	
Protocol	TIAS 11254	Various		
Canada[2]	TIAS 11087	Jan. 1, 1985	1986-2 C.B. 258	1987-2 C.B. 298.
Protocol	TIAS	Jan. 1, 1996		
China, People's Republic of [5]	TIAS	Jan. 1, 1987	1988-1 C.B. 414	1988-1 C.B. 447.
Commonwealth of Independent States[4]	TIAS 8225	Jan. 1, 1976	1976-2 C.B. 463	1976-2 C.B. 475.
Cyprus	TIAS 10965	Jan. 1, 1986	1989-2 C.B. 280	1989-2 C.B. 314.
Czech Republic	TIAS	Jan. 1, 1993		
Denmark	TIAS 1854	Jan. 1, 1948	1950-1 C.B. 77	T.D. 5692, 1949-1 C.B. 104; T.D. 5777, 1950-1 C.B. 76.
Egypt	TIAS 10149	Jan. 1, 1982	1982-1 C.B. 219	1982-1 C.B. 243.
Finland	TIAS	Jan. 1, 1991		
France	TIAS	Jan. 1, 1996		
Germany	TIAS	Jan. 1, 1990[3]		
Greece	TIAS 2902	Jan. 1, 1953	1958-2 C.B. 1054	T.D. 6109, 1954-2 C.B. 638.
Protocol	TIAS 2902	Jan. 1, 1953	1958-2 C.B. 1059	
Hungary	TIAS 9560	Jan. 1, 1980	1980-1 C.B. 333	1980-1 C.B. 354.
Iceland	TIAS 8151	Jan. 1, 1976	1976-1 C.B. 442	1976-1 C.B. 456.
India	TIAS	Jan. 1, 1991		
Indonesia	TIAS	Jan. 1, 1990		
Protocol	TIAS	Feb. 1, 1997		
Ireland	TIAS	Jan. 1, 1998		
Israel	TIAS	Feb. 1, 1995		
Italy	TIAS 11064	Jan. 1, 1985	1992-1 C.B. 442	1992-1 C.B. 473.
Jamaica	TIAS 10207	Jan. 1, 1982	1982-1 C.B. 257	1982-1 C.B. 291.
Japan	TIAS 7365	Jan. 1, 1973	1973-1 C.B. 630	1973-1 C.B. 653.
Kazakstan	TIAS	Jan. 1, 1996		
Korea, Republic of	TIAS 9506	Jan. 1, 1980	1979-2 C.B. 435	1979-2 C.B. 458.
Luxembourg	TIAS 5726	Jan. 1, 1964	1965-1 C.B. 615	1965-1 C.B. 642.
Mexico	TIAS	Jan. 1, 1994	1994-2 C.B. 424	1994-2 C.B. 489.
Protocol	TIAS	Oct. 26, 1995		
Morocco	TIAS 10195	Jan. 1, 1981	1982-2 C.B. 405	1982-2 C.B. 427.
Netherlands	TIAS	Jan. 1, 1994		
New Zealand	TIAS 10772	Jan. 1, 1984	1990-2 C.B. 274	1990-2 C.B. 303.
Norway	TIAS 7474	Jan. 1, 1971	1973-1 C.B. 669	1973-1 C.B. 693.
Protocol	TIAS 10205	Jan. 1, 1982	1982-2 C.B. 440	1982-2 C.B. 454.
Pakistan	TIAS 4232	Jan. 1, 1959	1960-2 C.B. 646	T.D. 6431, 1960-1 C.B. 755.
Philippines	TIAS 10417	Jan. 1, 1983	1984-2 C.B. 384	1984-2 C.B. 412.
Poland	TIAS 8486	Jan. 1, 1974	1977-1 C.B. 416	1977-1 C.B. 427.
Portugal	TIAS	Jan. 1, 1996		
Romania	TIAS 8228	Jan. 1, 1974	1976-2 C.B. 492	1976-2 C.B. 504.
Russia	TIAS	Jan. 1, 1994		
Slovak Republic	TIAS	Jan. 1, 1993		
South Africa	TIAS	Jan. 1, 1998		
Spain	TIAS	Jan. 1, 1991		
Sweden	TIAS	Jan. 1, 1996		
Switzerland	TIAS	Jan. 1, 1998		
Thailand	TIAS	Jan. 1, 1998		
Trinidad and Tobago	TIAS 7047	Jan. 1, 1970	1971-2 C.B. 479	
Tunisia	TIAS	Jan. 1, 1990		
Turkey	TIAS	Jan. 1, 1998		
United Kingdom	TIAS 9682	Jan. 1, 1975	1980-1 C.B. 394	1980-1 C.B. 455.

[1] Treaties and Other International Act Series.
[2] Information on treaty can be found in Publication 597, *Information on the United States-Canada Income Tax Treaty*.
[3] The general effective date for the area that comprises the former German Democratic Republic is January 1, 1991.
[4] The U.S.—U.S.S.R. income tax treaty applies to the countries of Armenia, Azerbaijan, Belarus, Georgia, Kyrgyzstan, Moldova, Tajikistan, Turkmenistan, Ukraine, and Uzbekistan.
[5] The United States—People's Republic of China income tax treaty does not apply to Hong Kong.

Chapter 10

Planning for Foreign Operations

¶ 1001 INTRODUCTION

This chapter discusses general planning issues with respect to a U.S. company's foreign operations. More specific planning issues are discussed throughout the book. For example, Chapter 3 discusses strategies for eliminating excess foreign tax credits, Chapter 4 discusses planning for dividend repatriations, Chapter 5 discusses developing a transfer pricing strategy, and Chapter 7 discusses techniques for maximizing the benefits of an FSC.

¶ 1002 EVOLUTION OF A U.S. EXPORTER

Entering a Foreign Market

There are several options available to a U.S. company that wishes to market its products abroad. For example, a U.S. company may initially export its products through independent brokers or distributors. Smaller U.S. exporters, in particular, may find it advantageous to use independent intermediaries to market their goods abroad since they often lack technical expertise regarding foreign markets and international trade. There are costs to such an arrangement, however, including the need to share profits with the intermediary (either through commission costs or reduced sales revenues), and the loss of control over the sales and distribution functions.

As the exporter's sales volume grows and the exporter becomes more familiar with international trade, it may wish to bring the foreign marketing function in-house by having U.S. employees travel abroad in order to identify customers, display inventory, negotiate sales agreements, and provide technical support. Alternatively, the U.S. exporter could employ local foreign nationals to perform these functions.

The next logical step in the progression of a U.S. company's foreign marketing activities is to establish a liaison or branch sales office within the importing country. The activities of a liaison office usually are limited to advertising and promotion, storing or displaying merchandise, market research, and liaising with agents, distributors, and customers. As foreign sales volume increases, however, the U.S. company may wish to have its foreign office also negotiate and close sales agreements, and distribute its products. These activities would elevate the status of the foreign operation to that a branch sales office. A foreign presence often is required in the case of export sales of services. For example, an export sale of construction services usually requires that U.S. engineers and technicians travel abroad in order to provide on-site management of the project.

Licensing and franchising are more indirect methods of entering a foreign market. Both entail a two-step process, whereby a U.S. company that has a patent, trademark, or other intangible first acquires the legally protected right to own that intangible in a foreign country, and then licenses that right to a local company. In return, the exporter receives a percentage of the local sales of the licensed or franchised product in the form of a royalty. In essence, licensing and franchising are types of joint venture arrangements, which permit a U.S. company to enter a foreign market quickly, but may not produce the same profit margins that are potentially available from more direct forms of exporting. Moreover, the U.S. company may lose some control over the quality and image of its product.

Basic Tax Issues

Export sales. A major tax issue for U.S. companies that export their products through independent distributors is whether to establish and route export sales through a foreign sales corporation (or "FSC"). An FSC allows a U.S. exporter to exclude a portion of its export profits from U.S. tax. The amount of the exclusion usually is 15% of the net income from qualifying export sales. The benefits of an FSC generally are not available, however, with respect to exports of services.[1] As discussed in Chapter 7, domestic corporations that are most likely to benefit from an FSC are those which exhibit the following characteristics:

(i)   have a high volume of export sales,

(ii) enjoy a high profit margin on their export sales,

(iii) produce their products in the United States,

(iv) are not in a net operating loss position, and

(v)   do not have a binding foreign tax credit limitation in the general limitation category.

U.S. companies that export their products through independent distributors will not have a taxable presence within the importing country, and therefore foreign tax reduction planning is a moot issue. Nevertheless, foreign tax credit planning may still be worthwhile since the exporter may be subject to foreign taxation in the future, and excess foreign tax credits can be carried back two years. One relatively simple strategy is to pass title abroad on export sales, in which case export sales will generate foreign-source income to the extent of the related marketing profits.

A U.S. company that exports its products using its own sales force faces the same tax issues (FSC and title passage) as those faced by companies that export through independent distributors. In addition, the presence of employees in the importing country may expose the U.S. exporter to foreign taxation. As discussed in the next section, whether a U.S. exporter will be subject to host country taxation depends on the internal tax laws of the host country and the provisions of any applicable tax treaties. Typically, the U.S. exporter will be subject to host country taxation only if it has a permanent establishment within the host country.

A U.S. exporter that establishes a foreign sales office must decide whether to structure the foreign sales operation as a branch or a subsidiary. In addition, assuming the sales office constitutes a taxable presence within the host country, the U.S. exporter must determine its taxable income for foreign tax purposes. The profit of a foreign sales office usually is computed based on the fiction that the office is an independent enterprise dealing at arm's length with the U.S. home office. Therefore, the more functions performed and the greater the risks assumed by the foreign sales office, the more profit it should earn. For example, if the office operates as a buy-sell distributor that assumes inventory risk, credit risk, and warranty risk, then its profit

---

[1] Code Sec. 924(a). There are exceptions for engineering and architectural services for foreign construction projects, and services that are related and subsidiary to a sale or lease of export property.

should be greater than a sales office that functions as a mere commission agent which never takes title to the goods.

Table 10.1 summarizes the primary tax issues associated with the different stages of foreign marketing activities.

TABLE 10.1. EXPORT SALES—BASIC TAX ISSUES

Export sales activities	*Basic tax issues*
Export through independent distributors	• Title passage • Foreign sales corporation (FSC)
Export using company salespersons	• Title passage and FSC • Permanent establishment (PE)
Establish foreign sales office	• Title passage, FSC, and PE • Branch versus subsidiary • Profit allocable to sales office

---

Licensing and franchising. A principal tax issue associated with foreign licensing and franchising arrangements is the appropriate foreign withholding tax rate on the U.S. company's royalty income. Most income tax treaties provide for reduced withholding tax rates on royalties derived by a passive foreign investor. Typically, the rate is 10% or less, and in some treaties varies with whether the payment is an industrial royalty (e.g., a payment for the use of a patent, trade secret, or formula), a motion picture or television royalty, or some other type of royalty, such as a payment for the use of a copyright on a book. Table 10.2 presents the royalty withholding tax rates for some of our major trading partners.

TABLE 10.2. TREATY WITHHOLDING TAX RATES ON ROYALTIES DERIVED BY U.S. RESIDENTS [a]

	Treaty withholding rate		
Foreign payer's country of residence	*Industrial royalties*	*Motion pictures and television royalties*	*Other royalties*
Canada	0%	10%	0%
China	10%	10%	10%
France	5%	0%	0%
Germany	0%	0%	0%
Italy	10%	8%	5%
Japan	10%	10%	10%
Mexico	10%	10%	10%
United Kingdom	0%	0%	0%

[a] Taken from Table 1 of IRS Publication 515 (1999), which is reproduced in its entirety in the appendix to Chapter 9.

The benefits of an FSC ordinarily are not available with respect to licensing and franchising arrangements because the definition of qualified export property specifically excludes intangibles such as patents, trade secrets, copyrights, trademarks, trade brands and franchises. However, the FSC benefit is available for copyrighted films, tapes, records, or similar reproductions for commercial or home use, and copyrighted articles, such as a book or mass market computer software.[2]

¶ 1003   DETERMINANTS OF HOST COUNTRY TAXATION

Carrying on a Trade or Business in a Foreign Country

A central tax issue for a U.S. exporter is whether its export profits will be subject to foreign taxation. Host country taxation is an important issue for two reasons. First, complying with foreign tax laws always entails administrative costs. In addition, if the effective rate of host country taxation exceeds the U.S. rate, the resulting excess foreign tax credits represent an out-of-pocket tax cost. Whether a U.S. company's export activities are subject to host country taxation depends on several factors, including the precise nature of the taxpayer's activities within the host country, the internal tax laws of the host country, and the provisions of any income tax treaty between the host country and the United States.

As a general rule, most countries assert jurisdiction over all of the income derived from sources within their borders, regardless of the citizenship or residence of the person receiving that income. However, most tax treaties contain a permanent establishment provision under which a U.S. exporter's business profits are exempt from foreign taxation unless those profits are attributable to a permanent establishment located within the foreign country.[3] A permanent establishment includes a fixed place of business (e.g. a sales office), unless the fixed place of business is used solely for auxiliary functions (e.g., purchasing, storing, displaying, or delivering inventory), or activities of a preparatory nature (e.g., collecting information about potential customers).[4] A permanent establishment also exists if employees or other dependent agents habitually exercise in the foreign country an authority to conclude sales contracts in the taxpayer's name.[5] As a consequence, a U.S. exporter that sends executives or salespeople abroad to enter into contracts may create a permanent establishment even if those employ-

---

[2] Code Sec. 927(a)(2)(B).

[3] For example, see Article 7(1) of the U.S. Model Treaty.

[4] For example, see Article 5(1), (2), and (4) of the U.S. Model Treaty.

[5] For example, see Article 5(5) of the U.S. Model Treaty.

ees operate out of hotels and thus have no fixed place of business. Employees who limit their activities to auxiliary or preparatory activities, such as collecting information about potential customers, with sales concluded in the United States, will not create a permanent establishment. Marketing products abroad solely through independent foreign brokers or distributors also does not create a permanent establishment.[6]

In addition to a permanent establishment provision, most tax treaties also contain a separate independent services provision that governs the taxation of personal services income derived by self-employed professionals, such as accountants, doctors, engineers, and lawyers. Such income is exempt from host country taxation unless the services are performed in the host country, and the income is attributable to an office or other fixed place of business that is located in the host country and is regularly available to the taxpayer for purposes of performing the services.[7] This provision allows self-employed U.S. persons to provide services abroad free of foreign taxes, as long as they do not maintain an office in the foreign country.

Carrying on a Trade or Business in a Country that Does Not Respect the U.S. Limited Liability Company

The U.S. Limited Liability Company ("LLC"), although becoming a commonly used entity in the U.S., is not universally respected as a separate entity. For example, because the Canada Customs and Revenue Agency does not consider the U.S. LLC a resident of the U.S., it denies the branch of a U.S. LLC the opportunity to use the U.S.-Canada treaty. As a result, (i) a Canadian branch of a U.S. LLC will be subject to tax in Canada even if it does not have a permanent establishment in Canada, and (ii) the LLC will be subject to the branch profit tax at a rate of 25 percent instead of 5 percent.

Example 10.1: USAllc, a domestic limited liability company, markets its products abroad by mailing catalogs to potential Canadian customers. USAllc's salesman visits Toronto the first 3 days of each month to solicit orders that he faxes back to USAllc in the U.S. for confirmation. If the U.S.-Canadian treaty does not apply, the salesman's visits combined with the mailing of catalogs to Canada constitute carrying on a trade or business in Canada. If the U.S.-Canadian treaty applied, this activity would not be subject to tax under the treaty because this level of activity does not constitute a permanent establishment in Canada. Currently, the Canadian Customs and Revenue Agency does not consider USAllc

---

[6] For example, see Article 5(6) of the U.S. Model Treaty.

[7] For example, see Article 14 of the U.S. Model Treaty.

to be a resident of the United States. Therefore, USAllc would not receive treaty protection and would be subject to tax on income attributable to the carrying on of a trade or business in Canada.[8]

¶ 1004 STRUCTURING THE FOREIGN OPERATION

A U.S. company that is establishing a sales, distribution, service, or manufacturing facility abroad can structure that foreign operation as either a branch or a subsidiary. Therefore, a central tax issue in planning for foreign operations is determining the best legal structure.

Branches

An unincorporated foreign branch is simply an extension of the domestic corporation, as opposed to a separate legal entity. Assuming the branch constitutes a permanent establishment, it will be subject to host country taxation. Branch taxable income usually is determined on the basis of a separate accounting, whereby the branch reports a profit equal to the amount it would have earned if it were an independent enterprise. Foreign countries usually allow a domestic corporation to allocate all direct costs, such as the cost of goods sold abroad, against branch income. The host country also may allow charges against branch income for reasonable allocations of indirect expenses, such as interest expense and home office overhead.

From a U.S. tax perspective, the income derived by a foreign branch represents foreign-source income earned directly by the domestic corporation. The branch's income is therefore subject to U.S. tax at the regular corporate rates, with a credit allowed for the lesser of the related foreign income taxes or the applicable foreign tax credit limitation. Thus, the taxpayer may owe a residual U.S. tax on the income of a branch operating in a low-tax foreign jurisdiction, whereas a branch operating in a high-tax foreign jurisdiction may create excess foreign tax credits.

The remittance of branch profits back to the U.S. home office is not a taxable event for U.S. tax purposes, except to the extent it triggers the recognition of a currency exchange gain or loss (see Chapter 8). Whether the remittance impacts the domestic corporation's foreign taxes depends on whether the host country has some type of branch profits tax. Most foreign countries impose withholding taxes on dividends paid by a local subsidiary to its U.S. parent. Some countries also have a branch profits tax, which is a withholding-type tax that is imposed on branch remittances. For example, the United States im-

---

[8] *The Queen v. Crown Forest Industries*, Limited, 2 S.C.R. 802 [1995]; Revenue Canada, Reorganizations and Foreign Division, April 3, 1995, Revenue Canada File Number 9416455.

poses a branch profits tax on the dividend equivalent amounts of U.S. branches of foreign corporations.[9]

Subsidiaries

A foreign subsidiary is a corporation organized under the laws of the host country, and therefore is a separate legal entity from its U.S. parent. The subsidiary's earnings are usually subject to host country taxation by virtue of its foreign citizenship, as well as the source of its income. As with a branch, the subsidiary's taxable income should reflect the amount of income that it would earn if it were an independent enterprise. To achieve this result, the U.S. parent corporation must use arm's length transfer prices for intercompany transactions. For example, if a foreign marketing subsidiary purchases inventory from its U.S. parent for resale abroad, the transfer price should equal the sales price on comparable sales involving two unrelated entities.

The United States generally does not tax foreign business profits earned through a foreign subsidiary until the subsidiary distributes those earnings to the U.S. parent corporation as a dividend. This makes it possible for a domestic corporation to defer payment of the residual U.S. tax on the earnings of foreign subsidiaries operating in low-tax foreign jurisdictions.

> **Example 10.2:** USAco, a domestic corporation, earns $10 million of foreign-source income through a foreign sales office. Assume the U.S. tax rate is 35% and the foreign tax rate is 20%. If USAco structures the foreign sales office as a branch, the total tax burden on the $10 million of foreign-source income is $3.5 million, consisting of foreign taxes of $2 million [20% × $10 million], and a residual U.S. tax of $1.5 million [$3.5 million pre-credit U.S. tax − $2 million foreign tax credit]. On the other hand, if USAco structures the foreign sales office as a subsidiary, the only current year tax due on the $10 million of foreign-source income is the foreign tax of $2 million [20% × $10 million]. Payment of the $1.5 million residual U.S. tax is postponed until the subsidiary distributes its earnings to USAco in the form of a dividend.

As discussed in Chapter 6, certain types of unrepatriated income earned through a foreign subsidiary, such as passive investment income, are subject to immediate U.S. taxation.

One disadvantage of deferral is that net operating losses of foreign subsidiaries do not flow-through and offset the U.S. parent corporation's domestic profits. In contrast, a domestic corporation can deduct the losses of a foreign branch. A branch loss recapture rule prevents

---

[9] Code Sec. 884.

taxpayers from exploiting this advantage of the branch form by initially operating abroad as a branch, and then converting to the subsidiary form when the foreign operation becomes profitable. Under the branch loss recapture rule, a U.S. person must recognize a gain on the incorporation of a foreign branch to the extent it has previously deducted branch losses against its other taxable income.[10]

Branch versus Subsidiary

The choice between the branch and subsidiary forms must take into account not only U.S. and foreign tax laws, but also general business considerations. There is no simple rule that dictates the best structure in all cases. Tax advantages of the subsidiary form include the following:

(i) A subsidiary generally allows a U.S. company to defer the residual U.S. tax on low-tax foreign-source income.

(ii) The subsidiary form provides more control over the timing of income recognition, which may be useful in foreign tax credit planning. For example, a U.S. parent in an excess credit position may wish to avoid repatriating the earnings of a high-tax foreign subsidiary, and thereby store excess credits in that subsidiary until they can be used. This option is not available with a branch, since its earnings are always subject to immediate U.S. taxation.

(iii) Local tax incentives, such as a tax holiday, may be available only to a locally incorporated entity.

(iv) The sale of stock in a subsidiary results in a capital gain, which may be exempt from foreign taxation.

(v) The separate legal status of a subsidiary may make it easier to justify management fees and other intercompany charges to foreign tax authorities.

Tax advantages of the branch form include the following:

(i) A domestic corporation can deduct the foreign losses of a branch against its U.S. profits. These losses are recaptured, however, if the branch later incorporates.[11]

(ii) The transfer of assets to a branch is a nontaxable event. In contrast, tax-free transfers of appreciated property to a foreign subsidiary are restricted.[12]

(iii) S corporation shareholders, who are generally individuals, cannot claim a deemed paid credit for foreign taxes incurred by a

---

[10] Code Sec. 367(a)(3)(C). The branch loss recapture rule is discussed in detail in Chapter 6.

[11] Code Sec. 367(a)(3)(C).
[12] Code Sec. 367.

foreign subsidiary.[13] However, they can claim a direct credit for the foreign taxes incurred by a branch. This aspect of a branch form is also advantageous for individuals who are partners in a U.S. partnership, or members of a U.S. limited liability company that is classified as a partnership for U.S. tax purposes.

(iv) There may be no foreign taxes when a branch repatriates its profits, whereas dividends paid by a subsidiary normally attract foreign withholding taxes.

General business factors which should be considered when choosing between the branch and subsidiary form include:

(i) A subsidiary insulates the U.S. parent from legal liability issues in the host country.

(ii) A subsidiary may present a better local image to potential customers and employees.

(iii) A branch may be simpler to operate. For example, business registration and financial reporting requirements of a branch may be less onerous than those for a locally incorporated entity.

(iv) Local laws may require a subsidiary to have outside foreign shareholders or directors.

(v) A subsidiary may make it easier to involve foreigners in the venture, since it can issue additional shares to those foreign investors.

(vi) The use of a branch avoids the minimum capitalization requirements imposed by some countries.

Hybrid Entities

A hybrid entity is a legal entity whose characterization for U.S. tax purposes is different than that for foreign tax purposes. The typical hybrid is a foreign entity that is considered a corporation for foreign tax purposes, but a branch or partnership for U.S. tax purposes. Under the United States pre-1997 approach to entity classification, an entity (whether domestic or foreign) was classified as a branch or partnership if it lacked two or more of the four primary corporate characteristics: limited liability, free transferability of interests, continuity of life, and centralized management.[14] Under this approach, a taxpayer wishing to have an entity classified as a branch or partnership had to structure

---

[13] Code Sec. 902(a) and 1373(a).

[14] Reg. § 301.7701-2 (1960), before amendments made December 17, 1996.

the entity such that it failed at least two corporate characteristics. Typically, this involved failing the corporate characteristics of continuity of life and free transferability of interests.

Effective January 1, 1997, most foreign business entities with at least two members can elect to be treated as a corporation or a partnership, and those entities with only a single member can elect to be treated as a corporation or an unincorporated branch. This regime is now commonly known as "check-the-box" because the entity's owner merely checks the box on a Form 8832 to classify the entity (Form 8832 is reproduced in the Appendix to this chapter). A separate entity must actually exist before checking the box. Federal tax law controls for purposes of determining what constitutes an entity.[15] Although federal law is determinative, the regulatory rules reflect the common law partnership definition of an entity as a group of participants carrying on a trade, business, financial operation, or venture and dividing the profits therefrom.[16] A cost sharing arrangement does not constitute an entity.[17] This so-called "check-the-box" approach to entity classification is one of the more significant tax simplifications in recent years.

About 80 types of foreign business entities listed in Table 10.3 below are excluded from the elective system because the IRS determined that they should be treated as "per se" corporations. However, the regulations grandfathered pre-existing classifications of foreign business entities that would otherwise be treated as per se corporations if certain conditions are met. For example, a per se entity that qualified as a partnership under the old regulations may retain its status as a partnership under certain circumstances.[18] Furthermore, any foreign entity existing before to the effective date of the regulations may retain its prior status if that prior status was relevant on a previously filed return.[19]

---

[15] Reg. §§ 301.7701-1(a)(1) and -1(a)(3).

[16] Reg. § 301.7701-1(a)(2). These factors are based on the case of *Luna v. Commissioner*, 42 T.C. 1067, 1077-1078 (1964).

[17] Reg. §§ 301.7701-(a)(2) and -1(c).

[18] Reg. § 301.7701-2(d).

[19] Reg. §§ 301.7701-3(b)(3)(ii) and -3(d).

TABLE 10.3. LIST OF PER SE CORPORATE ENTITIES

American Samoa, Corporation

Argentina, Sociedad Anonima

Australia, Public Limited Company

Austria, Aktiengesellschaft

Barbados, Limited Company

Belgium, Societe Anonyme

Belize, Public Limited Company

Bolivia, Sociedad Anonima

Brazil, Sociedade Anonima

Canada, Corporation and Company

Chile, Sociedad Anonima

People's Republic of China, Gufen Youxian Gongsi

Republic of China (Taiwan), Ku-fen Yu-hsien Kung-szu

Colombia, Sociedad Anonima

Costa Rica, Sociedad Anonima

Cyprus, Public Limited Company

Czech Republic, Akciova Spolecnost

Denmark, Aktieselskab

Ecuador, Sociedad Anonima or Compania Anonima

Egypt, Sharikat Al-Mossahamah

El Salvador, Sociedad Anonima

Finland, Osakeyhtio/Aktiebolag

France, Societe Anonyme

Germany, Aktiengesellschaft

Greece, Anonymos Etairia

Guam, Corporation

Guatemala, Sociedad Anonima

Guyana, Public Limited Company

Honduras, Sociedad Anonima

Hong Kong, Public Limited Company

Hungary, Reszvenytarsasag

Iceland, Hlutafelag

India, Public Limited Company

Indonesia, Perseroan Terbuka

Ireland, Public Limited Company

Israel, Public Limited Company

Italy, Societa per Azioni

Jamaica, Public Limited Company

Japan, Kabushiki Kaisha

Kazakstan, Ashyk Aktsionerlik Kogham

Republic of Korea, Chusik Hoesa

Liberia, Corporation

Luxembourg, Societe Anonyme

Malaysia, Berhad

Malta, Partnership Anonyme

Mexico, Sociedad Anonima

Morocco, Societe Anonyme

The Netherlands, Naamloze Vennootschap

Peru, Sociedad Anonima

Philippines, Stock Corporation

Poland, Spolka Akcyjna

Portugal, Sociedade Anonima

Puerto Rico, Corporation

Romania, Societe pe Actiuni

New Zealand, Limited Company

Nicaragua, Compania Anonima

Nigeria, Public Limited Company

Northern Mariana Islands, Corporation

Norway, Aksjeselskap

Pakistan, Public Limited Company

Panama, Sociedad Anonima

Paraguay, Sociedad Anonima

Russia, Otkrytoye Aktsionernoy Obshchestvo

Saudi Arabia, Sharikat Al-Mossahamah

Singapore, Public Limited Company

Slovak Republic, Akciova Spolocnost

South Africa, Public Limited Company

Spain, Sociedad Anonima

Surinam, Naamloze Vennootschap

Sweden, Publika Aktiebolag

Switzerland, Aktiengesellschaft

Thailand, Borisat Chamkad (Machachon)

Trinidad and Tobago, Public Limited Company

Tunisia, Societe Anonyme

Turkey, Anonim Sirket

Ukraine, Aktsionerne Tovaristvo Vidkritogo Tipu

United Kingdom, Public Limited Company

United States Virgin Islands, Corporation

Uruguay, Sociedad Anonima

Venezuela, Sociedad Anonima or Compania Anonima

Three special default rules apply if a foreign eligible entity does not make an election.[20] First, if the foreign entity has two or more owners and at least one owner does not have limited liability, the foreign entity is a partnership. Second, if all the owners have limited liability, the foreign entity is a corporation. Finally, if the foreign entity has only one owner that does not have limited liability, the entity is a branch. An owner of a foreign entity has limited liability if ownership does not result in personal liability. This is purely a matter of the foreign country's local law, and requires a review of the foreign entity's organizational documents.[21] Finally, the mechanics for checking-the-box are relatively easy. An election can have an effective date of up to seventy-five days prior to the election date and up to one year after the election date. Once elected, an owner cannot re-elect for five years.[22]

Hybrid entities provide the tax advantages of the flow-through entity form (i.e., a branch or partnership), while still providing the U.S. parent corporation with limited liability and a "corporate" presence in the host country. For example, an entity that is considered a branch or a partnership for U.S. tax purposes allows foreign losses to flow-through and be deducted by the U.S. parent corporation. In contrast, losses of a foreign subsidiary are not deductible by the U.S. parent corporation. Second, whereas noncorporate shareholders can not claim a deemed paid foreign tax credit for the foreign income taxes incurred by a foreign corporation,[23] they can claim a direct credit for the foreign taxes incurred by a foreign branch or partnership.[24] Third, partnership status allows certain noncontrolling U.S. shareholder to apply a look-through rule in computing its foreign tax credit limitation, such that the foreign entity's active business income is assigned to the general limitation rather than a separate noncontrolled section 902 corporation limitation.[25] Fourth, hybrid entities allow U.S. companies to avoid Subpart F treatment of transfers between CFCs. Under Subpart F, interest and dividends payments between commonly controlled CFCs located in different countries constitute Subpart F income. One solution to this problem is the use of hybrid entities (e.g., single member branches) below a first-tier CFC holding company. This structure achieves the effective consolidation of the U.S. multinational's foreign operations, with the first-tier CFC, along with all the lower-tier hybrid entities, treated as a single taxable entity for U.S. purposes. This single

---

[20] Reg. § 301.7701-3(b). A different default rule applies for domestic entities, treating the entity as a partnership if the entity has multiple owners and a branch if the entity has only a single owner.

[21] Reg. § 301.7701-3(b)(2)(ii).

[22] Reg. § § 301.7701-3(b)(3)(iii) and (iv).

[23] Code Sec. 902(a) and 1373(a).

[24] Code Sec. 901(b)(5).

[25] Reg. § 1.904-5(h)(1).

corporate entity can move cash in and out of each country without U.S. tax consequences.[26]

Although hybrid entities have a number of benefits, there are significant tax costs associated with converting an existing foreign subsidiary into a foreign branch or partnership. In particular, "hybridizing" an existing foreign subsidiary is a two-part transaction, involving the inbound liquidation of the foreign corporation, followed by a contribution of those assets to a foreign branch or partnership. Taxpayers must carefully analyze such transactions since inbound repatriating liquidations are subject to a special toll charge tax,[27] and an outbound expatriating transfer to a foreign partnership may be subject to a special excise tax.[28]

Reverse Hybrid Entities

Reverse hybrid entities are treated as corporations by the U.S., but as flow-through entities by the foreign countries. From a U.S. perspective, operating as a reverse hybrid offers several tax planning opportunities. A foreign subsidiary generally will allow a U.S. company to defer the residual U.S. tax on foreign profits. Furthermore, a foreign subsidiary offers more control over the timing of income recognition, which is useful in foreign tax credit planning. To take advantage of these opportunities, but avoid local foreign tax, a U.S. company can create a reverse hybrid.

> **Example 10.3.** USAco operates in country L, a low tax country through a Limitata for which it checked the box as "corporate status." Limitata earns $1,000,000 in Country L. Because Country L does not impose any tax on the Limitata and does not impose a branch level tax, USAco does not incur any tax in country L on the Limitata. Furthermore, there will not be any U.S. tax until distributions of the $1,000,000 of earnings are made.

> **Example 10.4.** USAco operates in country L, a low tax country through a Limitata for which it checked the box as "corporate status." In each of its first 5 years, Limitata earns $1,000,000 in Country L, for accumulated earnings of $5,000,000 by the end of year 5. Because Country L does not impose any tax on the Limitata and does not impose a branch level tax, USAco does not incur any tax in country L on the Limitata. On December 31 of year 5,

---

[26] In Notice 98-11, 1998-6 IRB 18, the IRS announced its intention to publish regulations under Subpart F relating to perceived abuses regarding hybrid branch payments. In March 1998, the IRS released proposed and temporary regulations under Code Sec. 954, which addressed foreign tax reduction strategies involving foreign entities. However, in Notice 98-35, the IRS reversed itself, announcing that it will withdraw the temporary and proposed regula-tions, and in Notice 99-76 (July 1999), the IRS announced that it would essentially allow unrestricted use of foreign tax reduction planning arrangements involving hybrids by all corporations, at least until January 1, 2006.

[27] Code Sec. 367(b) and 1248(a). See discussion in Chapter 6.

[28] Code Sec. 721(c). See discussion in Chapter 6.

USAco receives a distribution from Limitata of $1,000,000. USAco pays tax at its U.S. marginal rate on the $1,000,000, but has effectively deferred the U.S. tax for 4 years.

¶ 1005   BASICS OF INTERNATIONAL TAX PLANNING

International tax planning involves the interplay of the tax laws of two or more countries. From a domestic corporation's perspective, the objective of international tax planning is to reduce the U.S. and foreign taxes on foreign-source income. Foreign taxes increase a domestic corporation's total tax costs only to the extent they are not creditable for U.S. tax purposes. Taxpayers can reduce these excess credits either through foreign tax reduction planning or planning that increases the allowable credit for U.S. tax purposes. With respect to U.S. taxes, the United States generally collects any residual U.S. taxes on low-tax foreign-source income. Nevertheless, foreign-source income can give rise to opportunities to defer or even permanently reduce U.S. taxes. These issues are discussed in more detail below.

U.S. Tax Incentives for Foreign Activities

The FSC provisions provide U.S. companies with an opportunity for permanently avoiding U.S. taxes on foreign-source income. The FSC provisions allow a U.S. company to exclude a portion of its export profits from U.S. tax. The amount of the exclusion usually is 15% of the net income from qualifying export sales. Chapter 7 discusses various strategies for maximizing the FSC benefit, including the use of transaction-by-transaction pricing in computing the export profits allocable to the FSC, and the use of special marginal costing rules and alternative methods of expense allocation in computing the combined taxable income of an FSC and its domestic parent corporation.

Prior to 1996, the possessions credit was another opportunity for U.S. companies to permanently avoid U.S. taxes on foreign-source income. Congress enacted the possessions credit to prevent U.S. taxes from nullifying the tax incentives offered by U.S. possessions, including Puerto Rico. For example, to induce U.S. companies to make investments in Puerto Rico, the Puerto Rican government grants low tax rates to U.S. companies that establish manufacturing operations in Puerto Rico. Without a special rule, however, the foreign tax savings from such tax holidays would be offset by a corresponding increase in the residual U.S. tax due on the low-tax foreign-source income. The possession credit prevents this result by allowing a qualifying domestic corporation to claim a credit equal to the amount of the U.S. tax that would otherwise be due on income derived from sources within a possession.[29] This practice is known as "tax sparing," since a credit is

---

[29] Code Sec. 936(a)(1).

granted even though no foreign taxes are paid. The net result is that a domestic corporation can enjoy a total tax rate on possession's income that is less than the U.S. corporate rate of 35%.

> **Example 10.5:** USAco is a qualified possession corporation that earns $100 million from manufacturing operations in Puerto Rico. After taking into account the special tax breaks provided by the Puerto Rican government, the Puerto Rican tax on USAco's profits is only $4 million. Because USAco is a U.S. corporation, the pre-credit U.S. tax on its possessions income is $35 million (assuming a 35% U.S. corporate tax rate). Despite having paid only $4 million in Puerto Rican tax, USAco can claim a possessions credit equal to the $35 million of U.S. tax that would otherwise be due on the $100 million of possessions income. Therefore, USAco's residual U.S. tax is $0, and its total tax equals the Puerto Rican tax of $4 million.

In 1996, Congress repealed the possessions credit for taxable years beginning after December 31, 1995. However, complex transitional rules allow pre-existing possessions corporations to claim the benefit through the year 2005.[30]

Operating in Low-tax Foreign Jurisdictions

The United States generally does not tax foreign business profits earned through a foreign subsidiary until the subsidiary repatriates those earnings through a dividend. Therefore, a U.S. multinational corporation may be able to reduce its total tax costs by shifting income producing assets and activities to a subsidiary located in a low-tax foreign jurisdiction. There are limitations on the tax benefits of this strategy, however. First, shifting income to a low-tax foreign subsidiary does not permanently avoid the residual U.S. tax on low-tax foreign earnings, but instead merely defers those taxes until the subsidiary repatriates its earnings through a dividend distribution. In addition, the eventual repatriation of those earnings may be subject to foreign withholding taxes, which increases the total foreign tax rate on those earnings.

There also are significant constraints on the ability of U.S. multinationals to shift income to low-tax foreign subsidiaries. For example, a domestic parent corporation must use arm's length transfer prices to compute its share of income arising from related party transactions,[31] and special penalties may apply if the IRS makes a significant transfer pricing adjustment.[32] Moreover, Congress has enacted a variety of anti-

---

[30] Code Sec. 936(j).
[31] Code Sec. 482.

[32] Code Sec. 6662. See discussion of transactional and net adjustment penalties in Chapter 5.

deferral provisions, including the Subpart F, passive foreign investment company, and foreign personal holding company provisions (see Chapter 6). Under these provisions, certain types of unrepatriated earnings of a foreign corporation, such as passive investment income, are subject to immediate U.S. taxation.

Operating in High-tax Foreign Jurisdictions

When a U.S. company conducts business in a high-tax foreign jurisdiction, the resulting excess foreign tax credits increase the total tax burden beyond what it would have been if only the United States had taxed the foreign-source income. One strategy for eliminating the excess credits is to increase the proportion of worldwide income that is classified as foreign-source for U.S. tax purpose. For example, by arranging for the passage of title abroad, export sales will generate foreign-source income to the extent of the marketing profit. Recharacterizing deductions also is an effective strategy for eliminating excess credits. For example, by using alternative apportionment bases for sourcing selling, general and administrative expenses, a taxpayer may be able to reduce the amount of these deductions allocated and apportioned to foreign-source income.

A second strategy for reducing excess credits is to blend low and high-tax foreign-source income within a single limitation. This allows the excess limitation on the low-tax foreign income to offset the excess credits on the high-tax foreign income. Under the current limitation system, a taxpayer must compute a separate limitation for each of nine separate categories of income.[33] Although this prevents cross-crediting between different types of income (e.g., passive versus general limitation income), cross-crediting is still allowed with respect to the same type of income derived from different foreign countries. The CFC look-through rule makes cross-crediting possible with respect to income derived from CFCs located in low and high-tax foreign jurisdictions, as long as the underlying earnings of the CFC are assigned to the same category of income limitation (e.g., the general limitation category).[34] On the other hand, dividends from each noncontrolled section 902 corporation comprise a separate limitation.[35] Therefore, excess credits on dividends from one noncontrolled section 902 corporation can not be used to offset the residual U.S. tax on dividends from another noncontrolled section 902 corporation. Chapter 4 discusses various strategies for avoiding this restriction. For example, by converting a noncontrolled section 902 corporation into an entity that is treated as a partner-

---

[33] Code Sec. 904(d)(1).
[34] Code Sec. 904(d)(3).

[35] Reg. § 1.904-4(g)(2)(i).

ship for U.S. tax purposes, the U.S. parent can take advantage of the look-through rule that applies to partnerships.[36]

A third strategy for eliminating the excess credits on high-tax foreign-source income is foreign tax reduction planning.

Foreign Tax Reduction Planning

Many of the techniques that a U.S. taxpayer can use to reduce foreign income taxes are essentially the same as those used to reduce income taxes in a purely domestic context. Examples include realizing income in a form that is taxed at a lower rate (such as a preferential rate for capital gains), deferring the recognition of gross income, and accelerating the recognition of deductions. Other foreign tax reduction techniques are unique to the international context, and include taking advantage of local tax incentives, debt financing, transfer pricing, and the use of tax treaties.

Local tax incentives. One way to reduce foreign taxes is to take advantage of the special tax exemptions and holidays that various countries offer as an incentive to locate particular types of operations within their borders. For example, Ireland taxes manufacturing profits at a reduced rate. Singapore offers tax breaks for the manufacture of advanced technologies. Puerto Rico grants tax exemptions to U.S. companies that establish manufacturing operations in Puerto Rico. Belgium offers tax breaks for distribution, service and coordination centers, and Switzerland offer low-tax rates for headquarters companies.

Debt financing. It may be advantageous to finance high-tax foreign subsidiaries in a way that maximizes interest deductions and minimizes dividend payments. The potential advantages of debt financing provided by a U.S. parent include a deduction in the high-tax foreign jurisdiction for interest paid to the U.S. parent, as well as the possibility of a lower foreign withholding taxes on interest payments, as opposed to dividend distributions.

Assuming the foreign subsidiary is a CFC, intercompany debt also increases the U.S. parent's foreign tax credit limitation by creating a stream of low-tax foreign-source income. Interest income derived from a CFC by a U.S. shareholder of that CFC is assigned to the passive income category to the extent of the CFC's foreign personal holding company income.[37] Any interest income in excess of the CFC's foreign personal holding company income is apportioned among the separate

---

[36] Reg. § 1.904-5(h)(1).   [37] Code Sec. 954(b)(5).

income categories other than passive income.[38] In contrast, only a portion of the U.S. parent's incremental interest expense, if any, caused by financing the CFC is allocable against foreign-source income under the asset-based apportionment rule for interest expense.[39] Nevertheless, a special rule (referred to as the "CFC netting rule") may require the U.S. parent to specifically allocate certain interest expense deductions against its foreign-source interest income in computing the foreign tax credit limitation.[40]

To secure the benefits of debt financing, the U.S. parent corporation must ensure that any intercompany payments meant to be interest qualify as such under the host country's tax laws. The rules for determining whether an investment in a local subsidiary is treated as debt and not equity vary from country to country. Some countries employ relatively objective standards (for example, a maximum debt to equity ratio of 3 to 1), while other countries employ more subjective facts and circumstances standards. To the extent that interest payments are limited by these standards, the taxpayer may wish to consider other methods of repatriating earnings that give rise to a deduction at the foreign subsidiary level, such as royalty payments.

Transfer pricing. By altering its transfer pricing policy, a U.S. multinational corporation may be able to allocate a smaller portion of its worldwide profits to subsidiaries located in high-tax foreign jurisdictions. For example, a U.S. parent can allocate a smaller share of the gross profit from intercompany inventory sales by charging foreign marketing subsidiaries a higher price, or paying foreign manufacturing subsidiaries a lower price. Another way to shift income is to charge foreign subsidiaries for the use of U.S.-owned manufacturing and marketing intangibles. If the subsidiary is a CFC, the resulting royalties also provide the U.S. parent with a stream of low-tax foreign-source income that has the same character for foreign tax credit limitation purposes as the underlying earnings of the CFC to which the royalty expense is properly allocable.[41] If a foreign jurisdiction does not allow a deduction for technology charges paid to a parent corporation, the taxpayer should consider using a cost-sharing arrangement (see discussion in Chapter 5). Charging a foreign subsidiary for management services provided by the U.S. home office also reduces the foreign income taxes of the subsidiary.

---

[38] Code Sec. 904(d)(3)(C). See Reg. § 1.904-5(c)(2)(ii) regarding the applicable apportionment method.

[39] Code Sec. 864(e)(2).
[40] Reg. § 1.861-10.
[41] Code Sec. 904(d)(3)(C) and Reg. § 1.904-5(c)(3).

As discussed in detail in Chapter 5, special penalties may apply if the IRS makes a significant transfer pricing adjustment.[42] Therefore, it is imperative for taxpayers to establish defensible positions for the transfer prices they use through contemporaneous documentation of their transfer pricing methodology.

Commission agents and contract manufacturing. A business entity's profits are determined by the functions it performs, the risk it bears, and the assets that it owns. As a consequence, a U.S. multinational may be able to reduce its foreign tax costs by structuring its foreign operations in a manner that minimizes the transfer of risks, responsibilities, and assets to high-tax foreign subsidiaries. Two strategies for achieving this result are the use of commissionaires (or stripped distributors) and contract manufacturing.

A traditional buy-sell foreign sales subsidiary purchases inventory from its U.S. parent for resale abroad. Such subsidiaries often assume responsibility not only for the advertising and selling functions, but also for inventory risks, credit risks, warranty administration, and technical services. As a result, arm's-length transfer prices allocate a significant portion of the U.S. multinational's total export profit to a foreign sales subsidiary. If the subsidiary is located in a high-tax foreign country, this can worsen the U.S. parent's excess credit problem. In contrast, if the U.S. parent holds title to its goods until their ultimate delivery to the foreign customer, with the foreign subsidiary acting as a mere commission agent for the U.S. parent, the subsidiary would earn a profit equal to an arm's-length commission determined under either a cost-plus approach or a percentage of sales revenue approach. A commission agent's profit is lower than that of a buy-sell distributor because the functions performed and risks assumed by such agents are typically limited to selling, compared to the much broader set of functions performed by a buy-sell distributor.

Another technique for minimizing the transfer of functions, risks and assets to a foreign operation is the use of contract manufacturing. The maquiladora operations of U.S. multinationals in Mexico are an example of contract manufacturing. Under this arrangement, a Mexican subsidiary processes materials using equipment owned and leased by the U.S. parent. The U.S. parent also provides the managerial and technical support personnel needed to manage the Mexican operation, and usually retains title to the raw materials, which are processed on a contract basis (hence, the name "contract manufacturer"). Histori-

---

[42] Code Sec. 6662.

cally, maquiladoras earn a profit equal to an arm's-length fee determined under a cost-plus approach.

Tax treaties. Taxpayers also can reduce foreign taxes by making use of permanent establishment provisions and the reduced withholding tax rates provided by tax treaties. Under most tax treaties, a domestic corporation's business profits are not subject to foreign taxation unless it conducts business through a permanent establishment located within the host country. A permanent establishment is a branch office, or the presence of dependent agents who habitually conclude sales contracts in the taxpayer's name. Marketing products abroad solely through independent brokers or distributors does not create a permanent establishment. Tax treaties also provide lower withholding tax rates on dividends, interest, and royalties derived from sources within the treaty country. As a consequence, a U.S. parent corporation may be able to reduce foreign withholding taxes by owning its foreign subsidiaries through strategically located holding companies (so-called "treaty shopping"). Chapter 9 discusses some of the restrictions on a taxpayer's ability to engage in treaty shopping.

Operating in Tax Haven Jurisdictions

U.S. taxpayers can achieve significant tax and nontax benefits from the use of tax haven related strategies. Each nation typically provides a definition of the term "tax haven." Although it may vary, a common factor is that the foreign jurisdiction imposes an income tax that is lower than the tax imposed by the home country. For example, in France, a tax haven is described as a country having a" privileged tax system," which is any country which levies a tax, equal to or less than two-thirds the tax France imposes.[43] The term tax haven, if applied literally, would include countries such as the U.S., since the U.S. does not tax interest earned by nonresident aliens on deposits in U.S. banks. It therefore constitutes a tax haven for those foreign investors who derive interest income from deposits in U.S. banks.

Although Congress has passed laws to limit the use of tax havens and other offshore sites for tax-savings purposes (e.g., Subpart F, Code Sec. 367 and the PFIC provisions), there is no U.S. statutory definition of the term "tax haven." However, for U.S. tax purposes, the IRS has identified a list of "tax haven" countries (Table 10.4) that either impose no tax or levy a tax that is low in comparison to the U.S. rates.[44]

---

[43] Code General des Impots Art. 238 A, paragraph 2.

[44] IRM 4233, Exhibit 500-8.

TABLE 10.4. LIST OF TAX HAVEN COUNTRIES [45]

Antigua	Isle of Man
Austria	Liberia
Bahamas	Liechtenstein
Bahrain	Luxembourg
Barbados	Monaco
Belize	Nauru
Bermuda	The Netherlands
British Virgin Islands	The Netherlands Antilles
Cayman Islands	Vanuatu
Cook Islands	Panama
Costa Rica	Singapore
Channels Islands	St. Kitts
Gibraltar	St. Vincent
Granada	Switzerland
Hong Kong	Turks and Caicos
Ireland	

In general, there are six principal characteristics of tax havens:

(i) A tax haven either imposes no income tax or imposes a tax on income that is small in comparison to the tax imposed by the home country.

(ii) A tax haven often protects the confidentiality of financial and commercial information. In so doing, it may adopt bank secrecy or similar internal laws that make it a crime to disclose this information to any person.

(iii) Financial institutions, such as banks, frequently assume a dominant role in the haven's trade or commerce, and its residents include those skilled in financial transactions, such as bankers, lawyers, and accountants.

(iv) A haven normally possesses modern communications facilities necessary to the conduct of financial and commercial affairs.

(v) A haven often does not impose currency controls or similar restrictions on foreign nationals.

(vi) If the haven has a treaty network, the haven may offer benefits such as reduced tax rates on income tax by its treaty partners.

---

[45] IRM 4233, Exhibit 500-8.

Tax haven incentives. A tax haven jurisdiction typically imposes a low or zero rate of tax on all or some class of income. The following list describes the special incentives that selected tax havens generally offer:

(i)   *Countries that impose zero tax*—These are jurisdictions that impose no tax on income, capital gains, gifts, inheritances, estates and trusts. Since these countries do not have treaty networks, they have no obligation to furnish tax information to other jurisdictions. Such countries generally charge an annual formation fee to registered companies. An example of this type of tax haven would be Bermuda.

(ii) *Countries that impose a low tax*—In order to compete with havens that impose a zero rate of tax, these jurisdictions offer a low rate of tax combined with a treaty network. The treaty networks are useful in adding some degree of flexibility to tax planning. An example of this type of tax haven would be the British Virgin Islands.

(iii) *Countries that impose no tax on foreign source income*—These tax havens do not impose any tax on income earned from sources outside of the particular jurisdiction. These havens are especially attractive to the transportation industry when, for example, the jurisdiction allows the registration of foreign flagships. An example of this type of tax haven would be Hong Kong.

(iv) *Countries that impose a reduced rate of tax on offshore finance and trade-oriented businesses*—These countries usually impose a minimal or token tax to resident companies that do not conduct business or trade within the haven. An example of this type of tax haven would be the British Virgin Islands.

(v)   *Countries that offer special inducements*—In order to attract certain companies, such as holding companies, some jurisdictions offer significant inducements that may include privileged treatment with respect to income taxes, import taxes, customs, duties, etc. An example of this type of tax haven would be the Netherlands. In order to attract manufacturing facilities to their countries, some jurisdictions, such as Singapore, provide for various tax holidays on profits earned on products manufactured for export.

Nontax factors. The laws of most countries provide for some degree of confidentiality with respect to banking and other commercial activities. However, most nations will not protect information from a legitimate inquiry initiated by a foreign government, especially if the request is made pursuant to a treaty provision. On the other hand, tax

¶ **1005**

havens with stringent secrecy laws typically refuse to breach their secrecy rules even when serious violations of another nation's law may have occurred. To do otherwise may seriously impair the jurisdiction's tax haven status with those persons who need the element of secrecy to plan their tax strategy.

Many jurisdictions, in order to maintain or improve their competitive position as a tax haven, have enacted legislation providing for criminal sanctions for breach of the secrecy laws. An example is the Cayman Islands. The Cayman Islands, which have had stringent bank secrecy laws since the 1960s when it tightened its common law through statute, passed additional legislation in 1976 providing for substantial sanctions against persons who either divulged or received confidential banking and commercial information.

Many tax havens have a dual currency control system that distinguishes between residents and nonresidents, and between local currency and foreign currency. Generally, residents are subject to currency controls while nonresidents are only subject to controls placed on the local currency. For currency control purposes, a company which is formed in the tax haven and which is beneficially owned by a resident and which conducts its business outside the haven is generally treated as a nonresident. Therefore, a tax haven company doing business solely in other jurisdictions cannot be subject to the haven's currency exchange controls provided it deals in the currency of other countries. These rules facilitate the use of a tax haven by a person wishing to establish a tax haven entity for purposes of doing business in other jurisdictions. The rules also offer the free movement of foreign currency abroad.

A tax haven enjoying a treaty network can provide a most attractive combination in the formation of a multi-national tax strategy. This combination offers increased flexibility in devising plans to reduce tax rates through treaty shopping. Many of the U.S. treaty partners have treaties with tax haven type countries.

Finally, in addition to selecting a particular tax haven for purposes such as low tax, secrecy, banking, currency control, communications, and treaty networks, taxpayers should also consider nontax factors. These factors include economic and political stability, geographic accessibility to markets, the availability of labor, the risk of nationalization of assets, and government cooperation.

¶ 1006 COMPREHENSIVE EXAMPLE

USAco, a domestic corporation, plans to locate a new factory in either country L or country H. USAco will structure the new facility as a wholly owned foreign subsidiary, FORco, and finance FORco solely with an equity investment. USAco projects that in FORco's first year of operations, it will generate $10 million of taxable income, all from active foreign manufacturing activities. Assume that the U.S. corporate tax rate is 35%. To simplify the analysis, further assume that USAco's only item of income during the year is that derived from FORco.

The total tax rate on FORco earnings will vary significantly, depending on a number of factors, including:

(i) whether FORco is located in a low-tax or high-tax foreign country,

(ii) the extent to which USAco repatriates FORco's earnings,

(iii) whether USAco repatriates FORco's earnings through dividend distributions, as opposed to interest, rental or royalty payments, and

(iv) the availability of favorable tax treaty withholding rates on dividends, interest, and other payments made by FORco to USAco.

The effect of these factors is illustrated below by computing the worldwide tax rate on FORco's earnings under a variety of assumptions.

Case 1: Low-tax country/No dividends. Country L has a corporate income tax rate of 25%, which is ten percentage points lower than the U.S. rate. If USAco locates FORco in country L and FORco pays no dividends, the total tax rate on its earnings will be 25%, computed as follows.

Foreign income tax
FORco's taxable income $10,000,000
Country L income tax rate . . . . ×   25%
Country L income tax . . . . $ 2,500,000

Foreign withholding taxes on repatriated earnings . . . . $ 0

U.S. tax on repatriated earnings . . . . $ 0

Total taxes [$2,500,000 + $0 + $0] . . . . $ 2,500,000

Worldwide effective tax rate [$2,500,000 ÷ $10,000,000] 25%

This example illustrates that USAco can reduce the current year worldwide tax rate on the new manufacturing facility below the U.S. tax rate of 35% by locating the factory in L, a low-tax foreign country.

Case 2: Low-tax country/Pays dividend/Tax treaty. Assume that country L has a tax treaty with the United States that provides a 10% withholding tax rate on dividends. If USAco locates FORco in country L and repatriates half of FORco's after-tax earnings through a dividend distribution, the total tax rate on its repatriated and unrepatriated earnings will be 30%, computed as follows.

Foreign income tax

FORco's taxable income	$	10,000,000
Country L income tax rate	×	25%
Country L income tax	$	2,500,000

Foreign withholding taxes on repatriated earnings

FORco's after-tax earnings [$10,000,000 − $2,500,000]	$	7,500,000
Percentage repatriated through dividend	×	50%
Dividend distribution	$	3,750,000
Withholding tax rate (per treaty)	×	10%
Country L withholding tax	$	375,000

U.S. tax on repatriated earnings

Dividend from FORco	$	3,750,000
Code Sec. 78 gross-up	+	1,250,000
USAco's taxable income	$	5,000,000
U.S. tax rate	×	35%
Pre-credit U.S. tax	$	1,750,000
Foreign tax credit	−	1,625,000

Foreign withholding taxes: $375,000
Deemed paid taxes: $2,500,000 × [$3,750,000 ÷ $7,500,000] = $1,250,000
Creditable foreign taxes: [$375,000 + $1,250,000] = $1,625,000

General limitation: $1,750,000 × [$5,000,000 ÷ $5,000,000] = $1,750,000

U.S. income tax	$	125,000

Total taxes [$2,500,000 + $375,000 + $125,000] .... $ 3,000,000

Worldwide effective tax rate [$3,000,000 ÷ $10,000,000] 30%

Thus, by repatriating half of FORco's earnings through a dividend distribution, USAco increases the worldwide tax rate on FORco's earnings from 25% in Case 1 to 30% in Case 2. The 30% rate is a blended rate, whereby the $5 million of income that USAco recognizes by virtue of the dividend is, in effect, taxed one time at the U.S. rate of 35%, and FORco's remaining $5 million of earnings is taxed one time at the country L rate of 25%.

Case 3: Low-tax country/Pays dividend/No tax treaty. An important assumption in Case 2 is that country L had a tax treaty with the United States that provided for a 10% withholding tax rate on dividends. Now assume that there is no tax treaty between the United States and country L, and that country L's statutory withholding rate on dividends is 30%. The lack of a favorable treaty withholding rate increases the total tax rate on FORco's repatriated and unrepatriated earnings from 30% in Case 2 to 36.25% in Case 3, computed as follows.

Foreign income tax

FORco's taxable income	$	10,000,000
Country L income tax rate	×	25%
Country L income tax	$	2,500,000

Foreign withholding taxes on repatriated earnings

FORco's after-tax earnings [$10,000,000 − $2,500,000]	$	7,500,000
Percentage repatriated through dividend	×	50%
Dividend distribution	$	3,750,000
Withholding tax rate (per statute)	×	30%
Country L withholding tax	$	1,125,000

U.S. tax on repatriated earnings

Dividend from FORco	$	3,750,000
Code Sec. 78 gross-up	+	1,250,000
USAco's taxable income	$	5,000,000
U.S. tax rate	×	35%
Pre-credit U.S. tax	$	1,750,000
Foreign tax credit	−	1,750,000

  Foreign withholding taxes: $1,125,000
  Deemed paid taxes: $2,500,000 × [$3,750,000 ÷
   $7,500,000] = $1,250,000
  Creditable foreign taxes: [$1,125,000 + $1,250,000] =
   $2,375,000

  General limitation: $1,750,000 × [$5,000,000 ÷
   $5,000,000] = $1,750,000

U.S. income tax	$	0

Total taxes [$2,500,000 + $1,125,000 + $0]	$	3,625,000

Worldwide effective tax rate [$3,625,000 ÷ $10,000,000]		36.25%

Thus, assuming USAco repatriates some of FORco's earnings through a dividend distribution, the availability of a favorable treaty withholding rate on dividends is critical to the ability of USAco to obtain the benefits of lower tax rates abroad.

Case 4: High-tax country/No dividends. Country H has a corporate income tax rate of 45%, which is ten percentage points higher than the U.S. rate. If USAco locates FORco in country H and FORco pays no dividends, the total tax rate on its earnings will be 45%, computed as follows.

Foreign income tax
FORco's taxable income $10,000,000
Country H income tax rate . . . . ×   45%
Country H income tax . . . . $ 4,500,000

Foreign withholding taxes on repatriated earnings . . . . $ 0

U.S. tax on repatriated earnings . . . . $ 0

Total taxes [$4,500,000 + $0 + $0] . . . . $ 4,500,000

Worldwide effective tax rate [$4,500,000 ÷ $10,000,000] 45%

The 45% worldwide tax rate indicates that the total tax rate on USAco new manufacturing facility will exceed the U.S. tax rate of 35% if USAco locates the factory in H, a high-tax foreign country.

Case 5: High-tax country/Pays dividend/Tax treaty. Assume that country H has a tax treaty with the United States that provides a 10% withholding tax rate on dividends. If USAco locates FORco in country H and repatriates half of FORco's after-tax earnings through a dividend distribution, the total tax rate on its repatriated and unrepatriated earnings will be 47.75%, computed as follows.

Foreign income tax
FORco's taxable income . . . . $ 10,000,000
Country H income tax rate . . . . ×   45%
Country H income tax . . . . $ 4,500,000

Foreign withholding taxes on repatriated earnings
FORco's after-tax earnings [$10,000,000 − $4,500,000] . . . . . $ 5,500,000
Percentage repatriated through dividend . . . . ×   50%
Dividend distribution . . . . $ 2,750,000
Withholding tax rate (per treaty) . . . . ×   10%
Country H withholding tax . . . . $ 275,000

U.S. tax on repatriated earnings

Dividend from FORco	$	2,750,000
Code Sec. 78 gross-up	+	2,250,000
USAco's taxable income	$	5,000,000
U.S. tax rate	×	35%
Pre-credit U.S. tax	$	1,750,000
Foreign tax credit	−	1,750,000

    Foreign withholding taxes: $275,000
    Deemed paid taxes: $4,500,000 × [$2,750,000 ÷
      $5,500,000] = $2,250,000
    Creditable foreign taxes: [$275,000 + $2,250,000] =
      $2,525,000

    General limitation: $1,750,000 × [$5,000,000 ÷
      $5,000,000] = $1,750,000

U.S. income tax	$	0
Total taxes [$4,500,000 + $275,000 + $0]	$	4,775,000
Worldwide effective tax rate [$4,775,000 ÷ $10,000,000]		47.75%

By repatriating half of FORco's earnings through a dividend distribution, USAco increases the worldwide tax rate on FORco's earnings from 45% in Case 4 to 47.75% in Case 5. The foreign withholding tax on the dividend distribution is responsible for the increase in the total tax rate.

Case 6: High-tax country/Pays dividend/No tax treaty. A comparison of Cases 4 and 5 indicates that repatriating half of FORco's earnings through a dividend distribution increases the worldwide tax rate on FORco's earnings from 45% to 47.75%. Now assume that there is no tax treaty between the United States and country H, and that country H's statutory withholding rate on dividends is 30%. The lack of a favorable treaty withholding rate increases the total tax rate on FORco's repatriated and unrepatriated earnings from 47.75% in Case 5 to 53.25% in Case 6, computed as follows.

Foreign income tax

FORco's taxable income		$10,000,000
Country H income tax rate	×	45%
Country H income tax	$	4,500,000

Foreign withholding taxes on repatriated earnings

FORco's after-tax earnings [$10,000,000 − $4,500,000]	$	5,500,000
Percentage repatriated through dividend	×	50%
Dividend distribution	$	2,750,000
Withholding tax rate (per statute)	×	30%
Country H withholding tax	$	825,000

U.S. tax on repatriated earnings

Dividend from FORco	$ 2,750,000
Code Sec. 78 gross-up	+ 2,250,000
USAco's taxable income	$ 5,000,000
U.S. tax rate	× 35%
Pre-credit U.S. tax	$ 1,750,000
Foreign tax credit	− 1,750,000

> Foreign withholding taxes: $825,000
> Deemed paid taxes: $4,500,000 × [$2,750,000 ÷ $5,500,000]
> = $2,250,000
> Creditable foreign taxes: [$825,000 + $2,250,000] =
> $3,075,000
>
> General limitation: $1,750,000 × [$5,000,000 ÷ $5,000,000]
> = $1,750,000

U.S. income tax	$ 0
Total taxes [$4,500,000 + $825,000 + $0]	$ 5,325,000
Worldwide effective tax rate [$5,325,000 ÷ $10,000,000]	53.25%

Case 7: High-tax country/Earnings stripping/Tax treaty. If USAco locates FORco in country H, one strategy for reducing the excess credits on FORco's earnings is to engage in earnings stripping, that is, to repatriate FORco's profits through deductible interest, rental, and royalty payments, rather than nondeductible dividend distributions. For example, assume that USAco modifies its plans for FORco, as follows:

(i) finance FORco with both debt and equity, such that FORco will pay USAco $3 million of interest each year,

(ii) charge FORco an annual royalty of $2 million for the use of USAco's patents and trade secrets, and

(iii) eliminate FORco's dividend distribution.

Assume that the applicable tax treaty withholding rate is 0% for both interest and royalties.

As the following computations indicate, debt financing and charges for technology transfers reduces the total tax rate on country H earnings from 47.75% in Case 5 to 40%, computed as follows.

Foreign income tax

FORco's income before interest and royalties	$ 10,000,000
Interest paid to USAco	− 3,000,000
Royalties paid to USAco	− 2,000,000
FORco's taxable income	$ 5,000,000
Country H income tax rate	× 45%
Country H income tax	$ 2,250,000

Foreign withholding taxes on repatriated earnings

Withholding tax on interest (per treaty)	$	0
Withholding tax on royalties (per treaty)		0
Country H withholding taxes	$	0

U.S. tax on repatriated earnings

Interest from FORco.....................................	$	3,000,000
Royalties from FORco	+	2,000,000
USAco's taxable income	$	5,000,000
U.S. tax rate	×	35%
Pre-credit U.S. tax.....................................	$	1,750,000
Foreign tax credit	−	0

Foreign withholding taxes: $0
Deemed paid taxes: $0 (no dividends)

U.S. income tax	$	1,750,000

Total taxes [$2,250,000 + $0 + $1,750,000].................. $ 4,000,000

Worldwide effective tax rate [$4,000,000 ÷ $10,000,000]....... 40%

The 40% worldwide tax rate on the country H earnings is a blended rate, whereby the $5 million of interest and royalties paid to USAco are, in effect, taxed one time at the U.S. rate of 35%, and the $5 million of unrepatriated earnings is taxed one time at the country H rate of 45%. Thus, earnings stripping can be an effective method for reducing the worldwide tax rate on the earnings of a high-tax foreign subsidiary.

Case 8: Low-tax country/Earnings stripping/Tax treaty. In contrast to the benefits illustrated in Case 7, debt financing and charges for technology transfers will have no effect on FORco's total tax rate if FORco is located in country L (the low-tax country). As in Case 2, where FORco repatriated its earnings through dividend distributions, the worldwide tax rate on FORco's repatriated and unrepatriated earnings is 30%, computed as follows.

Foreign income tax

FORco's income before interest and royalties	$	10,000,000
Interest paid to USAco	−	3,000,000
Royalties paid to USAco	−	2,000,000
FORco's taxable income	$	5,000,000
Country L income tax rate	×	25%
Country L income tax..................................	$	1,250,000

Foreign withholding taxes on repatriated earnings

Withholding tax on interest (per treaty).................	$	0
Withholding tax on royalties (per treaty)		0
Country L withholding taxes	$	0

U.S. tax on repatriated earnings

Interest from FORco	$	3,000,000
Royalties from FORco	+	2,000,000
USAco's taxable income	$	5,000,000
U.S. tax rate	×	35%
Pre-credit U.S. tax	$	1,750,000
Foreign tax credit	−	0

Foreign withholding taxes: $0
Deemed paid taxes: $0 (no dividends)

U.S. income tax	$	1,750,000

Total taxes [$1,250,000 + $0 + $1,750,000]	$	3,000,000

Worldwide effective tax rate [$3,000,000 ÷ $10,000,000]	30%

Case 9: Low-tax country/No dividends/Hybrid entity. Country L has a corporate income tax rate of 25%, which is ten percentage points lower than the U.S. rate. Country L does not impose a branch profits tax. If USAco locates FORco in country L and checks-the-box treating FORco as a pass through entity, i.e., a branch, USAco is deemed to receive all of FORco's earnings even though FORco does not pay any dividends. The total tax rate on its earnings will be 35%, computed as follows.

Foreign income tax

FORco's taxable income	$	10,000,000
Country L income tax rate	×	25%
Country L income tax	$	2,500,000

Foreign withholding taxes on repatriated earnings	$	0

U.S. tax on repatriated earnings

Earnings from FORco	$	10,000,000
U.S. tax rate	×	35%
Pre-credit U.S. tax	$	3,500,000
Foreign tax credit	−	2,500,000
U.S. income tax	$	1,000,000

Total taxes [$2,500,000 + $0 + $1,000,000]	$	3,500,000

Worldwide effective tax rate [$3,500,000 ÷ $10,000,000]	35%

This example illustrates that USAco cannot reduce the current year worldwide tax on the new manufacturing facility below the U.S. tax rate of 35% by locating the factory in L, and checking the box for hybrid status for FORco in country L. By forming a hybrid in country

L, a low tax country, USAco actually loses the opportunity to defer paying U.S. tax.

Case 10: Low-tax country/No dividends/Reverse hybrid entity. Country L has a corporate income tax rate of 25%, which is ten percentage points lower than the U.S. rate. Country L does not impose a branch profits tax. USAco owns FORlp, a limited partnership in country L and checks-the-box for corporate treatment. USAco is not deemed to receive any income because FORco is not treated as a pass through entity. The total tax rate on its earnings will be 25%, computed as follows.

Foreign income tax
FORlp's taxable income . . . . $ 10,000,000
Country L income tax rate . . . . ×   25%

Country L income tax. . . . . $ 2,500,000

Foreign withholding taxes on repatriated earnings . . . . $ 0

U.S. tax on repatriated earnings. . . . . $ 0

Total taxes [$2,500,000 + $0 + $0] . . . . $ 2,500,000

Worldwide effective tax rate [$2,500,000 ÷ $10,000,000] 25%

This example illustrates how USAco can reduce the current year worldwide tax rate on the new manufacturing facility below the U.S. tax rate of 35% by locating the factory in L, and checking the box for reverse hybrid status for FORlp in country L, a low-tax foreign country. By creating a reverse hybrid entity, USAco can control the time of reporting earnings on its U.S. return.

Case 11: High-tax country/No dividends/Hybrid entity. Country H has a corporate income tax rate of 45%, which is ten percentage points higher than the U.S. rate. Country H does not impose a branch profits tax. If USAco locates FORco in country H and checks-the-box treating FORco as a pass through entity, i.e., a branch, USAco is deemed to receive all of FORco's earnings even though FORco does not pay any dividends. The total tax rate on its earnings will be 45%, computed as follows.

Foreign income tax
FORco's taxable income . . . . $ 10,000,000
Country H income tax rate . . . . ×   45%

Country H income tax . . . . $ 4,500,000

Foreign withholding taxes on repatriated earnings. . . . . $ 0

U.S. tax on repatriated earnings

Earnings from FORco	$	10,000,000
U.S. tax rate	×	35%
Pre-credit U.S. tax	$	3,500,000
Foreign tax credit	−	3,500,000

   Creditable foreign taxes: = $4,500,000

   General limitation: $3,500,000 × [$10,000,000 ÷ $10,000,000] = $3,500,000

U.S. income tax	$	0

Total taxes [$4,500,000 + $0 + $0] .... $ 4,500,000

Worldwide effective tax rate [$4,500,000 ÷ $10,000,000]....... 45%

This example illustrates that if USAco locates the factory in H, a high-tax foreign country, the 45% worldwide tax rate on USAco new manufacturing facility will exceed the U.S. tax rate of 35%.

Case 12: High-tax country/No dividends/Reverse hybrid entity. USAco owns FORlp, a limited partnership in country H, which has an income tax rate of 45%, and checks-the-box for corporate treatment. Country H does not impose a branch profits tax. USAco is not deemed to receive any income because FORlp does not make any distributions. The total tax rate on its earnings will be 45%, computed as follows.

Foreign income tax

FORlp's taxable income	$	10,000,000
Country H income tax rate	×	45%
Country H income tax	$	4,500,000

Foreign withholding taxes on repatriated earnings.......... $ 0

U.S. tax on repatriated earnings........ $ 0

Total taxes [$4,500,000 + $0 + $0]..... $ 4,500,000

Worldwide effective tax rate [$4,500,000 ÷ $10,000,000]...... 45%

This example illustrates that regardless of the choice of entity in country H, USAco cannot reduce the current year worldwide tax rate on the new manufacturing facility below the country H tax rate of 45% by locating the factory in country H. However, by creating a reverse hybrid entity, USAco can control the time of reporting foreign earnings on its U.S. return.

Summary. Table 10.5 summarizes the results of the twelve case scenarios described above.

TABLE 10.5. COMPREHENSIVE EXAMPLE—SUMMARY

Case	U.S. tax rate	Host country tax rate	Percentage of earnings repatriated	Method of repatriating earnings	Foreign withholding tax rate	Current year worldwide effective tax rate
1	35%	25%	None	n.a.	n.a.	25%
2	35%	25%	50%	Dividend	10%	30%
3	35%	25%	50%	Dividend	30%	36.25%
4	35%	45%	None	n.a.	n.a.	45%
5	35%	45%	50%	Dividend	10%	47.75%
6	35%	45%	50%	Dividend	30%	53.25%
7	35%	45%	50%	Interest and royalties	0%	40%
8	35%	25%	50%	Interest and royalties	0%	30%
9	35%	25%	100%	Pass-through	n.a.	35%
10	35%	25%	None	n.a.	n.a.	25%
11	35%	45%	100%	Pass-through	n.a.	45%
12	35%	45%	None	n.a.	n.a.	45%

¶ 1007   FINANCIAL REPORTING IMPLICATIONS OF INTERNATIONAL TAX PLANNING

The globalization of U.S. business has increased the importance of understanding how a U.S. multinational corporation's foreign operations impact the effective tax rate it reports in its financial statements. Virtually all countries tax the income of corporations, and therefore the profits of a U.S. multinational corporation are typically subject to income taxation in a number of countries. A firm's worldwide effective tax rate provides a convenient metric for capturing the cumulative effect of these various income taxes on the corporation's profitability. For financial reporting purposes, a firm's effective tax rate is computed by dividing its total income tax expense by its pre-tax earnings. For example, if the sum of a U.S. corporation's federal, state and foreign income taxes is $100 million, and its pre-tax earnings is $300 million, the company has an effective tax rate of 33 percent.

When evaluating a U.S. corporation's effective tax rate, the de facto benchmark is the U.S. statutory rate. For large U.S. corporations, the statutory tax rate has been 35 percent since 1993.[46] However, a U.S. company's foreign operations can cause its effective tax rate to diverge from 35 percent. For example, operations in high-tax foreign jurisdictions can give rise to excess foreign tax credits that increase a firm's effective tax rate. Likewise, operations in low-tax foreign jurisdictions can reduce a firm's reported effective tax rate if management intends to permanently reinvest those earnings. Finally, a FSC allows a U.S. exporter to permanently exclude from U.S. tax a portion of the net

---

[46] Code Sec. 11.

profits from qualifying export sales, which reduces the firm's effective tax rate.

Operations in High Tax Foreign Jurisdictions

Corporate income tax rates exceed the U.S. statutory rate of 35 percent in a number of foreign jurisdictions, such as Canada, France, Germany, Italy and Japan. The foreign tax credit limitation prevents U.S. companies operating in such jurisdictions from claiming a credit for foreign taxes in excess of the U.S. statutory tax rate. These excess credits can increase the total tax burden on a U.S. company's foreign earnings beyond what it would have been if only the United States had taxed the income. Excess credits can be carried back up to two years and carried forward up to five years, and taken as a credit in a year that the limitation exceeds the amount of creditable foreign taxes.[47] Therefore, excess credits increase the reported effective tax rate only to the extent they cannot be utilized in one of the carryback or carryforward years.[48] The financial statements of U.S. oil companies illustrate the impact of excess credits on the effective tax rate of a U.S. multinational corporation. For example, in its 1998 annual report, Mobil Oil Corporation reported an effective tax rate of 44.3% on its worldwide earnings. Oil-producing countries often impose special taxes the profits of oil companies. For example, U.S. oil companies derive significant profits from operations in Norway, and Norway imposes a special 50 percent petroleum tax in addition to its general corporate income tax of 28 percent.

Operations in Low Tax Foreign Jurisdictions

There are also a number of foreign jurisdictions that offer corporate income tax rates that are lower than the U.S. statutory rate of 35 percent, such as Bermuda, Hong Kong, Singapore and Switzerland. Other countries have statutory rates comparable to the U.S. rate, but offer special tax breaks to U.S. multinational corporations that locate new facilities within their borders. For example, Belgium offers special tax incentives to U.S. multinationals that locate a distribution, service or coordination center in Belgium. Likewise, Ireland offers a ten percent rate to U.S. multinational companies that locate new manufacturing operations in Ireland. Because the U.S. generally does not tax the foreign profits of a foreign subsidiary until those earnings are remitted

---

[47] Code Sec. 905.

[48] If a company carries back its excess credits, it obtains an immediate tax benefit that is reflected in a lower current year income tax expense. The current year income tax expense is also reduced if the firm expects to use its excess credits in a carryforward year, in which case the firm establishes a deferred tax asset for the expected future tax benefit of the carryforward. Statement of Financial Accounting Standards No. 109, *Accounting for Income Taxes* (Financial Accounting Standards Board, 1992).

to the U.S. parent as a dividend, it is possible to defer payment of the "residual" U.S. tax on low-tax foreign earnings.

For financial reporting purposes, it is presumed that the U.S. parent will eventually repatriate all of a foreign subsidiary's undistributed earnings,[49] in which case the tax savings associated with deferral are accounted for as a temporary difference that has no effect on the firm's reported effective tax rate. However, if sufficient evidence shows that the firm has or will reinvest undistributed foreign earnings "indefinitely," it is not necessary to include the residual U.S tax on undistributed low-tax foreign earnings in the current year's income tax expense. This exception provides U.S. corporations with the ability to treat the benefit of operating in a low-tax foreign jurisdiction as a permanent difference that reduces both the income tax expense and the reported effective tax rate. The possessions credit, which is being currently being phased out over a ten-year period ending in 2005, has also historically provided a statutory mechanism for obtaining a financial statement benefit from low-tax foreign earnings.

The financial statements of U.S. pharmaceutical companies illustrate the impact of operations in low-tax jurisdiction on the effective tax rate of a U.S. multinational corporation. Unlike oil companies, drug companies have some flexibility in terms of where they can locate production activities. The effective tax rates of these pharmaceutical firms indicate that they are taking advantage of this flexibility by locating operations in low-tax foreign jurisdictions. For example, in its 1998 annual report, Pfizer, Inc. reported an effective tax rate of 24.8% on its worldwide earnings. The 10.2 percentage point reduction from the benchmark U.S. statutory rate was attributed to operations in low tax foreign countries, including Puerto Rico.

FSC Benefit

Finally, the foreign sales corporation provisions provides a basis for permanently excluding a pre-specified portion of a FSC's profits from U.S. tax. In addition, because a FSC is normally located in foreign countries that do not tax corporate income, such as Bermuda, the total tax burden on FSC income usually reduces the effective tax rate below 35%. Given the requirements for obtaining the FSC benefit, the major beneficiaries of this tax break are U.S. manufacturers with significant export sales. For example, in its 1998 annual report, Caterpillar Corporation reported an effective tax rate of 30.6% on its worldwide earnings. The reduction from the benchmark U.S. statutory rate was attributable primarily to the tax savings associated FSC benefit.

---

[49] Accounting Principles Board Opinion No. 23, *Accounting for Income Taxes—Special Areas* (1972).

¶ 1008   SURVEY OF FOREIGN ENTITY CLASSIFICATION

This survey (Tables 10.6, 10.7 and 10.8) lists entities in selected foreign countries, discusses whether the foreign country imposes an entity level tax, describes the treatment for U.S. tax purposes if an election is not made (whether the entity is a per se corporation or has default status as a corporation or flow through entity), and considers the possibility for treatment as a hybrid or reverse hybrid entity. In each listed country, U.S. owners may operate as a sole proprietorship or a branch, which is not treated as a separate entity under the check-the-box rules.

For example, in Hong Kong, the principle business forms are limited liability companies, whether referred to as public or private, partnerships and limited partnerships, branches of foreign companies, and sole proprietors. A public limited liability company is easy to classify because it is the only Hong Kong entity on the per se list.[50] Therefore, the shareholders of a public limited liability company must treat it as a corporation for U.S. tax purposes. As a public limited liability company, it must pay a corporate tax in Hong Kong,[51] and offers minimal planning opportunities.

A private limited liability company is an entity whose creditors are limited to pursuit of the company's assets.[52] As a result, the default rules treat the private limited liability company as a corporation. However, because the private limited liability company pays a Hong Kong corporate income tax,[53] it presents hybrid tax planning opportunities if its shareholders elect partnership or branch classification for U.S. purposes. The failure to elect will result in the default rules limiting planning opportunities.

Hong Kong law provides for both partnerships and limited partnerships. Under common law, a partnership constitutes a separate entity.[54] Since each partner is liable for all the debts and obligations of the partnership, the default rules treat the entity as a partnership for U.S. purposes. Similarly, the default rules also treat a Hong Kong limited partnership as a partnership because one or more partners have unlimited liability. Since Hong Kong taxes a partner's share of partnership income only once,[55] a reverse hybrid entity planning opportunity exists if the partnership's partners elect corporate classification for U.S. purposes. Failure to elect corporate status will result in a loss of this opportunity through partnership classification in both countries.

---

[50] Reg. § 301.7701-2(b)(8); Table 10.3.

[51] Chapter 112, Laws of Hong Kong, Section 41.

[52] Chapter 32, Laws of Hong Kong, Section 4(2)(a).

[53] chapter 112, Laws of Hong Kong, Section 45.

[54] Chapter 112, Laws of Hong Kong, Section 22(1).

[55] Chapter 112, Laws of Hong Kong, Section 22(1).

TABLE 10.6. CLASSIFICATION OF ENTITIES IN ASEAN COUNTRIES

	Foreign country tax	Status without checking-the-box election	Hybrid or reverse hybrid opportunity
Australia			
Public limited liability company	Yes	Per Se Corp	– – – –
Private limited liability company	Yes	Corporation	Hybrid
Partnership	No	Pass-through	Reverse
Hong Kong			
Public limited liability company	Yes	Per Se Corp	– – – –
Private limited liability company	Yes	Corporation	Hybrid
Partnerships	No	Pass-through	Reverse
Limited partnerships	No	Pass-through	Reverse
Japan			
Corporation (Kabushiki Kaisha)	Yes	Per Se Corp	– – – –
Limited liability company (Yugen Kaisha)	Yes	Corporation	Hybrid
Unlimited liability partnership company (Gomei Kaisha)	Yes	Pass-through	Hybrid
Limited liability partnership company (Goshi Kaisha)	Yes	Pass-through	Hybrid
Korea			
Stock corporation (chusik hoesa)	Yes	Per Se Corp	– – – –
Limited liability company (yuhan hoesa)	Yes	Corporation	Hybrid
Unlimited membership enterprise (hapmyong hoesa)	No	Pass-through	Reverse
Limited partnership (hapja hoesa)	No	Pass-through	Reverse
Singapore			
Private limited company	Yes	Corporation	Hybrid
Public limited company	Yes	Per Se Corp	– – – –

¶ **1008**

TABLE 10.7. CLASSIFICATION OF ENTITIES IN EUROPE

	Foreign country tax	Status without checking-the-box election	Hybrid or reverse hybrid opportunity
European Union			
European Economic Interest Grouping (EEIG)	No	Pass-through	Reverse
France			
Joint stock company "SA" (societe anonyme)	Yes	Per Se Corp	– – – –
Limited liability company "SARL" (societe a responsabilite limitee)	Yes	Corporation	Hybrid
Simplified limited liability company "SAS" (societe par actions simplifiee)	Yes	Corporation	Hybrid
General partnership "SNC" (societe en nom collectif)	No	Pass-through	Reverse
Limited partnership "SCS" (societe en commandite simple)	No	Pass-through	Reverse
Partnership limited by shares "SCPA" (societe en commandite par actions)	No	Pass-through	Reverse
Germany			
Limited liability company "GmbH" (Gesellschaft mit beschrankter Haftung)	Yes	Corporation	Hybrid
Stock corporation "AG" (Aktiengesellschaft)	Yes	Per Se Corp	– – – –
General commercial partnership "OHG" (Handelsgesellschaft)	No	Pass-through	Reverse
Limited partnership "KG" (Kommanditgesellschaft)	No	Pass-through	Reverse
Limited partnership with Transferable shares "KgaA" (Kommanditgesellschaft auf Aktien)	No	Pass-through	Reverse
Civil law partnership "GbR" (Gesellschaft burgerlichen Rechts)	No	Pass-through	Reverse
Silent partnership (Stile Gesellschaft)	No	Pass-through	Reverse

¶ 1008

TABLE 10.7. CLASSIFICATION OF ENTITIES IN EUROPE (CONTINUED)

	Foreign country tax	Status without checking-the-box election	Hybrid or reverse hybrid opportunity
Italy			
Corporation "SpA" (Societa per Azioni)	Yes	Per Se Corp	– – – –
Limited liability company "SRL" (Societa a Responsabilita Limitata)	Yes	Corporation	Hybrid
General partnership "SNC" (Societa in Nome Collettivo)	No	Pass-through	Reverse
Limited partnership "Sas" (Societa in Accomandita Semplice)	No	Pass-through	Reverse
Limited share partnership "SapA" (Societa in Accomandita per Azioni)	No	Pass-through	Reverse
The Netherlands			
Private limited liability company "BV" (Besloten Vennootschap Mat Beperkte Aansprakelijkheid)	Yes	Corporation	Hybrid
Public limited liability company "NV" (Naamlooze Vennootschap)	Yes	Per Se Corp	– – – –
General partnership "VOF" (Vennootschap Onder Firma)	No	Pass-through	Reverse
Limited partnership "CV" (Commanditaire Vennootschap)	No	Pass-through	Reverse
Switzerland			
Corporation "SA" (Societe Annonyme)	Yes	Per Se Corp	– – – –
Limited liability company "Sarl" (Societe a Responsabilite Limitee)	Yes	Corporation	Hybrid
General partnership (Societe en nom Collectif)	No	Pass-through	Reverse
Limited partnership (Societe en Commandite)	No	Pass-through	Reverse
The United Kingdom			
Private limited company	Yes	Corporation	Hybrid
Public limited company	Yes	Per Se Corp	– – – –
Partnership	No	Flow Through	Reverse
Limited partnership	No	Flow Through	Reverse

¶ 1008

TABLE 10.8. CLASSIFICATION OF ENTITIES IN NORTH AMERICA

	Foreign country tax	Status without checking-the-box election	Hybrid or reverse hybrid opportunity
Canada			
Corporation (federal and provincial)	Yes	Per Se Corp	– – – –
Nova Scotia Unlimited Liability Company (NSULC)	Yes	Corporation	Hybrid
General partnership	No	Pass-through	Reverse
Limited partnership	No	Pass-through	Reverse
Mexico			
Corporation with fixed capital (sociedad anomima)	Yes	Per Se Corp	– – – –
Corporation with variable capital (sociedad anomima de capital variable)	No	Per Se Corp	– – – –
Limited liability company (sociedad responsabilidad limitada)	Yes	Corporation	Hybrid
General partnerships (sociedad en nombre colectivo)	No	Pass-through	Reverse
Limited partnership with shares (sociedad en comandita simple)	No	Pass-through	Reverse
Limited partnership without shares (sociedad en comandita por acciones)	No	Pass-through	Reverse
Joint ventures (asociacion en participacion)	No	Pass-through	Reverse

¶ 1009   APPENDIX

Form **8832**
(December 1996)
Department of the Treasury
Internal Revenue Service

Entity Classification Election

OMB No. 1545-1516

Name of entity	**Employer identification number (EIN)**

Please Type or Print

Number, street, and room or suite no. If a P.O. box, see instructions.

City or town, state, and ZIP code. If a foreign address, enter city, province or state, postal code and country.

1   Type of election (see instructions):

a ☐ Initial classification by a newly-formed entity (or change in current classification of an existing entity to take effect on January 1, 1997)

b ☐ Change in current classification (to take effect later than January 1, 1997)

2   Form of entity (see instructions):

a ☐ A domestic eligible entity electing to be classified as an association taxable as a corporation.

b ☐ A domestic eligible entity electing to be classified as a partnership.

c ☐ A domestic eligible entity with a single owner electing to be disregarded as a separate entity.

d ☐ A foreign eligible entity electing to be classified as an association taxable as a corporation.

e ☐ A foreign eligible entity electing to be classified as a partnership.

f ☐ A foreign eligible entity with a single owner electing to be disregarded as a separate entity.

3   Election is to be effective beginning (month, day, year) (see instructions) . . . . ▶ ____ / ____ / ____

4 Name and title of person whom the IRS may call for more information	**5** That person's telephone number

Consent Statement and Signature(s) (see instructions)

Under penalties of perjury, I (we) declare that I (we) consent to the election of the above-named entity to be classified as indicated above, and that I (we) have examined this consent statement, and to the best of my (our) knowledge and belief, it is true, correct, and complete. If I am an officer, manager, or member signing for all members of the entity, I further declare that I am authorized to execute this consent statement on their behalf.

Signature(s)	Date	Title

For Paperwork Reduction Act Notice, see page 2.   Cat. No. 22598R   Form **8832** (12-96)

General Instructions

Section references are to the Internal Revenue Code unless otherwise noted.

Paperwork Reduction Act Notice

We ask for the information on this form to carry out the Internal Revenue laws of the United States. You are required to give us the information. We need it to ensure that you are complying with these laws and to allow us to figure and collect the right amount of tax.

You are not required to provide the information requested on a form that is subject to the Paperwork Reduction Act unless the form displays a valid OMB control number. Books or records relating to a form or its instructions must be retained as long as their contents may become material in the administration of any Internal Revenue law. Generally, tax returns and return information are confidential, as required by section 6103.

The time needed to complete and file this form will vary depending on individual circumstances. The estimated average time is:

Recordkeeping . . .1 hr., 20 min.
Learning about the law or the form . . .1 hr., 41 min.
Preparing and sending the form to the IRS . . . .17 min.

If you have comments concerning the accuracy of these time estimates or suggestions for making this form simpler, we would be happy to hear from you. You can write to the Tax Forms Committee, Western Area Distribution Center, Rancho Cordova, CA 95743-0001. **DO NOT** send the form to this address. Instead, see **Where To File** on page 3.

Purpose of Form

For Federal tax purposes, certain business entities automatically are classified as corporations. See items **1** and **3** through **8** under the definition of corporation on this page. Other business entities may choose how they are classified for Federal tax purposes. Except for a business entity automatically classified as a corporation, a business entity with at least two members can choose to be classified as either an association taxable as a corporation or a partnership, and a business entity with a single member can choose to be classified as either an association taxable as a corporation or disregarded as an entity separate from its owner.

Generally, an eligible entity that does not file this form will be classified under the default rules described below. An eligible entity that chooses not to be classified under the default rules or that wishes to change its current classification must file Form 8832 to elect a classification. The IRS will use the information entered on this form to establish the entity's filing and reporting requirements for Federal tax purposes.

Default Rules

Existing entity default rule.— Certain domestic and foreign entities that are already in existence before January 1, 1997, and have an established Federal tax classification, generally do not need to make an election to continue that classification. However, for an eligible entity with a single owner that claimed to be a partnership under the law in effect before January 1, 1997, that entity will now be disregarded as an entity separate from its owner. If an existing entity decides to change its classification, it may do so subject to the rules in Regulations section 301.7701-3(c)(1)(iv). A foreign eligible entity is treated as being in existence prior to the effective date of this section only if the entity's classification is relevant at any time during the 60 months prior to January 1, 1997.

Domestic default rule.— Unless an election is made on Form 8832, a domestic eligible entity is:

1. A partnership if it has two or more members.

2. Disregarded as an entity separate from its owner if it has a single owner.

Foreign default rule.— Unless an election is made on Form 8832, a foreign eligible entity is:

1. A partnership if it has two or more members and at least one member does not have limited liability.

2. An association if all members have limited liability.

3. Disregarded as an entity separate from its owner if it has a single owner that does not have limited liability.

Definitions

Business entity.— A business entity is any entity recognized for Federal tax purposes that is not properly classified as a trust under Regulations section 301.7701-4 or otherwise subject to special treatment under the Code. See Regulations section 301.7701-2(a).

Corporation.— For Federal tax purposes, a corporation is any of the following:

1. A business entity organized under a Federal or state statute, or under a statute of a federally recognized Indian tribe, if the statute describes or refers to the entity as incorporated or as a corporation, body corporate, or body politic.

2. An association (as determined under Regulations section 301.7701-3).

3. A business entity organized under a state statute, if the statute describes or refers to the entity as a joint-stock company or joint-stock association.

4. An insurance company.

5. A state-chartered business entity conducting banking activities, if any of its deposits are insured under the Federal Deposit Insurance Act, as amended, 12 U.S.C. 1811 et seq., or a similar Federal statute.

6. A business entity wholly owned by a state or any political subdivision thereof.

7. A business entity that is taxable as a corporation under a provision of the Code other than section 7701(a)(3).

8. A foreign business entity listed in Regulations section 301.7701-2(b)(8). However, a foreign business entity listed in those regulations generally will not be treated as a corporation if all of the following apply:

a. The entity was in existence on May 8, 1996.

Form 8832 (12-96)   Page **3**

b. The entity's classification was relevant (as defined below) on May 8, 1996.

c. No person (including the entity) for whom the entity's classification was relevant on May 8, 1996, treats the entity as a corporation for purposes of filing that person's Federal income tax returns, information returns, and withholding documents for the tax year including May 8, 1996.

d. Any change in the entity's claimed classification within the 60 months prior to May 8, 1996, was a result of a change in the organizational documents of the entity, and the entity and all members of the entity recognized the Federal tax consequences of any change in the entity's classification within the 60 months prior to May 8, 1996.

e. The entity had a reasonable basis (within the meaning of section 6662) for treating the entity as other than a corporation on May 8, 1996.

f. Neither the entity nor any member was notified in writing on or before May 8, 1996, that the classification of the entity was under examination (in which case the entity's classification will be determined in the examination).

Binding contract rule.—If a foreign business entity described in Regulations section 301.7701-2(b)(8)(i) is formed after May 8, 1996, under a written binding contract (including an accepted bid to develop a project) in effect on May 8, 1996, and at all times thereafter, in which the parties agreed to engage (directly or indirectly) in an active and substantial business operation in the jurisdiction in which the entity is formed, **8** on page 2 is applied by substituting the date of the entity's formation for May 8, 1996.

Eligible entity.—An eligible entity is a business entity that is not included in items **1** or **3** through **8** under the definition of corporation on page 2.

Limited liability.—A member of a foreign eligible entity has limited liability if the member has no personal liability for any debts of or claims against the entity by reason of being a member. This determination is based solely on the statute or law under which the entity is organized (and, if relevant, the entity's organizational documents). A member has personal liability if the creditors of the entity may seek satisfaction of all or any part of the debts or claims against the entity from the member as such. A member has personal liability even if the member makes an agreement under which another person (whether or not a member of the entity) assumes that liability or agrees to indemnify that member for that liability.

Partnership.—A partnership is a business entity that has **at least** two members and is not a corporation as defined on page 2.

Relevant.—A foreign eligible entity's classification is relevant when its classification affects the liability of any person for Federal tax or information purposes. The date the classification of a foreign eligible entity is relevant is the date an event occurs that creates an obligation to file a Federal tax return, information return, or statement for which the classification of the entity must be determined.

Effect of Election

The resulting tax consequences of a change in classification remain the same no matter how a change in entity classification is achieved. For example, if an organization classified as an association elects to be classified as a partnership, the organization and its owners must recognize gain, if any, under the rules applicable to liquidations of corporations.

Who Must File

File this form for an **eligible entity** that is one of the following:

● A domestic entity electing to be classified as an association taxable as a corporation.

● A domestic entity electing to change its current classification (even if it is currently classified under the default rule).

● A foreign entity that has more than one owner, all owners have limited liability, and it elects to be classified as a partnership.

● A foreign entity that has at least one owner without limited liability, and it elects to be classified as an association taxable as a corporation.

● A foreign entity with a single owner having limited liability, and it elects to have the entity disregarded as an entity separate from its owner.

● A foreign entity electing to change its current classification (even if it is currently classified under the default rule).

Do not file this form for an eligible entity that is:

● Tax-exempt under section 501(a), or

● A real estate investment trust (REIT), as defined in section 856.

When To File

See the instructions for line 3.

Where To File

File Form 8832 with the Internal Revenue Service Center, Philadelphia, PA 19255. Also attach a copy of Form 8832 to the entity's Federal income tax or information return for the tax year of the election. If the entity is not required to file a return for that year, a copy of its Form 8832 must be attached to the Federal income tax or information returns of all direct or indirect owners of the entity for the tax year of the owner that includes the date on which the election took effect. Although failure to attach a copy will not invalidate an otherwise valid election, each member of the entity is required to file returns that are consistent with the entity's election. In addition, penalties may be assessed against persons who are required to, but who do not, attach Form 8832 to their returns. Other penalties may apply for filing Federal income tax or information returns inconsistent with the entity's election.

Specific Instructions

Employer Identification Number (EIN)

Show the correct EIN on Form 8832. If the entity does not have an EIN, it generally must apply for one on **Form SS-4,** Application for Employer Identification Number. If the filing of Form 8832 is the only reason the entity is applying for an EIN, check the "Other" box on line 9 of Form SS-4 and write "Form 8832" to the right of that box. If the entity has not received an EIN by the time Form 8832 is due, write "Applied for" in the space for the EIN. **Do not** apply for a new EIN for an existing entity that is changing its classification. If you are electing to disregard an entity as separate from its owner, enter the owner's EIN.

Address

Include the suite, room, or other unit number after the street address. If the Post Office does not deliver mail to the street address and the entity has a P.O. box, show the box number instead of the street address.

Line 1

Check box 1a if the entity is choosing a classification for the first time **and** the entity does not want to be classified under the applicable default classification. **Do not** file this form if the entity wants to be classified under the default rules.

Check box 1b if the entity is changing its current classification to take effect later than January 1, 1997, whether or not the entity's current classification is the default classification. However, once an eligible entity makes an election to change its classification (other than an election made by an existing entity to change its classification as of January 1, 1997), the entity cannot change its classification by election again during the 60 months after the effective date of the election. However, the IRS may permit (by private letter ruling) the entity to change its classification by election within the 60-month period if more than 50% of the ownership interests in the entity as of the effective date of the election are owned by persons that did not own any interests in the entity on the effective date of the entity's prior election.

Line 2

Check the appropriate box if you are changing a current classification (no matter how achieved), or are electing out of a default classification. **Do not** file this form if you fall within a default classification that is the desired classification for the new entity.

Line 3

Generally, the election will take effect on the date you enter on line 3 of this form or on the date filed if no date is entered on line 3. However, an election specifying an entity's classification for Federal tax purposes can take effect no more than 75 days prior to the date the election is filed, nor can it take effect later than 12 months after the date on which the election is filed. If line 3 shows a date more than 75 days prior to the date on which the election is filed, the election will take effect 75 days before the date it is filed. If line 3 shows an effective date more than 12 months from the filing date, the election will take effect 12 months after the date the election was filed.

Regardless of the date filed, an election will in no event take effect before January 1, 1997.

Consent Statement and Signatures

Form 8832 must be signed by:

1. Each member of the electing entity who is an owner at the time the election is filed; or

2. Any officer, manager, or member of the electing entity who is authorized (under local law or the organizational documents) to make the election and who represents to having such authorization under penalties of perjury.

If an election is to be effective for any period prior to the time it is filed, each person who was an owner between the date the election is to be effective and the date the election is filed, and who is not an owner at the time the election is filed, must also sign.

If you need a continuation sheet or use a separate consent statement, attach it to Form 8832. The separate consent statement must contain the same information as shown on Form 8832.

Chapter 11

Foreign Persons Investing in the United States

¶ 1101   U.S. SYSTEM FOR TAXING FOREIGN PERSONS

Overview

U.S. tax law contains the following two-pronged territorial system for taxing the U.S.-source income of nonresident alien individuals and foreign corporations:

(i)   *U.S. trade or business profits*—If a nonresident alien individual or foreign corporation is engaged in a trade or business within the United States, the net amount of income effectively connected with the conduct of that U.S. trade or business is taxed at the regular graduated rates.[1]

(ii)   *U.S.-source nonbusiness income*—If a nonresident alien individual or foreign corporation derives nonbusiness (or investment-type) income from sources within the United States, the gross amount of that income is taxed at a flat rate of 30%.[2] In addition, the person controlling the payment of the income must deduct and withhold U.S. tax at the 30% rate.[3]

---

[1] Code Secs. 871(b) and 882(a).
[2] Code Secs. 871(a) and 881(a).

[3] Code Secs. 1441(a) and 1442(a).

There are several major exceptions to the general rules for taxing foreign persons. For example, income tax treaties usually reduce the withholding tax rate on U.S.-source interest, dividend, and royalty income from the statutory rate of 30% to 15% or less. In addition, the United States generally exempts from taxation portfolio interest income.[4] Capital gains also are generally exempt from U.S. taxation,[5] except for gains on the sale of U.S. real property interests, which are taxed in the same manner as income effectively connected with the conduct of a U.S. trade or business.[6] Finally, U.S. branch operations are subject to the branch profits tax and the tax on excess interest.[7]

Chapter 11 discusses the U.S. system for taxing the U.S.-source nonbusiness income of foreign persons, and Chapter 12 discusses the U.S. system for taxing a foreign person's income effectively connected with the conduct of a U.S. trade or business.

Impact of U.S. Taxes on Total Tax Costs

The effect of U.S. taxation on a foreign person's total tax costs depends on the type of system which the taxpayer's home country employs to mitigate international double taxation. For example, if a foreign person is a citizen or resident of a country that employs a territorial system, then the full amount of any U.S. taxes imposed on the taxpayer's U.S.-source income represents an out-of-pocket cost. In such situations, the foreign person's objective will be to minimize U.S. taxes, since every dollar of U.S. taxes saved reduces the taxpayer's total tax costs by a dollar. On the other hand, if a foreign person is a citizen or resident of a country that employs a credit system, then the taxpayer's U.S. tax costs may be either partially or fully offset by the tax savings associated with the home country credit.

> **Example 11.1:** FORco, a foreign corporation, has a branch sales office in the United States. During the current year, FORco's effectively connected income is $100 (all numbers in thousands). FORco's home country allows it to claim a credit for the U.S. taxes paid on its U.S.-source income. Assuming the U.S. corporate tax rate is 35% and FORco's home country rate is 40%, FORco can claim a credit for all of its U.S. income taxes, as follows.

---

[4] Code Secs. 871(h) and 881(c).
[5] Reg. § 1.1441-2(a)(3).

[6] Code Sec. 897(a)(1).
[7] Code Sec. 884.

Home country tax return	
Taxable income	$100
Tax rate	× .40
Pre-credit tax	$ 40
Credit	− 35
Tax	$ 5

U.S. tax return	
Taxable income	$100
U.S. tax rate	× .35
U.S. tax	$ 35

U.S. taxes do not represent an out-of-pocket tax cost in this case. For example, if FORco were able to reduce its U.S. tax from $35 to $34, the U.S. tax savings would be completely offset by an increase in home country taxes from $5 to $6.

In such situations, the foreign person's objective may not be to minimize U.S. taxes, but rather to maintain those taxes at a level which allows a full credit for home country tax purposes.

¶1102 WITHHOLDING ON U.S.-SOURCE NONBUSINESS INCOME

Introduction

The United States taxes the gross amount of a foreign person's U.S.-source nonbusiness (or investment-type) income at a flat rate of 30%.[8] In addition, the person controlling the payment of the income must deduct and withhold U.S. tax at the 30% rate.[9] Thus, once the appropriate amount of U.S. taxes is withheld, a passive foreign investor generally has no further U.S. tax obligations. Withholding is required because it is the only sure way to collect taxes from passive offshore investors. In order to withhold, the withholding agent must be able to readily ascertain both the tax base and the applicable tax rate. This explains both the gross basis taxation and the use of a flat tax rate since the U.S. withholding agent may have no way of determining a foreign person's allocable expenses and appropriate tax bracket based on worldwide income.

General Rules

Persons subject to withholding. The following types of persons are subject to U.S. withholding taxes:

    (i)   nonresident alien individuals,

    (ii) foreign corporations,

    (iii) foreign partnerships, and

---

[8] Code Secs. 871(a) and 881(a).   [9] Code Secs. 1441(a) and 1442(a).

(iv) foreign estates and trusts.[10]

A nonresident alien is an individual who is neither a citizen nor a resident of the United States.[11] An alien is considered a U.S. resident in any calendar year that he or she meets either the green card test or the substantial presence test.[12] A foreign corporation is a corporation organized or created under the laws of a foreign country or U.S. possession.[13] Likewise, a foreign partnership is a partnership organized or created under the laws of a foreign country or U.S. possession.[14] An estate is foreign if its foreign-source income, other than any income effectively connected with a U.S. trade or business, is not subject to U.S. taxation.[15] A trust is foreign if no U.S. court is able to exercise primary supervision over the administration of the trust, or no U.S. persons have the authority to control all substantial decisions of the trust.[16]

Income subject to withholding. Withholding is required with respect to any income that meets the following two tests:

(i) the income is fixed or determinable, annual, or periodical, and

(ii) the income is derived from sources within the United States.[17]

Fixed or determinable, annual, or periodical income includes interest (other than original issue discount), dividends, rents, royalties, salaries, wages, premiums, annuities, and other forms of compensation.[18] It is immaterial whether the income is received through a series of payments or in a single lump sum. For example, $50,000 in rental income is subject to withholding, whether it is paid in 10 payments of $5,000 each or in one payment of $50,000.[19] In addition, although original issue discount is specifically exempted from withholding, withholding is required with respect to certain accrued amounts upon the sale or exchange of an original issue discount obligation,[20] and on the imputed interest portion of an installment payment.[21]

Allowable deductions. No deductions are allowed for purposes of computing the amount of a foreign person's U.S.-source nonbusiness income subject to U.S. withholding taxes.[22]

Applicable tax rate. The statutory withholding rate on a foreign person's U.S.-source nonbusiness income generally is 30%.[23] However, special statutory rates apply to the following types of income:

---

[10] Reg. § § 1.1441-1(a) and 1.1441-3(f) and (g).

[11] Code Sec. 7701(b)(1)(B).

[12] Code Sec. 7701(b)(1)(A). The green card and substantial presence tests are discussed in Chapter 1.

[13] Code Sec. 7701(a)(5).

[14] Code Sec. 7701(a)(5).

[15] Code Sec. 7701(a)(31)(A).

[16] Code Sec. 7701(a)(30)(E) and (a)(31)(B).

[17] Code. Sec. 1441(a) and (b). For this purpose, the United States includes the 50 states and the District of Columbia, but not U.S. possessions. Code Sec. 7701(a)(9).

[18] Code. Sec. 1441(b).

[19] Reg. § 1.1441-2(a)(1).

[20] Code Secs. 871(a)(1)(C) and 881(a)(3).

[21] Reg. § 1.1441-2(a)(1) and Code Sec. 483(a).

[22] Reg. § § 1.871-7(a)(3) and 1.881-2(a)(3).

[23] Code Secs. 1441(a) and 1442(a).

(i) a 10% withholding rate applies to the amount realized on the disposition of a U.S. real property interest,[24]

(ii) the applicable withholding rate on a foreign partner's distributive share of a partnership's effectively connected taxable income is the maximum U.S. tax rate applicable to the type of taxpayer (corporate or noncorporate) in question,[25] and

(iii) a 14% withholding rate applies to scholarships and fellowships received by a nonresident alien individual.[26]

In addition, as discussed later in this chapter, tax treaties often reduce the withholding rate on dividends, interest, and royalties to 15% or less.

Withholding agent responsibilities. Any person having control, receipt, custody, disposal, or payment of an item of U.S.-source non-business income to a foreign person is obligated to withhold U.S. tax.[27] Examples of withholding agents include corporations distributing dividends, debtors paying interest, tenants paying rents, and licensees paying royalties. A withholding agent who fails to withhold is liable for the uncollected tax.[28] Therefore, potential withholding agents must carefully monitor any payments made to foreign persons to ensure that the appropriate amount of tax is being withheld.

In the case of dividend distributions, a corporate payer ordinarily may rely on a shareholder's address to determine whether the payee is a foreign person. Therefore, withholding is not required for dividends mailed to an address within the United States, unless the facts and circumstances indicate that the payee is a foreign person. On the other hand, withholding is required on dividends mailed to an address outside the United States, unless the recipient provides the withholding agent with a written statement that the recipient is a U.S. person.[29]

> **Example 11.2:** USAco, a domestic corporation, is preparing to distribute a dividend. One of USAco's shareholders is F, a nonresident alien individual. F's shares are held by a U.S. broker and are registered in the broker's name. Because a U.S. address appears in USAco's records for F's shares, USAco need not withhold tax on the dividend it pays to F, unless USAco has reason to believe that F is a nonresident alien. However, if F's U.S. broker knows F is a nonresident alien, the broker is obligated to withhold U.S. tax because it has custody of that dividend income. Another USAco shareholder is S, a U.S. citizen. S currently resides abroad and

---

[24] Code Sec. 1445(a).
[25] Code Sec. 1446(b).
[26] Code Sec. 1441(b).
[27] Code Secs. 1441(a) and 1442(a).
[28] Code Sec. 1461.
[29] Reg. § § 1.1441-3(b)(3) and 1.1441-5. If a shareholder's address changes from a foreign address to a

U.S. address, tax should be withheld unless proof is furnished that the shareholder is a U.S. person or the withholding agent is otherwise satisfied that the shareholder is not a foreign person.

therefore has a foreign address. Because a foreign address appears in USAco's records for S's shares, USAco must withhold tax on the dividend it pays to S. S can avoid withholding by furnishing USAco with a written statement that he or she is a U.S. citizen. However, even if S avoids withholding, the dividend is still subject to U.S. taxation by virtue of S's U.S. citizenship.

This address system applies only to dividends. Therefore, U.S. payers of interest, rents, royalties, and other types of U.S.-source nonbusiness income are not allowed to rely on the payee's address to determine if withholding is required. In such cases, the U.S. payer must consider all of the relevant facts and circumstances in determining whether a payee is a foreign person. Given the strict nature of a withholding agent's liability, when in doubt, the payer probably should withhold.[30]

A withholding agent must deposit any taxes withheld with a Federal Reserve bank or an authorized financial institution using Form 8109, Federal Tax Deposit Coupon.[31] The withholding agent also must file an annual informational return, Form 1042, Annual Withholding Tax Return for U.S. Source Income of Foreign Persons. When filing Form 1042, the withholding agent must attach a separate Form 1042-S, Foreign Person's U.S. Source Income Subject to Withholding, for each foreign payee.[32] A copy of Form 1042-S also must be provided to the payee.[33] (Forms 1042 and 1042-S are reproduced in the appendix to this chapter.)

Exemptions and Special Rules

At first glance, it would appear that the United States imposes a significant tax burden on U.S.-source nonbusiness income of foreign persons. After all, the statutory tax rate is 30% and stringent withholding requirements ensure collection. However, according to the most recent IRS statistics, the effective withholding tax rate on the U.S.-source nonbusiness income reported to the IRS in 1995 was only 2.8% (see Table 11.1). This low effective tax rate is due to various exemptions, in particular, the portfolio interest exemption as well as treaty exemptions and reduced treaty withholding rates for interest, dividends and royalties.

---

[30] Under regulations issued in 1997, the address system will be replaced by the requirement that a foreign payee claiming a reduced treaty rate provide the withholding agent with a beneficial owner withholding certificate. Treas. Reg. § 1.1441-6. These new regulations were originally scheduled to take effect January 1, 1999, but the effective date has been postponed twice, first to January 1, 2000 (Notice 98-16, 1998-15 IRB 12), and more recently to January 1, 2001 (Notice 99-25, 1999-20 IRB 75).

[31] Reg. § 1.6302-2.

[32] Reg. § 1.1461-2(b). Form 1042 is due by March 15 of the year following the end of the calendar year in which the tax was required to be withheld.

[33] Reg. § 1.1461-2(c).

TABLE 11.1. U.S.-SOURCE INCOME PAID TO FOREIGN PERSONS IN 1995

Type of U.S.-source income	Amount (in millions)
Interest..	$60,447
Dividends..	17,578
Rents and royalties	7,096
Other	10,707
Total foreign source taxable income	$95,828

U.S. withholding taxes	Amount (in millions)
Total income paid to foreign persons (A)	$95,828
Income exempt from withholding	$74,155
Income subject to withholding	$21,673
Total U.S. tax withhold (B)	$2,684
Effective withholding tax rate (B ÷ A)	2.8%

Source: "Foreign Recipients of U.S. Income, 1995," *IRS Statistics on Income Bulletin,* 1998.

Effectively connected income. Withholding is not required on any U.S.-source income that is effectively connected with the conduct of a U.S. trade or business.[34] Although such income is exempt from withholding, it is subject to U.S. taxes at the regular graduated rates.[35] Interest, dividends, rents, royalties, and other types of nonbusiness income are treated as effectively connected income if the income is derived from assets used in, or held for use in, the conduct of a U.S. trade or business, or the activities of the U.S. trade or business were a material factor in the realization of the income.[36] The exemption for effectively connected income also applies to any income received by a foreign partnership or a foreign corporation for the performance of services.[37] However, as discussed below, special rules apply to the effectively connected personal services income of a nonresident alien individual, as well as the effectively connected income of a partnership which is allocable to a foreign partner.

To obtain a withholding exemption for effectively connected income, the foreign person engaged in the U.S. trade or business must submit a Form 4224, Exemption from Withholding of Tax on Income Effectively Connected with the Conduct of a Trade or Business in the United States, to each withholding agent from whom amounts are to be received.[38] (Form 4224 is reproduced in the appendix to this chapter.)

---

[34] Code Sec. 1441(c)(1).

[35] Code Secs. 871(b) and 882(a).

[36] Code Sec. 864(c)(2). See discussion in Chapter 12.

[37] Reg. § 1.1441-4(a)(1).

[38] Reg. § 1.1441-4(a)(2).

Effectively connected personal services income. The withholding exemption for effectively connected income does not apply to the personal services income of a nonresident alien individual unless the income meets one of the following requirements:

(i) the compensation is subject to standard wage withholding under Code Sec. 3402 (which imposes a withholding obligation on employers with respect to wages paid to any employee),

(ii) the compensation is exempt from withholding under Code Sec. 3402,

(iii) the compensation is derived by a self-employed resident of Canada or Mexico who enters and leaves the United States at frequent intervals, or

(iv) the compensation is exempt from tax by reason of a treaty exemption.[39]

The treaty exemptions for personal services income are discussed later in this chapter.

Effectively connected income allocable to a foreign partner. As discussed under the general rules, a partnership must withhold tax on a foreign partner's distributive share of U.S.-source nonbusiness income, such as passive dividend and interest income.[40] In addition, a domestic or foreign partnership must withhold income tax at a specified rate on the portion of its effectively connected taxable income which is allocable to a foreign partner.[41] A foreign partner is any partner who is not a U.S. person, and thus includes nonresident alien individuals, foreign corporations, foreign partnerships, and foreign trusts or estates.[42] The amount of this special withholding tax equals the foreign partner's distributive share of effectively connected taxable income multiplied by the maximum U.S. tax rate applicable to individuals in the case of a noncorporate partner, and the maximum U.S. tax rate applicable to corporations in the case of a corporate partner.[43] The partnership must remit this withholding tax through quarterly estimated tax payments.[44]

Gains from the sale or exchange of property. Income derived from the sale in the United States of property, whether real or personal, is not subject to withholding.[45] This provision applies to all types of

---

[39] Reg. § 1.1441-4(b)(1) and Temp. Reg. § 1.1441-4T(b)(1).

[40] Reg. § 1.1441-3(f).

[41] Code Sec. 1446(a). This withholding requirement applies regardless of whether any distributions are actually made to such partners. The partnership must file a Form 8804 (Annual Return For Partnership Wtihholding Tax), Form 8805 (Foreign Partner's Information Statement), and a Form 8813 (Partnership Withholding Tax Payment).

[42] Code Sec. 1446(e).

[43] Code Sec. 1446(b). The maximum U.S. tax rate is currently 39.6% for individuals and 35% for corporations. Code Secs. 1 and 11.

[44] Rev. Proc. 89-31, 1989-1 C.B. 895, and Rev. Proc. 92-66, 1992-2 C.B. 428.

[45] Reg. § 1.1441-2(a)(3).

gains, both capital and ordinary. However, its main effect is to exempt from withholding capital gains realized by foreign persons from the sale of U.S. stocks and securities. One rationale for this exemption is the belief that the only way to enforce the taxation of passive foreign investors is through withholding, and that withholding on capital gains is not feasible. Taxing the gross amount realized on a sale is unfair if the net gain is small, and taxing the net gain may be impractical since the withholding agent may have no way of determining the foreign person's basis in the property.

Despite these administrative problems, withholding is required on the following types of gains:[46]

(i)   gains from the disposition of timber, coal, or domestic iron ore with a retained economic interest,[47]

(ii) gains from the sale or exchange of original issue discount obligations attributable to certain accrued amounts,[48]

(iii) gains from the sale or exchange of patents, copyrights, secret processes and formulas, goodwill, trademarks, trade brands, franchises, and other like property, to the extent such gains are derived from payments which are contingent on the productivity, use, or disposition of the property,[49] and

(iv) gains from dispositions of U.S. real property interests.[50]

Portfolio interest exemption. Portfolio interest received by a foreign corporation or nonresident alien individual is exempt from U.S. withholding tax.[51] Congress enacted the portfolio interest exemption in 1984, partly in recognition of the widespread avoidance of U.S. taxes on portfolio interest. Prior to 1984, passive foreign investors were able to avoid U.S. taxation of portfolio interest through treaty exemptions, or, in the case of foreign investors from nontreaty countries, treaty shopping. For example, a U.S. multinational corporation wishing to raise funds would organize a financing subsidiary in the Netherlands Antilles. The Netherlands Antilles subsidiary issued bonds to foreign investors which were guaranteed by the U.S. parent, and then re-lent the proceeds from the bond issuance to the U.S. parent at similar interest rates and terms. Due to the favorable treaty network of the Netherlands Antilles, this arrangement permitted foreign investors from nontreaty countries to derive what was in substance U.S.-source interest free of U.S. tax.

---

[46] Code Secs. 1441(b) and 1442(a). Reg. § 1.1441-3(d) discusses the procedures for withholding on gains.

[47] Code Secs. 871(a)(1)(B), 881(a)(2), and 631(b) and (c).

[48] Code Secs. 871(a)(1)(C) and 881(a)(3).

[49] Code Secs. 871(a)(1)(D) and 881(a)(4).

[50] Code Sec. 1445(a).

[51] Code Secs. 1441(c)(9) and 1442(a).

Generally speaking, portfolio interest is any U.S.-source interest (other than interest effectively connected with the conduct of a U.S. trade or business) paid or accrued on debt obligations issued after July 18, 1984. However, Congress has enacted various restrictions in order to protect against the unauthorized use of the portfolio interest exemption by U.S. persons. In the case of registered debt obligations, the exemption applies only if the U.S. withholding agent has received a statement that the beneficial owner of the obligation is not a U.S. person.[52]

In the case of unregistered (or bearer) debt obligations, the exemption applies only if the following requirements are met:

(i) there are arrangements reasonably designed to ensure that the obligation will be sold (or resold in connection with the original issue) only to a person who is not a U.S. person,

(ii) interest on the obligation is payable only outside the United States and its possessions, and

(iii) there is a statement on the face of the obligation that any U.S. person who holds the obligation will be subject to limitations under the U.S. income tax laws.[53]

In addition, consistent with the idea that the portfolio interest exemption is aimed at passive foreign investors, the following types of foreign lenders do not qualify for the exemption:

(i) *10% shareholders*—Interest received by a 10% shareholder does not qualify for the portfolio interest exemption.[54] In the case of an obligation issued by a corporation, a 10% shareholder is any person who owns, directly or constructively, 10% of more of the combined voting power of all classes of stock of such corporation.[55] In the case of an obligation issued by a partnership, a 10% shareholder is any person who owns 10% of more of the capital or profits interest in such partnership.[56]

(ii) *Foreign banks*—Any interest received by a foreign bank on a loan entered into in the ordinary course of its banking business (other than interest paid on an obligation of the U.S. government) does not qualify for the portfolio interest exemption.[57]

(iii) *Controlled foreign corporations*—Any interest received by a controlled foreign corporation from a related person does not qualify for the portfolio interest exemption.[58]

---

[52] Code Secs. 871(h)(2)(B) and 881(c)(2)(B). See Code Sec. 871(h)(5) regarding the requirements for this statement.

[53] Code Secs. 871(h)(2)(A), 881(c)(2)(A), and 163(f)(2)(B).

[54] Code Secs. 871(h)(3)(A) and 881(c)(3)(B).

[55] Code Secs. 871(h)(3)(B)(i) and (h)(3)(C).

[56] Code Sec. 871(h)(3)(B)(ii).

[57] Code Sec. 881(c)(3)(A).

[58] Code Sec. 881(c)(3)(C). Other special rules apply to portfolio interest received by a controlled foreign corporation (see Code Sec. 881(c)(5)).

In 1993, Congress repealed the portfolio interest exemption for so-called "contingent interest" in order to prevent a perceived abuse.[59] Since 1980, the United States has taxed gains realized by foreign investors on the disposition of equity interests in U.S. real property.[60] One method of avoiding the tax on U.S. real property interests is to use shared appreciation mortgages and other hybrid debt instruments to obtain debt characterization for what are, in substance, equity investments in U.S. real estate. The contingent interest rules close this loophole by taxing the interest income associated with such hybrid debt instruments. Contingent interest is defined as any interest, the amount of which is determined by reference to one of the following items:

(i)   the receipts, sales, or other cash flows of the debtor or a related person,

(ii) any income or profits of the debtor or a related person,

(iii) any change in the value of any property of the debtor or a related person, or

(iv) any dividend, partnership distribution, or similar payment made by the debtor or a related person.[61]

The contingent interest provisions do not apply to any interest paid or accrued with respect to fixed-term indebtedness issued on or before April 7, 1993.[62] In addition, any interest received by a foreign person that is exempt under an existing U.S. tax treaty is not subject to the tax on contingent interest.[63]

Other exemptions for interest and dividends. In addition to the portfolio interest exemption, the following types of interest and dividend income also are exempt from the 30% withholding tax:

(i)   interest on bank deposits or amounts held by an insurance company under an agreement to pay interest thereon,

(ii) a portion of any dividends distributed by a domestic corporation which, during the preceding three taxable years, derived 80% or more of its gross income from the active conduct of a foreign business, and

(iii) income derived by a foreign central bank of issue from banker's acceptances.[64]

Treaty reductions for dividends, interest, and royalties. Tax treaties usually reduce the 30% statutory withholding tax rate on dividend, interest, and royalty income to 15% or less, as long as the

---

[59] Code Secs. 871(h)(4) and 881(c)(4).

[60] Code Sec. 897(a)(1).

[61] Code Sec. 871(h)(4)(A). Various exceptions are provided in Code Sec. 871(h)(4)(C).

[62] Code Sec. 871(h)(4)(D). An exception also applies to any fixed-term indebtedness issued after April 7,

1993, pursuant to a binding written contract which was in effect on April 7, 1993, and at all times thereafter before such debt was issued.

[63] Notice 94-39, 1994-1 C.B. 350.

[64] Code Secs. 871(i) and 881(d).

income is not attributable to a permanent establishment which the taxpayer maintains within the United States.[65] In the case of dividends, the rate often is lower for controlling shareholders (e.g., a shareholder owning 10% or more of the payer's stock) than for noncontrolling shareholders. For example, under the U.S. Model Treaty, the withholding rate on dividends is 5% for taxpayers owning 10% or more of the corporation and 15% for all other shareholders.[66] Interest and royalties often are exempt from withholding tax.[67] In some treaties, the withholding rate on royalties varies with whether the payment is an industrial royalty (such as a payment for the use of a patent, trade secret, or formula), a motion picture or television royalty, or some other type of royalty (such as a payment for the use of a copyright on a book). The appendix in Chapter 9 provides a listing of treaty withholding rates for dividends, interest, and royalties, by country.

In the case of dividends, the corporate payer generally may rely on the payee's address of record as a basis for withholding at a lower treaty rate.[68]

> **Example 11.3:** USAco, a domestic corporation, is preparing to distribute a dividend. One of USAco's shareholders is F, whose address of record is a foreign country with which the United States has an income tax treaty. The treaty provides for a 15% withholding rate on dividends. Based on F's address of record, USAco may withhold tax at the lower treaty rate, unless it has reason to believe that F is not a resident of that treaty country.

This address system applies only to dividends. Therefore, U.S. payers of interest and royalties are not allowed to rely on the payee's address as a basis for withholding at a lower treaty rate. Instead, the withholding agent must receive from the payee a Form 1001, Ownership, Exemption, or Reduced Rate Certificate.[69] The withholding agent need not verify the accuracy of representations made by a payee on Form 1001, and is not liable for any underwithholding if the payee misrepresents the facts.[70] (Form 1001 is reproduced in the appendix to this chapter.) The IRS is in the process of issuing new forms for these situations in accordance with new withholding regulations scheduled to take effect January 1, 2001.[71]

---

[65] Generally speaking, a permanent establishment is an office or other fixed place of business (see Chapter 9 for a more detailed definition).

[66] Article 10(2) of the United States Model Income Tax Convention of September 20, 1996 (or "U.S. Model Treaty").

[67] See, for example, Articles 11(1) and 12(1) of the U.S. Model Treaty.

[68] Reg. § 1.1441-3(b)(3) and IRS Pub. No. 515 (1999). Under regulations issued in 1997, the address system will be replaced by the requirement that a foreign payee claiming a reduced treaty rate provide the withholding agent with a beneficial owner withholding certificate. Treas. Reg. § 1.1441-6. These new regulations were originally scheduled to take effect January 1, 1999, but the effective date has been postponed twice, first to January 1, 2000 (Notice 98-16, 1998-15 IRB 12), and more recently to January 1, 2001 (Notice 99-25, 1999-20 IRB 75).

[69] Reg. § 1.1441-6(b) and (c). Form 1001 is effective for three calendar years.

[70] Rev. Rul. 76-224, 1976-1 C.B. 268.

[71] Notice 99-25, 1999-20 IRB 75.

Treaty reductions for personal services income. Tax treaties usually provide a variety of tax exemptions for personal services income. For example, under the U.S. Model Treaty, income derived by a nonresident alien individual from dependent personal services performed in the United States is exempt from U.S. taxation if the following requirements are satisfied:

(i) the dependent agent is present in the United States for 183 days or less,

(ii) the agent's compensation is paid by, or on behalf of, an employer which is not a U.S. resident, and

(iii) the compensation is not borne by a permanent establishment or a fixed base which the employer maintains in the United States.[72]

A separate independent services provision usually governs the taxation of personal services income derived by self-employed professionals, such as accountants, doctors, engineers, and lawyers. Under the U.S. Model Treaty, such income is exempt from U.S. taxation unless the services are performed in the United States and the income is attributable to an office or other fixed place of business that is located in the United States and is regularly available to the taxpayer for purposes of performing the services.[73]

Finally, tax treaties often contain special rules governing personal services income derived by crew members of ships and aircraft operated in international traffic,[74] entertainers and athletes,[75] government workers,[76] and students and trainees.[77] The appendix to Chapter 9 provides a listing of the treaty provisions governing personal services income, by country.

To obtain a treaty exemption for independent services, a self-employed nonresident alien individual must submit a Form 8233, Exemption from Withholding on Compensation for Independent Personal Services of a Nonresident Alien Individual, to each withholding agent from whom amounts are to be received.[78] (Form 8233 is reproduced in the appendix to this chapter.) To obtain a treaty exemption for dependent services, the nonresident alien employee must file a statement with its employer.[79]

---

[72] Article 15(2) of the U.S. Model Treaty.

[73] Article 14 of the U.S. Model Treaty.

[74] See, for example, Article 15(3) of the U.S. Model Treaty.

[75] See, for example, Article 17 of the U.S. Model Treaty.

[76] See, for example, Article 19 of the U.S. Model Treaty.

[77] See, for example, Article 20 of the U.S. Model Treaty.

[78] Reg. § 1.1441-4(b)(2).

[79] Reg. § 1.1441-4(b)(2) and IRS Pub. No. 515 (1996).

Election to treat real property income as effectively connected income. A foreign corporation or nonresident alien individual who is a passive investor in a U.S. real property interest may elect to have the U.S.-source income derived from the investment taxed as if it were effectively connected income.[80] Since deductions are allowable against effectively connected income,[81] this election allows foreign persons to offset the gross income from investments in U.S. real property (e.g., gross rental income) with related deductions, such as depreciation, depletion, and interest expense.

> **Example 11.4:** T is a nonresident alien individual. T purchases an office building located in the United States. T does not manage the property, but instead leases the building to an unrelated and independent U.S. person who then subleases the building to the tenants. During the first year of operations, T has rental income of $400,000 and operating expenses (including depreciation and interest expense) of $340,000. Because T's U.S. activities are *de minimis*, T probably is not engaged in a U.S. trade or business. Therefore, under the general rules, T's U.S.-source rental income of $400,000 is subject to withholding tax at a 30% rate. As a consequence, T's U.S. tax would be $120,000 [30% × $400,000], even though T realizes only $60,000 of net income from the U.S. rental property. On the other hand, if T elects to have its U.S. real property income taxed as if it were income effectively connected with a U.S. trade or business, then T's net profit of $60,000 [$400,000 − $340,000] would be subject to U.S. tax at the regular graduated rates applicable to individual taxpayers.

To qualify for the election, the taxpayer must derive income during the taxable year from real property located within the United States and held for the production of income, including gains from the sale or exchange of real property, rents or royalties from mines, wells, or other natural deposits, and gains from the disposition of timber, coal, or domestic iron ore with a retained economic interest.[82] If made, the election applies to all of the taxpayer's income from U.S. real property which would not otherwise be treated as effectively connected income.[83] The election applies for all subsequent taxable years, and may be revoked only with the consent of the Commissioner.[84] If the election is revoked, a new election may not be made for five years, unless the Commissioner consents to an early re-election.[85]

---

[80] Code Secs. 871(d)(1) and 882(d)(1).

[81] Reg. §§ 1.873-1(a)(1) and 1.882-4(b)(1).

[82] Code Secs. 871(d)(1) and 882(d)(1).

[83] Reg. § 1.871-10(b)(1).

[84] Code Secs. 871(d)(1) and 882(d)(1). See Reg. § 1.871-10(d) regarding the procedures for making and revoking the election. To obtain a withholding exemption for the covered income, the taxpayer must submit a Form 4224, Exemption from Withholding of Tax on Income Effectively Connected with the Conduct of a Trade or Business in the United States, to each withholding agent from whom amounts are to be received. Reg. § 1.1441-4(a)(2). Form 4224 is reproduced in the appendix to this chapter.

[85] Code Secs. 871(d)(2) and 882(d)(2).

Foreign governments and international organizations. Income derived by a foreign government from investments in the United States in stocks, bonds, or other domestic securities, financial instruments held in execution of governmental financial or monetary policy, or interest on deposits in U.S. banks, is exempt from U.S. tax.[86] In the case of an international organization, income from investments in the United States in stocks, bonds, or other domestic securities, or from interest on deposits in U.S. banks, is exempt from U.S. tax.[87] The compensation of employees of foreign governments or international organizations also is exempt from U.S. tax under certain conditions.[88] Finally, any income derived by a foreign central bank of issue from obligations of the United States, or of any agency or instrumentality thereof, or from interest on bank deposits, is exempt from U.S. tax.[89]

Foreign tax-exempt organizations. A foreign tax-exempt organization is subject to withholding on any receipts of unrelated business taxable income, unless such income is effectively connected with the conduct of a U.S. trade or business.[90] The gross U.S.-source investment income of a foreign private foundation also is subject to withholding taxes, albeit at a reduced rate of 4%.[91] However, if a tax treaty provides for a withholding exemption with respect to a particular type of income (e.g., interest income), then that treaty exemption applies to the foreign private foundation's income.[92]

Social security benefits. One-half of the social security benefits received by a nonresident alien individual are subject to the 30% withholding tax.[93]

Gambling winnings. Withholding is not required on proceeds from a wager placed by a nonresident alien individual in playing blackjack, baccarat, craps, roulette, or big-6 wheel.[94] Other gambling winnings are subject to withholding tax if the amount of the winnings exceeds certain dollar thresholds.[95]

Tax on gross transportation income. The U.S.-source gross transportation income of a foreign corporation and a nonresident alien individual is subject to a special 4% tax.[96] Transportation income is income derived from the use or lease of a vessel or aircraft (including any container used in connection with a vessel or aircraft), or from the performance of services directly related to the use of a vessel of

---

[86] Code Sec. 892(a)(1). This exception does not apply to income derived by a foreign government from the conduct of a commercial activity, either directly or through a controlled commercial entity. Code Sec. 892(a)(2).

[87] Code Sec. 892(b).

[88] Code Sec. 893.

[89] Code Sec. 895. This exception does not apply to an obligation or deposit held for, or used in connection with, the conduct of a commercial activity.

[90] Reg. § 1.1443-1(a)(2).

[91] Reg. § 1.1443-1(b)(1)(i) and Code Sec. 4948(a).

[92] Reg. § 1.1443-1(b)(1)(ii).

[93] Code Sec. 871(a)(3).

[94] Code Secs. 1441(c)(11) and 871(j).

[95] Code Sec. 3402(q).

[96] Code Sec. 887(a).

aircraft.[97] A foreign person's U.S.-source gross transportation income equals 50% of the income from any transportation which begins in the United States and ends abroad or which begins abroad and ends in the United States.[98] The 4% tax does not apply to any income effectively connected with the conduct of a U.S. trade or business.[99] A foreign person's U.S.-source gross transportation income is considered to be effectively connected income if the following requirements are met:

(i) the taxpayer has a fixed place of business in the United States which is involved in the earning of the U.S.-source gross transportation income, and

(ii) substantially all of the taxpayer's U.S.-source gross transportation income is attributable to regularly scheduled transportation, or, in the case of the leasing of a vessel or aircraft, is attributable to a fixed place of business in the United States.[100]

Tax treaties often provide exemptions for income from the international operation of a vessel or aircraft.[101]

¶ 1103   TAXATION OF U.S. REAL PROPERTY INTERESTS

Introduction

When U.S. real estate became a popular investment with foreigners in the 1970s, the favorable tax treatment accorded foreign investors in U.S. real property became a domestic political issue. Congress responded in 1980 by enacting the Foreign Investment in Real Property Tax Act of 1980 (or "FIRPTA"), which better equates the tax treatment of real property gains realized by domestic and foreign investors. Prior to FIRPTA, foreign persons generally were not taxed on gains from the disposition of a U.S. real property interest.[102] Under FIRPTA, gains or losses realized by foreign corporations or nonresident alien individuals from any sale, exchange, or other disposition of a U.S. real property interest are taxed in the same manner as income effectively connected with the conduct of a U.S. trade or business.[103] This means that gains from dispositions of U.S. real property interests are taxed at the regular graduated rates, whereas losses are deductible from effectively connected income.[104]

---

[97] Code Sec. 863(c)(3).

[98] Code Sec. 863(c)(2)(A). This rule generally does not apply to transportation income derived from personal services performed by the taxpayer. Code Sec. 863(c)(2)(B).

[99] Code Sec. 887(b)(2). Certain possessions income also is exempt. Code Sec. 887(b)(3).

[100] Code Sec. 887(b)(4).

[101] See, for example, Article 8 of the U.S. Model Treaty.

[102] Reg. § 1.1441-2(a)(3).

[103] Code Sec. 897(a)(1). In addition, for purposes of computing a nonresident alien individual's alternative minimum tax, the taxable excess amount cannot be less than the individual's net U.S. real property gain for the taxable year. Code Sec. 897(a)(2).

[104] Code Secs. 871(b) and 882(a). However, a loss realized by a nonresident alien individual from the disposition of a U.S. real property interest held for personal use is deductible only if it arises from a fire, storm, or other casualty event. Code Secs. 897(b) and 165(c).

Example 11.5: F is a nonresident alien individual whose only connection with the United States is the ownership of some undeveloped land located in the United States. F holds the land as a passive investment. Prior to the enactment of FIRPTA, any gain realized by F on the sale of the land would be exempt from U.S. taxation. Under FIRPTA, the United States taxes F's gain on the sale of the land in the same manner as income effectively connected with the conduct of a U.S. trade or business, that is, on a net basis and at the regular graduated rates.

U.S. Real Property Interests

A U.S. real property interest includes interests in any of the following types of property located within the United States or the U.S. Virgin Islands:

(i)   land,

(ii) buildings, including a personal residence,

(iii) inherently permanent structures other than buildings (e.g., grain bins or broadcasting towers),

(iv) mines, wells, and other natural deposits,

(v)   growing crops and timber, and

(vi) personal property associated with the use of real property, such as mining equipment, farming equipment, or a hotel's furniture and fixtures.[105]

For this purpose, an "interest" in real property means any interest (other than an interest solely as a creditor), including fee ownership, co-ownership, a leasehold, an option to purchase or lease property, a time-sharing interest, a life estate, remainder, or reversionary interest, and any other direct or indirect right to share in the appreciation in value or proceeds from the sale of real property.[106]

A U.S. real property interest also includes any interest (other than an interest solely as a creditor) in a domestic corporation which was a U.S. real property holding corporation at any time during the five-year period ending on the date of the disposition of such interest, or, if shorter, the period the taxpayer held the interest.[107] This provision prevents foreign persons from avoiding the FIRPTA tax by incorporating their U.S. real estate investments, and then realizing the resulting gains through stock sales, which ordinarily are exempt from U.S. taxation.[108] A domestic corporation is a U.S. real property holding corporation if the market value of its U.S. real property interests equals

---

[105] Code Sec. 897(c)(1)(A)(i) and Reg. § 1.897-1(b).
[106] Code Sec. 897(c)(6)(A) and Reg. § 1.897-1(d)(2).
[107] Code Sec. 897(c)(1)(A)(ii).
[108] Reg. § 1.1441-2(a)(3).

50% or more of the market value of the sum of the corporation's following interests:

(i)   U.S. real property interests (including any interest in another U.S. real property holding corporation),

(ii) interests in foreign real property, and

(iii) any other property of the corporation which is used or held for use in a trade or business.[109]

For this purpose, a domestic corporation is treated as owning a proportionate share of the assets of any other corporation it controls, as well as a proportionate share of the assets of any partnership, trust, or estate, in which it is a partner or beneficiary.[110]

The following types of interests are exempted from the U.S. real property holding corporation taint:

(i)   *Publicly traded corporations*—Stock which is regularly traded on an established securities market generally is not treated as a U.S. real property interest.[111] Without this exception, some major U.S. industrial companies would be treated as U.S. real property holding corporations.

(ii) *Corporations that have disposed of all U.S. real property interests*—U.S. real property interests do not include an interest in a corporation that has previously disposed of all of its U.S. real property interests in transactions in which the full amount of gain, if any, was recognized.[112]

(iii) *Domestically controlled real estate investment trusts*—An interest in a real estate investment trust is not a U.S. real property interest if foreign persons directly or indirectly own less than 50% of the value of the stock of the real estate investment trust.[113]

Special Rules for Certain Dispositions

Congress has enacted a variety of special rules in order to apply the FIRPTA tax to the following types of dispositions:

(i)   a distribution by a foreign corporation of a U.S. real property interest to its shareholders, either as a dividend, in redemption of stock, or in liquidation,[114]

---

[109] Code Sec. 897(c)(2). For this purpose, a U.S. real property holding corporation includes any interests in a foreign corporation which would qualify as a U.S. real property holding corporation if that foreign corporation were a domestic corporation. Code Sec. 897(c)(4)(A).

[110] Code Sec. 897(c)(4)(B) and (c)(5).

[111] Code Sec. 897(c)(3). An exception applies to a person who owns, directly or constructively, more than 5% of the stock in question. Code Sec. 897(c)(3) and (c)(6)(C).

[112] Code Sec. 897(c)(1)(B).

[113] Code Sec. 897(h)(2) and (h)(4)(B).

[114] Code Sec. 897(d) and Temp. Reg. § 1.897-5T(c).

(ii) a disposition of a U.S. real property interest that would otherwise qualify as a nontaxable transaction (e.g., a like-kind exchange),[115]

(iii) a sale or other disposition of an interest in a partnership, trust, or estate which holds a U.S. real property interest,[116]

(iv) a distribution by a real estate investment trust which holds a U.S. real property interest,[117] and

(v) a transfer of a U.S. real property interest to a foreign corporation as a contribution to capital.[118]

Withholding Requirements

To ensure collection of the FIRPTA tax, any transferee acquiring a U.S. real property interest must deduct and withhold a tax equal to 10% of the amount realized on the disposition.[119] A transferee is any person, foreign or domestic, that acquires a U.S. real property interest by purchase, exchange, gift, or any other type of transfer.[120] The amount realized is the sum of the cash paid or to be paid (excluding interest), the market value of other property transferred or to be transferred, the amount of liabilities assumed by the transferee, and the amount of liabilities which the transferred property was taken subject to.[121] Withholding requirements also apply to distributions made by a domestic or foreign corporation, partnership, estate, or trust, to the extent the distribution involves a U.S. real property interest, as well as to dispositions of interests in a partnership, trust, or estate that has a U.S. real property interest.[122]

As with withholding taxes in general, a transferee that fails to withhold is liable for any uncollected taxes.[123] Therefore, any transferee of U.S. real property must be careful to determine whether withholding is required. To ease the withholding burden, withholding is not required in the following situations:

(i) the transferee receives an affidavit from the transferor which states, under penalty of perjury, that the transferor is not a foreign person or, in the case of the disposition of an interest in a domestic corporation, that the domestic corporation is not and has not been a U.S. real property holding company,

---

[115] Code Sec. 897(e) and Temp. Reg. § 1.897-6T.

[116] Code Sec. 897(g).

[117] Code Sec. 897(h)(1) and (h)(3).

[118] Code Sec. 897(j).

[119] Code Sec. 1445(a). A transferee must file Forms 8288 and 8288-A to report and deposit any tax withheld within 20 days of withholding. Reg. § 1.1445-1(c)(1).

[120] Reg. § 1.1445-1(g)(4).

[121] Reg. § 1.1445-1(g)(5).

[122] Code Sec. 1445(e) and Reg. § 1.1445-5.

[123] Code Sec. 1461. However, the transferee's liability for a failure to withhold the FIRPTA tax is limited to the transferor's maximum tax liability. Code Sec. 1445(c)(1)(A).

   (ii) the transferee receives a withholding certificate issued by the IRS, which notifies the transferee that no withholding is required,

  (iii) the transferee receives a notice from the transferor that no recognition of gain or loss on the transfer is required because a nonrecognition provision applies,

  (iv) the transferee acquires the property for use as a personal residence and the purchase price does not exceed $300,000, or

  (v) the transferee acquires stock that is regularly traded on an established securities market.[124]

The administrative burden also is eased by a procedure whereby the IRS will issue a withholding certificate which provides for a reduced level of withholding, and a procedure whereby a foreign person may obtain an early refund of any excess withholding taxes.[125]

---

[124] Code Sec. 1445(b) and Reg. § 1.1445-2. An agent of the transferee or transferor, such as a real estate broker or attorney, who has actual knowledge that an affidavit regarding the status of the transferor is false, but fails to notify the transferee that it is false, may be liable for the withholding tax to the extent of the agent's compensation from the transaction. Code Sec. 1445(d) and Reg. § 1.1445-4.

[125] Reg. § 1.1445-3.

¶ 1104 APPENDIX

Form **1001** (Rev. July 1998) Department of the Treasury Internal Revenue Service	**Ownership, Exemption, or** **Reduced Rate Certificate** ▶ File this form with your withholding agent.	OMB No. 1545-0055

Please Type or Print

Name of beneficial owner	U.S. identifying number, if any
Address (number and street). See instructions.	Recipient's country of residence for tax purposes
City and province or state. Enter postal code where appropriate.	Country

1 Check type of income to which this certificate applies. *(If you check box **a**, you do not have to check any other box.)*

- **a** ☐ Income from a trust, estate, or investment account
- **b** ☐ Coupon bond interest (including tax-free covenant bonds)
- **c** ☐ Interest, other than coupon bond interest
- **d** ☐ Rents
- **e** ☐ Natural resource royalties and income from real property

- **f** ☐ Royalties from use of patents, secret processes, etc.
- **g** ☐ Royalties from use of films, television tapes, etc.
- **h** ☐ Annuities
- **i** ☐ Other income (specify)_____

*If you checked box **b**, complete items 2a through 2h and, if applicable, line 4 or line 5.*
*If you checked any box other than **b**, complete either line 3 or line 4, whichever applies. Also complete line 5 if applicable.*
Note: *Before completing line **4** or line **5**, see instructions.*

2 Information on coupon bonds
a Name and address of obligor of bonds

b Identification of bond	**c** Date of issue

d Date interest due	**e** Date interest paid	**f** Gross amount of interest paid	**g** Rate of tax (see instructions)	**h** Amount of tax withheld
		$	%	$

3 Calendar years for which the reduced rate of tax or exemption from tax applies to other than coupon bond interest:

First year	Second year	Third year

4 Withheld tax requested to be released (see instructions) . . . . $

5 **Qualified resident status.** If you are a corporation claiming treaty benefits for dividends you received from another foreign corporation, or interest you received from a U.S. trade or business of another foreign corporation, explain how you meet qualified resident status (see instructions).

I certify that the information entered above is correct; and, if a reduced rate of tax or exemption from tax applies, I further certify that I have complied with all requirements to qualify for the reduced rate of tax or exemption from tax.

Sign Here ▶ _____   _____
                  (Signature of beneficial owner, fiduciary, trustee, or agent)   (Date)

_____
(If trust or estate, enter name)

_____
(Address of fiduciary, trustee, or agent)

General Instructions

Section references are to the Internal Revenue Code unless otherwise noted.

Purpose of Form

Beneficial owners of certain types of income (or owners' trustees or agents) use this form to report to a withholding agent both the ownership of the income and the reduced rate of tax or exemption from tax on the income under tax conventions or treaties. The form can also be used to claim a release of tax withheld at source.

Instructions for Owners, Trustees, or Agents

Who must file. You must file Form 1001 if you are the beneficial owner of income subject to withholding under section 1441, 1442, or 1451 (or you are the trustee or agent of the beneficial owner) and the owner is a nonresident alien individual or fiduciary, a foreign partnership, or a foreign corporation or other foreign entity.

The term "beneficial owner" means the person ultimately entitled to control the income. A nominee or any person acting in a similar capacity is not the beneficial owner.

Who does not have to file. You do not have to file this form if you are:

1. A beneficial owner, trustee, or agent who receives only dividends, except as provided on page 2. The withholding agent may generally rely on an owner's address of record as the basis for allowing the benefit of any income tax treaty to dividends being paid to the owner.

(continued on back of form)

For Paperwork Reduction Act Notice, see back of form.   Cat. No. 17110L   Form **1001** (Rev. 7-98)

However, a foreign corporation that receives dividends from another foreign corporation that are treated as income from sources within the United States under section 861(a)(2)(B) must file Form 1001 unless the dividends are exempt from tax under section 884(e)(3) (relating to earnings and profits subject to the branch profits tax).

2. A beneficial owner, trustee, or agent who receives only income (other than coupon bond interest) and who **does not** claim the benefit of an income tax treaty.

3. A nonresident alien individual or fiduciary, foreign partnership, or foreign corporation engaged in a trade or business in the United States during the tax year, if the income is **(a)** effectively connected with the conduct of a trade or business in the United States by the individual, fiduciary, partnership, or corporation, and **(b)** exempt from withholding under section 1441 or 1442 because of Regulations section 1.1441-4(a). Instead, file **Form 4224,** Exemption From Withholding of Tax on Income Effectively Connected With the Conduct of a Trade or Business in the United States.

4. A nonresident alien individual who claims exemption from withholding on compensation for independent personal services based on a U.S. tax treaty or the personal exemption amount. Instead, file **Form 8233,** Exemption From Withholding on Compensation for Independent (and Certain Dependent) Personal Services of a Nonresident Alien Individual.

5. A nonresident alien individual or fiduciary, a foreign corporation, or a foreign partnership made up entirely of nonresident alien individuals and foreign corporations, if the interest is exempt from withholding under section 1441 or 1442 because of section 1441(c)(9) or (10).

6. A foreign partnership or foreign corporation engaged in a trade or business in the United States during the tax year, if the income is exempt from withholding under section 1441 or 1442 because of Regulations section 1.1441-4(f).

Where and when to file. Give this form to the withholding agent. When you do so depends on the type of income to which the Form 1001 applies, as specified in the box(es) you check in line 1:

Box 1b. For interest on coupon bonds, including tax-free covenant bonds, file the form each time you present a coupon for payment. Use a separate Form 1001 for each issue of bonds.

All other item 1 boxes. For all other types of income, file the form as soon as you can for any successive 3-calendar-year period during which you expect to receive the income. Use a separate Form 1001 for each type of income, except for income received from a trust, estate, or investment account (box 1a). For that type of income, use a separate Form 1001 for each different trust, estate, or investment account.

If, after filing a form, you become ineligible for benefits on the income under that tax treaty, you must notify the withholding agent in writing. If the beneficial ownership of the income changes hands, the new beneficial owner of record may receive the reduced or exempt rate of tax under the treaty **only** if entitled to it. In addition, the new beneficial owner must properly file Form 1001 with the withholding agent.

Specific Instructions

Address. Enter your address in the space provided. For an individual, your address is your permanent place of residence. For partnerships or corporations, the address is the principal office or place of business. For estates and trusts, the address is the permanent residence or principal office of the fiduciary. Enter a P.O. box only if mail is not delivered to the street address.

Note: *To qualify for treaty benefits, a taxpayer must be a resident of a treaty country. (In some cases, a corporate taxpayer must also be a "qualified resident." See the instructions for line 5.) The withholding agent may presume that the beneficial owner of the income is not a resident (or qualified resident) of a treaty country, and is not entitled to treaty benefits, if the owner does not have a residence address in that country. However, in that case, the beneficial owner of the income may demonstrate that he or she was a resident (or qualified resident) of the treaty country and was entitled to treaty benefits.*

Line 2g. Get **Pub. 901,** U.S. Tax Treaties, for the applicable rate, if any, to enter on line 2g. If the interest is exempt from tax, write "None."

Line 3. If you checked any box on line 1 other than box b, enter the years for which the reduced rate of tax or exemption from tax applies.

Line 4. If you use this form to claim a release of tax withheld at source, enter the amount claimed on line 4. In the space to the left of the dollar entry space on line 4, identify the income tax treaty and the rate of tax for items 1a and 1c through 1i as applicable.

The release is only available prior to the withholding agent's filing of **Form 1042,** Annual Withholding Tax Return for U.S. Source Income of Foreign Persons, for the calendar year (see Regulations section 1.1461-4).

Line 5. This line applies only to a corporation that claims treaty benefits for dividends paid to it by another foreign corporation, or interest paid to it by a U.S. trade or business of another foreign corporation. To obtain treaty benefits for these payments, the recipient corporation must generally be a "qualified resident" of a treaty country or meet the requirements of a "limitation on benefits" article that entered into force after 1986. (See section 884 and its regulations for the definition of interest paid by a U.S. trade or business and other applicable rules.)

In general, a foreign corporation is a qualified resident of a country if any of the following applies: **(a)** it meets a 50% ownership and base erosion test; **(b)** it is primarily and regularly traded on an established securities market in its country of residence or the United States; **(c)** it carries on an active trade or business in its country of residence; or **(d)** it obtains a ruling from the IRS that it is a qualified resident. See Regulations section 1.884-5 for the requirements that must be met to satisfy each of these tests. Complete this line by indicating which of these tests has been met (if you claim qualified resident status) or that you meet the requirements of a "limitation on benefits" article that entered into force after 1986.

Instructions for Withholding Agent

Do not send Form 1001 to the IRS. Instead, use it to prepare magnetic tape or paper document **Form(s) 1042-S,** Foreign Person's U.S. Source Income Subject to Withholding. Keep Form 1001 for at least 4 years after the end of the last calendar year in which all income to which the form pertains was paid.

Prepare a separate Form 1042-S for payment during the calendar year of each type of income (including coupon bond interest) checked on Form 1001. If you receive more than one Form 1001 for an owner during the calendar year, prepare only one Form 1042-S to show the total amount of each separate item paid to the owner for that year.

For withholding rates and other information, get **Pub. 515,** Withholding of Tax on Nonresident Aliens and Foreign Corporations.

Paperwork Reduction Act Notice. We ask for the information on this form to carry out the Internal Revenue laws of the United States. You are required to provide the information. It is needed to ensure that you are complying with these laws and to ensure that the correct amount of tax is withheld.

You are not required to provide the information requested on a form that is subject to the Paperwork Reduction Act unless the form displays a valid OMB control number. Books or records relating to a form or its instructions must be retained as long as their contents may become material in the administration of any Internal Revenue law. Generally, tax returns and return information are confidential, as required by section 6103.

The time needed to complete and file this form will vary depending on individual circumstances. The estimated average time is:

Recordkeeping		4 hr., 32 min.
Learning about the law or the form		1 hr., 5 min.
Preparing and sending the form		1 hr., 13 min.

If you have comments concerning the accuracy of these time estimates or suggestions for making this form simpler, we would be happy to hear from you. You can write to the Tax Forms Committee, Western Area Distribution Center, Rancho Cordova, CA 95743-0001.

DO NOT file this form with the IRS. Instead, file it with the withholding agent.

Form **1042**	**Annual Withholding Tax Return for U.S. Source Income of Foreign Persons**	OMB No. 1545-0096
Department of the Treasury Internal Revenue Service	▶ See instructions.	19**99**

If this is an Amended Return, check here . . ▶ ☐   If completing only Part II as a transmittal document, check here . . ▶ ☐

Name of withholding agent	Taxpayer identification number	For IRS Use Only	
		CC	FD
Number, street, and room or suite no. (if a P.O. box, see instructions)		RD	FF
		CAF	FP
City or town, state, and ZIP code		CR	I
		EDC	SIC

If you will not be liable for returns in the future, check here ▶ ☐   Enter date final income paid ▶ ....

Check here if you made quarter-monthly deposits using the 90% rule (see **Deposit Requirements** in the instructions) . . . . ▶ ☐

Part I	**Record of Federal Tax Liability (Do not show Federal tax deposits here.)**

Line No.	Period ending		Tax liability for period (including any taxes assumed on Form(s) 1000)	Line No.	Period ending		Tax liability for period (including any taxes assumed on Form(s) 1000)	Line No.	Period ending		Tax liability for period (including any taxes assumed on Form(s) 1000)
1	Jan.	7		21	May	7		41	Sept.	7	
2		15		22		15		42		15	
3		22		23		22		43		22	
4		31		24		31		44		30	
5	Jan. total			25	May total			45	Sept. total		
6	Feb.	7		26	June	7		46	Oct.	7	
7		15		27		15		47		15	
8		22		28		22		48		22	
9		28		29		30		49		31	
10	Feb. total			30	June total			50	Oct. total		
11	Mar.	7		31	July	7		51	Nov.	7	
12		15		32		15		52		15	
13		22		33		22		53		22	
14		31		34		31		54		30	
15	Mar. total			35	July total			55	Nov. total		
16	Apr.	7		36	Aug.	7		56	Dec.	7	
17		15		37		15		57		15	
18		22		38		22		58		22	
19		30		39		31		59		31	
20	Apr. total			40	Aug. total			60	Dec. total		

61a Total tax liability (add monthly total lines from above) **61a**

 b Adjustments (see instructions) **61b**

 c Total net tax liability (combine lines 61a and 61b) . . . . ▶ **61c**

62 No. of Forms 1042-S filed on **a** Magnetic tape............ **b** Paper with this form...........

 c Paper with previously filed Form(s) 1042 (Parts I or II)..

63 For **all** Form(s) 1042-S and 1000:

 a Gross income paid............................ **b** Taxes withheld or assumed.....................

64 Total paid by Federal tax deposit coupons or by electronic funds transfer (or with a request for an extension of time to file) for 1999 **64**

65 Enter overpayment applied as a credit from 1998 Form 1042 . **65**

66 **Total payments.** Add lines 64 and 65 . . . . ▶ **66**

67 If line 61c is larger than line 66, enter **BALANCE DUE** here **67**

68 If line 66 is larger than line 61c, enter **OVERPAYMENT** here **68**

69 Apply overpayment on line 68 to (check one): ☐ Credit on 2000 Form 1042; or ☐ Refund

Sign Here — Under penalties of perjury, I declare that I have examined this return, including accompanying schedules and statements, and to the best of my knowledge and belief, it is true, correct, and complete. Declaration of preparer (other than withholding agent) is based on all information of which preparer has any knowledge.

▶ Your signature	Date	▶ Capacity in which acting	

Paid Preparer's Use Only	Preparer's signature ▶	Date	Check if self-employed ▶ ☐	Preparer's SSN or PTIN
	Firm's name (or yours if self-employed) and address ▶		EIN ▶	
			ZIP code ▶	

For Privacy Act and Paperwork Reduction Act Notice, see the instructions.   Cat. No. 11384V   Form **1042** (1999)

¶ 1104

Form 1042 (1999)   Page **2**

Part II	**Transmittal of Paper Forms 1042-S**

▶ **DO NOT complete Part II if you are completing Part I of this Form 1042.**

Name of withholding agent	Taxpayer identification number

70 Complete this line **only** if you have **not yet filed** a 1999 Form 1042 (Part I).

Number of paper Forms 1042-S attached: **a** Original .... **b** Voided .... **c** Corrected ....

71 Complete this line if you have **already filed** a 1999 Form 1042 (Part I).
Caution: You cannot use Part II to transmit any Forms 1042-S that would cause the gross income or tax withheld information shown on your previously filed Form 1042 (Part I) to change. Instead, you must file an amended Form 1042 (Part I). See the instructions.

Number of paper Forms 1042-S attached: **a** Original .... **b** Voided .... **c** Corrected ....

72 Number of paper Forms 1042-S previously filed with Form 1042 (Parts I or II), if applicable ....

Form **1042** (1999)

¶ **1104**

General Instructions

Section references are to the Internal Revenue Code unless otherwise noted.

Changes To Note

1. You must make electronic deposits of all depository tax liabilities that occur after 1999 if during calendar year 1998 your total required Federal tax deposits were more than $200,000.

2. For deposits made by the Electronic Federal Tax Payment System (EFTPS) to be on time, you must initiate the transaction at least one business day before the date the deposit is due.

Purpose of Form

Use Form 1042 to report tax withheld on certain income of nonresident aliens, foreign partnerships, foreign corporations, and nonresident alien or foreign fiduciaries of estates or trusts, and to transmit paper **Forms 1042-S**, Foreign Person's U.S. Source Income Subject to Withholding.

Who Must File

Every U.S. withholding agent who receives, controls, has custody of, disposes of, or pays any fixed or determinable annual or periodic income must file an annual return for the preceding calendar year on Form 1042. Certain Canadian withholding agents must also file an annual return on Form 1042 (see below). The withholding agent must transmit with Form 1042 the information called for on Form 1042-S.

You must file Form 1042 if:

● You are required to file Form(s) 1042-S (whether or not any tax was withheld or was required to be withheld). File Form 1042 even if you file Forms 1042-S only on magnetic media or electronically.

● You pay gross investment income to foreign private foundations that are subject to tax under section 4948(a).

Who Is a Withholding Agent

Any person required to withhold tax is a withholding agent. A withholding agent may be an individual, trust, estate, partnership, corporation, government agency, association, or tax-exempt foundation, whether domestic or foreign.

Canadian withholding agent. If you are a nominee, representative, fiduciary, or partnership in Canada and you receive dividends from sources in the United States for the account of any person who is not entitled to the reduced rate granted under the tax treaty between the United States and Canada, you are a withholding agent and you must withhold the additional tax due on the income. Send the additional U.S. tax withheld, in U.S. dollars, with Form 1042 to the Internal Revenue Service Center, Philadelphia, PA 19255, by March 15, 2000.

Note: *Every person required to deduct and withhold any tax under Chapter 3 of the Code is liable for such tax. See section 1461.*

Where and When To File

File Form 1042 with any paper Forms 1042-S and other required forms and attachments with the Internal Revenue Service Center, Philadelphia, PA 19255, by March 15, 2000.

Also send amended returns and transmittal documents to this address.

Extension of time to file. If you need more time to file Form 1042, you may submit **Form 2758**, Application for Extension of Time To File Certain Excise, Income, Information, and Other Returns.

Form 2758 **does not** extend the time for payment of tax.

Additional Information

For details on withholding of tax, get **Pub. 515**, Withholding of Tax on Nonresident Aliens and Foreign Corporations, by calling 1-800-TAX-FORM (1-800-829-3676).

Income Tax Withholding on Wages, Pensions, Annuities, and Certain Other Deferred Income

Use **Form 941**, Employer's Quarterly Federal Tax Return, to report social security and Medicare taxes, and any income tax withheld, on wages paid to a nonresident alien employee.

Use **Form 945**, Annual Return of Withheld Federal Income Tax, to report income tax withheld under section 3405 from pensions, annuities, and certain other deferred income paid to a nonresident alien individual. However, if the recipient has elected under section 3405(a)(2) or (b)(2) not to have withholding under section 3405, these payments are subject to withholding under section 1441 and the tax withheld must be reported using Forms 1042 and 1042-S.

Use **Schedule H (Form 1040)**, Household Employment Taxes, to report social security and Medicare taxes, and any income tax withheld, on wages paid to a nonresident alien household employee.

For more information, see the instructions for these forms.

Deposit Requirements

Generally, if you are not required to use the Electronic Federal Tax Payment System (EFTPS), you must deposit the tax withheld and required to be shown on Form 1042 with an authorized financial institution or a Federal Reserve bank or branch using your preprinted **Form 8109**, Federal Tax Deposit Coupon. Do not use anyone else's coupons. If you do not have your coupons when a deposit is due, contact your IRS district office. To avoid a penalty, **do not** mail your deposits directly to the IRS.

How much tax you are required to withhold determines the frequency of your deposits. The following rules explain how often deposits must be made:

1. If at the end of any quarter-monthly period the total amount of undeposited taxes is $2,000 or more, you must deposit the taxes within 3 banking days after the end of the quarter-monthly period. (A quarter-monthly period ends on the 7th, 15th, 22nd, and last day of the month.) To determine banking days, do not count Saturdays, Sundays, legal holidays, or any local holidays observed by authorized financial institutions.

The deposit rules are considered met if:

● You deposit at least 90% of the actual tax liability for the deposit period, **and**

● If the quarter-monthly period is in a month other than December, you deposit any underpayment with your first deposit that is required to be made after the 15th day of the following month.

Any underpayment of $200 or more for a quarter-monthly period ending in December must be deposited by January 31.

2. If at the end of any month the total amount of undeposited taxes is at least $200 but less than $2,000, you must deposit the taxes within 15 days after the end of the month. If you make a deposit of $2,000 or more during any month **except December** under rule 1 above, carry over any end-of-the-month balance of less than $2,000 to the next month. If you make a deposit of $2,000 or more during December, any end-of-December balance of less than $2,000 should be paid directly to the IRS along with your Form 1042 by March 15, 2000.

3. If at the end of a calendar year the total amount of undeposited taxes is less than $200, you may either pay the taxes with your Form 1042 or deposit the entire amount by March 15, 2000.

Note: *If you are requesting an extension of time to file using Form 2758, follow the above rules to see if you must make a deposit of any balance due or if you can pay it with Form 2758. See Form 2758 and its instructions for more information.*

Electronic deposit requirement. You must make electronic deposits of all depository tax liabilities that occur after 1999 if the total of **all** your required Federal tax deposits exceeded $200,000 during calendar year 1998.

See Regulations section 31.6302-1(h) for more information.

The EFTPS must be used to make electronic deposits. If you are required to make electronic deposits and fail to do so, you may be subject to a 10% penalty.

Taxpayers who are not required to make electronic deposits may voluntarily participate in EFTPS. To enroll in EFTPS, call 1-800-945-8400 or 1-800-555-4477. For general information about EFTPS, call 1-800-829-1040.

Depositing on time. For deposits made by EFTPS to be on time, you must initiate the transaction at least one business day before the date the deposit is due.

Completing Form 8109. If you do not use EFTPS, deposit your income tax payments using Form 8109. In most cases, you will fill out a Form 8109 following the instructions in the coupon book. However, if a deposit liability arises from a distribution reportable on Form 1042 for the prior year, darken the 4th quarter box on Form 8109. If the distribution is reportable for the current year, darken the 1st quarter box. In all cases, follow the coupon book instructions for completing the rest of the deposit coupon. To ensure proper crediting, write your taxpayer identification number, the period to which the tax deposit applies, and "Form 1042" on the check or money order.

Deposits by foreign corporations. Fill in a preprinted Federal Tax Deposit Coupon showing the "Amount of Deposit" in U.S. dollars. Mail the completed coupon with a bank draft in U.S. dollars to:

Federal Reserve Bank of Philadelphia
Attn: Treasury Tax and Loan Unit
P.O. Box 44
Philadelphia, PA 19105 USA

Interest and Penalties

If you file Form 1042 late, or fail to pay or deposit the tax when due, you may be liable for penalties and interest unless you can show that the failure to file or pay was due to reasonable cause and not willful neglect.

1. Interest. Interest is charged on taxes not paid by the due date, even if an extension of time to file is granted. Interest is also charged on penalties imposed for failure to file, negligence, fraud, and substantial understatements of tax from the due date (including extensions) to the date of payment. Interest is figured at a rate determined under section 6621.

2. Late filing of Form 1042. The penalty for not filing Form 1042 when due (including extensions) is 5% of the unpaid tax for each month or part of a month the return is late, up to a maximum of 25% of the unpaid tax.

3. Late payment of tax. The penalty for not paying tax when due is usually ½ of 1% of the unpaid tax for each month or part of a month the tax is unpaid. The penalty cannot exceed 25% of the unpaid tax.

4. Failure to deposit tax when due. The penalty for failure to deposit tax when due is 2% for deposits not more than 5 days late, 5% for deposits more than 5 days late but not more than 15 days late, and 10% for deposits more than 15 days late. The penalty is increased to 15% if the tax is not deposited within 10 days after the date of the first delinquency notice sent to the taxpayer.

5. Other penalties. Penalties may be imposed for negligence, substantial understatement of tax, and fraud. See sections 6662 and 6663.

Specific Instructions

Part I

Note: *File only one Form 1042 (Part I) consolidating all Form 1042-S recipient information, regardless of the number of different clients, branches, divisions, or types of income for which you are the withholding agent. Show your name, address, and taxpayer identification number in the entity section.*

Address. Include the suite, room, or other unit number after the street address. If the Post Office does not deliver mail to the street address and you have a P.O. box, show the box number instead of the street address.

Lines 1 through 60. Do not enter any negative amounts on these lines.

Line 61a. The amount on line 61a must equal the sum of the monthly totals as listed on the Record of Federal Tax Liability. Do not make any adjustments on this line. Except for adjustments described in the instructions for line 61b, you may only make adjustments on the appropriate entry line in the Tax Liability column of the Record of Federal Tax Liability.

Line 61b. If you are a regulated investment company (RIC) or a real estate investment trust (REIT) that has paid a dividend in January subject to section 852(b)(7) or section 857(b)(8) (relating to certain dividends declared in the preceding October, November, or December), enter your additional tax liability on those dividends declared in 1999 but paid in January 2000 **less** any additional tax liability on those dividends declared in 1998 but paid in January 1999. Show any negative amount in brackets. Attach a statement showing your calculation.

Line 62a. Include the number of Forms 1042-S filed electronically.

Note: References to magnetic media forms in these instructions include forms filed electronically.

Line 63a. The amount on line 63a should equal the sum of all magnetic media and paper document Forms 1042-S, line 3, column (b), plus the amount shown on **Forms 1000**, Ownership Certificate, you have submitted to date.

Line 63b. The amount on line 63b should equal the sum of all Forms 1042-S, line 3, column (g) (less any tax released to the recipient before you file Form 1042), plus the tax assumed from Forms 1000. If it does not, attach a statement to Form 1042 explaining the difference.

Lines 68 and 69. You may claim an overpayment shown on line 68 as a refund or a credit. Check the applicable box on line 69 to show which you are claiming. If you claim a credit, it can reduce your required deposits of withheld tax for 2000.

Caution: *Be sure to reconcile amounts on Form 1042 with amounts on Forms 1042-S (including magnetic media files), to avoid unnecessary correspondence with the IRS.*

Part II

Use Part II in certain cases to transmit paper Forms 1042-S. Be sure to check the "Transmittal" box on the front of Form 1042. Complete your identifying information at the top of the form. Enter your name and taxpayer identification number in Part II. **Use of Part II to transmit paper Forms 1042-S does not affect your obligation to file Form 1042 (Part I) annually.**

Caution: *Do not use Part II if changes made to Forms 1042-S, or additional Forms 1042-S submitted, also change the gross income or tax information previously reported on Form 1042 (Part I). Instead, file an amended Form 1042 (Part I). See Amended Return below.*

Line 70. If you have **not yet filed** a Form 1042 (Part I) for 1999, you may complete Part II to:

• Submit original paper document Forms 1042-S; or

• Void or correct paper document Forms 1042-S previously submitted on a Part II transmittal document.

You may send in more than one Part II transmittal document to submit paper Forms 1042-S prior to filing your Form 1042 (Part I). You may submit corrected and voided Forms 1042-S even though changes reflect differences in gross income and tax withheld information on Forms 1042-S previously submitted with a Part II transmittal document.

Line 71. If you have **already filed** a Form 1042 (Part I) for 1999, you may use Part II to submit original, voided, or corrected paper document Forms 1042-S only if the corrections **do not change** the gross income or tax withheld information previously reported on line 63a or 63b of your Form 1042. For example, you may submit a Form 1042-S to change an income code in column (a) of a previously submitted Form 1042-S.

You are not required to sign at the bottom of page 1 when using Part II of this form.

Forms You Must Send With Form 1042

Send Copy A of all paper document Forms 1042-S when you file Form 1042 (Part I or II) even if income is exempt from tax withholding. Also, see **Magnetic Media/Electronic Reporting** in the Instructions for Form 1042-S.

Amended Return

If you have to make changes to your Form 1042 after you submit it, file an amended Form 1042. Use a Form 1042 for the year you are amending. Check the "Amended Return" box at the top of the form. You must complete all of Part I, including all filing information for the calendar year, and sign the return. Attach a statement explaining why you are filing an amended return (e.g., you are filing because the tax liability for May was incorrectly reported due to a mathematical error).

If you are also amending Form(s) 1042-S, see **Correcting Paper Forms 1042-S** in the Form 1042-S instructions.

Do not amend Form 1042 to recover taxes overwithheld in the prior year. For more information, see **Adjustment for Overwithholding** in Pub. 515.

Form **1042-S**	**Foreign Person's U.S. Source Income**	2000	OMB No. 1545-0096

Department of the Treasury
Internal Revenue Service

Subject to Withholding

► For Paperwork Reduction Act Notice, see page 6 of the separate instructions.

Copy A for
Internal Revenue Service

Line	(a) Income code	(b) Gross income paid	(c) Withholding allowances (for income code 15 or 16 only)	(d) Net income (column (b) minus column (c))	(e) Tax rate (%)	(f) Exemption code	(g) U.S. Federal tax withheld (net of any tax released)	(h) Country code
1								
2								
3	Total							

4 Recipient code ►

5 Recipient's U.S. taxpayer
identification number (TIN), if any ►

6 Account number (optional) ►

7 RECIPIENT'S name (first name, initial, and last name), street address, city or town, province or state, and country (including postal code)

9 WITHHOLDING AGENT'S name and address (including ZIP code)

10 Withholding agent's TIN

11 PAYER'S name and TIN (if different from withholding agent's)

12 State income tax withheld

8 Recipient's country of residence for tax purposes

13 Payer's state tax number

14 Name of state

☐ **VOID** ☐ **CORRECTED**   Cat. No. 11386R   Form **1042-S** (2000)

¶ 1104

U.S. Income Tax Filing Requirements

Every nonresident alien individual, nonresident alien fiduciary, and foreign corporation with United States income, including income that is effectively connected with the conduct of a trade or business in the United States, must file a United States income tax return. However, no return is required to be filed by a nonresident alien individual, nonresident alien fiduciary, or a foreign corporation if such person was not engaged in a trade or business in the United States at any time during the tax year and if the tax liability of such person was fully satisfied by the withholding of United States tax at the source. (Corporations file Form 1120-F; all others file Form 1040NR (or Form 1040NR-EZ if eligible).) You may get the return forms and instructions at any United States Embassy or consulate or by writing to: Eastern Area Distribution Center, P.O. Box 85074, Richmond, VA 23261-5074, U.S.A.

Tout étranger non-résident, tout organisme fidéicommissaire étranger non-résident et toute société étrangère percevant un revenu aux Etats-Unis, y compris tout revenu dérivé, en fait, du fonctionnement d'un commerce ou d'une affaire aux Etats-Unis, doit soumettre aux Etats-Unis, une déclaration d'impôt sur le revenu. Cependant aucune déclaration d'impôt sur le revenu n'est exigée d'un étranger non-résident, d'un organisme fidéicommissaire étrange non-résident, ou d'une société étrangère s'ils n'ont pris part à aucun commerce ou affaire aux Etats-Unis à aucun moment pendant l'année fiscale et si les impôts dont ils sont redevables, ont été entièrement acquittés par une retenue à la source, de leur montant. (Les sociétés doivent faire leur déclaration d'impôt en remplissant le formulaire 1120-F; tous les autres redevables doivent remplir le formulaire 1040NR (ou 1040NR-EZ si éligible).) On peut se procurer formulaires de déclarations d'impôts et instructions dans toutes les Ambassades et tous les Consulats des Etats-Unis. L'on peut également s'adresser pour tous renseignements a: Eastern Area Distribution Center, P.O. Box 85074, Richmond, VA 23261-5074, U.S.A.

Todo extranjero no residente, todo organismo fideicomisario extranjero no residente y toda sociedad anónima extranjera que reciba ingresos en los Estados Unidos, incluyendo ingresos relacionados con la conducción de un negocio o comercio dentro de los Estados Unidos, deberá presentar una declaración estadounidense de impuestos sobre ingreso. Sin embargo, no se requiere declaración alguna a un individuo extranjero, una sociedad anónima extranjera u organismo fideicomisario extranjero no residente, si tal persona no ha efectuado comercio o negocio en los Estados Unidos durante el año fiscal y si la responsabilidad con los impuestos de tal persona ha sido satisfecha plenamente mediante retencion del impuesto de los Estados Unidos en la fuente. (Las sociedades anónimas envian la Forma 1120-F; todos los demás contribuyentes envian la Forma 1040NR (o la Forma 1040NR-EZ si le corresponde).) Se podrán obtener formas e instrucciones en cualquier Embajada o Consulado de los Estados Unidos o escribiendo directamente a: Eastern Area Distribution Center, P.O. Box 85074, Richmond, VA 23261-5074, U.S.A.

Jede ausländische Einzelperson, jeder ausländische Bevollmächtigte und jede ausländische Gesellschaft mit Einkommen in den Vereinigten Staaten, einschliesslich des Einkommens, welches direkt mit der Ausübung von Handel oder Gewerbe innerhalb der Staaten verbunden ist, müssen eine Einkommensteuererklärung der Vereinigten Staaten abgeben. Eine Erklärung, muss jedoch nicht von Ausländern, ausländischen Bevollmächtigten oder ausländischen Gesellschaften in den Vereinigten Staaten eingereicht werden, falls eine solche Person während des Steuerjahres kein Gewerbe oder Handel in den Vereinigten Staaten ausgeübt hat und die Steuerschuld durch Einbehaltung der Steuern der Vereinigten Staaten durch die Einkommensquelle abgegolten ist. (Gesellschaften reichen den Vordruck 1120-F ein; alle anderen reichen das Formblatt 1040NR oder wenn passend das Formblatt 1040NR-EZ ein.) Einkommensteuererklärungen und Instruktionen können bei den Botschaften und Konsulaten der Vereinigten Staaten eingeholt werden. Um weitere Informationen wende man sich bitte an: Eastern Area Distribution Center, P.O. Box 85074, Richmond, VA 23261-5074, U.S.A.

¶ 1104

Explanation of Codes

Column (a). Income code.

Code	Type of Income
01	Interest paid by U.S. obligors—general
02	Interest on real property mortgages
03	Interest paid to controlling foreign corporations
04	Interest paid by foreign corporations
05	Interest on tax-free covenant bonds
06	Dividends paid by U.S. corporations—general
07	Dividends paid by U.S. subsidiaries to foreign parent corporations (including consent dividends)
08	Dividends paid by foreign corporations
09	Capital gains
10	Industrial royalties
11	Motion picture or television copyright royalties
12	Other royalties (e.g., copyright, recording, publishing)
13	Real property income and natural resources royalties
14	Pensions, annuities, alimony, and/or insurance premiums
15	Scholarship or fellowship grants
16	Compensation for independent personal services[1]
17	Compensation for dependent personal services[1]
18	Compensation for teaching[1]
19	Compensation during studying and training[1]
20	Earnings as an artist or athlete[2]
24	Real estate investment trust (REIT) distributions of capital gains
25	Trust distributions subject to IRC section 1445
26	Unsevered growing crops and timber distributions by a trust subject to IRC section 1445
27	Publicly traded partnership distributions subject to IRC section 1446
28	Gambling winnings
50	Other income

Column (f). Exemption code (applies if the tax rate entered in column (e) is 0%).

Code	Authority for Exemption
1	Income effectively connected with a U.S. trade or business
2	Exempt under an Internal Revenue Code section (income other than portfolio interest)
3	Income is not from U.S. sources[3]
4	Exempt under tax treaty
5	Portfolio interest exempt under an Internal Revenue Code section

Line 4. Recipient code.

Code	Type of Recipient
01	Individual[2]
02	Corporation[2]
03	Partnership[2]
04	Fiduciary (trust)
05	Nominee
06	Government or International Organization
07	Tax-Exempt Organization (IRC section 501(a))
08	Private Foundation
09	Artist or athlete[2]
10	Fiduciary (estate)
11	Fiduciary (other)
19	Other
20	Type of recipient unknown

[1] If compensation that otherwise would be covered under income codes 16–19 is directly attributable to the recipient's occupation as an artist or athlete, income code 20 should be used.

[2] If income code 20 is used, recipient code 09 (artist or athlete) should be used instead of recipient code 01 (individual), 02 (corporation), or 03 (partnership).

[3] Non-U.S. source income received by a nonresident alien is not subject to U.S. tax. This income amount is being furnished for information reporting purposes only.

Form **4224**
(Rev. August 1998)

Department of the Treasury
Internal Revenue Service

**Exemption From Withholding of Tax on
Income Effectively Connected With the
Conduct of a Trade or Business in the United States**
▶ File this form with your withholding agent.
(For use by a nonresident alien individual or fiduciary, foreign partnership, or foreign corporation.)

OMB No. 1545-0165

This exemption is applicable for calendar year _____ , or other tax year beginning _____ , and ending _____ ,

**Please
Type
or
Print**

Owner of income	U.S. taxpayer identification number
Foreign address (number, street, and apt. or suite no.)	
City or town, province or state. Include postal code where appropriate.	Country

Trade or Business in the United States

Name of trade or business	Type of business

Address (number and street) (Include apt. or suite no. or P.O. box if mail is not delivered to street address.)

City or town, state, and ZIP code

Describe each item of income that is, or is expected to be, effectively connected with the owner's U.S. trade or business: ....

....
....
....
....
....
....
....
....
....
....
....
....
....
....
....
....
....
....

Withholding Agent

Name of withholding agent	Employer identification number

U.S. address (number and street) (Include apt. or suite no. or P.O. box if mail is not delivered to street address.)

City or town, state, and ZIP code

I certify to the best of my knowledge and belief that the income described above is, or is expected to be, effectively connected with the conduct of the owner's trade or business in the United States and is includible in gross income for the tax year.

Signature of owner, fiduciary, trustee, or agent	Date

If an estate or trust, give name here

Address of fiduciary, trustee, or agent (number and street) (Include apt. or suite no. or P.O. box if mail is not delivered to street address.)

City or town, state, and ZIP code (If a foreign address, see instructions.)

For Paperwork Reduction Act Notice, see back of form.   Cat. No. 41460A   Form **4224** (Rev. 8-98)

Instructions

Section references are to the Internal Revenue Code.

General Information

Purpose of form. This form is used to obtain an exemption from withholding of tax under section 1441 or 1442 on certain income for nonresident alien individuals and fiduciaries, foreign partnerships, and foreign corporations. See **Pub. 519,** U.S. Tax Guide for Aliens, for details on alien status.

When exemption applies. File a new Form 4224 with the withholding agent for each tax year. The exemption applies only to income paid after the withholding agent receives the form, within the specified tax year of the owner (the person entitled to the income) whose name appears on the form. See **Pub. 515,** Withholding of Tax on Nonresident Aliens and Foreign Corporations, for further information.

Income eligible for exemption. In general, to be exempt from withholding, the income must be effectively connected with the conduct of the owner's trade or business in the United States, and must be included in the owner's gross income under section 871(b)(2), 842, or 882(a)(2) for the tax year. If these requirements are met, the following items of income may be exempt from withholding: interest, dividends, rents, royalties, salaries, wages, premiums, annuities, compensation, remuneration, emoluments, and other fixed or determinable annual or periodic gains, profits, and income; gains described in section 631(b) or (c); amounts subject to tax under section 871(a)(1)(C) or 881(a)(3); gains subject to tax under section 871(a)(1)(D) or 881(a)(4); and gains on transfers described in section 1235 made by October 4, 1966.

If a nonresident alien individual or foreign corporation is a partner in a foreign or domestic partnership, the exemption from withholding under section 1441 or 1442 only applies to the partner's distributive share of partnership income that is effectively connected with the conduct of a trade or business in the United States.

Income not eligible for exemption. The following are not eligible for exemption from withholding: compensation for personal services by a nonresident alien individual (but see **Form 8233,** Exemption From Withholding on Compensation for Independent (and Certain Dependent) Personal Services of a Nonresident Alien Individual), compensation described in section 543(a)(7) received by a foreign corporation that is a personal holding company, and income resulting from a section 897 disposition of an investment in U.S. real property.

Filing of tax return. All persons who have income effectively connected with the conduct of a trade or business in the United States are required to include that income on an annual U.S. income tax return. See **Pub. 519** for more information.

Filing Form 4224

Owner of income. Give Form 4224 to your withholding agent before payments are made to obtain exemption from withholding on any income to which it applies. You should keep a copy for your records. Promptly notify your agent in writing if the income to which the form applies is no longer effectively connected with the conduct of a trade or business in the United States.

U.S. taxpayer identification number. You are required to furnish a taxpayer identification number to obtain exemption from withholding on eligible income. You may use a social security number (SSN) or an employer identification number (EIN) if you have one.

Contact a Social Security Administration office to find out if you are eligible to get an SSN. If you do not have, **and are not eligible to obtain,** an SSN, you must apply for an IRS individual taxpayer identification number (ITIN), using **Form W-7,** Application for IRS Individual Taxpayer Identification Number.

Nonresident alien estates or trusts must use their employer identification number. See **Form SS-4,** Application for Employer Identification Number, for more information.

If you do not know the withholding agent's employer identification number, please get it from the withholding agent.

Withholding agent. Keep this form for your records. Do not attach Form 4224 to **Form 1042,** Annual Withholding Tax Return for U.S. Source Income of Foreign Persons, or to **Form 1042-S,** Foreign Person's U.S. Source Income Subject to Withholding.

Address of fiduciary, trustee, or agent. For a foreign address, enter the city or town, province or state, and country. **Do not** abbreviate the country name. Include the postal code where appropriate.

Paperwork Reduction Act Notice. We ask for the information on this form to carry out the Internal Revenue laws of the United States. You are required to give the information to the withholding agent. It is needed to ensure that you are complying with these laws and to allow the withholding agent to figure and collect the right amount of tax.

You are not required to provide the information requested on a form that is subject to the Paperwork Reduction Act unless the form displays a valid OMB control number. Books or records relating to a form or its instructions must be retained as long as their contents may become material in the administration of any Internal Revenue law. Generally, tax returns and return information are confidential, as required by Code section 6103.

The time needed to complete and file this form will vary depending on individual circumstances. The estimated average time is:

Recordkeeping . . . . 7 min.
Learning about the law or the form . . . . . . 13 min.
Preparing the form . . . . 14 min.
Copying and sending the form . . . . 20 min.

If you have comments concerning the accuracy of these time estimates or suggestions for making this form simpler, we would be happy to hear from you. You can write to the Tax Forms Committee, Western Area Distribution Center, Rancho Cordova, CA 95743-0001. **DO NOT** send the form to this address. Instead, see **Filing Form 4224** on this page.

Form **8233**
(Rev. October 1996)

Department of the Treasury
Internal Revenue Service

Exemption From Withholding on Compensation for Independent (and Certain Dependent) Personal Services of a Nonresident Alien Individual

▶ **See separate instructions.**

OMB No. 1545-0795

This exemption is applicable for compensation for calendar year 19 ...., or other tax year beginning ...., 19......., and ending ...., 19 .

Part I **Nonresident Alien Individual Identification (See Specific Instructions)**

Name

Taxpayer identification number ....

U.S. address (number and street) (Include apt. or suite no. or P.O. box)

United States visa type and number ....

City, state, and ZIP code

Citizens of Canada or Mexico complete either lines 1a and 1b or line 2 below; all other filers complete lines 1a, 1b, and 2.

1a Country issuing passport .... **2** Permanent foreign address
  b Passport number ....

3 Compensation is for services performed by me as a:
  ☐ Self-employed person (independent personal services) ☐ Foreign student ☐ Foreign professor/teacher
  ☐ Foreign researcher ☐ Business/vocational trainee

Caution: *If you are a foreign student, foreign professor/teacher, or foreign researcher, see the* **line 3 instructions** *for the required additional statement you must attach.*

4 Compensation for independent (and certain dependent) personal services:
  a Description of personal services you are providing..
  ....
  ....
  b Total compensation you expect to be paid for these services in this calendar or tax year $ ....

5 If compensation is exempt from withholding because of a U.S. tax treaty, provide:
  a Tax treaty **and treaty article** under which you are claiming exemption from withholding ....
  ....
  b Total compensation listed in 4b above that is exempt from tax under this treaty $ ....
  c Country of permanent residence ....

6 Additional facts to justify the exemption from withholding...
  ....
  ....
  ....

7 Number of personal exemptions claimed ▶   **8** How many days will you perform services in the United States during this tax year? ▶

Under penalties of perjury, I declare that I have examined this form and any accompanying statements, and, to the best of my knowledge and belief, they are true, correct, and complete. I also declare, under penalties of perjury, that I am not a citizen or resident of the United States.

Signature of nonresident alien individual ▶   Date ▶

Part II **Withholding Agent Certification**

Name

Employer identification number

Address (number and street) (Include apt. or suite no. or P.O. box, if applicable.)

City, state, and ZIP code

Telephone number
( )

Under penalties of perjury, I certify that I have examined this form and any accompanying statements, that I am satisfied that an exemption from withholding is warranted, and that I do not know or have reason to know that the nonresident alien individual's compensation is not entitled to the exemption or that the eligibility of the nonresident alien's compensation for the exemption cannot be readily determined.

Signature of withholding agent ▶   Date ▶

For Paperwork Reduction Act Notice, see separate instructions.   Cat. No. 62292k   Form **8233** (Rev. 10-96)

Department of the Treasury
Internal Revenue Service

Instructions for Form 8233

(Rev. October 1996)

Exemption From Withholding on Compensation for Independent (and Certain Dependent) Personal Services of a Nonresident Alien Individual

Section references are to the Internal Revenue Code unless otherwise noted.

Paperwork Reduction Act Notice.—We ask for the information on this form to carry out the Internal Revenue laws of the United States. If you want to receive exemption from withholding on compensation for independent (and certain dependent) personal services, you are required to give us the information. We need it to ensure that you are complying with these laws and to allow us to figure and collect the right amount of tax.

You are not required to provide the information requested on a form that is subject to the Paperwork Reduction Act unless the form displays a valid OMB control number. Books or records relating to a form or its instructions must be retained as long as their contents may become material in the administration of any Internal Revenue law. Generally, tax returns and return information are confidential, as required by Code section 6103.

The time needed to complete and file this form will vary depending on individual circumstances. The estimated average time is: **Recordkeeping**, 26 min.; **Learning about the law or the form**, 19 min.; **Preparing and sending the form to IRS**, 42 min.

If you have comments concerning the accuracy of these time estimates or suggestions for making this form simpler, we would be happy to hear from you. You can write to the Tax Forms Committee, Western Area Distribution Center, Rancho Cordova, CA 95743-0001. **DO NOT** send the tax form to this office. Instead, give it to your withholding agent.

Avoid Common Errors

To ensure that your Form 8233 is promptly accepted, be sure that you:

- Enter your complete name, address, and taxpayer identification number (TIN) in Part I.

- Answer all applicable questions completely.

- Are not trying to claim treaty benefits for a country with which the United States does not have a ratified tax treaty.

- Are not trying to claim a treaty exemption that does not exist in your treaty.

- Answer all parts of questions 4 and 5 in sufficient detail to allow the IRS to determine which tax treaty benefit you are claiming.

- Have claimed the proper number of personal exemptions in question 7.

- Have attached the required statement if you are a foreign student, professor/teacher, or researcher.

- Have fully completed the required certification in Part II if you are the withholding agent.

General Instructions

Purpose of Form.—In general, section 1441 requires 30% Federal income tax withholding on payments to nonresident aliens for independent personal services (self-employment). Sections 1441, 3401, and 3402 require withholding, sometimes at 30% and sometimes at graduated rates, on compensation for dependent personal services paid to nonresident alien students, professors/teachers, and researchers. However, some payments may be exempt from withholding because of a tax treaty or the personal exemption amount. Complete and give Form 8233 to your withholding agent if some or all of your compensation is exempt from withholding.

Who Should Use Form 8233.—A nonresident alien individual should use this form to claim exemption from withholding on some or all compensation paid for (1) independent personal services (self-employment) or (2) dependent personal services provided by a student, professor/teacher, researcher, or business/vocational trainee. For services in (1) above, use Form 8233 to claim a tax treaty exemption and/or the personal exemption amount. For services in (2) above, use Form 8233 only to claim a **tax treaty exemption** for any part of your compensation that is exempt from withholding; use **Form W-4**, Employee's Withholding Allowance Certificate, to claim the personal exemption amount.

Voluntary Use of Form 8233.—Certain resident aliens are eligible to exempt from Federal income tax their dependent personal service income under a tax treaty article covering students, professors/teachers, or researchers. These persons may (but are not required to) certify a claim for exemption from withholding by submitting a completed Form 8233 to their withholding agent. In such cases, the withholding agent **should not** submit Form 8233 to the IRS for approval.

Canadian students.—Canadian students performing dependent personal services who reasonably expect to earn $10,000 or less in a tax year may also use this form as described above to certify their exemption from withholding under Article XV of the U.S./Canada tax treaty. These students should check "Foreign student" on line 3 and write "Canadian" above the checkbox.

Giving Form 8233 to the Withholding Agent.—Complete a separate Form 8233 for each type of income and give it to each withholding agent for review. You must complete a Form 8233 for each tax year.

Example. A nonresident alien is primarily present in the United States as a professor, but also is occasionally invited to lecture at another educational institution. These lectures are not

connected with his teaching obligations but are in the nature of self-employment. The professor must complete two Forms 8233 and give one to each withholding agent to claim tax treaty benefits on the separate items of income.

If the withholding agent accepts your Form 8233, the withholding agent will sign it in Part II and will forward it to the IRS Office of the Assistant Commissioner (International). An accepted Form 8233 is effective only for the tax year shown on the form.

Do not use Form 8233 if you have an office in the United States regularly available to you for performing personal services. If you have an office in the United States regularly available to you, contact the IRS Office of the Assistant Commissioner (International). You may call 202-874-1460 or write to the address shown under Part II on page 2 for more information.

Definitions

Nonresident Alien Individual.—Any individual who is not a citizen or resident of the United States is a nonresident alien individual. An alien individual meeting either the "green card test" or the "substantial presence test" for the calendar year is a resident alien. Any person not meeting either test is a nonresident alien. The term "individual" also includes a nonresident alien fiduciary.

For more information on resident and nonresident alien status, the tests for residence, and common exceptions to them, see **Pub. 519**, U.S. Tax Guide for Aliens. You can get Pub. 519 by calling 1-800-TAX-FORM (1-800-829-3676).

Note: *Even though a nonresident alien individual married to a U.S. citizen or resident alien may choose to be treated as a resident alien for income tax purposes (e.g., for purposes of filing a joint income tax return), such individual is still treated as a nonresident alien for withholding tax purposes on all income except wages.*

Compensation for Independent Personal Services (Self-Employment Income).—Independent personal services are services performed in the United States by a nonresident alien individual who is an independent contractor (self-employed) rather than an employee. Such compensation includes payments for contract labor; payments for professional services, such as fees to an attorney, physician, or accountant, if the payments are made directly to the person performing the services; consulting fees; and generally, payments for performances by public entertainers, such as actors, musicians, artists, and athletes.

Compensation for Dependent Personal Services.—Dependent personal services are services performed in the United States by a nonresident alien individual employee. The name by which the compensation for these services is designated is immaterial. Thus, wages, salaries, fees, bonuses, commissions, and similar items paid to an employee are included in this definition.

Any part of a scholarship, fellowship, or grant paid for past, present, or future services to the institution paying the grant or fellowship is compensation for personal services.

Example. *G, a foreign graduate student, received a fellowship to a university to conduct advanced research in G's field. As part of this grant, G must teach a seminar 10 hours per week. The part of the grant that is payment for teaching is compensation for personal services.*

Withholding Agent.—Any person required to withhold tax on payments made to a nonresident alien individual is a withholding agent. The withholding agent may be an individual, corporation, partnership, trust, association, or

Cat. No. 22663B

any other entity. Generally, the person who pays or conveys the item of U.S. source income to the nonresident alien individual (or to his or her agent) must withhold. For further information, see **Pub. 515**, Withholding of Tax on Nonresident Aliens and Foreign Corporations.

Specific Instructions

Part I

Taxpayer Identification Number.—You are required to furnish a taxpayer identification number when completing this form. You may use a social security number (SSN) if you have one. If you do not have, **and are not eligible to obtain,** an SSN, you must apply for an IRS Individual Taxpayer Identification Number (ITIN), using **Form W-7**, Application for IRS Individual Taxpayer Identification Number.

Contact a Social Security Administration (SSA) office to find out if you are eligible to get an SSN. If you do not have an SSN but are required or eligible to get one, apply on **Form SS-5**, Application for a Social Security Card.

Nonresident alien estates or trusts must use their employer identification number or apply for one on **Form SS-4**, Application for Employer Identification Number.

Visa Type and Number.—Enter the visa type that is currently granted to you by the Immigration and Naturalization Service (INS). For example, foreign students are usually granted an "F-1" visa. Foreign professors, teachers, or researchers are usually granted a "J-1" visa. Business/vocational trainees are usually granted an "M-1" visa; however, some persons granted a "J-1" visa may also be considered business/vocational trainees, for example, a person admitted to complete a postgraduate residency in medicine. Also enter the serial number that was assigned to your visa at the time it was granted.

If you do not have, or do not require, a visa, write "None."

Note: *Spouses and dependents admitted on secondary visas (e.g., F-2, J-2, H-4, O-3) are* **not** *usually eligible to claim the same treaty benefits as the primary visa holder.*

Lines 1a, 1b, and 2.—Everyone must complete lines 1a, 1b, and 2, except citizens of Canada or Mexico, who can complete either lines 1a and 1b, or line 2.

Line 3.—Check the box that describes the **primary** reason you are in the United States. For example, if you have an "F-1" visa, the primary reason you are in the United States is as a student.

Caution: *Nonresident alien students, professors/teachers, and researchers using Form 8233 to claim exemption from withholding on compensation for personal services that is exempt from tax under a U.S. tax treaty* **must** *attach to Form 8233 the statement required by Revenue Procedure 87-8, 87-9, or 93-22. The format and contents of the required statements are contained in Pub. 519.*

For a newly ratified tax treaty not listed in the above revenue procedures, a nonresident alien student, professor/teacher, or researcher must attach a statement in a format similar to those contained in Pub. 519.

Line 4a.—If you are a nonresident alien individual performing independent personal services (self-employment) in the United States, fully describe the nature of the service, for example, "Consulting contract to design software," or "Give three lectures at XYZ University."

If you are a nonresident alien student or researcher who is also performing dependent personal services, fully describe the nature of your employment, for example, "Part-time library assistant," "Waiting on tables," or "Teaching one chemistry course per semester to undergraduate students."

If you are a nonresident alien professor/teacher, write "Teaching."

If you are a nonresident alien business/vocational trainee, fully describe the nature of your employment, for example, "Neurosurgical residency at ABC Hospital," or "One-year internship in hydraulic engineering at XYZ Corporation."

Line 4b.—Enter the total amount of compensation for personal services you will receive from this payer during the tax year. Enter an estimated amount if you do not know the exact amount.

Line 5a.—You must provide full information concerning the specific treaty and article on which you are basing your claim for exemption from withholding, for example, "U.S./Germany tax treaty, Article 20(1)."

Line 5b.—If all income received for the services performed to which this Form 8233 applies is exempt, write "All." If only part is exempt, enter the exact dollar amount that is exempt from withholding.

To avoid underwithholding of income taxes on amounts not exempt from tax, nonresident aliens completing Form W-4 should: (a) not claim exemption from income tax withholding; (b) request withholding as if they are single; (c) generally, claim only one personal exemption; and (d) request an additional income tax withholding amount of $4.00 per week.

Caution: *Special restrictions on exemption from or reduction of withholding apply to nonresident alien artists, athletes, entertainers, and similar individuals. Generally, such individuals are subject to 30% withholding from gross income paid for personal services performed unless a reduced rate of withholding under a withholding agreement prepared in accordance with Revenue Procedure 89-47, 1989-2 C.B. 598, has been approved by the IRS. For more information, contact the IRS Office of the Assistant Commissioner (International) at 202-874-1460, or write to the address shown under Part II below.*

Line 5c.—Generally, you may claim an exemption from Federal income tax only under a U.S. tax treaty with the country in which you claim permanent (or indefinite) foreign residence. This is the foreign country in which you live most of the time. It is not necessarily the country of your citizenship. For example, you are a citizen of Pakistan but have your home (where you live) in England. You **cannot** claim any exemption provisions under the U.S./Pakistan tax treaty. You can only use the U.S./United Kingdom tax treaty to claim exemption.

Line 6.—Enter any other information you believe may be necessary to clarify or explain your request for exemption from withholding.

Lines 7 and 8. For Independent Personal Services Only.

Line 7.—Generally, 30% must be withheld from your compensation after subtracting the value of one personal exemption. However, if you are a resident of Canada, Mexico, Japan, or the Republic of Korea, a student from India, or a U.S. national, you may be able to claim additional personal exemptions for your spouse and children. See Pub. 519 for more information.

Line 8.—Each allowable personal exemption must be prorated for the number of days during the tax year you will perform the personal

services identified on each Form 8233 in the United States. To figure the daily proration amount for each allowable exemption, divide the personal exemption amount (for example, $2,550 for tax year 1996) by 365 (366 for a leap year). Then multiply the result by the number of days you will perform these services in the United States. The amount allowed for each personal exemption changes from year to year, and may be obtained from the IRS.

Signature.—The nonresident alien individual or duly authorized representative must sign and date Form 8233.

Part II

Withholding Agent's Responsibilities.—When the nonresident alien individual gives you Form 8233, review it to see if you are satisfied that the exemption from withholding is warranted. If you are satisfied, based on the facts presented, complete and sign the certification in Part II.

You will need four copies of a completed Form 8233. Within 5 days of your acceptance, forward one copy to:

> Office of the Assistant Commissioner (International)
> Director, Office of International District Operations
> Attn: CP:IN:D:C:SS
> 950 L'Enfant Plaza South, S.W.
> Washington, DC 20024

Give one copy of the completed Form 8233 to the nonresident alien individual. Also attach a copy of the form to **Form 1042**, Annual Withholding Tax Return for U.S. Source Income of Foreign Persons, that you file with the IRS. Keep a copy for your records. Each copy of Form 8233 must include any attachments submitted by the nonresident alien individual.

The exemption from withholding is effective for payments made at least 10 days after you properly mail Form 8233 to the IRS.

You must not accept Form 8233, and you must withhold, if either of the following applies:

- You know or have reason to know that any of the facts or statements on Form 8233 may be false; or

- You know or have reason to know that the eligibility of the nonresident alien individual's compensation for the exemption cannot be readily determined (for example, if you know that the nonresident alien individual has an office in the United States regularly available for performing personal services).

If you accept Form 8233 and later find that either of the situations described above applies, you must promptly notify the IRS at the address above, in writing, and you must begin withholding on any amounts not yet paid. Also, if you are notified by the IRS that the eligibility for the exemption of the nonresident alien individual's compensation is in doubt or that the compensation is not eligible for exemption, you must begin withholding. See Regulations section 1.1441-4(b)(2)(iii) for examples illustrating these rules.

If you submit an incorrect Form 8233, you will be notified by the IRS that the form submitted is not acceptable and that you must begin withholding immediately. An incorrect Form 8233 is (a) any Form 8233 that claims a tax treaty benefit or exemption that does not exist or is obviously false; or (b) any Form 8233 that has not been completed in sufficient detail to allow determination of the correctness of the tax treaty benefit or exemption claimed.

Signature.—You or your duly authorized agent must sign and date Form 8233. See Regulations section 1.1441-7(b) for information about duly authorized agent.

Form **8288**		U.S. Withholding Tax Return for	

Form **8288**
(Rev. August 1998)
Department of the Treasury
Internal Revenue Service

U.S. Withholding Tax Return for Dispositions by Foreign Persons of U.S. Real Property Interests

OMB No. 1545-0902

Complete Part I or Part II. Also complete and attach Copies A and B of Form(s) 8288-A.
(Attach additional sheets if you need more space.)

Part I   **To Be Completed by the Buyer or Other Transferee Required To Withhold**

1   Name of withholding agent (buyer or other transferee)   Identification number

Street address (apt. or suite no., or rural route. Do not use a P.O. box.)

City or town, state, and ZIP code

2   Description and location of property acquired

3   Date of transfer   **4**   Number of Forms 8288-A attached   **5**   Amount realized on the transfer

6   Check applicable box.   **7**   Amount withheld
  a   Withholding is at 10% . . . . ☐
  b   Withholding is of a reduced amount . . . . ☐

Part II   **To Be Completed by a Corporation, Partnership, Trust, or Estate Subject to the Provisions of Section 1445(e)**

1   Name of withholding agent (corporation, partnership, or fiduciary)   Identification number

Street address (apt. or suite no., or rural route. Do not use a P.O. box.)

City or town, state, and ZIP code

2   Description of U.S. real property interest transferred or distributed

3   Date of transfer   **4**   Number of Forms 8288-A attached

5   Check all applicable boxes.   **6**   Total amount withheld
  a   Withholding is at 10% or 35% . . . . ☐
  b   Withholding is of a reduced amount . . . . ☐
  c   Large trust election to withhold at distribution . . . . ☐

Sign Here

Under penalties of perjury, I declare that I have examined this return, including accompanying schedules and statements, and to the best of my knowledge and belief, it is true, correct, and complete. Declaration of preparer (other than taxpayer) is based on all information of which preparer has any knowledge.

▶ Signature of withholding agent, partner, fiduciary, or corporate officer   Title (if applicable)   Date

Paid Preparer's Use Only

Preparer's signature ▶	Date	Check if self-employed ▶ ☐	Preparer's social security number
Firm's name (or yours if self-employed) and address ▶		EIN ▶	
		ZIP code ▶	

For Paperwork Reduction Act Notice, see instructions.   Cat. No. 62260A   Form **8288** (Rev. 8-98)

¶ 1104

General Instructions

Section references are to the Internal Revenue Code unless otherwise noted.

Purpose of Form

A withholding obligation is generally imposed on the buyer or other transferee (withholding agent) when a U.S. real property interest is acquired from a foreign person. The withholding obligation also applies to certain partnerships, foreign and domestic corporations, and the fiduciary of certain trusts and estates. This withholding serves to collect tax that may be owed by the foreign person. Use this form to report and transmit the amount withheld.

Note: *You are not required to withhold if any of the Exceptions listed on page 3 apply.*

Amount To Withhold

Generally, you must withhold 10% of the amount realized on the disposition by the transferor (see **Definitions** on this page).

See **Corporations, Partnerships, Trusts, and Estates Subject to Section 1445(e)** on page 4 for information about when withholding at 35% is required. Also see **Withholding Certificate Issued by the IRS** under **Exceptions** on page 3 for information about applying for reduction or elimination of withholding.

Joint transfers. If one or more foreign persons and one or more U.S. persons jointly transfer a U.S. real property interest, you must determine the amount subject to withholding in the following manner.

First, allocate the amount realized from the transfer among the transferors based on their capital contribution to the property. For this purpose, a husband and wife are treated as having contributed 50% each.

Second, withhold on the total amount allocated to foreign transferors.

Third, credit the amount withheld among the foreign transferors as they mutually agree. The transferors must request that the withholding be credited as agreed upon by the 10th day after the date of transfer. If no agreement is reached, credit the withholding by evenly dividing it among the foreign transferors.

Who Must File

A buyer or other transferee of a U.S. real property interest, and a corporation, partnership, or fiduciary that is required to withhold tax, must file Form 8288 to report and transmit the amount withheld. If two or more persons are joint transferees, each is obligated to withhold. However, the obligation of each will be met if one of the joint transferees withholds and transmits the required amount to the IRS.

Publicly traded partnerships, publicly traded trusts, and REITs. Distributions from a publicly traded partnership are generally subject to the withholding requirements of section 1446 and are not subject to the withholding requirements of section 1445. See Rev. Proc. 89-31, 1989-1 C.B. 895. Distributions from a trust that is regularly traded on an established securities market and distributions from a real estate investment trust (REIT) are subject to section 1445 and its regulations. However, for such partnerships and trusts, generally the method of paying over and reporting the withholding to the IRS is governed by section 1461 and its regulations and the deposit rules in Regulations section 1.6302-2. Use **Form 1042,** Annual Withholding Tax Return for U.S. Source Income of Foreign Persons, and **Form 1042-S,** Foreign Person's U.S. Source Income Subject to

Withholding, to report and pay over the withheld amounts. **Do not** use Forms 8288 and 8288-A for these distributions. See Regulations section 1.1445-8.

When To File

A transferee must file Form 8288 and transmit the tax withheld to the IRS by the 20th day after the date of transfer.

You must withhold even if an application for a withholding certificate is or has been submitted to the IRS on the date of transfer. However, you do not have to file Form 8288 and transmit the withholding until the 20th day after the day the IRS mails you a copy of the withholding certificate or notice of denial. But if the principal purpose for filing the application for a withholding certificate was to delay paying the IRS the amount withheld, interest and penalties will apply to the period after the 20th day after the date of transfer.

Installment payments. You must withhold the full amount at the time of the first installment payment. If you cannot because the payment does not involve sufficient cash or other liquid assets, you may obtain a withholding certificate from the IRS. See the instructions for **Form 8288-B,** Application For Withholding Certificate for Dispositions by Foreign Persons of U.S. Real Property Interests, for more information.

Where To File

Send Form 8288 with the amount withheld, and Copies A and B of Form(s) 8288-A to the Internal Revenue Service Center, P.O. Box 21086, d.p. 543 East Bldg./FIRPTA-X, Philadelphia, PA 19114-0586.

Forms 8288-A Must Be Attached

Anyone who completes Form 8288 must also complete a **Form 8288-A,** Statement of Withholding on Dispositions by Foreign Persons of U.S. Real Property Interests, for each person subject to withholding. Copies A and B of Form 8288-A must be attached to Form 8288. Copy C is for your records.

After receipt of Form 8288 and Form(s) 8288-A, the IRS will stamp Copy B of Form 8288-A to show receipt of the withholding and will forward the stamped copy to the foreign person subject to withholding at the address shown on Form 8288-A.

You are not required to furnish a copy of Form 8288 or 8288-A directly to the transferor. To receive credit for the withheld amount, the transferor generally must attach the stamped Copy B of Form 8288-A to a U.S. income tax return (e.g., Form 1040NR or 1120F) or application for early refund filed with the IRS.

Penalties

Under section 6651, penalties apply for failure to file Form 8288 when due and for failure to pay the withholding when due. In addition, if you are required to but do not withhold tax under section 1445, the tax, including interest, may be collected from you. Under section 7202, you may be subject to a penalty of up to $10,000 for willful failure to collect and pay over the tax. Corporate officers or other responsible persons may be subject to a penalty under section 6672 equal to the amount that should have been withheld and paid over to the IRS.

Definitions

Transferee. Any person, foreign or domestic, that acquires a U.S. real property interest by purchase, exchange, gift, or any other disposition.

Transferor. For purposes of this withholding, this means any foreign person that disposes of a U.S. real property interest by sale, exchange, gift, or any other disposition.

Withholding agent. For purposes of this return, this means the buyer or other transferee who acquires a U.S. real property interest from a foreign person.

Foreign person. A nonresident alien individual, a foreign corporation that does not have a valid election under section 897(i) to be treated as a domestic corporation, a foreign partnership, a foreign trust, or a foreign estate. A resident alien individual is **not** a foreign person.

U.S. real property interest. Any interest, other than an interest solely as a creditor, in:

1. Real property located in the United States or the Virgin Islands.

2. Certain personal property associated with the use of real property.

3. A domestic corporation, unless it is shown that the corporation was not a U.S. real property holding corporation during the previous 5 years (or during the period in which the transferor held the interest, if shorter).

A U.S. real property interest does not include:

1. An interest in a domestically controlled real estate investment trust (REIT).

2. An interest in a corporation that has disposed of all its U.S. real property interests in transactions in which the full amount of any gain was recognized as provided in section 897(c)(1)(B).

3. An interest in certain publicly traded corporations, partnerships, and trusts.

See Regulations sections 1.897-1 and -2 for more information. Also see **Transferred Property That Is Not a U.S. Real Property Interest** under **Exceptions** on page 3.

Amount realized. The sum of the cash paid or to be paid (not including interest or original issue discount), the fair market value of other property transferred or to be transferred, and the amount of any liability assumed by the transferee or to which the U.S. real property interest is subject immediately before and after the transfer. Generally, the amount realized for purposes of this withholding is the sales or contract price.

Date of transfer. The first date on which consideration is paid or a liability is assumed by the transferee. However, for purposes of sections 1445(e)(2), (3), and (4), and Regulations sections 1.1445-5(c)(1)(iii) and 1.1445-5(c)(3), the date of transfer is the date of distribution that creates the obligation to withhold. Payment of consideration does not include the payment before passage of legal or equitable title of earnest money (other than pursuant to an initial purchase contract), a good-faith deposit, or any similar amount primarily intended to bind the parties to the contract and subject to forfeiture. A payment that is not forfeitable may also be considered earnest money, a good-faith deposit, or a similar sum.

Exceptions

You are not required to withhold if any of the following applies:

1. You acquire the property for use as a residence and the amount realized (sales price) is not more than $300,000.

2. The transferor (seller) is not a foreign person.

3. You did not acquire a U.S. real property interest.

4. You receive a notice of nonrecognition of gain or loss from the transferor and you file a copy of the notice with the IRS.

5. You receive a withholding certificate from the IRS that excuses withholding.

6. The amount realized by the transferor is zero (e.g., the property is transferred as a gift and the recipient does not assume any liabilities or furnish any other consideration to the transferor).

7. An amount is realized by the grantor on the grant or lapse of an option to acquire a U.S. real property interest. However, withholding is required on the sale, exchange, or exercise of an option.

8. The property is acquired by the United States, a U.S. state or possession or political subdivision, or the District of Columbia.

For rules that apply to foreclosures, see Regulations section 1.1445-2(d)(3).

1. Purchase of residence for $300,000 or less. No withholding is required if one or more individuals acquire U.S. real property for use as a residence and the amount realized is not more than $300,000. A U.S. real property interest is acquired for use as a residence if you or a member of your family has definite plans to reside in the property for at least 50% of the number of days the property is used by any person during each of the first two 12-month periods following the date of transfer. Do not take into account the number of days the property will be vacant in making this determination. No form or other document is required to be filed with the IRS for this exception; however, if you do not in fact use the property as a residence, the withholding tax may be collected from you.

This exception applies whether or not the **transferor** is an individual, partnership, trust, corporation, or other transferor. However, this exception does not apply if the actual **transferee** is not an individual, even if the property is acquired for an individual.

2. Transferor not a foreign person. You are not required to withhold if you receive a certification of nonforeign status from the transferor, signed under penalties of perjury, stating that the transferor is not a foreign person and containing the transferor's name, address, and identification number (social security number (SSN) or employer identification number (EIN)). If you receive a certification, the withholding tax cannot be collected from you unless you knew that the certification was false or you received a notice from your agent or the transferor's agent that it was false. The certification must be signed by the individual, a responsible officer of a corporation, a general partner of a partnership, or the trustee, executor, or fiduciary of a trust or estate.

A foreign corporation electing to be treated as a domestic corporation under section 897(i) must attach to the certification a copy of the acknowledgment of the election received from the IRS. The acknowledgment must state that the information required by Regulations section 1.897-3 has been determined to be complete. If the acknowledgment is not attached, you may not rely on the certification. Keep any certification of nonforeign status you receive in your records for 5 years after the year of transfer.

You may also use other means to determine that the transferor is not a foreign person. But if you do, and it is later determined that the transferor is a foreign person, the withholding tax may be collected from you.

Late notice of false certification. If, after the date of transfer, you receive a notice from your agent or the transferor's agent that the certification of nonforeign status is false, you do not have to withhold on consideration paid before you received the notice. However, you must withhold the full 10% of the amount realized from any consideration that remains to be paid, if possible. You must do this by withholding and paying over the entire amount of each successive payment of consideration until the full 10% has been withheld and paid to the IRS. These amounts must be reported and transmitted to the IRS by the 20th day following the date of each payment.

3. Transferred property that is not a U.S. real property interest. No withholding is required if you acquire an interest in property that is not a U.S. real property interest. A U.S. real property interest includes certain interests in U.S. corporations, as well as direct interests in real property and certain associated personal property (see **Definitions** on page 2).

No withholding is required on the acquisition of an interest in a domestic corporation if **(1)** any class of stock of the corporation is regularly traded on an established securities market, or **(2)** the transferee receives a statement by the corporation that the interest is not a U.S. real property interest, unless you know that the statement is false or you receive a notice from your agent or the transferor's agent that the statement is false. A corporation's statement may be relied on only if it is dated not more than 30 days before the date of transfer.

Late notice of false statement. If after the date of transfer you receive a notice that an interest in a corporation is not a U.S. real property interest is false, follow the instructions under **Late notice of false certification** above.

Generally, no withholding is required on the acquisition of an interest in a foreign corporation. However, withholding may be required if the foreign corporation has made the election under section 897(i) to be treated as a domestic corporation.

4. Transferor's nonrecognition of gain or loss. You may receive a notice signed under penalties of perjury stating that the transferor is not required to recognize gain or loss on the transfer because of a nonrecognition provision of the Internal Revenue Code (see Temporary Regulations section 1.897-6T(a)(2)). You may rely on the transferor's notice unless **(1)** only part of the gain qualifies for nonrecognition, or **(2)** you know or have reason to know that the transferor is not entitled to the claimed nonrecognition treatment.

No particular form is required for this notice. By the 20th day after the date of transfer, you must send a copy of the notice of nonrecognition with a cover letter giving your name, identification number, and address to the address listed under **Where To File** on page 2. See Temporary Regulations section 1.1445-9T(b) for more information on the transferor's notice of nonrecognition.

5. Withholding certificate issued by the IRS. A withholding certificate may be issued by the IRS to reduce or eliminate withholding on dispositions of U.S. real property interests by foreign persons. Either a transferee or transferor may apply for the certificate. The certificate may be issued if:

1. Reduced withholding is appropriate because the 10% or 35% amount exceeds the transferor's maximum tax liability,

2. The transferor is exempt from U.S. tax or nonrecognition provisions apply, or

3. The transferee or transferor enters into an agreement with the IRS for the payment of the tax.

An application for a withholding certificate must comply with the provisions of Regulations sections 1.1445-3 and 1.1445-6 and Rev. Proc. 88-23, 1988-1 C.B. 787. In certain cases, you may use **Form 8288-B** to apply for a withholding certificate. The IRS will normally act on an application by the 90th day after a complete application is received.

If you receive a withholding certificate from the IRS that excuses withholding, you are not required to file Form 8288. However, if you receive a withholding certificate that reduces (rather than eliminates) withholding, there is **no** exception to withholding, and you are required to file Form 8288. Attach a copy of the withholding certificate to Form 8288. See **When To File** on page 2 for more information.

Liability of Agents

If the transferee or other withholding agent has received **(1)** a transferor's certification of nonforeign status, or **(2)** a corporation's statement that an interest is not a U.S. real property interest, and the transferee's or transferor's agent knows that the document is false, the agent must provide notice to the transferee or other withholding agent. If the notice is not provided, the agent will be liable for the tax that should have been withheld, but only to the extent of the agent's compensation from the transaction.

If you are the transferee or withholding agent and you receive a notice of false certification or statement from your agent or the transferor's agent, you must withhold tax as if you had not received a certification or statement. But see **Late notice of false certification** above.

The terms "transferor's agent" and "transferee's agent" mean any person who represents the transferor or transferee in any negotiation with another person (or another person's agent) relating to the transaction, or in settling the transaction. For purposes of section 1445(e), a transferor's or transferee's agent is any person who represents or advises an entity, a holder of an interest in an entity, or a fiduciary with respect to the planning, arrangement, or completion of a transaction described in sections 1445(e)(1) through (4).

A person is not treated as an agent if the person only performs one or more of the following acts in connection with the transaction:

1. Receiving and disbursing any part of the consideration.

2. Recording any document.

3. Typing, copying, and other clerical tasks.

4. Obtaining title insurance reports and reports concerning the condition of the property.

5. Transmitting documents between the parties.

6. Functioning exclusively in his or her capacity as a representative of a condominium association or cooperative housing corporation. This exemption includes the board of directors, the committee, or other governing body.

¶ **1104**

Corporations, Partnerships, Trusts, and Estates Subject to Section 1445(e)

Withholding is required on certain distributions and other transactions by domestic or foreign corporations, partnerships, trusts, and estates. A domestic trust or estate must withhold 35% of the amount distributed to a foreign beneficiary from a "U.S. real property interest account" that it is required to establish under Regulations section 1.1445-5(c)(1)(iii). A foreign corporation that has not made the election under section 897(i) must withhold 35% of the gain it recognizes on the distribution of a U.S. real property interest to its shareholders. Certain domestic corporations are required to withhold tax on distributions to foreign shareholders.

No withholding is required on the transfer of an interest in a domestic corporation if any class of stock of the corporation is regularly traded on an established securities market. Also, no withholding is required on the transfer of an interest in a publicly traded partnership or trust.

No withholding will be required with respect to an interest holder if the entity or fiduciary receives a certification of nonforeign status from the interest holder. An entity or fiduciary may also use other means to determine that an interest holder is not a foreign person, but if it does so and it is later determined that the interest holder is a foreign person, the withholding may be collected from the entity or fiduciary.

Section 1445(e)(1) Transactions

Partnerships. A domestic partnership that is not publicly traded must withhold tax under section 1446 on effectively connected income of its foreign partners and must file **Form 8804,** Annual Return for Partnership Withholding Tax (Section 1446), and **Form 8805,** Foreign Partner's Information Statement of Section 1446 Withholding Tax. A publicly traded partnership generally must withhold tax under section 1446 on distributions to its foreign partners and must file Forms 1042 and 1042-S. Because a domestic partnership that disposes of a U.S. real property interest is required to withhold under section 1446, it is not required to withhold under section 1445(e)(1).

Trusts and estates. If a domestic trust or estate disposes of a U.S. real property interest, the amount of gain realized must be paid into a separate "U.S. real property interest account." For these purposes, a domestic trust is one that does not make the "large trust election" (explained below), is not a REIT, and is not publicly traded. The fiduciary must withhold 35% of the amount distributed to a foreign person from the account during the tax year of the trust or estate in which the disposition occurred. The withholding must be paid over to the IRS within 20 days of the date of distribution. Special rules apply to grantor trusts. See Regulations section 1.1445-5 for more information and how to compute the amount subject to withholding.

Large trust election. Trusts with more than 100 beneficiaries may make an election to withhold upon distribution rather than at the time of transfer. The amount to be withheld from each distribution is 35% of the amount attributable to the foreign beneficiary's proportionate share of the current balance of the trust's section 1445(e)(1) account. This election does not apply to any REIT or to any publicly traded trust. Special rules apply to large trusts that make recurring sales of growing crops and timber.

A trust's section 1445(e)(1) account is the total net gain realized by the trust on all section 1445(e)(1) transactions after the date of the election, **minus** the total of all distributions made by the trust after the date of the election from such total net gain. See Regulations section 1.1445-5(c)(3) for more information.

Section 1445(e)(2) Transactions

A foreign corporation that distributes a U.S. real property interest must generally withhold 35% of the gain recognized by the corporation. No withholding or reduced withholding is required if the corporation receives a withholding certificate from the IRS.

Section 1445(e)(3) Transactions

Generally, a domestic corporation that distributes any property to a foreign person that holds an interest in the corporation must withhold 10% of the fair market value of the property distributed if:

1. The foreign person's interest in the corporation is a U.S. real property interest under section 897, and

2. The property is distributed either in redemption of stock under section 302 or in liquidation of the corporation under sections 331 through 341.

Similar rules apply in the case of any distribution to which section 301 applies and that is not made out of the earnings and profits of the corporation.

No withholding or reduced withholding is required if the corporation receives a withholding certificate from the IRS.

Section 1445(e)(4) Transactions

No withholding is required under section 1445(e)(4), relating to certain taxable distributions by domestic or foreign partnerships, trusts, and estates, until the effective date of a Treasury Decision under section 897(e)(2)(B)(ii) and (g).

Section 1445(e)(5) Transactions

The transferee of a partnership interest must withhold 10% of the amount realized on the disposition by a foreign partner of an interest in a domestic or foreign partnership in which at least 50% of the value of the gross assets consists of U.S. real property interests and at least 90% of the value of the gross assets consists of U.S. real property interests plus any cash or cash equivalents. However, no withholding is required under section 1445(e)(5) for dispositions of interests in other partnerships, trusts, or estates until the effective date of a Treasury Decision under section 897(g). No withholding is required if, no earlier than 30 days before the transfer, the transferee receives a statement signed by a general partner under penalties of perjury that at least 50% of the value of the gross assets of the partnership does not consist of U.S. real property interests or that at least 90% of the value of the gross assets does not consist of U.S. real property interests plus cash or cash equivalents. The transferee may rely on the statement unless the transferee knows it is false or the transferee receives a false statement notice pursuant to Regulations section 1.1445-4.

Specific Instructions

Lines 1. If you are a fiduciary, list your name and the name of the trust or estate. Enter the home address of an individual or the office address of an entity.

Identifying Number. The buyer or other withholding agent must provide its U.S. taxpayer identification number. For a U.S. individual, this is a social security number (SSN). For any entity other than an individual (e.g., corporation, estate, or trust), this is an employer identification number (EIN).

If you are a nonresident alien individual who is not eligible for a social security number and you have already obtained an IRS Individual Taxpayer Identification Number (ITIN), you must provide it on Form 8288. If you do not already have an ITIN, you must apply for one before filing Form 8288. If you have applied for an ITIN but you have not yet received it when you file Form 8288, write "Applied For" in the Identification Number box. You must provide your ITIN to the IRS as soon as you receive it. See **Form W-7,** Application for IRS Individual Taxpayer Identification Number, for more information.

Lines 2. Enter the location and a description of the property, including any substantial improvements (e.g., "12-unit apartment building"). In the case of interests in a corporation that constitute a U.S. real property interest, enter the class or type and amount of the interest (e.g., "10,000 shares Class A Preferred Stock XYZ Corporation").

Lines 4. Copies A and B of each Form 8288-A should be counted as one form.

Part II, line 3. If you are a domestic trust or estate or you make the large trust election, enter the date of distribution.

Paperwork Reduction Act Notice. We ask for the information on this form to carry out the Internal Revenue laws of the United States. You are required to give us the information. We need it to ensure that you are complying with these laws and to allow us to figure and collect the right amount of tax.

You are not required to provide the information requested on a form that is subject to the Paperwork Reduction Act unless the form displays a valid OMB control number. Books or records relating to a form or its instructions must be retained as long as their contents may become material in the administration of any Internal Revenue law. Generally, tax returns and return information are confidential, as required by section 6103.

The time needed to complete and file these forms will vary depending on individual circumstances. The estimated average times are:

	Form 8288	Form 8288-A
Recordkeeping	5 hr., 30 min.	2 hr., 52 min.
Learning about the law or the form	4 hr., 40 min.	12 min.
Preparing and sending the form to the IRS	4 hr., 58 min.	15 min.

If you have comments concerning the accuracy of these time estimates or suggestions for making these forms simpler, we would be happy to hear from you. You can write to the Tax Forms Committee, Western Area Distribution Center, Rancho Cordova, CA 95743-0001. **DO NOT** send the forms to this address. Instead, see **Where To File** on page 2.

Withholding agent's name, street address, city, state, and ZIP code	**1** Date of transfer	**Statement of Withholding on Dispositions by Foreign Persons of U.S. Real Property Interests**
	2 Federal income tax withheld	OMB No. 1545-0902

Withholding agent's Federal identification number	Identification number of foreign person subject to withholding (see instructions)	**3** Amount realized	**4** Gain recognized by foreign corporation	**Copy A For Internal Revenue Service Center**
Name of person subject to withholding		**5** Description of property transferred		For Paperwork Reduction Act Notice, see the instructions for Form 8288.
Foreign address (number, street, and apt. or suite no.)		**6** Person subject to withholding is: An individual ☐ A corporation ☐ Other (specify) ▶		
City, province or state, postal code, and country (not U.S.)		Mailing address of person subject to withholding (if different)		

Form **8288-A** (Rev. 8-98)   Cat. No. 62261L   **Attach Copies A and B to Form 8288**   Department of the Treasury - Internal Revenue Service

Instructions for the Withholding Agent

Prepare Form 8288-A for each foreign person subject to withholding. **Attach Copies A and B** to **Form 8288,** U.S. Withholding Tax Return for Dispositions by Foreign Persons of U.S. Real Property Interests. Copy B will be stamped by the IRS and sent to the person subject to withholding. Retain Copy C for your records. You do not have to give a copy of this form to the person subject to withholding.

Identification number. A Federal identification number is a social security number (SSN), employer identification number (EIN), or IRS individual taxpayer identification number (ITIN). The withholding agent must provide the transferor's TIN if the tranferor has, or is required to have, a TIN.

Address. You must enter the foreign home address (for an individual) or the foreign office address (for other than an individual) of the person subject to withholding. You may enter a separate mailing address in the space provided. If provided, the IRS will use the separate mailing address to forward Copy B to the person subject to withholding.

Note: *The home or office address of the person subject to withholding must be an address outside the United States. If the person does not have an address outside the United States, enter the country of residence of the foreign person in this section and provide a complete mailing address.*

Box 1. Enter the date of transfer. However, enter the date of distribution if you withheld under section 1445(e)(2) or (e)(3) or if you made the large trust election to withhold at the date of distribution.

Box 2. Enter the Federal income tax you withheld for the foreign person whose name appears on this form.

Box 3. Enter the amount realized by the foreign person whose name appears on this form.

Box 4. Complete only if you are a foreign corporation required to withhold under section 1445(e)(2).

Box 6. Check the applicable box to indicate whether the foreign person subject to withholding is an individual or a corporation. If "other," specify whether the person is a partnership, trust, or estate.

See the instructions for Form 8288 for more information.

Instructions for the Person Subject to Withholding

Generally, if you are a foreign person that disposes of real property located in the United States as seller or transferor, the buyer or other transferee must withhold 10% of the gross amount realized. Certain foreign interest holders that are beneficiaries or shareholders are also subject to Federal income tax withholding, but at a rate of 35%.

You must file a tax return (Form 1040NR, 1041, 1065, 1065-B or 1120F) to report the sale or other disposition as effectively connected with the conduct of a trade or business in the United States. To receive credit for any Federal income tax withheld shown in box 2, attach Form 8288-A to your tax return, unless you make a request for early refund. Foreign partnerships should report the withholding on **Form 8804,** Annual Return for Partnership Withholding Tax (Section 1446), and attach Form 8288-A. See **Pub. 515,** Withholding of Tax on Nonresident Aliens and Foreign Corporations, and **Pub. 519,** U.S. Tax Guide for Aliens, for more information.

Note: *If you do not already have one, you are required to get a Federal identification number before you file a tax return or a request for early refund. See Pub. 515 or 519 for more information.*

If the amount shown in box 2 is greater than your maximum tax liability, you may apply for an early refund. However, you must still file your tax return when due. To apply for an early refund, you must first get a withholding certificate. No particular form is required for an application for early refund, but it must include the following information in separate paragraphs numbered as shown below:

1. Your name, address, and Federal identification number,

2. The amount required to be withheld as stated in the withholding certificate issued by the IRS,

3. The amount withheld shown in box 2 (attach a copy of this Form 8288-A), and

4. The amount to be refunded.

Send your application for a withholding certificate and/or application for early refund to the Philadelphia Service Center, P.O. Box 21086, d.p. 543 East Bldg./FIRPTA-X, Philadelphia, PA, 19114-0586.

See Regulations sections 1.1445-3 and 1.1445-6, Rev. Proc. 88-23, and **Form 8288-B,** Application for Withholding Certificate for Dispositions by Foreign Persons of U.S. Real Property Interests, for information about withholding certificates.

Form **8288-B**
(Rev. August 1998)
Department of the Treasury
Internal Revenue Service

Application for Withholding Certificate for Dispositions by Foreign Persons of U.S. Real Property Interests

OMB No. 1545-1060

▶ **Please type or print.**

1 Names of all transferor(s) (attach additional sheets if more than one transferor)

Identification number

Street address, apt. or suite no., or rural route. Do not use a P.O. box.

City, state or province, and country (if not U.S.). Include ZIP code or postal code where appropriate.

2 Names of all transferee(s) (attach additional sheets if more than one transferee)

Identification number

Street address, apt. or suite no., or rural route. Do not use a P.O. box.

City, state or province, and country (if not U.S.). Include ZIP code or postal code where appropriate.

3 Applicant is: Transferee ☐   Transferor ☐

4 a Name of withholding agent (see instructions)   **b Identification number**

c Name of estate, trust, or entity (if applicable)   **d Identification number**

5 Address where you want withholding certificate sent (street address, apt. or suite no., P.O. box, or rural route number)   **Phone no.** (optional)
(   )

City, state or province, and country (if not U.S.). Include ZIP code or postal code where appropriate.

6 Description of U.S. real property transaction:
a Date of transfer (month, day, year) ....   **b** Contract price $ ....
c Type of interest transferred: ☐ Real property   ☐ Associated personal property
☐ Domestic U.S. real property holding corporation
d Use of property at time of sale: ☐ Rental or commercial   ☐ Personal   ☐ Other (attach explanation)
e Adjusted basis $ ....
f Location and general description of property (for a real property interest), description (for associated personal property), or the class or type and amount of the interest (for an interest in a U.S. real property holding corporation). See instructions.

....
....
....
....
....
....
....
....

7 Check the box to indicate the reason a withholding certificate should be issued. See the instructions for line 6 for information that must be attached to Form 8288-B.
a ☐ The transferor is exempt from U.S. tax or nonrecognition treatment applies.
b ☐ The transferor's maximum tax liability is less than the tax required to be withheld.
c ☐ The special installment sales rules described in Rev. Proc. 88-23 allow reduced withholding.

8 Does the transferor have any unsatisfied withholding liability under section 1445?. . . . .   ☐ Yes   ☐ No

9 Is this application for a withholding certificate made under section 1445(e)?. . . . .   ☐ Yes   ☐ No
If "Yes," check the applicable boxes below.
a Type of transaction: ☐ 1445(e)(1)   ☐ 1445(e)(2)   ☐ 1445(e)(3)   ☐ 1445(e)(5)
b Applicant is: ☐ Taxpayer   ☐ Other person required to withhold. Specify your title (e.g., trustee.) ▶ _____

Under penalties of perjury, I declare that I have examined this application and accompanying attachments, and, to the best of my knowledge and belief, they are true, correct, and complete.

Signature	Title (if applicable)	Date

For Paperwork Reduction Act Notice, see instructions.   Cat. No. 10128Z   Form **8288-B** (Rev. 8-98)

¶ 1104

General Instructions

Section references are to the Internal Revenue Code unless otherwise noted.

Purpose of form. Use Form 8288-B to apply for a withholding certificate to reduce or eliminate withholding on dispositions of U.S. real property interests by foreign persons, but **only** if the application is based on:

1. A claim that the transferor is entitled to nonrecognition treatment or is exempt from tax,

2. A calculation solely of the transferor's maximum tax liability, or

3. The special installment sales rules described in Rev. Proc. 88-23, 1988-1 C.B. 787.

Do not use this form for applications:

● Based on an agreement for the payment of tax with conforming security,

● For blanket withholding certificates under Rev. Proc. 88-23, or

● Other than the three types described above.

See Regulations sections 1.1445-3 and 1.1445-6 and Rev. Proc. 88-23 for information and procedures for applying for a withholding certificate.

Who can apply for a withholding certificate. Either the transferee or the transferor (or other authorized person) can file this application.

Withholding certificate. The IRS can issue a withholding certificate to reduce or eliminate withholding under section 1445. A certificate issued before the transfer notifies the transferee that reduced withholding or no withholding is required. A certificate issued after the transfer may authorize an early or a normal refund. If, on the date of transfer, an application for a withholding certificate is or has been submitted to the IRS, the applicable withholding is not required to be paid over to the IRS until the 20th day after the day that the IRS mails the withholding certificate or notice of denial.

The IRS will normally act on an application within 90 days of receipt of all information necessary to make a proper determination. The IRS will determine whether withholding should be reduced or eliminated or whether a withholding certificate should not be issued.

Identification number. The transferee, transferor, and agent (if applicable) must provide a Federal identification number (a TIN) on any application for a withholding certificate accompanied by a request for early refund filed with the IRS. For U.S. individuals, the TIN is a social security number (SSN). For all other entities, it is an employer identification number (EIN). If you are a nonresident alien individual who is required to have a TIN, but is not eligible to obtain an SSN, you must apply for an IRS individual taxpayer number (ITIN). Get **Form W-7**, Application for IRS Individual Taxpayer Identificatin Number, for more information.

Any withholding certificate issued by the IRS applies only for the limited purpose of determining the withholding obligation under section 1445 and does not apply to any substantive issue that may arise in connection with the transfer. The acceptance by the IRS of any evidence submitted in connection with this application is not binding on the IRS for any purpose other than issuing the withholding certificate. The information submitted in support of the application may be subject to verification by the IRS prior to issuance of a withholding certificate.

If you receive a withholding certificate from the IRS and withholding is still required, a copy of the withholding certificate must be attached to **Form 8288,** U.S. Withholding Tax Return for Dispositions by Foreign Persons of U.S. Real Property Interests.

Installment sales. A transferee is required to withhold on the full sales price regardless of the amount of the payment. However, if the transferor is not a dealer and will report gain using the installment method under section 453, a withholding certificate allowing reduced withholding may be obtained. Any withholding certificate based on the installment sale method will provide for payment of interest on the deferred tax liability under section 453A(c) when applicable.

For installment sales subject to withholding under section 1445(a) or (e), the IRS will consider applications for a withholding certificate based on the transferee's (or entity's or fiduciary's) agreement to all of the following:

1. Withhold and pay over 10% or lower amount determined by the IRS (or the amount the IRS determines to be appropriate under section 1445(e)) of the down payment. The amount paid over must include any liabilities of the transferor (entity in the case of section 1445(e)) assumed by the transferee, or liabilities to which the U.S. real property interest was subject immediately before and after the transfer.

2. Withhold 10% or lower amount determined by the IRS (or the amount the IRS determines to be appropriate under section 1445(e)) on each subsequent payment and, for withholding under section 1445(a), the interest on the deferred tax liability.

3. Use Forms 8288 and 8288-A (relating to withholding on dispositions by foreign persons of U.S. real property interests) to pay over all amounts withheld. The identification number of the transferor (or interest holder subject to withholding under section 1445(e)) must be included on Forms 8288 and 8288-A.

4. Notify the IRS before the disposition or encumbrance of the U.S. real property interest (of the installment obligation under section 1445(e)), and when it occurs, pay over the remaining amount to be withheld.

5. Continue to withhold under a reduced withholding certificate until an amended certificate is issued, even if the transferor pledges the installment obligation in exchange for all or part of the proceeds due on the obligation and includes in gross income under section 453A(d) the net proceeds of the secured indebtedness.

Where to send applications for a withholding certificate. Form 8288-B and other applications for a withholding certificate must be sent to the Internal Revenue Service Center, d.p. 543 East building/FIRPTA-X, P.O. Box 21086, Philadelphia, PA 19114-0586.

Required attachments to Form 8288-B. See the **Specific Instructions** below to find out what information must be attached to this form. Failure to include all the required information and documents with the application will cause it to be considered incomplete and may delay the issuance of the withholding certificate.

Specific Instructions

Read the following instructions carefully. In certain cases, attachments to this form are required.

Line 1. Enter the name, street address, and identification number of the transferor. If there are multiple transferors, attach additional sheets giving the required information about each one. For a transaction under section 1445(e), enter the required information for each foreign person who will bear substantive income tax liability because of the transaction for whom adjusted withholding is sought.

Line 2. Enter the name, street address, and identification number of the transferee. If there are multiple transferees, attach additional sheets giving the required information about each one.

Line 4a. The withholding agent will normally be the buyer or other transferee as described in section 1445(c)(4). For distributions under section 1445(e), the withholding agent also includes a trustee, executor, or other authorized person.

Line 4b. If you are not applying for this withholding certificate in your personal capacity, enter your SSN or ITIN (see *Identification number* under **General Instructions** for more information).

Line 4c. If you are acting on behalf of an estate or trust, or are signing as an authorized person for an entity other than an individual (e.g., a corporation or partnership), enter the name of the estate, trust, or entity.

Line 4d. Enter the EIN of the estate, trust, or entity.

Line 5. Enter the address you want the IRS to use for purposes of returning the withholding certificate.

Line 6c. "Associated personal property" means property (e.g., furniture) sold with a building. See Regulations section 1.897-1.

Line 6d. Check "Other" if the property was used for both personal and rental use and attach an explanation.

Line 6f. Enter the address and description of the property (e.g., "10-story, 100-unit luxury apartment building"). For a real estate holding corporation interest transferred, enter the class or type and amount of the interest (e.g., "10,000 shares Class A Preferred Stock XYZ Corporation").

Line 7a. If you checked 7a, attach:

1. A brief description of the transfer,

2. A summary of the law,

3. Facts supporting the claim of nonrecognition or exemption,

4. Evidence that the transferor has no unsatisfied withholding liability, **and**

5. The most recent assessed value for state or local property tax purposes of the interest to be transferred, or other estimate of its fair market value. You need not submit supporting evidence of the value of the property.

A nonresident alien or foreign corporation must also attach a statement of the adjusted basis of the property immediately before the distribution or transfer.

Line 7b. If you checked 7b, attach a calculation of the maximum tax that can be imposed on the disposition. You must also include a statement signed by the transferor under penalties of perjury that the calculation and all supporting evidence is true and correct to the best knowledge of the transferor.

The calculation of the maximum tax that can be imposed must include:

1. Evidence of the amount to be realized by the transferor, such as a copy of the signed contract of transfer,

2. Evidence of the adjusted basis of the property, such as closing statements, invoices for improvements, and depreciation schedules, or if no depreciation schedules are submitted, a statement of the nature of the use of the property and why depreciation was not allowed,

3. Amounts to be recaptured for accelerated depreciation, investment credit, or other items subject to recapture,

4. The maximum capital gain and/or ordinary income tax rates applicable to the transfer,

5. The tentative tax owed, **and**

6. Evidence showing the amount of any increase or reduction of tax to which the transferor is subject, including any reduction to which the transferor is entitled under a U.S. income tax treaty.

If you have a net operating loss, see section 4.06 of Rev. Proc. 88-23 for special rules about the maximum tax calculation.

If the purchase price includes personal property not subject to tax under section 897, for the calculation of maximum tax, the transferor must also include a statement listing each such item of personal property transferred and the fair market value attributable to each item. The fair market value claimed should be supported by an independent appraisal or other similar documentation.

Line 7c. If you checked 7c, see **Installment sales** on page 3.

Line 8. You must provide a calculation of the transferor's unsatisfied withholding liability or evidence that it does not exist. This liability is the amount of any tax the transferor was required to, but did not, withhold and pay over under section 1445 when the U.S. real property interest now being transferred was acquired, or upon a prior acquisition. The transferor's unsatisfied withholding liability is included in the calculation of maximum tax liability so that it can be satisfied by the withholding on the current transfer.

Evidence that there is no unsatisfied withholding liability includes any of the following:

1. Evidence that the transferor acquired the subject or prior real property interest before 1985;

2. A copy of Form 8288 filed and proof of payment;

3. A copy of a withholding certificate issued by the IRS plus a copy of Form 8288 and proof of payment of any amount required by that certificate;

4. A copy of the nonforeign certificate furnished by the person from whom the U.S. real property interest was acquired, executed at the time of that acquisition;

5. Evidence that the transferor purchased the subject or prior real property interest for $300,000 or less and a statement, signed by the transferor under penalties of perjury, that the transferor purchased the property for use as a residence within the meaning of Regulations section 1.1445-2(d)(1);

6. Evidence that the person from whom the transferor acquired the subject or prior U.S. real property interest fully paid any tax imposed on that transaction under section 897;

7. A copy of a notice of nonrecognition treatment provided to the transferor under Regulations section 1.1445-2(d)(2) by the person from whom the transferor acquired the subject or prior U.S. real property interest; or

8. A statement, signed by the transferor under penalties of perjury, explaining why the transferor was not required to withhold under section 1445(a) with regard to the transferor's acquisition of the subject or prior real property interest.

Line 9a. If the transaction is subject to withholding under section 1445(e), check the box to indicate which provision of section 1445(e) applies.

Line 9b. Indicate whether the applicant is the taxpayer or the person required to withhold, and in what capacity that person is required to withhold.

Signature. The application must be signed by an individual, a responsible corporate officer, a general partner of a partnership, or a trustee, executor, or other fiduciary of a trust or estate. The application may also be signed by an authorized agent with a power of attorney. **Form 2848,** Power of Attorney and Declaration of Representative, can be used for this purpose.

Paperwork Reduction Act Notice. We ask for the information on this form to carry out the Internal Revenue laws of the United States. You are required to give us the information. We need it to ensure that you are complying with these laws and to allow us to figure and collect the right amount of tax.

You are not required to provide the information requested on a form that is subject to the Paperwork Reduction Act unless the form displays a valid OMB control number. Books or records relating to a form or its instructions must be retained as long as their contents may become material in the administration of any Internal Revenue law. Generally, tax returns and return information are confidential, as required by Code section 6103.

The time needed to complete and file this form will vary depending on individual circumstances. The estimated average time is:

Recordkeeping . . . . .2 hr., 4 min.

Learning about the law or the form . . . . 1 hr., 48 min.

Preparing the form . . . . . . 53 min.

Copying, assembling, and sending the form to the IRS . . . . 20 min.

If you have comments concerning the accuracy of these time estimates or suggestions for making this form simpler, we would be happy to hear from you. You can write to the Tax Forms Committee, Western Area Distribution Center, Rancho Cordova, CA 95743-0001. **DO NOT** send this form to this office. Instead, see **Where to send applications for a withholding certificate** on page 3.

Form **8804**	**Annual Return for Partnership Withholding Tax (Section 1446)**	OMB No. 1545-1119

▶ See separate Instructions for Forms 8804, 8805, and 8813.

▶ Attach Form(s) 8805.

Department of the Treasury
Internal Revenue Service   For calendar year 1999 or tax year beginning   , 1999, and ending   ,

1999

Check this box if the partnership consisted entirely of nonresident alien partners during the tax year   . . . . ▶ ☐

Part I   **Partnership**

1a Name of partnership	b Employer identification number

c Number, street, and room or suite no. If a P.O. box, see page 4 of the instructions.	**For IRS Use Only**	
	CC	FD
	RD	FF
d City, state, and ZIP code. If a foreign address, see page 4 of the instructions.	CAF	FP
	CR	I
	EDC	

Part II   **Withholding Agent**

2a Name of withholding agent. If partnership is also the withholding agent, enter "SAME" and do not complete lines 2b–d.	b Withholding agent's U.S. identifying number

c Number, street, and room or suite no. If a P.O. box, see page 4 of the instructions.

d City, state, and ZIP code

Part III   **Section 1446 Tax Liability and Payments**

3a	Enter number of noncorporate foreign partners . . . . ▶		
b	Enter number of corporate foreign partners . . . . ▶		
4a	Total effectively connected taxable income allocable to noncorporate foreign partners	4a	
b	Multiply line 4a by 39.6% (.396)		4b
5a	Total effectively connected taxable income allocable to corporate foreign partners.	5a	
b	Multiply line 5a by 35% (.35)		5b
6	Total section 1446 tax owed. Add lines 4b and 5b		6
7a	Payments of section 1446 tax made by the partnership identified on line 1a during its tax year (or with a request for an extension of time to file) and amount credited from 1998 Form 8804 . .	7a	
b	Section 1446 tax paid or withheld by another partnership in which the partnership identified on line 1a was a partner during the tax year (attach Form(s) 1042-S or 8805)	7b	
c	Section 1445(a) or 1445(e)(1) tax withheld from the partnership identified on line 1a during the tax year for a disposition of a U.S. real property interest by that partnership. Attach Form(s) 1042-S or 8288-A. See page 5 of the instructions	7c	
8	Total payments. Add lines 7a through 7c		8
9	**Balance due.** If line 6 is more than line 8, subtract line 8 from line 6. Attach a check or money order for the full amount payable to the "United States Treasury." Write the partnership's employer identification number, tax year, and Form 8804 on it . .		9
10	**Overpayment.** If line 8 is more than line 6, subtract line 6 from line 8		10
11	Amount of line 10 you want **refunded to you.** . . . . ▶		11
12	Amount of line 10 you want **credited to next year's Form 8804**	12	

Please Sign Here

Under penalties of perjury, I declare that I have examined this return, including accompanying schedules and statements, and to the best of my knowledge and belief, it is true, correct, and complete. Declaration of preparer (other than general partner, limited liability company member, or withholding agent) is based on all information of which preparer has any knowledge.

▶ _____   _____   _____
    Signature of general partner, limited liability company   Title   Date
    member, or withholding agent

Paid Preparer's Use Only	Preparer's signature ▶		Date	Check if self-employed ☐	Preparer's SSN or PTIN
	Firm's name (or yours if self-employed) and address ▶			EIN	
				ZIP code	

For Paperwork Reduction Act Notice, see separate Instructions for Forms 8804, 8805, and 8813.   Cat. No. 10077T   Form **8804** (1999)

¶ **1104**

Form **8805**

Department of the Treasury
Internal Revenue Service

**Foreign Partner's Information Statement
of Section 1446 Withholding Tax**

▶ See separate Instructions for Forms 8804, 8805, and 8813.

For partnership's calendar year 1999, or tax year beginning , 1999, and ending ,

OMB No. 1545-1119

1999

Copy A for Internal Revenue Service
Attach to Form 8804.

1a Foreign partner's name

b Number, street, and room or suite no.

c City, state, and ZIP code. If a foreign address, see page 4 of the instructions.

2a U.S. identifying number of foreign partner subject to withholding

b Account number assigned by partnership (if any)

3 Type of partner: ☐ Individual ☐ Corporation ☐ Partnership ☐ Other (specify) ▶

4 Country code of partner. See page 7 of the instructions for a listing of codes.

5a Name of partnership

b Number, street, and room or suite no. If a P.O. box, see page 4 of the instructions.

c City, state, and ZIP code. If a foreign address, see page 4 of the instructions.

6 Partnership's U.S. employer identification number

7a Withholding agent's name. If partnership is also the withholding agent, enter "SAME" and do not complete line 7b.

b Withholding agent's U.S. identifying number

8a Check if the partnership identified on line 5a owns an interest in one or more partnerships . . . . ▶ ☐
b Check if the partnership income is exempt from U.S. tax for the partner identified on line 1a . . . . ▶ ☐

9 Partnership's effectively connected taxable income allocable to partner for the tax year . . | **9** |

10 Enter the applicable tax rate: .396 (noncorporate partner) or .35 (corporate partner) . . . . . . | **10** | . |

11 Total tax credit allowed to partner under section 1446. Multiply line 9 by line 10. **Individual and corporate partners:** Claim this amount as a credit against your U.S. income tax on Form 1040NR, 1120-F, etc. . . . | **11** |

For Paperwork Reduction Act Notice, see separate Instructions for Forms 8804, 8805, and 8813.   Cat. No. 10078E   Form **8805** (1999)

Form **8813** (Rev. November 1999) Department of the Treasury Internal Revenue Service	**Partnership Withholding Tax Payment (Section 1446)** ▶ See separate Instructions for Forms 8804, 8805, and 8813.	OMB No. 1545-1119

For calendar year _____ , or tax year beginning _____ , ____ , and ending _____ .

1	PARTNERSHIP'S name, address (number, street, and room or suite no.), city, state, and ZIP code. If a P.O. box or foreign address, see page 4 of the instructions.	2	Partnership's U.S. employer identification number

| 3 | Amount of this payment. Attach a check or money order payable to the "United States Treasury." Write the partnership's employer identification number, tax year, and Form 8813 on it . . . . | **3** | |

For Paperwork Reduction Act Notice, see separate Instructions for Forms 8804, 8805, and 8813.   Cat. No. 10681H   Form **8813** (Rev. 11-99)

Chapter 12

Foreign Persons Doing Business in the United States

¶ 1201 TAXATION OF A U.S. TRADE OR BUSINESS

A foreign company may initially market its products in the United States through the use of independent U.S. brokers or distributors. As the importer's U.S. sales volume grows, it may wish to bring the U.S. marketing function in-house by having its employees travel to the United States in order to identify customers, display inventory, negotiate sales agreements, and provide technical support. The next logical step in the progression of the foreign company's U.S. marketing activities is to establish a U.S. sales office, which could be structured as a branch or a subsidiary.[1] A threshold issue for a foreign company importing its products into the United States is whether the company's U.S. activities are subject to U.S. taxation. As discussed below, the answer to this question depends on both U.S. tax law and the provisions of any income tax treaty between the United States and the importer's home country.

---

[1] A U.S. subsidiary is a corporation organized under the laws of one of the 50 states or the District of Columbia, and therefore is a separate legal entity from its foreign parent corporation. A U.S. branch is simply an extension of the foreign corporation, as opposed to a separate legal entity.

Determinants of U.S. Taxation

U.S. trade or business. The United States taxes foreign corporations and nonresident alien individuals on the net amount of income effectively connected with the conduct of a trade or business within the United States.[2] Therefore, under the Internal Revenue Code, the existence of a U.S. trade or business is the touchstone of U.S. taxation of a foreign person's business profits. Despite its importance, there is no comprehensive definition of the term "trade or business" in the Code or the Regulations. The relevant case law suggests that a U.S. trade or business exists only if the activities of either the taxpayer or the taxpayer's dependent agents within the United States are considerable, continuous, and regular.[3] This determination is made based on the facts and circumstances of each case.

The conduct of a U.S. trade or business by an independent agent generally is not imputed to the principal.[4] An independent agent is one who is both legally and economically independent of the principal, and who is willing to act on behalf of more than one principal. Likewise, the conduct of a U.S. trade or business by a domestic corporation is not imputed to a foreign shareholder, even if the shareholder owns 100% of the stock of the domestic corporation. However, if a partnership, estate, or trust is engaged in a U.S. trade or business, then each partner or beneficiary is considered to be engaged in a U.S. trade or business.[5]

A U.S. trade or business ordinarily includes the performance of personal services in the United States.[6] However, under a *de minimis* rule, the performance of dependent personal services by a nonresident alien individual does not constitute a U.S. trade or business if the following requirements are met:

(i) the nonresident alien is present in the United States for 90 days or less during the taxable year,

(ii) the nonresident alien receives no more than $3,000 for his or her U.S. services, and

(iii) the nonresident alien works as an employee or under contract for either a foreign person who is not engaged in a U.S. trade or business or the foreign office of a U.S. person.[7]

This exception allows nonresident aliens to make short business trips to the United States free of U.S. taxes. As discussed later in this chapter,

---

[2] Code Secs. 871(b) and 882(a). For this purpose, the United States includes the 50 states and the District of Columbia, but not U.S. possessions. Code Sec. 7701(a)(9).

[3] See, for example, *I. Balanovski v. U.S.*, 236 F2d 298 (2nd Cir., 1956).

[4] See, for example, *British Timken, Ltd. v. Comm'r*, 12 TC 880 (1949).

[5] Code Sec. 875.

[6] Code Sec. 864(b).

[7] Code Sec. 864(b)(1) and Reg. § 1.864-2(b). The compensation of a nonresident alien who meets these requirements is treated as foreign-source income. Code Sec. 861(a)(3).

¶ 1201

income tax treaties often contain more generous exemptions which allow for longer stays and increase or eliminate the limitation on earnings for business travelers from treaty countries.

In addition to the *de minimis* rule for dependent personal services, the following safe harbor exceptions are provided for foreign persons engaged in the trading of stocks, securities, and certain commodities: [8]

 (i) *Broker-dealers*—Trading for the account of another through an independent agent located in the United States does not constitute a U.S. trade or business.[9] This exception does not apply, however, if, at any time during the taxable year, the taxpayer has an office or other fixed place of business in the United States through which, or by the direction of which, the trades are made.[10]

 (ii) *Trading for own account*—Trading by taxpayers for their own account does not constitute a U.S. trade or business, regardless of whether the trades are made by the taxpayer, the taxpayer's employee, or an independent agent. This exception does not apply to dealers.[11]

Taxpayers whose trading activities do not qualify for one of these safe harbor provisions are not necessarily considered to be engaged in a U.S. trade or business. Instead, that determination is made based on the facts and circumstances of each case.[12]

Treaty exemptions. Income tax treaties to which the United States is a party ordinarily contain a provision which exempts a foreign person's business profits from U.S. tax, unless those profits are attributable to a permanent establishment which the taxpayer maintains within the United States.[13] A permanent establishment includes a fixed place of business (e.g., a sales office), unless the fixed place of business is used solely for auxiliary functions (e.g., purchasing, storing, displaying, or delivering inventory), or activities of a preparatory nature (e.g., collecting information about potential customers).[14] A permanent establishment also exists if employees or other dependent agents habitually exercise in the United States an authority to conclude sales contracts in the taxpayer's name.[15] As a consequence, a foreign company that sends executives or salespeople to the United States to enter into contracts may create a permanent establishment even if those

---

[8] Code Sec. 862(b)(2). These exceptions apply only to commodities of the kind customarily dealt in on an organized commodity exchange (e.g., grain), and then only to transactions of the kind customarily consummated at such an exchange (e.g., futures). Code Sec. 864(b)(2)(B)(iii).

[9] Code Sec. 864(b)(2)(A)(i) and (b)(2)(B)(i). For purposes of this exception, the volume of stock, security, or commodity transactions effected during the taxable year is irrelevant. Reg. §1.864-2(c)(1).

[10] Code Sec. 864(b)(2)(C).

[11] Code Sec. 864(b)(2)(A)(ii) and (b)(2)(B)(ii).

[12] Reg. § 1.864-2(e).

[13] For example, Article 7(1) of the United States Model Income Tax Convention of September 20, 1996 (or "U.S. Model Treaty").

[14] See, for example, Article 5(1) and (4) of the U.S. Model Treaty.

[15] See, for example, Article 5(5) of the U.S. Model Treaty.

employees operate out of hotels and thus have no fixed place of business. Employees who limit their U.S. activities to auxiliary or preparatory functions, with sales concluded in a foreign country, will not create a permanent establishment. Marketing products in the United States solely through independent U.S. brokers or distributors also does not create a permanent establishment.[16]

Tax treaties also usually provide various exemptions for personal services income. These provisions allow nonresident alien individuals to perform personal services within the United States and avoid U.S. taxation, as long as their U.S. activities do not exceed a specified level of intensity. A common approach is to exempt income derived by nonresident alien individuals from dependent services performed in the United States if the following requirements are satisfied:

(i)   the dependent agent is present in the United States for 183 days or less,

(ii) the agent's compensation is paid by an employer which is not a U.S. resident, and

(iii) the compensation is not borne by a permanent establishment which the employer maintains in the United States.[17]

Most tax treaties also contain a separate exemption for personal services income derived by self-employed professionals, such as accountants, doctors, engineers, and lawyers. Such income ordinarily is exempt from U.S. taxation unless the services are performed in the United States, and the income is attributable to an office or other fixed place of business that is located in the United States and is regularly available to the taxpayer for purposes of performing the services.[18] Finally, tax treaties often contain special rules governing personal services income derived by crew members of ships and aircraft operated in international traffic,[19] entertainers and athletes,[20] government workers,[21] and students and trainees.[22] The appendix to Chapter 9 provides a listing of the treaty provisions governing personal services income, by country.

Effectively Connected Income

Overview. If a foreign corporation or nonresident alien individual is engaged in a U.S. trade or business, it is subject to U.S. taxation on the income effectively connected with the conduct of that U.S. trade or

---

[16] See, for example, Article 5(6) of the U.S. Model Treaty.

[17] See, for example, Article 15(2) of the U.S. Model Treaty.

[18] See, for example, Article 14 of the U.S. Model Treaty. U.S.-source service fees derived by self-employed nonresident alien individuals are not subject to U.S. self-employment taxes. Reg. § 1.1401-1(c).

[19] See, for example, Article 15(3) of the U.S. Model Treaty.

[20] See, for example, Article 17 of the U.S. Model Treaty.

[21] See, for example, Article 19 of the U.S. Model Treaty.

[22] See, for example, Article 20 of the U.S. Model Treaty.

business.[23] Effectively connected income includes the following five categories of income:

(i) certain types of U.S.-source income,[24]

(ii) certain types of foreign-source income attributable to a U.S. office,[25]

(iii) certain types of deferred income which is recognized in a year that the foreign person is not engaged in a U.S. trade or business, but which would have been effectively connected income if the recognition of the income had not been postponed,[26]

(iv) income from an interest in U.S. real property which a passive foreign investor has elected to treat as effectively connected income,[27] and

(v) interest income derived from U.S. obligations by a bank organized and doing business in a U.S. possession.[28]

Categories (i), (ii), and (iii) are discussed in detail below. Category (iv) is discussed in Chapter 11, and category (v) obviously impacts only a relatively small number of taxpayers.

U.S.-source income. Effectively connected income includes all of the U.S.-source income of a foreign corporation or nonresident alien individual engaged in a U.S. trade or business, other than U.S. source nonbusiness (or investment-type) income which ordinarily is subject to the 30% withholding tax.[29] Common examples of such income include income derived by a U.S. branch from the sale of inventory, or from providing services.[30]

U.S.-source dividends, interest, rents, and royalties also are included in effectively connected income if the item of income meets one of the following tests:

(i) *Asset-use test*—The income is derived from assets used in, or held for use in, the conduct of the U.S. trade or business.

(ii) *Business-activities test*—The activities of the U.S. trade or business were a material factor in the realization of the income.[31]

---

[23] Code Secs. 871(b) and 882(a).

[24] Code Sec. 864(c)(2) and (3).

[25] Code Sec. 864(c)(4).

[26] Code Sec. 864(c)(6) and (7).

[27] Code Secs. 871(d) and 882(d).

[28] Code Sec. 882(e).

[29] Code Sec. 864(c)(3). Chapter 11 discusses the types of U.S.-source income ordinarily subject to the 30% withholding tax.

[30] Whether the U.S.-source income is actually derived from the taxpayer's U.S. trade or business is irrelevant for this purpose. Reg. § 1.864-4(b). How-

ever, tax treaty provisions regarding permanent establishments usually prohibit the United States from taxing a foreign person's business profits unless those profits are attributable to a permanent establishment. See, for example, Article 7(1) of the U.S. Model Treaty.

[31] Code Sec. 864(c)(2). In determining whether an item of income satisfies either the asset-use and business-activities tests, due regard is given to how the asset or income is reflected in the foreign corporation's books and records. Code Sec. 864(c)(2) and Reg. § 1.864-4(c)(4).

Both tests are designed to include in effectively connected income any interest, dividends, rents, and royalties which are in substance business income. Examples include interest income derived from an account or note receivable arising from the trade or business, dividends and interest derived by a dealer in securities, and rents or royalties derived from an active leasing or licensing business.[32]

Foreign-source income attributable to a U.S. office. Effectively connected income ordinarily includes only U.S.-source income.[33] However, certain types of foreign-source income are treated as effectively connected income if the foreign person maintains an office or other fixed base in the United States, and the U.S. office is a material factor in producing the income and regularly carries on activities of the type which produce such income.[34] This exception applies to the following types of foreign-source income:

(i) rents or royalties for the use of, or for the privilege of using, any patent, copyright, secret process or formula, goodwill, trademark, trade brand, franchise, or other like property, derived from the active conduct of a U.S. trade or business,

(ii) dividend and interest income derived from the active conduct of a banking, financing, or similar business within the United States, or received by a corporation, the principal business of which is trading in stocks and securities for its own account, and

(iii) gains from the sale or exchange of inventory sold through the U.S. office or other fixed base of business, unless the inventory is sold for use, disposition, or consumption outside the United States and a foreign office of the taxpayer materially participates in the sale.[35]

In the case of a foreign corporation engaged in the life insurance business, any foreign-source income which is attributable to the foreign corporation's U.S. life insurance business is treated as effectively connected income.[36]

Look-back rules. Generally, only income recognized in the year that the foreign person is engaged in a U.S. trade or business is treated as effectively connected income.[37] However, there are two exceptions which are designed to prevent foreign persons from avoiding the effectively connected income taint by deferring income. Under the first

---

[32] Reg. § 1.864-4(c)(2) and (c)(3). Special rules apply to foreign persons engaged in a banking, financing, or similar business within the United States. Reg. § 1.864-4(c)(5).

[33] Code Sec. 864(c)(4)(A).

[34] Code Sec. 864(c)(4)(B).

[35] Code Sec. 864(c)(4)(B). However, effectively connected income does not include any Subpart F in-

come, or any dividend, interest, or royalty income derived from a foreign corporation in which the taxpayer owns directly, indirectly, or constructively more than 50% of the combined voting power of all voting stock. Code Sec. 864(c)(4)(D).

[36] Code Sec. 864(c)(4)(C).

[37] Code Sec. 864(c)(1)(B).

exception, income which is recognized in one taxable year, but is attributable to a disposition of property or the performance of services in a prior taxable year, is treated as effectively connected income if that is the treatment which would have resulted had the income been recognized in that prior taxable year.[38] An example of such income is a deferred gain from an installment sale of business equipment made in the last taxable year in which the foreign person was engaged in a U.S. trade or business. Under the second exception, a gain from the disposition of property which was withdrawn from a U.S. trade or business and is disposed of within 10 years after the withdrawal is treated as effectively connected income if that is the treatment which would have resulted had the disposition occurred immediately before the property was withdrawn from the U.S. trade or business.[39]

Allowable deductions. A foreign corporation or nonresident alien individual engaged in the conduct of a U.S. trade or business can claim the following deductions against its effectively connected gross income:

(i)   expenses, losses, and other deductions which are directly related to effectively connected gross income (e.g., cost of goods sold), as well as a ratable portion of any deductions which are not definitely related to any specific item of gross income (e.g., interest expense),[40]

(ii) foreign income taxes imposed on either foreign-source effectively connected income or U.S.-source effectively connected income which is subject to foreign taxation by reason of the income's source rather than the taxpayer's citizenship, residence, or domicile,[41]

(iii) charitable contributions made to domestic charitable organizations,[42] and

(iv) in the case of a nonresident alien individual, casualty and theft losses with respect to personal use property located within the United States, and a personal exemption deduction.[43]

Special rules govern the allocation of a foreign corporation's interest expense deduction against effectively connected gross income. Under these rules, the interest expense deduction is generally computed using a three-step process based on the value of the corporation's U.S. assets, its worldwide debt-to-assets ratio, and the liabilities recorded on the books of the U.S. business.[44] These regulations are based on the idea

---

[38] Code Sec. 864(c)(6).

[39] Code Sec. 864(c)(7).

[40] Reg. §§ 1.873-1(a)(1), 1.882-4(b)(1), and 1.861-8.

[41] Code Secs. 873(a) and 882(c)(1)(A), as modified by Code Sec. 906(b)(1).

[42] Code Secs. 873(b)(2) and 882(c)(1)(B).

[43] Reg. § 1.873-1(b)(2)(ii) and (b)(3). Residents of Mexico or Canada may qualify for an additional exemption deduction.

[44] Reg. § 1.882-5.

that, within a single corporate entity with operations in two or more countries, borrowing (and the related interest expense) can be artificially allocated between different countries. Therefore, the regulations adopt an objective, formulary approach, for computing interest expense deductions.

Step one of this process is to compute the amount of the foreign corporation U.S. assets. Step two involves computing the total amount of the foreign corporation's U.S. connected liabilities. This is accomplished by multiplying the foreign corporation's U.S. assets (determined in step one) by its debt-to-asset ratio for the year. The corporation's debt-to-asset ratio equals the total amount of the foreign corporation's worldwide liabilities divided by the total value of its worldwide assets. In lieu of determining its actual ratio, a foreign corporation may elect to use a fixed ratio of 50%, which is increased to 93% in the case of a corporation that is a bank. Step three of the process involves a comparison of the amount of the foreign corporation's U.S. connected liabilities (determined in step two) to its U.S. booked liabilities, the latter being those liabilities that are properly reflected on the books of a taxpayer's U.S. trade or business. If the corporation's U.S. booked liabilities exceeds its U.S. connected liabilities, the corporation's U.S. interest expense equals the interest accrued on U.S. book liabilities multiplied by the ratio of U.S. connected liabilities to U.S. booked liabilities. On the other hand, if the corporation's U.S. booked liabilities are less than its U.S. connected liabilities, then the foreign corporation is allowed to increase its interest expense deduction beyond the amount of interest accrued on U.S. book liabilities.[45]

Applicable Tax Rates

The progressive rate schedules applicable to U.S. persons also apply to the effectively connected income of foreign persons.[46] Therefore, the applicable rates range from 15% to 35% in the case of a foreign corporation[47] and 15% to 39.6% in the case of a nonresident alien individual.[48] For nonresident aliens, the applicable schedules include those for single taxpayers, married individuals filing separately, and surviving spouses.[49] Nonresident aliens generally cannot use the head of household or married filing jointly rate schedules.[50]

---

[45] Reg. § 1.882-5. In *National Westminster Bank, PLC v. U.S.*, 44 Fed. Cl. 120 (1999), the court ruled that Article 7 of the U.S.-U.K. treaty overrides the formulary approach of Reg. § 1.882-5 insofar as the U.S. branch of a banking corporation is concerned.

[46] Code Secs. 871(b)(1) and 882(a)(1).
[47] Code Sec. 11.
[48] Code Sec. 1.
[49] Reg. § 1.1-1(a)(1).
[50] Code Secs. 2(b)(3)(A) and 6013(a)(1).

Foreign Tax Credit

A foreign corporation or nonresident alien individual engaged in a U.S. trade or business can, in lieu of a deduction, claim a credit for any foreign income taxes imposed on the following two types of income:

(i)   foreign-source effectively connected income, and

(ii) U.S.-source effectively connected income which is subject to foreign taxation by reason of the income's source rather than the taxpayer's citizenship, residence, or domicile.[51]

The credit is allowable only against U.S. taxes on effectively connected income and cannot offset U.S. withholding taxes or the branch profits tax.[52] In addition, only the taxpayer's effectively connected income is taken into account for purposes of computing the foreign tax credit limitation.[53]

Alternative Minimum Tax

The effectively connected income of a foreign corporation or nonresident alien individual is subject to the alternative minimum tax if the taxpayer's tentative minimum tax exceeds the regular tax for the year.[54] A corporate taxpayer's tentative minimum tax equals 20% (in the case of noncorporate taxpayers, a two-tiered rate schedule of 26% and 28% applies) of the taxpayer's alternative minimum taxable income less an exemption amount, and reduced by the alternative minimum foreign tax credit.[55] Alternative minimum taxable income equals a taxpayer's regular taxable income, determined with certain adjustments, and increased by the amount of the taxpayer's tax preferences.[56]

¶ 1202   BRANCH PROFITS TAX

Introduction

Prior to the enactment of the branch profits tax in 1986, there was a substantial disparity between the tax treatment of earnings repatriations from U.S. branch and subsidiary operations. U.S. withholding taxes were imposed on dividend distributions from a U.S. subsidiary, but no U.S. tax was imposed on earnings remittances from a U.S. branch. Therefore, foreign corporations could avoid the shareholder-level U.S. tax on their U.S.-source business profits merely by operating in the United States through a branch rather than a subsidiary.

---

[51] Code Sec. 906(a) and (b)(1). A foreign corporation which receives a dividend from a 10%-or-more-owned foreign corporation also may qualify for a deemed paid foreign tax credit if the dividend income is effectively connected with the recipient's U.S. trade or business.

[52] Code Sec. 906(b)(3) and (7).

[53] Code Sec. 906(b)(2).

[54] Code Secs. 871(b)(1), 882(a)(1), and 55.

[55] Code Sec. 55(b)(1).

[56] Code Sec. 55(b)(2).

Example 12.1: FORco, a foreign corporation, owns 100% of USAco, a domestic corporation which derives all of its income from U.S. business operations. During its first year of operations, USAco has taxable income of $10 million, and distributes all of its after-tax earnings to FORco as a dividend. Assume the U.S. corporate tax rate is 35% and that the applicable treaty withholding rate for U.S.-source dividends is 5%.

USAco pays $3.5 million of U.S. tax on its $10 million of taxable income and then distributes a dividend to FORco of $6.5 million [$10 million of taxable income − $3.5 million of U.S. income taxes]. The dividend is subject to $325,000 of U.S. withholding tax [$6.5 million dividend × 5% withholding tax rate], which makes the total U.S. tax burden on USAco's repatriated earnings equal to $3,825,000 [$3.5 million of U.S. income tax + $325,000 of U.S. withholding tax].

If FORco had structured its U.S. operation as a branch rather than as a subsidiary, it would still pay $3.5 million of U.S. income tax on its $10 million of income effectively connected with the U.S. branch operation. However, ignoring the branch profits tax, the repatriation of branch profits would be an internal fund transfer that is not subject to U.S. withholding tax. Thus, without a branch profits tax, FORco could avoid $325,000 of U.S. withholding taxes merely by operating in the United States through a branch rather than a subsidiary.

The branch profits tax better equates the tax treatment of branch and subsidiary operations by imposing a tax equal to 30% of a foreign corporation's dividend equivalent amount for the taxable year, subject to treaty reductions.[57] The dividend equivalent amount is an estimate of the amount of U.S. earnings and profits that a U.S. branch remits to its foreign home office during the year. Therefore, like the withholding tax imposed on a U.S. subsidiary's dividend distributions, the branch profits tax represents a second layer of U.S. taxes imposed on a foreign corporation's U.S.-source business profits.

Example 12.2: The facts are the same as Example 12.1, except now take into account the effects of the branch profits tax. If FORco had structured its U.S. operation as a branch rather than as a subsidiary, it would pay $3.5 million of U.S. income tax on its $10 million of effectively connected income [$10 million × 35% U.S. tax rate]. In addition, assuming the U.S. branch's dividend equivalent amount equals the branch's after-tax earnings of $6.5 million [$10 million of taxable income − $3.5 million of U.S. income taxes], FORco also would be subject to a branch profits tax

---

[57] Code Sec. 884(a).

of $325,000 [$6.5 million dividend equivalent amount $\times$ 5% tax rate]. Thus, the branch profits tax creates a shareholder-level U.S. tax that is equivalent to the U.S. withholding tax imposed on dividends.

The branch profits tax is payable in the same manner as a foreign corporation's regular income tax (see discussion later in this chapter), except that no estimated tax payments are required with respect to the branch profits tax.[58]

Dividend Equivalent Amount

The tax base for the branch profits tax is the dividend equivalent amount, which is an estimate of the amount of U.S. earnings and profits that a branch remits to its foreign home office during the year. Such an estimate must take into account the earnings and profits generated by the U.S. branch during the year, as well as any changes in the branch's accumulated earnings and profits during the year. Consistent with this reasoning, a foreign corporation's dividend equivalent amount for a taxable year is computed using the following two-step procedure: [59]

Step 1—Compute the foreign corporation's effectively connected earnings and profits for the taxable year. Effectively connected earnings and profits equals the earnings and profits attributable to income effectively connected with the foreign corporation's U.S. trade or business, before any reductions for dividend distributions, the branch profits tax, or the tax on excess interest.[60]

Step 2—Adjust the effectively connected earnings and profits amount for any changes in the foreign corporation's U.S. net equity during the year. The effectively connected earnings and profits amount from Step 1 is reduced by the amount of any increase in U.S. net equity for the year (but not below zero), and is increased by the amount of any reduction in U.S. net equity for the year.[61] In other words, an increase in U.S. net equity during the year is treated as a reinvestment of earnings and profits in the U.S. branch operation, whereas a reduction in U.S. net equity during

---

[58] Reg. § 1.884-1(a).

[59] Code Sec. 884(b).

[60] Code Sec. 884(d)(1) and Reg. § 1.884-1(f)(1). A corporation's earnings and profits equals its taxable income, plus or minus various adjustments designed to make earnings and profits a better measure of the corporation's economic income. Examples of the required adjustments include adding back tax-exempt income, adding back the excess of accelerated depreciation over straight-line depreciation, and subtracting income taxes. Code Sec. 312. Certain types of earn-

ings and profits are excluded from effectively connected earnings and profits (see Code Sec. 884(d)(2)).

[61] Code Sec. 884(b). A positive adjustment for a reduction in U.S. net equity for the year cannot exceed an amount equal to the excess of the aggregate amount of effectively connected earnings and profits accumulated in taxable years beginning after December 31, 1986, over the aggregate amount of dividend equivalent amounts from prior taxable years. Code Sec. 884(b)(2)(B). This limitation prevents the taxation of returns of capital.

the year is treated as a repatriation of prior year earnings and profits.

Example 12.3: FORco, a foreign corporation, operates a branch sales office in the United States. During its first year of operations, FORco's effectively connected earnings and profits are $250,000, and its U.S. net equity is $500,000 at the beginning of the year and $750,000 at the end of the year. Therefore, FORco's dividend equivalent amount for year 1 is $0, computed as follows:

(A) *Effectively connected earnings and profits*		$250,000
(B) *Increase in U.S. net equity:*		
End of the year U.S. net equity	$750,000	
Beginning of the year U.S. net equity . .	−$500,000	
Increase in U.S. net equity		$250,000
Dividend equivalent amount [A − B]		None

During year 2, FORco has no effectively connected earnings and profits, and its U.S. net equity is $750,000 at the beginning of the year and $600,000 at the end of the year. Therefore, FORco's dividend equivalent amount for year 2 is $150,000, computed as follows:

(A) *Effectively connected earnings and profits*		$ 0
(B) *Decrease in U.S. net equity:*		
Beginning of the year U.S. net equity	$750,000	
End of the year U.S. net equity . . .	$600,000	
Decrease in U.S. net equity		$150,000
Dividend equivalent amount [A + B]		$150,000

The determination of U.S. net equity is made as of the last day of the foreign corporation's taxable year.[62] U.S. net equity equals the aggregate amount of money and the adjusted basis of the property of the foreign corporation connected with the U.S. trade or business, reduced (including below zero) by the amount of liabilities connected with the U.S. trade or business.[63] The amount of U.S.-connected liabilities is determined by applying the same formula used to determine a foreign corporation's interest expense deduction (discussed earlier in this chapter), except that the asset value and liability amounts are based on end of year totals rather than annual averages.[64] Roughly speaking, an asset is considered to be "connected" with a U.S. trade or business to the extent the income produced by the asset or a gain from the disposition of the asset is effectively connected income. Various

---

[62] Reg. § 1.884-1(c)(3).

[63] Code Sec. 884(c).

[64] Reg. §§ 1.884-1(e)(1) and 1.882-5. An election is available whereby the foreign corporation can reduce its U.S.-connected liabilities by the excess of the formulary amount over a books and records amount. Reg. § 1.884-1(e)(3).

special rules are provided for applying this principle to specific types of assets, such as depreciable property, inventory, installment obligations, accounts receivable, bank deposits, and debt instruments.[65]

Finally, special rules apply to the computation of the branch profits tax for a taxable year in which a termination occurs. A termination includes the incorporation of a branch, the repatriation of all branch assets, a sale of all branch's assets, or the liquidation or reorganization of the foreign corporation. The basic thrust of these provisions is to mimic the tax consequences that the foreign corporation would experience if it had structured its U.S. operations as a subsidiary rather than as a branch.[66]

Treaty Reductions and Exemptions

If a tax treaty with the country of which the foreign corporation is a resident provides an exemption from the branch profits tax or a reduced rate of tax, that treaty relief can be taken into account if the taxpayer satisfies certain requirements.[67] Examples of U.S. tax treaties that provide an exemption or a reduced rate of tax include those with Belgium, Canada, France, Germany, the Netherlands, Japan, and the United Kingdom.[68] In the case of treaties that provide neither an exemption from the branch profits tax nor a reduced branch profits tax rate, the applicable treaty rate shall be the rate applicable to dividends paid to the foreign corporation by a wholly owned domestic corporation.[69]

Impact on Dividend Withholding Tax

The 30% U.S. withholding tax is imposed only on income derived from sources within the United States.[70] Dividends paid by a foreign corporation generally are foreign-source income,[71] and therefore usually are exempt from U.S. withholding taxes. However, if 25% or more of a foreign corporation's gross income during the preceding three taxable years was effectively connected with the conduct of a U.S. trade or business, a portion of any dividends it pays is recharacterized as U.S.-source income.[72] One effect of this special source rule is to make foreign shareholders of such foreign corporations liable for U.S. withholding taxes on the U.S.-source portion of the dividends. U.S. withholding taxes are not due, however, if the foreign corporation is distributing

---

[65] Reg. § 1.884-1(c)(2) and (d).

[66] Reg. § 1.884-2 and Temp Reg. § 1.884-2T.

[67] Code Sec. 884(e)(2) and Reg. § 1.884-1(g)(1) and (g)(2).

[68] Reg. § 1.884-1(g)(3) and (g)(4). Special rules apply to Canadian corporations. Reg. § 1.884-1(g)(4)(iv).

[69] Code Sec. 884(3)(2)(A)(ii) and Reg. § 1.884-1(g)(4)(i)(A).

[70] Code Secs. 1441(a) and 1442(a).

[71] Code Secs. 861(a)(2) and 862(a)(2).

[72] Code Sec. 861(a)(2)(B). The U.S.-source portion equals the amount of the dividend times the ratio of gross income that was effectively connected with a U.S. trade or business during the three-year test period to the foreign corporation's total gross income for that period.

earnings and profits from a taxable year in which it paid a U.S. branch profits tax on its effectively connected earnings and profits.[73]

Taxes on Branch Interest

Branch interest withholding tax. The rationale for the branch profits tax is to place U.S. branch and subsidiary operations on a tax parity. The branch interest withholding tax is designed to further this objective. Under the branch interest withholding tax, any interest paid by a foreign corporation's U.S. branch is treated as if it were paid by a domestic corporation.[74] The effect of this rule is to recharacterize the interest payment as U.S.-source income, and thereby subject any interest received by a foreign person from a U.S. branch to the 30% withholding tax which ordinarily applies to U.S.-source interest income.[75] Generally speaking, interest is considered to be "paid by" a U.S. branch if either the underlying liability is designated by the taxpayer as a branch liability or the liability has a particular connection with the branch operation. Examples include a liability which is reflected in the books and records of the U.S. trade or business, a liability secured predominantly by a U.S. asset, or a liability specifically identified by the taxpayer as a liability of the U.S. trade or business.[76]

The branch interest withholding tax is not imposed on interest that qualifies for one of the following withholding tax exemptions (each of which is discussed in Chapter 11): [77]

(i)   the portfolio interest exemption,[78]

(ii) the exemption for interest paid on a U.S. bank deposit,[79] or

(iii) the exemption for interest income that is effectively connected with the conduct of a U.S. trade or business.[80]

In addition, if the applicable tax treaty provides an exemption or reduced withholding rate for interest income, that treaty relief can be taken into account if the taxpayer satisfies certain requirements.[81]

Example 12.4:[82] FORco, a foreign manufacturer of industrial equipment, has a branch sales office in the United States. During the current year, the following items of interest were paid by FORco:

(i) $55,000 of portfolio interest paid to B, an unrelated non-resident alien individual,

---

[73] Code Sec. 884(e)(3)(A).

[74] Code Sec. 884(f)(1)(A).

[75] Reg. § 1.884-4(a)(1). Unlike the branch profits tax, the branch interest withholding tax is borne by the foreign person receiving the interest income, not the foreign corporation making the interest payment.

[76] Reg. § 1.884-4(b).

[77] Reg. § 1.884-4(a)(1).

[78] Code Secs. 871(h) and 881(c).

[79] Code Secs. 871(i)(2)(A) and 881(d).

[80] Code Sec. 1441(c)(1).

[81] Code Sec. 884(f)(3) and Reg. § 1.884-4(b)(8).

[82] Compare Reg. § 1.884-4(a)(4), Example 1.

(ii) $25,000 of interest paid to C, a foreign corporation which owns 15% of the combined voting power of FORco's stock, and

(iii) $20,000 of interest paid to D, a domestic corporation.

Neither B nor C is engaged in the conduct of a U.S. trade or business. The $55,000 of interest paid to B is not subject to the branch interest withholding tax because it qualifies for the portfolio interest exemption. The $20,000 of interest paid to D also is not subject to the branch interest withholding tax because D is a U.S. person. However, the $25,000 of interest paid to C is subject to the branch interest withholding tax because C is a 10%-or-more shareholder of FORco, and therefore does not qualify for the portfolio interest exemption. The amount of C's withholding tax liability is $7,500 [$25,000 of U.S.-source interest income × 30% statutory withholding rate], assuming a tax treaty does not provide for a reduced withholding rate for interest.

Tax on excess interest. In addition to the branch interest withholding tax, the branch profits tax regime also imposes a tax on excess interest. The idea behind the excess interest tax is that any interest expense which is deductible against the branch's U.S. taxable income also should give rise to an income inclusion, which is analogous to what happens when a U.S. subsidiary corporation makes an interest payment. A foreign corporation's excess interest equals the excess of:

(i)   the amount of interest expense which is deducted against the foreign corporation's effectively connected income, over

(ii) the amount of interest deemed paid by the foreign corporation for purposes of the branch interest withholding tax.

Under this provision, on the last day of the foreign corporation's taxable year, the foreign corporation is deemed to have received a payment of interest from a wholly owned domestic corporation equal to the foreign corporation's excess interest.[83] The effect of this provision is to subject the foreign corporation's excess interest to the 30% withholding tax which ordinarily applies to U.S.-source interest income.[84] However, if a tax treaty with the country of which the foreign corporation is a resident provides an exemption or reduced withholding rate for interest income, that treaty relief can be taken into account if the taxpayer satisfies certain requirements.[85] In all cases, the tax due on

---

[83] Code Sec. 884(f)(1)(B) and Reg. § 1.884-4(a)(2). A special exemption applies to interest on deposits with U.S. branches of foreign banks.

[84] Unlike the branch interest withholding tax, the tax on excess interest is borne by the foreign corporation operating the U.S. branch.

[85] Reg. § 1.884-4(c)(3)(i).

excess interest must be reported on the foreign corporation's income tax return, and estimated tax payments are required.[86]

> **Example 12.5:**[87] FORco, a foreign manufacturer of industrial equipment, has a branch sales office in the United States. During the current year, FORco apportions $120,000 of interest expense against the branch's effectively connected gross income. However, only $100,000 of this amount is considered to be paid by FORco's U.S. branch for purposes of the branch interest withholding tax. Therefore, FORco has excess interest of $20,000 [$120,000 − $100,000]. FORco's tax on this excess interest is $6,000 [$20,000 of excess interest × 30% statutory withholding rate], assuming a tax treaty does not provide for a reduced withholding rate for interest.

¶ 1203   ANTI-EARNINGS STRIPPING PROVISIONS

What Is Earnings Stripping?

Determining the most tax-efficient way for a foreign parent corporation to repatriate profits from a U.S. subsidiary requires an analysis of both subsidiary-level and parent-level U.S. taxes. At the subsidiary level, the U.S. subsidiary's total taxable income is subject to U.S. taxation at the regular graduated rates. At the foreign parent corporation level, any earnings which are repatriated through a dividend distribution are subject to U.S. withholding taxes at either the 30% statutory rate or a reduced treaty rate. Therefore, the total U.S. tax burden on the earnings of a U.S. subsidiary which are repatriated through a dividend distribution equals the sum of the subsidiary-level corporate income tax and the shareholder-level withholding tax. In contrast to a dividend distribution, repatriating a U.S. subsidiary's earnings through interest payments raises the possibility of both a deduction at the subsidiary level and a lower treaty withholding tax rate at the shareholder level. Therefore, by "stripping" the earnings of a U.S. subsidiary through intercompany interest payments, a foreign parent may be able to reduce or eliminate both levels of U.S. taxation.

> **Example 12.6:** FORco, a foreign corporation, owns 100% of USAco, a domestic corporation which derives all of its income from U.S. business operations. During its first year of operations, USAco has taxable income of $10 million. Assume the U.S. corporate tax rate is 35% and that the applicable treaty withholding rate is 5% for dividends and 0% for interest.
>
> *Case 1—Repatriate earnings through dividend distribution:* Given the 35% U.S. tax rate, USAco pays $3.5 million of U.S. tax on its $10 million of taxable income. As a consequence, if FORco repatriates all of USAco's after-tax earnings through a dividend, FORco

---

[86] Reg. § 1.884-4(a)(2)(iv).   [87] Compare Reg. § 1.884-4(a)(4), Example 1.

would receive a $6.5 million dividend [$10 million of pre-tax earnings − $3.5 million of corporate income tax], and would incur $325,000 of U.S. withholding tax [$6.5 million dividend × 5% treaty withholding rate]. Thus, the total effective U.S. tax on USAco's repatriated profits is 38.25% [($3.5 million of corporate income tax + $325,000 of withholding tax) ÷ $10 million of taxable income].

Case 2—Repatriate earnings through interest payments: Now assume that FORco has a creditor interest in USAco such that USAco makes annual interest payments of $10 million to FORco. Ignoring the anti-earnings stripping provisions, the $10 million of interest expense would shelter the entire amount of USAco's profits from U.S. income taxes. In addition, FORco is not subject to U.S. withholding taxes on the interest payments because of the treaty exemption. As a consequence, by repatriating USAco's earnings through interest payments rather than a dividend distribution, FORco is able to reduce the total effective U.S. tax rate on USAco's repatriated earning from 38.25% to 0%.

Foreign parent corporations engaging in earnings stripping must ensure that any intercompany payments meant to be interest qualify as such under U.S. tax laws. Historically, the IRS's only alternatives for attacking earnings stripping schemes were to attempt to recharacterize a portion of the U.S. subsidiary's intercompany debt as disguised equity, or to argue that the amount of interest paid on the intercompany debt did not represent an arm's-length charge. During the 1980s, Congress became concerned that U.S. tax collections from foreign corporations were not keeping pace with the growth in their U.S. business activities, and attributed part of this shortfall to the use of excessive debt by foreign multinationals to finance their U.S. subsidiaries. As a consequence, in 1989 Congress enacted the anti-earnings stripping provisions in order to provide the IRS with a more powerful weapon for attacking earnings stripping schemes.

Before discussing the details of the anti-earnings stripping provisions, it is important to restate a core principle of international tax planning, which is that both U.S. and foreign tax consequences must be considered when analyzing any cross-border transaction. In the present context, the issue is determining the most tax efficient method for a foreign parent corporation to repatriate profits from a U.S. subsidiary. Interest payments received by a foreign parent corporation from a U.S. subsidiary are generally subject to taxation in a foreign parent's home country. However, some countries, such as Germany and the Netherlands, generally do not tax dividends that a parent company receives from an operating subsidiary located in another country. Thus, although interest payments may be the optimal approach for minimizing

¶ **1203**

U.S. taxes, in the case of parent corporations based in selected foreign countries, these U.S. tax savings may be offset by higher foreign taxes.

Anti-earnings Stripping Provisions

The mechanism Congress chose to prevent earnings stripping is to deny the domestic subsidiary corporation a deduction for any disqualified interest.[88] Disqualified interest includes the following two types of interest:

(i) *Related-person debt*—Interest which is paid or accrued by a corporation (directly or indirectly) to a related person, and is not subject to U.S. tax.[89]

(ii) *Guaranteed debt*—Disqualified interest also includes any interest paid or accrued by the taxpayer to an unrelated person if a related foreign person or a related tax-exempt entity guarantees the debt, and the interest income is not subject to gross-basis U.S. taxation.[90] A disqualifying guarantee includes virtually any form of credit support.[91] Gross-basis U.S. taxation is a reference to the 30% withholding tax imposed on any U.S.-source nonbusiness (or investment-type) income derived by a foreign person.[92]

For purposes of both related person debt and guaranteed debt, interest which is subject to a reduced rate of U.S. tax under a tax treaty is treated as interest not subject to U.S. tax in proportion to the amount of the treaty reduction. For example, if the statutory withholding rate is 30% and the treaty rate is 10%, then two-thirds of the interest is considered to be interest not subject to U.S. tax.[93]

The following exceptions and special rules mitigate the effects of the anti-earnings stripping provisions:

(i) *Excess interest limitation*—The amount of disallowed interest deductions is limited to a corporation's excess interest expense for the taxable year.[94] Excess interest expense equals the excess of the corporation's net interest expense (interest expense minus interest income) over 50% of the corporation's

---

[88] Code Sec. 163(j)(1)(A). Members of an affiliated group generally are treated as a single corporation for purposes of applying the anti-earnings stripping provisions. Prop. Reg. § 1.163(j)-5.

[89] Code Sec. 163(j)(3)(A). For a definition of "related" person for this purpose, see Code Sec. 163(j)(4).

[90] Code Sec. 163(j)(3)(B) and (j)(6)(D)(i). Exceptions apply (i) if the corporation paying the interest owns a controlling interest in the guarantor, or (ii) in any circumstances identified by regulations, where the interest would have been subject to net-basis U.S. taxation if the interest had been paid to the guarantor. Code Sec. 163(j)(6)(D)(ii).

[91] Code Sec. 163(j)(6)(D)(iii).

[92] Code Sec. 163(j)(6)(E)(i). If no gross-basis tax is imposed, interest is disqualified even if the interest is subject to net-basis U.S. taxation. For example, interest paid to a U.S. bank on a loan guaranteed by a related person is disqualified interest even though the bank's interest income is subject to net-basis U.S. taxation.

[93] Code Sec. 163(j)(5)(B) and Prop. Reg. § 1.163(j)-4(b).

[94] Code Sec. 163(j)(1)(A).

adjusted taxable income.[95] Adjusted taxable income equals a corporation's taxable income, with numerous adjustments designed to produce a better measure of the corporation's net cash flow from operations before interest income or expense. Examples of the required adjustments include adding back to taxable income net interest expense, net operating losses, depreciation, amortization, and depletion.[96]

(ii) *Debt-to-equity safe harbor*—A corporation can deduct the full amount of its disqualified interest if its debt-to-equity ratio on the last day of its taxable year is less than or equals 1.5 to 1.[97]

(iii) *Carryforward of disallowed interest*—Any disallowed interest can be carried forward indefinitely and deducted in a year the taxpayer has an excess limitation.[98] A taxpayer has an excess limitation in any year that its net interest expense is less than 50% of its adjusted taxable income.[99]

(iv) *Carryforward of excess limitation*—An excess limitation in one year can be carried forward three years and used to reduce excess interest expense in a carryforward year.[100]

Example 12.7: FORco, a foreign corporation, owns 100% of USAco, a domestic corporation which derives all of its income from U.S. business operations. FORco also has a creditor interest in USAco, such that USAco's debt to equity ratio is 2 to 1, and USAco makes annual interest payments of $20 million to FORco. The results from USAco's first year of operations are as follows:

Sales...	$60 million
Interest income	$ 2 million
Interest expense (paid to FORco)..............	<$20 million>
Depreciation expense	<$10 million>
Other operating expenses	<$27 million>
Pre-tax income	$ 5 million

Assume the U.S. corporate tax rate is 35% and that the applicable treaty exempts interest income from withholding tax.

Because USAco's debt to equity ratio exceeds 1.5 to 1 and USAco has excess interest expense, USAco's deduction for its $20 million of disqualified interest is limited. USAco's excess interest expense equals its net interest expense of $18 million [$20 million of interest expense − $2 million of interest income] less 50% of its adjusted taxable income of $33 million [$5 million of pre-tax

---

[95] Code Sec. 163(j)(2)(B)(i) and (j)(6)(B).

[96] Code Sec. 163(j)(6)(A). Prop. Reg. § 1.163(j)-2(f) lists a total of 12 addition modifications and nine subtraction modifications.

[97] Code Sec. 163(j)(2)(A). See Prop. Reg. § 1.163(j)-3 regarding the computation of debt to equity, including various provisions designed to prevent taxpayers from manipulating the ratio at year-end.

[98] Code Sec. 163(j)(1)(B).

[99] Code Sec. 163(j)(2)(B)(iii).

[100] Code Sec. 163(j)(2)(B)(i) and (ii).

income + $18 million of net interest expense + $10 million of depreciation]. Therefore, $1.5 million of interest expense [$18 million − (50% × $33 million)] is disallowed, and USAco's taxable income after taking into account the disallowed interest deductions is $6.5 million [$5 million of pre-tax income + $1.5 million of disallowed interest deductions]. The $1.5 million of disallowed interest can be carried forward and deducted in a year that USAco has an excess limitation.

¶ 1204 ADMINISTRATIVE REQUIREMENTS

Returns and Payment of Tax

A foreign corporation which is engaged in a U.S. trade or business at any time during a taxable year must file Form 1120-F, U.S. Income Tax Return of a Foreign Corporation. This requirement applies even if the foreign corporation has no effectively connected income, has no U.S.-source income, or all of the corporation's income is exempt from U.S. tax by reason of a treaty provision.[101] A foreign corporation which is not engaged in a U.S. trade or business but which has income that is subject to U.S. withholding taxes also must file Form 1120-F, unless its liability for the year is fully satisfied by the withholding tax.[102] (Form 1120-F is reproduced in the appendix to this chapter.[103]) A foreign corporation engaged in a U.S. trade or business must make quarterly estimated tax payments of its tax liability.[104] However, no estimated tax payments are required with respect to the branch profits tax.[105]

A nonresident alien individual who is engaged in a U.S. trade or business must file Form 1040NR, U.S. Nonresident Alien Income Tax Return. This requirement applies even if the nonresident alien has no effectively connected income, has no U.S.-source income, or all of its income is exempt from U.S. tax by reason of a treaty provision.[106] A nonresident alien who is not engaged in a U.S. trade or business but who has income that is subject to U.S. withholding taxes also must file Form 1040NR, unless his or her liability for the year is fully satisfied by the withholding tax.[107] (Form 1040NR is reproduced in the appen-

---

[101] Reg. § 1.6012-2(g)(1)(i). A foreign corporation must timely file a true and accurate Form 1120-F in order to claim a deduction or credit. Reg. § 1.882-4(a)(2). For an example, see *InverWorld Inc. v. Comm'r,* 71 TCM 3231 (1996).

[102] Reg. § 1.6012-2(g)(2).

[103] Form 1120-F is due by the 15th day of the third month following the close of the taxable year if the foreign corporation has a U.S. office, and by the 15th day of the sixth month following the close of the taxable year if the foreign corporation does not have a U.S. office. Reg. § 1.6072-2(a) and (b). However, a foreign corporation can obtain a six-month extension of time for filing Form 1120-F. Reg. § 1.6081-3(a).

[104] Code Sec. 6655. A foreign corporation that has a U.S. office is required to deposit the amount of U.S. taxes due with a Federal Reserve bank or an authorized financial institution using Form 8109, Federal Tax Deposit Coupon. Reg. § 1.6302-1. A foreign corporation that does not have a U.S. office remits any taxes due by mailing a check or money order to the IRS (see instructions to Form 1120-F).

[105] Reg. § 1.884-1(a).

[106] Reg. § 1.6012-1(b)(1)(i). A nonresident alien individual must timely file a true and accurate Form 1040NR in order to claim a deduction or credit. Reg. § 1.874-1(a).

[107] Reg. § 1.6012-1(b)(2).

dix to this chapter.[108]) A nonresident alien whose tax exceeds the amount of any withholding must make estimated tax payments.[109]

Any partnership engaged in a U.S. trade or business, or that has income from U.S. sources, is required to file Form 1065, U.S. Partnership Return of Income, which is an informational return.[110] As discussed in Chapter 11, the partnership must also withhold on a foreign partner's distributive share of effectively connected income. The partnership must file a Form 8804 (Annual Return For Partnership Withholding Tax), Form 8805 (Foreign Partner's Information Statement), and a Form 8813 (Partnership Withholding Tax Payment). A partnership that is not engaged in a U.S. trade or business and has no U.S.-source income need not file either a Form 1065 or any other type of partnership return.[111]

Special Information Reporting and Record Maintenance Requirements

In order to effectively audit the transfer prices used by a U.S. subsidiary of a foreign corporation, the IRS often must examine the books and records of the foreign parent corporation. Historically, foreign parties have resisted making their records available to the IRS, or have not maintained records sufficient to determine arm's-length transfer prices. In response, Congress enacted the requirement that each year certain reporting corporations must file Form 5472, Information Return of a 25% Foreign-Owned U.S. Corporation or a Foreign Corporation Engaged in a U.S. Trade or Business, and maintain certain books and records.[112] A domestic corporation is a reporting corporation if, at any time during the taxable year, 25% or more of its stock, by vote or value, is owned directly or indirectly by one foreign person. A foreign corporation is a reporting corporation if, at any time during the taxable year, it is engaged in a U.S. trade or business, and 25% or more of its stock, by vote or value, is owned directly or indirectly by one foreign person.[113] In filing a Form 5472, the reporting corporation must provide information regarding its foreign shareholders, certain other related parties, and the dollar amounts of transactions that it entered into during the taxable year with foreign related parties.[114] A separate Form 5472 is filed for each foreign or domestic related party with which the reporting corporation engaged in reportable transactions

---

[108] Form 1040NR is due by the 15th day of the sixth month following the close of the taxable year, unless the income includes wages subject to withholding, in which case the return is due by the 15th day of the fourth month following the close of the taxable year. Reg. § 1.6072-1(c). A nonresident alien can obtain a four-month extension of time for filing Form 1040NR. Reg. § 1.6081-4(a).

[109] Code Sec. 6654.
[110] Reg. § 1.6031-1(c). Form 1065 generally is due by the 15th day of the fourth month after the close of the partnership's taxable year. Reg. § 1.6031-1(e)(2).
[111] Reg. § 1.6031-1(d)(1).
[112] See generally, Code Secs. 6038A and 6038C.
[113] Reg. § 1.6038A-1(c).
[114] Reg. § 1.6038A-2(b).

during the year.[115] The practical importance of Form 5472 is that the IRS often uses this form as a starting point for conducting a transfer pricing examination.[116] (Form 5472 is reproduced in the appendix to this chapter.)

In addition to filing Form 5472, a reporting corporation also must maintain permanent books and records sufficient to establish the correctness of the reporting corporation's U.S. tax liability, with an emphasis on transactions with related parties.[117] Certain reporting corporations are exempted from these special record maintenance requirements, but still must file Form 5472. These include reporting corporations whose annual U.S. gross receipts are less than $10 million,[118] and reporting corporations whose annual payments to and from foreign related persons with respect to related-party transactions are not more than $5 million and are less than 10% of the reporting corporation's U.S. gross income.[119] Any reporting corporation that fails to either file Form 5472 or maintain the requisite records may be subject to an annual penalty of $10,000.[120]

---

[115] Reg. § 1.6038A-2(a).

[116] See Internal Revenue Manual Audit Guidelines for Transfer Pricing Cases, dated June 14, 1994, § 522.1(2).

[117] Reg. § 1.6038A-3(a)(1).

[118] Reg. § 1.6038A-1(h).

[119] Reg. § 1.6038A-1(i).

[120] Reg. § 1.6038A-4(a).

¶ 1205 APPENDIX

Form **1040NR**	**U.S. Nonresident Alien Income Tax Return**	OMB No. 1545-0089
Department of the Treasury Internal Revenue Service	For the year January 1–December 31, 1999, or other tax year beginning , 1999, and ending ,	19**99**

Your first name and initial	Last name	Identifying number (see page 5 of inst.)

Present home address (number, street, and apt. no., or rural route). If you have a P.O. box, see page 5.

Check if: ☐ Individual   ☐ Estate or Trust

City, town or post office, state, and ZIP code. If you have a foreign address, see page 5.

For Disclosure and Paperwork Reduction Act Notice, see page 18.

Country ▶   Of what country were you a **citizen** or national during the tax year? ▶

Give address **outside the United States** to which you want any refund check mailed. If same as above, write "Same."

Give address in the country where you are a **permanent resident.** If same as above, write "Same."

(Please print or type.)
(Attach Copy B of your Forms W-2 and W-2G here. Also attach Form(s) 1099-R if tax was withheld.)

Filing Status and Exemptions for Individuals (See page 6.)

		7a Yourself	7b Spouse

Filing status. Check only one box (1–6 below).

1. ☐ Single resident of Canada or Mexico, or a single U.S. national
2. ☐ Other single nonresident alien
3. ☐ Married resident of Canada or Mexico, or a married U.S. national   } If you check box 7b, enter your spouse's identifying number ▶ ....
4. ☐ Married resident of Japan or the Republic of Korea
5. ☐ Other married nonresident alien
6. ☐ Qualifying widow(er) with dependent child (year spouse died ▶ 19   ). (See page 6.)

Caution: *Do not check box 7a if your parent (or someone else) can claim you as a dependent.*
Do not check box 7b if your spouse had any U.S. gross income.

No. of boxes checked on 7a and 7b ▶

7c Dependents:*		(2) Dependent's identifying number	(3) Dependent's relationship to you	(4)✓ if qualifying child for child tax credit (see page 6)
(1) First name	Last name			☐
				☐
				☐
				☐

No. of your children on 7c who:
*lived with you ▶
**did not live with you due to divorce or separation ▶
**Dependents on 7c not entered above ▶
Add numbers entered on lines above ▶

*Applies generally only to residents of Canada, Mexico, Japan, and the Republic of Korea and to U.S. nationals. (See page 6.)
**Applies generally only to residents of Canada and Mexico and to U.S. nationals. (See page 6.)

d Total number of exemptions claimed

(Income Effectively Connected With U.S. Trade/Business)

8	Wages, salaries, tips, etc. Attach Form(s) W-2	8	
9a	**Taxable** interest	9a	
b	**Tax-exempt** interest. DO NOT include on line 9a 9b		
10	Ordinary dividends	10	
11	Taxable refunds, credits, or offsets of state and local income taxes (see page 7)	11	
12	Scholarship and fellowship grants. Attach explanation (see page 7)	12	
13	Business income or (loss). Attach Schedule C or C-EZ (Form 1040)	13	
14	Capital gain or (loss). Attach Schedule D (Form 1040) if required. If not required, check here ☐	14	
15	Other gains or (losses). Attach Form 4797	15	
16a	Total IRA distributions . . . 16a	16b Taxable amount (see page 8)	16b	
17a	Total pensions and annuities 17a	17b Taxable amount (see page 8)	17b	
18	Rental real estate, royalties, partnerships, trusts, etc. Attach Schedule E (Form 1040)	18	
19	Farm income or (loss). Attach Schedule F (Form 1040)	19	
20	Unemployment compensation	20	
21	Other income. List type and amount (see page 9)	21	
22	Total income exempt by a treaty from page 5, Item M 22		
23	Add lines 8, 9a, 10–15, 16b, and 17b–21. This is your **total effectively connected income**. ▶	23	

(Adjusted Gross Income)

24	IRA deduction (see page 9)	24			
25	Student loan interest deduction (see page 10)	25			
26	Medical savings account deduction. Attach Form 8853	26			
27	Moving expenses. Attach Form 3903	27			
28	Self-employed health insurance deduction (see page 10)	28			
29	Keogh and self-employed SEP and SIMPLE plans	29			
30	Penalty on early withdrawal of savings	30			
31	Scholarship and fellowship grants excluded	31			
32	Add lines 24 through 31			32	
33	Subtract line 32 from line 23. Enter here and on line 34. This is your **adjusted gross income** ▶			33	

(Enclose, but do not staple, any payment with your return.)

Cat. No. 11364D   Form **1040NR** (1999)

Form 1040NR (1999)   Page 2

Tax Computation

34	Amount from line 33 (adjusted gross income)	34
35	**Itemized deductions** from page 3, Schedule A, line 17	35
36	Subtract line 35 from line 34	36
37	Exemptions (see page 11)	37
38	**Taxable income.** Subtract line 37 from line 36. If line 37 is more than line 36, enter -0-	38
39	**Tax** (see page 11). Check if any tax is from a ☐ Form(s) 8814 b ☐ Form 4972, ▶	39

Credits

40	Credit for child and dependent care expenses. Attach Form 2441	40	
41	Child tax credit (see page 11)	41	
42	Adoption credit. Attach Form 8839	42	
43	Foreign tax credit. Attach Form 1116 if required	43	
44	Other. Check if from a ☐ Form 3800 b ☐ Form 8396		
	c ☐ Form 8801 d ☐ Form (specify) _____	44	
45	Add lines 40 through 44. These are your **total credits**		45
46	Subtract line 45 from line 39. If line 45 is more than line 39, enter -0- ▶		46

Other Taxes

47	Alternative minimum tax. Attach Form 6251	47
48	Tax on income not effectively connected with a U.S. trade or business from page 4, line 82	48
49	Social security and Medicare tax on tip income not reported to employer. Attach Form 4137	49
50	Tax on IRAs, other retirement plans, and MSAs. Attach Form 5329 if required.	50
51	Transportation tax (see page 13)	51
52	Household employment taxes. Attach Schedule H (Form 1040)	52
53	Add lines 46 through 52. This is your **total tax** ▶	53

Payments

54	Federal income tax withheld from Forms W-2, 1099, 1042-S, etc.	54	
55	1999 estimated tax payments and amount applied from 1998 return	55	
56	Additional child tax credit. Attach Form 8812	56	
57	Amount paid with Form 4868 (request for extension)	57	
58	Excess social security and RRTA tax withheld (see page 13)	58	
59	Other payments. Check if from a ☐ Form 2439 b ☐ Form 4136	59	
60	Credit for amount paid with Form 1040-C	60	
61	U.S. tax withheld at source:		
a	From page 4, line 79	61a	
b	By partnerships under section 1446 (from Form(s) 8805 or 1042-S)	61b	
62	U.S. tax withheld on dispositions of U.S. real property interests:		
a	From Form(s) 8288-A	62a	
b	From Form(s) 1042-S	62b	
63	Add lines 54 through 62b. These are your **total payments** ▶		63

Refund

64	If line 63 is more than line 53, subtract line 53 from line 63. This is the amount you **OVERPAID**	64
65a	Amount of line 64 you want **REFUNDED TO YOU.** If you want it directly deposited, see page 14 and fill in 65b, c, and d ▶	65a
b	Routing number [ ][ ][ ][ ][ ][ ][ ][ ][ ] c Type: ☐ Checking ☐ Savings	
d	Account number [ ][ ][ ][ ][ ][ ][ ][ ][ ][ ][ ][ ][ ][ ][ ][ ][ ]	
66	Amount of line 64 you want **APPLIED TO YOUR 2000 ESTIMATED TAX** ▶	66

Amount You Owe

67	If line 53 is more than line 63, subtract line 63 from line 53. This is the **AMOUNT YOU OWE.** For details on how to pay, including what to write on your payment, see page 14 ▶	67
68	Estimated tax penalty. Also include on line 67	68

Sign Here

Keep a copy of this return for your records.

Under penalties of perjury, I declare that I have examined this return and accompanying schedules and statements, and to the best of my knowledge and belief, they are true, correct, and complete. Declaration of preparer (other than taxpayer) is based on all information of which preparer has any knowledge.

Your signature ▶	Date	Your occupation in the United States

Paid Preparer's Use Only

Preparer's signature ▶	Date	Check if self-employed ☐	Preparer's SSN or PTIN
Firm's name (or yours if self-employed) and address ▶		EIN	
		ZIP code	

Form **1040NR** (1999)

Form 1040NR (1999)   Page **3**

Schedule A—Itemized Deductions (See pages 14, 15, and 16.)   07

State and Local Income Taxes	**1** State income taxes	**1**	
	2 Local income taxes	**2**	
	3 Add lines 1 and 2		**3**
Gifts to U.S. Charities	**Caution:** *If you made a gift and received a benefit in return, see page 15.*		
	4 Gifts by cash or check. If you made any gift of $250 or more, see page 15.	**4**	
	5 Other than by cash or check. If you made any gift of $250 or more, see page 15. You **MUST** attach Form 8283 if "the amount of your deduction" (see definition on page 15) is more than $500	**5**	
	6 Carryover from prior year	**6**	
	7 Add lines 4 through 6		**7**
Casualty and Theft Losses	**8** Casualty or theft loss(es). Attach Form 4684		**8**
Job Expenses and Most Other Miscellaneous Deductions	**9** Unreimbursed employee expenses—job travel, union dues, job education, etc. You **MUST** attach Form 2106 or Form 2106-EZ if required. See page 16 ▶	**9**	
	10 Tax preparation fees	**10**	
	11 Other expenses. See page 16 for expenses to deduct here. List type and amount ▶	**11**	
	12 Add lines 9 through 11	**12**	
	13 Enter the amount from Form 1040NR, line 34. . . . . . **13**		
	14 Multiply line 13 by 2% (.02)	**14**	
	15 Subtract line 14 from line 12. If line 14 is more than line 12, enter -0-	**15**	
Other Miscellaneous Deductions	**16** Other—certain expenses of disabled employees, estate tax on income of decedent, etc. List type and amount ▶	**16**	
Total Itemized Deductions	**17** Is Form 1040NR, line 34, over $126,600 (over $63,300 if you checked filing status box 3, 4, or 5 on page 1 of Form 1040NR)?		
	No. Your deduction is not limited. Add the amounts in the far right column for lines 3 through 16. Also enter this amount on Form 1040NR, line 35.		
	Yes. Your deduction may be limited. See page 16 for the amount to enter here and on Form 1040NR, line 35.	▶ **17**	

Form **1040NR** (1999)

¶ **1205**

Form 1040NR (1999)   Page **4**

Tax on Income Not Effectively Connected With a U.S. Trade or Business

Attach Forms 1042-S, SSA-1042S, RRB-1042S, 1001 or similar form.

Nature of income	(a) U.S. tax withheld at source	Enter amount of income under the appropriate rate of tax (see pages 16 and 17)			
		(b) 10%	(c) 15%	(d) 30%	(e) Other (specify) ___% ___%
69 Dividends paid by:					
a U.S. corporations **69a**					
b Foreign corporations **69b**					
70 Interest:					
a Mortgage **70a**					
b Paid by foreign corporations **70b**					
c Other **70c**					
71 Industrial royalties (patents, trademarks, etc.) **71**					
72 Motion picture or T.V. copyright royalties . **72**					
73 Other royalties (copyrights, recording, publishing, etc.) **73**					
74 Real property income and natural resources royalties . **74**					
75 Pensions and annuities **75**					
76 Social security benefits **76**					
77 Gains (include capital gain from line 85 below) . **77**					
78 Other (specify) ▶ _____ **78**					
79 Total U.S. tax withheld at source. Add column (a) of lines 69a through 78. Enter the total here and on Form 1040NR, line 61a . . . . ▶ **79**					
80 Add lines 69a through 78 in columns (b)–(e) **80**					

81 Multiply line 80 by rate of tax at top of each column **81**

82 Tax on income not effectively connected with a U.S. trade or business. Add columns (b)–(e) of line 81. Enter the total here and on Form 1040NR, line 48 . . . . ▶ **82**

Capital Gains and Losses From Sales or Exchanges of Property

83 (a) Kind of property and description (if necessary, attach statement of descriptive details not shown below)	(b) Date acquired (mo., day, yr.)	(c) Date sold (mo., day, yr.)	(d) Sales price	(e) Cost or other basis	(f) LOSS If (e) is more than (d), subtract (d) from (e)	(g) GAIN If (d) is more than (e), subtract (e) from (d)
Enter only the capital gains and losses from property sales or exchanges that are from sources within the United States and not effectively connected with a U.S. business. Do not include a gain or loss on disposing of a U.S. real property interest; report these gains and losses on Schedule D (Form 1040).						
Report property sales or exchanges that are effectively connected with a U.S. business on Schedule D (Form 1040), Form 4797, or both.						
84 Add columns (f) and (g) of line 83 . . . . **84**					( )	
85 Capital gain. Combine columns (f) and (g) of line 84. Enter the net gain here and on line 77 above (if a loss, enter -0-) . . ▶ **85**						

Form **1040NR** (1999)

Other Information (If an item does not apply to you, enter "N/A.")

A What country issued your passport? ....

B Were you ever a U.S. citizen? . . . . . ☐ Yes ☐ No

C Give the purpose of your visit to the United States ▶ ......

....

....

D Type of entry visa and visa number ▶ ....
.... and type of current visa and date
of change ▶ ....

E Date you first entered the United States ▶ ....

F Did you give up your permanent
residence as an immigrant in the United
States this year? . . . . ☐ Yes ☐ No

G Dates you entered and left the United States during the
year. Residents of Canada or Mexico entering and leaving
the United States at frequent intervals, give name of country
only. ▶_____

H Give number of days (including vacation and nonwork
days) you were present in the United States during:
1997 .... , 1998 .... , and 1999 ....

I If you are a resident of Canada, Mexico,
Japan, or the Republic of Korea, or a U.S.
national, did your spouse contribute to the
support of any child claimed on Form
1040NR, line 7c? . . . . ☐ Yes ☐ No
If "Yes," enter amount ▶ $_____

If you were a resident of Japan or the Republic of Korea
for any part of the tax year, enter in the space below your
total foreign source income not effectively connected with
a U.S. trade or business. This information is needed so that
the exemption for your spouse and dependents residing in
the United States (if applicable) may be allowed in
accordance with Article 4 of the income tax treaties
between the United States and Japan or the United States
and the Republic of Korea.

Total foreign source income not effectively connected
with a U.S. trade or business ▶ $..............................

J Did you file a U.S. income tax return for
any year before 1999?. . . . . . . ☐ Yes ☐ No
If "Yes," give the latest year and form number ▶.........

....

K To which Internal Revenue office did you pay any amounts
claimed on Form 1040NR, lines 55, 57, and 60? ....

....

L Have you excluded any gross income other
than foreign source income not effectively
connected with a U.S. trade or business? . ☐ Yes ☐ No

If "Yes," show the amount, nature, and source of the
excluded income. Also, give the reason it was excluded.
(Do not include amounts shown in item M.) ▶..............

....

M If you are claiming the benefits of a U.S. income tax treaty
with a foreign country, give the following information. See
page 17 for additional information.
● Country ▶...

● Type and amount of effectively connected income exempt
from tax. Also, identify the applicable tax treaty article. Do
not enter exempt income on lines 8–15, 16b, and 17b–21
of Form 1040NR:
For 1999 (also, include this exempt income on
line 22 of Form 1040NR) ▶........._____

....

....

For 1998 ▶......_____

....

● Type and amount of income not effectively connected that
is exempt from or subject to a reduced rate of tax. Also,
identify the applicable tax treaty article:
For 1999 ▶...

....

For 1998 ▶...

....

● Were you subject to tax in that country
on any of the income you claim is entitled
to the treaty benefits? . . . . ☐ Yes ☐ No

● Did you have a permanent establishment
or fixed base (as defined by the tax treaty)
in the United States at any time during
1999? . . . . ☐ Yes ☐ No

N If you file this return to report community income, give your
spouse's name, address, and identifying number.

....

....

O If you file this return for a trust, does the
trust have a U.S. business? . . . . . ☐ Yes ☐ No
If "Yes," give name and address ▶_____

....

P Is this an "expatriation return" (see
page 17)? . . . . ☐ Yes ☐ No

If "Yes," you must attach Form 8854 **OR**
attach an explanation as to why you are
not submitting that form.

Q During 1999, did you apply for, or take
other affirmative steps to apply for, lawful
permanent resident status in the United
States or have an application pending to
adjust your status to that of a lawful
permanent resident of the United States? ☐ Yes ☐ No

If "Yes," explain ▶_____

....

Form **1040NR** (1999)

¶ **1205**

Form **1120-F**	**U.S. Income Tax Return of a Foreign Corporation**	OMB No. 1545-0126
Department of the Treasury Internal Revenue Service	For calendar year 1999, or tax year beginning .... , 1999, and ending .... , ... ► **See separate instructions.**	19**99**

Please type or print

Name		Employer identification number
Number, street, and room or suite no. (see page 6 of instructions)		**Check applicable boxes:** ☐ Initial return ☐ Amended return
City or town, state and ZIP code, or country (see page 6 of instructions)		☐ Final return ☐ Change of address

A Country of incorporation ....

B Foreign country under whose laws the income reported on this return is subject to tax ....

C Date incorporated ....

D Location of corporation's primary books and records (city, state, and country) ....

Principal location of business ....

If the corporation maintains an office or place of business in the U.S. check here . . . . ► ☐

E If the corporation had an agent in the United States at any time during the tax year, enter:

Kind of agent ....

Name ....

Address ....

F Refer to the list beginning on page 18 of the instructions and state the corporation's principal:

(1) Business activity code number ► ....

(2) Business activity ► ....

(3) Product or service ► ....

G Check method of accounting: (1) ☐ Cash (2) ☐ Accrual

(3) ☐ Other (specify) ► ....

		Yes	No
H	Did the corporation file a U.S. income tax return for the preceding tax year?		
I	At any time during the tax year, was the corporation engaged in a trade or business in the United States?		
J	At any time during the tax year, did the corporation have a permanent establishment in the United States for purposes of applying section 894(b) and any applicable tax treaty between the United States and a foreign country? . .		

If "Yes," enter the name of the foreign country:

....

K Is the corporation a foreign personal holding company? (See section 552 for definition.)

If "Yes," have you filed Form 5471? (Sec. 6035) (See page 3 of the instructions.). . . . .

L Did the corporation have any transactions with related parties? . . . .

If "Yes," you may have to file Form 5472 (section 6038A and section 6038C). (See page 3 of the instructions.)

Enter number of Forms 5472 attached ► ....

Note: *Additional information is required at the bottom of pages 2 and 5.*

Computation of Tax Due or Overpayment

1	Tax from Section I, line 11, page 2	**1**	
2	Tax from Section II, Schedule J, line 11, page 4	**2**	
3	Tax from Section III (add lines 6 and 10 on page 5)	**3**	
4	Personal holding company tax (attach Schedule PH (Form 1120))—see page 6 of instructions . . .	**4**	
5	**Total tax.** Add lines 1 through 4	**5**	
6	**Payments:**		
a	1998 overpayment credited to 1999 **6a**		
b	1999 estimated tax payments . . **6b**		
c	Less 1999 refund applied for on Form 4466 **6c** ( ) **Bal** ► **6d**		
e	Tax deposited with Form 7004 . . . **6e**		
f	Credit for tax paid on undistributed capital gains (attach Form 2439) . . . **6f**		
g	Credit for Federal tax on fuels (attach Form 4136). See instructions . . . **6g**		
h	U.S. income tax paid or withheld at source (add line 12, page 2, and amounts from Forms 8288-A and 8805 (attach Forms 8288-A and 8805)) **6h**		
i	Total payments. Add lines 6d through 6h	**6i**	
7	Estimated tax penalty (see page 6 of instructions). Check if Form 2220 is attached . . . . . . ► ☐	**7**	
8	**Tax due.** If line 6i is smaller than the total of lines 5 and 7, enter amount owed	**8**	
9	**Overpayment.** If line 6i is larger than the total of lines 5 and 7, enter amount overpaid	**9**	
10	Enter amount of line 9 you want: **Credited to 2000 estimated tax** ► **Refunded** ►	**10**	

Sign Here

Under penalties of perjury, I declare that I have examined this return, including accompanying schedules and statements, and to the best of my knowledge and belief, it is true, correct, and complete. Declaration of preparer (other than taxpayer) is based on all information of which preparer has any knowledge.

► Signature of officer   Date   ► Title

Paid Preparer's Use Only

Preparer's signature ►	Date	Check if self-employed ► ☐	Preparer's SSN or PTIN
Firm's name (or yours if self-employed) and address ►		EIN ►	
		ZIP code ►	

For Paperwork Reduction Act Notice, see page 17 of separate instructions.   Cat. No. 11470I   Form **1120-F** (1999)

Form 1120-F (1999) Page **2**

SECTION I.—Certain Gains, Profits, and Income From U.S. Sources That Are NOT Effectively Connected With the Conduct of a Trade or Business in the United States (See page 6 of instructions.)

If you are required to complete Section II or are using Form 1120-F as a claim for refund of tax withheld at source, include below **ALL** income from U.S. sources that is **NOT** effectively connected with the conduct of a trade or business in the United States. Otherwise, include only those items of income on which the U.S. income tax was not fully paid at the source. The rate of tax on each item of **gross** income listed below is 30% (4% for the gross transportation tax) or such lower rate specified by tax treaty. No deductions are allowed against these types of income. Fill in treaty rates where applicable. **If the corporation claimed a lower treaty rate, also complete Item W, page 5.**

Name of treaty country, if any ▶

(a) Nature of income	(b) Gross income	(c) Rate of tax (%)	(d) Amount of tax	(e) Amount of U.S. income tax paid or withheld at the source
1 Interest				
2 Dividends				
3 Rents				
4 Royalties				
5 Annuities				
6 Gains from disposal of timber, coal, or domestic iron ore with a retained economic interest (attach supporting schedule)				
7 Gains from sale or exchange of patents, copyrights, etc.				
8 Fiduciary distributions (attach supporting schedule)				
9 Gross transportation income (see page 6 of instructions).		4		
10 Other fixed or determinable annual or periodic gains, profits, and income				
11 Total. Enter here and on line 1, page 1 . . . . ▶				

12 Total. Enter here and include on line 6h, page 1. . . . . ▶

Additional Information Required *(continued from page 1)*

	Yes	No
M Is the corporation a personal holding company? (See section 542 for definition.).		
N Is the corporation a controlled foreign corporation? (See section 957 for definition.)		
O Is the corporation a personal service corporation? (See page 7 of instructions for definition.)		

P Enter tax-exempt interest received or accrued during the tax year (see instructions) ▶ $ ....

Q At the end of the tax year, did the corporation own, directly or indirectly, 50% or more of the voting stock of a U.S. corporation? (See section 267(c) for rules of attribution.) . . . .

If "Yes," attach a schedule showing (1) name and identifying number of such U.S. corporation; (2) percentage owned; and (3) taxable income or (loss) before NOL and special deductions of such U.S. corporation for the tax year ending with or within your tax year.

R If the corporation has a net operating loss (NOL) for the tax year and is electing to forego the carryback period, check here . . . . ▶ ☐

	Yes	No
S Enter the available NOL carryover from prior tax years. (Do not reduce it by any deduction on line 30a, page 3.) ▶ $		
T Is the corporation a subsidiary in a parent-subsidiary controlled group?		

If "Yes," enter the name and employer identification number of the parent corporation ▶ ....
....

U At the end of the tax year, did any individual, partnership, corporation, estate, or trust own, directly or indirectly, 50% or more of the corporation's voting stock? (See section 267(c) for attribution rules.) . .

If "Yes," attach a schedule showing the name and identifying number. (Do not include any information already entered in T above).

Enter percentage owned ▶..........................

Note: *Additional information is required at the bottom of page 5.*

Form **1120-F** (1999)

Form 1120-F (1999) Page 3

SECTION II.—Income Effectively Connected With the Conduct of a Trade or Business in the United States (See page 7 of instructions.)

IMPORTANT—Fill in all applicable lines and schedules. If you need more space, see **Attachments** on page 3 of instructions.

Income	**1a** Gross receipts or sales ____ **b** Less returns and allowances ____ **c** Bal ▶	1c		
	2 Cost of goods sold (Schedule A, line 8)	2		
	3 Gross profit (subtract line 2 from line 1c)	3		
	4 Dividends (Schedule C, line 14)	4		
	5 Interest	5		
	6 Gross rents	6		
	7 Gross royalties	7		
	8 Capital gain net income (attach Schedule D (Form 1120))	8		
	9 Net gain or (loss) from Form 4797, Part II, line 18 (attach Form 4797)	9		
	10 Other income (see page 8 of instructions—attach schedule)	10		
	11 **Total income.** Add lines 3 through 10 ▶	11		
Deductions (See instructions for limitations on deductions.)	**12** Compensation of officers (Schedule E, line 4). Deduct only amounts connected with a U.S. business	12		
	13 Salaries and wages (less employment credits)	13		
	14 Repairs and maintenance	14		
	15 Bad debts	15		
	16 Rents	16		
	17 Taxes and licenses	17		
	18 Interest allowable under Regulations section 1.882-5 (see page 10 of instructions—attach schedule)	18		
	19 Charitable contributions (see page 10 of instructions for 10% limitation)	19		
	20 Depreciation (attach Form 4562) — 20			
	21 Less depreciation claimed on Schedule A and elsewhere on return — 21			
	22 Balance (subtract line 21 from line 20)	22		
	23 Depletion	23		
	24 Advertising	24		
	25 Pension, profit-sharing, etc., plans	25		
	26 Employee benefit programs	26		
	27 Other deductions (see page 11 of instructions—attach schedule)	27		
	28 **Total deductions.** Add lines 12 through 27 ▶	28		
	29 Taxable income before NOL deduction and special deductions (subtract line 28 from line 11)	29		
	30 **Less:** **a** Net operating loss deduction (see page 12 of instructions) — 30a			
	b Special deductions (Schedule C, line 15) — 30b	30c		
	31 Taxable income or (loss). Subtract line 30c from line 29	31		

Schedule A **Cost of Goods Sold** (See page 12 of instructions.)

1 Inventory at beginning of year	1		
2 Purchases	2		
3 Cost of labor	3		
4 Additional section 263A costs (see instructions—attach schedule)	4		
5 Other costs (attach schedule)	5		
6 Add lines 1 through 5	6		
7 Inventory at end of year	7		
8 **Cost of goods sold.** Subtract line 7 from line 6. Enter here and on Section II, line 2 above	8		

9a Check all methods used for valuing closing inventory:

(1) ☐ Cost as described in Regulations section 1.471-3

(2) ☐ Lower of cost or market as described in Regulations section 1.471-4

(3) ☐ Other (Specify method used and attach explanation.) ▶ ....

b Check if there was a writedown of subnormal goods as described in Regulations section 1.471-2(c) ▶ ☐

c Check if the LIFO inventory method was adopted this tax year for any goods ▶ ☐
If checked, attach Form 970.

d If the LIFO inventory method was used for this tax year, enter percentage (or amounts) of closing inventory computed under LIFO — 9d

e Do the rules of section 263A (for property produced or acquired for resale) apply to the corporation? ☐ **Yes** ☐ **No**

f Was there any change in determining quantities, cost, or valuations between opening and closing inventory? ☐ **Yes** ☐ **No**
If "Yes," attach explanation.

Form **1120-F** (1999)

Form 1120-F (1999)   Page **4**

Schedule C — Dividends and Special Deductions (See instructions.)

	(a) Dividends received	(b) %	(c) Special deductions: (a) × (b)
1 Dividends from less-than-20%-owned domestic corporations that are subject to the 70% deduction (other than debt-financed stock)		70	
2 Dividends from 20%-or-more-owned domestic corporations that are subject to the 80% deduction (other than debt-financed stock)		80	
3 Dividends on debt-financed stock of domestic and foreign corporations (section 246A)		see instructions	
4 Dividends on certain preferred stock of less-than-20%-owned public utilities		42	
5 Dividends on certain preferred stock of 20%-or-more-owned public utilities		48	
6 Dividends from less-than-20%-owned foreign corporations that are subject to the 70% deduction		70	
7 Dividends from 20%-or-more-owned foreign corporations that are subject to the 80% deduction		80	
8 **Total.** Add lines 1 through 7. See page 13 of instructions for limitation			
9 Other dividends from foreign corporations not included on lines 3, 6, and 7			
10 Foreign dividend gross-up (section 78)			
11 IC-DISC and former DISC dividends not included on lines 1, 2, or 3 (section 246(d))			
12 Other dividends			
13 Deduction for dividends paid on certain preferred stock of a public utility			
14 Total dividends. Add lines 1 through 12. Enter here and on line 4, page 3			
15 Total deductions. Add lines 8 and 13. Enter here and on line 30b, page 3			

Schedule E — Compensation of Officers (Complete Schedule E only if total receipts (line 1a plus lines 4 through 10 of Section II) are $500,000 or more. See **Line 12. Compensation of officers** on page 9 of instructions.)

(a) Name of officer	(b) Social security number	(c) Percent of time devoted to business	Percent of corporation stock owned (d) Common	(e) Preferred	(f) Amount of compensation
1		%	%	%	
		%	%	%	
		%	%	%	
		%	%	%	
		%	%	%	
		%	%	%	

2 Total compensation of officers

3 Compensation of officers claimed on Schedule A and elsewhere on this return

4 Subtract line 3 from line 2. Enter the result here and on line 12, page 3

Schedule J — Tax Computation (See page 14 of instructions.)

1 Check if the corporation is a member of a controlled group (see sections 1561 and 1563) ▶ ☐
Important: Members of a controlled group, see instructions.

2a If the box on line 1 is checked, enter the corporation's share of the $50,000, $25,000, and $9,925,000 taxable income bracket amounts (in that order):
(1) $ **(2)** $ **(3)** $

b Enter the corporation's share of:
(1) Additional 5% tax (not more than $11,750) $
(2) Additional 3% tax (not more than $100,000) $

3 Income tax. Check this box if the corporation is a qualified personal service corporation (see instructions) ▶ ☐   **3**

4a Foreign tax credit (attach Form 1118)   **4a**
b Check: ☐ Nonconventional source fuel credit
    ☐ QEV credit (attach Form 8834)   **4b**
c General business credit. Enter here and check which forms are attached:
☐ 3800 ☐ 3468 ☐ 5884 ☐ 6478 ☐ 6765
☐ 8586 ☐ 8830 ☐ 8826 ☐ 8835 ☐ 8844
☐ 8845 ☐ 8846 ☐ 8820 ☐ 8847 ☐ 8861   **4c**
d Credit for prior year minimum tax (attach Form 8827)   **4d**

5 **Total credits.** Add lines 4a through 4d   **5**
6 Subtract line 5 from line 3   **6**
7 Recapture taxes. Check if from: ☐ Form 4255 ☐ Form 8611   **7**
8 Alternative minimum tax (attach Form 4626)   **8**
9 Add lines 6 through 8   **9**
10 Qualified zone academy bond credit (attach Form 8860)   **10**
11 **Total tax.** Subtract line 10 from line 9. Enter here and on line 2, page 1   **11**

Form **1120-F** (1999)

¶ **1205**

SECTION III.—Branch Profits Tax and Tax on Excess Interest (See instructions beginning on page 15.)

Part I—Branch Profits Tax

1 Enter the amount from Section II, line 29	**1**	
2 Enter total adjustments made to get effectively connected earnings and profits. (Attach a schedule showing the nature and amount of adjustments.) (See page 16 of instructions.) . .	**2**	
3 Effectively connected earnings and profits. Combine line 1 and line 2. Enter the result here . .	**3**	
4a Enter U.S. net equity at the end of the current tax year. (Attach schedule.)	**4a**	
b Enter U.S. net equity at the end of the prior tax year. (Attach schedule.).	**4b**	
c Increase in U.S. net equity. If line 4a is greater than or equal to line 4b, subtract line 4b from line 4a. Enter the result here and skip to line 4e	**4c**	
d Decrease in U.S. net equity. If line 4b is greater than line 4a, subtract line 4a from line 4b. Enter the result here	**4d**	
e Non-previously taxed accumulated effectively connected earnings and profits. Enter excess, if any, of effectively connected earnings and profits for preceding tax years beginning after 1986 over any dividend equivalent amounts for those tax years	**4e**	
5 Dividend equivalent amount. Subtract line 4c from line 3. Enter the result here. If zero or less, enter -0-. If no amount is entered on line 4c, add the lesser of line 4d or line 4e to line 3 and enter the total here	**5**	
6 **Branch profits tax.** Multiply line 5 by 30% (or lower treaty rate if the corporation is a qualified resident or otherwise qualifies for treaty benefits). Enter here and include on line 3, page 1. (See instructions.) **Also complete Items W and X below**	**6**	

Part II—Tax on Excess Interest

7a Enter the interest from Section II, line 18	**7a**	
b Enter the interest apportioned to the effectively connected income of the foreign corporation that is capitalized or otherwise nondeductible.	**7b**	
c Add lines 7a and 7b	**7c**	
8 Enter the branch interest (including capitalized and other nondeductible interest). (See instructions for definition.) If the interest paid by the foreign corporation's U.S. trade or business was increased because 80% or more of the foreign corporation's assets are U.S. assets, check this box ▶ ☐	**8**	
9a Excess interest. Subtract line 8 from line 7c. If zero or less, enter -0-.	**9a**	
b If the foreign corporation is a bank, enter the excess interest treated as interest on deposits. Otherwise, enter -0-. (See page 17 of instructions.).	**9b**	
c Subtract line 9b from line 9a	**9c**	
10 **Tax on excess interest.** Multiply line 9c by 30% or lower treaty rate (if the corporation is a qualified resident or otherwise qualifies for treaty benefits). (See page 17 of instructions.) Enter here and include on line 3, page 1. **Also complete Items W and X below**	**10**	

Additional Information Required *(continued from page 2)*

	Yes	No			Yes	No
V Is the corporation claiming a reduction in, or exemption from, the branch profits tax due to:			**W** Is the corporation taking a position on this return that a U.S. tax treaty overrules or modifies an Internal Revenue law of the United States thereby causing a reduction of tax?		

V Is the corporation claiming a reduction in, or exemption from, the branch profits tax due to:

(1) A complete termination of all U.S. trades or businesses? . . . .

(2) The tax-free liquidation or reorganization of a foreign corporation?. . . . .

(3) The tax-free incorporation of a U.S. trade or business?. . . . .

If **(1)** applies or **(2)** applies and the transferee is domestic, attach Form 8848.

If **(3)** applies, attach the statement required by Regulations section 1.884-2T(d)(5).

W Is the corporation taking a position on this return that a U.S. tax treaty overrules or modifies an Internal Revenue law of the United States thereby causing a reduction of tax? . . . .
If "Yes," complete and attach Form 8833.

Note: *Failure to disclose a treaty-based return position may result in a $10,000 penalty (see section 6712).*

X If the corporation is claiming it is a qualified resident of its country of residence for purposes of computing its branch profits tax and excess interest tax, check the basis for that claim:

Stock ownership and base erosion test . . . . . . ☐
Publicly traded test . . . . ☐
Active trade or business test . . . . ☐
Private letter ruling . . . . ☐

Form **1120-F** (1999)

Additional schedules to be completed for Section II or Section III (See page 17 of instructions.)

Schedule L — Balance Sheets per Books

ASSETS	Beginning of tax year		End of tax year	
	(a)	(b)	(c)	(d)
1 Cash				
2a Trade notes and accounts receivable				
b Less allowance for bad debts . . .	( )		( )	
3 Inventories				
4 U.S. government obligations . . .				
5 Tax-exempt securities (see instructions)				
6 Other current assets (attach schedule)				
7 Loans to stockholders				
8 Mortgage and real estate loans . .				
9 Other investments (attach schedule) .				
10a Buildings and other fixed depreciable assets				
b Less accumulated depreciation . .	( )		( )	
11a Depletable assets				
b Less accumulated depletion . . .	( )		( )	
12 Land (net of any amortization) . .				
13a Intangible assets (amortizable only) .				
b Less accumulated amortization . .	( )		( )	
14 Other assets (attach schedule). . .				
15 Total assets				
LIABILITIES AND STOCKHOLDERS' EQUITY				
16 Accounts payable				
17 Mtges., notes, bonds payable in less than 1 year				
18 Other current liabilities (attach schedule)				
19 Loans from stockholders				
20 Mtges., notes, bonds payable in 1 year or more				
21 Other liabilities (attach schedule) . .				
22 Capital stock: a Preferred stock . .				
b Common stock . .				
23 Additional paid-in capital				
24 Retained earnings—Appropriated (attach schedule)				
25 Retained earnings—Unappropriated .				
26 Adjustments to shareholders' equity (attach schedule)				
27 Less cost of treasury stock. . . .		( )		( )
28 Total liabilities and stockholders' equity				

Note: *The corporation is not required to complete Schedules M-1 and M-2 below if the total assets on Schedule L, line 15, column (d) are less than $25,000.*

Schedule M-1 — Reconciliation of Income (Loss) per Books With Income per Return

1 Net income (loss) per books . . .		7 Income recorded on books this year not included on this return (itemize):	
2 Federal income tax		a Tax-exempt interest . $	
3 Excess of capital losses over capital gains		....	
4 Income subject to tax not recorded on books this year (itemize):		8 Deductions on this return not charged against book income this year (itemize):	
....		a Depreciation . . . $	
5 Expenses recorded on books this year not deducted on this return (itemize):		b Contributions carryover $	
a Depreciation . . . $		9 Add lines 7 and 8	
b Contributions carryover $		10 Income (line 29, page 3)—line 6 less line 9	
c Travel and entertainment $			
6 Add lines 1 through 5			

Schedule M-2 — Analysis of Unappropriated Retained Earnings per Books (Schedule L, line 25)

1 Balance at beginning of year . . .		5 Distributions: a Cash	
2 Net income (loss) per books . . .		b Stock	
3 Other increases (itemize):		c Property	
....		6 Other decreases (itemize):	
		7 Add lines 5a through 6	
4 Add lines 1, 2, and 3		8 Balance at end of year (line 4 less line 7)	

Form **1120-F** (1999)

¶ **1205**

Form **5472**
(Rev. June 1997)

Department of the Treasury
Internal Revenue Service

Information Return of a 25% Foreign-Owned U.S. Corporation or a Foreign Corporation Engaged in a U.S. Trade or Business
(Under Sections 6038A and 6038C of the Internal Revenue Code)

For tax year of the reporting corporation beginning ...., 19 ....., and ending .... , 19 .....

Note: Enter all information in English and money items in U.S. dollars.

OMB No. 1545-0805

Part I   Reporting Corporation (See instructions.) All reporting corporations must complete Part I.

1a Name of reporting corporation

Number, street, and room or suite no. (if a P.O. box, see instructions)

City, state or province, ZIP or postal code, and country

1b   Employer identification number

1c Total assets
$

1d Principal business activity

1e Total value of gross payments made or received (see instructions)
$

1f Total number of Forms 5472 filed for the tax year

1g Check here if this is a consolidated filing of Form 5472 . . . ▶ ☐

1h Country of incorporation

1i Country(ies) under whose laws the reporting corporation files an income tax return as a resident

1j Principal country(ies) where business is conducted

Part II   25% Foreign Shareholder (See instructions.)

1a Name and address of direct 25% foreign shareholder

1b U.S. identifying number, if any

1c Principal country(ies) where business is conducted

1d Country of citizenship, organization, or incorporation

1e Country(ies) under whose laws the direct 25% foreign shareholder files an income tax return as a resident

2a Name and address of direct 25% foreign shareholder

2b U.S. identifying number, if any

2c Principal country(ies) where business is conducted

2d Country of citizenship, organization, or incorporation

2e Country(ies) under whose laws the direct 25% foreign shareholder files an income tax return as a resident

3a Name and address of ultimate indirect 25% foreign shareholder

3b U.S. identifying number, if any

3c Principal country(ies) where business is conducted

3d Country of citizenship, organization, or incorporation

3e Country(ies) under whose laws the ultimate indirect 25% foreign shareholder files an income tax return as a resident

4a Name and address of ultimate indirect 25% foreign shareholder

4b U.S. identifying number, if any

4c Principal country(ies) where business is conducted

4d Country of citizenship, organization, or incorporation

4e Country(ies) under whose laws the ultimate indirect 25% foreign shareholder files an income tax return as a resident

Part III   Related Party (See instructions.)

Check applicable box: Is the related party a ☐ foreign person or ☐ U.S. person?
All reporting corporations must complete this question and the rest of Part III.

1a Name and address of related party

1b U.S. identifying number, if any

1c Principal business activity

1d Relationship—Check boxes that apply: ☐ Related to reporting corporation ☐ Related to 25% foreign shareholder ☐ 25% foreign shareholder

1e Principal country(ies) where business is conducted

1f Country(ies) under whose laws the related party files an income tax return as a resident

For Paperwork Reduction Act Notice, see page 2.   Cat. No. 49987Y   Form **5472** (Rev. 6-97)

¶ 1205

Form 5472 (Rev. 6-97)   Page **2**

Part IV Monetary Transactions Between Reporting Corporations and Foreign Related Party

If reasonable estimates are used, check here ▶ ☐ . (See instructions.)

1	Sales of stock in trade (inventory)	**1**
2	Sales of tangible property other than stock in trade	**2**
3	Rents and royalties received (for other than intangible property rights)	**3**
4	Sales, leases, licenses, etc., of intangible property rights (e.g., patents, trademarks, secret formulas) . . .	**4**
5	Consideration received for technical, managerial, engineering, construction, scientific, or like services . . .	**5**
6	Commissions received	**6**
7	Amounts borrowed (see instructions) a Beginning balance _____ b Ending balance or monthly average ▶	**7b**
8	Interest received	**8**
9	Premiums received for insurance or reinsurance	**9**
10	Other amounts received (see instructions)	**10**
11	**Total.** Combine amounts on lines 1 through 10	**11**
12	Purchases of stock in trade (inventory)	**12**
13	Purchases of tangible property other than stock in trade	**13**
14	Rents and royalties paid (for other than intangible property rights)	**14**
15	Purchases, leases, licenses, etc., of intangible property rights (e.g., patents, trademarks, secret formulas) .	**15**
16	Consideration paid for technical, managerial, engineering, construction, scientific, or like services	**16**
17	Commissions paid	**17**
18	Amounts loaned (see instructions) a Beginning balance _____ b Ending balance or monthly average ▶	**18b**
19	Interest paid	**19**
20	Premiums paid for insurance or reinsurance	**20**
21	Other amounts paid (see instructions)	**21**
22	**Total.** Combine amounts on lines 12 through 21	**22**

Part V Describe All Nonmonetary and Less-Than-Full Consideration Transactions Between the Reporting Corporation and the Foreign Related Party

(Attach separate sheet and check here. ▶ ☐) (See instructions.)

Part VI Additional Information

All reporting corporations must complete Part VI.

1 Does the reporting corporation import goods from a foreign related party? . . . . ☐ Yes ☐ No

2a If "Yes," is the basis or inventory costs of the goods valued at greater than the customs value of the imported goods? ☐ Yes ☐ No
  If "No," do not complete the rest of Part VI.

b If "Yes," attach a statement explaining the reason or reasons for such difference.

c If the answers to questions 1 and 2a are "Yes," were the documents used to support this treatment of the imported goods in existence and available in the United States at the time of filing Form 5472? . . . . ☐ Yes ☐ No

Paperwork Reduction Act Notice

We ask for the information on this form to carry out the Internal Revenue laws of the United States. You are required to give us the information. We need it to ensure that you are complying with these laws and to allow us to figure and collect the right amount of tax.

You are not required to provide the information requested on a form that is subject to the Paperwork Reduction Act unless the form displays a valid OMB control number. Books or records relating to a form or its instructions must be retained as long as their contents may become material in the administration of any Internal Revenue law. Generally, tax returns and return information are confidential, as required by section 6103.

The time needed to complete and file this form will vary depending on individual circumstances. The estimated average time is:

Recordkeeping . . . . 17 hr., 13 min.

Learning about the law or the form . . . . . 1 hr., 47 min.

Preparing and sending the form to the IRS . . . 2 hr., 9 min.

If you have comments concerning the accuracy of these time estimates or suggestions for making this form simpler, we would be happy to hear from you. See the instructions for the tax return with which this form is filed.

General Instructions

Section references are to the Internal Revenue Code unless otherwise noted.

Purpose of Form

Use Form 5472 to provide information required under sections 6038A and 6038C whenever transactions occur between a reporting corporation and a foreign or domestic related party.

A transaction with a foreign entity that is subject to reporting under section 6038A may also be a section 1491 transfer. **Form 926,** Return by a U.S. Transferor of Property To a Foreign Corporation, Foreign Estate or Trust, or Foreign Partnership, is used to report a section 1491 transfer. However, if no excise tax applies, the section 1491 reporting requirement will be

satisfied if the transferor complies with the section 6038A reporting requirements by filing Form 5472. See Notice 97-18, 1997-10, I.R.B. 35 for more details.

Definitions

Reporting corporation.—A reporting corporation is either:

- a 25% foreign-owned U.S. corporation, or

- a foreign corporation engaged in a trade or business within the United States.

Note: *Only reporting corporations that engage in* **reportable transactions** *during the tax year must file Form 5472. See page 3 for definition of a reportable transaction.*

25% foreign owned.—A corporation is 25% foreign owned if it has at least one direct or indirect 25% foreign shareholder at any time during the tax year.

25% foreign shareholder.—Generally, a foreign person is a 25% foreign shareholder if the person owns, directly or indirectly, at least 25% of either:

- the total voting power of all classes of stock entitled to vote, or

- the total value of all classes of stock of the corporation.

¶ **1205**

The constructive ownership rules of section 318 apply with the following modifications to determine if a corporation is 25% foreign owned. Substitute "10%" for "50%" in section 318(a)(2)(C). Do not apply sections 318(a)(3)(A), (B), and (C) so as to consider a U.S. person as owning stock that is owned by foreign person.

Related party.—A related party is either:

• any direct or indirect 25% foreign shareholder of the reporting corporation,

• any person who is related (within the meaning of section 267(b) or 707(b)(1)) to the reporting corporation,

• any person who is related (within the meaning of section 267(b) or 707(b)(1)) to a 25% foreign shareholder of the reporting corporation, or

• any other person who is related to the reporting corporation within the meaning of section 482 and the related regulations.

"Related party" does not include any corporation filing a consolidated Federal income tax return with the reporting corporation.

The rules contained in section 318 apply to the definition of related party with the modifications listed under the definition of **25% foreign shareholder** on page 2.

Reportable transaction.—A reportable transaction is:

• any type of transaction listed in Part IV of the form (e.g., sales, rents, etc.) for which monetary consideration (including U.S. and foreign currency) was the sole consideration paid or received during the reporting corporation's tax year, or

• any transaction or group of transactions listed in Part IV of the form, if

—any part of the consideration paid or received was not monetary consideration, or

—if less than full consideration was paid or received.

Transactions with a U.S. related party, however, are not required to be specifically identified in Parts IV and V.

Direct 25% foreign shareholder.—A foreign person is a direct 25% foreign shareholder if it owns directly at least 25% of the stock of the reporting corporation by vote or value.

Ultimate indirect 25% foreign shareholder.—An ultimate indirect 25% foreign shareholder is a 25% foreign shareholder whose ownership of stock of the reporting corporation is not attributed (under the principles of section 958(a)(1) and (2)) to any other 25% foreign shareholder. See Rev. Proc. 91-55, 1991-2 C.B. 784.

Foreign person.—A foreign person is:

• an individual who is not a citizen or resident of the United States,

• an individual who is a citizen or resident of a U.S. possession who is not otherwise a citizen or resident of the United States,

• any partnership, association, company, or corporation that is not created or organized in the United States,

• any foreign estate or foreign trust described in section 7701(a)(31), or

• any foreign government (or agency or instrumentality thereof) to the extent that the foreign government is engaged in the conduct of a commercial activity as defined in section 892.

However, the term "foreign person" does not include any foreign person who consents to the filing of a joint income tax return.

Who Must File

Generally, a reporting corporation must file Form 5472 if it had a reportable transaction with a foreign or domestic related party. See **Definitions,** which starts on page 2.

Exceptions from filing.—A reporting corporation is not required to file Form 5472 if any of the following apply:

1. It had no reportable transactions of the types listed in Parts IV and V of the form.

2. A U.S. person that controls the foreign related corporation files **Form 5471,** Information Return of U.S. Persons With Respect To Certain Foreign Corporations, for the tax year to report information under section 6038. To qualify for this exception, Form 5471 must contain information required by Regulations section 1.6038-2(f)(11) concerning the reportable transactions between the reporting corporation and the related party for the tax year.

3. The related corporation qualifies as a foreign sales corporation for the tax year and files **Form 1120-FSC,** U.S. Income Tax Return of a Foreign Sales Corporation.

4. It is a foreign corporation that does not have a permanent establishment in the United States under an applicable income tax treaty and timely files the notice required under section 6114.

5. It is a foreign corporation all of whose gross income is exempt from taxation under section 883 and it timely and fully complies with the reporting requirements of sections 883 and 887.

6. Both the reporting corporation and the related party are not U.S. persons as defined in section 7701(a)(30) and the transactions will not generate in any tax year:

• gross income from sources within the United States or income effectively connected, or treated as effectively connected, with the conduct of a trade or business within the United States, or

• any expense, loss, or other deduction that is allocable or apportionable to such income.

Consolidated returns.—If a reporting corporation is a member of an affiliated group filing a consolidated income tax return, Regulations section 1.6038A-2 may be satisfied by filing a U.S. consolidated Form 5472. The common parent must attach to Form 5472 a schedule stating which members of the U.S. affiliated group are reporting corporations under section 6038A, and which of those members are joining in the consolidated filing of Form 5472. The schedule must show the name, address, and employer identification number of each member who is including transactions on the consolidated Form 5472.

Note: *A member is not required to join in filing a consolidated Form 5472 just because the other members of the group choose to file one or more Forms 5472 on a consolidated basis.*

When and Where To File

File Form 5472 by the due date of the reporting corporation's income tax return (including extensions). A separate Form 5472 must be filed for each foreign or domestic related party with which the reporting corporation had a reportable transaction during the tax year. Attach Form 5472 to the income tax return and file a copy of Form 5472 with the Internal Revenue Service Center, Philadelphia, PA 19255. If the reporting corporation's income tax return is not filed when due, file a timely Form 5472 (with a copy to Philadelphia) separately with the service center where the tax return is due. When the tax return is filed, attach a copy of the previously filed Form 5472.

Penalties

Penalties for failure to file Form 5472.— A penalty of $10,000 will be assessed on any reporting corporation that fails to file Form 5472 when due and in the manner prescribed. The penalty also applies for failure to maintain records as required by Regulations section 1.6038A-3.

Note: *Filing a substantially incomplete Form 5472 constitutes a failure to file Form 5472.*

Each member of a group of corporations filing a consolidated information return is a separate reporting corporation subject to a separate $10,000 penalty and each member is jointly and severally liable.

If the failure continues for more than 90 days after notification by the IRS, an additional penalty of $10,000 will apply. This penalty applies with respect to each related party for which a failure occurs for each 30-day period (or part of a 30-day period) during which the failure continues after the 90-day period ends.

Criminal penalties under sections 7203, 7206, and 7207 may also apply for failure to submit information or for filing false or fraudulent information.

Record Maintenance Requirements

A reporting corporation must keep the permanent books of account or records as required by section 6001. These books must be sufficient to establish the correctness of the reporting corporation's Federal income tax return, including information or records that might be relevant to determine the correct treatment of transactions with related parties. See Regulations section 1.6038A-3 for more detailed information. Also see Regulations section 1.6038A-1(h) and Regulations section 1.6038A-1(i) for special rules that apply to small corporations and reporting corporations with related party transactions of de minimis value.

Specific Instructions

Part I

Line 1a—Address.—Include the suite, room, or other unit number after the street address.

If the Post Office does not deliver mail to the street address and the corporation has a P.O. box, show the box number instead of the street address.

Line 1c—Total assets.—Domestic reporting corporations enter the total assets from item D, page 1, Form 1120. Foreign reporting corporations enter the amount from line 15, column (d), Schedule L, Form 1120-F.

Line 1d—Principal business activity.—See the instructions for Form 1120 or Form 1120-F for a list of principal business activities.

Line 1e.—Enter on line 1e the total value in U.S. dollars of all foreign related party transactions reported in Parts IV and V of this Form 5472. This is the total of the amounts entered on lines 11 and 22 of Part IV plus the fair market value of the nonmonetary and less-than-full consideration transactions reported in Part V. Do not complete line 1e if the reportable transaction is with a U.S. related party.

Line 1f.—File a separate Form 5472 for each foreign or each U.S. person who is a related party with which the reporting corporation had a reportable transaction. Enter the total number of Forms 5472 (including this one) being filed for the tax year.

Line 1j.—Provide the principal country(ies) where business is conducted. Do not include a country(ies) in which business is conducted solely through a subsidiary. Do not enter "worldwide" instead of listing the country(ies). These rules also apply to lines 2c, 3c, 4c, Part II, and line 1e, Part III.

Part II

Only 25% foreign-owned U.S. corporations complete Part II.

The form provides sufficient space to report information on two direct 25% foreign shareholders and two ultimate indirect 25% foreign shareholders. If more space is needed, show the information called for in Part II on an attached sheet.

Report in lines 1a through 1e information about the direct 25% foreign shareholder who owns (by vote or value) the largest percentage of the stock of the U.S. reporting corporation.

Report in lines 2a through 2e information about the direct 25% foreign shareholder who owns (by vote or value) the second-largest percentage of the stock of the U.S. reporting corporation.

Report in lines 3a through 3e information about the ultimate indirect 25% foreign shareholder who owns (by vote or value) the largest percentage of the stock of the U.S. reporting corporation.

Report in lines 4a through 4e information about the ultimate indirect 25% foreign shareholder who owns (by vote or value) the second-largest percentage of the stock of the U.S. reporting corporation.

Lines 3a through 3e and lines 4a through 4e.—Attach an explanation of the attribution of ownership. See Rev. Proc. 91-55 and Regulations section 1.6038A-1(e).

Part III

All filers (foreign and domestic) must complete Part III, even if the related party has been identified in Part II as a 25% foreign shareholder. Report in Part III information about the related party with which the reporting corporation had reportable transactions during the tax year.

Part IV

Do not complete Part IV if the reportable transactions are with a domestic related party.

When completing Part IV or Part V, the terms "paid" and "received" include accrued payments and accrued receipts. State all amounts in U.S. dollars and attach a schedule showing the exchange rates used.

If the related party transactions occur between a related party and a partnership that is, in whole or in part, owned by a reporting corporation, the reporting corporation reports only the percentage of the value of the transaction(s) equal to the percentage of its partnership interest. This rule does not apply if the reporting corporation owns a less-than-25% interest in the partnership. The rules of attribution apply when determining the reporting corporation's percentage of partnership interest.

Generally, all reportable transactions between the reporting corporation and a related foreign party must be entered on Part IV.

Reasonable estimates.—When actual amounts are not determinable, enter reasonable estimates (see below) of the total dollar amount of each of the categories of transactions conducted between the reporting corporation and the related person in which monetary consideration (U.S. currency or foreign currency) was the sole consideration paid or received during the tax year of the reporting corporation.

A reasonable estimate is any amount reported on Form 5472 that is at least 75% but not more than 125% of the actual amount required to be reported.

Small amounts.—If any actual amount in a transaction or a series of transactions between a foreign related party and the reporting corporation does not exceed a total of $50,000, the amount may be reported as "$50,000 or less."

Line 7—Amounts borrowed.—Report amounts borrowed using either the outstanding balance method or the monthly average method. If the outstanding balance method is used, enter the beginning and ending outstanding balance for the tax year on lines 7a and 7b. If the monthly average method is used, skip line 7a and enter the monthly average for the tax year on line 7b.

Line 10—Other amounts received.—Enter on line 10 amounts received that are not specifically reported in lines 1 through 9. Include amounts in line 10 to the extent that these amounts are taken into account in determining the taxable income of the reporting corporation.

Line 18—Amounts loaned.—Report amounts loaned using either the outstanding balance method or the monthly average method. If the outstanding balance method is used, enter the beginning and ending outstanding balance for the tax year on lines 18a and 18b. If the monthly average method is used, skip line 18a and enter the monthly average for the tax year on line 18b.

Line 21—Other amounts paid.—Enter on line 21 amounts paid that are not specifically reported on lines 12 through 20. Include amounts in line 21 to the extent that these amounts are taken into account in determining the taxable income of the reporting corporation.

Part V

If the related party is a domestic entity, the reporting corporation is not required to attach the information called for in Part V.

If the related party is a foreign person, the reporting corporation must attach a schedule describing each reportable transaction, or group of reportable transactions, listed in Part IV of the form. The description must include sufficient information so that the nature and approximate monetary value of the transaction or group of transactions can be determined. The schedule should include:

1. A description of all property (including monetary consideration), rights, or obligations transferred from the reporting corporation to the foreign related party and from the foreign related party to the reporting corporation;

2. A description of all services performed by the reporting corporation for the foreign related party and by the foreign related party for the reporting corporation; and

3. A reasonable estimate of the fair market value of all properties and services exchanged, if possible, or some other reasonable indicator of value.

If the entire consideration received for any transaction includes both tangible and intangible property and the consideration paid is solely monetary consideration, report the transaction in Part IV instead of Part V if the intangible property was related and incidental to the transfer of the tangible property (e.g., a right to warranty services).

See the instructions for Part IV above for information on reasonable estimates and small amounts.

Chapter 13

International Tax Practice and Procedure

As the major economies of the world have become global in nature, the frequency and complexity of cross-border transactions have increased significantly. While many of the same procedural issues present in audits of domestic businesses are germane, there are other unique problems facing U.S.-based multinationals (outbound investment) as well as U.S. subsidiaries of foreign parent companies (inbound investment).

¶ 1301 INTERNATIONAL EXAMINATIONS

Given the extraordinary complexity of the international provisions of the Internal Revenue Code, the importance and involvement of the international examiner has increased in multinational corporation audits. Recognizing this, the IRS has retrained many of its agents as international examiners. Whereas previously they were located only in large metropolitan districts, many audits of small and medium-sized corporations with international operations now have international examiners assigned.

Due to the increased emphasis by the IRS on intercompany transfer pricing, IRS economists are also becoming involved in the audit process at the field agent level. Their role is to identify potential transfer pricing issues early in the examination process as well as assist in gathering factual information in support of the service position.

The IRS has also developed a "survey" procedure for returns with international issues, either before or after assignment to examiners, when their workload is excessive or no significant tax adjustment would result from an audit.[1] A taxpayer who (i) is a domestic corporation at least twenty-five-percent foreign-owned, or (ii) is a foreign corporation twenty-five-percent foreign-owned and engaged in a trade or business with the U.S. or (iii) is a foreign corporation engaged in a trade or business within the U.S. at any time during the taxable year, will not be subject to the survey procedure. Those returns not surveyed are subject to analysis to determine whether referral to the District Program Manager is appropriate. Eleven reasons exist for referral including the presence of tax haven issues, Subpart F income, foreign tax credit claims in excess of $25,000, Puerto Rican related entities, Domestic International Sales (DISC) or Foreign Sales Corporation (FSC) status, Interest-Charge DISC status and international boycott issues.

Coordinated Examination Program

The IRS established the Coordinated Examination Program (CEP) to provide a team approach to the examination of very large corporate cases that meet specific criteria for size and complexity of audit.[2] The large case program brings together as one unit for audit purposes the primary taxpayer and all of the taxpayer's effectively controlled corporations and other entities. A CEP case, therefore, will usually involve a large group of closely affiliated, centrally controlled, widely dispersed and highly diversified business entities. Domestic and foreign corporations, partnerships, joint ventures, syndicates, unincorporated businesses, individual, trusts, estates, foundations, pension and profit sharing trusts and other exempt organizations may be included within the coordinated audit group.[3]

CEP Process

The CEP case manager is responsible for organizing, controlling and directing the team examination. The supporting team usually includes not only groups of revenue agents in other districts throughout the country, but also industry and other specialists, such as international examiners, economists, engineer revenue agents, excise tax agents, computer audit specialists, employment tax agents and em-

---

[1] IRM 222 (Rev. 10-22-92).

[2] Certain variable factors, including total assets, gross receipts, number of controlled entities diversity of industries and audit staff requirements, are assigned point values in accordance with a fixed formula to determine if the final point total qualifies for the large case program. IRM Exhibit 42(11)0-2.

[3] IRM 42(11)8, *Handbook for Field Examination Case Managers*, 122, 123.

ployee and exempt organization specialists.[4] The case manager organizes and sets the scope of the examination in a three-step process. In the first step, the general scope and depth of the examination is established by reviewing all of the related returns, reviewing the planning files of previous CEP examinations and discussing the case with the case managers of previous CEP examinations.[5] The second step involves the review of certain taxpayer records in order to aid in (i) determining the procedures to be employed in examining noncompliance areas, (ii) determining other areas or issues not apparent in the preliminary review and (iii) modifying decisions made during the preliminary review.[6] In the third step, questionable items are further defined and audit procedures are developed with respect to specific accounts.[7] After this three-step initial review has taken place, a pre-examination conference is held with representatives of the taxpayer. The meeting permits the parties to discuss the scope of the audit and to consider any accommodations that may be possible to facilitate the audit or minimize the disruption to business operations.[8]

Scope of CEP Pre-Examination

The scope of any CEP examination should consider concurrently all returns of the various entities included in the CEP group. In addition to income tax returns, this may encompass employment and excise tax returns and pension and profit sharing plans.[9] The CEP case manager may include in the examination plan any other areas that are believed to require compliance checks.

Improper payments by corporations relating to bribes, kickbacks, illegal political contributions and the use of slush funds and secret bank accounts also may be given special attention during a large case audit. When considered appropriate, selected officers and key employees are asked five specific questions concerning these matters. If any of the questions are answered in the affirmative, the IRS will continue to probe until all details have been obtained. If the questions are not answered voluntarily, the IRS will issue an administrative summons to compel such testimony.

During the pre-examination conference, the conferees may also discuss the accuracy related penalty for either negligence or a substantial understatement of tax.[10] The taxpayer is allowed to make any corrections to the return or make adequate disclosure as to items that may cause the taxpayer to be subject to the negligence and the

---

4 IRM 42(11)3(14)(Rev. 3-15-95).

5 IRM 42(11)8 Sec. 621 (Rev. 2-28-95).

6 IRM 42(11)8 Sec. 622 (Rev. 10-13-93). The records to be reviewed in this step include the Schedule M, corporate minutes, internal management reports and accounting manuals and systems analysis.

7 IRM 42(11)8 Sec. 623 (Rev. 10-13-93).

8 IRM 42(11)3(7) (Rev. 3-15-95).

9 IRM 42(11)7.5 (Rev. 3-150-95).

10 Code Sec. 6662.

substantial understatement penalty. Under these special procedures the penalty will be waived if the taxpayer makes adequate disclosure within fifteen days of a request for such a statement by the IRS.[11]

Written Plan

Following the pre-examination conference, The IRS formulates a written plant that it provides to the taxpayer. The purpose of this document is twofold. First, it formalizes the general examination procedures to be followed. Second, it prevents any misunderstanding as to agreements reached between the taxpayer and the IRS. To avoid misunderstanding, agreements reached during the pre-examination conference should be included in the plan.[12] This written plan provides for the general scope of the examination and it clearly apprises the taxpayer that it may be modified to meet the needs of the examination.

District Counsel

During CEP examinations, IRS attorneys in the District Counsel's office are more directly involved. Officially, they are available to offer legal advice on complex issues and to provide assistance in the development of such intimate involvement by District Counsel during the examination phase, the IRS maintains that such involvement promotes early development and resolution of the significant legal issues.[13] If the international issue is sufficiently complex, the District Counsel attorney may seek informal field service advice from the Office of the Associate Chief Counsel (International) in Washington, D.C.

The Tax Court has been critical of the active participation by an IRS attorney in an ongoing CEP examination at the same time the attorney was acting as trial counsel in a docketed case against the same taxpayer for earlier years involving identical issues. In *Westreco, Inc. v. Commissioner*,[14] the Tax Court ordered the IRS trial attorney to discontinue participating in the CEP audit.

Large Business Examination

Where the taxpayer is not large enough to be classified as a CEP audit a pre-examination conference should still be held between the taxpayer and the examination team. During this meeting, similar to a CEP audit, the taxpayer should meet with the case manager for purposes of providing basic data, establishing the scope and depth of the examination and arranging for computer assistance.[15] The taxpayer will also learn who has been assigned to its audit, and may want to

---

[11] Rev. Proc. 94-69, 1994-2 CBS 804.
[12] IRM 42(11)8 Sec. 61 (Rev. 2-28-95).
[13] Daily Tax Report, BNA, at E-1 (Mar. 4, 1991).
[14] 60 TCM. 924 (1990), CCH Dec. 46,882(M).

[15] The IRS's goals for the pre-audit conference often include reaching an agreement with the taxpayer regarding (i) the lines of communication between the IRS and the taxpayer, (ii) the use of

begin its own investigation to better prepare for the audit. Also at this meeting, if not before, taxpayers should agree, preferably in writing,[16] to procedures to be followed during the course of the audit regarding international issues.

¶ 1302   IRS PROCEDURAL TOOLS

The primary authority for recordkeeping requirements of an entity potentially liable for U.S. tax is Code Sec. 6001 of the Internal Revenue Code and the related Regulations.[17] The IRS also has the specific authority to examine any books, papers, records or other data that may be relevant or material to ascertaining the correctness of any return, determining the tax liability of any person or collecting any tax.[18] Since most taxpayers and other individuals voluntarily produce records and answer questions when requested to do so by the IRS, this authority in itself is normally sufficient to obtain the necessary information.

Information Document Requests

An Information Document Request ("IDR") is designed to request information or documents from taxpayers when there are voluminous records to be examined, or when it is desirable to document requests. Requested on Form 4564, the IDR provides a convenient means to request information, and simultaneously yields a permanent record of what was requested, received, and returned to the taxpayer.[19] (Form 4564 is reproduced in the appendix to this chapter.)

An international examiner in both CEP and non CEP audits will often begin by issuing IDRs for information relevant to the scope of the review. For example, if intercompany purchases or sales of inventory exist, a typical IDR would request a copy of any intercompany pricing agreements as well as any contemporaneous documentation of methodology.[20] If the examination involved a substantial foreign tax credit, the international examiner would generally request copies of the appropriate foreign tax returns and allocation and apportionment schedules.

(Footnote Continued)

taxpayer resources, such as office space, (iii) the procedures for providing the IRS with returns of related parties, (iv) the procedures for the taxpayer to present documentation of items that may reduce its tax liability, (v) the procedures for resolving questions regarding the content of IDRs, (vi) the periods of time for submitting and responding to IDRs, and (vii) procedures and timing of the examination of off-site records and facilities.

[16] In many IRS districts, there appears to be an objective to have a written audit agreement with every taxpayer under audit.

[17] The Regulations may require generally that any person subject to tax under subtitle A of the Code . . . or an person required to file a return of information

with respect to income, shall keep such permanent books or account or records . . . as are sufficient to establish the amount of gross income, deductions, credits, or other matters required to be shown by such person in any return of such tax or information. Reg. § 1.6001-1(21)(a). Additionally, '[t]he district director may require any person, by notice served upon him, to make such returns, render such statements, or keep such specific records as will enable the district director to determine whether or not such person is liable for tax under subtitle A of the Code.'

[18] Code Sec. 7602(a)(1).

[19] IRM 403(23).

[20] Code Sec. 6662(e)(3)(B)(i)(III).

After reviewing the information gathered from these initial IDRs, the examiner will focus on those areas with the largest potential for possible adjustments. As the examination progresses, IDRs generally become more narrow in scope and tend to focus on specific items or transactions.

In addition to this authority, the IRS can employ several procedural tools to obtain information beyond that obtained via IDRs. These include on site inspection, formal document requests, summons, designated summons, Code Sec. 6038A, and exchanges of information under treaties.

On Site Inspections

In addition to IDRs, International Examiners appear to have taken an increased interest in foreign site visits and plant tours over the past few years. While recent IRS budget constraints may affect the number or duration of such visits, taxpayers should expect such requests and prepare to respond. Taxpayers should remember that it is a request, not an order, and that any request may be negotiated in terms of choosing the facility to visit (taxpayer may want to substitute a domestic plant for a foreign one), the duration of the visit, the timing of the visit, and the number of IRS employees involved. Careful planning of any such trip may result in an opportunity to present, in effect, key facts supporting the taxpayer's position. Finally, the taxpayer should prepare the plant personnel for the visit. Pre-screen the tour and determine if it covers processes or procedures relevant to the audit cycle. Pre-interview all involved personnel and sensitize them to the potential issues. International examiners have the following instruction for plant tours:[21]

(i)   Obtain information about departmental cost sheets or schedules.

(ii)   Learn the training requirements of each type of production employee.

(iii) Obtain any records regarding sales to all customers.

(iv)   Ascertain the extent of product development performed at the plant.

(v)   Interview plant employees. Plant interviews will bring a sense of reality to the case. Interviews should flush out the employee's ability to alter the production process and the technical training each production employee received.

---

[21] IRS International Continuing Professional Education materials, Chicago, Illinois, May 1995.

(vi)   If the company is a controlled foreign corporation, determine how and to whom it sells its products.

(vii)   Obtain all company manuals regarding the operations of the plant.

(viii) Obtain all job descriptions prior to the plant tour.

(ix)   Obtain all annual evaluations of the employees to be interviewed.

(x)   Obtain all company "programmer" manuals. This manual offers guidance to the programmer to construct his program, so that software can be readily translated and localized.

Formal Document Requests

If the IRS is unable to gather through IDRs the foreign information it considers necessary to conduct its examination, it may issue a formal document request (FDR). The FDR is not intended to be used as a routine tool at the beginning of an examination, but instead as a mechanism for securing information that could not be obtained through normal IDRs. The rare use of the FDR is indicated by the fact that the IRS does not have a specific form for the FDR. Instead, the IRS will issue a Form 4564 entitled "Information Document Request" with the notation "Formal Document Request." The FDR must be mailed by registered or certified mail and provide:

(i)   the time and place for the production of the documentation,

(ii) a statement of the reason the documentation previously produced (if any) is not sufficient,

(iii) the consequences to the taxpayer of the failure to produce the documentation described in subparagraph (iii).[22]

(iv) the consequences to the taxpayer of the failure to produce the documentation described in subparagraph (iii).[23]

If the taxpayer does not furnish the requested information within 90 days of the mailing of the FDR, the taxpayer will be prevented from later introducing the requested documentation. Foreign-based documentation is "any documentation which is located outside the U.S. and which may be relevant or material to the tax treatment of the examined item."[24] Thus, the IRS has broad authority to request virtually any relevant information. The purpose of this section is to discourage taxpayers from delaying or refusing disclosure of certain foreign-based documentation. To avoid the application of this section, the taxpayer must substantially comply with the FDR.

---

[22] Code Sec. 982(c)(1).
[23] Reg. § 982(c)(1).

[24] Code Sec. 982(d).

Whether there has been substantial compliance will depend on all the facts and circumstances. For example, if the taxpayer submits nine out of ten requested items and the court believes the missing item is the most substantial, the taxpayer could be found to have failed to comply substantially with the FDR. Accordingly, the taxpayer could be prevented from later introducing the missing documentation. The FDR is not intended to be used as a routine beginning to an examination but instead as a mechanism for securing information which could not be obtained through normal request procedures.[25]

Any taxpayer that receives a FDR has the right to begin proceedings to quash the request within ninety days after the request was mailed. In this proceeding the taxpayer may contend, for example, that the information requested is irrelevant, that the requested information is available in the U.S., or that reasonable cause exists for the failure to produce or delay in producing the information.

Reasonable cause does not exist where a foreign jurisdiction would impose a civil or criminal penalty on the taxpayer for disclosing the requested documentation.[26] In a proceeding to quash, the Commissioner has the burden of proof to show the relevance and materiality of the information requested. During the period that a proceeding to quash or any appeal from that proceeding is pending, the statute of limitations is suspended.[27]

The legislative history to Code Sec. 982 specifies that three factors should be considered in determining whether there is reasonable cause for failure to furnish the requested documentation. These factors are: (i) whether the request is reasonable in scope; (ii) whether the requested documents are available within the U.S.; and (iii) the reasonableness of the requested place of production within the U.S.

For the first factor, an example of an unreasonable scope may be a request "for all the books and records and all the supporting documents for all the entries made in such books or records" for a particular foreign entity that is controlled by a taxpayer. However, a request for the general ledger, an analysis of an account, supporting documents for a particular transaction of such foreign entity should be declared by a court as reasonable in scope. The second factor indicates that the IRS may not seek original documents if copies of such documents are available in the U.S. Finally, the place of production of records is generally at the taxpayer's place of business or the agent's office. Production of records in New York City by a taxpayer that is residing in and engages in a trade or business in Los Angeles may be considered

[25] See Joint Committee on Taxation, General Explanation of the Tax Equity and Fiscal Responsibility Act of 1982.
[26] Code Sec. 982(e).
[27] Code Sec. 982(e).

an unreasonable place for the production of records. The key to the reasonableness of the place for production is that such a place should be mutually convenient to both the taxpayer and the IRS.

If the taxpayer initiates proceedings to quash the FDR, the proper forum is the U.S. District Court. If a domestic taxpayer initiates quash proceedings, it must file suit in the District Court where the taxpayer resides. If the FDR is issued to a foreign taxpayer, it must file quash proceedings in the U.S. District Court for the District of Columbia.

The Summons Power

To give force and meaning to this general authority to examine, the IRS has been granted the power to compel a taxpayer or any other person to produce records and to testify under oath. This compulsory process is authorization to the IRS to issue an administrative summons.[28] The IRS may summon any person to appear at a time and place named in the summons for the purpose of giving testimony under oath and producing books, papers, records or other data. The authority to issue summonses has been delegated generally to those agents and other personnel within the IRS who are responsible for the examination of returns, collection of taxes, and investigation of tax offenses.[29] Thus, international examiners, revenue agents, tax auditors, revenue officers and special agents are all permitted to issue a summons.

When a corporation is under examination, the summons may be directed to either a specific corporate officer or the corporation itself.[30] The summons should indicate the officer's corporate position or title. When a summons is directed to the corporation, service must be made upon an officer, director, managing agent or other person authorized to accept service of process on behalf of the corporation.

After service of the summons, the individual serving the summons prepares and signs a certificate of service on the reverse side of the Form 2039 retained by the IRS. The date, time and manner of service are entered on the certificate. The signed certificate of service is evidence of the facts it states in any proceeding to enforce the summons.[31] (Form 2039 is reproduced in the appendix to this chapter.)

Scope of the summons power. The scope of the summons power extends to the production of records stored on magnetic tape.[32] It has also been held to require the production of videotapes [33] and microfiche

---

[28] Code Sec. 7602(a)(2).

[29] TD 6421 (approved October 23, 1959); Delegation Order No. 4 (as revised).

[30] IRM 4022.7(4) and (5) (Rev. 7-28-87).

[31] Code Sec. 7603.

[32] *U.S. v. Davey*, 543 F.2d 996 (2d Cir. 1976), 76-1 USTC ¶ 9724.

[33] *U.S. v. Schenk*, 581 F. Supp. 218 (S.D. Ind. 1984), 84-1 USTC ¶ 9197; *U.S. v. Norton*, 81-1 USTC ¶ 9398 (N.D. Cal. 1981).

copies of records.[34] The Supreme Court has even approved the use of a summons to compel handwriting exemplars.[35] However, the summons cannot require the creation of any documents, such as lists or schedules of factual information, which did not exist at the time the summons was issued.[36]

Although the authority to summon and to examine books and records is very extensive, it is not without limits. No taxpayer shall be subjected to unnecessary examination and prohibits more than one inspection of the taxpayer's books for each taxable year, unless the taxpayer requests otherwise or unless the IRS notifies the taxpayer in writing that an additional inspection is necessary.[37] The courts, as well as the IRS, generally have taken the position that there is no second inspection, even though the requested records were inspected previously, if the examination or investigation for the taxable year has not been completed or closed.[38]

The date fixed in the summons for compliance cannot be less than ten days from the date of the summons.[39] Agents are instructed that the time set for appearance should not be less than eleven full calendar days from the date the summons is served.[40] This minimum allowable time for compliance is for the benefit of the summoned party and may be waived by an earlier voluntary compliance.

Proper use of IRS summons. An IRS summons may be used only for the purposes set forth in Code Sec. 7602. These purposes include the verification, determination and collection of the tax liability of any person. Since 1982, the IRS also has specific authorization to issue summonses for the purpose of investigating any criminal tax offense.[41]

The Supreme Court has stated that a summons will not be enforced if it has been issued for an improper purpose, such as to harass the taxpayer, pressure settlement of a collateral dispute or for any other purpose reflecting on the good faith of the particular investigation.[42] Enforcement of such a summons constitutes an abuse of the court's process.[43]

Use of summonses in Tax Court proceedings. The use of administrative summonses by the IRS during Tax Court proceedings

---

[34] *U.S. v. Mobil Corp.*, 543 F. Supp. 507 (N.D. Tex. 1982), 82-1 USTC ¶ 9242.

[35] *U.S. v. Euge*, 444 U.S. 707 (1980), 80-1 USTC ¶ 9222.

[36] *U.S. v. Davey, supra,* note 7; IRM 4022.64(4) (Rev. 6-12-80).

[37] Code Sec. 7605(b).

[38] IRM 9781, Special Agents Handbook ¶ 367.33 (Rev. 10-19-92); *U.S. v. Gilpin*, 542 F.2d 38 (7th Cir. 1976), 76-2 USTC ¶ 9636; *U.S. v. Silvestain*, 668 F.2d 1161 (10th Cir. 1982), 82-1 USTC ¶ 9159.

[39] Code Sec. 7605(a). A longer period is required for third-party recordkeeper summonses. See ¶ 615, *infra.*

[40] IRM 4022.65 (Rev. 5-11-94).

[41] Code Sec. 7602(b).

[42] *U.S. v. Powell*, 379 U.S. 48 (1964), 64-2 USTC ¶ 9858.

[43] For an excellent discussion of the possible abuse of process and improper use of an IRS summons demanding appearance at a police station for the taking of fingerprints, see *U.S. v. Michaud*, 907 F.2d 750 (7th Cir. 1990), 90-2 USTC ¶ 50,425.

has raised objections by taxpayers. The Tax Court discovery rules permitting both parties to obtain relevant information before trial are much more restricted in their scope than the summons power available to the IRS. In certain situations, the Tax Court has held that to allow the IRS in a pending case to use evidence obtained by the issuance of a summons would give the government an unfair advantage over the taxpayer. In substance, such use of the summons would permit the IRS to circumvent the limitations of the Tax Court's discovery rules. The Tax Court will issue protective orders to preclude the IRS from using information obtained by such abusive use of the administrative summons.[44]

In *Ash v. Commissioner*,[45] the Tax Court set forth guidelines which it would follow in determining whether such a protective order should be issued when the IRS obtains information during a pending case by means of a summons. Where litigation has commenced by the filing of a petition by the taxpayer, and a summons is then issued with regard to the same taxpayer and taxable year involved in the case, the Tax Court will issue a protective order to prevent the IRS from using any of the summoned evidence in the litigation.[46] However, in such a situation, the Court will not issue a protective order if the IRS can show that the summons was issued for a sufficient reason that was independent of the pending litigation.

In those cases where the summons is issued before the taxpayer files a Tax Court petition, no order will be issued with respect to any information obtained as a result of the summons. The Tax Court in *Ash* explained that, before a petition is filed, the Court has no jurisdiction and there is no basis for viewing the summons as an attempt to undermine the Court's discovery rules.

In the third situation dealt with in *Ash*, where litigation has commenced, and an administrative summons is issued with regard to a different taxpayer or a different taxable year, the Tax Court normally will not issue a protective order.[47] However, the Court stated that it would do so if the taxpayer could show that the IRS lacked an independent and sufficient reason for the summons.

Designated Summonses

If, after issuing a summons, the IRS does not obtain the desired information in a timely manner, the IRS may consider issuing a designated summons.[48]

---

[44] Tax Court Rule 103.

[45] 96 T.C. 459 (1991).

[46] The Tax Court issued such an order in *Universal Manufacturing Co. v. Commissioner*, 93 TC 589 (1989), CCH Dec. 46,154.

[47] In an earlier case involving this type of situation, the issuance of a protective order was justified by the "compelling facts." *Westreco, Inc. v. Commissioner*, 60 TCM 824 (1990), CCH Dec. 46,882(M).

[48] Code Sec. 6503(j).

A designated summons tolls the running of the statute of limitations during the period in which judicial enforcement proceedings are pending, and for either 60 or 120 days thereafter, depending on whether or not the court orders compliance with the summons. The legislative history indicates Congress was concerned that taxpayers made a practice of responding slowly to IRS requests for information without extending the statute of limitations. Congress did not intend to extend the statute of limitations in a large number of cases, but to encourage taxpayers to provide requested information on a timely basis by realizing that the IRS had this tool available. The internal procedures the IRS personnel have to follow to issue a designated summons are a major impediment to their issuance. In addition to the International Examiner and the case manager, a designated summons is generally approved by the District Counsel, Regional Counsel, and Associate Chief Counsel (International).

> **Example 13.1:** A distributor of computers, USAco is a subsidiary of ASIAco. USAco buys computers from ASIAco and resells them in the U.S. The IRS's International Examiner conducts a transfer pricing audit of USAco. After USAco fails to respond to the International Examiner's IDR requesting all agreements between USAco and ASIAco, only 45 days remain on the statute of limitations. USAco will not sign a consent to extend the statute of limitations. As a result, the International Examiner issues a designated summons for the agreements. The designated summons tolls the statute of limitations during enforcement proceedings and for a short time thereafter.

Code Sec. 6038A

Congressional perception that foreign-owned U.S. subsidiaries were not paying their proper share of U.S. tax and the inability of the IRS to obtain foreign-based documentation caused Congress to expand greatly the application of Code Sec. 6038A. The section places the reporting burden for intercompany transactions on the 25 percent or greater foreign-owned corporation with a U.S. branch. These U.S. taxpayers, the "reporting corporations," must furnish certain information annually and maintain records necessary to determine the correctness of the intercompany transactions. In addition, the reporting corporation must furnish the required information by filing Form 5472 on an annual basis.

Reg. § 1.6038A-3(a)(1) provides that "[a] reporting corporation must keep the permanent books of account or records as required by Code Sec. 6001 that are sufficient to establish the correctness of the federal income tax return of the corporation, including information, documents, or records ('records') to the extent they may be relevant to determine the correct U.S. tax treatment of transactions with related parties." Such records may include cost data, if appropriate, to determine the profit or loss on intercompany products and services.

Failure to maintain or timely furnish the required information may result in a penalty of $10,000 for each taxable year in which the failure occurs for each related party.[49] If any failure continues for more than ninety days after notice of the failure to the reporting corporation, an additional penalty of $10,000 per thirty-day period is imposed while the failure continues. Additional penalties can be levied if it is determined the taxpayer failed to maintain records after the ninety-day notification.[50]

Within thirty days after a request by the IRS, a foreign-related party must appoint the reporting corporation as its limited agent. Failure to appoint such an agent can result in penalties for noncompliance.[51] In such a case, the District Director in his or her sole discretion shall determine the amount of the relevant deduction or the cost to the reporting corporation.

The IRS is prepared to follow the letter of the law as shown in *Asat, Inc. v. Commissioner*.[52] Code Sec. 6038A(e) allows the IRS to reduce the cost of goods sold when a taxpayer does not obtain its foreign parent's permission to be an agent for the request of certain documents. In *Asat*, the Tax Court literally applied Code Sec. 6038A(e) against the taxpayer, upholding the IRS's reduction to the cost of goods sold. Adhering to the legislative history, the Tax Court further found irrelevant that the foreign parent during the year in issue was not the parent at the time of the audit.

One of the largest Code Sec. 6038A problems for foreign owned U.S. taxpayers is that most foreign corporations do not have records that are in a usable format. Records are often stated in foreign currency and prepared in foreign languages. Therefore, the U.S. taxpayer must spend a large amount of time and money translating and explaining the documents to the IRS.

This problem was confronted in the case of *Nissei Sangyo America, Ltd. v. U.S.*[53] *Nissei* involved the audit of a U.S. subsidiary of a Japanese parent. The U.S. subsidiary, in response to a summons, had randomly selected documents relating to the issue under examination and provided full translations. The Japanese parent had also randomly selected and translated documents. In addition, it translated the subject matter headings or titles of 1,441 pages of Japanese correspondence

---

[49] Reg. § 1.6038A-4(a)(1) (1990).

[50] *Id.* Reg. § 1.6038A-4(d)(1).

[51] *Id.* Reg. § 1.6038A-5. The inability of a reporting corporation to obtain authorization from its twenty-five percent foreign shareholder will not abate the penalty. *ASAT, Inc. v. Commissioner*, 108 TC 147 (1997).

[52] 108 T.C. 147 (1997).

[53] 95-2 USTC ¶ 50,327 (N.D. Il).

and prepared English translation keys for the travel expense authorization forms. The IRS demanded that all documents described in the summonses be translated into English, which the company estimated would cost from $850,000 to $1.5 million. The court held that the general summons standard [54] applied and thus the IRS could not compel the translation of documents that were not relevant to the tax liability or that the IRS already had in its possession. Although the IRS lost, this case clearly indicates that the IRS will aggressively pursue documents and their translation.

> **Example 13.2:** A distributor of toy dolls, USAco is a subsidiary of ASIAco. USAco buys toy dolls from ASIAco and resells them in the U.S. The IRS's International Examiner conducts a transfer pricing audit of USAco. Pursuant to Code Sec. 6038A, the International Examiner requests any pricing studies that ASIAco conducted. If ASIAco does not give them to USAco to provide the International Examiner, the IRS can reduce USAco's cost of goods sold to $0.

Exchanges of Information Under Treaties

Under the exchange of information provisions of a treaty, the IRS can generally request information from a foreign country that is either in the foreign country's possession or available under the respective taxation laws of that foreign country. These provisions generally do not require the exchange of information that would disclose any trade or business secret.

The IRS exercises discretion and judgment in both requesting and furnishing of information. In general, the IRS will not request information from another country unless: (i) there is a good reason to believe that the information is necessary in the determination of the tax liability of a specific taxpayer; (ii) the information is not otherwise available to the IRS; and (iii) the IRS is reasonably sure that requested information is in the possession of, or available to, the foreign government from whom the information is being requested.

> **Example 13.3:** A distributor of sports shoes, USAco is a subsidiary of ASIAco. USAco buys sports shoes from ASIAco and resells them in the U.S. The IRS's International Examiner conducts a transfer pricing audit of USAco. After USAco fails to respond to the International Examiner's IDR requesting all agreements between USAco and ASIAco, the International Examiner requests the information from ASIA country's tax authority pursuant to the exchange of information provision in the U.S.-ASIA treaty.

---

[54] *U.S. v. Powell,* 379 U.S. 48 (1964).

The IRS's internal guidelines require that information sought from another competent authority must specifically describe the information desired and the reason why the information is necessary.[55]

¶ 1303   CONCLUSION OF AN EXAMINATION

At the conclusion of the examination, the international examiner will prepare a report summarizing the findings. The report is then incorporated into the field agent's report. Any disputed issues from the international examiner's report may be pursued with the Appeals Office along with other domestic issues raised during the examination.

Settling Issues

Certain issues over which there is disagreement may be settled by the case manager under the authority of Code Sec. 7121. This authority exists where the Appeals Office has previously approved a settlement agreement involving the same issue in a CEP examination in a prior year involving the same taxpayer or a taxpayer directly involved in the taxable transaction.[56] The following conditions must be present for the case manager to have jurisdiction to settle an issue: (i) substantially the same facts must be involved in both examination years, (ii) the legal authority must not have changed, (iii) the issue must have been settled on its merits and not have been settled in exchange for the taxpayer's concession on another issue and (iv) the issue must concern the same taxpayer or a taxpayer who was directly involved in the settled transaction.

Accelerated Issue Resolution

Another option available in CEP cases for unresolved issues is the accelerated issue resolution (AIR) program. The purpose of this program is to advance the resolution of issues from one tax period to another. Under this program, the taxpayer enters into an AIR agreement that acts as a closing agreement with respect to one or more issues present in a CEP examination for one or more periods ending before the date of the agreement.[57] Revenue procedure 94-67 explains the scope and procedure for obtaining an AIR agreement. An AIR agreement may only be entered into for issues which fall under the jurisdiction of the District Director and which relate to other items in another tax period. An AIR agreement may not be entered into for transfer pricing transactions, partnership items or any item designated for litigation by the Office of Chief Counsel.[58] Because the AIR program is voluntary, the taxpayer must submit a written request to the case manager in the District Director's office which has jurisdiction over the taxpayer's

---

[55] IRM § 42(10n)(10n).
[56] IRM 42(11)8 and 14(23) (Rev. 2-28-95).

[57] Rev. Proc. 94-67, 1994-2; CB 800.
[58] *Id.*

returns. If the request is denied, the taxpayer has no right to appeal an AIR determination.

Early Appeals Referral

If the issue is one that is not within the case manager's settlement jurisdiction, the taxpayer may elect to use the early appeals referral procedures and have the issue considered by the Appeals Office while the audit work continues in other areas. The IRS has instituted the early referral program for CEP cases in order to expedite the resolution of unagreed issues. Early referral is optional, it must be initiated by the taxpayer and it is subject to the approval of both the District Director and the Assistant Regional Director of Appeals-large Case.[59] Early referral cannot be requested for issues that have been designated for litigation. The early referral request must be submitted in writing, slating the issues and positions involved. It must contain a perjury statement and it must be signed by the CEP taxpayer or an authorized representative.[60] The taxpayer will be notified within forty-five days whether the early referral was granted. If the request is granted, the file is forwarded to the Appeals Office. The taxpayer cannot appeal a refusal to grant early referral.

¶ 1304   APPEALS DIVISION OF IRS

Protest Requirements

Upon completion of an international examination, the District Office may issue the taxpayer a thirty-day letter proposing a deficiency. The taxpayer may object to any proposed tax adjustments and request a conference with the Appeals Office by filing a protest with the Appeals Office. Where the deficiency resulted from a field examination of the taxpayer's return, more formalized procedures are required to obtain Appeals Office review. The taxpayer must formally request the conference by means of a document known as a protest. The protest must be in writing and must include certain elements to meet the requirements of the Appeals Office.[61]

Procedure at the Appeals Division

Proceedings before the Appeals Office are informal. Testimony is not taken under oath, although the Appeals Office may require matters alleged to be true to be submitted in the form of affidavits or declarations under the penalties of perjury. The taxpayer or the representative will meet with the appeals officer and informally discuss the pros and

---

[59] Rev. Proc. 96-9.
[60] Rev. Proc. 96-9.

[61] Statement of Procedural Rules § 601.106(a)(iii).

cons of the various positions taken by the taxpayer and the IRS. Rule I of the Conference and Practice requirements of the Appeals Division:[62]

> An appeals representative in his or her conclusions of fact or application of law shall hew to the law and the recognized standards of legal construction. It shall be his or her duty to determine the correct amount of tax, with strict impartiality as between the taxpayer and the Government and without favoritism or discrimination as between taxpayers.

Although an appeals officer is to maintain the standard of impartiality set forth in the Conference and Practice rules, he or she must, nevertheless, protect the rights of the IRS and act as an advocate on its behalf. Therefore, an appeals officer can raise a new issue or propose a new theory in support of the examining agent's proposed adjustment. However, an appeals officer generally will not do so unless the grounds for raising such new issues are substantial and the effect on the tax liability is material.

Appeals Process For a CEP Case

Unlike normal audit and appeal procedures, however, in a CEP case, personnel from the offices of Examination and Appeals are authorized and, in some instances, required to hold a conference before Appeals Office personnel meet with the taxpayer.[63] The purpose of this unique pre-conference is to discuss the issues, the taxpayer's protest and the written rebuttal to the protest prepared by the Office of Examination. Such a conference also serves to identify the need for additional information and development of issues.

It is expected at this pre-conference that lines of communication will be established between the Offices of appeals and examination that will be maintained throughout the case. Although the Office of Examination is encouraged during this meeting to share its views on the issues, including its assessment of litigating hazards, the parties are specifically instructed that the conference is not to be used as a means for securing a commitment from the Office of Appeals that any particular issue should be defended or the manner in which the case should be settled.[64] In substance, despite such intimate discussions of the case, the parties to the pre-conference are reminded that the detached objectivity of the Office of Appeals is not to be compromised. District Counsel must be invited to attend in other CEP cases.

---

[62] Reg. 601.106(f)(1).
[63] IRM 8628 (Rev. 8-1-91).
[64] *Id.*

Settlement Agreements

The IRS describes the "appeals mission" as one to resolve tax controversies without litigation, on a basis that is fair and impartial to both the government and the taxpayer and in a manner that will enhance voluntary compliance and public confidence in the integrity and efficiency of the IRS.[65] Thus, the appeals officer can split or trade issues where there are substantial uncertainties as to the law, the facts or both. In splitting a "legal issue," the appeals officer will ordinarily consider the hazards which would exist if the case were litigated. He will weigh the testimony of the proposed witnesses, judge the trends that the court has been following in similar cases and generally try to predict the outcome of the matter if the case were actually tried. Where a case involves concessions by both the government and the taxpayer "for purposes of settlement," and where there is substantial uncertainty as to how the courts would interpret and apply the law or what facts the court would find, a settlement is classified as a "mutual concession settlement." According to the regulations, no settlement is to be made simply on nuisance value.

Where a taxpayer and the appeals officer have reached an agreement as to some or all of the issues in controversy, generally the appeals officer will request the taxpayer to sign a Form 870, the same agreement used at the district level. However, when neither party with justification is willing to concede in full the unresolved area of disagreement and a resolution of the dispute involves concessions for the purposes of settlement by both parties based on the relative strengths of the opposing positions, a "mutual concession settlement" is reached, and a Form 870-AD type of agreement is to be used.[66] (Forms 870 and 870-AD are reproduced in the appendix to this chapter.)

The special appeals Form 870-AD differs from the normal Form 870 in several ways. The Form 870-AD agreement contains pledges against reopening which the usual agreement does not. Furthermore, the normal 870 becomes effective as a Waiver of Restrictions on Assessment when received by the IRS, whereas the special 870-AD is effective only upon acceptance by or on behalf of the Commissioner of Internal Revenue. Finally, the running of interest is suspended thirty days after a Form 870 is received,[67] whereas with a Form 870-AD, interest is not suspended until thirty days after the agreement is executed by the government.

The finality of the Form 870-AD has been the subject of substantial litigation. The form provides that upon acceptance by or on behalf of the Commissioner,

---

[65] IRM 1175.11.
[66] IRM 1218, P-8-47.

[67] Code Sec. 6601(c).

the case shall not be reopened in the absence of fraud, malfeasance, concealment or misrepresentation of material fact, [or] an important mistake in mathematical calculation . . . and no claim for refund or credit shall be filed or prosecuted for the year(s) stated . . .

Furthermore, the form states in language similar to that contained in a normal 870 that it is not a final closing agreement under Code Sec. 7121 and does not extend the statutory period of limitations on refund, assessment or collection of tax. A controversy may arise where a taxpayer, after executing a Form 870-AD, pays the tax, files a claim for refund and brings suit in the district court or the Court of Federal Claims. Under this scenario, the taxpayer takes the position that Code Sec. 7121 of the Internal Revenue Code is the exclusive method by which the IRS may enter into a final and binding agreement and since the Form 870-AD specifically repudiates reference to this section, the taxpayer is not bound by the agreement.

¶ 1305   COMPETENT AUTHORITY PROCESS

Generally, if the taxpayer has been unable to agree with the Appeals office on an adjustment which results in double taxation, the next course of action is to seek competent authority relief. An integral part of all U.S. Income Tax Treaties is a mutual agreement procedure which provides a mechanism for relief from double taxation. The Association Commissioner (International) acts as the U.S. competent authority. The competent authority's primary objective is to make a reasonable effort to resolve double taxation cases and situations in which U.S. taxpayers have been denied benefits provided for by a treaty.[68] The taxpayer may request competent authority when the actions of the U.S., the treaty country or both will result in taxation that is contrary to provisions of an applicable tax treaty. Revenue Procedure 96-13 [69] explains how to request assistance of the U.S. competent authority in resolving conflicts between treaty partners. (An outline of Revenue Procedure 96-13 is reproduced in the appendix to this chapter.) To the extent a treaty partner proposes an adjustment which appears inconsistent with a treaty provision or would result in double taxation, competent authority assistance should be sought as soon as is practical after the issue is developed by the treaty country.

When the IRS proposes adjustments that are inconsistent with a treaty provision or would result in double taxation, the taxpayer is encouraged to seek competent authority relief after the amount of the proposed adjustment is determined and communicated to the taxpayer

[68] IRM 8113; ch. 8700 at 2155 (Rev. 6-9-92).
[69] Rev. Proc. 96-13, 1996-1 CB 616 (modified by Rev. Proc. 96-53, 1996-49 IRB).

in writing. Generally, taxpayers must use the Appeals process to try to resolve the adjustments before competent authority assistance is sought. Were it is in the best interests of both parties, competent authority assistance may begin prior to consideration by the Appeals office. However the U.S. competent authority may require the taxpayer to waive the right to the appeals process at any time during the competent authority process.

The opportunities to resolve disputes at Competent Authority have increased from the traditional Mutual Agreement Procedure to include the Simultaneous Appeals Procedure and the Accelerated Competent Authority Procedure. All these methods have the potential to resolve disputes of international tax issues in a manner that avoid litigation.

Mutual Agreement Procedure

The mutual agreement procedure ("MAP") articles generally apply when the actions of the U.S. or foreign income tax authorities result in taxation not in accordance with the provisions of the applicable treaty. Distribution, apportionment, or allocation under transfer pricing rules may subject a taxpayer to U.S. federal income taxation on income that the taxpayer had attributed to a foreign country. Without an offsetting decrease in income reported to the foreign country, the taxpayer may be subject to double taxation of the same income.

> **Example 13.4:** A distributor, USAco is a subsidiary of ASIAco. USAco buys widgets from ASIAco for $100 and resells them in the U.S. for $105. The IRS argues that the arm's length price from ASIAco to USAco should be $90 and makes an assessment. Because $10 of income (the difference between the $100 ASIAco charged and the $90 the IRS believes is arm's length) is taxed by both the IRS and ASIA's tax administration, either USAco or ASIAco can request relief from their respective competent authorities. The competent authorities will negotiate with each other to determine who will tax the $10.

Before 1996, taxpayers had to use the Appeals process to try to resolve the adjustment before Competent Authority assistance is sought. However, where it is in the best interest of both parties, Competent Authority assistance may begin prior to consideration by the Appeals Office.

Simultaneous Appeals Procedure

Under the Simultaneous Appeals Procedure ("SAP"), taxpayers may seek simultaneous Appeals and Competent Authority consideration of an issue.[70] This procedure allows taxpayers to obtain Appeals

---

[70] Rev. Proc. 96-13, 1996-1 C.B. 616.

involvement in a manner consistent with the ensuing Competent Authority process and should reduce the time required to resolve disputes by allowing taxpayers more proactive involvement in the process. By informally approaching Competent Authority before submitting a formal request, the Competent Authority effectively becomes the taxpayer's advocate. SAP further opens the possibility of developing strategies to explore the view likely to be taken by the other country.

Taxpayers may request SAP with Competent Authority in three situations:

(i)   after Examination has proposed an adjustment with respect to an issue that the taxpayer wishes to submit to Competent Authority;[71]

(ii) after Examination has issued a 30-day letter. The taxpayer can file a protest and decide to sever the issue and seek Competent Authority assistance while other issues are referred to or remain in Appeals;[72] or

(iii) after the taxpayer is in Appeals and it is evident that the taxpayer will request Competent Authority assistance on an issue.[73]

The taxpayer also can request SAP with Appeals after a Competent Authority request is made.[74] Generally, the request will be denied if the U.S. position paper has already been communicated to the foreign Competent Authority. The U.S. Competent Authority also can request the procedure.[75]

SAP is a two-part process. First, the Appeals representative will prepare an Appeals Case Memorandum ("ACM") on the issue. The ACM is shared with the Competent Authority representative, but not with the taxpayer. The ACM is a tentative resolution that is considered by the U.S. Competent Authority in preparing the U.S. position paper for presentation to the foreign Competent Authority.[76] Second, the U.S. Competent Authority prepares and presents the U.S. position paper to the foreign Competent Authority. The U.S. Competent Authority meets with the taxpayer to discuss the technical issue to be presented to the foreign Competent Authority and the Appeals representative may be asked to participate. If the Competent Authorities fail to agree or the taxpayer does not accept the mutual agreement reached, the taxpayer is allowed to refer the issue to Appeals for further consideration.[77]

---

[71] 1996-3 I.R.B. 31 at § 8.02(a)(1).
[72] Id. at § 8.02(a)(2).
[73] Id. at § 8.02(a)(3).
[74] Id. at § 8.02(b).
[75] Id. at § 8.01.

[76] This situation is analogous to the APA process. The Appeals representative will be a team chief, international specialist, or Appeals officer with international experience.
[77] Rev. Proc. 96-13, at Section 8.07.

Accelerated Competent Authority Procedure

The Accelerated Competent Authority Procedure ("ACAP") shortens the time required to complete a case.[78] A taxpayer requesting ACAP assistance with respect to an issue raised by the IRS may request that the competent authorities resolve the issue for subsequent tax years ending prior to the date of the request for the assistance.[79] In such a request, the taxpayer must agree that the inspection of books and/or records under the procedure will not preclude or impede a later examination or inspection for any period covered in the request; and the IRS need not comply with any procedural restrictions before beginning such examination or inspection. The U.S. Competent Authority will contact the appropriate district to determine whether the issue should be resolved for subsequent tax years. If the district consents, the U.S. Competent Authority will present the request to the foreign Competent Authority.[80]

¶ 1306   CIVIL ACTIONS BY TAXPAYERS

A taxpayer may contest an adverse IRS determination in one of three tribunals. A petition may be filed with the U.S. Tax Court, and assessment and collection of the deficiency will be stayed until the Court's decision becomes final. Alternatively, the taxpayer may pay the deficiency including interest and penalties and sue for a refund in a U.S. District Court or the U.S. Court of Federal Claims.[81]

Filing a Petition in the U.S. Tax Court does not require payment of any tax, penalties or interest until the taxpayer's liability has been finally determined. If, on the other hand, the taxpayer sues for a refund in the district court or the U.S. Court of Federal Claims, the taxpayer must initially pay the tax including interest and penalties.

In a suit brought in the district court the taxpayer may request that a jury determine factual issues.[82] A jury trial *cannot* be obtained before the U.S. Tax Court or the U.S. Court of Federal Claims. Many factors must be taken into consideration in selecting the forum, including previous rulings on the particular issue by the particular court and whether the issue is one that will affect tax liability for future years. A tax refund suit arising out of a tax treaty may be brought against the U.S. in either the U.S. Court of Federal Claims or the District Court.[83]

---

[78] *Id.* at § 7.06.

[79] *Id.* at § 7.06.

[80] *Id.*

[81] Judicial Code Sec. 1346; Code Sec. 7422.

[82] 28 U.S.C. Sec. 2402.

[83] Code Sec. 7422(f)(1).

¶ 1307   APPENDIX

Form **870** (Rev. March 1992)	Department of the Treasury — Internal Revenue Service **Waiver of Restrictions on Assessment and Collection of Deficiency in Tax and Acceptance of Overassessment**	Date received by Internal Revenue Service
Names and address of taxpayers *(Number, street, city or town, State, ZIP code)*		Social security or employer identification number

	Increase (Decrease) in Tax and Penalties				
Tax year ended	Tax	Penalties			
	$	$	$	$	$
	$	$	$	$	$
	$	$	$	$	$
	$	$	$	$	$
	$	$	$	$	$
	$	$	$	$	$
	$	$	$	$	$

(For instructions, see back of form)

Consent to Assessment and Collection

I consent to the immediate assessment and collection of any deficiencies *(increase in tax and penalties)* and accept any overassessment *(decrease in tax and penalties)* shown above, plus any interest provided by law. I understand that by signing this waiver, I will not be able to contest these years in the United States Tax Court, unless additional deficiencies are determined for these years.

YOUR SIGNATURE → HERE		Date
SPOUSE'S SIGNATURE →		Date
TAXPAYER'S REPRESENTATIVE HERE →		Date
CORPORATE NAME →		
CORPORATE OFFICER(S) SIGN HERE		Title	Date
		Title	Date

Catalog Number 16894U   Form **870** (Rev. 3-92)

Form **870-AD** (Rev. April 1992)	Department of the Treasury—Internal Revenue Service **Offer to Waive Restrictions on Assessment and Collection of Tax** **Deficiency and to Accept Overassessment**		
Symbols	Name of Taxpayer		SSN or EIN

Under the provisions of section 6213(d) of the Internal Revenue Code of 1986 (the Code), or corresponding provisions of prior internal revenue laws, the undersigned offers to waive the restrictions provided in section 6213(a) of the Code or corresponding provisions of prior internal revenue laws, and to consent to the assessment and collection of the following deficiencies and additions to tax, if any, with interest as provided by law. The undersigned offers also to accept the following overassessments, if any, as correct. Any waiver or acceptance of an overassessment is subject to any terms and conditions stated below and on the reverse side of this form.

		Deficiencies (Overassessments) and Additions to Tax				
Year Ended	Kind of Tax	Tax				
		$	$	$		
		$	$	$		
		$	$	$		
		$	$	$		
		$	$	$		
		$	$	$		

Signature of Taxpayer	Date
Signature of Taxpayer	Date
Signature of Taxpayer's Representative	Date
Corporate Name	Date
By Corporate Officer　　　　　　　　　　Title	Date

For Internal Revenue Use Only	Date Accepted for Commissioner	Signature
	Office	Title

Cat. No. 16896Q　　　　　　　　(See Reverse Side)　　　　　　　　Form **870-AD** (Rev. 4-92)

This offer must be accepted for the Commissioner of Internal Revenue and will take effect on the date it is accepted. Unless and until it is accepted, it will have no force or effect.

If this offer is accepted, the case will not be reopened by the Commissioner unless there was:

* fraud, malfeasance, concealment or misrepresentation of a material fact
* an important mistake in mathematical calculation
* a deficiency or overassessment resulting from adjustments made under Subchapters C and D of Chapter 63 concerning the tax treatment of partnership and subchapter S items determined at the partnership and corporate level
* an excessive tentative allowance of a carryback provided by law

No claim for refund or credit will be filed or prosecuted by the taxpayer for the years stated on this form, other than for amounts attributed to carrybacks provided by law.

The proper filing of this offer, when accepted, will expedite assessment and billing (or overassessment, credit or refund) by adjusting the tax liability. This offer, when executed and timely submitted, will be considered a claim for refund for the above overassessment(s), if any.

This offer may be executed by the taxpayer's attorney, certified public accountant, or agent provided this is specifically authorized by a power of attorney which, if not previously filed, must accompany this form. If this offer is signed by a person acting in a fiduciary capacity (for example: an executor, administrator, or a trustee) Form 56, Notice Concerning Fiduciary Relationship, must accompany this form, unless previously filed.

If this offer is executed for a year for which a joint return was filed, it must be signed by both spouses unless one spouse, acting under a power of attorney, signs as agent for the other.

If this offer is executed by a corporation, it must be signed with the corporate name followed by the signature and title of the officer(s) authorized to sign. If the offer is accepted, as a condition of acceptance, any signature by or for a corporate officer will be considered a representation by that person and the corporation, to induce reliance, that such signature is binding under law for the corporation to be assessed the deficiencies or receive credit or refund under this agreement. If the corporation later contests the signature as being unauthorized on its behalf, the person who signed may be subject to criminal penalties for representing that he or she had authority to sign this agreement on behalf of the corporation.

*U.S. GPO: 1992-617-016/49236

Form **870-AD** (Rev. 4-92)

Summons

In the matter of _____

Internal Revenue District of _____ Periods _____

The Commissioner of Internal Revenue

To: _____

At: _____

_____

You are hereby summoned and required to appear before _____,
an officer of the Internal Revenue Service, to give testimony and to bring with you and to produce for examination the following books, records, papers, and other data relating to the tax liability or the collection of the tax liability or for the purpose of inquiring into any offense connected with the administration or enforcement of the internal revenue laws concerning the person identified above for the periods shown.

Do not write in this space

Business address and telephone number of IRS officer before whom you are to appear:

_____

Place and time for appearance at _____

IRS

Department of the Treasury
Internal Revenue Service

www.irs.ustreas.gov

Form 2039 (Rev. 9-1999)
Catalog Number 21405J

on the _____ day of _____ , _____ at _____ o'clock _____ m.
                                              (year)

Issued under authority of the Internal Revenue Code this_____ **day of** _____ , _____ .
                                                                                              (year)

_____   _____
Signature of issuing officer   Title

_____   _____
Signature of approving officer *(if applicable)*   Title

Original — to be kept by IRS

Service of Summons, Notice and Recordkeeper Certificates
(Pursuant to section 7603, Internal Revenue Code)

I certify that I served the summons shown on the front of this form on:

Date	Time

How Summons Was Served

1. ☐ I certify that I handed a copy of the summons, which contained the attestation required by § 7603, to the person to whom it was directed.

2. ☐ I certify that I left a copy of the summons, which contained the attestation required by § 7603, at the last and usual place of abode of the person to whom it was directed. I left the copy with the following person (if any):_____

3. ☐ I certify that I sent a copy of the summons, which contained the attestation required by § 7603, by certified or registered mail to the last known address of the person to whom it was directed, that person being a third-party recordkeeper within the meaning of § 7603(b). I sent the summons to the following address:_____

Signature	Title

4. This certificate is made to show compliance with IRC Section 7609. This certificate does not apply to summonses served on any officer or employee of the person to whose liability the summons relates nor to summonses in aid of collection, to determine the identity of a person having a numbered account or similar arrangement, or to determine whether or not records of the business transactions or affairs of an identified person have been made or kept.

I certify that, within 3 days of serving the summons, I gave notice (Part D of Form 2039) to the person named below on the date and in the manner indicated.

Date of giving Notice: _____   Time: _____

Name of Noticee: _____

Address of Noticee (if mailed): _____

How Notice Was Given

☐ I gave notice by certified or registered mail to the last known address of the noticee.

☐ I left the notice at the last and usual place of abode of the noticee. I left the copy with the following person (if any).

☐ I gave notice by handing it to the noticee.

☐ In the absence of a last known address of the noticee, I left the notice with the person summoned.

☐ No notice is required.

Signature	Title

I certify that the period prescribed for beginning a proceeding to quash this summons has expired and that no such proceeding was instituted or that the noticee consents to the examination.

Signature	Title

Form **2039** (Rev. 9-1999)

Formal Document Request

Form **4564** (Rev. June 1988)	Department of the Treasury — Internal Revenue Service ~~Information Document Request~~		Request number
To: *(Name of Taxpayer and Company Division or Branch)*		Subject	
		SAIN number	Submitted to:
		Dates of previous requests	

Please return Part 2 with listed documents to requester identified below

Description of documents requested

Information due by _____	At next appointment ☐	Mail in ☐	
From:	Name and title of requester	Employee ID number	Date
	Office location		Telephone number

Catalog No. 23145K

Form **4564** (Rev. 6-1988)

Your Appeal Rights and How To Prepare a Protest If You Don't Agree

Department of the Treasury
Internal Revenue Service

www.irs.ustreas.gov

Publication 5 (Rev. 01-1999)
Catalog Number 46074I

Introduction

This Publication tells you how to appeal your tax case if you don't agree with the Internal Revenue Service (IRS) findings.

If You Don't Agree

If you don't agree with any or all of the IRS findings given you, you may request a meeting or a telephone conference with the supervisor of the person who issued the findings. If you still don't agree, you may appeal your case to the Appeals Office of IRS.

If you decide to do nothing and your case involves an examination of your income, estate, gift, and certain excise taxes or penalties, you will receive a formal Notice of Deficiency. The Notice of Deficiency allows you to go to the Tax Court and tells you the procedure to follow. If you do not go to the Tax Court, we will send you a bill for the amount due.

If you decide to do nothing and your case involves a trust fund recovery penalty, or certain employment tax liabilities, the IRS will send you a bill for the penalty. If you do not appeal a denial of an offer in compromise or a denial of a penalty abatement, the IRS will continue collection action.

If you don't agree, we urge you to appeal your case to the Appeals Office of IRS. The Office of Appeals can settle most differences without expensive and time-consuming court trials. [Note: Appeals can not consider your reasons for not agreeing if they don't come within the scope of the tax laws (for example, if you disagree solely on moral, religious, political, constitutional, conscientious, or similar grounds.)]

The following general rules tell you how to appeal your case.

Appeals Within the IRS

Appeals is the administrative appeals office for the IRS. You may appeal most IRS decisions with your local Appeals Office. The Appeals Office is separate from - and independent of - the IRS Office taking the action you disagree with. The Appeals Office is the only level of administrative appeal within the IRS.

Conferences with Appeals Office personnel are held in an informal manner by correspondence, by telephone or at a personal conference. There is no need for you to have representation for an Appeals conference, but if you choose to have a representative, see the requirements under *Representation.*

If you want an Appeals conference, follow the instructions in our letter to you. Your request will be sent to the Appeals Office to arrange a conference at a convenient time and place. You or your representative should prepare to discuss all issues you don't agree with at the conference. Most differences are settled at this level.

In most instances, you may be eligible to take your case to court if you don't reach an agreement at your Appeals conference, or if you don't want to appeal your case to the IRS Office of Appeals. See the later section *Appeals To The Courts.*

Protests

When you request an appeals conference, you may also need to file a formal written protest or a small case request with the office named in our letter to you. Also, see the special appeal request procedures in Publication 1660, Collection Appeal Rights, if you disagree with lien, levy, seizure, or denial or termination of an installment agreement.

You need to file a written protest:

- In all employee plan and exempt organization cases without regard to the dollar amount at issue.

- In all partnership and S corporation cases without regard to the dollar amount at issue.

- In all other cases, unless you qualify for the small case request procedure, or other special appeal procedures such as requesting Appeals consideration of liens, levies, seizures, or installment agreements. See Publication 1660.

How to prepare a protest:

When a protest is required, **send it within the time limit specified in the letter you received.** Include in your protest:

1) Your name and address, and a daytime telephone number,

2) A statement that you want to appeal the IRS findings to the Appeals Office,

3) A copy of the letter showing the proposed changes and findings you don't agree with (or the date and symbols from the letter),

4) The tax periods or years involved,

5) A list of the changes that you don't agree with, and why you don't agree.

6) The facts supporting your position on any issue that you don't agree with,

7) The law or authority, if any, on which you are relying.

8) You must sign the written protest, stating that it is true, under the penalties of perjury as follows:

"Under the penalties of perjury, I declare that I examined the facts stated in this protest, including any accompanying documents, and, to the best of my knowledge and belief, they are true, correct, and complete."

If your representative prepares and signs the protest for you, he or she must substitute a declaration stating:

1) That he or she submitted the protest and accompanying documents and

2) Whether he or she knows personally that the facts stated in the protest and accompanying documents are true and correct.

We urge you to provide as much information as you can, as this will help us speed up your appeal. This will save you both time and money.

Small Case Request:

If the total amount for any tax period is not more than $25,000, you may make a small case request instead of filing a formal written protest. In computing the total amount, include a proposed increase or decrease in tax (including penalties), or claimed refund. For an offer in compromise, in calculating the total amount, include total unpaid tax, penalty and interest due. For a small case request, follow the instructions in our letter to you by: sending a letter requesting Appeals consideration, indicating the changes you don't agree with, and the reasons why you don't agree.

Representation

You may represent yourself at your appeals conference, or you may have an attorney, certified public accountant, or an individual enrolled to practice before the IRS represent you. Your representative must be qualified to practice before the IRS. If you want your representative to appear without you, you must provide a properly completed power of attorney to the IRS before the representative can receive or inspect confidential information. Form 2848, Power of Attorney and Declaration of Representative, or any other properly written power of attorney or authorization may be used for this purpose. You can get copies of Form 2848 from an IRS office, or by calling 1-800-TAX-FORM (1-800-829-3676).

You may also bring another person(s) with you to support your position.

Appeals To The Courts

If you and Appeals don't agree on some or all of the issues after your Appeals conference, or if you skipped our appeals system, you may take your case to the United States Tax Court, the United States Court of Federal Claims, or your United States District Court, after satisfying certain procedural and jurisdictional requirements as described below under each court. (However, if you are a nonresident alien, you cannot take your case to a United States District Court.) These courts are independent judicial bodies and have no connection with the IRS.

Tax Court

If your disagreement with the IRS is over whether you owe additional income tax, estate tax, gift tax, certain excise taxes or penalties related to these proposed liabilities, you can go to the United States Tax Court. (Other types of tax controversies, such as those involving some employment tax issues or manufacturers' excise taxes, cannot be heard by the Tax Court.) You can do this after the IRS issues a formal letter, stating the amounts that the IRS believes you owe. This letter is called a notice of deficiency. You have 90 days from the date this notice is mailed to you to file a petition with the Tax Court (or 150 days if the notice is addressed to you outside the United States). The last date to file your petition will be entered on the notice of deficiency issued to you by the IRS. If you don't file the petition within the 90-day period (or 150 days, as the case may be), we will assess the proposed liability and send you a bill. You may also have the right to take your case to the Tax Court in some other situations, for example, following collection action by the IRS in certain cases. See Publication 1660.

If you discuss your case with the IRS during the 90-day period (150-day period), the discussion will not extend the period in which you may file a petition with the Tax Court.

The court will schedule your case for trial at a location convenient to you. You may represent yourself before the Tax Court, or you may be represented by anyone permitted to practice before that court.

Note: If you don't choose to go to the IRS Appeals Office before going to court, normally you will have an opportunity to attempt settlement with Appeals before your trial date.

If you dispute not more than $50,000 for any one tax year, there are simplified procedures. You can get information about these procedures and other matters from the Clerk of the Tax Court, 400 Second St. NW, Washington, DC 20217.

Frivolous Filing Penalty

Caution: If the Tax Court determines that your case is intended primarily to cause a delay, or that your position is frivolous or groundless, the Tax Court may award a penalty of up to $25,000 to the United States in its decision.

District Court and Court of Federal Claims

If your claim is for a refund of any type of tax, you may take your case to your United States District Court or to the United States Court of Federal Claims. Certain types of cases, such as those involving some employment tax issues or manufacturers' excise taxes, can be heard only by these courts.

Generally, your District Court and the Court of Federal Claims hear tax cases only after you have paid the tax and filed a claim for refund with the IRS. You can get information about procedures for filing suit in either court by contacting the Clerk of your District Court or the Clerk of the Court of Federal Claims.

If you file a formal refund claim with the IRS, and we haven't responded to you on your claim within 6 months from the date you filed it, you may file suit for a refund immediately in your District Court or the Court of Federal Claims. If we send you a letter that proposes disallowing or disallows your claim, you may request Appeals review of the disallowance. If you wish to file a refund suit, you must file your suit no later than 2 years from the date of our notice of claim disallowance letter.

Note: Appeals review of a disallowed claim doesn't extend the 2 year period for filing suit. However, it may be extended by mutual agreement.

Recovering Administrative and Litigation Costs

You may be able to recover your reasonable litigation and administrative costs if you are the prevailing party, and if you meet the other requirements. You must exhaust your administrative remedies within the IRS to receive reasonable litigation costs. You must not unreasonably delay the administrative or court proceedings.

Administrative costs include costs incurred on or after the date you receive the Appeals decision letter, the date of the first letter of proposed deficiency, or the date of the notice of deficiency, whichever is earliest.

Recoverable litigation or administrative costs may include:

- Attorney fees that generally do not exceed $125 per hour. This amount will be indexed for a cost of living adjustment.

- Reasonable amounts for court costs or any administrative fees or similar charges by the IRS.

- Reasonable expenses of expert witnesses.

- Reasonable costs of studies, analyses, tests, or engineering reports that are necessary to prepare your case.

You are the prevailing party if you meet all the following requirements:

- You substantially prevailed on the amount in controversy, or on the most significant tax issue or issues in question.

- You meet the net worth requirement. For individuals or estates, the net worth cannot exceed $2,000,000 on the date from which costs are recoverable. Charities and certain cooperatives must not have more than 500 employees on the date from which costs are recoverable. And taxpayers other than the two categories listed above must not have net worth exceeding $7,000,000 and cannot have more than 500 employees on the date from which costs are recoverable.

You are not the prevailing party if:

- The United States establishes that its position was substantially justified. If the IRS does not follow applicable published guidance, the United States is presumed to not be substantially justified. This presumption is rebuttable. Applicable published guidance means regulations, revenue rulings, revenue procedures, information releases, notices, announcements, and, if they are issued to you, private letter rulings, technical advice memoranda and determination letters. The court will also take into account whether the Government has won or lost in the courts of appeals for other circuits on substantially similar issues, in determining if the United States is substantially justified.

You are also the prevailing party if:

- The final judgment on your case is less than or equal to a "qualified offer" which the IRS rejected, and if you meet the net worth requirements referred to above.

A court will generally decide who is the prevailing party, but the IRS makes a final determination of liability at the administrative level. This means you may receive administrative costs from the IRS without going to court. You must file your claim for administrative costs no later than the 90th day after the final determination of tax, penalty or interest is mailed to you. The Appeals Office makes determinations for the IRS on administrative costs. A denial of administrative costs may be appealed to the Tax Court no later than the 90th day after the denial.

Rev. Proc. 96-13

Topical Index

References are to paragraph (¶) numbers.

FOR

FOR